# LIFE INSURANCE & MODIFIED ENDOWMENTS

*Under Internal Revenue Code Sections 7702 and 7702A*

*Second Edition*

CHRISTIAN J. DESROCHERS, FSA, MAAA
JOHN T. ADNEY, ESQ.
BRIAN G. KING, FSA, MAAA
CRAIG R. SPRINGFIELD, ESQ.

Published By:

475 North Martingale Rd., Suite 600
Schaumburg, IL 60173

Copyright © 2015. Society of Actuaries. All rights reserved under U.S. and international laws.

No part of this publication may be reproduced or distributed in any form without the express written permission of the Society of Actuaries.

This publication is provided for informational and educational purposes only. The Society of Actuaries makes no representation or guarantee with regard to its content, and disclaims any responsibility or liability in connection with the use or misuse of any information provided herein. This publication should not be construed as professional or financial advice. Statements of fact and opinions expressed herein are those of the individual author and are not necessarily those of the Society of Actuaries or its officers, directors, staff or representatives.

The Society of Actuaries does not endorse or make any guarantee with regard to any products, services or procedures mentioned or advertised herein.

**Library of Congress Cataloging-in-Publication Data**

Life insurance & modified endowments : under internal revenue code sections 7702 and 7702a / Christian J. DesRochers, FSA, MAAA, John T. Adney, Esq., Brian G. King, FSA, MAAA, Craig R. Springfield, Esq. -- Second edition.
    pages cm
 ISBN 978-0-9913363-1-9
 1. Life insurance--Taxation--Law and legislation--United States. I. DesRochers, Christian J., author.
 KF6428.L5L54 2015
 343.7305'24--dc23
                     2015029482

ISBN 978-0-9913363-1-9
Second Edition

Printed in the United States of America

19 18 17 16 15     1 2 3 4 5

# LIFE INSURANCE & MODIFIED ENDOWMENTS

*Under Internal Revenue Code Sections 7702 and 7702A*

Second Edition

# DEDICATION

**In memoriam**
Christian J. DesRochers, FSA, MAAA
1949–2013

We dedicate this second edition of *Life Insurance & Modified Endowments Under Internal Revenue Code Sections 7702 and 7702A* to our colleague and friend, the late Chris DesRochers. In the fall of 2002, Chris observed that the IRS had not finalized a single regulation, and had published very little other authority, to provide guidance on the tax statutes defining life insurance and modified endowment contracts, sections 7702 and 7702A of the Internal Revenue Code. This was the case even though the two statutes then were, respectively, 18 and 14 years old, and section 7702's predecessor defining flexible premium life insurance contracts, section 101(f), had been enacted two decades prior. So Chris proposed that the Society of Actuaries should publish a textbook to fill in the gap, educating life insurance product designers and tax practitioners on the subject. The SOA agreed, and to join in the writing, Chris recruited two actuaries, Douglas Hertz and Brian King, and one lawyer, John Adney.

Even as the initial copies of this text's first edition were printed in the fall of 2004, significant change was setting in for life product taxation. Perhaps most importantly for the future of product tax compliance, while the first edition had been drafted with practitioners in mind, the SOA began using it as course material for students seeking the FSA credential. Hence, some three years ago, the SOA asked Chris to consider a revision of the text to reflect the changing circumstances, with particular focus on the needs of actuarial students. With the retirement of Doug Hertz, Chris turned to the three co-authors of this second edition to join him in producing a thoroughly revised text. Chris proceeded to map out the re-worked chapter structure of the new edition and to create the first draft of its student-focused initial chapters.

Then in the fall of 2013, as preparation of the new edition began under Chris's guidance, tragedy struck. Chris's sudden and untimely death in mid-September of that year left his three co-authors and many others in mourning, and left this text facing an uncertain future. But soon thereafter his three co-authors resolved to push forward with production of the planned new text, not least as a means of honoring his memory. Fittingly, Chris's name remains on the second edition, as the lead author, since it was all his idea in the first place.

J.T.A.
B.G.K
C.R.S.

# TABLE OF CONTENTS

Foreword . . . . . . . . . . . . . . . . . . . . . . . . . . . . . . . . . . . . . . . . . . . . . . . . . . . . . . . . . . . . . . . . . . . . xv
Preface . . . . . . . . . . . . . . . . . . . . . . . . . . . . . . . . . . . . . . . . . . . . . . . . . . . . . . . . . . . . . . . . . . . . . xvii
Acknowledgements . . . . . . . . . . . . . . . . . . . . . . . . . . . . . . . . . . . . . . . . . . . . . . . . . . . . . . . xxi
About the Authors . . . . . . . . . . . . . . . . . . . . . . . . . . . . . . . . . . . . . . . . . . . . . . . . . . . . . . . xxiii
List of Figures and Tables . . . . . . . . . . . . . . . . . . . . . . . . . . . . . . . . . . . . . . . . . . . . . . . . xxvii

## Chapter 1. Introduction — 1

In the Beginning . . . . . . . . . . . . . . . . . . . . . . . . . . . . . . . . . . . . . . . . . . . . . . . . . . . . . . . . . . . 1
Income Tax Treatment of Life Insurance Contracts . . . . . . . . . . . . . . . . . . . . . . . . . . . . 1
    Death Benefits . . . . . . . . . . . . . . . . . . . . . . . . . . . . . . . . . . . . . . . . . . . . . . . . . . . . . . . . 2
    Inside Buildup and Lifetime Distributions . . . . . . . . . . . . . . . . . . . . . . . . . . . . . . . . 2
    Other Rules . . . . . . . . . . . . . . . . . . . . . . . . . . . . . . . . . . . . . . . . . . . . . . . . . . . . . . . . . . 2
Life Insurance Defined . . . . . . . . . . . . . . . . . . . . . . . . . . . . . . . . . . . . . . . . . . . . . . . . . . . . 3
    Common Law Rules . . . . . . . . . . . . . . . . . . . . . . . . . . . . . . . . . . . . . . . . . . . . . . . . . . 3
    TEFRA: Section 101(f) . . . . . . . . . . . . . . . . . . . . . . . . . . . . . . . . . . . . . . . . . . . . . . . 4
    DEFRA: Section 7702 . . . . . . . . . . . . . . . . . . . . . . . . . . . . . . . . . . . . . . . . . . . . . . . . 4
    Tax Reform Act of 1986 . . . . . . . . . . . . . . . . . . . . . . . . . . . . . . . . . . . . . . . . . . . . . . 4
    TAMRA: Section 7702A . . . . . . . . . . . . . . . . . . . . . . . . . . . . . . . . . . . . . . . . . . . . . . 5
The Role of Sections 7702 and 7702A in Life Insurance Taxation . . . . . . . . . . . . . . . 5
"Applicable Law" Requirement of Section 7702 . . . . . . . . . . . . . . . . . . . . . . . . . . . . . . 6
    Insurable Interest . . . . . . . . . . . . . . . . . . . . . . . . . . . . . . . . . . . . . . . . . . . . . . . . . . . . 7
    Alternative Forms of Life Insurance . . . . . . . . . . . . . . . . . . . . . . . . . . . . . . . . . . . . 8
Foreign-Issued Life Insurance Contracts . . . . . . . . . . . . . . . . . . . . . . . . . . . . . . . . . . . . 9
    Canadian Requirements . . . . . . . . . . . . . . . . . . . . . . . . . . . . . . . . . . . . . . . . . . . . . . 9
    Foreign Account Tax Compliance Act . . . . . . . . . . . . . . . . . . . . . . . . . . . . . . . . . . 10
Appendix 1.1. Summary of Other Life Insurance Tax Rules . . . . . . . . . . . . . . . . . . . 10
    Death Benefits . . . . . . . . . . . . . . . . . . . . . . . . . . . . . . . . . . . . . . . . . . . . . . . . . . . . . . 10
    Inside Buildup and Lifetime Distributions . . . . . . . . . . . . . . . . . . . . . . . . . . . . . . 13
    Other Rules . . . . . . . . . . . . . . . . . . . . . . . . . . . . . . . . . . . . . . . . . . . . . . . . . . . . . . . . 15
    Continued Reading . . . . . . . . . . . . . . . . . . . . . . . . . . . . . . . . . . . . . . . . . . . . . . . . . . 18
Appendix 1.2. A Note on Tax Authorities . . . . . . . . . . . . . . . . . . . . . . . . . . . . . . . . . . . 18

## Chapter 2. Introduction to Sections 7702 and 7702A — 21

Chapter Overview . . . . . . . . . . . . . . . . . . . . . . . . . . . . . . . . . . . . . . . . . . . . . . . . . . . . . . . 21
The Model or Test Plan Concept . . . . . . . . . . . . . . . . . . . . . . . . . . . . . . . . . . . . . . . . . . 21
Cash Value Accumulation Test . . . . . . . . . . . . . . . . . . . . . . . . . . . . . . . . . . . . . . . . . . . 23
    Net Single Premium . . . . . . . . . . . . . . . . . . . . . . . . . . . . . . . . . . . . . . . . . . . . . . . . . 24
    Cash Surrender Value . . . . . . . . . . . . . . . . . . . . . . . . . . . . . . . . . . . . . . . . . . . . . . . 25
    Terms of the Contract . . . . . . . . . . . . . . . . . . . . . . . . . . . . . . . . . . . . . . . . . . . . . . . 25

| | |
|---|---:|
| Guideline Premium/Cash Value Corridor Test | 26 |
|     Guideline Single and Guideline Level Premiums | 26 |
|     Section 7702(d) Cash Value Corridor | 28 |
|     Premiums Paid | 29 |
|     Treatment of Premiums Returned to Policyholders to Comply With the GPT | 30 |
|     Applying the Guideline Premium Test | 31 |
| Choice of Tests Under Section 7702 | 32 |
| Modified Endowment Contracts Under Section 7702A | 34 |
|     The 7-Pay Test | 34 |
|     $75 Per Policy and Modal Premium Expense Allowances | 35 |
|     Amount Paid Under Section 7702A | 35 |
|     Applying the 7-Pay Test | 36 |
| Interest | 37 |
|     Treatment of Initial Guarantees | 38 |
|     Short-Term Guarantees | 38 |
|     Policyholder Dividends and Interest Guarantees | 39 |
|     Relationship of Statutory Rates to Contractual Guarantees | 40 |
|     Monthly Interest Assumption and Death Benefit Discount Rate | 40 |
|     Implied Guarantees | 41 |
| Mortality | 41 |
|     Reasonable Mortality Standard | 42 |
|     The Permanent Mortality Rule | 42 |
|     The Interim Mortality Rule | 43 |
|     Reasonable Mortality, Prevailing Commissioners' Standard Tables and IRS Notice 88-128 | 43 |
|     IRS Notices 2004-61 and 2006-95 | 44 |
|     Monthly Mortality Assumption | 47 |
|     Cost of Insurance Rates | 48 |
| Expense Charges | 49 |
|     Defining Reasonable Expense Charges | 49 |
|     Expense Charges Used in Calculating Guideline Premiums | 50 |
| Future Benefits | 50 |
|     Packwood-Baucus Colloquy | 51 |
|     Computational Rules | 51 |
|     Qualified Additional Benefits | 53 |
| Adjustments | 53 |
|     CVAT Adjustments | 54 |
|     Guideline Premium Test Adjustments | 54 |
|     7-Pay Test Adjustments | 55 |
| Appendix 2.1. Sample At-Issue Calculations | 57 |
|     An Illustration: Application of the Test Plan to Term Insurance | 59 |
| Appendix 2.2. Calculation Methods | 59 |
|     Basic Actuarial Principles | 59 |
|     Commutation Functions | 60 |
|     Projection-Based Methods | 61 |
|     Processing Frequency | 62 |
|     Equivalence of Methods | 62 |
|     Rounding of Values | 63 |
| Appendix 2.3. Payment of Death Claims Assumptions | 63 |
| Appendix 2.4. IRS Notice 88-128 | 65 |
| Appendix 2.5. Proposed Regulation on "Reasonable" Mortality | 66 |

## Chapter 3. Components of Section 7702 and 7702A Calculations — 69

| | |
|---|---|
| Chapter Overview | 69 |
| Defining Cash Value and Cash Surrender Value | 69 |
|     1992 Proposed Regulation Defining Cash Surrender Value | 70 |
|     Private Letter Rulings Defining Cash Surrender Value | 71 |
|     Additional Considerations Regarding Cash Surrender Value | 72 |
| Defining "Age" | 72 |
| Computational Rules: Limiting "Future Benefits" | 76 |
|     Background: Section 101(f) Computational Rules | 76 |
|     Section 7702 | 77 |
| Section 7702(e)(2)(A) and (B) Alternative Death Benefit Rules | 79 |
|     Net Level Reserve Test | 80 |
|     Least Endowment Rule | 81 |
|     Treatment of the Initial Premium Under Option 2 Contracts | 81 |
| Computational Rules for the 7-Pay Premium | 82 |
|     Future Benefits Under Section 7702A | 83 |
|     Option 2 Death Benefits Under Section 7702A | 83 |
| Summary of Computational Rules Under Sections 7702 and 7702A | 84 |
| Reinstatements | 84 |
| Qualified Additional Benefits | 84 |
|     Reflecting QABs in the GLP | 87 |
|     Deletion of QAB Coverage | 89 |
|     Treatment of Additional Benefits That Are Not QABs (non-QABs) | 89 |
|     Treatment of Riders Under 7702A | 90 |
| Term Insurance Riders on the Insured: Death Benefit Versus QAB Treatment | 91 |
|     Section 7702 | 91 |
|     Section 7702A | 91 |
|     Both Statutes | 92 |
|     Summary and Import of the Rulings | 92 |
| Mortality Rates Beyond Age 100 | 92 |
|     Age 121 Terminal Values | 92 |
|     Revenue Procedure 2010-28 | 93 |
|     Some Observations on Revenue Procedure 2010-28 | 95 |
| Substandard Mortality | 97 |
|     Methods of Computing Substandard Values | 97 |
|     Temporary or Flat Extras | 99 |
|     Age Adjustments | 99 |
|     Terminal Age of Substandard Tables | 99 |
|     Simplified Underwriting | 100 |
| Application of Reasonable Expense Charge Limitations to QABs | 100 |

## Chapter 4. Adjusting the Limitations Under Sections 7702 and 7702A — 103

| | |
|---|---|
| Chapter Overview | 103 |
| Adjustments Under Section 7702 | 103 |
| CVAT Adjustments | 104 |
| Guideline Premium Test Adjustments | 105 |
|     Background: Section 101(f) Adjustment Events and Methods | 105 |
|     Section 7702 Adjustment Events | 107 |
|     Section 7702 Adjustment Method: The Attained-Age Increment and Decrement Rule | 109 |

| | |
|---|---:|
| Observations on the Attained-Age Increment and Decrement Method | 111 |
| Timing of Adjustments to the Guideline Premiums | 112 |
| Sample Adjustment Calculations | 114 |
| Problems in Applying Guideline Premium Test Adjustments | 119 |
| Reinstatements | 120 |
| Adjustments Under Section 7702A | 122 |
| Reduction in Benefits | 122 |
| Material Changes | 124 |
| The Rollover Rule | 127 |
| Material Change Example | 128 |
| Necessary Premiums | 129 |
| Necessary Premiums Under the Guideline Test | 131 |
| Necessary Premiums Under the CVAT | 133 |
| CVAT Necessary Premium Example | 135 |
| Summary of Adjustment Rules Under Sections 7702 and 7702A | 137 |
| Option 2 and Death Benefit Option Changes | 138 |
| Treatment of the Guideline Single Premium Under Option 2 Plans | 138 |
| Sample Option Change Calculations | 139 |
| Death Benefit Option Change Example 1: Level (Option 1) to Increasing (Option 2) | 139 |
| Death Benefit Option Change Example 2: Increasing (Option 2) to Level (Option 1) | 142 |
| Recapture Ceiling Rules Under Section 7702(f)(7)(B)–(E) | 145 |
| Rev. Rul. 2003-95 | 147 |

## Chapter 5. Statutory Effective Dates and the Impact of Material Changes — 151

| | |
|---|---:|
| Chapter Overview | 151 |
| Contract Changes and New-Issuance Treatment: An Introduction | 151 |
| Contract Exchanges | 152 |
| The Issue Date of a Contract | 154 |
| Material Changes and the Section 7702 Effective Date Rule | 155 |
| Reapplying Section 7702: New Issue Treatment of Contracts and the Role of the Adjustment Rules | 159 |
| Absence of an Option or Right | 159 |
| Fundamental Change | 161 |
| Role of the Adjustment Rules | 162 |
| TAMRA: Reasonable Charges, Section 7702A and the TAMRA Effective Date Rules | 162 |
| Reapplication of Section 7702's Reasonable Mortality Rule | 164 |
| The Special Case of Insurance Company Rehabilitations | 167 |
| Administering the Effective Date and Material Change Rules | 167 |
| Rule Eras and Assumption Eras | 168 |
| Material Changes, Effective Date Rules and Contract Adjustments | 169 |
| A Concluding Comment | 174 |

## Chapter 6. Product-Specific Issues — 175

| | |
|---|---:|
| Chapter Overview | 175 |
| Variable Life | 175 |
| Diversification Rules | 176 |
| Offshore and Private Placement Products | 176 |
| M&E and Asset-Based Expenses | 177 |
| Guaranteed Minimum Withdrawal Benefits | 178 |

| | |
|---|---|
| Equity-Indexed Contracts | 179 |
| Multiple-Life Plans | 180 |
|     Joint Life | 180 |
|     Survivorship | 181 |
|     Determining the Insureds' "Age" | 182 |
|     Reduction in Benefits Under Survivorship Contracts | 184 |
| Paid-Up Additions Riders | 184 |
| Combination Plans | 185 |
| Interest-Sensitive Whole Life and Fixed-Premium Universal Life: The Challenge of Dual Cash Surrender Values | 186 |
|     Application of DEFRA Blue Book Footnote 53 | 186 |
|     Observations On and Issues in Using the Footnote 53 Process | 190 |
| Group Universal Life | 192 |
| Single Premium Net Rate Products | 193 |
| Burial or Preneed Contracts | 195 |
| Reversionary Annuity Plans | 198 |
| Church-Related Death Benefit Plans | 198 |
| Issues in Special Product Features | 198 |
|     Cash Value Bonuses | 198 |
|     Decreasing Face Amount Plans | 199 |
|     Intentionally Failed Contracts | 200 |
|     Life Insurance and Annuity Combinations | 200 |
|     No-Lapse Guarantees | 200 |
|     Premium Deposit Funds | 201 |
|     Return of Premium Plans | 201 |

## Chapter 7. Long-Term Care Insurance Riders and Accelerated Death Benefits   205

| | |
|---|---|
| Chapter Overview | 205 |
| Origin and Characteristics of Accelerated Death Benefits | 205 |
| Federal Tax Rules for ADBs: Introduction to Sections 101(g) and 7702B | 207 |
|     Chronic Illness ADBs | 207 |
|     Terminal Illness ADBs | 211 |
|     Critical Illness and Other ADBs | 212 |
| Qualified Long-Term Care Insurance: Tax Treatment of Premiums and Charges | 213 |
|     Premiums and Charges in General: Limited or No Deduction | 213 |
|     Health Savings Accounts | 214 |
|     Charges for QLTCI Riders: Special Rule of Section 72(e)(11) | 215 |
| Qualified Long-Term Care Insurance: Tax Treatment of Benefits | 215 |
|     In General: A&H Tax Treatment of Benefits Under Section 7702B | 215 |
|     Per Diem Benefits | 217 |
|     Refunds from QLTCI Riders | 222 |
| Definition of a Qualified Long-Term Care Insurance Contract | 223 |
|     Introduction | 223 |
|     Section 7702B(b)(1): Insurance Contract Requirement | 224 |
|     Section 7702B(b)(1)(A): Coverage of Only QLTC Services | 225 |
|     Section 7702B(b)(1)(B): Coordination with Medicare | 232 |
|     Section 7702B(b)(1)(C): Guaranteed Renewability | 232 |
|     Section 7702B(b)(1)(D), (E) and (2)(C): Limitations on Cash and Loan Values and Allowance of Return of Premium Benefits | 233 |
|     Section 7702B(b)(2)(A): Special Rule for Per Diem Benefits | 234 |

| | |
|---|---|
| Section 7702B(e): Special Rules for Long-Term Care Riders | 235 |
| Sections 7702B(g) and 4980C: Consumer Protection Rules for QLTCI | 236 |
| Section 101(g) Chronic Illness Riders | 240 |
| Tax Treatment of Chronic Illness Benefits from Section 101(g) Riders | 241 |
| Requirements for Chronic Illness Benefits Under Section 101(g) | 241 |
| Comparison of QLTCI Riders with Section 101(g) Riders That Are Not QLTCI | 244 |
| Reporting Requirements for Chronic Illness Riders | 246 |
| Consequences of ADB Riders Under Sections 7702, 7702A and 72 | 247 |
| Section 7702: Accounting for ADB Riders | 247 |
| Section 7702A: Accounting for ADB Riders | 250 |
| Section 72: Accounting for ADB Riders | 250 |
| Grandfather Considerations | 251 |
| Section 1035 Exchanges Involving ADB Riders | 251 |
| Appendix 7.1. Consumer Protection Rules Imposed by Cross-Reference to 1993 LTC Model Rules | 252 |

## Chapter 8. Failed Contracts and Inadvertent Modified Endowment Contracts: Corrections of Errors, Waivers and Closing Agreements — 261

| | |
|---|---|
| Chapter Overview | 261 |
| "Self-Help" Corrections | 261 |
| Section 101(f) and 7702 Failures | 262 |
| Calculation of the Income on the Contract | 263 |
| Introduction to Remediation Processes | 265 |
| Waiver and Closing Agreement Processes | 266 |
| Correction of Failed Contracts | 268 |
| Waivable Errors and the Causes of Noncompliance | 269 |
| Programming or Systems Errors | 270 |
| Errors in Contract Administration | 271 |
| Manual Calculation and Input Errors | 274 |
| The Remediation Revolution (Part 1): Failed Contracts | 274 |
| Rev. Proc. 2008-38: Correcting the QAB Error | 276 |
| Rev. Proc. 2008-40: Correcting Failed Contracts Generally | 278 |
| Rev. Proc. 2008-42: Automatic Waivers | 283 |
| The Remediation Revolution (Part 2): Inadvertent MECs | 284 |
| Treatment of Failed Contracts or Inadvertent MECs in an Acquisition | 292 |
| Presale Due Diligence | 292 |
| Product and Contract Review | 292 |
| Remediation Plan | 293 |

## Chapter 9. The Development of the Tax Law's Limitations on Life Insurance: History and Precedents — 295

| | |
|---|---|
| Chapter Overview | 295 |
| Development of Cash Surrender Values and Their Tax Treatment | 296 |
| The Insurance Value Concept | 296 |
| The Development of Cash Surrender Values | 297 |
| The Revenue Act of 1913 | 298 |
| Developments After 1913 | 300 |
| Supplee-Biddle Hardware | 301 |
| Early Cases and the Treatment of Cash Surrender Values | 302 |

The Development of an Economic Definition of Life Insurance ... 302
   *Le Gierse* and the Estate Tax Exemption ... 303
   Cecile Le Gierse and Anna Keller ... 303
   Developments after *Le Gierse* ... 305
The Limitations on Financed Life Insurance ... 306
   High Early Cash Value Contracts and Minimum Deposit Life Insurance Plans ... 308
Universal Life and the Product Revolution: The Rise of a Statutory Definition of Life Insurance ... 309
   Variable Life ... 310
   Universal Life ... 310
   The Hutton Life Rulings ... 311
   GCM 38934 ... 312
Section 101(f) ... 312
   GCM 39022 ... 313
Section 7702 ... 314
   Stark-Moore Proposal ... 314
   DEFRA ... 315
Section 7702A ... 315
   The Stark-Gradison Bill ... 316
   The NALU-AALU Proposal ... 316
   The ACLI Proposal ... 317
   The Joint Industry Proposal ... 317
   TAMRA ... 318

# Chapter 10. Tax Policy and the Taxation of Life Insurance Contracts — 321

Chapter Overview ... 321
Tax Policy and the Ideal of a Comprehensive Income Tax ... 321
   Tax Treatment of Life Insurance ... 322
Inside Buildup of Permanent Life Insurance Contracts ... 323
   Economic Income Associated with the Inside Buildup ... 323
   Reasons for Tax Deferral on the Inside Buildup ... 324
The Limitations on Inside Buildup ... 326
   The Roads Not Taken ... 326
   Sections 7702 and 7702A ... 327
   Relationship Between Section 7702 and State Nonforfeiture Law for Life Insurance ... 331
   The Nonforfeiture Law for Life Insurance as a Safety Net ... 333
   Potential Future Limitations on the Inside Buildup ... 334

# Glossary — 337

# Appendices — 353

Appendix A
IRC Section 7702 ... 353

Appendix B
IRC Section 7702A ... 365

Appendix C
IRC Section 7702B ... 371

Appendix D
IRC Section 101(f) .................................................................. 381

Appendix E
IRC Section 101(g) .................................................................. 385

Appendix F
IRC Section 4980C .................................................................. 389

Appendix G
DEFRA Blue Book: General Explanation of the Revenue Provisions of the Deficit Reduction
Act of 1984 ........................................................................... 393

Appendix H
TAMRA House Report: Miscellaneous Revenue Act of 1988—Report of the Committee on
Ways and Means ..................................................................... 409

Appendix I
TAMRA Conference Report: Technical and Miscellaneous Revenue Act of 1988—
Conference Report ................................................................... 425

Appendix J
1989 OBRA House Report: Omnibus Budget Reconciliation Act of 1989—
Report of the Committee on the Budget .................................... 441

Appendix K
1986 Technical Corrections Blue Book: Explanation of Technical Corrections to the
Tax Reform Act of 1984 and Other Recent Tax Legislation .......... 447

Appendix L
TEFRA Blue Book: General Explanation of the Revenue Provisions of the Tax Equity and
Fiscal Responsibility Act of 1982 .............................................. 457

Appendix M
104th Congress Blue Book: General Explanation of Tax Legislation Enacted in the 104th
Congress ................................................................................ 471

# Index 489

# FOREWORD

Messrs. Adney, King and Springfield have done a masterful job in taking a complex and arcane subject and boiling it down into bite-sized chunks to make it comprehensible.

The subject of qualification of a life insurance contract under Internal Revenue Code section 7702 is vitally important to the life insurance industry. First, there are the requirements to design a policy so that it does not run afoul of the life insurance qualification requirements from the start. Further, the administrative requirements to keep it qualified—through both the normal course of the policy over the years, let alone through policyholder-initiated changes—are complex but must be followed in order to continue to enjoy the tax advantages of a life insurance contract. The consequences of failure can involve not only the policyholder but also the company's reputation, the regulators and agents, and can be costly to remedy. Indeed, there have been events where a portfolio of failed contracts has caused pending company acquisitions to go off the rails.

The additional subject of Modified Endowment Contracts (MECs), contracts that qualify under section 7702 but contain onerous tax rules on non-death distributions, is easily as complex, and many companies have experienced the consequences of inadvertently creating MECs by not complying with the rules of Code section 7702A. Similarly to the section 7702 environment, a MEC can be created either by poor policy design or by faulty administrative practices, and the remediation process can involve the company, regulators and agents in a similarly costly process.

The requirements under these two Code sections are not only complex but involve disparate sources of guidance above and beyond the Code (legislative history, notices, rulings, etc.). This book is unique in that it pulls those disparate sources together in one relatively compact book to create complete explanations of the concepts.

The chapters have been designed so that the inexperienced reader can get a general understanding of the concepts while the experienced practitioner can find relatively complete discussions of the complex technical issues and rigorous reference citations to support statements and positions.

There was one other co-author in addition to the above three: Chris DesRochers. Chris was the foremost actuarial authority in the 1984 formation of section 7702 and its later interpretative phases. Later on, he served in a similar interpretive role for section 7702A. Before he passed away in 2013 he was heavily involved in the writing of the original drafts of the chapters of this book. We will dearly miss him and his substantial contributions to professional knowledge.

Edward L. Robbins, FSA, MAAA

# PREFACE

## Introduction

This textbook addresses issues surrounding the federal income tax treatment of life insurance contracts in the United States. It describes in great detail the statutory definition of "life insurance contract" found in section 7702 of the Internal Revenue Code as its precursor, section 101(f), as well as the "modified endowment contract" rules of section 7702A. Although these definitional limitations on life insurance contracts have existed in the Code for more than a quarter of a century—33 years in the case of section 101(f)—no textbooks other than this one and its 2004 predecessor have focused on them. We hope this book will provide guidance to those who must deal with the day-to-day tax compliance problems faced by life insurers and also serve as an introduction to students new to the subject. (That said, we would advise our readers to consult a qualified tax advisor on matters of statutory interpretation.)

This text is intended, in particular, to provide sufficient background and historical information so that those charged with the compliance of life insurance products with the tax law will have an appreciation of the context in which the Code's definitional limitations were developed. This background includes the historical precedents that led up to the enactment of the definitional limitations as well as the tensions that exist between the current tax treatment of life insurance and the views of some that life insurance is imbued with a tax benefit, or a tax preference, when compared to the treatment of other financial instruments. Moreover, many of the changes that have been made to the tax treatment of life insurance over the years, including adoption of the definitional limitations, were made in response to the introduction of new products. In this respect, it is important for the reader to appreciate that Congress and the courts have periodically been called upon to engage in what could be characterized as line drawing in reaction to life insurance products that were seen as straying over the tax policy line separating life insurance from other financial instruments.

As documented in Chapter 9, life insurance and the federal income tax have been connected since the first income tax was imposed in the United States to finance the Civil War. The tax treatment of life insurance contracts was debated during the enactment of the modern income tax in 1913, and the current tax treatment (including deferral of tax on the increase in cash values and the receipt of death benefits free of income tax to the beneficiary) is largely unchanged from that provided under the Revenue Act of 1913. In more recent years, sections 7702 and 7702A were added to the Internal Revenue Code to impose a comprehensive limitation on the investment orientation of contracts that qualify as life insurance for federal income tax purposes. These provisions seek to do so by controlling, through the limitation of actuarial assumptions, the relationship of death benefits and cash surrender values within a life insurance contract. To this end, the guideline premium test (GPT) and the cash value accumulation test (CVAT) were added to the Code, first in 1982 and then, on a permanent basis, in 1984. In 1988, the modified endowment contract (MEC) rules and further restrictions on the actuarial assumptions under section 7702 were added. It is important to note these definitional limitations were intended to provide certainty in the tax treatment of many of the new life insurance products then entering the market.

## Audience

This text was written by two actuaries, the late Chris DesRochers (see our Dedication page) and Brian King, and two attorneys, John Adney and Craig Springfield. It reflects the actuarial theory, tax law and policy, and political compromise underlying the statutory limitations. Thus, its content is neither purely actuarial nor purely legal, but combines elements of both. While attorneys with tax compliance responsibilities rely on statutes, legislative history and written determinations of the Internal Revenue Service, the actuarial materials provide necessary contextual background. Thus, formulas and sample calculations are provided, as well as extensive legal analysis and citations. In this respect, the text parallels the statutes under discussion, which contain significant actuarial elements. We have endeavored to balance the actuarial and legal content so that both attorneys and actuaries, as well as others who have compliance responsibilities with respect to sections 7702 and 7702A, will find the text a useful resource. At the very least, the authors expect to cure the insomnia of both the legal and actuarial audiences.

This second edition of the text looks rather different from the first because of an attempted improvement that its student readers may appreciate. Namely, an introduction to the entirety of the definitional limitations (well, most of it) is now encompassed in the first two chapters. Unfortunately, those charged with tax compliance responsibility in insurance companies and their supporting firms must read on.

## Organization

As just noted, Chapters 1 and 2 present a fairly comprehensive introduction to the definitional limitations, documenting the development of the limitations in response to the emergence of universal life and similar products and providing an exposition of the statutory requirements; those seeking an introduction to sections 7702 and 7702A can find it in these two chapters. More specifically, following an overview of and background on the subject in Chapter 1, Chapter 2 catalogues most of the requirements for a contract to be treated as life insurance under the Internal Revenue Code, introducing the CVAT, the GPT and the section 7702A 7-pay test. In doing so, Chapter 2 addresses many of the features of the definitional limitations and describes the key concepts underlying them, including the fact that the limitations are actuarial in nature, based on the net premium required to fund the contractual benefits. In addition, Chapter 2 discusses actuarial methods that can be used in computing the values which underlie the definitional limitations.

While chapters 1 and 2 provide a basic but relatively detailed discussion of the definitional limitations, Chapter 3 fills in other fundamental information that is perhaps of more interest to practitioners than to students. This information spans the evolving definition of "cash surrender value" under section 7702, the direction provided by the sole regulation under the statute for determining an insured's age, and the limitations imposed and opportunities presented by the statute's primary and alternate computational rules. Also discussed in Chapter 3 are considerations in performing post-age-100 and substandard mortality calculations and the rules for reflecting "qualified additional benefits" in the statutory premium limits.

Next, the sometime mysteries of the "adjustment" rules of the statutes and of the Code's general material change rules as they may apply to life insurance contracts are the focus, respectively, of Chapters 4 and 5. Chapter 4 describes the manner in which section 7702's adjustment provisions apply under the CVAT and apply differently under the GPT, and it also lays out the reduction-in-benefit and material change rules of section 7702A, providing illustrations of their application that are updated from those in the book's first edition. New in this chapter is an expanded discussion of the "necessary premium" test embedded in section 7702A(c)(3), a challenging concept that has been the focus of insurers' programming efforts in recent years. Chapter 5, also containing much new discussion, undertakes a highly detailed treatment of the concept of a material change in the broadest sense of the tax law, examining a set of authorities that, where applicable, can significantly disrupt insurers' efforts to comply with the definitional limitations by forfeiting "grandfathering" of pre-existing rules. In addressing post-issue changes in contracts, these two chapters detail the source of much of the complexity in implementing the limitations.

Chapter 6 in this book's first edition described the manner in which sections 7702 and 7702A apply to special products and special features of products, including variable life products and multiple life plans. Chapter 6 of the second edition continues this description and elaborates on these topics, providing new discussions of guaranteed minimum withdrawal benefits, equity-indexed contracts and no-lapse guarantees along with enhanced discussion of cash value bonuses, return-of-premium benefits and preneed contracts.

A completely new chapter, Chapter 7, introduces a robust treatment of "accelerated death benefits," covering qualified long-term care insurance riders subject to the section 7702B rules and chronic and terminal illness riders governed by section 101(g). This is followed by the completely revamped chapter on the remediation of contracts that do not comply with the definitional limitations, Chapter 8. The series of revenue procedures the Internal Revenue Service issued in 2008 that revolutionized contract remediation are presented in detail in this chapter.

The new edition's two concluding chapters carry forward, with updating, the messages of the first edition's final chapters, describing the history and tax policy relative to the definitional limitations. Chapter 9 documents four key developments that have helped shape these limitations:

- The emergence of a "savings element" in life insurance through the introduction of cash surrender values in the early 20th century

- The development of an "economic" definition of life insurance through case law in the 1940s

- The evolution of the Code's various limitations on financed life insurance

- The development of new life insurance products during the product revolution that began in the late 1970s

Chapter 10 presents the policy issues related to the taxation of life insurance and documents the relationship of the definitional limitations to the requirements of the standard nonforfeiture law for life insurance. This chapter makes the point that the "inside buildup," the interest credited to the cash value of permanent life insurance, is seen as properly tax-deferred so long as it is needed to fund a contract's future benefits. Thus, while Chapters 1–8 address the "hows" of compliance with the definitional limitations, Chapters 9 and 10 address the "whys."

Finally, the textbook concludes with a glossary of terms and a series of appendices containing reprints of the statutes themselves and the legislative history that has been key to their interpretation. In this connection, the reader will see that certain terms in this book appear in **bold type**. These are significant terms, the definitions of which appear in the book's Glossary or in the text itself.

## Interpretations and Reliance

Tax law is a dynamic area, and interpretations are subject to change. The discussions found in this text are based solely on the views of the authors and the state of the tax law related to the definitional limitations as we currently find it. In writing the text, we were surprised as to how close our individual views were on many subjects. We do not expect that every reader will agree with all of our interpretations, however. Where there is uncertainty, which is not in short supply, we have attempted to present a fair and balanced picture.

JOHN T. ADNEY, ESQ.
BRIAN G. KING, FSA, MAAA
CRAIG R. SPRINGFIELD, ESQ.

JUNE 2015

# ACKNOWLEDGEMENTS

*If you steal from one author, it's plagiarism;
if you steal from many, it's research.*
Wilson Mizner (1876–1933)

As was true of this textbook's first edition, there are a great many people to thank for their contributions to the writing of this second edition of *Life Insurance & Modified Endowments Under Internal Revenue Code Sections 7702 and 7702A*. In the spirit of Wilson Mizner, we have quoted everyone from Yogi Berra to Elizur Wright. It is a tribute to all those who have contributed to the tax treatment of life insurance that we can take two sections of the Internal Revenue Code and write a textbook. Or, as one of our colleagues commented, "That's a big book for such a small section of the Code."

In some ways, the history of this text goes back to the experiences of two of the authors with the development of the definitional limitations in the late 1970s, when universal life insurance was in its infancy. More recently, the text's history can be traced to discussions among the authors of the need to assemble and interpret the official and semiofficial materials available with respect to the limitations. Perhaps it was fitting that the initial discussions leading to the book's first edition followed a Society of Actuaries seminar at Disney World in late 2002. After a nice bottle of wine, the idea for the book was born. A decade later, the Society of Actuaries asked us for an update, prompting the major revision of the text that constitutes this second edition.

We must first acknowledge the contributions of our spouses, Sue Adney, Amber King and Kathy Springfield, along with Carolyn DesRochers, the spouse of our late co-author, who put up with this nonsense in the first place. Then, we must acknowledge the many reviewers who provided useful input to the process. First among these is Daniel Stringham, tax counsel at the Prudential Insurance Co. of America, who (with Barbara Gold, the former chief tax actuary at Prudential) served as a lead reviewer of the first edition and continued in that role for this one. Accompanying Dan in this work were Mitzi Brandon, Lynne Gandy, Jeremy Goodwin, Christopher Malfara and Julie Terranova, all of Prudential's Corporate Tax Group. Larry Hirsch of Pacific Life provided thorough comments on the newest chapter of the book, Chapter 7 (long-term care and accelerated death benefits). Also, as the revision of the original text was still in contemplation, Sue Schechter and the actuarial and legal staffs at MassMutual provided valuable input. In addition to these individuals, we would like to thank the Society of Actuaries, the SOA's publications manager, Karen Perry, and Jennifer Hull, who served as the editor for this second edition.

A great deal of support was provided at our respective firms: Ernst & Young LLP and Davis & Harman LLP. Reviewers at EY included Ed Robbins (who also graciously wrote the foreword for the second edition), Kristin Norberg, Kennedy Kilale and Giedre Delgado, and work that Mark Biglow performed on the first edition still survives. A number of people at Davis & Harman contributed substantially to the writing: Daniela Stoia, who reviewed the thoroughly revised chapter on contract remediation (Chapter 8); Janis McClintock, who tracked down aging and elusive congressional materials and citations; Bryan Keene, who provided *inter alia* the innovative citation to a quotation on a baseball; and the late William B. Harman Jr., who was there from the very beginning of the definitional limitations and wrote the foreword for the first edition.

Finally, we would be remiss if we did not acknowledge Douglas N. Hertz, co-author of the book's first edition, whose strong substantive contributions and sense of humor permeated that edition and continue in the new one. Still others who provided input to the text's foundation included Tom Herget as well as Jim Hickman, whose idea it was to create the flowchart in Chapter 1.

It is with deep gratitude that we acknowledge all of the foregoing, although as the book's authors, we accept full responsibility for the entirety of the writing and for any and all errors that may appear therein. The responsibility for the provisions of the Internal Revenue Code, however, must rest solely with the Congress of the United States.

# ABOUT THE AUTHORS

*Christian J. DesRochers, FSA, MAAA*

At his untimely death in the fall of 2013, Chris DesRochers was an executive director with the Insurance and Actuarial Advisory Services practice of Ernst & Young LLP's Financial Services Office. He provided consulting assistance to the life insurance industry, specializing in taxation matters related to life insurance products, life insurance and annuity product development, as well as the financial analysis of life insurance companies, including mergers and acquisitions, special ventures and rehabilitations. Other areas of expertise included expert witness assignments related to a variety of life insurance company and product taxation issues, including cases involving the deduction of policy loan interest by corporate policyholders.

Prior to joining Ernst & Young LLP in 2011, Mr. DesRochers was employed as senior managing director with Smart Business Advisory and Consulting LLP, which merged with LECG in 2010. Before joining Smart, he was a partner of Avon Consulting Group LLP, a life actuarial consulting firm started in 1993 and acquired by Aon in 2001. Prior to this, Mr. DesRochers served as director of the Consulting Division of Chalke Inc., where he managed consulting operations, including a team of financial and actuarial consultants.

Mr. DesRochers served on numerous committees of the Society of Actuaries, including the Board of Governors, holding the office of secretary/treasurer. He chaired the Taxation, Life Insurance and Annuity Product Development, and Smaller Life Insurance Company sections of the Society of Actuaries, and was a frequent speaker at seminars and conferences. Mr. DesRochers authored numerous articles and papers, including "The Definition of Life Insurance Under Section 7702 of the Internal Revenue Code," *Society of Actuaries' Transactions* (1988), and was a contributing author to the *Annuities Answer Book* (4th ed. 2005).

A graduate of the University of Connecticut with a Bachelor of Arts degree, Mr. DesRochers is a fellow of the Society of Actuaries and a member of the American Academy of Actuaries.

Mr. DesRochers was lead author of the first edition of the Society of Actuaries' textbook *Life Insurance & Modified Endowments Under Internal Revenue Code Sections 7702 and 7702A*.

*John T. Adney, Esq.*

John T. Adney is a partner in the law firm of Davis & Harman LLP, practicing primarily in the areas of taxation and insurance law. Mr. Adney received his B.A. summa cum laude from Millikin University in 1972 and his J.D. from Yale Law School in 1975. He served as a law clerk for the Trial Division of the U.S. Court of Claims in 1975–76 and clerked for Judge Marion T. Bennett of the U.S. Court of Claims in 1976–77. From 1977 to 1985, Mr. Adney was an associate and then a partner in the Washington office of Sutherland, Asbill & Brennan. In 1985, he helped organize Davis & Harman, serving as the firm's first managing partner.

Since 1977, Mr. Adney has engaged in an insurance product taxation advisory, ruling and regulatory practice, covering universal life insurance, variable life insurance, group-term life insurance, corporate-owned life insurance, fixed and variable annuities, and long-term care insurance. During the same period, he engaged in extensive advisory and ruling work relating to insurance company taxation. In addition, since 1981, Mr. Adney has been involved in legislative representation of insurance companies on tax matters relating to the companies and their products, including the enactment or revision of Internal Revenue Code sections 72, 101(f), 101(g), 101(j), 801–18, 832, 846, 848, 1035, 7702, 7702A and 7702B.

Mr. Adney is a member of the bars of the District of Columbia and the U.S. Supreme Court. He is a member of the American Bar Association and its Section of Taxation, is past chair of the Section's Committee on Insurance Companies, is a member of the Association of Life Insurance Counsel, and currently serves as a member of the Council of the Taxation Section of the Society of Actuaries. Mr. Adney is co-editor of the *Annuities Answer Book* (4th ed. 2005) and is co-author of the chapters titled "Using Life Insurance in Executive Compensation" in *Executive Compensation* (2011) and "The Tax Treatment of Variable Contracts" in *Variable Annuities & Variable Life Insurance Regulation* (2015). He also has authored a number of articles on the taxation of insurance companies and products, serves on the editorial board of the *Taxing Times* newsletter of the Society of Actuaries' Taxation Section, and is an associate editor of the *Journal of Financial Services Professional*s. Mr. Adney has been a frequent speaker at programs of the Insurance Tax Conference, the Society of Actuaries and the American Bar Association. He is chair emeritus of the Board of Trustees of Millikin University.

Mr. Adney was a co-author of the first edition of the Society of Actuaries' textbook *Life Insurance & Modified Endowments Under Internal Revenue Code Sections 7702 and 7702A*.

### *Brian G. King, FSA, MAAA*

Brian King is an executive director with the Insurance and Actuarial Advisory Services practice of Ernst & Young LLP's Financial Services Office. He provides consulting assistance to the insurance industry, with extensive experience in the federal income taxation of life insurance companies and products, including compliance under Internal Revenue Code sections 72, 101, 7702 and 7702A. He has extensive experience with the design and development of life insurance and annuity products, as well as the administrative requirements for maintaining compliance with sections 7702 and 7702A. He has assisted numerous companies with the remediation of failed life insurance contracts and inadvertent modified endowment contracts under IRS Rev. Procs. 2008-39 and 2008-40 and their predecessor correction programs.

Prior to joining Ernst & Young LLP in 2011, Mr. King was employed as managing director with Smart Business Advisory and Consulting LLP, which merged with LECG in 2010. Before joining Smart, Mr. King was a consulting actuary with Avon Consulting Group LLP, which was acquired by Aon in 2001. Prior to this, he was with The Travelers Insurance Cos., where as an actuarial student he held various positions in several departments.

Mr. King has authored numerous articles on life insurance taxation issues and is a frequent speaker at industry seminars and conferences, including meetings of the Society of Actuaries and various regional actuarial clubs. He is a previous council member of the Society of Actuaries' Taxation Section and is currently serving on the editorial board of its newsletter *Taxing Times*.

An honors graduate of the University of Connecticut, with a Bachelor of Science degree in mathematics, Mr. King is a fellow of the Society of Actuaries and a member of the American Academy of Actuaries.

Mr. King was a co-author of the first edition of the Society of Actuaries' textbook *Life Insurance & Modified Endowments Under Internal Revenue Code Sections 7702 and 7702A*.

## *Craig R. Springfield, Esq.*

Craig R. Springfield is a partner with Davis & Harman LLP, practicing primarily in the areas of taxation and insurance law. His practice covers annuity, life insurance and long-term care insurance product taxation as well as tax issues associated with variable insurance products. Mr. Springfield works extensively before the National Office of the Internal Revenue Service and the Department of the Treasury to address tax compliance-related issues, including under sections 72, 101, 1035, 7702, 7702A and 7702B, and under Subchapter L of the Internal Revenue Code. He has worked on Affordable Care Act implementation and related health insurance issues and on various legislative matters, e.g., the tax treatment of combination insurance products and the Medicaid rules governing qualified state long-term care insurance partnerships.

A native of Florida, Mr. Springfield received his BSBA, magna cum laude, and M.S. in accounting from the University of Central Florida. In 1990, he earned his J.D., with honors, from the University of Florida, and in 1991 he received an LL.M. in Taxation from New York University.

Mr. Springfield is a frequent speaker and author. Articles he has co-authored include: "They Go Bump in the Night: Life Insurance Policies and the Law of Material Change," *Taxing Times* supplement (May 2012); "A Mystery Partially Unveiled: The IRS Rules on Section 7702A's Necessary Premium Test," *Taxing Times* (February 2012); "The CLASS Act: What Does it Mean for Private Long-Term Care Insurance," *Journal of Financial Service Professionals* (September 2010); "New Closing Agreement Procedure for Failed Life Insurance Contracts – Rev. Proc. 2008-40," *Taxing Times* (February 2009); "Private Rulings Regarding 'Cash Surrender Value' Under Section 7702," *Taxing Times* (September 2006); "Determining Guideline Premiums for Fixed-Premium Universal Life Insurance Contracts," *Taxing Times* (December 2005); and "The New Tax Rules Governing Long-Term Care Insurance," *Journal of the American Society of CLU and ChFC* (September 1997, November 1997 and January 1998).

Mr. Springfield is a member of the District of Columbia Bar. He also is a member of the American Bar Association's Section of Taxation and is a past chair of the section's Committee on Insurance Companies. He also has previously served as managing partner of Davis & Harman LLP.

# LIST OF FIGURES AND TABLES

## Figures

| | | |
|---|---|---:|
| 1.1 | Qualification under IRC 7702 and 7702A | 7 |
| 2.1 | CVAT limitations: net single premium; $1,000 death benefit | 24 |
| 2.2 | Guideline premium limitation per $1,000 of death benefit | 26 |
| 2.3 | Minimum death benefit per $1 of CSV | 29 |
| 3.1 | QAB example 1: cash surrender value | 87 |
| 3.2 | Cash value per $1,000 of face amount, option 1 death benefit | 95 |
| 3.3 | Cash value per $1,000 of face amount, option 2 death benefit | 96 |
| 4.1 | Guideline premium limitation | 110 |
| 4.2 | Decrease in face amount: attained-age decrement | 119 |
| 6.1 | $936.33 fixed annual premium | 188 |
| 6.2 | $800 fixed annual premium | 189 |
| 6.3 | $900 fixed annual premium | 190 |
| 10.1 | Selected interest rates 1982–2014 | 330 |
| 10.2 | CVAT maximum and nonforfeiture minimum values | 331 |

## Tables

| | | |
|---|---|---:|
| 1.1 | Summary of taxation of distributions under IRC section 72 | 15 |
| 1.2 | Taxation of a policy loan to pay premiums: non-MEC | 16 |
| 1.3 | Taxation of a policy loan to pay premiums: MEC | 16 |
| 2.1 | NSP per $1,000 | 25 |
| 2.2 | Guideline premium limitation per $1,000 | 28 |
| 2.3 | Section 7702(d) corridor factors | 28 |
| 2.4 | Seven-pay limitation per $1,000 of death benefit | 36 |
| 2.5 | Premiums for a male age 45 | 37 |
| 2.6 | Comparison of mortality assumptions, 2001 CSO male aggregate | 48 |
| 2.7 | Basic at-issue calculations, male age 45 | 57 |
| 2.8 | Processing for various claims payment assumptions | 64 |
| 2.9 | Male age 45, $100,000 face amount, 2001 CSO ANB, endowment at age 100 | 64 |
| 2.10 | Male age 45, $100,000 face amount, 1980 CSO aggregate, ANB, endowment at age 100 | 65 |
| 3.1 | Universal life options 1 and 2 premium limitations | 80 |
| 3.2 | TEFRA Blue Book option 2 example | 82 |
| 3.3 | Sections 7702 and 7702A computational rules | 84 |
| 3.4 | Reflecting QABs in the guideline level premium, QAB example 2 | 88 |
| 3.5 | Standard premiums, male age 45 whole life, Table D (100%) | 98 |
| 4.1 | Guideline premium examples, TEFRA Blue Book, male age 35 | 107 |
| 4.2 | $100,000 on-anniversary increase at age 50 | 115 |
| 4.3 | Effect of off-anniversary increase in the sum of the guideline level premiums | 116 |
| 4.4 | $50,000 decrease at age 70 | 118 |
| 4.5 | Reduction in benefits under section 7702A | 123 |
| 4.6 | Section 7702A rollover calculation | 129 |
| 4.7 | CVAT necessary premium example | 136 |
| 4.8 | Sections 7702 and 7702A adjustment rules | 137 |
| 4.9 | Death benefit option change: option 1 to option 2 | 140 |
| 4.10 | Option change at 50, constant specified amount | 140 |

| | | |
|---|---|---:|
| 4.11 | Option change at 50, constant net amount at risk | 141 |
| 4.12 | Death benefit option change: option 2 to option 1 | 143 |
| 4.13 | Option change at 50, constant specified amount | 143 |
| 4.14 | Option change at 50, constant net amount at risk | 144 |
| 4.15 | Rev. Rul. 2003-95, assumptions | 147 |
| 4.16 | Rev. Rul. 2003-95, Situation 1: CVAT 4 years after issue | 148 |
| 4.17 | Rev. Rul. 2003-95, Situation 2: guideline 4 years after issue | 148 |
| 4.18 | Rev. Rul. 2003-95, Situation 3: 4 years after issue | 149 |
| 5.1 | Life insurance contract rule and assumption eras | 169 |
| 6.1 | Single and multi-life NSPs | 182 |
| 6.2 | Example 2 guaranteed assumptions under footnote 53 | 189 |
| 6.3 | Example 3 guaranteed assumptions under footnote 53 | 190 |
| 6.4 | Implicit interest rates under gross-up rule | 194 |
| 7.1 | Indexed eligible long-term care premiums | 214 |
| 7.2 | Comparison of QLTCI riders and section 101(g) riders | 245 |
| 8.1 | Sample section 7702(g) income on the contract calculation | 264 |
| 8.2 | Toll charges under Rev. Rul. 2005-6 | 278 |
| 8.3 | Earnings rates to be used to calculate either excess earnings or overage earnings | 290 |
| 8.4 | Sample calculations of overage earnings, Rev. Proc. 2008-39 closing agreement | 291 |
| 9.1 | Le Gierse contract values | 304 |
| 9.2 | Financed insurance economics | 307 |
| 10.1 | Maximum nonforfeiture interest rates | 330 |
| 10.2 | Comparison of nonforfeiture minimum and section 7702 maximum requirements | 332 |
| 10.3 | Pretax equivalent rates of return | 334 |

# Chapter 1

# INTRODUCTION

## In the Beginning …

This chapter presents a broad overview of the federal income tax treatment of the owners and beneficiaries of **life insurance** contracts. The chapter begins with a brief discussion of the tax treatment of death benefits and lifetime distributions from such contracts, e.g., full and partial surrenders and policy loans. The chapter then describes the development and structure of the federal tax law's definition of life insurance found in section 7702[1] and in the earlier temporary provisions of section 101(f) and introduces the **modified endowment contract (MEC)** rules of section 7702A. The chapter includes an overview of other rules in the Code pertaining to life insurance and a detailed discussion of the foundational rule for the application of sections 7702 and 7702A, i.e., the "applicable law" rule appearing at the beginning of section 7702(a). This chapter concludes with two appendices: the first provides additional information on the Code's life insurance rules other than those of sections 7702 and 7702A, and the second explains the significance of the various tax authorities cited throughout the book.

The in-depth discussion of these statutes begins in Chapter 2, which addresses the requirements for qualification as a life insurance contract and the rules for classification of a contract as a modified endowment contract. Chapter 2 describes the key concepts underlying these requirements (referred to as the "definitional limitations"), and this continues in Chapter 3, which sets out more specifics on calculation procedures (the "definitional calculations") and related issues under the statutes. Chapters 4 and 5 then provide detail on the treatment of contractual changes under the statutes, followed by discussions of product-specific issues in Chapter 6 and the tax rules governing accelerated death benefits in Chapter 7. The remediation of noncompliance with sections 7702 and 7702A (and section 101(f) before them) is the subject of Chapter 8, after which the book concludes with a brief history of life insurance taxation (Chapter 9) and a discussion of the federal income tax policy behind the statutes and the related tax rules governing the uses of life insurance (Chapter 10). The book's appendices include reprints of the statutes, their legislative histories and certain other official materials.

## Income Tax Treatment of Life Insurance Contracts

For as long as there has been an income tax in the United States (see Chapter 9), life insurance death benefits paid to the beneficiary generally have been free of federal income tax. Also, absent a distribution while the insured is alive, the increments in the cash surrender value of permanent life insurance contracts—such as whole life, universal life and variable life—due to the crediting of interest, earnings and policyholder **dividends** generally have not been currently includible in the gross income of policyholders for federal tax purposes. This treatment is called the tax-deferred inside buildup, or simply the **inside buildup**. Today, sections 7702 and 7702A define the actuarially based limitations that, if complied with, serve as the gateway for a life insurance contract to receive the tax treatment just referenced. This is described further below. The computation of these limitations is the subject of much of what follows in this book.

Even apart from sections 7702 and 7702A, the federal income tax treatment associated with life insurance contracts is not without complexity. Immediately following is a list of some of the Code's rules specific to life insurance (apart from its use in the employment context, including qualified retirement plans), assuming a contract's compliance with section 7702; additional detail appears in Appendix 1.1.

---

[1] Unless otherwise indicated, references in this book to "section" are to the provisions of the Internal Revenue Code of 1986, as amended (also referred to as "IRC" or the "Code").

## Death Benefits

**Death benefit exclusion, section 101(a)(1):** Proceeds from a life insurance contract payable on the death of the insured are generally excludable from the gross income of the beneficiary.

**Transfer for value rule, section 101(a)(2):** The exclusion of the death benefit proceeds from gross income is denied in the case of a contract's "transfer for value," such as a sale, subject to stated exceptions.

**Payout of death benefit over time, section 101(d):** Death benefit proceeds received in the form of an annuity are prorated between excludable and includible components.

**Accelerated death benefits, sections 101(g) and 7702B(e):** Death benefits paid from a life insurance contract prior to the death of a "terminally ill" or "chronically ill" insured generally are excludable from gross income, subject to certain qualification requirements and consumer protections. These rules are discussed in detail in Chapter 7.

**Employer-owned life insurance, section 101(j):** The full death benefit exclusion is denied to an employer who receives death benefit proceeds from a contract on the life of an employee unless there is compliance with special rules that limit coverage to certain classes of employees and impose employee notice and consent requirements.

## Inside Buildup and Lifetime Distributions

**Inside buildup:** As noted above, as a general rule, the increments in the cash surrender value of permanent life insurance contracts due to the crediting of interest, earnings and dividends that remain inside the contracts—again, the inside buildup—are not currently includible in the gross income of policyholders for federal tax purposes. Moreover, these increments are permanently excluded from income when paid out as part of an otherwise excludable death benefit.

**Lifetime distributions, sections 72(e) and 7702A:** Distributions from a life insurance contract prior to the death of the insured (lifetime distributions) may be includible in gross income, depending on the gain in the contract (generally the cash value in excess of the investment in the contract) and whether it is classified as a MEC—a highly investment-oriented contract as defined in section 7702A—or not (i.e., a non-MEC).

- **In the case of a MEC,** lifetime distributions—**partial withdrawals**, full surrenders, **policy loans**, assignments or pledges to secure borrowing, and dividends received by the policyholder (e.g., paid in cash or applied to pay off a loan)—are includible in gross income to the extent of gain in the contract, and may be subjected to a 10 percent **penalty tax**. Also, certain MECs are aggregated, i.e., treated as a single contract, in determining the amount of the gain received in a distribution.

- **In the case of a non-MEC,** in contrast, lifetime distributions generally are subject to a more favorable income tax regime, e.g., a partial withdrawal generally is includible in gross income only to the extent it exceeds the investment in the contract; policy loans, assignments and pledges generally are not treated as distributions; and no 10 percent penalty tax applies.

## Other Rules

**Premium and interest deduction limits, sections 163, 263, and 264(a) and (f):** Premiums paid for life insurance and interest paid or accrued on policy loans are generally not deductible by individuals. A business policyholder typically cannot deduct premiums if it can benefit from the contract, cannot deduct policy loan interest except in limited circumstances and may lose other interest deductions simply by holding a contract.

**Contract exchanges, section 1035:** The exchange of an existing life insurance contract for a new life insurance contract, an annuity or a qualified long-term care insurance contract may be accomplished tax-free.

**Contract sales and gifts, section 1001:** The sale of a life insurance contract is taxable to the policyholder to the extent of the gain in the contract. The gift of a contract, on the other hand, does not trigger income tax for either the donor or the donee.

**Deduction of loss on surrender or sale, section 165:** A policyholder generally cannot deduct a loss incurred on the surrender or sale of a contract.

**Variable contracts, section 817(h) and investor control:** A variable contract will lose the benefit of inside buildup tax deferral or exemption if the separate account investments underlying it are not "adequately diversified" as required by tax regulations or if the policyholder is considered to exercise excessive control over such investments.

## Life Insurance Defined

Until 1982, no statutory rule defined the characteristics of contracts that constituted life insurance for most federal tax purposes.[2] Rather, recognition as life insurance generally was based on the contractual form of the coverage provided. As the sole exception in the Code, the term "life insurance contract" was defined in section 1035, but only for purposes of applying the tax-free exchange rules of that provision. A brief, general reference to life insurance also existed under Treasury regulations,[3] but this served mainly to clarify that death benefits having the character of life insurance proceeds paid under worker's compensation contracts, endowment contracts, and accident and health insurance contracts are covered by the section 101(a)(1) death benefit exclusion. However, beginning in the early 1980s and motivated by the development of a new generation of life insurance products including universal life, Congress adopted temporary definitional rules of limited scope in section 101(f); it followed this with the enactment of section 7702, adding a formal definition of life insurance to the Code. Before that time, the determination of what was a life insurance contract for federal income tax purposes was based on common law rules, i.e., those established by judicial precedent.

### Common Law Rules

Early case law definitions of life insurance focused on the contractual form of the death benefits provided and the presence of an **insurable interest**.[4] The baseline definition of a life insurance contract under federal law was a contractual one—life insurance was an agreement to pay a certain sum of money upon the death of the insured in consideration of the payment of premiums.[5]

Beginning in the early 1940s, an actuarial or economic definition of life insurance emerged for federal tax purposes, focusing on the shifting and distribution of risk. The landmark case of *Helvering v. Le Gierse*[6] (and similar cases) presented the courts with a choice of continuing the contract-based definition for commercial insurance contracts or supplementing that definition by applying an actuarial or economic analysis in matters related to the federal tax treatment of life insurance. Ultimately, in the *Le Gierse* case, the Supreme Court chose to apply an economic approach, ruling that the simultaneous purchase of a single premium life insurance contract and a nonrefund life annuity from the same insurer had eliminated any meaningful risk undertaking on the part of the insurer. Thus, the contract under the arrangement was not eligible for tax treatment as life insurance. *Le Gierse* established the principle that although a contract (or a combination of contracts) is in the form of a standard commercial life insurance contract, it is not treated as a life insurance contract for purposes of federal tax law unless it provides for risk shifting and risk distributing (or pooling). Essentially, the court took these as descriptive of the essential characteristics of insurance. One court explained the concept as follows:

> Risk shifting emphasizes the individual aspect of insurance: the effecting of a contract between the insurer and the insured each of whom gamble on the time the latter will die. Risk distribution, on the other hand, emphasizes the broader, social aspect of insurance as a method of dispelling the danger of the potential loss by spreading its cost throughout the group.[7]

---

[2] No general statutory definition of life insurance exists for contracts issued prior to January 1, 1985. However, pre-January 1, 1985, "flexible premium contracts" qualify for the IRC § 101(a)(1) death benefit exclusion only if the statutory requirements of IRC § 101(f) are met.
[3] Treas. Reg. § 1.101-1(a)(1).
[4] *See, e.g., United States v. Supplee-Biddle Hardware Co.*, 265 U.S. 189 (1924), *aff'g* 58 Ct. Cl. 343 (1923).
[5] *Central Bank of Washington v. Hume*, 128 U.S. 195, 209 (1888).
[6] 312 U.S. 531 (1941).
[7] *Comm'r v. Treganowan*, 183 F.2d 288, 291 (2d Cir. 1950) [citing *The New York Stock Exchange Gratuity Fund: Insurance That Isn't Insurance*, 59 YALE L.J. 780, 784 (1950)], *cert. denied sub nom. Strauss's Estate v. Comm'r*, 340 U.S. 853 (1950).

The object of the simultaneous purchase of a single premium life insurance contract and a nonrefund life annuity was to provide an otherwise uninsurable client the use of an exemption (since repealed) for up to $40,000 of life insurance death benefits from the federal estate tax. While *Le Gierse* and related cases established an economic standard for a contract to be defined as life insurance for federal tax purposes, requiring the presence of insurance risk, the cases did not endeavor to quantify either the amount of risk needed or the period over which it was necessary for the risk to exist for a contract to be accorded life insurance tax treatment. However, these cases marked a first step on the path to a modern tax definition of a life insurance contract. The *Le Gierse* case is discussed further in Chapter 9.

## *TEFRA: Section 101(f)*

**Section 101(f)**, enacted by the Tax Equity and Fiscal Responsibility Act of 1982 (TEFRA),[8] provided the first statutory definition of life insurance for federal income tax purposes, albeit only for a limited period and for a class of contracts referred to as flexible premium life insurance contracts.[9] A flexible premium contract was defined in the statute as a contract under which one or more premium payments were not fixed by the insurer as to both timing and amount. By imposing maximum premium and minimum risk limitations, section 101(f) sought to deny life insurance tax treatment to flexible premium life insurance contracts used primarily for investment purposes (i.e., contracts that had large cash values in relation to the death benefit), while providing a degree of certainty in the tax treatment of flexible premium contracts issued before January 1, 1984 (later extended to January 1, 1985). Section 101(f) was expressly made temporary in that it applied only to contracts issued prior to the specified date; thus the provision was limited in its application pending a more permanent and comprehensive solution. However, section 101(f) confirmed the treatment of universal life as life insurance for federal income tax purposes—the death benefit was excluded from the beneficiary's income and the inside buildup was not currently taxed—removing uncertainty resulting from a change in the ruling position of the Internal Revenue Service (IRS). (The events leading to the enactment of section 101(f) are documented in Chapter 9.)

## *DEFRA: Section 7702*

In 1984, Congress enacted **section 7702** as part of the Deficit Reduction Act of 1984 (DEFRA).[10] Section 7702 generally extended to all life insurance contracts issued after December 31, 1984, rules similar (but not identical) to the rules contained in section 101(f).[11] Following the approach used in section 101(f), section 7702 restricts life insurance tax treatment to those contracts that provide at least a specified minimum amount of pure insurance protection (or net amount at risk) in relation to the contract cash value. In this manner, Congress sought to limit the **investment orientation** of all life insurance contracts, allowing life insurance tax treatment only for a contract that, in very general terms, does not have a cash value greater than a comparable single premium, level-face endowment at the insured's age 95. More precisely, section 7702 constrains, by way of alternative actuarial tests, the cash value that may support, or the amount of premiums that may be paid for, the future benefits provided under a life insurance contract. The specifics of these actuarial tests will be the focus of later chapters.

## *Tax Reform Act of 1986*

The Tax Reform Act of 1986 (TRA 1986)[12] was notable in that one element of the Reagan administration's proposal for a broader tax base was to impose current taxation on the inside buildup of life insurance contracts. Although the administration's proposal to tax inside buildup was not adopted by Congress, the act did, indirectly, affect life insurance products. In *Two Decades of Insurance Tax Reform*, William B. Harman Jr. wrote:

---

[8] Pub. L. No. 97-248, § 266(a).
[9] These contracts included flexible premium universal life insurance as well as the adjustable life insurance contracts issued by Minnesota Mutual Life (later Minnesota Life) and Bankers Life of Iowa (later Principal Life).
[10] Pub. L. No. 98-369, § 221(a).
[11] *See* H.R. Rep. No. 98-432, pt. 2, at 1443 (1984) (hereinafter DEFRA House Report); S. Prt. No. 98-169, vol. I, at 572 (1984) (hereinafter DEFRA Senate Report); H.R. Rep. No. 98-861, at 1074-1075 (1984) (Conf. Rep.) (hereinafter DEFRA Conference Report). The DEFRA effective date and transition rules are described in Chapter 5.
[12] Pub. L. No. 99-514.

> The Tax Reform Act of 1986 … was largely premised upon a broadening of the income tax base in return for lower marginal tax rates. This movement towards a broader tax base carried with it, in President Reagan's proposal in May, 1985, an initiative to tax the inside buildup of life insurance contracts.
>
> The 1984 Act [i.e., DEFRA] … had already substantially addressed the issue raised by this proposal, rejecting it in favor of defining what was, and was not, life insurance for tax purposes. The Administration's proposal to tax inside buildup was subsequently dropped for a variety of reasons, not the least of which was that Congress had only recently considered and resolved the issue, albeit with a different result.[13]

TRA 1986 closed down many tax-favored investments and tax shelters, increasing the attractiveness of life insurance. Thus, in the wake of the act, life insurance sales benefited from changes affecting other financial instruments. After 1986, single premium life insurance plans gained in popularity because inside buildup was tax-deferred and policy loans for the full cash value could be obtained without adverse tax consequences if the contracts remained in force until the insured's death. Sales of single premium products exploded, with some very aggressive advertising promoting single premium life insurance as "the last great tax shelter," catching the attention of Congress (again, see Chapter 9). This led to the enactment in 1988 of section 7702A and also of amendments to section 7702.

## *TAMRA: Section 7702A*

In the Technical and Miscellaneous Revenue Act of 1988 (TAMRA),[14] Congress enacted section 7702A, which defined and prescribed less favorable tax treatment for MECs. Specifically, Congress substantially altered the tax treatment of predeath distributions from those life insurance contracts it considered to be funded at too fast a rate and, thus, providing significant tax-deferred inside buildup. Thus, under section 7702A, a contract entered into after June 20, 1988, that meets the requirements of section 7702, and thus is a life insurance contract, will be characterized as a MEC[15] if it fails to meet a so-called **7-pay test**. For a MEC, distributions are taxed on an income-first basis (that is, the gain in the contract's inside buildup is deemed to be distributed before any recovery of the investment in the contract); policy loans are treated for this purpose as distributions, contrary to their treatment under non-MECs; and in many circumstances there is a 10 percent additional tax imposed on the amount of income thus subjected to tax.[16] The contract, however, is still treated as a life insurance contract, with tax-deferred inside buildup and tax-free death benefits.

Beyond the modified endowment contract rules, TAMRA made a substantial change affecting section 7702. As noted above, sections 7702 and 7702A operate by use of actuarially computed limitations. TAMRA amended section 7702 to require contracts "entered into" after October 20, 1988, to use only "reasonable" mortality and expense charge assumptions used in the definitional calculations.[17] Prior law had allowed the use of mortality and expense charges specified in the contract, in the expectation that market forces would compel a reasonable relation between the contractual maximum mortality and expense charges and those actually charged to the policyholder. This expectation was not uniformly realized.[18]

## The Role of Sections 7702 and 7702A in Life Insurance Taxation

Sections 7702 and 7702A (and section 101(f) before them) serve as the foundation for the Code's comprehensive framework governing the tax treatment of life insurance contracts. As noted above, section 101(f) provides a definitional limitation applicable to flexible premium contracts issued in 1984 and earlier. Section 7702 pro-

---

[13] William B. Harman Jr., *Two Decades of Insurance Tax Reform*, 6 Ins. Tax Rev. 1089, 1091 (1992) (citations omitted) (hereinafter Harman).
[14] Pub. L. No. 100-647, § 5012.
[15] The phrase modified endowment contract is defined in IRC § 7702A. It has no significance in the U.S. market outside the Code, although a contract by that name (providing periodic payments over the insured's lifetime as well as a maturity payment) is sold in some other countries. Kenneth Black Jr., Harold D. Skipper Jr. and Kenneth Black III, Life Insurance 91 (14th ed. 2013) (hereinafter Black, Skipper and Black). For example, single premium whole life insurance contracts are generally MECs but are not endowment contracts in the traditional sense.
[16] *See* IRC §§ 7702A, 72(e)(5)(C), 72(e)(10) and 72(v). See Appendix 1.1 for a discussion of this additional tax.
[17] Pub. L. No. 100-647, § 5011; IRC § 7702(c)(3)(B)(i) and (ii).
[18] For more detailed discussion of the history of the definition of life insurance for federal tax purposes, see Chapter 9.

vides a definition of life insurance for all life insurance contracts issued after 1984; failure to meet its definitional limitations results in the taxation of the life insurance policyholder on the inside buildup as it is credited, although the **net amount at risk** continues to be received by the beneficiary of the death benefit free of federal income tax. Section 7702A, for its part, defines the MEC subclass of life insurance contracts. As is often typical of legislative changes, contracts issued prior to the enactment of these statutes generally are "grandfathered" from the application of the statutes, provided the contracts themselves are not materially changed.

Through the definitional limitations imposed by sections 7702 and 7702A, Congress has created three classes of life insurance contracts for purposes of determining their tax treatment:

- Life insurance contracts that comply with section 7702 and are not MECs (non-MECs), to which the traditional tax treatment of lifetime (i.e., predeath) distributions applies in full
- MECs, which are subject to the more adverse tax treatment of predeath distributions previously described
- Contracts considered life insurance under applicable (e.g., state) law but that fail to comply with section 7702 (e.g., certain short-term endowments) for which the increase in cash surrender value is currently taxable in a manner prescribed by the Code (**failed contracts**)[19]

Together, these two sections contain the standards Congress has imposed on the design and operation of life insurance contracts for entitlement to income tax-free death benefits, deferral of tax on the inside buildup and the income tax treatment of distributions (including loans) from contracts.

Section 7702 imposes two requirements that a contract must satisfy to be treated as a life insurance contract for federal tax purposes. First, the contract must be a life insurance contract under **applicable law**. Second, the contract must meet at least one of two alternative actuarial tests, either (1) the **cash value accumulation test** (CVAT) or (2) the **guideline premium limitation** and **cash value corridor** requirements. These tests regulate the relationship among the premiums, death benefits and cash values of a given contract. A simplified flow chart of the operation of sections 7702 and 7702A is provided in Figure 1.1.

## "Applicable Law" Requirement of Section 7702

Before turning in the ensuing chapters to the actuarial requirements applicable to a contract under section 7702, it is important to note that the definitional provision begins, in subsection (a), with the applicable law requirement. This requirement is in turn defined in the statute's **legislative history** to mean that the contract in question must be one of life insurance under state or foreign law, i.e., the governing law of the jurisdiction in which the contract is issued.[20] The requirement thus extends to all contracts intended to qualify as life insurance for federal income tax purposes, whether issued in the United States or in another jurisdiction (i.e., offshore). It is therefore possible for an insurance contract to be governed by non-U.S. insurance law and still qualify as life insurance under the Code.

The applicable law requirement relies on state statutes and regulations (or their counterparts under foreign law) to define the scope of the contract under consideration, thereby subjecting it—whatever its scope is—to the actuarial tests of section 7702. As noted in the DEFRA legislative history:

> [A]ny life insurance contract that is treated under State law as a single, integrated life insurance contract and that satisfies these guidelines [the section 7702 numerical tests] will be treated for Federal tax purposes as a single contract of life insurance and not as a contract that provides separate life insurance and annuity benefits. For example, for purposes of this definition, a whole life insurance contract that provides for the purchase of paid-up or deferred additions will be treated as a single life insurance contract.[21]

---

[19] *See* IRC § 7702(g). However, such noncompliant life contracts generally are not offered for sale.

[20] DEFRA House Report, *supra* note 11, at 1443; DEFRA Senate Report, *supra* note 11, at 572; STAFF OF JT. COMM. ON TAX'N, 98TH CONG., GENERAL EXPLANATION OF THE REVENUE PROVISIONS OF THE DEFICIT REDUCTION ACT OF 1984, at 646 (Comm. Print 1984) (hereinafter DEFRA Blue Book). See Appendix 1.2 for a discussion of the term "legislative history" as used here.

[21] DEFRA Senate Report, *supra* note 11, at 572; DEFRA Blue Book, *supra* note 20, at 647. The first sentence of the quoted language also appears in the DEFRA House Report, *supra* note 11, at 1443.

**Figure 1.1.** Qualification under IRC 7702 and 7702A

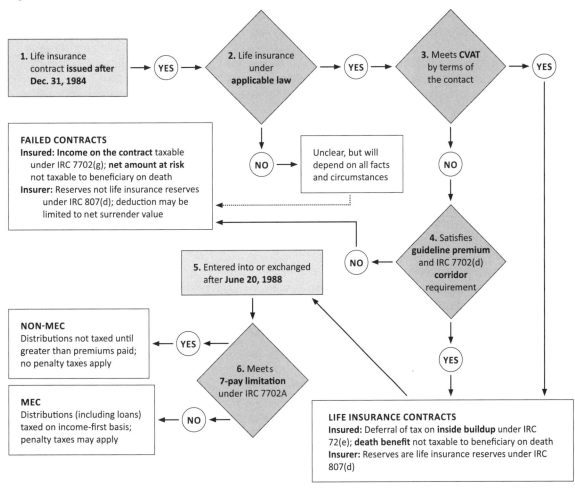

Applying this rule, the IRS has held that a contract marketed as a reversionary annuity constituted life insurance for tax purposes, as the insurer involved in the IRS ruling could demonstrate that the regulatory authorities in the states in which the contract would be issued considered it to be life insurance.[22] However, as noted in the legislative history, a combination of term life insurance with an annuity contract would not be considered an integrated contract of life insurance because all of the elements are not treated under state law as providing a single integrated contract of life insurance.[23]

*Insurable Interest*

At times, the issue of insurable interest has been raised with respect to the applicable law requirement under section 7702, particularly with respect to corporate-owned life insurance (COLI) policies.[24] As a general rule, an insurable interest, which exists when a policyholder has an interest in the continued life of the insured as distinguished from profiting on the insured's death, is required to be present at a contract's inception for it to be

---

[22] PLR 9717033 (Jan. 27, 1997). A reversionary annuity provides for annuity payments to a specified beneficiary on the death of the insured. Thus, the death benefits under a reversionary annuity generally are payable only if the beneficiary survives the insured. As a general matter, reversionary annuities are specifically excluded from life insurance nonforfeiture requirements under state law.

[23] DEFRA House Report, *supra* note 11, at 1443; DEFRA Senate Report, *supra* note 11, at 572; DEFRA Blue Book, *supra* note 20, at 646. *See also* PLR 200022003 (Dec. 9, 1999) and PLR 9552016 (Sept. 27, 1995).

[24] COLI policies sold to banks are known by the acronym BOLI, while similar policies owned by trusts are known as TOLI.

treated as a valid life insurance contract.[25] Under case law predating the development of the statutory definition of life insurance, the exclusion of death proceeds from gross income under section 101(a)(1) was denied if the owner of a contract did not possess an insurable interest in the insured since the contract was viewed merely as a wagering contract.[26] Although there is no evidence in the legislative history of a specific congressional intent to do so, the common law requirement that an insurable interest exist may have been codified, in effect, in section 7702 via the applicable law requirement. Notably, the IRS and the Department of Justice have advanced this position in rulings and litigation. In a technical advice memorandum (TAM) on COLI, the IRS stated:

> If [the] Taxpayer did not have an insurable interest in the employees covered by the COLI program when the contracts were issued under the law of State A, the contracts insuring those lives would not be life insurance under applicable law and would fail to qualify as life insurance under section 7702.[27]

The issue also was addressed in litigation related to the deduction of policy loan interest on COLI. In *Dow Chemical Co. v. United States*, the government contended that one of Dow's COLI plans did not constitute "life insurance" under Michigan law, on the theory that Dow did not have an insurable interest in all of the employees under the plan.[28] As a consequence, the government argued, the Dow policies did not comply with the applicable law requirement of section 7702(a) and therefore were not entitled to deferral of tax on the inside buildup or to the deduction of the interest paid on policy loans under section 163.[29] (The contracts otherwise met the actuarial requirements of section 7702.) In finding the existence of an insurable interest, the district court commented that "[i]t appears, therefore, that the presence of an insurable interest is a necessary component of a life insurance contract [to be] valid under state law and, therefore, IRC section 7702(a) as well."[30]

## *Alternative Forms of Life Insurance*

The applicable law requirement does not mandate that a contract be in the form of a commercial life insurance contract to be treated as life insurance under the Code. In this regard, the precise effect of the applicable law requirement is less than perfectly clear. In the United States, life insurance companies are generally organized under state law and are closely regulated by the states on issues regarding market conduct, allowable or required contract provisions, and financial condition. Whether a contract to which state law does not apply—say, because of pre-emption by federal law such as ERISA[31]—can meet the applicable law requirement while avoiding state regulation is not clear.

Historically, both the courts and the IRS have, from time to time, found life insurance to exist in situations where there is no commercial life insurance contract between the insured and the insurer. The standards generally applied in these cases to determine whether life insurance exists include the presence of risk shifting and risk distribution under the *Le Gierse* standard as well as the actuarial soundness of the (reserve) fund from which benefits are to be paid. Payments made by members of a stock exchange to deceased members, funded by a fixed initiation fee and assessments upon a member's death, were held to be life insurance death benefits excludable from gross income under section 101(a)(1) and its 1939 Code predecessor.[32] Similarly, payments from a state-established survivors' benefit program for state employees to the employees' designated beneficiaries were held to be payments of life insurance death benefits excludable from gross income under section 101(a).[33] Both of these arrangements long predated the enactment of the statutory definition of life insurance found in section 7702.

---

[25] Insurable interest is governed by state law, typically including both statutory provisions and case law. The insurable interest requirement, which is a feature of U.S. law as well as the law in Canada and the United Kingdom, dates back to an act of the British Parliament, the Life Assurance Act of 1774. The latter was enacted to discourage wagering on human lives.
[26] *See, e.g., Atl. Oil Co. v. Patterson*, 331 F.2d 516, 517 (5th Cir. 1964); *Ducros v. Comm'r*, 272 F.2d 49, 50 (6th Cir. 1959).
[27] TAM 199901005 (Sept. 29, 1998).
[28] *Dow Chem. Co. v. United States*, 250 F. Supp. 2d 748, 753 (E.D. Mich. 2003), *rev'd on other grounds*, 435 F.3d 594 (6th Cir. 2006), *cert. denied*, 549 U.S. 1205 (2007).
[29] *Id.*
[30] *Id.* at 821. The district court held in Dow's favor. However, as indicated above, the district court's decision in *Dow* was reversed, albeit on other grounds, by the U.S. Court of Appeals for the Sixth Circuit. *Dow Chem. Co. v. United States*, *supra* note 28.
[31] The Employee Retirement Income Security Act of 1974, 29 USCA § 1001 *et seq.*
[32] *Comm'r v. Treganowan*, *supra* note 7; *Estate of Moyer v. Comm'r*, 32 T.C. 515, 527 (1959), *acq.*, 1960-2 C.B. 6.
[33] *Ross v. Odom*, 401 F.2d 464, 474 (5th Cir. 1968).

In a 1998 **private letter ruling**,[34] the IRS held that certain death benefits were paid under a "life insurance contract" within the meaning of section 7702(a), even though they were paid under the mandate of a federal statute rather than under the provisions of a commercial life insurance contract. In the ruling, the IRS concluded that the "applicable law" for purposes of determining whether the taxpayer's death benefit coverage was a life insurance contract under section 7702(a) was federal law, because state law was pre-empted by federal statutes and foreign law was irrelevant. The IRS went on to note that the source of federal law in this case was the federal common law summarized above, so that under the case law criteria, the taxpayer's death benefit coverage constituted a life insurance contract. As the coverage involved had no cash surrender value, the IRS held that it satisfied the CVAT of section 7702(a)(1) and thus complied with section 7702, thereby providing an income tax-free death benefit.[35] This ruling also indicates the IRS continues to apply the risk-shifting/risk-distribution standard of *Le Gierse* in determining whether a contract is, fundamentally, one of insurance; this is the case whether or not the contract complies with the actuarial tests of section 7702.

It is also noteworthy the regulations under section 101(a)(1) provide that "death benefit payments having the character of life insurance proceeds payable by reason of death under contracts, such as worker's compensation insurance contracts, endowment contracts, or accident and health insurance contracts, are covered by" the death benefit exclusion.[36] While the rule just quoted predates the enactment of section 7702, it should remain valid today even though certain of the referenced contracts do not qualify as life insurance under applicable law and, therefore, section 7702(a). The regulations, implementing the intent of Congress under section 101(a)(1), certainly have the authority to specify the scope of the death benefit exclusion, expanding it as may be appropriate beyond contracts that technically qualify under the statutory definition. When it enacted section 7702, Congress presumably was aware of the rule—statutory construction principles would so presume—and yet said nothing in derogation of it in the DEFRA legislative history. The IRS, too, has been silent on the matter during the three decades since section 7702's enactment, simply leaving the rule in place.

## Foreign-Issued Life Insurance Contracts

By their terms, sections 7702 and 7702A apply to all contracts treated as life insurance under the applicable law regardless of whether the policyholders are U.S. taxpayers. Hence, if a life insurance contract is issued by an insurer outside the United States, the two sections technically apply to it, although in most instances the foreign-issued contract's probable noncompliance (or at most accidental compliance) with these sections would not matter to the policyholder, who likely would not be a U.S. taxpayer. However, in cases where a U.S. taxpayer purchases a contract outside the United States, or a foreign policyholder becomes a U.S. resident (and therefore a U.S. taxpayer), the compliance or noncompliance of the contract with sections 7702 and 7702A certainly will matter. In such cases, it will be important to test the contract for compliance with the two sections, and to do so from the inception of the contract, although that may not be an easy matter where the issuing insurer is not set up to perform the testing.[37]

### *Canadian Requirements*

Like the United States, Canada imposes restrictions on life insurance contracts as a condition to receiving favorable income tax treatment of the inside buildup. The policyholder tax rules in Canada create two classes of insurance policies: exempt and nonexempt. Exempt policies are considered as providing primarily insurance protection. A life insurance policy is an exempt policy if it satisfies the exempt test found in section 306(1) of the Canadian Income Tax Regulations. This test limits the amount of a contract's cash value relative to its death benefit through a comparison of the cash values (the accumulating fund) of the actual contract to the accumu-

---

[34] PLR 9840040 (July 6, 1998).
[35] *See also* PLR 200002030 (Oct. 15, 1999) and 199921036 (Feb. 26, 1999) (holding that death benefit coverage provided under a plan to which state law did not apply because of its pre-emption by ERISA qualified as a life insurance contract). It is uncertain whether the IRS would continue to adopt this ruling position. Section 5.01(2) of Rev. Proc. 2014-3, 2014-1 I.R.B. 111, provides that life insurance not issued by an insurance company is under study and that the IRS will not issue rulings as to its tax treatment, including for purposes of IRC §§ 101 and 7702.
[36] Treas. Reg. § 1.101-1(a)(1).
[37] *See* Philip Friedlan and John T. Adney, *Cross-Border Life Insurance: Differing Definitions in an Age of International Tax Reporting*, 10 Taxing Times, no. 2, May 2014, at 19; Philip Friedlan and John T. Adney, *Life Insurance on the Move: Cross-Border Tax Implications and Opportunities for Canadian and U.S. Policyholders*, 28 Ins. Tax Rev., no. 5, May 2005.

lating fund of one or more standard contracts known as exemption test policies. The effect of the exempt test is to limit the amount of income that can be accumulated in a contract on a tax-deferred basis, similarly to the CVAT. If a contract does not satisfy the requirements to be an exempt policy, then it will be a nonexempt policy, and the policyholder will be subject to taxation on the annual income earned under it.[38]

The existence of a tax-based definition of life insurance in Canada that differs substantially from the U.S. definition poses a particular compliance challenge for policyholders of one jurisdiction who establish residence in the other, even temporarily. It appears the United States and Canada are the only countries that define life insurance in their tax laws.[39]

## Foreign Account Tax Compliance Act

In 2010, Congress enacted a group of Code provisions known as the Foreign Account Tax Compliance Act (FATCA) to combat income tax evasion by U.S. persons who maintain assets in foreign financial accounts.[40] In general, FATCA imposes a 30 percent withholding tax on most types of U.S.-source income paid to (among other entities) a foreign financial institution (FFI), but the tax is not imposed if the FFI agrees to report to the IRS on the financial accounts it maintains for U.S. persons. To enable this reporting by their resident FFIs, a number of foreign governments have entered into "inter-governmental agreements" (IGAs) with the United States, often with a promise of reciprocal reporting on the U.S.-based financial accounts of those governments' nationals. According to the regulations under FATCA (and the applicable IGAs), FFIs agreeing to report to the IRS on their U.S. account holders include "specified" insurance companies, defined as insurers that issue cash value life insurance (and annuity) contracts. These companies are required to report each contract's cash value as of the annual reporting date, together with any distributions made during the reporting period, along with information identifying the U.S. policyholder. Exceptions from the reporting requirements exclude smaller life insurance contracts.

The upshot of FATCA's reporting requirements is that the IRS will be apprised of the cash values of foreign-issued contracts owned by or for the benefit of U.S. persons. The reports will not include any indication whether these contracts meet the requirements of section 7702 or 7702A, but they ultimately will provide IRS auditors with information about the existence of the contracts and the size of the cash values, information the IRS now lacks unless it is furnished by the policyholders on foreign asset reporting forms (FinCen Form 114 and IRS Form 8938).[41]

---

# Appendix 1.1. Summary of Other Life Insurance Tax Rules

The following represent simplified descriptions of some of the federal income tax rules specific to life insurance, apart from sections 7702 and 7702A but assuming compliance with section 7702, with citations to supporting authorities and references to texts providing additional detail. Note that these descriptions do not take into account the use of life insurance in the employment context, including qualified retirement plans.

## Death Benefits

**Death benefit exclusion, section 101(a)(1):** Proceeds from a life insurance contract payable on the death of the insured are generally excludable from the gross income of the beneficiary. This exclusion, a distinguishing feature of the federal income tax treatment of life insurance and one of the oldest rules in the Code, is available regardless of the party who owns the contract, pays the premiums for it or is named as death beneficiary.[42] Hence, a corporation, a partnership or a trust as well as an individual may own a life insurance contract or be named as death beneficiary without forfeiting the exclusion.[43] However, as discussed above, the availability of

---

[38] *See id.*
[39] *See id.* A number of changes in the exempt test rules became effective in 2015.
[40] Pub. L. No. 111-147, § 501(a); IRC §§ 1471–74.
[41] The IRS may have some information on the policies' existence if the premium payors report on and pay their excise tax liability under IRC § 4371, but this information does not include cash value amounts.
[42] IRC § 101(a)(1); Treas. Reg. § 1.101-1.
[43] IRC § 101(a)(1); Treas. Reg. § 1.101-1(a); *United States v. Supplee-Biddle Hardware Co., supra* note 4.

the exclusion depends upon the existence of a valid "insurable interest." An insurable interest is generally defined as the contract applicant's lawful and substantial interest in the continuing life (as opposed to the death) of the insured as established at the time of contract issuance.[44] In limited circumstances, the exclusion also may be denied on the ground that the beneficiary is receiving the proceeds for a reason other than the death of the insured, e.g., a business may receive the proceeds to liquidate an obligation of the insured.[45]

**Transfer for value rule, section 101(a)(2):** The exclusion of the death benefit proceeds is denied in the case of a "transfer for value" of an interest in the life insurance contract.[46] There are exceptions to this denial, however, where the transfer is made to the insured, a partner of the insured, a partnership in which the insured is a partner or a corporation in which the insured is an officer or shareholder.[47] Other exceptions include a transfer made in connection with a tax-free corporate reorganization, or in any other circumstance in which the contract's tax basis in the hands of the transferee is determined in whole or part by reference to the transferor's basis in the contract; a transfer to a spouse or a former spouse;[48] a transfer that is partly for value and partly by gift; and a transfer to a grantor trust of which the insured is the grantor.[49]

**Payout of death benefit over time, section 101(d):** Death benefit proceeds may be received in the form of an annuity under one of a life insurance contract's standard settlement options. Annuitized death proceeds are treated for tax purposes in a manner somewhat akin to periodic payments under a payout annuity as provided in section 72(b) and the related regulations. In brief, an "amount held by the insurer with respect to any beneficiary" is determined as of the date of the insured's death (e.g., the death benefit if there is an option to pay such amount in a lump sum at death), and this amount—which is akin to "investment in the contract"—is then prorated over the annuity payout period, as adjusted for any refund feature, in order to determine the portion of each payment excludable from income.[50] As a result, the death benefit effectively is recovered income tax-free through a portion of each payment received and the remainder of each payment is includible in gross income. The includible amounts may also be taxable as "net investment income" under section 1411, which took effect on January 1, 2013, and imposes an additional tax at a 3.8 percent rate on "annuities," among other items, subject to certain thresholds. In addition, interest credited on death benefit amounts left on deposit with the insurer is fully includible in gross income in the year credited[51] and is includible as net investment income for purposes of the tax under section 1411.

**Accelerated death benefits, sections 101(g) and 7702B(e):** The Health Insurance Portability and Accountability Act of 1996 (HIPAA)[52] amended the Code to extend the death benefit exclusion to benefits that are "accelerated," or paid prior to the insured's death, in the event the insured becomes "terminally ill" or "chronically ill," subject to meeting certain qualification requirements (including a variety of consumer protections). Such benefits typically are provided under life insurance-based "combination" products. As enacted by HIPAA, section 101(g) provides this exclusion by treating accelerated death benefits paid because of the insured's terminal or chronic illness as if they were made at the insured's death, subject to limitations applicable to per diem amounts in the case of chronic illness payments.[53] The exclusion by reason of section

---

[44] *Atl. Oil Co. v. Patterson, supra* note 26; *Dow Chem. Co. v. United States, supra* note 28. *See also United States v. Supplee-Biddle Hardware Co., supra* note 4; Black, Skipper and Black, *supra* note 15, at 455; McGill's Life Insurance 777–785 (Edward E. Graves ed., 4th ed. 2002) (hereinafter McGill). In addition, an individual has an insurable interest in his or her own life. See Black, Skipper and Black, *supra* note 15, at 458; McGill at 779. In several states, insurable interest also must be established at the time of the transfer of a contract.

[45] *See, e.g., Landfield Fin. Co. v. United States,* 418 F.2d 172 (7th Cir. 1969); Rev. Rul. 70-254, 1970-1 C.B. 31.

[46] IRC § 101(a)(2); Treas. Reg. § 1.101-1(b).

[47] *Id.*

[48] IRC § 1041. This result under IRC § 101(a)(2) is achieved by virtue of the IRC § 1041 rule treating the transferee as succeeding to the transferor's adjusted basis. The transfer to the former spouse must be incident to divorce within the meaning of IRC § 1041.

[49] IRC § 101(a)(2)(A); Rev. Rul. 2007-13, 2007-11 I.R.B. 684 (transfer to grantor trust); Rev. Rul. 69-187, 1969-1 C.B. 45 (transfer in part for valuable consideration and in part as gift); PLR 201332001 (May 10, 2013) (purchase of a contract by a grantor trust of which the insured was grantor from another irrevocable trust falls within the exception for a transfer to the insured). The IRS also has ruled that no transfer of life insurance contracts occurred where interests in an entity taxed as a partnership that owned such contracts were themselves transferred. *See* PLR 201308019 (Aug. 23, 2012) and PLR 200826009 (Dec. 20, 2007).

[50] IRC § 101(d); Treas. Reg. § 1.101-4.

[51] IRC § 101(c); Treas. Reg. § 1.101-3.

[52] Pub. L. No. 104-191.

[53] IRC § 101(g), as added by § 331 of Pub. L. No. 104-191. The provision defines "terminal illness" as a condition expected to result in death within 24 months, as certified by a physician, and it relies on the long-term care insurance definition provided by IRC § 7702B.

101(g) does not apply, however, if the benefits are payable to the insured's employer.[54] As an alternative, section 7702B(e) and related rules for qualified long-term care (LTC) insurance provide an exclusion for LTC-based accelerated death benefits by treating them in the same manner as accident and health insurance benefits.[55] These rules are discussed in detail in Chapter 7.

**Employer-owned life insurance, section 101(j):** The full death benefit exclusion is denied to an employer who receives death benefit proceeds from a contract on the life of an employee unless there is compliance with special "employer-owned life insurance" rules that limit coverage to certain classes of employees and impose employee notice and consent requirements.[56] Under these "COLI best practices" rules,[57] the full exclusion is available only in the case of a contract:

- covering the life of an insured who was an employee of the contract owner within the 12-month period prior to the insured's death,

- under which the death benefits are payable to beneficiaries designated by the insured or are used to purchase an equity interest in the employer from such beneficiaries or from certain other heirs of the insured, or

- insuring an individual who is:
  - a director of the contract owner,
  - a "highly compensated employee" within the meaning of the Code's qualified retirement plan non-discrimination rules, or
  - a "highly compensated individual" within the meaning of the Code's self-funded employer health plan nondiscrimination rules.[58]

Also, the statute's notice and consent requirements condition the exclusion on the employee:

- being notified in writing that the employer intends to purchase the coverage, with the notification disclosing the "maximum face amount for which the employee could be insured at the time the contract was issued,"

- providing written consent to the coverage and to its continuation after the insured's employment is terminated, and

- being informed in writing that the death benefits will be payable to the employer.[59]

These requirements must be met prior to the issuance of coverage; the ability to cure a failure to do so is very limited.

---

[54] IRC § 101(g)(1) and (5).

[55] *See* IRC § 7702B(b) and (e).

[56] IRC § 101(j)(1). An employer-owned life insurance contract is generally defined as a life insurance contract owned by a trade or business, directly or indirectly benefits that trade or business (or a related party), and covers the life of an insured (other than a nonresident alien) who is an employee with respect to the trade or business of the contract owner on the date the contract is issued. *See* IRC § 101(j)(3)(A) and (5). For this purpose, the contract owner—technically, the "applicable policyholder" under the statute—is broadly defined as the employer and its affiliates. If there is noncompliance, the death benefit exclusion is limited to the premiums the owner paid for the contract.

[57] These rules appear in IRC § 101(j), effective for contracts entered into or materially changed after June 17, 2006. There is an exception for contracts received in a tax-free exchange under IRC § 1035, provided the contracts are not otherwise materially changed. See § 863(d) of the Pension Protection Act of 2006, Pub. L. No. 109-280; Notice 2009-48, 2009-24 I.R.B. 1085; John T. Adney, Bryan W. Keene and Kirk Van Brunt, *COLI in Congress: New Tax Rules Address Concerns and the Product's Future*, 61 J. OF FIN. SERV. PROF., no. 2, March 2007 (hereinafter *COLI in Congress*).

[58] IRC § 101(j)(2)(A)(ii). Specifically, IRC § 101(j) cross-references IRC § 414(q) in defining the term "highly compensated employee," disregarding paragraph (1)(B)(ii) thereof, and cross-references IRC § 105(h)(5) in defining a "highly compensated individual." IRC § 414(q), as specially incorporated into IRC § 101(j)(2), defines a highly compensated employee as any employee who was a 5 percent owner at any time during the year or the preceding year as defined in IRC § 416(i)(1)(B)(i) or had compensation from the employer in excess of $100,000 (indexed for inflation since 2006) for the preceding year. IRC § 105(h)(5), as specially incorporated into IRC § 101(j)(2), defines a highly compensated individual as an individual who is (1) one of the five highest paid officers, (2) a shareholder who owns (or constructively owns under IRC § 318) more than 10 percent in value of the stock of the employer, or (3) among the highest paid 35 percent of all employees.

[59] IRC § 101(j)(4). Compliance with the notice and consent requirements was the subject of PLR 201217017 (Jan. 20, 2012). For contracts subject to the COLI best-practices rules, there is also an employer reporting requirement. See IRS Form 8925, which is filed with the employer's federal income tax return. For additional information on the COLI best-practices rules, see IRS Notice 2009-48 and *COLI in Congress*, both *supra* note 57.

## Inside Buildup and Lifetime Distributions

**Inside buildup:** As a general rule, the increments in the cash surrender value of permanent life insurance contracts—again, the inside buildup—are not currently includible in the gross income of policyholders for federal tax purposes. This includes interest credited to cash values and, in the case of variable contracts, earnings and gains under investment options to which cash values are allocated. In the latter case, cash values may be allocated or reallocated among the investment options without giving rise to a taxable event. The nontaxation of the inside buildup is not found in a particular Code provision but rather is embedded in the tax law's doctrine of constructive receipt[60] as well as in the Code's structure; the Code's rules (e.g., section 72(e)) relating to the tax treatment of distributions from a life insurance contract while the insured is living (lifetime distributions) and to tax-free exchanges of contracts, discussed below, would not make sense if the inside buildup were currently taxable.[61] The interest or earnings increments constituting the inside buildup become includible in gross income, if at all, when received as lifetime distributions under a contract or in connection with the sale or exchange of a contract. Moreover, the increments are permanently excluded from income when paid out as part of an otherwise excludable death benefit. There are, however, two exceptions to this general rule: the inside buildup of a corporate-owned contract is currently taxable under the alternative minimum tax,[62] and if the contract fails to satisfy either of the two actuarial tests of section 7702, its inside buildup (as specially defined) is currently taxable under section 7702(g).

**Lifetime distributions, sections 72(e) and 7702A:** The tax treatment of a predeath, i.e., lifetime, distribution from a life insurance contract depends, in the first instance, on the status of the contract as a modified endowment contract (MEC) or not (i.e., a non-MEC). The classification of a contract as a MEC or non-MEC is the sole function of section 7702A; while the operation of that statute is discussed in great depth hereafter, a MEC is essentially a highly investment-oriented life insurance contract that complies with section 7702—one generally funded at a rate exceeding that necessary to become paid-up within seven years—whereas a non-MEC is any other section 7702-compliant life insurance contract. MEC status carries with it more adverse tax treatment of lifetime distributions, including potential imposition of a penalty tax. More specifically:

- **In the case of a non-MEC,** lifetime distributions—partial withdrawals or surrenders, full surrenders, policy loans, assignments or pledges to secure borrowing, and dividends received by the policyholder (e.g., paid in cash)—are subject to relatively favorable tax treatment. While the proceeds of a full surrender are includible in gross income in the amount by which they exceed the "investment in the contract" (the premiums paid for the contract less any amounts previously received under the contract that were not includible in income),[63] a partial withdrawal or surrender generally is includible in gross income only to the extent it exceeds such investment.[64] This treatment also applies to policyholder dividends paid in cash or, e.g., to pay down a loan.[65] In the case of a contract with a surrender charge, the amount considered distributed (the "amount received" in the language of section 72) is net of any surrender charge imposed. All such amounts, insofar as they are includible in gross income, are

---

[60] An amount generally is not includible in a taxpayer's gross income until it is actually or constructively received, and income is not constructively received if the taxpayer's control of its receipt is subject to substantial limitations or restrictions. Loss of insurance protection upon a contract's surrender is such a substantial restriction. IRC § 451(a); Treas. Reg. § 1.451-2(a); *Cohen v. Comm'r*, 39 T.C. 1055 (1963); *Nesbitt v. Comm'r*, 43 T.C. 629 (1965).

[61] *See, e.g.*, IRC § 72(e); IRC § 1035; IRC § 7702(g) (discussed in Chapter 8); PLR 200151038 (Dec. 21, 2001); General Counsel Memorandum (GCM) 38934 (Dec. 8, 1982).

[62] IRC § 56(g)(4)(B)(i) and (ii). For this purpose, the inside buildup is technically referred to as the income on the contract as defined in IRC § 7702(g). IRC § 56(g)(4)(B)(ii)(I). Also, the "portion of any premium which is attributable to insurance coverage" is deductible for alternative minimum tax purposes. IRC § 56(g)(4)(B)(ii)(II).

[63] IRC § 72(e)(5). This treatment also applies to proceeds paid upon policy maturity while the insured remains alive. As previously noted, death proceeds may be received in the form of an annuity under one of the policy's standard settlement options, and this is also the case with surrender proceeds. Pursuant to IRC § 72(h), if the annuity is elected within 60 days after the proceeds become available, the annuity payment tax rules of IRC § 72(b) will govern in lieu of the rules cited above.

[64] IRC § 72(e)(5) and (6). This investment-recovery-first treatment under the IRC § 72 **stacking rules** is informally called **FIFO taxation** or simply **FIFO**, since the first amount entering the contract (the premium) is deemed to be returned first via a lifetime distribution, or first in, first out. The investment in the contract is sometimes referred to, informally, as "basis," although it is technically distinguishable from tax basis as prescribed in IRC § 1011 *et seq*. While this basis-first rule generally applies, there is a contrary "recapture ceiling" rule—deeming income to come out first—that may apply in some situations. The latter rule, which appears in IRC § 7702(f)(7)(B)–(E) and applies during the first 15 years of a contract, is discussed in Chapter 4. As discussed below, the investment-first ordering rule also is reversed in the case of a MEC.

[65] IRC § 72(e)(5)(C); *Brown v. Comm'r*, 693 F.3d 765 (7th Cir. 2012), *aff'g* T.C. Memo. 2011-83 (April 12, 2011).

taxed as ordinary income, not capital gain, even if attributable to the appreciation of assets underlying variable contracts.[66] On the other hand, if the cash surrender value is accessed by policy loan or by assignment or pledge of the contract, the tax law does not even deem this to be a taxable event,[67] although the amount of any cash value serving as collateral for a policy loan unpaid at the time of contract termination before the insured's death is treated as a distribution at that time.[68] Finally, if surrender proceeds are taken in the form of an annuity under a settlement option, a portion of each payment is includible in income pursuant to the section 72(b) rules governing "amounts received as an annuity," and the taxable amount also is included in net investment income and potentially subject to the tax under section 1411.[69]

- **In the case of a MEC,** in contrast, lifetime distributions are taxable to the extent there is gain in the contract. Specifically, the amount of any partial withdrawal or surrender is includible in gross income if it is considered a distribution of the "income on the contract," defined as the excess of the contract's cash value (disregarding any surrender charges) over the investment in the contract.[70] This income-first treatment also applies to dividends received by the policyholder (e.g., paid in cash or applied to pay off a loan), although dividends used to reduce future premiums or purchase additional coverage are not treated as income under an **amounts retained rule**.[71] Further, the amount of a policy loan, or of any assignment or pledge of the contract, is treated in the same manner as a partial withdrawal,[72] including any amounts of policy loan interest that accrue on a loan balance (i.e., capitalized interest). All such distributions, moreover, including any full surrenders, are subjected to a 10 percent penalty tax (i.e., an additional tax equal to 10 percent of the amount includible in income) unless they are received:

  ○ after the taxpayer attains age 59 1/2,

  ○ due to the taxpayer becoming disabled, or

  ○ in a series of substantially equal payments over the taxpayer's life or life expectancy or over the joint lives or life expectancies of the taxpayer and his or her beneficiary.[73]

In addition, to prevent the purchase of a series of contracts in an effort to circumvent this income-first treatment, an **aggregation rule** requires the amount includible in gross income to be determined by aggregating all MECs issued by the same insurance company (or its affiliates) to the same policyholder during any calendar year, essentially treating them as a single contract.[74] These relatively onerous rules serve either to maintain the cash value "inside" the contract until death, when it is paid out income tax free as under a non-MEC, or else to treat the lifetime distributions in a manner similar to premature distributions from nonqualified deferred annuity contracts.[75] Finally, as in the case of a non-MEC, where

---

[66] *Gallun v. Comm'r*, 327 F.2d 809 (7th Cir. 1964); *First Nat'l Bank of Kan. City v. Comm'r*, 309 F.2d 587 (8th Cir. 1962); Rev. Rul. 2009-13, 2009-21 I.R.B. 1029 (situation 1).

[67] *See, e.g., Minnis v. Comm'r*, 71 T.C. 1049 (1979).

[68] *See, e.g., Brown v. Comm'r, supra* note 65; *Atwood v. Comm'r*, T.C. Memo 1999-61. Many recent cases have reached this same conclusion. In an effort to preclude taxation of amounts previously borrowed when a contract terminates, some insurers offer an "overloan protection" rider, which prevents a contract from terminating when the borrowed amount approaches the contract's cash value if certain conditions are met. Such a rider can present "adjustment" issues under IRC §§ 7702 and 7702A (discussed in Chapter 4) as well as other tax issues warranting consideration.

[69] *See also* IRC § 72(h).

[70] IRC § 72(e)(10). This income-first treatment is informally called **LIFO taxation** since the last amount entering the contract (the interest or earnings) is deemed to be returned first via a lifetime distribution, or last in, first out. In the case of a MEC, full recovery of the investment in the contract generally is delayed until a full surrender occurs.

[71] IRC § 72(e)(4)(B).

[72] IRC § 72(e)(4)(A) and (10). Again, the amounts includible in income are considered ordinary income, not capital gain. To the extent a policy loan is included in income, it increases the investment in the contract. Since the cash value of a life insurance contract is not reduced by the making of a policy loan, in the case of a MEC, the taxed loan amount is converted from gain to basis. (As discussed in Chapter 6, an exception from the general income inclusion rule is provided for the assignment or pledge of a MEC to cover burial or prearranged funeral expenses if the death benefit does not exceed $25,000.) The repayment of a policy loan or the payment of policy loan interest does not affect the calculation of gain under a MEC.

[73] IRC § 72(v). None of these exceptions can apply in the case of a taxpayer that is not a natural person, such as the owner of a COLI contract.

[74] *See* IRC § 72(e)(12).

[75] For a more complete explanation of this point and the associated income tax rules, see John T. Adney and Mark E. Griffin, *The Great Single Premium Life Insurance Controversy: Past and Prologue*, XLIII J. OF AMER. SOC'Y OF CLU AND ChFC, no. 3, May 1989, at 64; no. 4, July 1989, at 74 (hereinafter Adney and Griffin, part 2); and no. 5, September 1989, at 70 (hereinafter Adney and Griffin, part 3).

surrender proceeds from a MEC are taken in the form of an annuity, a portion of each payment is includible in income under the section 72(b) rules, and the taxable amount also is included in net investment income for purposes of the section 1411 tax.

Table 1.1 breaks down the section 72 distributions.

| Table 1.1. Summary of taxation of distributions under IRC section 72 | | | |
|---|---|---|---|
| | Timing of tax | Policy loans | Penalty tax |
| Non-MEC life insurance | Generally investment first | Not taxed when made | None |
| MECs | Income first | Taxed with investment adjustment | 10% with exceptions |

Properly monitoring life insurance contracts for compliance with the section 7702 and 7702A requirements (i.e., ensuring that a contract is a life insurance contract and classifying it as either a MEC or non-MEC) is necessary for purposes of determining the appropriate income tax withholding and reporting requirements that will apply to distributions. These requirements differ as between distributions made to U.S. citizens or residents and those made to foreign persons (nonresident aliens).[76]

## Other Rules

**Premium and interest deduction limits, sections 163, 263, and 264(a) and (f):** Premiums paid for life insurance and interest paid or accrued on policy loans are generally not deductible by individuals.[77] A business policyholder generally cannot deduct premiums if it owns or can benefit from the contract.[78] Further, it cannot deduct policy loan interest (including interest on loans collateralized by the assignment or pledge of the contract) except in limited circumstances relating to the coverage of "key" employees.[79] A business policyholder's deductions for interest on indebtedness unrelated to life insurance contracts also are disallowed on a pro rata basis to the extent allocable to unborrowed policy cash values, although this disallowance does not apply to coverage insuring the life of a person who, at the time first covered, was a 20 percent owner of the policyholder or an officer, director or employee of the policyholder's trade or business.[80]

**Policy loans applied to pay premiums:** If a policy loan is applied to pay a premium, the investment in the contract is increased by any taxed portion of the loan and further increased by the amount applied as premium (just as any premium payment increases investment in the contract). This is illustrated in Tables 1.2 (non-MEC) and 1.3 (MEC) below, which involve a life insurance contract with a $10,000 cash surrender value from which a $1,000 loan is taken and then used to pay a premium.

---

[76] IRC §§ 3405 and 6047(d) address the withholding and reporting requirements for distributions to U.S. citizens and residents. IRC §§ 1441 and 1442 address these requirements for distributions to foreign persons. In the case of distributions to foreign entities, the requirements of FATCA are implicated. *See* IRC §§ 1471–74 and discussion in text *supra* at note 41. Further, in some circumstances (such as where there has been a transfer for value), withholding and reporting requirements also may apply to payments of the death benefit.

[77] *See* IRC § 163(h) (personal interest not deductible); IRC § 262 (personal expenses generally not deductible); IRC § 264(a)(1) (premiums not deductible if the taxpayer possesses interest in or benefits from a life insurance contract).

[78] IRC § 264(a)(1). *But see* Rev. Rul. 70-254, 1970-1 C.B. 31 (premiums paid by the corporation on life insurance covering the lives of purchasers of home sites are ordinary and necessary business expenses deductible under IRC § 162(a); death proceeds constitute ordinary income, citing *Landfield Fin. Co. v. United States*, *supra* note 45).

[79] The interest deduction, which is provided by IRC § 163(a), is limited by the rules of IRC § 264(a)(2)–(4) and (d). In essence, the interest deduction is allowed on borrowing of no more than $50,000 on each of a small number of "key employee" insured lives, and the borrowing must not be done with respect to a single premium contract (as defined in IRC § 264(c)) or on more than three of the first seven annual premiums due for a contract.

[80] *See* IRC § 264(f)(1) (pro rata disallowance rule); IRC § 264(f)(4)(A) (exception for coverage of employees, etc.). *See also* Rev. Rul. 2011-9, 2011-12 I.R.B. 554 (applying the interest expense disallowance rule of IRC § 264(f) in the context of an IRC § 1035 exchange of life insurance contracts). The disallowance rule includes an aggregation rule for affiliated businesses. Special rules apply to insurance companies that own COLI.

## Table 1.2. Taxation of a policy loan to pay premiums: non-MEC

|  | Section 7702 cash surrender value | Section 72(e) investment in contract | Section 72(e) gain | Section 7702 premiums |
|---|---|---|---|---|
| Starting policy values | $10,000 | $7,000 | $3,000 | $7,000 |
| Policy loan | — | — | — | — |
| Values "after" loan | $10,000 | $7,000 | $3,000 | $7,000 |
| Loan proceeds applied as premium payment | $1,000 | $1,000 | — | $1,000 |
| Vales "after" proceeds applied as premium | $11,000 | $8,000 | $3,000 | $8,000 |

## Table 1.3. Taxation of a policy loan to pay premiums: MEC

|  | Section 7702 cash surrender value | Section 72(e) investment in contract | Section 72(e) gain | Section 7702 premiums |
|---|---|---|---|---|
| Starting policy values | $10,000 | $7,000 | $3,000 | $7,000 |
| Policy loan | — | $1,000 | -$1,000 | — |
| Values "after" loan | $10,000 | $8,000 | $2,000 | $7,000 |
| Loan proceeds applied as premium payment | $1,000 | $1,000 | — | $1,000 |
| Vales "after" proceeds applied as premium | $11,000 | $9,000 | $2,000 | $8,000 |

**Contract exchanges, section 1035:** The exchange of an existing life insurance contract for a new life insurance contract, an annuity contract or a qualified long-term care insurance contract, whether the new contract is issued by the same insurer or a different one, may be accomplished without surrendering the existing contract for cash and without incurring tax. A life insurance contract is defined generally in section 1035, for purposes of that section, as a contract with an insurance company that depends in part on the life expectancy of the insured and is not ordinarily payable in full during the insured's lifetime.[81] Such an exchange will be tax-free so long as the existing contract is transferred to the insurer by an assignment, not surrendered for cash, and both contracts cover the same insured and owner.[82] In theory, the tax-free exchange can involve only a portion of a contract,[83]

---

[81] More technically, IRC § 1035(b)(1) defines an endowment contract as "a contract with an insurance company which depends in part on the life expectancy of the insured, but which may be payable in full in a single payment during his life." In turn, IRC § 1035(b)(3) defines a contract of life insurance as "a contract to which paragraph [(b)](1) applies but which is not ordinarily payable in full during the life of the insured." IRC § 1035(b)(3) goes on to provide that a life insurance contract may contain a qualified long-term care insurance contract (by rider or otherwise) and still fall within the statute's definition of a life insurance contract (i.e., for tax-free exchange purposes).

[82] IRC § 1035(a); Treas. Reg. § 1.1035-1; Rev. Rul. 2007-24, 2007-1 C.B. 1282 (holding that where a taxpayer receives a check from a life insurance company for an annuity contract and endorses the check to a second life insurance company for a second annuity contract, the transaction does not qualify as a tax-free exchange under IRC § 1035); Rev. Rul. 90-109, 1990-2 C.B. 191 (substitution of one insured for another under a "key person" contract held to be a taxable exchange). Although IRC § 1035 refers to the exchange of endowment contracts, such as contracts that mature for their full death benefit before the insured's age 95, such contracts are not usually issued today insofar as they cannot satisfy the limitations imposed by IRC § 7702. The extent to which exchanges qualify for IRC § 1035 treatment has been the subject of a number of rulings by the IRS. See, e.g., PLR 201304003 (Oct. 15, 2012) (exchange of a survivorship life contract having one surviving insured for a contract insuring only the survivor qualifies as a tax-free exchange); PLR 9248013 (Aug. 28, 1992) (same); PLR 200801001 (Oct. 1, 2007) (exchange of interests in group and individual bank-owned fixed life insurance contracts for individual variable life insurance contracts qualifies); PLR 9708016 (Nov. 20, 1996) (exchange of two life insurance contracts for one annuity contract qualifies).

[83] See Rev. Proc. 2011-38, 2011-30 I.R.B. 66 (superseding and modifying Rev. Proc. 2008-24, 2008-1 C.B. 684); see also Conway v. Comm'r, 111 T.C. 350 (1998), acq. 1999-2 C.B. xvi; Rev. Rul. 2003-76, 2003-2 C.B. 355. According to Rev. Proc. 2011-38, dealing with partial exchanges of annuity contracts, a partial exchange will be respected as completely tax free if no distribution from either the old contract or the new contract occurs within 180 days of the exchange or distributions are made pursuant to a partial annuitization. Otherwise, the revenue procedure indicates the IRS will treat the distribution, depending upon the circumstances, as "boot" received in connection with an exchange (see below) or as a partial withdrawal subject to tax under the LIFO rule.

although the manner of applying the "partial exchange" concept to a life insurance contract is not well defined, and some insurers do not accept such an interpretation of the statute. Where an exchange qualifies as tax free, the basis of the replaced contract is carried over to the new contract.[84] If cash is received during the exchange, the cash (referred to as "boot" by tax practitioners) will be includible in income up to the gain in the contract, but its receipt will not detract from the otherwise tax-free nature of the transaction.[85] For more on exchanges, see Chapter 5.

**Contract sales, section 1001:** The sale of a life insurance contract is taxable to the policyholder to the extent of the gain in the contract. The amount includible in income equals the sales proceeds received by the seller in excess of the seller's basis in the contract. A taxpayer's basis in a life insurance contract, comparably to the investment in the contract, is typically the amount of the premiums paid for the contract less any prior untaxed distributions. There is an issue, however, whether this basis should also be reduced by any cost of insurance provided through the date of the sale of the contract. In a highly controversial ruling, the IRS has stated that it should in many instances.[86] The gain recognized by the seller can be ordinary income or capital gain, depending on the circumstances; the gain is ordinary to the extent it would have been realized under section 72 upon a surrender of the contract, while the remaining gain is capital.[87] The portion of the sales proceeds includible in income also is considered net investment income for purposes of the additional tax imposed under section 1411. The purchaser's investment in the contract is deemed to equal the purchase price paid to acquire the contract plus any future premiums paid (less any future untaxed distributions).[88] The gift of a life insurance contract, on the other hand, does not trigger income tax for either the donor or the donee.[89] This is true in the case of a MEC as well as a non-MEC.

**Deduction of loss on surrender or sale, section 165:** A policyholder generally cannot deduct a loss incurred on the surrender or sale of a life insurance contract.[90] The IRS has ruled, however, that in the case of a business which owned and then surrendered a variable life insurance contract, a loss on the surrender is deductible under section 165, but only to the extent that the amount received on surrender is less than the investment in the contract as reduced by the cost of insurance and certain other contract charges.[91]

**Variable contracts, section 817(h) and investor control:** A variable contract will lose the benefit of inside buildup tax deferral or exemption (i.e., section 7702(g) treatment will apply) if the separate account investments underlying it are not "adequately diversified" as required by tax regulations or if the policyholder is considered to exercise excessive control over such investments, i.e., if the "investor control doctrine" is violated. The investment **diversification rules** for a variable contract separate account (technically, a "segregated asset account"), which are set forth in detailed regulations, generally require that no more than 55 percent of an account's investments be in the securities or other assets of any one issuer, no more than 70 percent in those of any two issuers, no more than 80 percent for any three and no more than 90 percent for any four.[92] A special rule for variable life insurance permits unlimited investments in U.S. Treasury securities.[93] The investor control doctrine, which is largely the creature of IRS rulings, generally prohibits policyholder influence over separate account investment decisions (including choosing specific investments or communicating with investment

---

[84] IRC § 1031(d). Interestingly, the Code is silent on the carry-over of the investment in the contract under IRC § 72(e)(6), but it is widely assumed that this also carries over in the exchange as well as an attribute from the first contract. In contrast, see the adjustment under IRC § 72(g) in the case of a sale, discussed below.
[85] *See* IRC §§ 1031(b) and 1035(c); Treas. Reg. § 1.1031(d)-2. On the other hand, no loss may be recognized in connection with a tax-free exchange. IRC § 1031(c).
[86] Rev. Rul. 2009-13, 2009-21 I.R.B. 1029 (situation 2). However, if the seller has no insurable interest or would suffer no loss on the insured's death, the IRS has ruled that the seller's basis is not reduced by the cost of insurance. Rev. Rul. 2009-14, 2009-21 I.R.B. 1031 (situation 2).
[87] Rev. Rul. 2009-13, 2009-21 I.R.B. 1029 (situations 2 and 3); Rev. Rul. 2009-14, 2009-21 I.R.B. 1031 (situation 2).
[88] *See* IRC § 72(g).
[89] IRC § 102 (gift generally not includible in income of donee); IRC § 72(e)(4)(C) (complete gift of deferred annuity contract triggers donor's taxation on gain; life insurance contracts not mentioned).
[90] *See London Shoe Co. v. Comm'r*, 80 F.2d 230 (2d Cir. 1935), *cert. denied*, 298 U.S. 663 (1936); *Century Wood Preserving Co. v. Comm'r*, 69 F.2d 967 (3d Cir. 1934).
[91] PLR 201351020 (Sept. 23, 2013); PLR 200945032 (July 17, 2009). The losses allowed by the IRS in these rulings appeared to have been generated by losses in the value of the securities underlying the variable contracts involved.
[92] IRC § 817(h); Treas. Reg. § 1.817-5.
[93] IRC § 817(h)(3).

managers regarding such investments) apart from allocating premiums and cash values among broad, general investment options offered by the insurers issuing variable contracts.[94] Importantly, the IRS does not view the investment diversification regulations as supplanting the investor control doctrine, even though the Code provision authorizing those regulations was enacted to prevent policyholder control over separate account investments. Rather, the IRS considers the investor control doctrine to represent an application of the tax law's substance-over-form doctrine, under which the substance of an arrangement controls its tax treatment and not the arrangement's form when inconsistent with its substance.

## *Continued Reading*

As indicated as the outset of this appendix, the foregoing represent simplified descriptions of some of the federal income tax rules specific to life insurance. For additional and more detailed information, the reader is referred to the following:

- KIRK VAN BRUNT AND MARK E. GRIFFIN, INCOME TAXATION OF LIFE INSURANCE AND ANNUITY CONTRACTS (2012). This volume of *BNA Tax Management Portfolios* focuses on the federal income tax treatment of life insurance and nonqualified annuity products in the nonemployment setting, although it also contains some discussion of the uses of life insurance in business and employment contexts.

- KENNETH BLACK JR., HAROLD D. SKIPPER JR. and KENNETH BLACK III, LIFE INSURANCE, Chapter 22 (Lucretian 2013). Chapter 22 of this definitive text on life insurance provides a readable overview of the federal income tax rules relating to life insurance. Also, Chapter 23 of the text addresses life insurance-related federal estate and gift tax considerations.

- JOHN T. ADNEY AND JOSEPH F. MCKEEVER III, *Tax Treatment of Variable Contracts*, in VARIABLE ANNUITIES & VARIABLE LIFE INSURANCE REGULATION (Clifford Kirsch, ed., 2015). This treatise, which focuses on variable contracts, contains a detailed discussion of the various federal income tax rules affecting life insurance and nonqualified annuity products, including the investment diversification requirements applicable to such contracts and the investor control doctrine.

- JOHN T. ADNEY AND JASON BORTZ, *Using Life Insurance in Executive Compensation*, in EXECUTIVE COMPENSATION (Michael Sirkin, ed., 2011). This treatise principally addresses nonqualified executive compensation and contains a discussion of life insurance as used in that context, including the related federal income tax and ERISA rules.

- TAXING TIMES, the newsletter of the Taxation Section of the Society of Actuaries. This newsletter, published in three issues each year, functions as a journal recording and commenting on current income tax developments affecting life insurance and annuity products as well as the tax treatment of life insurance companies.

## Appendix 1.2. A Note on Tax Authorities

In this and later chapters, reference is made to a variety of authorities that establish or interpret the federal tax laws. The statutes, enacted by Congress and codified as sections of the Internal Revenue Code of 1986, as amended (and prior laws), are the primary source of the federal tax laws, including the life insurance definitional requirements. Explanations of congressional intent at the time the statutes were enacted can be found in the legislative history. Formal legislative history consists of House Ways and Means Committee, Senate Finance Committee and Conference Committee reports issued prior to the enactment of legislation. It also includes floor statements of the members of Congress who are managing legislation and so-called **colloquies**, which are orchestrated discussions that occur on the floor of the House or Senate between the chairman of the commit-

---

[94] *See* Rev. Rul. 2003-92, 2003-2 C.B. 350; Rev. Rul. 2003-91, 2003-2 C.B. 347; Rev. Proc. 99-44, 1999-2 C.B. 598; Rev. Rul. 82-55, 1982-1 C.B. 12; Rev. Rul. 82-54, 1982-1 C.B. 11; Rev. Rul. 81-225, 1981-2 C.B. 13; Rev. Rul. 80-274, 1980-2 C.B. 27; Rev. Rul. 77-85, 1977-1 C.B. 12. *See also Christoffersen v. United States*, 749 F.2d 513 (8th Cir. 1984), *cert. denied*, 473 U.S. 905 (1985); *Webber v. Comm'r*, 144 T.C. No. 17 (2015). The IRS has issued many private letter rulings addressing the application of the investor control doctrine to a variety of variable contract designs. *See also* PLR 200244001 (May 2, 2002) (holding that the investor control doctrine was not pre-empted by the enactment of IRC §§ 817(h) and 7702); *Webber v. Comm'r*, (same).

tee of jurisdiction and another committee member for the purpose of clarifying or expanding on the wording of the legislation. These floor statements are preserved in the Congressional Record, the official journal of the proceedings of Congress. In addition, materials prepared by the Joint Committee on Taxation are useful as being reflective of (but not official) legislative history. These include background materials prepared as a part of the legislative process as well as general explanations, or **Blue Books** (so named because of their color), which are prepared after the passage of major tax legislation. The 1982 legislation, or TEFRA, which introduced section 101(f), and the 1984 legislation, or DEFRA, which introduced section 7702, were accompanied by Blue Books.[95] The 1988 TAMRA legislation, which introduced the MEC rules, does not have a Blue Book. Note that because of their status as after-the-fact summaries, Blue Books do not have the same authoritative standing as contemporary legislative history.[96] However, for convenience, this text refers to all congressional materials, including Blue Books, as legislative history. Other background materials include reports by the General Accounting Office and the Treasury Department. (The statutes and selected legislative history are included as appendices at the end of this book.)

Once tax legislation is enacted, it is administered by the IRS. As a part of the administration process, the IRS may issue a variety of pronouncements. Regulations interpreting the Code's provisions, which are issued by the IRS pursuant to statutory authority and concurred in by the Treasury Department, generally are accorded the force and effect of law by the courts. Although several regulations have been proposed under sections 7702 and 7702A, only one, relating to the "attained age" of the insured, has been finalized at the time of this writing. Other IRS pronouncements include revenue rulings, revenue procedures and notices, all of which are published in the Internal Revenue Bulletin and can be relied on by taxpayers as statements of IRS positions. A revenue ruling states the IRS's view of how the tax law should be interpreted and applied to specific facts; a revenue procedure describes the process a taxpayer can use to obtain a particular tax treatment, e.g., to change a method of accounting or correct a life insurance contract that violated applicable tax rules; a notice makes an important announcement, such as outlining what future regulations will say or asking public input on a tax administration issue. In litigation involving whether IRS positions are correct, the courts will not necessarily defer to this class of pronouncements but will examine the issues independently.

In addition, the IRS issues rulings relating to a single taxpayer, including private letter rulings (PLRs) requested by taxpayers[97] and technical advice memoranda (TAMs) requested in the course of an audit.[98] PLRs and TAMs are issued by the IRS chief counsel's office in Washington, address the facts placed in front of the IRS and have no precedential value beyond the taxpayers involved in them. However, they are disclosed to the public (after redacting taxpayer-identifying information), and tax practitioners read them because they serve to indicate the IRS's thinking on the subject involved at the time they are issued. Private letter rulings constitute a significant source of information regarding the IRS's views on sections 7702 and 7702A, particularly as they are the means by which waivers of noncompliance have been granted under section 7702(f)(8) (see Chapter 8). It is important to remember that a PLR is binding on the IRS only as to the taxpayer who received it; in future circumstances, the IRS can change its mind. Still other forms of nonprecedential pronouncements appear from time to time, including field service advice (FSA) and general information letters from chief counsel office lawyers.

Case law, particularly addressing the principles of risk shifting and risk distribution, still serves as the basis for the fundamental definition of insurance under federal tax law. A taxpayer who disputes legal or factual determinations made by the IRS in an audit has the right to ask a federal court to review those determinations and reach an independent judgment as to the tax liability in question. A taxpayer may bring such a dispute to the Tax Court, a federal district court or the Court of Federal Claims, and occasionally such a dispute can

---

[95] Staff of the Jt. Comm. on Tax'n, 97th Cong., General Explanation of the Revenue Provisions of the Tax Equity and Fiscal Responsibility Act of 1982, beginning at 366 (Comm. Print 1982) (hereinafter TEFRA Blue Book); DEFRA Blue Book, *supra* note 20, beginning at 646.

[96] *United States v. Woods*, 571 U.S. ___, 134 S. Ct. 557 (2013).

[97] A private letter ruling is an official communication sent by the IRS in response to a request by a taxpayer for clarification of federal tax law as it applies to a specific factual situation involving the taxpayer. PLRs do not constitute legal precedent and may be relied upon only by the taxpayers to whom they are issued. *See* IRC § 6110(k)(3). However, they are widely read as indicating the views of the IRS's National Office on the issues presented when the rulings are issued.

[98] A technical advice memorandum represents an expression of the views of the IRS National Office as to the application of law, regulations, and precedents to the facts of a specific case, and is issued primarily as a means of assisting IRS field agents and officials in the examination and closing of the case involved (i.e., in an audit context).

even reach the U.S. Supreme Court. The courts' decisions typically are explained in opinions, sometimes called case law. Case law will usually have value as legal precedent and may be binding on the IRS and other courts depending on the circumstances. If and when called upon to interpret sections 7702 and 7702A, courts will look first to the statute, then to regulations (if any exist) and then to the statute's legislative history, and they will follow any prior case law that is binding in the matter. As noted above, IRS rulings and like pronouncements will be accorded a lesser status in judicial proceedings.

# Chapter 2

# INTRODUCTION TO SECTIONS 7702 AND 7702A

## Chapter Overview

This chapter sets out the basic principles of sections 7702 and 7702A,[1] examining the two tests that define "life insurance contract" for federal tax purposes and the test which determines whether a contract is a modified endowment contract (MEC). The chapter begins with a discussion of the concept of a model or test plan that forms the basis for computing **net single premiums (NSPs)** and guideline premiums under section 7702 and **7-pay premiums** under section 7702A—also collectively referred to as the definitional calculations or the definitional limitations. The test plan concept begins with a general discussion of the calculation of an actuarial premium, which is based on the actuarial present value of future policy benefits or of the premiums needed to fund such benefits. This is appropriate, since both statutes require the calculation of a premium, on their face relying on the customary mechanics of an actuarial premium calculation. A broad overview of the statutory provisions is presented next, covering the operation of the NSPs and guideline premiums under section 7702 and the 7-pay premiums under section 7702A. This overview will describe the concepts involved in computing these limitations, including the statutory restrictions imposed on the **actuarial assumptions** (i.e., interest, mortality and expenses) and **future benefits** used in determining them, and the adjustment of the limitations due to contract changes. The chapter concludes with a series of appendices providing additional information, including a summary example outlining sample at-issue calculations of the guideline single, guideline level, net single and 7-pay premiums, and a discussion of calculation methods and payments of claims assumptions used in the definitional calculations.

## The Model or Test Plan Concept

A common and fundamental element in the calculation of all of the limitations under sections 7702 and 7702A (and section 101(f)) is the concept of an actuarial or **net premium**. The net premium is the mechanism by which the relationship between the **cash surrender value** of a contract and its net amount at risk is controlled, directly or indirectly, through the imposition of the definitional limitations. As expressed by the net premium formula, the cost of a life insurance contract is a function of assumed mortality, interest and expenses.

The NSP for a whole life insurance contract is given by the term $A_x$. The actuarial symbol $A_x$ denotes the expected present value of life insurance of $1 payable on the death of an insured age $(x)$:

$$A_x = \sum_{t=0}^{\omega-1} v^{t+1} \times {}_{t|}q_x. \qquad (2.1)$$

That is, $A_x$ is equal to the weighted summation of the present value of $1 to be paid at the end of the year of death for an insured age $(x)$ at issue, where the weights are the discounted probabilities of death. More precisely:

- $v = \dfrac{1}{1+i}$ where $i$ is the assumed interest rate
- $q_x = 1 - p_x$ = the probability that an insured age $(x)$ will die within one year, where $p_x$ is the probability of surviving from age $x$ to age $x+1$
- ${}_{t|}q_x = {}_tp_x \times q_{x+t}$ = the probability an insured age $(x)$ will survive for $t$ years and die in year $t+1$
- ${}_tp_x$ = the probability an insured age $(x)$ survives for $t$ years (for $t = 0$, ${}_tp_x = 1$)

---

[1] Unless otherwise indicated, references in this book to "section" are to the provisions of the Internal Revenue Code of 1986, as amended (also referred to as "IRC" or the "Code").

- $\omega$ = is the limiting duration for the summation, which for a whole life insurance contract generally corresponds to the duration when the mortality table ends (as discussed below, **computational rules** imposed by sections 7702 and 7702A may alter the limiting duration)

For any life insurance contract, the NSP is the amount needed at any time, under a given set of actuarial assumptions, to provide for the future benefits under the contract, whether payable because of death or survival. It is always the sum of the present values of the expected future benefits; if the actual experience conforms to the expected experience, the NSP will exactly fund the total of all future claims.

The actuarial symbol $P_x$ represents the net level annual premium for a whole life insurance contract issued to an insured age $(x)$. The present value for these premiums, payable at the beginning of each year the insured is alive, is $P_x \ddot{a}_x$, where $\ddot{a}_x$ denotes the present value of \$1 payable at the beginning of each year for as long as the insured is alive. The calculation of the definitional limitations is derived from the basic principle that at contract issuance the present value of expected net premiums (i.e., excluding contract expenses) equals the present value of the future benefits expected to be provided. For level premium whole life coverage:

$$A_x = P_x \times \ddot{a}_x \tag{2.2}$$

where $P_x$ = the level annual premium for an insurance benefit payable at the end of the year of death for an insured age $(x)$, and

$$\ddot{a}_x = \sum_{t=0}^{\omega-1} v^t \times {}_tp_x. \tag{2.3}$$

A pure endowment is an amount payable at the end of year $(t)$ if the insured is then alive. The general formula for a pure endowment at duration $(t)$ for an insured age $(x)$, denoted as $({}_tE_x)$, is as follows:

$$EA \times {}_tE_x = EA \times \left( v^t \times {}_tp_x \right) \tag{2.4}$$

where $EA$ = the amount of the endowment benefit.

Using the concept of a net premium as the basis for the actuarial limitations, sections 7702 and 7702A operate to restrict the assumptions in the calculation of the statutes' limitations, thereby determining the limiting values at the core of the statutory rules. Under section 7702, a level benefit single premium life plan is the **model** for defining the maximum permissible investment orientation. That is, in section 7702, Congress provided definitional rules that expressly permit a level benefit life insurance contract to be funded on a single premium basis and be recognized as life insurance for federal income tax purposes. Also, a 7-payment plan, similar to the level benefit single premium plan, serves as the model for determining the status of the contract as a MEC under section 7702A. By explicitly limiting the actuarial assumptions and the pattern of future benefits to be used in the calculation, Congress prohibited the use of certain assumptions, such as very low interest rates, highly **substandard mortality** on standard cases, short endowment periods, and increasing death benefits that would increase the **cash value** relative to the death benefit and thereby undermine the purpose of the statutory tests, i.e., requiring at least certain minimum pure insurance elements to be provided by contracts.

Conceptually, the assumptions set forth in sections 7702 and 7702A are used to create **model-plan** or **test-plan values** that are compared to the contract values to determine if the definitional limitations are met. This test plan is the combination of contractual benefits and statutory restrictions on assumptions that form the basis for the calculation of the values of the applicable limitations. For example, a contract may provide for a maturity age of 85, but in calculating the definitional limitations, a maturity age of 95 to 100 must be used (this is discussed later in this chapter). Therefore, the test-plan value for maturity age, rather than the contract value for maturity age, would be used in the computation of the limitations. In this manner, the test plan provides both premium and cash value limitations under these statutes that reflect assumptions that may differ from, and ultimately constrain, the operation of the actual contract. The NSP, guideline premiums and 7-pay premiums each are "premiums," which, subject to the test plan, should be calculated consistently with reasonable actuarial practices appropriate to the contract design and mechanics.

In defining their limits, sections 7702 and 7702A provide safeguards as a part of the test plan to protect against the manipulation of contract designs to produce highly investment-oriented contracts.[2] In his paper on the federal tax definition of life insurance, Professor Andrew Pike notes that the "extraordinarily technical and arcane" provisions of section 7702 were viewed as necessary by the drafters to prevent avoidance of the statute by product designers.[3] He went on to say that section 7702 "incorporates explicit, and complicated, safeguards to preclude the use of actuarial techniques designed to frustrate the statutory purpose."[4]

Note that under the test-plan concept, the actuarial limitations imposed do not directly limit actual contract provisions. That is, the test-plan assumptions need not be a part of the contract being tested. However, these limitations may restrict the product design indirectly by restricting the allowable cash surrender values or **premiums paid**. According to the staff of the Joint Committee on Taxation:

> These rules restrict the actual provisions and benefits that can be offered in a life insurance contract only to the extent that they restrict the allowable cash surrender value (under the cash value accumulation test) or the allowable funding pattern (under the guideline premium limitation). By prescribing computation assumptions for purposes of the definitional limitations, Congress limited the investment orientation of contracts while avoiding the regulation of the actual terms of insurance contracts.[5]

While it is still possible, for example, to design a 10-year full-face endowment contract at issue age 45, such a contract would not qualify as a life insurance contract for federal tax purposes as it falls outside the test-plan parameters. Such a contract would fall into the category of life insurance contracts for which the annual increase in cash values is currently taxable. Thus, while the section 7702 rules do not, in theory, directly restrict contract provisions, in practice an insurer will not generally (knowingly) market a product that does not qualify under section 7702. The discussions under the headings that follow describe the restrictions on the actuarial assumptions imposed by sections 7702 and 7702A in calculating the NSPs, guideline premiums and 7-pay premiums. These discussions are then followed by a description of the restrictions imposed on the future benefits that may be taken in account in these calculations, including the computational rules of sections 7702 and 7702A. The application of these rules is illustrated in Appendix 2.1, Sample At-Issue Calculations. See also Appendix 2.2, Calculation Methods, and Appendix 2.3, Payment of Death Claims Assumptions, which bear on the manner in which the definitional calculations are performed.

## Cash Value Accumulation Test

The cash value accumulation test (CVAT) is the first of the two alternative, quantitative tests prescribed in section 7702. To meet the requirements of the CVAT, a life insurance contract's cash surrender value can never exceed the NSP required to fund its "future benefits." As illustrated in Figure 2.1,[6] under the CVAT, a contract's net amount at risk (i.e., the excess of the death benefit over the cash surrender value) always must at least equal the net amount at risk provided by a single premium contract computed in accordance with the statutory requirements. Further, the contract must be structured so that it complies with this restriction, or to state this point in the words of the statute, the requirements of the CVAT must be satisfied "by the terms of the contract." Each of these key concepts (i.e., the NSP, the cash surrender value and the qualification "by the terms of the contract") is considered in the discussion below. The concept of future benefits is defined briefly below and in greater detail later in this chapter and in Chapter 3.

---

[2] Andrew D. Pike, *Reflections on the Meaning of Life: An Analysis of Section 7702 and the Taxation of Cash Value Life Insurance*, 43 Tax L. Rev. 491, 545 (1988) (hereinafter Pike). Pike notes, "Similarly, the statutory 'computational rules' prevent actuarial gimmicks from upsetting the intended balance between the investment and current insurance components of life insurance contracts." *See id.*
[3] *Id.* at 495.
[4] *Id.* at 508.
[5] DEFRA Blue Book, *supra* Chapter 1, note 20, at 651. *See also* DEFRA House Report, *supra* Chapter 1, note 11, at 1447; DEFRA Senate Report, *supra* Chapter 1, note 11, at 576.
[6] The illustration in Figure 2.1 is based on the 2001 Commissioners Standard Ordinary (CSO) tables, age nearest birthday (ANB).

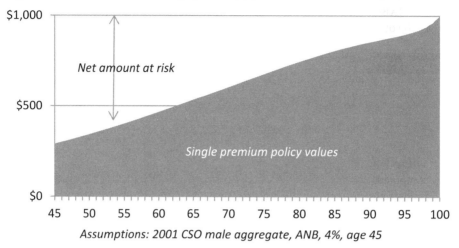

**Figure 2.1.** CVAT limitations: net single premium; $1,000 death benefit

Assumptions: 2001 CSO male aggregate, ANB, 4%, age 45

## *Net Single Premium*

The NSP is the premium needed at any time to fund the contract's future benefits at that time. This premium is a net premium, that is, it disregards expenses (loading) unrelated to mortality. The NSP calculation for a whole life contract for an insured age ($x$) assuming maturity at age 100 ($\omega = 100 - x$) is given by the following formula (definitions of the formulaic terms appear in the discussion of the model- or test-plan concept above):

$$NSP = Face\,Amount \times A_x$$

$$NSP = Face\,Amount \times \sum_{t=0}^{\omega-1} v^{t+1} \times {}_{t|}q_x$$

Under the CVAT, as noted above, the NSP represents the maximum cash surrender value permissible in a qualifying contract. The NSP under the CVAT is determined, according to section 7702(b)(2), assuming

- an annual effective interest rate of 4 percent or, if greater, the rate or rates guaranteed on issuance of the contract;
- for **contracts entered into before October 21, 1988,** the mortality charges specified in the contract or, if none is specified, the mortality charges used in determining the reserves for the contract; and
- for **contracts entered into on or after October 21, 1988,** "reasonable" mortality charges that, except as provided in regulations, do not exceed the mortality charges specified in the "prevailing commissioners' standard tables" as defined in section 807(d)(5) as of the time the contract is issued.

As noted in the test-plan discussion earlier in this chapter, the determination of the NSP is based in part on the interest and mortality rates guaranteed in the contract, subject to further rules in section 7702 that place restrictions on these assumptions. The interest rate rule appears in section 7702(b)(2)(A), while the mortality charge rule appears in section 7702(c)(3)(B)(i).[7] As for the benefits underlying the determination of the NSP, a similar comparison is made in the test plan between those provided in the contract and the future benefits permitted for use under section 7702. Sections 7702(f)(4) and (f)(5)(A)–(B) define the term "future benefits" to mean death benefits, endowment benefits and the **charges for qualified additional benefits (QABs)**. Additionally, rules set forth in section 7702(e)—generally referred to as the "computational rules"—restrict the fu-

---

[7] Clause (i) of IRC § 7702(c)(3)(B) was amended by the Technical and Miscellaneous Revenue Act of 1988 (TAMRA) to impose the "reasonable" mortality charge requirement in lieu of the use of the mortality rates specified in the contract or used in the contract's reserves. While the mortality charge rule appears in the portion of IRC § 7702 dealing with the guideline premium test, it applies as well to the CVAT, and by virtue of IRC § 7702A(b), it also applies to the 7-pay test.

ture benefits that may be taken into account in the NSP calculation. The computational rules, and the description and treatment of QABs, are addressed later in this chapter and in detail in Chapter 3. Table 2.1 illustrates sample NSPs per $1,000 of death benefit computed in conformity with the rules of the CVAT.[8]

| Table 2.1. NSP per $1,000 | | | | | |
|---|---|---|---|---|---|
| Age | 25 | 35 | 45 | 55 | 65 |
| NSP | 147.21 | 206.64 | 291.24 | 402.11 | 534.82 |
| Assumptions: 2001 CSO male aggregate, ANB, endowment at 100, 4%, curtate | | | | | |

## Cash Surrender Value

Once the NSP is computed, it is compared to the **cash surrender value (CSV)** of a contract to determine whether the CVAT requirements are met for that contract (i.e., that the NSP always must equal or exceed the CSV). Specifically, subparagraphs (A) and (B) of section 7702(f)(2), respectively, provide the following definitions of cash surrender value and **net surrender value** for use in the section 7702 determinations:

- "The cash surrender value of any contract shall be its cash value determined *without regard* to any surrender charge, policy loan, or reasonable *termination dividends*" (emphasis added).[9]

- "The net surrender value of any contract shall be the contract's cash value determined with regard to surrender charges but without regard to any policy loan."[10]

Note that the term "cash surrender value" is often used in life insurance contracts to refer to the cash value of the contract, less any remaining surrender charges and less outstanding policy loans and accrued policy loan interest due, which differs markedly from the statutory definition just quoted. In the balance of this book, "CSV" will be used to refer to the cash surrender value as defined for section 7702 purposes. A more in-depth look at CSV appears in Chapter 3.

## Terms of the Contract

The third element of the CVAT is that compliance must be **by the terms of the contract**. The CVAT has its roots in the cash value test under section 101(f), which applied to flexible premium contracts issued prior to January 1, 1985. According to the legislative history of section 7702, the CVAT was intended to allow "traditional whole life insurance policies, with cash values that accumulate based on reasonable interest rates, to continue to qualify as life insurance contracts."[11] Under both the cash value test of section 101(f) and the CVAT of section 7702, compliance must be guaranteed "by the terms of the contract." As a result, the CVAT is a prospective test that must be met at all times. That is, one should be able to read the contract at issuance and know whether the requirement is satisfied (provided the contract is in fact subsequently administered in accordance with its terms). Thus, a contract that would not meet the CVAT at some future date will be considered to have failed the test at issue. A contract need not affirmatively indicate the intent to comply with the CVAT to meet this requirement, however. Compliance may be assured by restrictions on the cash value in the contract and the uses to which dividends may be put, as in traditional contracts, or by a provision that increases death benefits automatically as cash values threaten to exceed the **attained age** NSP for the then-current face amount.

---

[8] The NSPs in Table 2.1 have been computed assuming that the contract does not guarantee an interest rate in excess of 4 percent and **reasonable** mortality is equal to the 2001 CSO. Further, they have been truncated rather than rounded, a practice that prevents slight overstatements of the limits. For a discussion of the "rounding rule" discussed in the DEFRA legislative history, see Appendix 2.2. Curtate values have been used in computing these examples. In practice, there are many choices of actuarial functions possible, including curtate, semicontinuous (immediate payment of claims) and others. See the discussion in Appendix 2.3.
[9] IRC § 7702(f)(2)(A).
[10] IRC § 7702(f)(2)(B). Note that the term net surrender value is also used in IRC § 807(d)(1)(A) as it relates to the permissible life insurance reserve deduction for a life insurance company and in IRC § 7702(g) for determining the income on a failed contract, as discussed in Chapter 8.
[11] DEFRA House Report, *supra* Chapter 1, note 11, at 1444; DEFRA Senate Report, *supra* Chapter 1, note 11, at 573; DEFRA Blue Book, *supra* Chapter 1, note 20, at 647.

## Guideline Premium/Cash Value Corridor Test

The alternative to the CVAT is the **guideline premium test (GPT)** found in section 7702(c)(1). The guideline premium test is a dual-element test that must be met at all times up to any given date for the contract to be treated as complying with section 7702 through that date. In this respect, the GPT is the statute's residual test: A contract satisfies section 7702 if it satisfies the CVAT, and if not, then it must satisfy the GPT to be treated as a life insurance contract under the Code. Compliance with the GPT need not be assured by the terms of the contract; it is sufficient if the contract is operated in compliance with the GPT in fact.

The guideline premium test is met if:

- the total of the gross premiums paid under the contract as of any time does not exceed the **guideline premium limitation** for the contract at that time, and
- the statutory **cash value corridor** requirement is satisfied at all times.

The guideline premium limitation at any time equals the greater of the **guideline single premium (GSP)** or the sum of the **guideline level premiums (GLPs)** to that time.[12] The operation of the guideline premium limitation is illustrated for a level death benefit contract in Figure 2.2. The cash value corridor requirement is satisfied if the death benefit (as defined in section 7702(f)(3)) under the contract at any time is at least equal to the applicable percentage of the CSV of the contract at that time. These applicable percentages are set forth in section 7702(d) and are shown later in Table 2.3.

### *Guideline Single and Guideline Level Premiums*

The GSP is defined in section 7702(c)(3) as the premium at contract issuance for the contract's future benefits and expenses and is generally given by the following formulas for an insured age (x) at issue:[13]

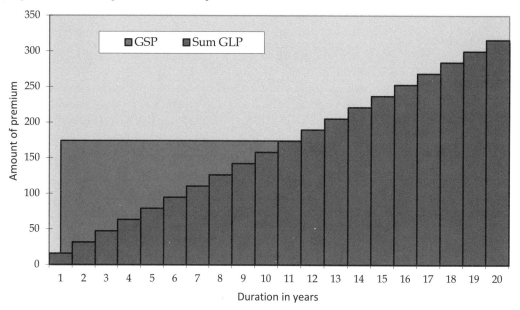

**Figure 2.2.** Guideline premium limitation per $1,000 of death benefit

*Assumptions: 2001 CSO male aggregate, 4% GLP, 6% GSP, age 45, endowment at age 100*

---

[12] In this regard, the sum of the GLPs up to a certain point in time is discrete by whole year integers. For example, the sum of the GLPs at time one year and six months would be equal to the sum of the first two year's GLPs, rather than the first year's GLP plus half of the second year's GLP.

[13] The formulas for the GSP and GLP are based on a contract design that provides for level annual expense charges (Expenses) and a level percentage of premium load (Premium Load %) that applies to all premiums paid.

$$GSP = \left[NSP + Expenses \times \ddot{a}_x\right] \div \left[1 - Premium\ Load\ \%\right]$$

$$GSP = \left[NSP + Expenses \times \sum_{t=0}^{\omega-1} v^t \times {}_t p_x\right] \div \left[1 - Premium\ Load\ \%\right]$$

As with the CVAT, future benefits assumed in the calculation of the GSP include death benefits, endowment benefits and charges for qualified additional benefits. However, unlike the case with the CVAT NSP, **expense charges** can be reflected in determining the guideline premiums, in recognition of the fact that the guideline premium limitation applies to gross premiums rather than net premiums. The GSP is computed assuming:

- an annual effective interest rate of 6 percent or, if greater, the rate or rates guaranteed on issuance of the contract;
- for **contracts entered into before October 21, 1988:**
  - the mortality charges specified in the contract, or, if none is specified, the mortality charges used in determining the reserves for the contract; and
  - any charges other than mortality charges—generally referred to as expense charges and qualified additional benefit charges—specified in the contract (the amount of any charge not so specified is treated as zero);[14] and
- for **contracts entered into on or after October 21, 1988:**
  - reasonable mortality charges that, except as provided in regulations, do not exceed the mortality charges specified in the "prevailing commissioners' standard tables" as defined in section 807(d)(5) as of the time the contract is issued; and
  - any reasonable charges other than mortality charges (i.e., reasonable expense and QAB charges) that are "reasonably expected to be actually paid" based on the insurance company's experience with similar products (if any).[15] Again, if any nonmortality charge is not specified, it is treated as zero.[16]

The interest rate rule appears in clause (iii) of section 7702(c)(3)(B), while the mortality charge and expense charge rules appear in clauses (i) and (ii) of that section, respectively.

The GLP, defined in section 7702(c)(4), is the level annual amount, assumed to be payable over a period not ending before the insured attains age 95, computed on the same basis as the GSP, except that a 4 percent interest rate minimum is substituted for the 6 percent minimum rate used to determine the GSP. Also unlike the GSP, the GLP may be computed by taking into account certain limited increases in a contract's death benefit. As such, the GLP may be computed either for an **option 1** (level) death benefit or for an **option 2** (face amount plus cash value) death benefit. The GLP is thus given by:

$$GLP^{DBO1} = \left[\left(Face\ Amount \times \frac{A_x}{\ddot{a}_x}\right) + Expenses\right] \div \left[1 - Premium\ Load\ \%\right]$$

$$GLP^{DBO2} = \frac{\left[\left(Face\ Amount \times \frac{\left\{\sum_{t=0}^{\omega-1} v^{t+1} \times q_{x+t}\right\} + v^{\omega-x}}{\sum_{t=0}^{\omega-1} v^t}\right) + Expenses\right]}{1 - Premium\ Load\ \%}$$

---

[14] Clause (ii) of IRC § 7702(c)(3)(B) was amended by TAMRA to impose the "reasonable" expense charge requirement in lieu of the use of the charges specified in the contract.
[15] IRC § 7702(c)(3)(D) provides that if a company does not have adequate experience for purposes of the determination under IRC § 7702(c)(3)(B)(ii), then to the extent provided in regulations, such determination is to be made on the basis of industrywide experience. No such regulations have been issued.
[16] IRC § 7702(c)(3)(D).

Sample GSPs, GLPs for option 1 death benefits, and CVAT NSPs are shown in Table 2.2.[17]

### Table 2.2. Guideline premium limitation per $1,000

| Age | 25 | 35 | 45 | 55 | 65 |
|---|---|---|---|---|---|
| GSP | 67.63 | 107.40 | 174.09 | 274.20 | 409.45 |
| GLP | 6.64 | 10.02 | 15.80 | 25.87 | 44.22 |
| GSP to GLP ratio | 10.19 | 10.72 | 11.02 | 10.60 | 9.26 |
| NSP | 147.21 | 206.64 | 291.24 | 402.11 | 534.82 |
| GSP to NSP | 45.9% | 52.0% | 59.8% | 68.2% | 76.6% |

*Assumptions: 2001 CSO male aggregate, ANB, 4% GLP ad NSP, 6% GSP, endowment at age 100, curtate*

The computational rules of section 7702(e) (again, discussed later in this chapter and in Chapter 3) also apply to the calculation of the GSP and the GLP.

## *Section 7702(d) Cash Value Corridor*

The guideline premium test, as noted above, imposes a dual limitation on qualifying life insurance contracts. Not only are the gross premiums payable for a contract limited by it, but the ongoing relationship of the contract's CSV and its death benefit also is limited—the latter by the cash value corridor factors set forth in section 7702(d). The cash value corridor is satisfied if the death benefit is always equal to or greater than the applicable percentage (as set forth in the statute) of the CSV at any given time. These applicable percentages are shown in Table 2.3.

### Table 2.3. Section 7702(d) corridor factors

| In the case of an insured with an attained age as of the beginning of the contract year of: | | The applicable percentage decreases by a ratable portion for each full year: | | | | | |
|---|---|---|---|---|---|---|---|
| More than | But not more than | Annual decrement | From | | | | To |
| 0 | 40 | 0% | 250 | 250 | 250 | 250 | 250 | 250 |
| 40 | 45 | 7% | 250 | 243 | 236 | 229 | 222 | 215 |
| 45 | 50 | 6% | 215 | 209 | 203 | 197 | 191 | 185 |
| 50 | 55 | 7% | 185 | 178 | 171 | 164 | 157 | 150 |
| 55 | 60 | 4% | 150 | 146 | 142 | 138 | 134 | 130 |
| 60 | 65 | 2% | 130 | 128 | 126 | 124 | 122 | 120 |
| 65 | 70 | 1% | 120 | 119 | 118 | 117 | 116 | 115 |
| 70 | 75 | 2% | 115 | 113 | 111 | 109 | 107 | 105 |
| 75 | 90 | 0% | 105 | 105 | 105 | 105 | 105 | 105 |
| 90 | 95 | 1% | 105 | 104 | 103 | 102 | 101 | 100 |

---

[17] The guideline premiums in Table 2.2 were computed with no allowance for expenses. As shown in the column **GSP to GLP ratio**, the GSP is approximately 10 to 11 times the GLP for an option 1 death benefit at ages up to 55. Comparison of the GSP in Table 2.2 with the net single premiums (NSPs) from Table 2.1 (GSP to NSP) shows how very much the shift from a 4 percent minimum rate to a 6 percent minimum affects the results. GSP values range from about half of the NSP at age 25 to about 75 percent of the NSP at age 65.

According to the legislative history, the cash value corridor is intended to regulate the buildup of cash value relative to the insurance risk present under the contract,[18] although to a lesser degree than the CVAT. This is because the guideline premium limitation component of the dual element test already places a more stringent limitation on gross premium payments than does the CVAT. Said differently, the lower **minimum interest rate** under the CVAT (4 percent as compared with 6 percent for the GSP) results in a lower permitted amount at risk under the CVAT in a contract's earlier durations. Later, minimum amounts at risk are higher under the CVAT than those permitted under the guideline premium test when the death benefit is determined by the cash value corridor percentages.

The actual corridor percentages resulted from political considerations during the writing of section 7702 and, as a result, the annual decrements in the percentages do not follow a smooth progression from age to age. Rather, the corridor factors are organized in brackets based on the "attained age" of the insured (the age of the insured for section 7702 purposes, and the related regulation, are discussed in Chapter 3).

The cash value corridor factors limit the relationship of the cash value to the death benefit in a manner similar to the operation of the CVAT. However, as the factors operate in tandem with the guideline premium limitation, the section 7702(d) factors, as noted just above, are intended to be less than the minimum ratio of death benefit to cash value allowed under the CVAT for a standard risk. The effective corridor provided by the CVAT can be expressed as the reciprocal of the NSP for a death benefit of $1.00. Figure 2.3 compares the section 7702(d) corridor with the (implicit) corridor provided by the CVAT under the 2001 Commissioners Standard Ordinary (CSO) male aggregate table with 4 percent interest. Note that the effective corridor in the CVAT varies with the assumed mortality table and interest rate, while the section 7702(d) corridor does not.[19] Thus, under the CVAT, the minimum required death benefit in relation to the cash value is a function of interest and mortality assumptions, whereas under the guideline premium test, it is fixed by statute.

## Premiums Paid

The determination of the premiums paid under a life insurance contract is important both in terms of determining compliance with section 7702's guideline premium test and measuring the taxable gain on contract surrender or maturity under section 72(e). The term **premiums paid** used in these two sections may have different meanings, however.

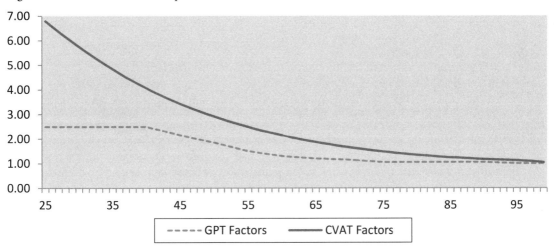

**Figure 2.3.** Minimum death benefit per $1 of CSV

CVAT assumptions: 2001 CSO male aggregate, ANB, 4% interest, endowment at age 100

---

[18] DEFRA House Report, *supra* Chapter 1, note 11, at 1445; DEFRA Senate Report, *supra* Chapter 1, note 11, at 574; DEFRA Blue Book, *supra* Chapter 1, note 20, at 650.

[19] As the 2001 CSO tables became the "reasonable" mortality standard, the effective "corridor" under the CVAT generally increased (as the mortality rates are generally lower than the corresponding rates under the 1980 CSO tables). The IRC § 7702(d) corridor, however, does not change.

For purposes of the guideline premium test, the term "premiums paid" is defined in section 7702(f)(1) to mean the premiums paid under the contract less:

- distributions, other than amounts included in gross income, to which section 72(e) applies (e.g., policyholder dividends and partial withdrawals treated as recovering investment in the contract);
- any excess premiums with respect to which there is a distribution described in section 7702(f)(7)(B) or (f)(7)(E) (this rule is described in Chapter 4);
- any amounts returned to the policyholder—with interest—within 60 days of the end of a **contract year** in order to comply with the guideline premium test, as described in the discussion of section 7702(f)(1)(B) below; and
- any other amounts received with regard to the contract that are specified in regulations (to date, none have been issued).

One circumstance in which premiums paid for purposes of the guideline premium test will differ from the premiums paid that govern the income tax treatment of predeath distributions from life insurance contracts occurs when an existing contract in a gain position (i.e., the cash surrender value exceeds the investment in the contract) is exchanged for a new contract in a tax-free transaction under section 1035. In a section 1035 exchange, the cash surrender value of the replaced contract that is transferred to the new contract—in this case, net of any surrender charges and paid-off loans under the replaced contract—is included in premiums paid for the new contract under section 7702(f)(1), regardless of whether that cash surrender value is greater than or less than the premiums paid for the replaced contract; the prior premiums paid are irrelevant for this purpose. For purposes of determining the section 72(e) taxable gain, however, the prior premiums paid (less any prior untaxed distributions from the replaced contract) make up the initial investment in the new contract under section 72(e)(6). Other examples of a difference between the definition of premiums paid for purposes of section 7702 and section 72(e)(6) occur where the 60-day rule of section 7702(f)(1)(B) noted above applies, and also where loans, assignments or pledges (or agreements to assign or pledge) result in an amount received under a MEC that triggers gain recognition under section 72(e)(4)(A). In other circumstances, however, the treatment of premiums paid may be the same under the two statutes. For example, in a 1990 private letter ruling, the IRS concluded that the waiver of the monthly deduction for mortality and other charges under a universal life contract due to the insured's disability do not affect either the investment in the contract under section 72(e)(6) or the premiums paid under section 7702(f)(1)(A).[20]

## *Treatment of Premiums Returned to Policyholders to Comply With the GPT*

Under section 7702(f)(1)(B), the premiums paid quantity is reduced by amounts returned within 60 days of the end of the contract year in order to comply with the guideline premium test, provided they are returned with interest (which is taxable). The statutory language provides that:

> If, in order to comply with the requirements of subsection (a)(2)(A), any portion of any premium paid during any contract year is returned by the insurance company (with interest) within 60 days after the end of a contract year, the amount so returned (excluding interest) shall be deemed to reduce the sum of the premiums paid under the contract during such year.

Read literally, if a premium must be returned to comply with the guideline premium test, any such amount returned during a year (net of the interest) will reduce the premiums paid during that year. Note that as the statute refers to the return of "any premium paid during any contract year," the premium returned need not be

---

[20] PLR 9106050 (Nov. 16, 1990). *See also* Rev. Rul. 55-349, 1955-1 C.B. 232 (stating that premiums separately paid for waiver of premium, etc., are not included in cost basis). This revenue ruling may have been made obsolete by IRC § 7702. Waiver of premium (and any other QAB) is part of the life insurance contract as defined by IRC § 7702, and premium paid for the contract is the starting point for determining "investment in the contract" under IRC § 72(c)(1) and (e)(6). At the same time, a QAB has a dual nature, in that its funding generally is regulated by IRC § 7702 together with the related life insurance contract, but it otherwise provides coverage that in some cases may be accorded separate treatment for income tax purposes. *See* PLRs 200339015 and 200339016 (June 17, 2003) (treating certain disability income benefits as accident or health insurance under IRC § 104(a)(3) but expressly not addressing whether such benefits were QABs).

an amount paid during the year in which it is returned. For example, if the guideline premiums are reduced as the result of a decrease in a contract's face value (see the discussion of section 7702(f)(7)(A) "adjustments" later in this chapter and in Chapter 4), an amount of premium could be **forced out** of the contract to comply with the guideline premium test. The amount forced out would reduce premiums paid under the guideline premium test in the year in which the amount was returned to the policyholder. For a MEC, this characterization of such forced-out amounts as a return of premiums may conflict with the income-first characterization of distributions that normally would apply under section 72(e), although section 7702(f)(1)(B) could be interpreted to mean that such a distribution was treated as premium for the guideline premium test but as potentially giving rise to income under section 72(e). More broadly, section 7702(f)(1)(B) arguably might be read to mean that forced-out premiums are simply treated as premiums returned and thus recover investment in the contract even if the contract is a MEC.

While section 7702(f)(1)(B) requires the returned premium to be accompanied by a payment of interest to the policyholder (who must pay income tax thereon), there is no guidance on the determination of the amount of such interest. The concept underlying the requirement is a simple one: where "excess" premiums paid during a contract year are returned at or just following the end of that year, the inside buildup (interest) credited to those excess premiums during the period when excess existed must be disgorged and taxed to the policyholder. The problem posed by this rule, in the absence of guidance, is that the required interest amount is not clearly defined when premiums need to be returned under the section 7702(f)(1)(B) rule, either due to a section 7702(f)(7)(A) adjustment or due to the need to correct a contract's noncompliance with section 7702 (as discussed in Chapter 8). In such cases, a variety of practices have been pursued. One approach, for example, has been to base the interest amount on the contract's interest crediting rate in the year of the premium return and the number of days the excess premium remained in the contract after the adjustment reduced the guideline premium limitation. Other approaches would be to use the contract's minimum guaranteed interest crediting rate or the interest rate applied to the delayed payment of proceeds on contract surrender or the death of the insured.

As a final observation on the section 7702(f)(1)(B) rule, it should be noted that the rule (comparably with other terms of the statute) depends upon action within a specific time period after the end of the "contract year." Section 7702 does not define this term, but the insurance industry has understood the statute's reference to a contract year to coincide with the concept of the "policy year," which is the one-year period following from the policy date or issue date placed on the contract's specification pages by the issuing insurer and from the anniversaries of that date. The legislative history of section 7702 appears to accept this understanding.[21] However, as discussed below, a potentially different "contract year" applies under section 7702A.

## *Applying the Guideline Premium Test*

Unlike the CVAT, which must be met prospectively by the terms of the contract, the guideline premium test need only be met by the operation of the contract. The GPT is a retrospective fact test under which a contract is viewed as being in compliance with section 7702 until noncompliance with the guideline premium limitation actually occurs. Thus, a contract tested under the guideline premium test may initially be in compliance with section 7702 even though by its terms it must ultimately fail. For example, a fixed premium contract with an annual premium exceeding the GLP will ultimately fail the guideline premium test, but it may be protected from failure for an initial period by the GSP. Such a contract is considered to fail only at the time the actual premiums paid exceed the GSP. In addition, a contract can actually fail to comply with the guideline premium test during a contract year and later be brought into compliance, within 60 days of the end of that contract year, using the premium refund provision of section 7702(f)(1)(B) described above.

More specifically, during the first year after a contract is issued, the guideline premium test is satisfied as long as the premiums paid (as defined above) do not exceed the GSP. If there is no change to a contract's terms or benefits after issue, the GSP will be the prevailing limit under the test for a number of contract durations—

---

[21] *See* DEFRA Blue Book, *supra* Chapter 1, note 20, at 655, stating, in the context of the effective date rule for IRC § 7702, that "the issue date of a contract is generally the date on the policy assigned by the insurance company, which is on or after the date the application was signed." This was subject to the proviso that the date on the policy would not be respected if the period between the application date and the policy date was unusually long. No comparable statement appears in the formal DEFRA legislative history.

approximately 8-12 years for an option 1 death benefit contract, and roughly four to six years in the case of an option 2 death benefit—after which the sum of the GLPs will constitute the prevailing limit. Under either death benefit option, as previously illustrated in Figure 2.2, at the beginning of year 13, the guideline premium limitation will increase over the amount of the limitation at the end of year 12 by one GLP, for the reason that the sum of the GLPs in year 13 (i.e., 13 GLPs) will exceed that sum for year 12 (i.e., 12 GLPs) by that one GLP. Hence, the guideline premium limitation will be satisfied in year 12 if the premiums paid do not exceed the sum of 12 GLPs, and it will be satisfied in year 13 as well if the premiums paid do not exceed the sum of 13 GLPs. In this connection, note that the contract year is as defined above.

Finally, section 7702(f)(6) provides that a premium payment that causes the sum of the premiums paid to exceed the guideline premium limitation will not result in disqualification of the contract if:

- the payment was necessary to prevent the termination of the contract on or before the end of the contract year, and
- the contract will have no CSV at the contract year-end.

This rule, an exception to the general proposition that there must be compliance with the guideline premium test (or the CVAT) at all times, was framed to address the circumstance of a contract that was insufficiently funded and therefore would terminate during a contract year absent payment of the additional premium. The important condition placed on the use of the section 7702(f)(6) exception to the general rule of the guideline premium test is that the contract must end the contract year with no CSV. Thus, a premium in excess of the limitation seemingly could be applied to a universal life contract under this rule on a monthly deduction date only if it is expected that no CSV will remain at the contract year-end. In this situation, it is necessary to adopt measures to manage the amount of the cash value so that it reaches zero by the year-end.

## Choice of Tests Under Section 7702

There is nothing in section 7702 that limits whether a contract is tested for compliance under the CVAT or the guideline premium/cash value corridor test, and there are advantages and disadvantages to using either approach. The notion of alternative tests, one designed for universal life and the other for traditional life insurance, was carried over into section 7702 from section 101(f). Conceptually, the CVAT can be thought of as modeled on a traditional participating contract, with dividends applied to purchase paid-up additions. The CVAT was intended to allow traditional life insurance contracts to continue to qualify as life insurance contracts without any significant changes in the plan design. Based on the two tests' origins, it is assumed, but not required, that the CVAT will generally be applied to traditional permanent contracts and that the guideline premium test will be applied to universal life. However, many universal life plans have been designed to comply with the CVAT.

By its nature, the guideline premium test is better suited to flexible premium contracts (although it has been applied to fixed premium plans). Basing the limitation on the greater of the GSP or the sum of the GLPs allows a flexible premium contract to be funded in a variety of ways and still qualify as life insurance. However, problems can arise when the guideline premium test is applied to flexible premium contracts that are not funded adequately, particularly in a low interest rate environment, or when the test is applied to contracts that have a fixed premium structure and cash value scale. The former is a result of the fact that the test is not sensitive to the amounts of the actual premium payments (as long as they do not exceed the guideline premium limitation), while the latter results from the inherent inconsistency between the attained-age-based adjustment rules of the guideline premium test and the requirements of the *Standard Nonforfeiture Law for Life Insurance*[22] (which operate on an issue-age basis).

As demonstrated in an analysis of IRS rulings waiving compliance failures under section 7702(f)(8) (see Chapter 8), errors can occur in the application of both tests. Noncompliance may result from errors made in plan design, systems and programming errors, contract administration errors and clerical errors. The failure to meet the CVAT by the terms of the contract can result in the failure of an entire group of contracts at issue. However, even though a contract may be intended to qualify under the CVAT, it does not fail to comply with

---

[22] NATIONAL ASSOCIATION OF INSURANCE COMMISSIONERS, *Standard Nonforfeiture Law for Life Insurance*, NAIC MODEL LAWS, REGULATIONS AND GUIDELINES, Vol. 6, Model 808 (January 2014).

section 7702 until it also fails the guideline premium test. As stated before, the latter is the residual test under the statute, and the presumption is made that unless a contract passes the CVAT, it must be considered under the guideline premium test. In contrast to CVAT errors, those made in computing the guideline premiums will only result in the failure of those contracts whose premiums paid actually exceed a properly computed guideline premium limitation, and only as of the date the limitation is exceeded. In this sense, the guideline premium test is more "forgiving."

One difference between the two tests is the need to maintain accurate policy transaction history (e.g., face amounts increases or decreases), as the GSP and GLP resulting from policy changes or adjustments are based in part on historical GSPs and GLPs. As such, the guideline premium test is prone to systems and administrative errors. Having access to historical transaction history is necessary should errors arise that require a recalculation of guideline premiums. This problem is not present under the CVAT, the calculations for which are based only on a contract's future benefits. However, errors in the basic design of a contract are simpler to correct under the guideline premium test as compared with the CVAT, and, as just noted, a contract will not fail the guideline premium test until the premiums paid actually exceed a correct guideline premium limitation. Thus, although one of the appeals of the CVAT is its apparent simplicity, it too is not without challenges, and waivers have been issued on CVAT contracts that were not administered in accordance with the contract terms.[23]

According to the Deficit Reduction Act of 1984 (DEFRA) legislative history, while a contract need not refer to the specific test under which it is intended to qualify, the choice of the test made for a contract would be evident from the face or form of the contract.[24] That is, the plan design underlying a life insurance contract will generally determine which of the two tests under section 7702 should apply to that contract. The prospective nature of the CVAT and the corresponding retrospective nature of the guideline premium test, often disregarded by product designers, represent a fundamental difference in approach to be considered in determining which test should apply to a particular plan. DesRochers notes:

> The prospective focus of the cash value accumulation test was seen as more appropriate to traditional forms with fixed premiums and policy values, while the retrospective nature of the guideline test was seen as better suited to universal life and other flexible coverage, where the contract values are not fixed at issue.[25]

In practice, a contract typically will state the basis on which it endeavors to qualify with section 7702, and often will also include a **fail-safe provision** empowering the company to construe and/or modify the contract to maintain qualification with the definitional limits. Traditional life insurance contracts may well comply with the CVAT in the way they operate, omitting any specific qualifying language. Universal life and other accumulation-type contracts seeking to qualify with the CVAT typically provide that the death benefit will at all times be at least equal to the CSV (again, as defined in section 7702(f)(2)(A)) divided by the appropriate NSP factor (determined in accordance with the section 7702 rules) to assure the contract meets the test by its terms. For these plans, the CVAT limitation is often expressed as a "corridor" minimum death benefit equal to the reciprocal of the NSP for $1 of death benefit multiplied by the CSV at death. If factors are incorporated into the contract, care should be taken in rounding. Where the factors are rounded down, it is possible that the CSV multiplied by the factor will produce a death benefit that does not satisfy the requirements of the CVAT.[26] (Additional discussion of rounding in the definitional calculations appears in Appendix 2.2.) For contracts seeking to comply with the guideline premium test, the section 7702(d) corridor factors are generally provided in the contract.

The method of qualification at issue is generally required to continue over the life of a contract. That is, once a contract satisfies section 7702 through reliance on one test, it generally must continue to rely on that test at

---

[23] See PLR 9625046 (March 27, 1996).
[24] DEFRA Blue Book, *supra* Chapter 1, note 20, at 646. No comparable statement appears in the formal DEFRA legislative history.
[25] Christian J. DesRochers, *The Definition of Life Insurance Under Section 7702 of the Internal Revenue Code*, 40 SOC'Y ACTUARIES TRANSACTIONS 209, 216 (1988) (hereinafter DesRochers).
[26] This can be illustrated by an example. At age 55, the NSP per $1,000 of death benefit (as shown in Table 2.1) is $402.11. The reciprocal of the NSP results in a corridor factor of 2.48688. If this is rounded down to 248 percent, the product of the corridor factor (248 percent) and the NSP ($402.11) is $997.23, instead of $1,000. Thus, the actual death benefit of $997.23 is less than the required death benefit ($1,000) needed to meet the CVAT. The application of a 249 percent factor results in a death benefit of $1,001.25. (To paraphrase Wilkins Micawber in Charles Dickens' DAVID COPPERFIELD: Corridor 249 percent, result happiness; corridor 248 percent, result misery.)

all times thereafter.[27] An exception to this is mentioned in the legislative history, permitting contracts using the guideline premium test to switch to the CVAT upon election of a nonforfeiture option.[28] Absent such relief, a guideline premium-tested contract for which a reduced paid-up election is made could easily fail the guideline premium limitation after the adjustment calculation. In **waiver rulings** and **closing agreements** addressing contracts' compliance failures, the IRS also has permitted contracts to be amended to change from the guideline premium test to the CVAT as the means of curing the failures.[29]

As there is no provision made in section 7702 for dividing a contract for purposes of applying the definitional test, whatever test is chosen should be applied consistently to the entire contract. This is reflected, for example, by the legislative history of section 7702, which states that for purposes of section 7702, "a whole life insurance contract that provides for the purchase of paid-up or deferred additions will be treated as a single life insurance contract."[30] Thus, a paid-up addition under a participating contract is included in both the CSV and the death benefit for purposes of applying section 7702. Under this rule it would be inappropriate to attach a rider tested under the CVAT to a guideline base plan, and vice versa.

## Modified Endowment Contracts Under Section 7702A

The term modified endowment contract is defined in section 7702A(a). A MEC is a contract entered into on or after June 21, 1988, that:

- qualifies as a life insurance contract within the meaning of section 7702 but fails to meet the "7-pay test" prescribed in section 7702A(b), or
- is received in exchange for a MEC.

As described in Chapter 1, predeath distributions from MECs (e.g., policy loans, partial withdrawals and policyholder dividends) are subject to more restrictive tax rules than distributions from contracts that are not MECs. The 7-pay test acts to slow the permissible funding during the first seven contract years (or for seven years following a **material change**, as described below and in Chapter 4), in effect requiring additional amounts at risk during that time relative to the minimum permitted under section 7702. Apart from predeath distributions, MECs are accorded the same tax treatment as all other life insurance contracts.

The 7-pay test is set forth in section 7702A(b) in these words: "a contract fails to meet the 7-pay test ... if the accumulated amount paid under the contract at any time during the $1^{st}$ 7 contract years exceeds the sum of the net level premiums which would have been paid on or before such time if the contract provided for paid-up future benefits after the payment of 7 level annual premiums."

Applying this definition, two components are involved in the application of the 7-pay test. First, the amount of each of the "7 [net] level annual premiums"—usually referred to as the "7-pay premium"—must be calculated. This premium is based on the contract's future benefits. Second, the cumulative amount of premium paid, known in the statutory terminology as the **amount paid**, during the first seven years of a contract's existence (or seven years following a material change) must be compared to the cumulative 7-pay premiums at each point in time. The rules applicable to the calculation of the NSP under the CVAT generally apply to the calculation of the 7-pay premium.

### *The 7-Pay Test*

In the same way that the NSP serves as the model for the CVAT, the 7-pay premium is the basis for the section 7702A limitation and is given by

---

[27] DEFRA House Report, *supra* Chapter 1, note 11, at 1443; DEFRA Senate Report, *supra* Chapter 1, note 11, at 572; DEFRA Blue Book, *supra* Chapter 1, note 20, at 646.

[28] DEFRA Blue Book, *supra* Chapter 1, note 20, at 646, n. 50. No comparable statement appears in the formal DEFRA legislative history.

[29] PLR 200329040 (April 16, 2003); PLR 200328027 (April 10, 2003) and PLR 200230037 (April 30, 2002). In PLR 200329040, the company added a CVAT endorsement to all in-force contracts (including failed contracts) effective retroactively to each contract's issue date. The ruling provided that the CVAT endorsement would not result in a loss of grandfathering under IRC §§ 72, 264, 7702 or 7702A. IRS closing agreements (discussed in Chapter 8) are not disclosed to the public.

[30] DEFRA Senate Report, *supra* Chapter 1, note 11, at 572.

$$7Pay = Face\ Amount \times \frac{A_x}{\ddot{a}_{x:\overline{7}|}}$$

$$7Pay = Face\ Amount \times \frac{\sum_{t=0}^{\omega-1} v^{t+1} \times {}_t p_x \times q_{x+t}}{\sum_{t=0}^{6} v^t \times {}_t p_x}$$

In describing the calculation of the 7-pay premium, section 7702A(c)(1) references the CVAT rules under section 7702(b)(2). Hence, like the NSP, the 7-pay premium for a contract is determined using

- an annual effective interest of 4 percent or, if greater, the rate or rates guaranteed on issuance of the contract;
- **reasonable mortality charges** that, except as provided in regulations, do not exceed the mortality charges specified in the prevailing commissioners' standard tables as defined in section 807(d)(5) as of the time the contract is issued;[31] and
- **reasonable expense charges** for QABs that are reasonably expected to be actually paid.

The "computational rules" for the 7-pay premium, set forth in section 7702A(c)(1), are discussed later in this chapter and in greater detail in Chapter 3.

With the exception of a $75 allowance for small contracts discussed subsequently, the 7-pay test does not permit other contractual expenses to be recognized in the calculation of its limitation, much like the CVAT in the calculation of the NSP. It does so despite the fact that the 7-pay test's limitation is imposed on the gross premiums paid for a contract.

## *$75 Per Policy and Modal Premium Expense Allowances*

While the general rule of the 7-pay test is that no expenses are recognized in computing the 7-pay premium, an exception to this was granted for small face amount contracts. For contracts with an initial death benefit of $10,000 or less that require payment of at least 7 nondecreasing premiums, each 7-pay premium is increased by $75. To prevent abuse of this allowance, all contracts previously issued by the same insurance company to the same policyholder are to be aggregated in determining whether this rule may be applied to a contract. For example, a policyholder may opt to buy two contracts each with a face amount of $10,000. For purposes solely of determining whether this exception applies, the contracts would be aggregated. The result would be an amount of death benefit not eligible for the exception, rather than two separate contracts, each of which was eligible.

As another potential exception, section 7702A(c)(5) grants the Secretary of the Treasury authority to issue regulations to allow expenses to be taken into account in calculating the 7-pay premium, provided they are attributable solely to the collection of premiums more frequently than annually (i.e., modal premiums). As no such regulation has been proposed, much less made final, these modal premium loads cannot be taken into account in computing the 7-pay premium, pending any future action by the Treasury.

## *Amount Paid Under Section 7702A*

The 7-pay test is applied by determining whether the **amount paid** at any time ever exceeds the 7-pay limit at that time. Under section 7702A(e)(1)(A), the amount paid means "(i) the premiums paid under the contract reduced by (ii) amounts to which section 72(e) applies (without regard to section 72(e)(4)(A)), but not including amounts includible in gross income." Because of the parenthetical phrase in the above quote, the receipt of a loan, repayment of a loan and payment of loan interest all have no effect on amounts paid under section 7702A. According to Adney and Griffin:

> This definition, which is modeled on but does not precisely follow the language of section 7702(f)(1)'s definition of "premiums paid," was intended to count as premiums all amounts paid for the

---

[31] The MEC rules apply to contracts entered into beginning on June 21, 1988, while the reasonable mortality rules apply to contracts issued beginning on October 21, 1988. For contracts issued in the period between June 21 and October 21, 1988, the contract mortality guarantees may be appropriate for computing the 7-pay premium.

policy being tested, though net of amounts, such as policyholder dividends and partial withdrawals, typically returned or removed from a policy without taxation (assuming that the policy is not already a modified endowment).[32]

Section 7702A(e)(1)(B) and (C) contains rules comparable to the 60-day return-of-premium rules for the guideline premium test described above. By returning, with interest, premium paid during a contract year in excess of the 7-pay limit for that year, MEC status can be avoided. The section 7702(e)(1)(B) rule, however, is of more limited utility in the case of certain contract changes than is the case with the guideline premium test. Where a contract undergoes a reduction in benefits during a 7-pay testing period, with a concomitant retroactive testing of the amount paid against a reduced 7-pay limit (as discussed below under "adjustments"), use of the rule will not provide the help needed to avoid MEC status in most cases because it does not operate to reduce the amount paid in prior years.

## *Applying the 7-Pay Test*

During the first year after a contract is issued, the contract will fail to meet the 7-pay test if the amount paid under the contract, at any time during that contract year, exceeds the 7-pay premium. During the second through seventh contract years, the accumulated amounts paid under the contract are compared to the sum of the 7-pay premiums through the start of that contract year (e.g., four 7-pay premiums in the fourth year). The sum of the 7-pay premiums, contract year by contract year, thus establishes a "7-pay limit." It is important to note that section 7702A(e)(2) defines "contract year," differently than section 7702, as "the 12-month period beginning with the 1st month for which the contract is in effect, and the 12-month period beginning with the corresponding month in subsequent calendar years." Thus, the contract year for section 7702A purposes will not necessarily be coextensive with the section 7702 contract year (i.e., generally the policy year established by the issuing insurer), although in most circumstances (barring a material change, as discussed below) it is reasonable to treat a contract's issue date as the date it goes into effect.

Contracts designed to be funded at the level of the 7-pay premium typically can qualify with the definition of life insurance under the CVAT. As can be seen in the **GSP to 7-pay ratio** row of Table 2.4, the GSP is about three times the 7-pay premium at age 25, a ratio that increases to about 4.5 at age 65. This means that, for a contract to be a non-MEC, only three or four of the allowed 7-pay premiums can be paid into a guideline premium-tested contract until such time as the sum of the GLPs becomes the effective limit for any additional funding of the contract (see Table 2.2). This result, which stems from the 6 percent interest rate minimum in computing the GSP and the absence of expenses in computing the 7-pay premium, can be an important consideration in choosing which definitional test a contract should be designed to meet.

| Table 2.4. Seven-pay limitation per $1,000 of death benefit | | | | | |
|---|---|---|---|---|---|
| Age | 25 | 35 | 45 | 55 | 65 |
| 7-pay | 23.66 | 33.23 | 47.06 | 65.77 | 90.55 |
| NSP | 147.21 | 206.64 | 291.24 | 402.11 | 534.82 |
| GSP | 67.63 | 107.40 | 174.09 | 274.20 | 409.45 |
| GSP to 7-pay ratio | 2.9 | 3.2 | 3.7 | 4.2 | 4.5 |
| GLP | 8.33 | 12.60 | 19.87 | 32.49 | 55.63 |

*Assumptions: 2001 CSO male aggregate; ANB; 4% GLP, NSP and 7-pay; 6% GSP; endowment at age 100; curtate*

Even after a 7-pay testing period ends with a contract passing (as opposed to failing) the 7-pay test, concern with the test does not cease. If a material change occurs, as explained in the "adjustments" discussion below, the 7-pay test applies anew beginning on the date of the change.

---

[32] Adney and Griffin, part 2, *supra* Chapter 1, note 75, at 74, 80.

## Interest

The statutory restriction on the rates of interest permitted in the calculation of the limitations under sections 7702 and 7702A (and previously section 101(f)) is that the greater of the **rate or rates guaranteed on issuance** of a contract or the statutory minimum rates must be used. In the calculation of the NSP, the GLP and the 7-pay premium as each pertains to its respective compliance test, a minimum annual effective interest rate of 4 percent is prescribed, while in calculating the GSP, a **floor interest rate** of 6 percent is to be used. Selection of the interest assumption to be used in computing these limitations is generally a relatively straightforward exercise, although the identification of the appropriate interest rate has occasionally created issues.

Interest rates are subject to statutory minimums because increases in the net premium can be realized by reducing the assumed rate of interest. Thus, a lower assumed rate of interest can result in a lower net amount at risk, creating a more highly investment-oriented contract. Where a low minimum assumed rate is combined with a significantly higher actual credited rate, significant amounts of inside buildup can be generated. To prevent too high an NSP, guideline premium or 7-pay premium per $1,000 of death benefit, sections 7702 and 7702A (like section 101(f) beforehand) impose minimums on the rates of interest that could be assumed in the calculations, consistently with the concept of the net premium as a control mechanism.

As illustrated in Table 2.5, for a male insured at age 45, the NSPs and 7-pay premiums per $1,000 of death benefit are reduced by approximately 20 to 25 percent for each 1 percent increase in the assumed interest rate, while the net level premium (used, for example, in determining the GLP) is reduced by approximately 15 percent for each 1 percent increase. The ratio columns are computed as the ratio of the NSP, net level premium or 7-pay to the corresponding value at a rate 1 percent lower.

### Table 2.5. Premiums for a male age 45

| Interest | NSP | Ratio | NLP | Ratio | 7-pay | Ratio |
| --- | --- | --- | --- | --- | --- | --- |
| 3% | 386.50 | — | 18.35 | — | 60.67 | — |
| 4% | 291.24 | 75.4% | 15.80 | 86.1% | 47.06 | 77.6% |
| 5% | 223.25 | 76.7% | 13.69 | 86.6% | 37.06 | 78.8% |
| 6% | 174.09 | 78.0% | 11.93 | 87.1% | 29.67 | 80.1% |

*Assumptions: 2001 CSO aggregate, ANB, endowment at age 100, curtate*

The DEFRA legislative history defined the reference to the "rate or rates guaranteed on issuance" in section 7702 to mean, in general, the floor rate of interest guaranteed at issue of the contract, i.e., the rate below which the interest credited to the contract for the period cannot fall.[33] In this connection, the legislative history noted that although an insurer may guarantee a higher interest rate from time to time after contract issuance, either by contractual declaration or by operation of a formula or index, the "rate … guaranteed at issuance" still should be taken to be the floor rate.[34] Thus, where a contract provides a long-term guaranteed rate of 4 percent, that rate is the guaranteed rate applicable to calculations under the statute, even though the company may, from time to time, declare a higher rate. In this connection, the legislative history also indicates that the statutory reference to the "rate or rates of interest guaranteed on issuance of the contract" should be interpreted in the same manner for purposes of both the guideline premium limitation and the CVAT.[35]

Contracts may also guarantee different floor rates for different periods of the contract. For example, a universal life contract may guarantee 5 percent for the first 10 contract years, and 4.5 percent thereafter. When this occurs, the guaranteed rate in each duration is compared to the statutory minimum, and the higher of the two rates is used for that duration. In computing the GLP for this contract, calculations would reflect both the 5 percent and the 4.5 percent interest rates for the durations in which the respective guarantees applied (i.e., 5 percent for contract years one through 10 and 4.5 percent for contract years 11 and later). However, the GSP

---

[33] DEFRA Blue Book, *supra* Chapter 1, note 20, at 648. No comparable statement appears in the formal DEFRA legislative history.
[34] *Id.*
[35] *Id.* n. 51.

would be computed using the 6 percent statutory minimum rate, since in all years that rate would be greater than the contractually guaranteed rates.

## *Treatment of Initial Guarantees*

By virtue of the reference to the rate or rates guaranteed at issuance and the equation of this to the floor rate(s) below which contractual crediting rates cannot fall, section 7702 (and sections 7702A and 101(f)) requires this to include any **initial guarantee** of interest made at issue that was enforceable by the policyholder, whether made specifically in the contract or otherwise. Initial interest guarantees (e.g., for the first 12 months) are common in many life insurance contracts today. Under universal life-type contracts, the contract's account value typically is guaranteed at issue to be credited with interest at a rate in excess of the contract's floor rate for at least some initial period of time. When the initial credited rate is guaranteed and exceeds the otherwise applicable guaranteed floor rate, the initial rate is considered a part of the rate(s) guaranteed at issuance and must be reflected for the duration of the initial guarantee period in the definitional calculations. However, as discussed below, short-term interest rate guarantees that become contractually enforceable only after issuance are generally not reflected in the calculations.

In determining the guaranteed interest rates for purposes of the calculations, any higher interest amounts (such as bonuses), to be credited at contract issuance or in subsequent durations, that are guaranteed in the contract and cause the interest rate or rates guaranteed at issue to exceed the greater of the floor rate(s) and the statutory minimum rates in one or more durations, must be taken into account. The effect of such a bonus can be reflected in the calculations by adjusting the guaranteed interest rate. (These plans are discussed in Chapter 6).

## *Short-Term Guarantees*

The DEFRA legislative history noted that *de minimis* guarantees in excess of the otherwise assumed floor rates may sometimes be disregarded.[36] According to the legislative history, **short-term interest guarantees** (those extending no more than one year) generally are considered *de minimis* in the calculation of the GLP but not in the calculation of the NSP or the GSP.[37] In other words, the NSP and the GSP generally must reflect all interest guarantees at issuance. Because section 7702A references the rules of section 7702(b)(2) (i.e., rules applicable to the calculation of the NSP) for purposes of computing the 7-pay premium, the *de minimis* rule contained in the DEFRA Blue Book seemingly would not allow short-term guarantees to be disregarded in the initial 7-pay premium computations.

The treatment of short-term guarantees made after contract issuance was addressed by the IRS in a 1999 private letter ruling.[38] In the ruling, the IRS was asked whether interest crediting guarantees lasting for 12 months that come into effect after a contract's issue date need to be taken into account for purposes of determining the NSP for the contract. The life insurance company issuing the contract involved in the ruling declared a current credited rate each year and guaranteed the crediting rate for a 12-month period based on an index formula set out in an endorsement. The IRS held that such annual interest rate declarations were in the nature of policyholder dividends and not "interest rate guarantees." The IRS reached this conclusion because, under the terms of the endorsement, the interest rate was guaranteed for periods of one year or less and subject to change after completion of each guarantee period pursuant to the endorsement's formula. Accordingly, the annual rates established under the endorsement, which could not be known in advance, were not required to be taken into account in determining the NSP for the contract after the first contract year.

The 1999 private letter ruling dealt with contracts guaranteeing future crediting rates based on a predetermined interest rate index. Applying the reasoning of the ruling (which cannot be relied on as precedent), a contract under which a minimum interest rate (if any) above the contract's floor rate is set from year to year by an index would generally have its definitional limitations calculated using the contract's floor rate, except that the initial index value would be used for the duration of the initial guarantee if it is higher than that rate (and assuming that all of the interest guarantees are not *de minimis* and equal or exceed the statutory minimums).

---

[36] DEFRA Blue Book, *supra* Chapter 1, note 20, at 649. No comparable statement appears in the formal DEFRA legislative history.
[37] *Id.*
[38] PLR 199929028 (April 27, 1999).

Significantly, in performing the calculations for an **adjustment event** or a material change after contract issuance (see Chapter 4), this logic suggests that annual short-term interest guarantees may be disregarded. However, the guidance in this area is limited, and the treatment of a short-term interest guarantee, as it relates to computations made to reflect an adjustment to a contract initiated by the policyholder, has not been addressed.

In an earlier (1997) private letter ruling, the IRS addressed the treatment of **excess interest** in the course of waiving the failure of an insurer to take certain interest guarantees into account in the computation of the guideline premiums.[39] In this ruling, the IRS noted that "one can reasonably infer that the drafters of section 101(f) may have viewed excess interest credits that vary from year to year as economically equivalent to policyholder dividends" and that "one also might reasonably infer that the annual declaration of an excess interest rate should not have any effect on a contract's guideline premium limitation." However, the IRS also indicated that, where an insurer obligates itself to credit excess interest (i.e., amounts above the floor rate) after contract issuance for a period of several years, the excess interest credits may not be economically equivalent to discretionary policyholder dividend distributions and thus should be reflected in the definitional calculations. Further, any excess interest guaranteed in the first contract year generally must be reflected in the calculations.

## *Policyholder Dividends and Interest Guarantees*

The phrase **economically equivalent to policyholder dividends** used in the 1997 ruling has a particular connotation under the Internal Revenue Code and is relevant to identification of contract guarantees for purposes of computing the definitional limits. In general, contractual guarantees are required to be reflected in the section 7702 and 7702A calculations, but policyholder dividends, broadly defined, are not. Thus, it is important in computing the limitations under sections 7702 and 7702A to distinguish between contract guarantees and what the federal income tax law views as policyholder dividends.

The definition of a policyholder dividend has a long and somewhat contentious history in the federal income taxation of the life insurance industry. The traditional, or textbook, definition of such dividends is that they are amounts paid out of a company's surplus by virtue of experience under its contracts (interest earnings, mortality costs and expenses) being better than anticipated or guaranteed to policyholders. In this view, dividends are conceptually earned first, then apportioned out of company surplus as divisible surplus, and then allocated among policies and paid or credited. The dividend is retrospective in this view, as it is paid out of past favorable experience.

The product revolution of the late 1970s and early 1980s saw a proliferation of life insurance and annuity products designed with significant nonguaranteed policy elements.[40] Universal life, indeterminate premium life, current assumption life insurance and excess interest annuities were all examples of this phenomenon. The Life Insurance Company Income Tax Act of 1959—essentially intact until 1984—effectively limited the deductibility of policyholder dividends by the life insurance company in some situations. This led many insurers to seek to avoid classification of these nonguaranteed elements as dividends, which might not be deductible in computing their federal income tax. The argument that these extra benefits or reduced premiums to policyholders were not "traditional dividends" under the Code ultimately proved futile, as the IRS announced in Revenue Ruling 82-133[41] that it viewed the concept of a policyholder dividend in tax law to be very broad. According to the ruling, policyholder dividends encompassed traditional dividends (paid or credited depending on the experience of the company or the discretion of management) as well as excess interest, mortality charge reductions, premium reductions, experience refunds or rate credits, and generally any benefit not guaranteed in the contract.

In 1984, as part of a sweeping revision of the taxation of life insurance companies that also brought section 7702 into the Code, the IRS interpretation of the meaning of policyholder dividend was explicitly enacted into law (at the same time, such dividends were generally made deductible by life insurers). Today, under section

---

[39] PLR 9723040 (March 11, 1997).
[40] Actuarial Standard of Practice No. 2 defines a nonguaranteed charge or benefit as: "Any element within a policy ... other than policy dividends, which affects policyholder costs or value, and which may be changed at the discretion of the insurer after issue. Examples of nonguaranteed charges or benefits include excess interest, mortality charges or expense charges lower than those guaranteed in the policy, indeterminate premiums, and participation rates for equity-indexed products." *See* ACTUARIAL STANDARDS BOARD, *Nonguaranteed Charges or Benefits for Life Insurance Policies and Annuity Contracts*, ACTUARIAL STANDARD OF PRACTICE NO. 2, at 2 (March 2013).
[41] 1982-2 C.B. 119.

808, "policyholder dividend" is a broadly construed concept for tax purposes, not being bound by the traditional textbook definition. A wide variety of creative methods of granting policyholders benefits not guaranteed in the contract have emerged in life insurance products, but the fact is, whether prospective or retrospective, and however or whenever paid or credited, they typically are all policyholder dividends for tax purposes.

While the foregoing does not answer the question under sections 7702 and 7702A in all circumstances, the treatment of post-issuance nonguaranteed benefits and other certain amounts as dividends within the meaning of section 808 often should provide comfort that such benefits and amounts do not involve guarantees which need to be taken into account in the definitional calculations, especially in cases where specific guidance under the statutes is lacking.

## *Relationship of Statutory Rates to Contractual Guarantees*

The statutory minimum interest rates do not constrain the actual contract guarantees directly, but they may serve to impose an indirect limitation, particularly for traditional contracts that qualify under the CVAT. As previously noted, the CVAT must be met by the terms of the contract, and a CVAT contract's CSV must not, at any time, be able to exceed the NSP computed at 4 percent interest. A CVAT contract that provides CSVs based on a nonforfeiture interest rate lower than 4 percent could not meet this requirement at the time the contract becomes paid up. Thus, such a contract could not simultaneously meet the requirements of the nonforfeiture law if paid-up values had to be based on an assumed nonforfeiture rate lower than 4 percent (e.g., 3 percent) and the requirements of the CVAT where CSVs are effectively limited to lower amounts dictated by a 4 percent NSP.

An accumulation-type contract such as a universal life insurance contract that is intended to qualify under the CVAT could provide a guaranteed interest rate less than 4 percent, but care should be taken that, if the contract offers a paid-up value, that value be computed at a 4 percent minimum rate so that the election of a nonforfeiture option does not cause the contract to fail the CVAT. On the other hand, such considerations do not carry over to contracts intended to comply with the guideline premium test. However, if such a contract provides a nonforfeiture value in the form of a paid-up benefit, upon election of the benefit it appears that the 4 percent NSP limitation could apply under the CVAT.[42] Whether the presence of a lower guaranteed nonforfeiture rate for such a benefit would create an issue under the "terms of the contract" requirement until it is actually elected is more problematic, and has not been the subject of guidance. In this regard, there is an argument that calculations of values under the definitional limitations must generally follow the basic benefit structure or "main track" of the policy.[43]

## *Monthly Interest Assumption and Death Benefit Discount Rate*

Universal life and other accumulation-type contracts often incorporate two distinct interest rate components, one for determining the amount of interest to be credited to the contract's cash surrender value (a varying rate depending on current rates, subject to a guaranteed minimum), and a second rate—a discount rate—for determining the net amount at risk for purposes of assessing mortality charges under the contract's accumulation value formula (a locked-in rate). Many contract forms explicitly define the first as a monthly interest rate factor. The interest rate generally assumed for monthly calculations is based on compound interest theory and is defined by the formula:

$$i^{(12)} = (1+i)^{1/12} - 1 \qquad (2.5)$$

where $i$ is the current annual effective rate of interest.

The discounting rate is incorporated into the determination of the net amount at risk, where:

$$NAR = \frac{SA}{(1+i)} \times CV \qquad (2.6)$$

---

[42] *See* the discussion of the "choice of tests" at the beginning of Chapter 3.
[43] DesRochers, *supra* note 25.

Here, *i* is different than that used in (2.5) and can be referred to as the **death benefit discount rate**. For most contract designs, the death benefit discount rate (if separately defined) and the guaranteed minimum interest rate are the same. However, because the death benefit discount rate is used only to determine the net amount at risk and does not directly affect cash value growth, it is typically considered to be a mortality-related element that is not an interest rate guaranteed on issuance of the contract for purposes of the definitional calculations.

### *Implied Guarantees*

For certain contract designs, the interest rate or rates guaranteed in the contract for purposes of the section 7702 and 7702A calculations may differ from the rates explicitly stated in the contract. Instead, the guarantees may be implied by a guarantee of a particular cash value scale (e.g., the nonforfeiture cash value). Such **implied guarantees** exist in plan designs commonly referred to as **net rate products**. Under the net rate plan design, premiums (generally single premiums) are credited to the contract's accumulation account. The gross premiums per $1,000 for these plans are typically based on the current mortality table and the minimum statutory interest rate. However, the contract provides guaranteed cash values based on the accumulation of premiums at a specified interest rate with no explicit deduction for mortality. As a result, the guaranteed cash values exceed those that would be provided if the premiums were accumulated reflecting both the specified interest rate and mortality costs.

Conceptually, the increased cash values that occur in these plan designs can be thought of as incorporating an interest guarantee at which those values accumulate that reflects the netting of two elements: an otherwise higher implicit interest crediting rate and the forgone mortality cost. The legislative history of section 7702 indicates that statutory reference to interest guaranteed on issuance of the contract means "the interest rate or rates reflected in the contract's nonforfeiture values assuming the use of the method in the Standard Nonforfeiture Law."[44] For these contracts, the DEFRA legislative history suggests a method of determining this implicit interest rate, referred to as the **gross-up rule**, requiring the contractually guaranteed interest rate for any period to be grossed-up or increased by the amount of the implicit mortality charges for that period. That is, the interest rate treated as guaranteed for purposes of the section 7702 and 7702A calculations must be increased by the implicit mortality charges. For example, where the cash value is $10,000 and the contract guarantees a net credited rate each year of 5 percent (i.e., the cash value in any year is 105 percent of the prior year's value), the interest rate assumed in the calculation must be increased to reflect the forgone (missing) mortality charges.

There is considerable uncertainty regarding the manner of applying the gross-up rule, due to both the absence of guidance and differences in and complexity of contract designs. However, in this simplified example, if the implicit **cost of insurance (COI)** for a given year were $200, then the 5 percent interest rate in the example would be increased to 7 percent in that year. In the absence of the gross-up, the resulting contract would be an increasing death benefit single premium contract that would mature on its guarantees for its initial face amount at an age earlier than 95, thus violating the section 7702(e) computational rules (discussed below). This occurs because the definitional limitations are typically computed assuming both interest and mortality, while the cash values reflect the accumulation of premiums at interest only. These single premium plans were the subject of a series of private letter rulings and are addressed in more detail in Chapter 6.[45]

## Mortality

Mortality rates reflect the probability that an insured attaining a particular age will die at that age. Since mortality rates generally increase with age (i.e., there is an increase in probability of death), so too will the premiums (or required cash values) necessary to fund future death benefits. Universal life and other accumulation-type contracts use both a **guaranteed mortality** table, generally tied to state approved nonforfeiture tables (e.g., the 1980 or 2001 CSO tables), and a lower "current" COI charge. While the minimum contractual guarantees are based on the guaranteed COI rates, the actual cash values reflect the current COI charges. Cash values for traditional life insurance contracts, on the other hand, are based directly on the applicable nonforfeiture table.

---

[44] DEFRA Senate Report, *supra* Chapter 1, note 11, at 573–74; DEFRA Blue Book, *supra* Chapter 1, note 20, at 648–49. *See also* DEFRA House Report, *supra* Chapter 1, note 11, at 1444 (1984).

[45] *See* PLRs 9833033 (May 21, 1998), 8846018 (Aug. 19, 1988), 8843008 (July 26, 1988), 8827012 (March 31, 1988), and 8816047 (Jan. 25, 1988). All except for PLR 8827012 were waiver rulings.

For participating traditional contracts, current mortality cost is reflected as one component of policyholder dividends.

As mentioned previously, for a contract entered into before October 21, 1988, the definitional calculations are based on the mortality charges specified (i.e., guaranteed) in the contract, or if none are specified, the mortality charges used in determining the reserves for the contract.[46] This standard, which was employed in section 101(f) and in the original version of section 7702, was changed by TAMRA. Specifically, under section 7702(c)(3)(B)(i), the definitional calculations for a contract entered into on or after October 21, 1988, generally are based on mortality charges that are "reasonable" and, except as allowed in regulations, do not exceed the mortality charges specified in the "prevailing commissioners' standard tables (as defined in section 807(d)(5)) as of the time the contract is issued."[47] For a standard risk contract issued today (2015), this generally means the mortality charges assumed in the calculations cannot exceed 100 percent of the applicable charges in the 2001 CSO tables. Section 4.03 of Notice 2006-95 provides that charges guaranteed under a contract that do not exceed 100 percent of the 2001 CSO tables satisfy the requirements of section 7702(c)(3)(B)(i), i.e., they are treated as both reasonable and as falling within the prevailing commissioners' standard tables.[48] The notice thus creates a "safe harbor" rule for insurers to use in performing the definitional calculations. As a condition of using it, however, this safe harbor requires that if a contract guarantees mortality charges that are less than those based on 100 percent of the 2001 CSO tables, the lower guaranteed charges must be employed in the definitional calculations. Notice 2006-95 also sets out rules governing the application of its safe harbor to pre-2001 CSO contracts that undergo changes, as discussed further below.

While the mortality charges used in the definitional calculations today must meet the statutory reasonableness standard, no specific calculation method is prescribed. Consequently, a variety of actuarial practices are applied in the calculations. In addition, the imposition of the reasonableness standard has created a great deal of uncertainty in the treatment of substandard risk charges, resulting in significant variations in how life insurers reflect such charges in the calculations; in contrast, under prior law, the treatment of substandard mortality was relatively straightforward, particularly under the guideline premium test.[49] The actuarial practices used in the reasonable mortality calculations, together with the role of the prevailing commissioners' standard table and the treatment of substandard mortality, are discussed in the following sections.

## *Reasonable Mortality Standard*

In 1988, as part of TAMRA, Congress responded to the perceived abuse of single premium plans and certain other life insurance products by enacting legislation that substantially altered the tax treatment of life insurance contracts viewed as heavily investment-oriented (i.e., contracts that came to be defined as MECs). In addition, to curb the use of what Congress considered to be overly generous assumptions used in the definitional calculations for such contracts, TAMRA imposed restrictions on the mortality and expense charge assumptions permitted to be used in the calculations.[50] As described next, the reasonable mortality requirements imposed on contracts under section 7702(c)(3)(B)(i) can be viewed as having both a **permanent mortality rule** and an **interim mortality rule**.

## *The Permanent Mortality Rule*

The permanent mortality rule refers to the standard specified in section 7702(c)(3)(B)(i). While requiring that mortality charges used in the section 7702 (and 7702A) calculations be reasonable, this provision does not define what is reasonable, leaving that task to regulations. However, the permanent rule does impose a limitation on the level of mortality that would be considered reasonable, i.e., that absent an exception provided in regula-

---

[46] If the contract is "materially changed" after October 20, 1988, the rule described next may apply.
[47] This definition is discussed below.
[48] See 2006-2 C.B. 848.
[49] In some early discussions of the IRC § 7702 tests, concern was expressed with respect to the use of substandard mortality in connection with the CVAT, in that the use of a substandard NSP was not consistent with prevailing industry practice in the determination of reserves and cash values under traditional life insurance plans. It was more common practice for traditional plans to charge a higher premium for a given death benefit for a substandard insured, and provide cash values equivalent to those in a standard risk contract. In other words, the substandard element of the contract was reflected through an otherwise higher premium that had no resulting effect on the contract's cash value.
[50] See Adney and Griffin, part 3, *supra* Chapter 1, note 75, at 70, 78.

tions, reasonable mortality cannot exceed the rates in the prevailing commissioners' standard tables at the time the contract is issued. The prevailing commissioners' standard tables, with respect to any contract, are generally defined in section 807(d)(5) to be the most recent commissioners' standard tables prescribed by the National Association of Insurance Commissioners (NAIC) and permitted to be used in computing reserves for that type of contract under the insurance laws of at least 26 states when the contract was issued. When this concept was introduced into the federal tax law in 1984, the 1980 CSO tables were the prevailing commissioners' standard tables for life insurance.[51] Therefore, under the permanent rule as enacted in 1988, 100 percent of the sex-distinct 1980 CSO tables generally provided an upper bound on reasonable mortality during the time those tables were prevailing. Since their adoption by the NAIC, the 2001 CSO tables[52] have been the most recent standard tables prescribed by the NAIC, and they became the **prevailing tables** after adoption by 26 states in July 2004. (This transition, including a statutory and administrative delay, is discussed further below.)

Section 5011(c)(1) of TAMRA directed the Secretary of the Treasury to issue regulations under section 7702(c)(3)(B)(i) by January 1, 1990, setting forth standards for determining the reasonableness of assumed mortality charges. In response, **proposed mortality regulations** were issued in 1991, as discussed below, although the Treasury Department and IRS have yet to issue final regulations. As a consequence, the permanent rule provides a ceiling on the assumed mortality charges at the level of the prevailing commissioners' standard tables in effect on the issue date of the contract, at least for standard cases, and there remains considerable uncertainty regarding what mortality charges otherwise should be considered "reasonable" under the statute. For a description of the proposed regulations, which are not in effect, see Appendix 2.5.

### *The Interim Mortality Rule*

Section 5011(c)(2) of TAMRA provides an interim rule for contracts entered into on or after October 21, 1988, but before the effective date of temporary or final regulations on the reasonable mortality standard. Because such regulations have yet to be issued, the interim rule can be used to satisfy section 7702(c)(3)(B)(i). The interim rule states that "mortality charges which do not differ materially from the charges actually expected to be imposed by the company (taking into account any relevant characteristics of the insured of which the company is aware) shall be treated as meeting the requirements" of section 7702(c)(3)(B)(i).

Although simple in concept, the interim mortality rule creates a rather vague standard for measuring compliance, one dependent in part on the interpretation of the phrase "mortality charges which do not differ materially from the charges actually expected to be imposed." Beginning with the enactment of TAMRA, the life insurance industry expressed its concerns to the IRS over the ambiguity it viewed as embedded in both the permanent and interim rules, focusing on possible interpretations that would require the use of current mortality charges under these rules. In particular, the industry sought guidance in the form of safe harbors that would allow the use of 100 percent of the 1958 and 1980 CSO tables in meeting the section 7702(c)(3)(B)(i) requirements for standard risks, as the use of these tables was believed to be necessary to allow traditional contracts, tested under the CVAT, to satisfy the *Standard Nonforfeiture Law for Life Insurance*.[53]

### *Reasonable Mortality, Prevailing Commissioners' Standard Tables and IRS Notice 88-128*

The "prevailing commissioners' standard tables" are the mortality tables used in the calculation of the deduction allowed to an insurer for its life insurance reserves under section 807(d). As previously noted, they are, with respect to a given contract, the most recent commissioners' standard tables prescribed by the NAIC and permitted to be used for valuing the reserves under the contract under the insurance laws of at least 26 states at the time the contract is issued. The 2001 CSO tables currently meet this standard.

---

[51] Rev. Rul. 87-26, 1987-1 C.B. 158, defined the Commissioners' 1980 Standard Ordinary male or female table, as appropriate, without select factors, as the prevailing table.

[52] NATIONAL ASSOCIATION OF INSURANCE COMMISSIONERS, *Recognition of the 2001 CSO Mortality Table for Use in Determining Minimum Reserve Liabilities and Nonforfeiture Benefits Model Regulation*, NAIC MODEL LAWS, REGULATIONS AND GUIDELINES, Vol. 6, Model 814 (January 2003). The status of the 2001 CSO tables as the prevailing tables was recognized in Notice 2006-95, discussed *infra*.

[53] For traditional life insurance plans, a safe harbor of the nonforfeiture table is needed because there are only two key actuarial assumptions used in computing the CVAT, namely, interest and mortality. As the interest rate implicit in the development of a contract's cash values, subject to the 4 percent statutory floor under the CVAT, is used in determining the NSP, the mortality assumption used in the development of those cash values must necessarily also be used, so that a contract can satisfy both the definitional limits and the nonforfeiture law (in circumstances where the maturity assumption associated with the mortality table is consistent with the computational rules of IRC § 7702).

Under the permanent mortality rule, the "reasonable mortality charges" for a contract generally cannot exceed the mortality charges specified in the "prevailing" tables at the time the contract is issued. At the time the reasonable mortality standards were imposed in October 1988, the 1980 CSO tables were the prevailing tables, as they were permitted in all states and were to be mandatory nationwide just 10 weeks later. Hence, at that time there was little need for transition rules, provided companies were performing the definitional calculations using the 1980 CSO tables rather than the 1958 CSO tables. IRS Notice 88-128, issued late in 1988, confirmed that regulations to be issued would provide that the male and female 1980 CSO mortality rates would satisfy the reasonable mortality requirement of 7702(c)(3)(B)(i), providing life insurers with the safe harbor they sought. The notice also allowed the use of the 1958 CSO tables for non-MECs issued through the end of 1988. Since regulations have not been issued, Notice 88-128 (as supplemented by Notice 2006-95, discussed next) remains in effect today for 1980 CSO contracts issued before January 1, 2009, the date on which the 2001 CSO tables became mandatory under state law. For a more detailed description of Notice 88-128, see Appendix 2.5.

## *IRS Notices 2004-61 and 2006-95*

In the fall of 2004 and again in the fall of 2006, the Treasury Department and the IRS issued notices in response to the life insurance industry's request for guidance on the transition to the 2001 CSO tables. First, Notice 2004-61[54] provided a set of safe harbor rules intended to enable an orderly transition to the new tables. The safe harbors under this notice addressed both 1980 and 2001 CSO contracts, permitting each set of tables to be used under section 7702 and 7702A in specified time periods. Then, reacting to industry comments concerning uncertainties raised by this notice, the government issued Notice 2006-95,[55] reiterating the prior notice's safe harbors but removing some troublesome wording. According to its terms, Notice 2006-95 "supplements" Notice 88-128 and "modifies and supersedes" Notice 2004-61.

**Safe harbors:** Notice 2006-95, like its 2004 predecessor, provides three safe harbors with respect to the reasonable mortality charge requirement of section 7702(c)(3)(B)(i), although these are not identical to those of Notice 2004-61.

- The first safe harbor, set forth in section 4.01 of Notice 2006-95, provides that the "interim rules" described in Notice 88-128 remain in effect "except as otherwise modified by the notice." Notice 88-128 allowed, as noted above, use of mortality charges that do not exceed 100 percent of the applicable mortality charges set forth in the 1980 CSO tables. One modification to the interim rules of the 1988 notice made by Notice 2006-95 (and previously by Notice 2004-61) results from the change in the prevailing tables to the 2001 CSO tables in 2004.[56] Reflecting this change, and taking into account the transition rules of the NAIC model regulation implementing the new tables, section 2 of Notice 2006-95 observes: "The 1980 CSO tables may still be used in all states for contracts issued in calendar years through 2008. For contracts issued after 2008, use of the 2001 CSO tables will be mandatory."

- The second safe harbor, set forth in section 4.02 of Notice 2006-95, provides that a mortality charge with respect to a life insurance contract will satisfy the requirements of section 7702(c)(3)(B)(i) so long as:
    - the charge does not exceed 100 percent of the applicable mortality charge set forth in the 1980 CSO tables;
    - the contract is issued in a state that permits or requires the use of the 1980 CSO tables at the time the contract is issued; and
    - the contract is issued before January 1, 2009.

    It is unclear what situations might satisfy this second safe harbor that would not satisfy the first safe harbor. It may be that this safe harbor simply represents a restatement of the second safe harbor of Notice

---
[54] 2004-2 C.B. 596.
[55] 2006-2 C.B. 848. Notice 2006-95 is effective Oct. 12, 2006. The notice states, however, that its provisions will not be applied adversely to taxpayers who issued, changed or modified contracts in compliance with Notice 2004-61 (without regard to the modifications to Notice 2004-61 made by Notice 2006-95).
[56] For the special case of burial or preneed life insurance contracts issued beginning in 2009, see the discussion in Chapter 6.

2004-61 with a modification—an important one—which removes a requirement added by Notice 2004-61 that the mortality charges assumed in the section 7702 calculations for a contract could not exceed the mortality charges specified in the contract at issuance. Section 3 of Notice 2006-95 expressly states that this change was made to ensure it does not subject 1980 CSO contracts to more stringent standards, retroactively, than applied under Notice 88–128. It may also be that this second safe harbor was intended to implement the "sunset" statement, made in section 2 of Notice 2006-95, that for contracts issued after 2008, use of the 1980 CSO tables will no longer be allowed.

- The third safe harbor, set forth in section 4.03 of Notice 2006-95, provides that a mortality charge with respect to a life insurance contract will satisfy the requirements of section 7702(c)(3)(B)(i) so long as:
    - the charge does not exceed 100 percent of the applicable mortality charge set forth in the 2001 CSO tables;
    - the charge does not exceed the mortality charge specified in the contract at issuance; and
    - either (a) the contract is issued after December 31, 2008, or (b) the contract is issued before January 1, 2009, in a state that permits or requires the use of the 2001 CSO tables at the time the contract is issued.

In this manner, the notice (like its predecessor) follows the adoption dates provided by the NAIC in its model regulation adopting the 2001 CSO tables. The model regulation provides that the 2001 CSO tables can be applied at the option of a company until January 1, 2009, by which time all products offered for sale must be 2001 CSO compliant. In following the NAIC model regulation, the notices, in effect, adopted through these safe harbors the same transition rules for compliance with the definitional limits as the states have provided for contract nonforfeiture values, thus removing the inherent conflict between state law and the definitional requirements.

**The importance of meeting one of the safe harbors:** There are at least two reasons why it is important for the section 7702 and 7702A calculations for a contract to make use of one of the safe harbors—a transient reason and a permanent one. First, the permanent reasonable mortality charge requirement, apart from guidance such as Notice 2006-95 and its predecessors, is tied to the prevailing commissioners' standard tables as defined in section 807(d)(5). Since, as noted above, the 2001 CSO tables became "prevailing" during 2004, the mortality tables' "year of change" within the meaning of the section 807(d)(5)(B) transition rule was 2005, so that under that rule—barring other guidance—the 1980 CSO tables would continue to be permitted to be used as the prevailing tables for "the 3-year period beginning with the first day of the year of change," i.e., only through December 31, 2007. Thus, looking solely at the statutory rules, use of the 2001 CSO tables would be required under the permanent rule for contracts issued beginning in 2008. It is therefore critical that 1980 CSO contracts meet a safe harbor if they are issued during 2008, since it may not otherwise be possible for such designs to comply with the statute. Second, the requirement of section 7702(c)(3)(B)(i) is not primarily that mortality charges assumed in the calculations be limited to the prevailing tables' charges. Rather, the primary requirement is that the charges be "reasonable," yet that term is not defined in the statute or in any other authority—the TAMRA interim rule excepted—apart from the safe harbors. Further, as discussed above, the TAMRA interim rule's standard is itself vague. Hence, certainty that the mortality charges used in the calculations are "reasonable" is obtained by falling within the safe harbors.

**A re-awakened role for contract guarantees:** As insurers design products with the intention of complying with the third safe harbor of Notice 2006-95, special care should be paid to ensuring the contract does not in some way guarantee mortality charges less than charges based on 100 percent of the 2001 CSO tables, such as through a secondary guarantee of cash values contained in the contract. If there were a more liberal mortality rate guarantee, it would be necessary to reflect it in the calculations under section 7702 and 7702A to come within the ambit of this safe harbor. Interestingly, in limiting the "reasonable" mortality charges to those specified in the contract, the third safe harbor engages in a "look back to the future," at least for charges up to those based on the prevailing table. The use of charges not greater than those specified in the contract was the original rule in section 7702, and in section 101(f) before it, prior to the advent of TAMRA. On the other hand, where a mortality charge reduction is not guaranteed but is discretionary with the insurer, it need not be reflected in the calculations.[57]

**Rules for smoker-distinct and gender-blended tables:** Notice 2004-61 had expressly permitted the use of smoker-distinct and gender-blended mortality tables, but only if a consistency requirement (foreshadowed in the 1991 proposed regulations on reasonable mortality) was met. In particular, if a state permitted the use of 1980 CSO or 2001 CSO unisex tables in determining minimum nonforfeiture values, Notice 2004-61 allowed such tables to be used in the definitional calculations for female insureds provided the same tables were used for male insureds. Similarly, if a state permitted the use of 1980 CSO or 2001 CSO smoker and nonsmoker tables in determining minimum nonforfeiture values, Notice 2004-61 allowed such smoker tables to be used in the definitional calculations for smoker insureds provided nonsmoker tables were used for nonsmokers. Notice 2006-95 retains these rules, but on its face does so only for purposes of the 2001 CSO tables under the notice's third safe harbor.

Section 3 of Notice 2006-95 describes this change as intended to help ensure that Notice 2006-95 does not subject 1980 CSO contracts to more stringent standards, retroactively, than applied under Notice 88-128. Apparently, the express consistency requirement applicable under Notice 2004-61 for the use of smoker-distinct and gender-blended tables was considered to be a restriction potentially being applied retroactively.

**Substandard risks:** Notice 2006-95 states that neither it nor notices 88-128 and 2004-61 address the reasonable mortality charge requirement in the case of substandard risks. Thus, reasonable mortality charges for contracts with substandard mortality rate guarantees generally will continue to be governed by the interim rule of section 5011(c)(2) of TAMRA. Under that rule, as noted above, a contract issued before the effective date of temporary or final regulations will be deemed to satisfy the reasonable mortality charge requirement of section 7702(c)(3)(B)(i) if the mortality charges assumed in the calculations "do not differ materially from the charges actually expected to be imposed by the company (taking into account any relevant characteristic of the insured of which the company is aware)." The use of substandard risk charges in the section 7702 and 7702A calculations is discussed in detail in Chapter 3.

**Contract changes:** The effective date language in section 5.01 of Notice 2006-95 (as well as of Notice 2004-61) uses a contract's issue date to determine whether the 1980 or 2001 CSO tables apply where changes are made to a contract on or after January 1, 2009, i.e., the mandatory effective date of the 2001 CSO. In describing the "date on which a contract was issued," Notice 2006-95 refers to the "standards that applied for purposes of the original effective date of section 7702."[58] As described in the legislative history of section 7702, the original transition rules followed the principle that "contracts received in exchange for existing contracts are to be considered new contracts issued on the date of the exchange."[59]

While this language clearly would apply to a 2001 CSO contract issued to replace a 1980 CSO contract, it may also sweep in changes made to existing contracts, depending on the nature and the extent of the change. In this regard, both the legislative history for the effective date of section 7702 and Notice 2006-95 state: "for these purposes, a change in an existing contract is not considered to result in an exchange if the terms of the resulting contract (that is, the amount and pattern of death benefit, the premium pattern, the [interest] rate or rates guaranteed on issuance of the contract, and mortality and expense charges) are the same as the terms of the contract prior to the change."[60]

Notice 2006-95 goes on to provide guidance regarding changes that, even though significant, also will not cause a contract to be newly issued for purposes of applying the reasonable mortality charge requirement. In particular, section 5.02 of Notice 2006-95 states that if a life insurance contract satisfied the 1980 CSO safe

---

[57] *See* PLR 200906001 (Oct. 17, 2008) (reduced mortality charges based on compliance with the terms of a "wellness rider" need not be reflected in the IRC § 7702 and 7702A calculations where the reduction was not guaranteed by the insurer).

[58] In this connection, the notice contained the following citation: "*See* H.R. Conf. Rep. No. 861, 98th Cong., 2d Sess. 1076 (1984), 1984-3 (Vol. 2) C.B. 330; *see also* 1 Staff of Senate Comm. on Finance, 98th Cong., 2d Sess., *Deficit Reduction Act of 1984, Explanation of Provisions Approved by the Committee on March 21, 1984*, at 579 (Comm. Print 1984)." These are references to the DEFRA Conference Report and the DEFRA Senate Report, respectively.

[59] DEFRA House Report, *supra* Chapter 1, note 11, at 1449; DEFRA Senate Report, *supra* Chapter 1, note 11, at 579; DEFRA Blue Book, *supra* Chapter 1, note 20, at 656. See Chapter 5 for additional detail on this rule.

[60] DEFRA Senate Report, *supra* Chapter 1, note 11, at 597; DEFRA Blue Book, *supra* Chapter 1, note 20, at 656; Notice 2006-95, *supra* note 55.

harbor when originally issued, a change from previous tables to the 2001 CSO tables is not required—that is, the 1980 CSO "grandfather" is not lost—if:

> (1) the change, modification, or exercise of a right to modify, add or delete benefits is *pursuant to the terms of the contract*; (2) the state in which the contract is issued does not require use of the 2001 CSO tables for that contract under its standard valuation and nonforfeiture laws; and (3) the contract continues upon the same policy form or blank [emphasis added].

Notice 2006-95 further states, in section 5.03, that:

> The changes, modifications, or exercises of contractual provisions referred to in section 5.02 include (1) the addition or removal of a rider; (2) the addition or removal of a qualified additional benefit (QAB); (3) an increase or decrease in death benefit (whether or not the change is underwritten); (4) a change in death benefit option (such as a change from an option 1 to option 2 contract or vice versa); (5) reinstatement of a policy within 90 days after its lapse; and (6) reconsideration of ratings based on rated condition, lifestyle or activity (such as a change from smoker to nonsmoker status).

The italicized phrase in the first condition of section 5.02 of the notice is of considerable importance. The IRS has stated in a private letter ruling that the changes referenced in section 5.03 assume the existence of a contractual right to make the change.[61]

In describing the changes being made to the rules of Notice 2004-61 with respect to the identification of the issue date of a contract, Notice 2006-95 provided two comments that are noteworthy.

- First, referring to the change made to an earlier reference to underwriting in the third example (formerly the second example) of section 5.03, Notice 2006-95 observes that "the rule for determining the issue date of a contract that undergoes an increase or decrease in death benefit is simplified by eliminating the concept of 'underwriting.' This change broadens the grandfather rule of Notice 2004-61 to encompass many routine transactions, but does not wholly defer to an issuer's administrative practices and procedures."

- Second, referring to the addition of the second, fifth and sixth examples to the list in section 5.03, Notice 2006-95 states that "additional examples are provided of changes, modifications, or exercises of contractual provisions that will not require a change from previous tables to the 2001 CSO tables." Interestingly, while seemingly intended as a liberalization, the inclusion of the fifth example—relating to reinstatement of a policy within 90 days after its lapse, apparently modeled on the rule of section 7702A(c)(2)(B)—could be read as an indirect form of restriction. Since a right to reinstate typically applies under a contract for a period considerably longer than 90 days, should reinstatements beyond 90 days result in a loss of grandfathered status for purposes of the notice's safe harbors? In such a case, it would seem the general rule of section 5.02 would apply, and the fact that a reinstatement is not specifically identified in the list of examples in section 5.03 should not alter this result.

## *Monthly Mortality Assumption*

While the method of defining a monthly interest rate factor is rather universal in its application, variations exist in the method used to define **monthly mortality** rates. These variations are exemplified by two approaches.

**Arithmetic method:** The monthly mortality rate under an arithmetic approach is simply defined by dividing the annual rate by 12:

$$q^{monthly} = \frac{q}{12} \tag{2.7}$$

In practice, many universal life insurance contracts provide a table of guaranteed maximum monthly mortality rates using this approach. If the resulting monthly rates are annualized, the results will be marginally lower than

---

[61] PLR 201230009 (Jan. 30, 2012). This ruling, a controversial one in the view of the life insurance industry, is discussed further in Chapter 5.

## 48 Life Insurance and Modified Endowments

the original annual rates at most ages. However, at the older ages, the annualized rates begin to diverge more from the annual rates, creating a greater discrepancy between the two rates. At least for option 1 (level death benefit) and traditional contracts, the effect of using the $q/12$ approach is to produce lower defining premiums than would otherwise be obtained.

**Exponential method:** Using an exponential formula to convert annual mortality rates to monthly rates has the benefit of producing consistency between the annualized rates and the original annual rates. A monthly exponential rate is derived as follows:

$$q^{monthly} = 1 - (1-q)^{\left(\frac{1}{12}\right)} \tag{2.8}$$

Table 2.6 compares the effect of the arithmetic and exponential methods at selected ages for males under the 2001 CSO table. For ages 55 and under, there is virtually no difference in values. The rates diverge as the ages increase, however.

### Table 2.6. Comparison of mortality assumptions, 2001 CSO male aggregate

| Age | Annual mortality rate (1) | Monthly mortality rates | | Annualized mortality rates | | Ratio annualized arithmetic to exponential (4)/(5) |
|---|---|---|---|---|---|---|
| | | Arithmetic method (2) | Exponential method (3) | Arithmetic method (4) | Exponential method (5) | |
| 25 | 0.001070 | 0.000089 | 0.000089 | 0.001069 | 0.001070 | 100.0% |
| 35 | 0.001210 | 0.000101 | 0.000101 | 0.001209 | 0.001210 | 99.9% |
| 45 | 0.002650 | 0.000221 | 0.000221 | 0.002647 | 0.002650 | 99.9% |
| 55 | 0.006170 | 0.000516 | 0.000516 | 0.006153 | 0.006170 | 99.7% |
| 65 | 0.016850 | 0.001404 | 0.001415 | 0.016720 | 0.016850 | 99.2% |
| 75 | 0.041910 | 0.003493 | 0.003561 | 0.041114 | 0.041910 | 98.1% |
| 85 | 0.116570 | 0.009714 | 0.010275 | 0.110539 | 0.116570 | 94.8% |
| 95 | 0.269170 | 0.022431 | 0.025793 | 0.238325 | 0.269170 | 88.5% |

### Cost of Insurance Rates

Universal life and other accumulation-type plans typically use a COI rate rather than a mortality rate in computing their policy or accumulation values. Thus, in determining the limitations under sections 7702 and 7702A, attention should be given to the distinction between these two rates.

- **Mortality rates**, $q_x$, represent the probability of death over the year following attainment of age x and are the appropriate rates for use in discounting future benefits under a retrospective type computation (e.g., basic principles or commutation function approaches).

- **COI rates** form the basis of determining the mortality cost assessed against an insurance contract to pay for the expected death benefits; a COI charge is assumed to be paid at the beginning of a period. COI rates are appropriate to use in prospective or projection-based computations where values are generated through an **illustration-based projection** of **policy values** or determined based on policy value formulas.

Although mortality and COI rates are related, they are not interchangeable, and care should be taken to ensure that the definitional calculations employ the appropriate rate. Using COI rates (in place of the mortality rates) in a basic principles calculation will overstate the mortality for a particular contract, potentially resulting in too large a definitional limit for a contract.

Mortality rates are converted to COI rates in a variety of ways. For example, for monthly rates:

$$\text{Arithmetic COI} = \frac{\frac{q}{12}}{1 - \frac{q}{12}} \tag{2.9}$$

$$\text{Exponential COI} = \frac{1 - (1-q)^{\left(\frac{1}{12}\right)}}{1 - \left[1 - (1-q)^{\left(\frac{1}{12}\right)}\right]} \tag{2.10}$$

See Formula (2.21) in Appendix 2.2 for a description of how COI rates and mortality rates are properly reflected in the prospective and retrospective methods for calculating successive cash values.

## Expense Charges

Expense charges in a life insurance contract can take a variety of forms, including (but not limited to) per policy, per year, per $1,000 of face amount and percentage of premium charges. Use of the contractual expense charges was permitted in section 101(f) and later section 7702, which allowed nonmortality charges "specified in the contract" to be used in determining the guideline premiums.[62] Section 7702 added the rule that any charge not so specified would be treated as zero. Note that the term **other charges** also includes the charges for qualified additional benefits, which (again) are discussed later in this chapter and in Chapter 3.

Parallels exist in the legislative history regarding the treatment of expense charges and mortality charges under section 7702. For contracts issued prior to October 21, 1988, there was no express statutory limitation on expense charges (unlike the statutory minimums imposed on interest rates). Like mortality, companies were permitted to use the maximum expense charges guaranteed at issuance of the contract. In 1988, congressional concern over the potential use of inflated mortality charges to increase the investment orientation of life insurance also extended to the treatment of expenses. Thus, in addition to requiring the use of reasonable mortality, section 5011(a) of TAMRA amended section 7702(c)(3)(B)(ii) to provide that, for contracts entered into on or after October 21, 1988, the guideline premiums must be computed assuming "any reasonable charges (other than mortality charges) which (on the basis of the company's experience, if any, with respect to similar contacts) are reasonably expected to be actually paid."

In describing the TAMRA change, the Joint Committee on Taxation commented that the "expense charges taken into account for purposes of the guideline premium requirement would be required to be reasonable based on the experience of the company and other insurance companies with respect to similar life insurance contracts."[63] The TAMRA Conference Report elaborated that "[i]f any company does not have adequate experience to determine whether expense charges are reasonably expected to be paid, then to the extent provided in regulations, the determination is to be made on the basis of industry-wide experience."[64] The conference report further stated that it was not intended that companies be required under this rule to make an independent determination with respect to industrywide experience.[65] Rather, regulations should provide guidance on what constitutes reasonable expense charges for similar contracts. This guidance has yet to appear. Thus, one key difference between the treatment of mortality charges and the treatment of expense charges is that safe harbors are provided for mortality charges in Notice 2006-95 and its predecessors, but there are no analogous safe harbors for expense charges.

### *Defining Reasonable Expense Charges*

No IRS guidance or other specific authorities currently apply to determine whether the expense loads on a contract are reasonable. Thus, any test applied necessarily will be in the manner of a facts and circumstances

---

[62] DEFRA House Report, *supra* Chapter 1, note 11, at 1445; DEFRA Senate Report, *supra* Chapter 1, note 11, at 574; DEFRA Blue Book, *supra* Chapter 1, note 20, at 650. The DEFRA legislative history also noted that such charges could be either for expenses or for "qualified supplemental benefits," presumably referring to QABs.
[63] STAFF OF THE JT. COMM. ON TAX'N, 100TH CONG., DESCRIPTION OF POSSIBLE COMMITTEE AMENDMENT PROPOSED BY CHAIRMAN ROSTENKOWSKI TO H.R. 4333, at 90 (Comm. Print 1988).
[64] H.R. REP. NO. 100-1104, pt. 2, at 108 (1988) (Conf. Rep.) (hereinafter TAMRA Conference Report).
[65] Id.

analysis. As regulations have yet to address reasonable expenses and other guidance is lacking, various interpretations of the terms **reasonable** and **reasonably expected to be actually paid** would seem possible.

In a 2003 private letter ruling addressing the treatment of qualified additional benefits (discussed in more detail in Chapter 3), the IRS compared the treatment of "reasonable" mortality charges with that of "reasonable" expense charges, noting:

> [Mortality] Charges contemplated by section 7702(c)(3)(B)(i) are deemed reasonable if they do not exceed the charges set forth in the 1980 CSO Mortality Table, regardless of whether the charges actually set forth in the contract are less than the 1980 CSO amount. In contrast, [expense] charges contemplated by section 7702(c)(3)(B)(ii) are deemed reasonable only if they reflect the amount expected to be actually paid, which typically correlates to a company's actual charges.[66]

Consistently with this observation, insurers commonly use as the reasonable expense charges in guideline premium calculations for a contract the charges they actually impose on issuance of the contract and show in the current or nonguaranteed illustration of values for the contract. Further, if the scale of current expense charges is altered after a contract is issued, the then-current charges are appropriately used in an adjustment calculation if and when an adjustment event (e.g., a policyholder-initiated increase in benefits) occurs.

### *Expense Charges Used in Calculating Guideline Premiums*

In view of the above, an insurer is faced with a limited number of choices in deciding which expense charges to incorporate into the determination of guideline premiums. The most notable choice involves expense structures designed with both a current scale and a guaranteed maximum scale. For example, a contract may specify a percentage of premium expense charge guaranteed not to exceed 10 percent of all premiums paid. On a current basis, however, the company has elected to impose a 5 percent expense charge on all premiums paid, even though the company has a contractual right to impose a higher expense charge. The statutory language would suggest that the use of a 10 percent expense load in the determination of guideline premiums would be appropriate for contracts issued before October 21, 1988. However, for contracts issued on or after that date, the 5 percent expense load would be an appropriate expense charge to assume in the determination of guideline premiums because it is the rate the company currently actually expects to be paid. It is unclear what expense charges above this level may be assumed, but again the facts and circumstances may offer an appropriate basis for assuming higher amounts in certain cases. Also, more complex contract designs, such as those in which the amount of expenses imposed depends upon a contingency that cannot be readily predicted, present further uncertainty with respect to the application of the reasonable expense charge requirements.

## Future Benefits

As previously indicated, the term **future benefits** as used in sections 7702 and 7702A has particular meaning and is defined, for both statutes, in section 7702(f)(4) and (f)(5)(B) to mean:

- death benefits (i.e., the amount payable due to the insured's death, determined without regard to any QABs);
- endowment benefits (i.e., the amount payable if the insured survives to the maturity date of the contract); and
- **charges** for any QABs, but not the QABs' benefits themselves (as explained below, the reasonable expense charge requirements apply for purposes of ascertaining which QAB charges may be reflected in calculations under sections 7702 and 7702A).

The legislative history of section 7702A states that, for purposes of the 7-pay test, riders to a life insurance contract are not tested separately but are to be considered part of the underlying or base contract for purposes

---

[66] PLR 200320020 (Feb. 6, 2003). The facts of the ruling dealt specifically with the application of the reasonable expense charge rule in the context of QABs. The IRS position on the treatment of QABs under this rule was subsumed in Rev. Rul. 2005-6, as described in Chapter 3.

of the 7-pay test.[69] This approach—which generally applies to riders providing death benefits or QABs—avoids any need to allocate each premium payment between or among the base contract and any riders in applying the 7-pay test. Instead, the future benefits under the base contract and the future benefits under each rider are aggregated, and a 7-pay premium is determined for the aggregate future benefits under the entire contract. However, this approach may result in differences in the treatment of term insurance riders on the insured under the base contract—as QABs under section 7702 and as death benefits under section 7702A. This is discussed in detail in Chapter 3.

## *Computational Rules*

Beginning with section 101(f) and carrying through to sections 7702 and 7702A, both the timing and the magnitude of the future benefits that may be assumed in the definitional calculations have been restricted by the **computational rules**. According to the staff of the Joint Committee on Taxation, the computational rules "are directed, generally, at preventing insurance companies from avoiding the definitional limitations by creative product design."[70]

Under the computational rules, limitations are imposed, solely for purposes of the definitional calculations, on:

- the pattern of assumed future death benefits and QABs (in this case, the QABs' benefits, not the charges) under a contract,

### Packwood-Baucus Colloquy

When the reasonable expense requirements were introduced in 1988, it was expected regulations would be issued defining the terms **reasonable** charges and **reasonably expected to be paid**. The Packwood-Baucus colloquy,[67] a discussion during the Senate floor debate on TAMRA between Finance Committee Chairman Bob Packwood and Ranking Member Max Baucus, indicated that regulations interpreting the expense charge rule should be issued to provide guidance for life insurers and that they should permit the amendment or exchange of contracts, without prejudice to pre-existing contracts (so that they are not treated as failing to meet the requirements of section 7702), if that is necessary to comply with the regulations. According to the colloquy:

> *Mr. Packwood:* Mr. President, the conference agreement includes a provision amending the definition of life insurance, section 7702 of the code, to limit the charges, other than for mortality, which may be assumed in calculating guideline premiums for a life insurance contract. Specifically, these charges are limited to "reasonable charges" which, based on an insurance company's experience with respect to any similar contract, are "reasonably expected to be actually paid." It seems to me that these new limitations may be subject to differing interpretations, and that additional guidance is needed before life insurance companies can interpret and apply them. Could the Senator please expand on what is intended by these references to the term "reasonable," and what a company is expected to do prior to any further guidance?
>
> *Mr. Baucus:* The Senator is correct that this new rule may be subject to differing interpretations. It is our intention that regulations are to be issued providing the necessary guidance as to the circumstances in which the charges to which the Senator refers should be considered reasonable and reasonably expected to be actually paid. It is our further intention that, in the case of any contract to which this new rule applies which is issued before regulatory guidance as to the meaning of the rule first becomes available, the regulations would permit, as appropriate, such contract to be amended, or exchanged for a new contract, if that is necessary to maintain compliance with amended section 7702 as interpreted by those regulations. Such an amendment or exchange should be allowed without prejudice to the pre-existing contract, so that it is not treated as a contract that fails the section 7702 tests.[68]

---

[67] For the definition of a colloquy, see Appendix 1.1.
[68] 134 Cong. Rec. S17,208 (1988).
[69] *See* 134 Cong. Rec. S12,353 (daily ed. Sept. 12, 1988) (statement of Sen. Baucus); TAMRA Conference Report, *supra* note 64, at 100 (conference agreement follows Senate amendment). The Senate was asked to include this clarification, in part, so "paid-up additions riders" would be tested as a part of the base contracts to which they were added. Note that paid-up additions (from dividends) are a part of the contract under IRC § 7702 and treatment automatically carries over to IRC § 7702A.
[70] Staff of the Jt. Comm. on Tax'n, 98th Cong., Description of Provisions of S. 1992 Relating to Life Insurance Products and Policyholders, 10 (Comm. Print 1984).

- the contract's assumed maturity value (i.e., the endowment value or cash surrender value at maturity), and
- its assumed maturity date.

These limitations on the assumed future benefits of a contract constitute a principal element in restricting NSPs, guideline premiums and 7-pay premiums, thereby precluding excessive investment orientation as well as potential manipulation of the premium amounts by assuming in the calculation, for example, increasing future benefits that may never actually arise. This is consistent with the overall approach in the design of the definitional limits, which seek to control investment-oriented product designs through the imposition of safeguards on the permissible assumptions.

Specifically, four computational rules are prescribed in section 7702(e)(1)(A)–(D) for use in computing the NSPs and guideline premiums:

- The death benefit used in computing the guideline premiums or NSP is assumed not to increase.
- The maturity date assumed in the calculations can be no earlier than the day on which the insured attains age 95 and no later than the day on which the insured attains age 100.
- Death benefits are assumed to be provided until the "deemed" maturity date.
- The amount of any endowment benefit (or sum of endowment benefits) taken into account cannot exceed the least amount payable as a death benefit at any time under the contract.[71]

In general, the computational rules applicable to the 7-pay premium under section 7702A(c)(1) follow the section 7702(e)(1) rules above, with one exception. The exception: the death benefit pattern used in calculating the 7-pay premium is subject to the rule set forth in section 7702A(c)(1)(B), which requires that the death benefit provided for in the first contract year be assumed to be provided until the contract's **deemed maturity date** without regard to any scheduled reduction after the first seven contract years. This rule parallels section 7702(e)(1)(C), which deems the death benefit at the inception of a contract to continue until the contract's maturity date.

As an exception to the general rule of section 7702(e)(1) prohibiting the reflection of increasing death benefits in the definitional calculations, certain limited increases in death benefits are permitted under two **alternate death benefit rules** that appear in section 7702(e)(2). First, under section 7702(e)(2)(A), in computing the GLP, an increasing death benefit may be taken into account, but only to the extent necessary to prevent a decrease in the excess of the death benefit of a contract over its CSV (i.e., to maintain a constant net amount at risk). According to the DEFRA legislative history, this exception generally is intended to permit GLPs to be adequate to fund, on a guaranteed basis, a death benefit equal to the CSV plus a fixed amount of insurance benefit (i.e., an option 2-type death benefit pattern).[72] However, the use of the section 7702(e)(2)(A) computational rule is not limited to an option 2 death benefit but may be applied to any increasing death benefit pattern, so long as that increase is provided in the contract and is recognized only to the extent necessary to prevent a decrease in the net amount at risk.

The second alternative death benefit rule, section 7702(e)(2)(B), allows for similar death benefit increases to be reflected under the requirements of the CVAT if the contract satisfies the test using a "net level premium reserve," rather than an NSP, as the basis for section 7702 compliance. Specifically, section 7702(e)(2)(B) permits an increase in the death benefit provided under a contract to be recognized in the CVAT calculations "assuming that the net level reserve (determined as if level annual premiums were paid for the contract over a period not ending before the insured attains age 95) is substituted for the net single premium," provided there

---

[71] IRC § 101(f)(2)(D) provided three computational rules for determining the GSP and GLP for "flexible premium contracts":
  ○ The net amount at risk assumed in the calculations cannot exceed the net amount at risk at issue.
  ○ The maturity date of the contract is assumed to be the latest date permitted under the contract, but not less than 20 years from issue, or age 95, if earlier.
  ○ The amount of any assumed endowment benefit cannot exceed the smallest death benefit (without regard to any QAB) at any time.
The NSP under IRC § 101(f)'s cash value test is also computed under these rules, except that the maturity date of the contract cannot be earlier than age 95. The enactment of IRC § 7702 carried over many of the requirements imposed by IRC § 101(f) on flexible premium life insurance contracts. However, certain changes were made to the computational rules contained in IRC § 7702(e), generally rendering IRC § 7702 more restrictive than IRC § 101(f).

[72] DEFRA Senate Report, *supra* Chapter 1, note 11, at 577; DEFRA Blue Book, *supra* Chapter 1, note 20, at 652–53.

is no increase in the net amount risk. Use of the net level reserve test may be problematic for contracts with adjustment events, as the net level reserve following an adjustment is not defined, and for participating contracts that permit dividends to purchase paid-up additions, as there is no guidance on whether the net level reserve test may be applied to a base plan, while, at the same time, the CVAT based on the NSP is applied to a paid-up addition. It is important to note that neither of these alternative rules allows relief from section 7702(e)(1)(D), which limits the guaranteed funding for the endowment benefit (including the CSV on the deemed maturity date) to the least death benefit payable under the contract.

The 7-pay premium usually is computed without taking increasing benefits into account. The wording of section 7702A(c)(1)(B) arguably permits certain increasing benefits to be recognized in the computation of the 7-pay premium. However, as section 7702(e)(2)(B) refers to a net level reserve, and not a premium, it is unclear how the 7-pay premium would be computed under a net level (annual premium) reserve method. Also, death benefit increases under the 7-pay test may result in material changes, as discussed in Chapter 4.

These computational rules are discussed in greater detail in Chapter 3, and a special computational rules relating to "preneed" contracts is discussed in Chapter 6.

### *Qualified Additional Benefits*

Section 7702(f)(5)(A) (like section 101(f)(3)(E) before it) defines QABs to mean certain benefits that typically accompany life insurance coverage. The QABs listed in the statute are:

- Guaranteed insurability
- Accidental death or disability benefits
- Family term coverage
- Disability waiver benefit

The statute also permits expansion of this list by regulations, but to date no benefits have been added to it.

Only those benefits deemed to be "qualified" are eligible to be incorporated into the definitional calculations and, thus, to be prefunded in the maximum permitted CSVs and premiums of the related life insurance contract. Generally, when a QAB is present in a life insurance contract, the definitional limitations for the contract may be increased to reflect the charges imposed for the benefit that satisfy the reasonable expense charge requirements, by virtue of section 7702(f)(1)(B)'s characterization of such charges as "future benefits."

A contract may also contain an "additional benefit" that is not a QAB, sometimes referred to as a **non-QAB**. Examples of non-QABs are term coverage on a nonfamily member, such as an unrelated business partner, or long-term care insurance provided by accelerating the base plan's death benefit. According to section 7702(f)(5)(C)(ii), the charge for a non-QAB is not included in the future benefits under the contract, and so the definitional limitations are not increased to reflect the cost of the benefit. Consistently with this treatment, a premium paid for the non-QAB is not considered a "premium paid" or an "amount paid" for purposes of section 7702 and section 7702A, respectively, provided that the payment never enters into the CSV of the underlying contract. However, if the payment for the non-QAB is credited to the CSV, even for a brief period of time, this is considered "prefunding," and the rule disregarding the payment does not apply. The presence of non-QABs may affect how compliance is measured under the CVAT as well as the section 7702(d) cash value corridor. Compliance with the CVAT or the corridor is based on the entire CSV of a contract, including any amounts attributable to the prefunding of the non-QAB.

## Adjustments

As the section 7702 and 7702A calculations generally are required to be performed originally at contract issuance, some procedures are necessary to reflect contract changes that alter the future benefits. Changes made after a life insurance contract is first issued are commonplace, and indeed were contemplated by Congress when the statutes were enacted. Contract changes include increases or decreases in coverage or the addition or deletion of a rider. They may also include changes to the structure of the contract, including a change in underwriting class (e.g., from a smoker to a nonsmoker), or in unusual cases, a change in expense or interest factors. Broadly defined, contractual changes can as well include an exchange of contracts (perhaps under section 1035) in which one life insurance contract replaces another.

Failure to adjust the definitional limitations for increases in future benefits could lead to situations in which the benefits could not be funded adequately, while failure to reflect decreases could permit overfunding and excessive inside buildup. Beginning with section 101(f) and continuing in section 7702 (in section 7702(f)(7)(A) in particular), the **adjustment rules** have permitted a degree of flexibility—to allow for increases and decreases in future benefits—while still maintaining the definitional limitations. Section 7702A, for its part, employs somewhat different rules under which events defined as "material changes" are reflected by restarting the 7-pay test for a contract and reductions in benefits within a 7-pay testing period (or at any time, in the case of a second-to-die contract) can cause the 7-pay premium to be recomputed and applied retroactively. As discussed in detail in Chapter 4, some of the more complex computational issues under sections 7702 and 7702A arise from adjustments and material changes.

Contractual changes have two potential effects regarding definitional limits. First, they can subject a contract to one or more of the adjustment rules noted just above and summarized below. Second, it is possible they can result in the loss of "grandfathered" status, thus causing the contract to be treated for section 7702 and 7702A purposes as if it were newly issued altogether. This, in turn, can in some circumstances require the application of the TAMRA rules on allowed mortality and expense assumptions to a contract issued before the advent of those rules.

## CVAT Adjustments

Under the CVAT, *any* change in future benefits must be reflected in the NSP, which is recalculated in its entirety at the time of the change based on the attained age of the insured. In this connection, it may be noted that while the adjustment and material change rules, as well as the potential for new issuance treatment, apply to contracts subject to the CVAT, a special rule in section 7702(b)(2)(C) affects the manner in which the CVAT operates. Unlike the guideline and 7-pay premiums, the NSPs are calculated and applied "at any time" (meaning at all times in this context) rather than "at issue," and a CVAT-tested contract must assure that the contract's CSV will never exceed the NSP.[73] This difference presents the question of how to reconcile these requirements for a contract with nonguaranteed elements, such as dividends or excess interest, that increase the contract's benefits with the two computational rules that forbid the assumption of increasing death benefits or an endowment benefit or maturity value greater than the lowest death benefit provided. Section 7702(b)(2)(C) addresses this by providing that the at-any-time NSP calculations are to be made "only" by taking account of "current and future death benefits and qualified additional benefits." As further explained in Chapter 4, this enables the CVAT to be "self-adjusting" under the section 7702(f)(7)(A) adjustment rule: Because the CVAT is applied at any time as an attained age NSP for only the future benefits at that time, benefit increases (and decreases) are handled automatically. In effect, the section 7702(b)(2)(C) mandate to use only the "current and future benefits" overcomes the limits otherwise imposed by these two computational rules, at least as they might otherwise constrain use of a contract's current benefits.

## Guideline Premium Test Adjustments

The changes in future benefits that must be reflected in the guideline premiums at and after the time of change are more limited than in the CVAT case. According to the legislative history of section 7702 (repeating elements of the **Dole-Bentsen colloquy**[74] in connection with section 101(f)), adjustments are required, and permitted, only in the case of (1) a change initiated by the policyholder to alter the amount or pattern of the future benefits previously reflected in the guideline premiums, and (2) an increase in benefits that was previously scheduled but could not be reflected in the guideline premiums due to restrictions imposed by the computational rules. Thus, such "adjustment events" can include:

- changes in death or endowment benefits made at the request of the policyholder,

---
[73] *See* IRC § 7702(b)(1).
[74] 128 Cong. Rec. S10,943 (daily ed. Aug. 19, 1982) (hereinafter Dole-Bentsen colloquy).

- certain changes in death or endowment benefits that result from the operation of the contract and that have not previously been reflected in the calculation of the limits (presumably because of the computational rules, as noted in (2) above),
- the purchase of a paid-up addition (or its equivalent),
- the addition or termination of a QAB,
- a change between a level (option 1) and an increasing (option 2) death benefit pattern, and
- the removal of a substandard rating or a change in the mortality charge guarantee from smoker to non-smoker.

On the other hand, changes that do not trigger adjustments generally include changes initiated by the company and changes resulting from the growth of the contract's cash value (whether by the crediting of excess interest or the payment of premiums up to the level of the pre-existing guideline premium limitation). That said, long-term changes to basic interest or other guarantees made by the company may trigger adjustments.

The adjustments of the guideline premiums are also made in a manner different from the recalculation of the NSPs under the CVAT. Specifically, an attained age layering approach is utilized, sometimes referred to as the **attained age increment and decrement method**. Thus, an increase or decrease in a contract's face amount is treated separately from the pre-existing guideline premiums: separate guideline premiums are computed to reflect the increase or decrease in face amount. Equivalent "before and after" calculations based on the attained age of the insured at the time of the change can be used to implement this. Under this method, attained age layers of guideline premium values are added to the existing GSP and GLP. In symbols:

$$\textit{Incremental Guideline Single Premium}_{x+t} = GSP(After)_{x+t} - GSP(Before)_{x+t} \qquad (2.11)$$

$$\textit{Incremental Guideline Level Premium}_{x+t} = GLP(After)_{x+t} - GLP(Before)_{x+t} \qquad (2.12)$$

Computing guidelines at attained age for the entire after contract (i.e., the characteristics of the contract following the change event) and subtracting the guidelines at attained age for the entire before contract (i.e., the characteristics of the contract immediately preceding the change event) has the same effect for benefit increases and decreases, and also the virtue of working where there are changes unrelated to a change in benefit, such as where a substandard rating reflected in the guideline premiums is permanently removed.

## *7-Pay Test Adjustments*

Changes in future benefits are addressed in yet a different manner under section 7702A. There are two adjustment-type rules that appear in paragraphs (2) and (3) of section 7702A(c)—dealing, respectively, with reductions in benefits and with "material changes"—supplemented by a special rule in section 7702A(c)(6) applicable to benefit reductions in **survivorship contracts** (i.e., second-to-die).

**Reductions in benefits.** The **reduction-in-benefits rule** of section 7702A(c)(2)(A) provides that if benefits under the contract are reduced during the first seven contract years (or the seven years following a material change), then section 7702A is applied as if the contract had originally been issued at the reduced benefit level, and the new reduced limitation is retroactively applied to the cumulative amount paid under the contract for each of the first seven years. Further, section 7702A(c)(6) extends the reduction in benefit rule beyond the end of the 7-pay testing period for the entire life of a survivorship contract (as discussed in Chapter 6). In determining whether a reduction in benefits has occurred, the benefits involved are the future benefits previously reflected in the 7-pay premium calculation. Under an exception provided in section 7702A(c)(2)(B), a benefit reduction due to nonpayment of premiums is disregarded if the contract is reinstated within 90 days of the reduction.

If under these rules a contract fails to satisfy the 7-pay test for any prior contract year, the contract is considered a MEC for:

- distributions that occur during the contract year the benefit reduction occurs and during any subsequent contract year and
- distributions that occur in anticipation of the benefit reduction.

The second of these rules treats any distributions made within two years before a reduction as made in anticipation of the reduction, although regulations (which have not been issued) can modify this period.

**Material changes.** When changes occur in a contract other than a reduction in benefits, the material change rule of section 7702A(c)(3) may apply. It is important to note that the material change rule applies throughout the life of a contract, i.e., it does not cease applying after a contract passes through a 7-pay testing period without becoming a MEC.

The statute does not provide a definition of "material change," but simply refers in section 7702A(c)(3)(A) to "a material change in the benefits under (or in other terms of) the contract which was not reflected in any previous determination under this section." However, section 7702A(c)(3)(B) generally provides that any increase in a contract's death benefit, or any increase in or addition of a QAB, constitutes a material change. Further, the legislative history of TAMRA, tracking the statutory wording, suggests that a change in a contract's benefits or terms not previously taken into account in the 7-pay calculations is a material change, along with a contract exchange whether or not it is tax free under section 1035. Thus, many changes in the benefits or terms under a contract (other than benefit reductions) that would be considered adjustment events under section 7702 would be treated as section 7702A material changes. Of great importance, in this connection, is the exception provided in clause (i) of 7702A(c)(3)(B), which excludes from material change treatment benefit increases attributable to "necessary" premium payments—a segue into a complex of rules that virtually constitute a fourth test under the definitional limitations. Detail on these "necessary premium test" rules appears in Chapter 4.

Upon the occurrence of a material change, a contract is treated for 7-pay test purposes as a new contract entered into on the day the material change takes effect. Consequently, the contract is tested from that point forward, over the ensuing seven years, to determine whether it will meet a new 7-pay test. For this testing (but not section 7702 testing), following the material change the contract year is measured from the date of the change rather than the contract's issue date. Also for this testing, a new 7-pay premium is computed reflecting the contract's CSV at the time of the change under the **rollover rule**. Under this rule, the face amount of the changed contract that is not funded by the existing CSV applied as an NSP serves as the basis for the new 7-pay premiums. (For the treatment of a material change that is a section 1035 exchange, see the discussion in Chapter 4.)

$$7Pay(Adj) = \left[\frac{NSP - CV}{\ddot{a}_{x:\overline{7}}}\right] \tag{2.13}$$

To compute the rollover adjustment to the 7-pay premium, the cash surrender value as of the date of the change is multiplied by a fraction, the numerator of which is the full 7-pay premium for the future benefits under the changed contract, and the denominator of which is the NSP for such benefits computed using the same assumptions used in determining that 7-pay premium. The result is then subtracted from the full 7-pay premium to produce the adjusted 7-pay premium.

$$7Pay(Adj) = 7Pay - CV \times \left[\frac{7Pay}{NSP}\right] \tag{2.14}$$

$$7Pay(Adj) = \left[\frac{NSP}{\ddot{a}_{x:\overline{7}}}\right] \times \left[1 - \frac{CV}{NSP}\right] \tag{2.15}$$

The above explanation of adjustments under sections 7702 and 7702A represents only a very general summary of the rules that comprise some of the most complex elements of the definitional limitations. A more complete treatment of this subject is provided in Chapter 4. ♥

## Appendix 2.1. Sample At-Issue Calculations

For this and subsequent chapters, a sample plan has been developed to illustrate the calculation of the section 7702 and 7702A limitations for a contract. This section presents the calculations that would be made at issuance of the contract. The at-issue calculations presented in Table 2.7 below are based on an assumed endowment age of 100 and an assumption that death claims are paid immediately (see Appendix 2.3 regarding timing assumptions), with the following at-issue characteristics (DBO1 and DBO2 refer to death benefit options 1 and 2, respectively):

- Sex: Male
- Age: 45
- Face amount: $100,000
- Mortality: 2001 CSO aggregate ANB
- Interest rate: 4.5 percent
- Expenses: 5 percent of premium load plus $60 annual administrative fee

### Table 2.7. Basic at-issue calculations, male age 45

|  | GSP | GLP-DBO1 | GLP-DBO2 | NSP | 7-pay |
|---|---|---|---|---|---|
| Net single premium | 17,925.21 | 26,011.25 | 79,424.76 | 26,011.25 | 26,011.25 |
| Annuity factor | — | 17.313 | 21.159 | — | 6.105 |
| Net premium | 17,925.21 | 1,502.37 | 3,753.68 | 26,011.25 | 4,260.34 |
| Expense factor | 1,864.98 | 142.23 | 260.72 | — | — |
| Limitation | 19,790.19 | 1,644.60 | 4,014.40 | 26,011.25 | 4,260.34 |

All formulas below incorporate a 4.5 percent interest rate assumption, with the exception of the GSP formulas, which are based on a 6 percent interest rate assumption.

$$GSP = \frac{\left[Face\ Amount \times \left(\frac{i}{\delta} \times A^1_{45:55} + A_{45:55}^{\ \ 1}\right)\right] + Admin\ Fee \times \ddot{a}_{45}}{1 - \%\ Premium\ Load}$$

$$GSP = \frac{\left[100{,}000 \times \left(\frac{i}{\delta} \times \left\{\sum_{t=0}^{54} v^{t+1} \times {}_{t|}q_{45}\right\} + v^{55} \times {}_{55}p_{45}\right)\right] + 60 \times \sum_{t=0}^{54} v^t \times {}_t p_{45}}{.95}$$

$$GSP = \frac{\left[100{,}000 \times .1792521\right] + 60 \times 14.59110}{.95}$$

$$GSP = 19{,}790.19$$

$$GLP^{DBO1} = \frac{\left[\dfrac{Face\ Amount \times \left(\frac{i}{\delta} \times A^1_{45:55} + A_{45:55}^{\ \ 1}\right)}{\ddot{a}_{45}}\right] + Admin\ Fee}{1 - \%\ Premium\ Load}$$

$$GLP^{DBO1} = \frac{\left[100{,}000 \times \left(\frac{i}{\delta} \times \left\{\sum_{t=0}^{54} v^{t+1} \times {}_{t|}q_{45}\right\} + v^{55} \times {}_{55}p_{45}\right)\right] + 60}{\sum_{t=0}^{54} v^t \times {}_t p_{45}}$$

$$GLP^{DBO1} = \frac{\left[\frac{100{,}000 \times .2601125}{17.313478}\right] + 60}{.95}$$

$$GLP^{DBO1} = \mathbf{1{,}644.60}$$

$$GLP^{DBO2} = \frac{\left[\frac{\text{Face Amount} \times \left(\frac{i}{\delta} \times \left\{\sum_{t=0}^{54} v^{t+1} \times q_{45+t}\right\} + v^{55}\right)}{\sum_{t=0}^{54} v^t}\right] + \text{Admin Fee}}{1 - \% \text{ Premium Load}}$$

$$GLP^{DBO2} = \frac{\left[\frac{100{,}000 \times (0.7034243 + .090823290)}{21.1591815}\right] + 60}{.95}$$

$$GLP^{DBO2} = \mathbf{4{,}104{,}40}$$

$$NSP = \left[\text{Face Amount} \times \left(\frac{i}{\delta} \times A^1_{45:55} + A_{45:\overset{1}{55}}\right)\right]$$

$$NSP = \left[100{,}000 \times \left(\frac{i}{\delta} \times \left\{\sum_{t=0}^{54} v^{t+1} \times {}_{t|}q_{45}\right\} + v^{55} \times {}_{55}p_{45}\right)\right]$$

$$NSP = 100{,}000 \times .2601125$$

$$NSP = \mathbf{26{,}011.25}$$

$$7Pay = \left[\frac{\text{Face Amount} \times \left(\frac{i}{\delta} \times A^1_{45:55} + A_{45:\overset{1}{55}}\right)}{\ddot{a}_{45:\overline{7}|}}\right]$$

$$7Pay = \left[\frac{100{,}000 \times \left(\frac{i}{\delta} \times \left\{\sum_{t=0}^{54} v^{t+1} \times {}_{t|}q_{45}\right\} + v^{55} \times {}_{55}p_{45}\right)}{\sum_{t=0}^{6} v^t \times {}_t p_{45}}\right]$$

$$7Pay = \left[\frac{100{,}000 \times .2601125}{6.105441}\right]$$

$$7Pay = \mathbf{4{,}260.34}$$

For the sample plan, a policyholder could pay up to $19,790.19 as a single premium under the guideline premium test, or pay a premium that would produce an initial cash value of up to $26,011.25 under the CVAT for a contract designed to comply by its terms with that test. Payments of premiums in excess of $4,260.34 per year (cumulative) in any of the first seven contract years would result in the contract being treated as a MEC.

## An Illustration: Application of the Test Plan to Term Insurance

Under the computational rules, the test plan against which qualification is measured is an endowment at age 95 even where the policy tested is a term insurance plan that expires before age 95. The definitional limitations are computed under the assumption that benefits are deemed to continue to a date which is no earlier than the day on which the insured attains age 95 and no later than the day on which the insured attains age 100. The DEFRA Blue Book noted: "In applying this rule to contracts that are scheduled to automatically mature or terminate prior to age 95, the benefits should also be deemed to continue to age 95 for purposes of computing both the net single premium and the guideline premium limitations. ... A contract written with a termination date before age 95 (e.g., term life insurance to age 65), which otherwise satisfies the requirements of section 7702, will qualify as a life insurance contract for tax purposes."[75] Thus, in the case of a level benefit term policy with a CSV (e.g., a return of premium plan), the test plan standard against which qualification is measured presumably is an endowment at 95, not a plan that continues only to the end of the term period. This would seem a necessary adjunct to allowing a partial endowment before age 95 to qualify as life insurance under section 7702.[76]

# Appendix 2.2. Calculation Methods

While the limitations imposed on premiums and cash surrender values under section 101(f), 7702 and 7702A are defined in terms of actuarial values, the statutes and the official guidance relating to them leave the methods by which those values are to be computed largely unspecified. Following accepted actuarial practice, there are several approaches that can be used to compute such values, each with its own advantages and disadvantages. However, in practice, two principal methods are commonly applied to the calculation of values: **basic actuarial principles** (including the use of **commutation functions**) and a **projection-based** (or **illustration system**) **approach**. Such values may also be determined based on policy value formulas.[77]

## Basic Actuarial Principles

The basic principles approach utilizes the basic techniques of actuarial mathematics for defining insurance premiums, relying on the fundamental relationship that equates the present value of future premiums with the present value of future benefits and expenses (and other charges). This method provides considerable flexibility in accommodating unique product designs and contract features, particularly for such matters as contract adjustments under the guideline premium test (see Chapter 4 for details on the attained age increment and decrement method of guideline premium adjustments). In this respect, independent calculations following basic actuarial principles can be performed to account for both the before and after calculations of the attained age adjustment formula employed under the guideline premium test.

For a whole life form with an option 1 (level) death benefit, the CSV limit under the CVAT is based on the classical actuarial formula for a level face amount NSP ($A_x$) and can be expressed as:

$$NSP^{DBO1} = SA \times A_x = SA \times \left( \sum_{t=0}^{\omega-x-1} v^{t+1} \times {}_tp_x \times q_{x+t} \right) \qquad (2.16)$$

where:

- $SA$ = the face or **specified amount**
- $v = 1/(1+i)$
- ${}_tp_x$ = the probability of a life age x surviving for t years

---

[75] DEFRA Blue Book, *supra* Chapter 1, note 20, at 652. No comparable statement appears in the formal DEFRA legislative history, but the amendment made to IRC § 7702(e)(1)(C) by the Tax Reform Act of 1986 (TRA) clarified that this statement describes the operative rule.

[76] *See* PLR 200910001 (Sept. 8, 2008) (IRC § 7702(e)(1)(C) construed to mean that benefits are deemed to continue to age 100 for certificates under CVAT-tested employer-owned group life insurance policy covering employees even though the employer may terminate certificate coverage when employees retire).

[77] Calvin D. Cherry, *Calculating Funding Premiums for Universal Life Insurance*, 4 N. Am. Actuarial J., no. 2, 20–27 (2000).

- $q_{x+t}$ = the probability of dying at age $x+t$, given that age $x+t$ has been attained

The expression above can be used to compute the section 7702 (or section 101(f)) NSP and, when certain expenses are reflected, the GSP. When divided by the appropriate annuity factor ($\ddot{a}_x$ or $\ddot{a}_{x:\overline{7}|}$), it can be used to compute the GLP or the 7-pay premium.

For an option 2 (face or specified amount plus cash value) death benefit, the analogous NSP expression is:

$$NSP^{DBO2} = A_x^{DBO2} = SA \times \left( \sum_{t=0}^{\omega-x-1} v^{t+1} \times q_{x+t} \right) + SA \times v^{\omega-x} \tag{2.17}$$

To determine the GLP for an option 2 death benefit under section 7702(e)(2)(A), the NSP in Formula (2.17) can be divided by an annuity factor equal to $\ddot{a}_{100-x}$. Note that a fundamental difference between option 1 and option 2 is that option 1 values are discounted with interest and survivorship, while the option 2 values are discounted at interest only.

## *Commutation Functions*

A related approach to the basic actuarial principles approach is one that involves the development of tables of actuarial functions known as **commutation functions**. These functions are labor-saving devices that, before the widespread use of computers, simplified the construction and manipulation of actuarial values.[78] Commutation functions commonly used in computing insurance and annuity values are as follows:

$$D_x = v^x \times l_x \qquad N_x = \sum_{t=1}^{\omega-x} D_{x+t}$$
$$C_x = v^{t+1} \times d_x \qquad M_x = \sum_{t=1}^{\omega-x} C_{x+t} \tag{2.18}$$

where $l_x$ is the number of people alive at age x and $d_x$ is the number of people who die between ages x and x+1. These computed functions remove much of the computational complexity inherent in determining test limits.

While each commutation function may not have particular meaning by itself, they can be combined to provide a different approach for defining insurance and annuity values.

$$A_x = \sum_{t=0}^{\omega-1} v^{t+1} \times {}_{t|}q_x = \frac{M_x}{D_x}$$

$$\ddot{a}_x = \sum_{t=0}^{\omega-1} v^t \times {}_tp_x = \frac{N_x}{D_x}$$

Using tables of various commutation values, NSPs, guideline premiums and 7-pay premiums can be derived by simply performing a table lookup to access the appropriate values. option 2 death benefits (for determining the GLP) can be accommodated by defining special commutation functions $D_x^{DBO2}$ and $C_x^{DBO2}$ etc., where:[79]

$$D_x^{DBO2} = v^t \qquad N_x^{DBO2} = \sum_{t=1}^{\omega-x} D_{x+t-1}^{DBO2}$$

$$C_x^{DBO2} = v^{t+1} \times q_x \qquad M_x^{DBO2} = \sum_{t=1}^{\omega-x} C_{x+t-1}^{DBO2}$$

The corresponding insurance and annuity values for an option 2 death benefit would be defined similarly to the option 1 death benefit values above by combining option 2 commutation factors.

$$A_x^{DBO2} = \frac{M_x^{DBO2}}{D_x^{DBO2}} + v^{\omega-x}$$

---

[78] Commutation functions are disadvantaged in that they work only with attained-age functions. Note that monthly factors can be approximated using commutation functions. For example, a monthly life annuity at age x = ((Nx ÷ Dx) − 11 ÷ 12). While commutation functions recognizing monthly transactions can be developed, they are highly complex and are not commonly found in practice.

[79] See Franklin C. Smith, *A General Treatment of Insurance for Face Amount Plus Reserve or Cash Value*, 16 SOC'Y ACTUARIES TRANSACTIONS 218, 230–31 (1964) (discussion by Cecil J. Nesbitt).

$$\ddot{a}_x^{DBO2} = \frac{N_x^{DBO2}}{D_x^{DBO2}}$$

Although simple in design and easily programmable, a commutation-based approach is best used for simple product designs. Difficulties can be encountered, for example, when applying a commutation-based approach for contracts with complex expense structures. Problems may also arise in adapting this approach to contracts with a nonlevel interest rate guarantee or QABs with nonlevel charges.

## *Projection-Based Methods*

The second principal method of computing values of the definitional limitations is a projection-based or illustration system approach. A projection-based method simulates the monthly contract mechanics. Applying the test plan concept, the values of the NSPs, guideline premiums and 7-pay premiums are the premiums that will endow the contract on the assumed maturity date using the actuarial assumptions and future benefits required or permitted in the definitional calculations.

A projection-based approach has the appeal of following contract mechanics for most types of flexible premium products, as the process of iterating for the desired premium involves crediting premium to a policy account, to which interest is credited and from which mortality and other expense charges are deducted. The calculation of universal life contract values (CVs) is generally based on an accumulation of net premiums less the cost of insurance and expenses, often on a monthly basis, according to a formula contained in the contract. The CV formula is recursive in nature in that it defines the CV on a given valuation date in terms of the comparable value on the previous valuation date.

| (2.19) Example of a cash value formula under a projection-based method | | |
|---|---|---|
| (1) | Start with the initial cash value | $_tCV$ |
| (2) | Add in a net payment, where $E^{PREMIUM}$ is the expense rate related to expenses that vary directly with the premium | $GP \times (1 - E^{PREMIUM})$ |
| (3) | Deduct any beginning-of-the-month contract related expenses | $E^{CONTRACT}$ |
| (4) | The net amount at risk can be obtained by adjusting the specified amount of insurance (SA) by the guaranteed interest factor ($i_g$), and subtracting the beginning fund value after the net payment has been added and expenses subtracted[80] | $NAR = (SA/(1+i_g)) - [(_tCV + (GP \times (1-E^{PREMIUM})) - (E^{CONTRACT})]$ |
| (5) | Deduct a monthly mortality charge based on the net amount at risk (NAR x COI rate) | $COI\ rate = q^{(m)}/(1-q^{(m)})$ |
| (6) | Credit interest for one month | $i_t$ |
| (7) | Equals the next month's cash value | $_{t+1}CV = [_tCV + GP \times (1 - E^{PREMIUM}) - E^{CONTRACT} - (NAR \times COI\ rate)] \times (1+i_r)$ |

Under a projection-based approach, successive CVs are computed with an iterative procedure to determine the definitional limitations. The definitional limitations are determined based on successive approximations of the premium needed to fund the benefits and produce the contract's endowment value permitted under the statutes (i.e., when the successive iterations have converged to a value within the tolerance set under the calculation approach). The resulting premium for the applicable limitation is the amount required to fund the future benefits provided by the contract and to endow the contract, while applying the actuarial assumptions required by the statutes.

---

[80] Several different methods are used in practice, including simultaneous equations that solve for the net amount at risk at the end of the month.

## Processing Frequency

The term **processing frequency** refers to the time interval over which discrete policy level events are assumed to occur. In determining the processing frequency to be assumed in the calculation of the definitional limitations, it is important to note that the decision regarding processing frequency does not affect the interval over which premiums are assumed payable for purposes of computing the GLP and the 7-pay premium. The GLP and the 7-pay premium are defined by sections 7702 and 7702A as level annual amounts. As such, it is inappropriate to compute these values assuming a more frequent premium payment assumption (e.g., monthly or continuous premiums). The choice of processing frequency generally comes down to a choice between annual and monthly processing. In choosing an interval that is other than annual, certain options (noted elsewhere) exist as to how interest and mortality rates are converted to an other-than-annual basis.

## Equivalence of Methods

Although the methods may be in different forms, each of the methods, consistently applied, will result in equivalent values. Algebraically, it can be demonstrated that the prospective (projection or illustration-based) approach and the retrospective approach (using basic principles and commutation functions) are equivalent.

| (2.20) Equivalence of prospective (projection) and retrospective (basic principles) methods | | |
|---|---|---|
| (1) | Start with the formula for successive cash values in an accumulation-type product under a projection-based method (i.e., Formula (2.20) excluding expenses) | $_{t+1}CV = \{_tCV + P_t - (NAR \times COI\,rate)\} \times (1+i)$ |
| (2) | Substitute values for $NAR \times COI$ rate where $NAR = SA/(1+i) - {}_tCV + P_t$ and COI rate $= (q_t/1-q_t)$ | $_{t+1}CV = \left\{_tCV + P_t - \left[(SA \times v) - (_tCV + P_t)\right] \times \frac{q_t}{1-q_t}\right\} \times (1+i)$ |
| (3) | Multiply both sides of the equation by $(1/1+i)$, or $v$ | $_{t+1}CV \times v = {}_tCV + P_t - \left[(SA \times v) - (_tCV + P_t)\right] \times \frac{q_t}{1-q_t}$ |
| (4) | Expand $(SA \times v - (_tCV+P_t)) \times (q_t/1-q_t)$ | $_{t+1}CV \times v = {}_tCV + P_t - \left((SA \times v) \times \frac{q_t}{1-q_t}\right) + \left((_tCV + P_t) \times \frac{q_t}{1-q_t}\right)$ |
| (5) | Combine terms with $CV_t$ | $_{t+1}CV \times v = \left((_tCV + P_t) \times \left(1 + \frac{q_t}{1-q_t}\right)\right) - \left((SA \times v) \times \frac{q_t}{1-q_t}\right)$ |
| (6) | Multiply both sides of the equation by $(1-q_t) \times (1+i)$ | $_{t+1}CV \times (1-q_t) = (_tCV + P_t) \times (1+i) - (SA \times q_t)$ |
| (7) | Equals the "classical" Fackler accumulation formula[81] | $_{t+1}CV \times p_t = (_tCV + P_t) \times (1+i) - (SA \times q_t)$ |

Although the mathematics of demonstrating the equivalence between the prospective method and the retrospective method increases in complexity with the inclusion of expense charges or QABs, the basic equivalence between these two methods still holds, provided the mechanics of the calculations are defined in a consistent manner. Note that an additional condition necessary to maintain equivalence between the two approaches is that the implicit risk amount in the prospective approach be permitted to go negative, if necessary. The need for a negative risk amount generally arises, as discussed earlier, only where there is significant prefunding of charges associated with a large QAB. The treatment of the death benefit discount rate as a

---

[81] CHESTER WALLACE JORDAN, JR., SOCIETY OF ACTUARIES' TEXTBOOK ON LIFE CONTINGENCIES 115 (2nd ed. 1967).

contract factor, rather than an assumed interest rate, also complicates the demonstration of equivalence of the methods.

## *Rounding of Values*

The legislative history of section 7702 observes:

> [I]t has been standard practice for most companies to round all cash values up to the next whole dollar per thousand of face amounts. This simplifies displays and assures compliance with minimum nonforfeiture standards under State law. Thus, it is expected that ... reasonable approximations (e.g., $1 per $1,000 of face amount) in the calculation of the net single premium or guideline premiums will be permitted.[82]

The concept just described is generally known as the "rounding rule." While this rule is often applied in practice and has been acknowledged by the IRS as an acceptable approach in performing the definitional calculations, its application in various contexts is not always clear. It has been the subject of a number of private letter rulings waiving errors.[83]

The rounding rule is perhaps best understood by reviewing its source: tabular cash values in whole life insurance contracts. As the legislative history quoted above indicates, these cash values typically are displayed, in terms of U.S. currency, in whole dollars per $1,000 of face amount of coverage. The rounding of NSPs for such contracts up to the nearest whole dollar per $1,000 of face amount enables them to "cover" the similarly rounded up cash values that typically are stated in whole life insurance contracts. When the rounding rule is applied outside this specific context, such as in the computation of guideline premiums and 7-pay premiums, it is important to keep its origin in mind. While the rounding of the GSP per $1,000 of coverage in the same manner as the NSP should be acceptable, care should be taken in applying the rule to level annual premiums.

It is also clear that the rounding rule does not impart a license simply to add $1.00 to the definitional limitations otherwise computed for each $1,000 of death benefit. The rule does not support use of such a tolerance factor in the definitional computations; apart from the computational choices discussed elsewhere in these appendices or specific directions in the statutes and their legislative histories, there is no tolerance allowed. The collection and crediting of a premium one cent above the guideline premium limitation constitutes a compliance error, absent use of the 60-day rule to remove it from the contract.

## Appendix 2.3. Payment of Death Claims Assumptions

Calculations of life insurance premiums and cash surrender values that assume events (e.g., payment of premiums, expense and mortality deductions, or the payment of a death claim) occur at discrete points in time are referred to as **curtate** calculations. Absent an adjustment in the calculations for the immediate payment of a death claim, an underlying assumption in a curtate calculation is that deaths occur (or more precisely, death claims are assumed payable) at the end of the contract month or year of death, depending on the processing frequency assumed in the calculation. In reality, deaths occur on a continuous, and arguably uniform, basis. Insurance companies generally pay death claims as they occur, and do not defer the payment to an otherwise discrete point in time, such as a contract "monthiversary" or anniversary.

To accommodate the practice of paying death claims when they occur, insurance companies have incorporated an **immediate payment of claims (IPC)** assumption in the determination of values under sections 7702 and 7702A. This results in a marginal increase in values to offset the forgone interest otherwise accruing to the company from the actual date of death to the assumed date of death in the curtate calculation (i.e., from the date of death to the end of the month or year of death). Adjusting values for an immediate payment of claims assumption will result in a semicontinuous calculation (i.e., death claims and the corresponding payment of a death benefit occur on a continuous basis, while other events, including the payment of premiums and the deduction of expense and other charges, occur on a discrete or curtate basis). While occasionally applied in prac-

---

[82] DEFRA Blue Book, *supra* Chapter 1, note 20, at 653. No comparable statement appears in the formal DEFRA legislative history.
[83] *See* PLRs 200143008 (July 17, 2001), 9436037 (June 13, 1994), 9144020 (July 31, 1991) and 9144009 (July 26, 1991).

tice, the use of fully continuous functions effectively assumes that premiums are paid continuously throughout the year, which is inconsistent with the test plan concept of single or level annual premiums.

The overall effect that an immediate payment of claims assumption will have on values will depend on the processing frequency underlying the calculation. The adjustment will be greater for annual calculations than for monthly calculations, as the period between the expected date of death and the assumed date of death is approximately six months under an annual calculation compared with one-half month for a monthly calculation. For an annual calculation, multiplying the curtate value by $[i \div ln(1+i)$ or $\frac{i}{\delta}]$, where $ln$ is the natural logarithm, produces a value appropriate for the assumption of a uniform distribution of deaths (and claim payments). The factor here is slightly smaller than $1 + i/2$. Note that the adjustment is purely interest-rate-driven. Care should be taken in applying an immediate payment of claims adjustment to the maturity or endowment benefit. Only death benefits should be adjusted under an immediate payment of claims assumption. The present value of the endowment benefit should not be adjusted in this calculation, as it is paid at the end of the year in which the contract matures. Table 2.8 summarizes the assumptions for various claims payment assumptions and processing methods.

## Table 2.8. Processing for various claims payment assumptions

| | Processing assumed | Benefits assumed payable | Mortality | Interest adjustment factor |
|---|---|---|---|---|
| Annual curtate | Annual | End of year | $q$ | — |
| Annual IPC | Annual | Continuously | $q$ | $i \div (ln(1+i))$ |
| Monthly arithmetic curtate | Monthly | End of month | $q/12$ | — |
| Monthly arithmetic IPC | Monthly | Continuously | $q/12$ | $i^{(12)} \div (ln(1+i^{(12)}))$ |
| Monthly exponential curtate | Monthly | End of month | $1-(1-q)^{(1/12)}$ | — |
| Monthly exponential IPC | Monthly | Continuously | $1-(1-q)^{(1/12)}$ | $i^{(12)} \div (ln(1+i^{(12)}))$ |

Caution needs to be exercised in choosing the assumption set used to compute the definitional limitations. Simply selecting an assumption set without appreciating the implications of the calculation method can create potential exposure to unrealistic or possibly unsupportable assumptions. Table 2.9 below illustrates the at-issue calculations under different processing and payment of claims assumptions. The values shown in Table 2.9 for annual curtate are based on the sample at-issue calculation presented in Appendix 2.1.

## Table 2.9. Male age 45, $100,000 face amount, 2001 CSO ANB, endowment at age 100

| | GSP | GLP-DBO1 | GLP-DBO2 | NSP | 7-pay |
|---|---|---|---|---|---|
| Annual curtate | 19,246.67 | 1,610.13 | 3,982.08 | 25,444.35 | 4,167.49 |
| Annual IPC | 19,790.19 | 1,644.60 | 4,014.40 | 26,011.05 | 4,260.34 |
| Monthly arithmetic curtate | 19,589.46 | 1,626.99 | 3,996.86 | 25,804.72 | 4,226.46 |
| Monthly arithmetic IPC | 19,634.81 | 1,629.85 | 4,004.08 | 25,851.92 | 4,234.17 |
| Monthly exponential curtate | 19,719.88 | 1,640.37 | 4,278.39 | 25,969.58 | 4,253.51 |
| Monthly exponential IPC | 19,765.59 | 1,643.27 | 4,286.14 | 26,017.15 | 4,261.31 |

Any potential distortion in values created under the arithmetic method for defining monthly mortality rates for option 1 death benefits will be eliminated under the exponential approach. However, despite this theoretical nicety, the exponential method seems sometimes in practice to produce odd results for the option 2 death benefit, particularly for 1980 CSO contracts, and it should be used with caution in situations involving monthly processed contracts. Note that when $q = 1$, the application of the exponential formula produces the result that $q^{monthly} = 1$ while the arithmetic method produces a $q^{monthly} = 1/12$. Table 2.10 provides comparative values for the GLP (DBO1 and DBO2) based on 1980 CSO mortality where the calculations are based on an age 100 endowment.

Table 2.10. Male age 45, $100,000 face amount, 1980 CSO aggregate, ANB, endowment at age 100

|  | GLP-DBO1 | GLP-DBO2 |
|---|---|---|
| Annual curtate | 2,035.42 | 5,556.59 |
| Annual IPC | 2,079.47 | 5,669.41 |
| Monthly arithmetic curtate | 2,055.37 | 5,658.69 |
| Monthly arithmetic IPC | 2,059.03 | 5,668.16 |
| Monthly exponential curtate | 2,074.42 | 11,193.83 |
| Monthly exponential IPC | 2,078.12 | 11,214.27 |

The option 2 GLP based on a monthly exponential mortality assumption is over twice the GLP that results from the arithmetic method (based on the $q/12$ approach). This is caused by the differing nature of option 2 death benefits. While the exponential computation is theoretically appropriate for option 1, it appears the arithmetic calculation is appropriate to option 2. The difference is greatest for mortality at advanced ages. The desire to avoid such issues in the later years of the mortality table was one of the reasons earlier designers of universal life contracts choose an endowment at 95 as the "standard" for design.

## Appendix 2.4. IRS Notice 88-128

IRS Notice 88-128,[84] issued in the fall of 1988 and applicable to contracts entered into on or after October 21, 1988, previewed rules interpreting the reasonable mortality charge requirements it said would be published in future regulations. This notice, which pursuant to Notice 2006-95 remains in effect for contracts entered into before January 1, 2009, also provides certain assurances regarding ongoing compliance with section 7702(c)(3)(B)(i) to insurers whose contracts satisfy the interim rules contained in the notice. Notice 88-128 does not attempt to define reasonable mortality, instead providing that use of certain safe harbor mortality tables will satisfy the requirements of section 7702(c)(3)(B)(i). According to the notice, the safe harbor mortality tables for contracts entered into after October 20, 1988, are the sex-distinct 1980 CSO tables, consistently with the tables' characterization as the prevailing commissioners' standard tables. Specifically, Notice 88-128 provides that "a mortality charge meets the requirements of section 7702(c)(3)(B)(i) if such mortality charge does not exceed 100 percent of the applicable mortality charge set forth in the 1980 CSO tables." It goes on to say that, to the extent a state requires the use of unisex tables, thereby imposing, for female insureds, mortality charges that exceed the (sex-distinct) 1980 CSO tables for males, the increased mortality charges may be taken into account with respect to contracts to which that unisex requirement applies.

Notice 88-128 generally treats use of sex-distinct, aggregate mortality rates under the 1980 CSO tables as reasonable. It does not, however, address the use of the smoker and nonsmoker versions of the 1980 CSO tables, nor does it appear to provide a safe harbor for the voluntary use of the unisex versions of the table. Thus, the notice raises a question as to whether unisex versions of the 1980 CSO tables could be looked to as a safe harbor in circumstances other than when required by state law (e.g., in Montana and, for a period of time, Massachusetts). In particular, the issue presented is whether group life insurance or other worksite or voluntary employee contracts, insofar as they are required to be on a unisex basis under federal requirements, *can* rely on unisex versions of the 1980 CSO tables as a safe harbor.[85] A related question is whether the unisex tables constitute a safe harbor for contracts issued on a unisex basis in absence of state or federal requirements. These questions

---

[84] 1988-2 C.B. 540.
[85] *See, e.g., Arizona Governing Comm. for Tax Deferred Annuity and Deferred Compensation Plans v. Norris*, 463 U.S. 1073 (1983) (holding Arizona's deferred compensation plan, which paid lower retirement benefits to women than men who paid the same contributions, violated federal law by discriminating based on gender).

are perhaps most critical for 1980 CSO contracts issued during 2008 covering standard risks, since satisfaction of the notice's safe harbor generally is necessary to meet the reasonable mortality charge rule, in that, apart from the safe harbor, this rule requires use of the 2001 CSO tables in the definitional calculations for such contracts.

Notice 88-128 also provides a second interim safe harbor for use of the 1958 CSO tables, provided a contract is not a MEC, was issued prior to December 31, 1988, and was issued on a contract form based on the 1958 CSO table approved by state regulatory authorities no later than October 21, 1988. The notice does not indicate how this safe harbor should apply to a contract that was not a MEC when it was issued but subsequently became a MEC.

The safe harbors provided by Notice 88-128 apply to contracts issued on or before 90 days after the issuance of temporary regulations on reasonable mortality (which the IRS has never issued). The notice also provides that, if the charges specified in the prevailing commissioners' standard tables exceed the allowable charges under the standards set forth in the regulations, the future regulations would apply prospectively to the extent of the excess. This is consistent with the TAMRA legislative history, which expressed the intent of Congress that any "[s]tandards set forth in such regulations that limit mortality charges to amounts less than those specified in the prevailing commissioners' standard tables are to be prospective in application."[86]

## Appendix 2.5. Proposed Regulation on "Reasonable" Mortality

In 1991, several years after the issuance of Notice 88-128, the IRS issued proposed regulations to define reasonable mortality charges for use in computations under sections 7702 and 7702A. Unlike Notice 88-128, which merely provided certain safe harbor mortality tables for satisfying the reasonable mortality requirements, Prop. Reg. sec. 1.7702-1 actually defined reasonable mortality. In the proposed regulations, which never have been finalized, reasonable mortality charges were defined to be "those amounts that an insurance company actually expects to impose as consideration for assuming the risk of the insured's death (regardless of the designation used for those charges), taking into account any relevant characteristics of the insured of which the company is aware."[87]

Like the permanent rule contained in section 7702(c)(3)(B)(i), the proposed regulations also placed an upper bound on what constitutes reasonable mortality. In particular, reasonable mortality charges could not exceed the lesser of the mortality charges specified in the prevailing commissioners' standard tables in effect when the contract was issued or the guaranteed mortality charges specified in the contract. This dual limit on reasonable mortality would have prevented the use of the prevailing table for those contracts that explicitly guaranteed lower mortality charges. In this respect, the limitation in the proposed regulations differed from that in Notice 88-128, which did not limit mortality based on the charges in the contract, and is comparable to the safe harbor in Notice 2006-95 for 2001 CSO contracts.

Subject to this dual limit, the proposed regulations included three safe harbors under which mortality charges for contracts with only one insured are deemed to be reasonable, as follows:

- The first safe harbor provides that mortality charges that do not exceed the applicable charges set forth in the 1980 CSO tables for male or female insureds are reasonable mortality charges.

- The second safe harbor addresses variations of the 1980 CSO tables, provided certain requirements are satisfied. This would extend the 1980 CSO safe harbor to unisex contracts, regardless of whether the use of unisex mortality was mandated under state or federal law.

- The third safe harbor provides that mortality charges not in excess of the applicable charges specified in the 1958 CSO tables are reasonable, subject to a number of conditions, namely, that the contract cannot be a MEC and must have been issued before 1989 under a plan of insurance or policy blank based on those tables and approved by the applicable state regulatory authority by October 21, 1988.

---

[86] TAMRA Conference Report, *supra* note 64, at 108.
[87] Prop. Treas. Reg. § 1.7702-1(b).

The proposed regulations permitted far greater leeway than did Notice 88-128 for life contracts covering a single life, subject to a consistency or "anti-whipsaw" rule. Under the proposed regulations, 1980 CSO-based mortality rates were deemed reasonable if consistently applied within a class of contracts, whether or not distinctions were made according to the insured's sex or tobacco use. In keeping with this consistency rule, it would not be reasonable, within the same plan of insurance, to use the 1980 CSO aggregate table for nonsmokers and use the smoker table for smokers.

Although issued in 1991, the proposed regulations would have applied to contracts entered into on or after October 21, 1988. This attempt at retroactivity is of no import, however, as the proposed regulations have not been adopted and thus do not embody legal requirements.

**Chapter 3**

# COMPONENTS OF SECTION 7702 AND 7702A CALCULATIONS

## Chapter Overview

This chapter examines certain components of the definitional calculations in more detail. Chapter 3 begins with a discussion of the definition of the term "cash surrender value" that is important to compliance under both the cash value accumulation test (CVAT) and the guideline premium/cash value corridor test as well as section 7702A.[1] Following this are an examination of the regulations applied to identify an insured's age, a more detailed review of the computational rules under sections 7702 and 7702A, a discussion of the treatment of contract reinstatements, and additional information on qualified additional benefits. The chapter concludes by addressing a variety of issues relating to the reasonable mortality and expense charge rules.

## Defining Cash Value and Cash Surrender Value

When testing a life insurance contract for compliance with the CVAT, the net single premium (NSP) computed for a contract is compared against the contract's **cash surrender value (CSV)** within the meaning of section 7702. In most life insurance contracts, "cash surrender value" refers to the cash value of the contract less any remaining surrender charges and less outstanding policy loans and accrued policy loan interest due (i.e., the net amount of cash payable to a surrendering policy owner). In section 7702 terms, however, the cash surrender value of a contract is more akin to the cash value of a traditional life insurance contract or to the policy value, accumulation value or account value of a universal life-type contract. In other words, the cash surrender value under section 7702 refers to the cash value determined *without regard to* any surrender charge, policy loan or reasonable termination dividends. The term "cash surrender value" thus has a specific meaning as it applies under the definitional limitations and should not be confused with the term as it may be defined by specific contractual language. (As noted in Chapter 2, CSV is used in this book to refer to the cash surrender value as specially defined for section 7702 purposes.)

As discussed in Chapter 2, under the CVAT, the CSV of a contract must never be able to exceed the NSP. Properly identifying a contract's cash surrender value and its root term, cash value, within the meaning of section 7702(f)(2)(A) is of critical importance for purposes of complying with the CVAT since this test must be met by the contract's terms. Identifying it is similarly important to satisfaction of the guideline premium test's cash value corridor, which requires the death benefit of a contract to be at least a certain percentage, varying by age, of the contract's CSV.

In the legislative history of the Deficit Reduction Act of 1984 (DEFRA), the definition of CSV is further amplified to refer to "the cash value of any contract (i.e., any amount to which the policyholder is entitled upon surrender and against which the policyholder can borrow) determined without regard to any surrender charge, policy loan, or a reasonable termination dividend."[2] The commentary in the legislative history goes on to observe that, whether a termination dividend is reasonable in amount (and thus may be excluded from the contract's CSV) is to be determined with reference to the historical practice of the industry, giving as an ex-

---

[1] Unless otherwise indicated, references in this book to "section" are to the provisions of the Internal Revenue Code of 1986, as amended (also referred to as "IRC" or the "Code").

[2] DEFRA House Report, *supra* Chapter 1, note 11, at 1444; DEFRA Senate Report, *supra* Chapter 1, note 11, at 573. Interestingly, the DEFRA Blue Book added the modifier "generally" between the phrase relating to the surrender value and the phrase relating to borrowing. See DEFRA Blue Book, *supra* Chapter 1, note 20, at 647.

ample the New York insurance law's maximum of $35 per $1,000 of face amount of coverage.[3] However, as this amount is stated as an example, it may not be an absolute maximum. Also, according to the legislative history, a contract's CSV does not include dividends on deposit (dividends held outside the contract that accumulate taxable interest) and certain amounts returned upon the termination of a credit life insurance policy.[4]

In testing for compliance under section 7702, the CSV of a contract is not reduced by any outstanding policy loans. Thus, both the CVAT and the section 7702(d) corridor apply to the CSV of a contract without reduction for policy loans.[5] Note that policy loans likewise do not reduce the CSV for material change rollovers under section 7702A, nor are they taken into account under the adjustment rules of section 7702(f)(7). These transactions are addressed in Chapter 4.

## *1992 Proposed Regulation Defining Cash Surrender Value*

While never finalized, a **proposed regulation defining cash value** that the IRS issued in 1992 relating to the treatment of accelerated death benefits (see Chapter 7) sheds some light on the government's then view of the scope of the term "cash surrender value" as it applies in section 7702.[6] The definitions section of the proposed regulation defined the term **cash value** as equal to the greater of

- the "maximum amount payable" under the contract (determined without regard to any surrender charge or policy loan), or
- the maximum amount the policyholder can borrow under the contract.

As the proposed regulation's definition of cash value was so comprehensive, particularly in its use of the phrase "maximum amount payable" under the contract, the proposed regulation also provided specific exemptions from inclusion in the cash value, as follows:

- The amount of any death benefit or qualified accelerated death benefit (a new concept the regulation was proposed to define, basically meaning terminal illness accelerated death benefits)
- The amount of a qualified additional benefit (QAB)
- Certain "morbidity risk" additional benefits, e.g., long-term care accelerated death benefits, under certain conditions
- Amounts returned to the insured upon termination of a credit life insurance contract due to a full repayment of the debt covered by the contract
- Reasonable termination dividends not in excess of $35 for each $1,000 of the face amount of the contract

Thus, under the proposed regulation, any amount payable under a life insurance contract not specifically excluded from the definition of cash value would be treated as CSV under the definitional limitations.

This proposed regulation was highly controversial, partly due to its divergence from the common life insurance industry understanding of CSV, and partly because it changed one significant word used in the DEFRA legislative history. The legislative history had defined CSV to mean "any amount to which the policyholder is entitled upon surrender *and* against which the policyholder can borrow" (emphasis added). In a departure from that history, the proposed regulation changed "and" to "or." The life insurance industry strongly objected to the approach taken in the proposed regulation.

---

[3] *See* DEFRA House Report, *supra* Chapter 1, note 11, at 1444; DEFRA Senate Report, *supra* Chapter 1, note 11, at 573; DEFRA Blue Book, *supra* Chapter 1, note 20, at 647.

[4] DEFRA House Report, *supra* Chapter 1, note 11, at 1444; DEFRA Senate Report, *supra* Chapter 1, note 11, at 573; DEFRA Blue Book, *supra* Chapter 1, note 20, at 647–48.

[5] In testimony to Congress in 1988 related to single premium life insurance, the General Accounting Office (GAO) recommended that a change in the definitional requirements be made to require that the net death benefit (the death benefit minus loans) be compared to the contract's account value minus loans to determine qualification. However, the GAO's recommendation was never enacted and the basis of comparison remains the death benefit and the CSV unadjusted by policy loans. *See* U.S. GEN. ACCOUNTING OFFICE, GAO/GGD-88-95, TAX POLICY: MORTALITY CHARGES ON SINGLE PREMIUM LIFE INSURANCE SHOULD BE RESTRICTED, 6 (1988).

[6] Qualified Accelerated Death Benefits Under Life Insurance Contracts, 57 Fed. Reg. 59,319 (proposed Dec. 15, 1992).

Since the proposed regulation was not finalized, it does not have the force and effect of law. Further, reflecting the controversy raised by the proposed regulation, in Notice 93-37[7] the IRS announced that the effective date of any new rules in this respect would be no earlier than the date of publication of final regulations in the Federal Register (which has not yet occurred).[8]

## *Private Letter Rulings Defining Cash Surrender Value*

The IRS has issued a number of private letter rulings addressing the meaning of the term cash surrender value as used in section 7702.[9] The contracts involved in these rulings provided for payment of an amount upon full surrender of the contracts in addition to the policy value generally payable upon surrender. The IRS concluded that the additional amount represented cash surrender value within the meaning of section 7702(f)(2)(A), and it further concluded that the failure of the taxpayers to reflect such amount as CSV was a reasonable error under section 7702(f)(8). In one of the rulings, the IRS held that an additional amount available upon surrender through a rider was part of the section 7702 CSV.

**Common facts of the rulings:** The contracts involved in the rulings were designed to comply either with the CVAT or the guideline premium/cash value corridor test. The contracts provided policy values computed in a typical manner that were available on surrender. The amounts in question in the rulings, styled the "remittance" in the majority of the PLRs, were not part of these policy values. Rather, they represented additional amounts payable on surrender, often added where the surrender occurred early in the life of a contract.[10] It appeared that the policyholder could not borrow against the additional amount in any of the rulings.

As an illustrative example, think of a contract that provides for a surrender benefit which is the greater of the policy value and a return of premiums paid. If premiums paid exceeded the policy value on the date of surrender, the policyholder would receive the policy value plus the excess of premiums paid over the policy value. This excess of policy value over premiums paid is analogous to the remittance described in several of the private letter rulings.

**The IRS analysis:** The rulings, most of which concluded with the IRS granting waivers of errors under section 7702(f)(8), began with a discussion of the common meaning of cash surrender value and cash value as described in certain insurance texts. One such text defined cash surrender value as "the amount made available contractually, to a withdrawing policyowner who is terminating his or her protection."[11] Another cited text defined cash value as the "amount available to the policyholder upon the surrender of the life insurance contract."[12] The IRS next cited the legislative history of section 7702, which as previously noted describes cash surrender value within the meaning of the statute as "the cash value of any contract (i.e., any amount to which the policyholder is entitled upon surrender and against which the policyholder can borrow) determined without regard to any surrender charge, policy loan, or a reasonable termination dividend."[13] Finally, the rulings discussed the proposed regulation defining cash value.

Based on these considerations, the IRS concluded that the remittances and other additional amounts constituted part of the CSV of the contracts, thus causing contracts designed to comply with the CVAT to fail this test because the contract forms did not specifically consider these remittances as CSV for purposes of defining the contract's death benefit. In addressing whether the insurer's error (in most of the rulings) of not treating the additional amounts as CSV was reasonable within the meaning of section 7702(f)(8), the IRS noted that pursuant to Notice 93-37, the proposed regulation was not then in effect (as it still is not), and also that it did not contain language identical to the CSV definition in the DEFRA legislative history. For these reasons, the IRS concluded that the error was waivable.

---

[7] 1993-2 C.B. 331.
[8] Notice 93-37 also outlined a relief provision that was anticipated for the final regulations, if and when published. Specifically, the notice states, "[it] is anticipated that insurance companies generally will be allowed a period of time after final regulations are published to bring their policy forms into compliance with any new rules."
[9] In chronological order, these are PLRs 200521009 (Feb. 22, 2005), 200528018 (Apr. 12, 2005), 200745006 (Aug. 9, 2007), 200841043 (March 28, 2008), and 200901028 (Sept. 29, 2008).
[10] The rulings involving the remittances do not explain what was meant by "early" surrenders.
[11] Kenneth Black Jr. and Harold D. Skipper Jr., Life and Health Insurance 46 (13th ed. 2000) (hereinafter Black and Skipper).
[12] John H. Magee, Life Insurance 599 (3rd ed. 1958).
[13] See *supra* note 2.

**Implications of the rulings:** The question remains as to how insurers should construe the meaning of cash surrender value under current law. Significantly, the holdings of the private letter rulings appear *not* to follow the official legislative history of section 7702 (as the IRS seems to have recognized), and instead appear to be more in line with the proposed regulation that is not in effect.[14] In the case of contracts designed to comply with the CVAT especially, given that the terms of the contract must ensure compliance with the test at all times, even minor errors in accurately identifying CSV can result in noncompliance with this test.

A conclusion that an amount apart from a traditional cash surrender value is properly treated as CSV for section 7702 purposes necessarily raises concern about insurers' ability to identify the proper amount to use in testing for compliance with the definitional limitations. In particular, the additional amounts involved in the rulings seemed to be returning portions of premiums paid for the contracts. This presents an important question: How should return-of-premium benefits available on contract surrender be treated under section 7702? There is reason to believe the IRS construes such benefits as constituting CSV, including in circumstances where they are provided under term life insurance contracts that otherwise have no such value and that rely on the CVAT for their compliance with section 7702.

Further, a conclusion that an amount constitutes CSV may have additional consequences under sections 7702 and 7702A that should be considered. Specifically, if an amount constitutes CSV and is provided on a guaranteed basis, does this affect the guarantees under a contract that are taken into account in calculating the NSPs, guideline premiums and 7-pay premiums under the statutes? The presence of an additional guaranteed CSV arguably could be viewed as resulting in an increased interest rate guarantee in certain circumstances. Also, if the additional CSV returns to the policyowner certain expenses that have been charged, this may imply such expenses are so contingent that they should not be taken into account in calculating guideline premiums in the first instance, e.g., if it is expected that policyholders likely will receive such additional CSV.

### *Additional Considerations Regarding Cash Surrender Value*

**Legislative history relating to cash surrender value under section 7702A:** In connection with explaining certain amendments to section 7702A made in 2002, the staff of the Joint Committee on Taxation commented that the definition of cash surrender value under the "rollover rule" of section 7702A(c)(3)(A)(ii) was, by cross-reference, the same as that in section 7702. The Joint Committee staff then stated that, for purposes of applying this rule, "it is intended that the fair market value of the contract be used as the cash surrender value under this provision, if the amount of the putative cash surrender value of the contract is artificially depressed."[15] This legislative history seems to have little relevance for purposes of generally defining cash surrender value since it appears to function solely as an anti-abuse rule directed at limited situations. It is interesting to note, however, that the cited passage refers to a putative cash surrender value, and this reference arguably is viewing a contract's putative amount, i.e., its policy value, as being the same as its CSV.

**A new regulation in the future?:** At the date of this writing (in 2015), the issuance of a new proposed regulation defining cash surrender value is on the Treasury-IRS "Priority Guidance Plan." This item has appeared on this plan for a number of years, and it is uncertain when it will be forthcoming. The presence of an item on the plan does not assure that such guidance will be issued.

## Defining "Age"

An insured's attained age is relevant in a number of contexts under the definitional limitations. In general, the section 7702 and 7702A calculations at any given time require knowledge of, or an assumption as to, the age(s) of the insured(s) at that time. More particularly, section 7702(e)(1)(B) generally requires the calculations to assume that a contract's maturity date is no earlier than the day on which the insured attains age 95 and no later

---

[14] There may have been a procedural reason for this. It is certainly noteworthy that the IRS made use of the proposed regulation in assessing both the existence and the reasonableness of the error even though the 1993 notice had provided assurance that a regulation defining cash surrender value would not be effective until finalized. This was apparently an artifact of internal IRS procedures, which require the agency to abide by its proposed rules in the context of private letter rulings. The private letter rulings discussed here were seeking waivers of noncompliance, and the taxpayers were likely relieved to receive them. Even so, the IRS did not need to focus on the proposed regulation in deciding to issue the requested waivers. The fact that it did should not be discounted.

[15] STAFF OF THE JT. COMM. ON TAX'N, 107TH CONG., TECHNICAL EXPLANATION OF THE JOB CREATION AND WORKER ASSISTANCE ACT OF 2002, at 45–46 (Comm. Print 2002) (hereinafter Technical Explanation of 2002 Act).

than the day on which the insured attains age 100. Also, under section 7702(e)(1)(C), death benefits are deemed to be provided until this maturity date, and under section 7702(e)(1)(D), the amount of any endowment benefit (or sum of endowment benefits, including any CSV on the maturity date) is deemed not to exceed the least amount payable as a death benefit at any time under the contract. The insured's attained age also is pertinent to application of the cash value corridor requirement of section 7702(d), which must be satisfied by contracts intended to comply with the guideline premium test.

In 2005, the Treasury Department and the IRS proposed regulations explaining how to determine the attained age of an insured for purposes of testing whether a contract satisfies the definitional limitations. Prior to that time, the sole official information relating to the determination of attained age was found in the DEFRA legislative history's statement that in applying the cash value corridor, the guideline premium limitation and the computational rules, "the attained age of the insured means the insured's age determined by reference to contract anniversaries (rather than the individual's actual birthdays), so long as the age assumed under the contract is within 12 months of the actual age."[16] As described below, the proposed regulations elaborated on this rule, and in 2006, subject to several changes, the proposal was finalized and now appears as Treas. Reg. section 1.7702-2. It is at this writing (in 2015) the sole final regulation under the definitional limitations.

The final **attained-age regulation,** consistently with the proposed regulations, establishes a general rule for determining an insured's attained age for purposes of calculating the guideline level premium (GLP) under section 7702(c)(4), applying the cash value corridor of section 7702(d) and utilizing the computational rules of section 7702(e). Significantly, the preamble to the final regulation states it does not, nor is it intended to, "endorse or prohibit any methodology for determining reasonable mortality charges under section 7702(c)." This limitation on the scope of the new rules was reiterated, and emphasized, by representatives of the Treasury and the IRS during discussion of the subject at the Society of Actuaries' Product Tax Seminar on Sept. 13, 2006, the day after the final regulation was published. Hence, the new attained-age rules apply for limited, specific purposes:

- Determining the level premium payment period under section 7702(c)(4), which refers to payments until at least age 95

- Applying the section 7702(d) corridor factors, which are age specific

- Making the various calculations in accordance with the endowment or maturity date rules of section 7702(e), which reference ages 95 and 100

The computational rules apply to the CVAT as well as the guideline premium test, and they also apply, derivatively, in determining the 7-pay premiums.

With respect to a contract insuring a **single life,** Treas. Reg. section 1.7702-2(b)(1) provides that the attained age of the insured under a contract is either:

- the insured's age determined by reference to the individual's actual birthday as of the date of determination (actual age), or

- the insured's age determined by reference to contract anniversary (rather than the insured's actual birthday)—sometimes called the "insurance age"—so long as the age assumed under the contract is within 12 months of the actual age as of that date.

Under these rules, age-last-birthday and age-nearest-birthday assumptions continue to be permitted. This is illustrated in examples 1 and 2 of Treas. Reg. section 1.7702-2(e), which may be summarized as follows:

- **Example 1:** An insured born on May 1, 1947, becomes 60 years old on May 1, 2007. On January 1, 2008, the insured purchases an insurance contract on his or her life. January 1 is the contract anniversary date for future years.[17] The insurance company determines the insured's premiums (or cost of insurance)

---

[16] DEFRA House Report, *supra* Chapter 1, note 11, at 1447; DEFRA Senate Report, *supra* Chapter 1, note 11, at 576; DEFRA Blue Book, *supra* Chapter 1, note 20, at 651.

[17] The regulation appears to use the hypothetical "purchase" date as the date the contract is "issued" or "entered into." This approach has the benefit of sidestepping questions that may arise as to exactly what a contract's issue date or entered-into date is.

based on an age-last-birthday method. Under this method, the insured has an attained age of 60 for the first contract year, 61 for the second contract year and so on.

- **Example 2:** The facts are the same as under example 1, except that the insurance company determines the insured's premiums based on an age-nearest-birthday method. Under this method, the insured's nearest birthday to January 1, 2008, is May 1, 2008, when the insured will be 61 years old. Thus, in this example, the insured has an attained age of 61 for the first contract year, 62 for the second contract year and so on.

In addition to addressing contracts covering a single insured's life, the regulation addresses the permissible attained-age assumptions that may be used under **joint life** insurance contracts, both those that cover the first of multiple insureds to die and those providing last-to-die coverage. The same set of requirements governing a single life contract also applies in determining the GLPs, in identifying the applicable cash value corridor percentage and in applying the computational rules for a multiple-life contract, although with two significant exceptions. In particular, Treas. Reg. section 1.7702-2(c)(1) and (d) provide, respectively, that for these purposes:

- The attained age of the insured under a contract insuring multiple lives on a last-to-die basis—joint and last survivor contracts—is the attained age of the youngest insured
- The attained age of the insured under a contract insuring multiple lives on a first-to-die basis is the attained age of the oldest insured

In response to a comment letter on the proposed regulation, the final regulation includes a rule specifically addressing a last-to-die contract that undergoes a change in both its cash value and its future mortality charges as a result of the death of an insured (i.e., the contract is not based on "frasierized"[18] mortality and reverts to a single life structure upon the death of an insured). According to Treas. Reg. section 1.7702-2(c)(2), if the youngest insured under such a contract should die, the attained age used for testing after that death is the attained age of the "youngest surviving insured." In this way, the attained age used for federal income tax purposes is consistent with that used under the terms of the contract.

Examples 4, 5 and 6 of Treas. Reg. section 1.7702-2(e) illustrate attained-age determinations for multiple-life contracts and may be summarized as follows:

- **Example 4:** An insured born on May 1, 1947, becomes 60 years old on May 1, 2007. In addition, a second insured covered by the contract was born on September 1, 1942, and becomes 65 years old on September 1, 2007. On January 1, 2008, the insureds purchase a last-to-die insurance contract, and the insurer uses the age-last-birthday method for measuring attained age. Because the insured born in 1947 is the younger insured, the attained age of 60 must be used for purposes of sections 7702(c)(4), 7702(d) and 7702(e), as applicable.

- **Example 5:** The facts are the same as under example 4, except that the younger of the two insureds dies in 2012. After the death of the younger insured, both the cash value and the (nonfrasierized) mortality charges of the contract are adjusted to take into account only the life of the surviving insured. Because of this adjustment, the attained age of the only surviving insured is taken into account (after the younger insured's death) for purposes of sections 7702(c)(4), 7702(d) and 7702(e), as applicable.

- **Example 6:** An insured born on May 1, 1947, becomes 60 years old on May 1, 2007. In addition, a second insured covered by the contract was born on September 1, 1952, and becomes 55 years old on September 1, 2007. On January 1, 2008, the insureds purchase a first-to-die insurance contract, and the insurer uses the age-last-birthday method for measuring attained age. Because the insured born in 1947 is the older insured, the attained age of 60 must be used for purposes of sections 7702(c)(4), 7702(d) and 7702(e), as applicable.

The treatment of contracts covering multiple lives is addressed further in Chapter 6.

---

[18] Named after William M. Frasier, the actuary who described the method. *See* William M. Frasier, *Second to Die Joint Life Cash Values and Reserves*, 12 THE ACTUARY 4 (March 1978) (hereinafter Frasier). This method is discussed further in Chapter 6.

**Consistency rule and changes in benefits between anniversaries:** The regulation contains a consistency requirement. Specifically, Treas. Reg. section 1.7702-2(b)(2) states: "Once determined ... the attained age with respect to an individual insured under a contract changes annually. Moreover, the same attained age must be used for purposes of applying sections 7702(c)(4), 7702(d), and 7702(e), as applicable." Example 3 of Treas. Reg. section 1.7702-2(e), summarized below, details and clarifies the intent of the regulation in dealing with benefit changes off-anniversary.

- **Example 3:** An insured born on May 1, 1947, purchases a contract on January 1, 2008. January 1 is the contract anniversary date for future years. The face amount of the contract is increased on May 15, 2011. During the contract year beginning January 1, 2011, the age assumed under the contract on an age-last-birthday basis is 63 years. However, at the time of the face amount increase, the insured's actual age is 64. Treas. Reg. section 1.7702-2(b)(2) provides that, once the attained age is determined, it remains that age until the next policy anniversary. Thus, the insured continues to be 63 years old throughout the contract year beginning January 1, 2011, for purposes of sections 7702(c)(4), 7702(d) and 7702(e), as applicable, even though the insured is age 64 at the time of the increase based on an age-last-birthday determination.

It is important to note that this approach runs contrary to a common insurance industry practice with regard to off-anniversary death benefit increases. Many administrative systems apply a "segment approach" to death benefit increases, where each segment, or layer, of additional death benefit is administered independently from the base contract. Each segment is assigned its own issue date, coverage amount, issue age, etc., and the system calculates, e.g., guideline premiums according to the characteristics assigned to each segment. Under a segment approach, the system would aggregate guideline premiums for each segment to determine the guideline premiums applicable to the contract. A common practice under this approach is to determine issue age for the segment as if the segment were viewed as a newly issued contract. Therefore, if the contract defines age on an age-last-birthday basis, the segment issue age would be determined on an age-last-birthday basis as of the segment issue date; under the facts of example 3 above, the insured would have a segment issue age of 64 years. Thus, the segment issue age under an age-last-birthday determination would be greater than the attained age permitted under the final regulations, resulting in a potential overstatement of guideline premiums.

This result was deliberate on the part of the Treasury Department and the IRS. A comment letter submitted on the proposed regulation characterized its language as unclear with respect to the attained age that should be used for a death benefit change occurring between contract anniversary dates. The letter requested flexibility in determining which attained age to use in this instance. The final regulation provided a clarification, but in a manner contrary to the request made, determining that the attained age of the insured, once established, remains constant until the next anniversary. Again, however, the new attained-age rules apply for the limited purposes of section 7702(c)(4), (d) and (e)—they do not govern "reasonable" mortality charges, according to the preamble. Off-anniversary changes, then, cannot alter the insured's attained age for purposes of determining the level premium payment period, applying the corridor factors and making calculations in accordance with the section 7702(e) maturity date rules.

One question that has arisen concerns the application of the final regulation when there is a material change under section 7702A(c)(3)(A)(i). Upon a material change in benefits under a contract that was not reflected in any previous determination under section 7702A, section 7702A(c)(3)(A)(i) requires the contract to be treated as "a new contract entered into on the day on which such material change takes effect." In example 3 above, if the contract is considered newly entered into on the date of the face amount increase (May 15, 2011), is it then appropriate to determine age as if the contract were newly entered into on that date for purposes of section 7702A(c)(3)(A)? It would seem so, in which case the attained age for the 7-pay premium calculation in the example is 64. While calculations of 7-pay premiums under section 7702A are made, in part, using the computational rules of section 7702(e), section 7702A(c)(3)(A)(i) appears to be the more specific statutory rule governing the date when calculations are made and an insured's age is identified. It would be helpful for this to be clarified in future guidance.

**Contractual assumptions:** A further question under the final regulation is whether the age assumptions contained within a contract (used, for example, for purposes of determining guaranteed mortality charges) must be used under section 7702, e.g., if a contract sets forth mortality guarantees based on an age-last-birthday assumption, is it permissible to calculate guideline premiums using an age-nearest-birthday assumption? Generally speaking, where section 7702 does not prescribe a particular treatment for an aspect of the calculations, it is appropriate to follow the mechanics of a contract, since such a practice usually will be actuarially reasonable in the circumstance. The statute does not, however, expressly require this, and thus the extent to which variations in practice are permitted is unclear in some respects. The second example of Treas. Reg. section 1.7702-2(e) describes use of an age-nearest-birthday assumption and notes that "under the contract" premiums were determined on this basis. In addition, the third of the safe harbors with respect to the reasonable mortality charge rule set forth in Notice 2006-95, described in Chapter 2, limits the mortality charges that can be reflected under section 7702 to those guaranteed under the contract, and thus insurers intending to utilize this safe harbor generally will need to reflect contractual age assumptions in their guideline premium calculations.

**Effective date:** The final regulation is effective September 13, 2006, and applies to contracts either issued on or after October 1, 2007, and based on the 2001 CSO tables, or issued after December 31, 2008. A taxpayer may choose, however, to apply the final regulation to contracts issued prior to October 1, 2007, provided the taxpayer does not later determine the contracts' qualification in a manner that conflicts with the regulation.

Given the prospective application of the regulation's guidance, questions have been asked about the appropriateness of practices, such as joint equal age assumptions and age rate-ups (discussed in Chapter 6), which insurers have used and continue to use with respect to contracts issued before the above-described effective date. Technically, the regulation does not in any way address such contracts or the appropriateness of any particular practices applied to determine their compliance (apart from the effective date rule permitting a taxpayer to apply the guidance retroactively to such contracts). Thus, the appropriateness of any particular interpretation of section 7702 and associated practice must be determined based on the requirements as set forth in the statute and other authorities such as legislative histories pertinent to such requirements. They must be judged, in other words, based on the law as it existed without regard to the final regulation.

## Computational Rules: Limiting "Future Benefits"

As previously noted, restriction of the actuarial assumptions is a key to the operation of the definitional limitations. Together with the interest, mortality and expense assumptions, actuarial mathematics defines the concept of an NSP in terms of the present value of future benefits. This discussion considers the restrictions on the future benefits that may be taken into account in the definitional calculations.

Recall from Chapter 2 that the term **future benefits** has particular meaning in section 7702 (and section 7702A) and is defined in section 7702(f)(4) and (f)(5)(B) to mean:

- Death benefits (i.e., the amount payable due to the insured's death, determined without regard to any QABs)

- Endowment benefits (i.e., the amount payable if the insured survives to the maturity date of the contract)

- Charges for any QABs that satisfy the reasonable expense charge rule, but not the QABs' benefits themselves

The definitional limitations include "computational rules" restricting the timing and magnitude of these benefits that may be assumed in the calculations. Specifically, under these rules, limitations are imposed on the pattern of the assumed future death benefits and QABs, maturity value and maturity date of a contract.

### *Background: Section 101(f) Computational Rules*

A review of the computational rules under the predecessor statute, section 101(f), provides background helpful to understanding the comparable rules applicable under section 7702 (and section 7702A). Section 101(f)(2)(D) provides three computational rules for determining the guideline single or level premiums:

- The net amount at risk assumed in the calculations cannot exceed the net amount at risk at issue.
- The maturity date of the contract is assumed to be the latest date permitted under the contract, but not less than 20 years from issue or, if earlier, the insured's age 95.
- The amount of any assumed endowment benefit cannot exceed the smallest death benefit (without regard to any QAB) at any time.

The NSP under the section 101(f) cash value test is also computed using these rules, except that the maturity date of the contract cannot be earlier than age 95, i.e., eliminating the earlier endowment permitted under the section 101(f) guideline premium limitation.

Because both the NSPs and the guideline premiums under section 101(f) are computed with respect to future benefits under the contract, application of the first computational rule will vary with the product design. A level death benefit assumption (with a declining net amount at risk) would underlie the calculation of values for a traditional option 1 design, where the death benefit generally is defined to equal the contract's "face amount" or "specified amount" of insurance. For contracts that provide for a traditional option 2 design (increasing death benefit, generally defined as the sum of a contract's face or specified amount plus its cash value), the section 101(f)(2)(D) rules allow the reflection of the increasing benefit in both the NSPs and the guideline premiums.[19] By limiting the net amount at risk and not the death benefit, the section 101(f)(2)(D) rules permit the funding of a universal life option 2 contract on a single premium basis. By comparison with the section 7702 computational rules discussed below, this is a generous provision.

Under the second section 101(f) computational rule, the definitional limitations for contracts maturing prior to age 95 must be measured by assuming that benefits continue to age 95 or, if shorter, for 20 years. This prevents the increase in the investment orientation of a life insurance contract that would result from assuming an earlier maturity date for the contract. By enacting the second computational rule, Congress established the precedent of eliminating life insurance tax treatment for short-term full endowments (i.e., less than 20 years in the case of the guideline premium test). This was extended from the flexible premium plans governed by section 101(f) to all endowments (for the full face amount of coverage) at ages less than 95 under the section 7702 rules, discussed below.

Under the third section 101(f) computational rule, the endowment benefit (or sum of endowment benefits) taken into account cannot exceed the least amount payable as a death benefit at any time under the contract. For this purpose, the term "endowment benefit" includes the CSV of the contract on the deemed maturity date. This rule is aimed at limiting the endowment benefit for contracts that might otherwise incorporate an endowment benefit that is excessively large relative to the death benefit.

## *Section 7702*

As discussed briefly in Chapter 1, the enactment of section 7702 carried over many of the requirements imposed by section 101(f) on flexible premium life insurance contracts. However, certain changes were made to the computational rules, now contained in section 7702(e), effectively rendering section 7702 more restrictive than section 101(f). For universal life plans, perhaps the most significant change was that option 2 death benefits could no longer be prefunded fully under the guideline single premium (GSP), as the level-amount-at-risk rule of section 101(f) was replaced with a nonincreasing death benefit rule. Without such a limitation, there was concern that an increasing death benefit contract could result in either a GSP or an NSP that would be a high percentage of the contract's initial death benefit, even for younger insureds. The legislative history also points out that the limit on increases in the death benefit prohibits a contract from assuming a death benefit that decreases in earlier years and increases in later years in order to increase the guideline premium limit artificially.[20] This curtailed a potential abuse of the section 101(f) rule.

---

[19] The use of option 1 to denote a level death benefit and option 2 to denote a level net amount at risk is used by some, but not all, life insurance companies to describe death benefit options provided under a universal life insurance contract. Option 1 and option 2 are used in this text consistently with the meanings ascribed above but may have different meanings with respect to the products offered by a specific life insurance company.

[20] DEFRA Blue Book, *supra* Chapter 1, note 20, at 652.

As originally enacted, section 7702 contained three computational rules, all of which applied to the calculation of both the NSPs and the guideline premiums:

- In computing the premiums, the death benefit is assumed not to increase.
- The maturity date (including the date on which any endowment benefit is payable) can be no earlier than age 95, nor later than age 100.
- The amount of any endowment benefit cannot exceed the least amount payable as a death benefit at any time.

In 1986, a technical correction clarified the import of the second computational rule, providing that the maturity date is "deemed" to be no earlier than age 95 and no later than age 100.[21] Also, as a further clarification, Tax Reform Act of 1986 (TRA) added a computational rule under which a contract's death benefits are "deemed" until the assumed maturity date, thus enabling a contract to mature prior to age 95 for a partial endowment benefit.[22] According to the DEFRA legislative history, these "deeming" rules reflected the congressional purpose of limiting investment orientation while not directly regulating the terms of qualifying contracts.[23]

Currently, four computational rules are prescribed under section 7702(e)(1)(A)–(D):

- **Nonincreasing death benefit:** Under section 7702(e)(1)(A), the death benefit used in computing the NSPs or guideline premiums is assumed not to increase. The basic intent of this rule is to reflect the benefits in the contract, but only as limited by the computational rule. Under this construction, contractually decreasing death benefits seemingly should be reflected in the computations at issue, although section 7702(e)(1)(C) (below) suggests that this may not be required.

- **Deemed maturity date:** Section 7702(e)(1)(B) provides that the maturity date assumed in the calculations can be no earlier than the day on which the insured attains age 95, and no later than the day on which the insured attains age 100. The DEFRA Senate Report, accompanying the enactment of section 7702, addressed the choice of a maturity date, noting that "the maturity date (including the date on which any endowment benefit is payable) shall be deemed to be no earlier than the day on which the insured attains age 95 and no later than the day on which the insured attains age 100. Thus, the deemed maturity date is generally the termination date set forth in the contract or the end of the mortality table."[24] The DEFRA House Report had no such comment on an upper limit on maturity date for computational purposes, presumably because the House bill (like section 101(f)) contained only the lower limit at age 95. However, in discussing the lower limit, the House report says, "For these purposes, the term maturity date generally means the termination date set forth in the contract or the end of the mortality table."[25] The age 100 termination date in section 7702(e)(1)(B) reflects the fact that the 1980 CSO tables assumed no survivorship after age 99 as well as the concern that the use of a maturity date later than age 100 would enable excessive investment orientation in increasing benefit contracts (see the discussion of the "alternative" death benefit rules below) and possibly other abuses.

- **Death benefits provided until deemed maturity date:** Section 7702(e)(1)(C) provides that death benefits are assumed to continue until the deemed maturity date. The purpose of the third rule, according to the legislative history of the 1986 amendment that added it, is to allow partial face endowments at ages before 95.[26] The language, however, does not seem to be limited to this purpose, and some have construed it to mean that contractually decreasing death benefits need not be reflected in the at-issue computations, but only need to be dealt with as the decreases occur. (See the discussion in Chapter 6 on

---

[21] Staff of the Jt. Comm. on Tax'n, 99th Cong., Explanation of Technical Corrections to the Tax Reform Act of 1984 and Other Recent Legislation, at 104 (Comm. Print 1987) (hereinafter Technical Corrections Blue Book).
[22] *Id. See* IRC § 7702(e)(1)(C). This change was made effective as if it were originally included in the enactment of IRC § 7702.
[23] *See* DEFRA House Report, *supra* Chapter 1, note 11, at 1447; DEFRA Senate Report, *supra* Chapter 1, note 11, at 576; DEFRA Blue Book, *supra* Chapter 1, note 20, at 651.
[24] DEFRA Senate Report, *supra* Chapter 1, note 11, at 576. *See also* DEFRA Blue Book, *supra* Chapter 1, note 20, at 652.
[25] DEFRA House Report, *supra* Chapter 1, note 11, at 1447.
[26] H.R. Rep. No. 99-426, at 965 (1985) (hereinafter TRA 1986 House Report); S. Rep. No. 99-313, at 986-987 (1986) (hereinafter TRA 1986 Senate Report); Technical Corrections Blue Book, *supra* note 21, at 104-105.

decreasing face amount plans.) The IRS itself, while not endorsing such a construction in the context of rulings on QABs (discussed below), has acknowledged that such a reading is possible. In particular, in a private letter ruling addressing certificates under an employer-owned group variable universal life insurance contract under which the insurer was obligated to continue coverage of the insured employees even though the employer could and was likely to terminate certificate coverage when employees retired, the IRS construed section 7702(e)(1)(C) to mean that the death benefits were deemed to continue to age 100 for purposes of the CVAT computations.[27]

- **Least endowment:** Section 7702(e)(1)(D) states that the amount of any endowment benefit (or sum of endowment benefits) taken into account cannot exceed the least amount payable as a death benefit at any time under the contract. For this purpose, the endowment benefit includes any CSV on the deemed maturity date. Like its section 101(f) counterpart, this limit is included to prevent the calculation of NSPs and guideline premiums based on CSVs that exceed what would otherwise be a contract's death benefit.

Similarly to their purpose under section 101(f)(2)(D), then, the computational rules of section 7702(e)(1) are designed to limit the extent to which the assumed future benefits under the contract or the assumed maturity date could potentially (and in some cases artificially) increase the investment orientation of the contract.

The cash value corridor of the guideline premium test may require an increase in the death benefit under a contract in order to maintain the contract's compliance with the requirements of section 7702. In a typical guideline premium calculation, the cash value corridor generally does not come into play. However, where a QAB of significant cost (such as a large amount of term coverage on a family member) is present on a contract, there may be a question about how to reconcile the section 7702(d) corridor requirements with the 7702(e)(1)(A) level-assumed-death-benefit computational rule. This is discussed below in addressing QABs.

It should be noted that the DEFRA legislative history provides for "reasonable" approximations and rounding in performing the definitional computations, subject to a prescribed limitation on which the IRS has issued a number of private letter rulings. This is discussed in Appendix 2.2.

## Section 7702(e)(2)(A) and (B) Alternative Death Benefit Rules

Although the section 7702(e)(1) computational rules eliminated the ability to reflect increasing death benefits in the calculation of the NSP and GSP as previously permitted under section 101(f), certain limited increases in death benefits continue to be permitted under the alternative death benefit rules set forth in section 7702(e)(2). Specifically, in computing the GLP, an increasing death benefit may be taken into account under section 7702(e)(2)(A), but only to the extent necessary to prevent a decrease in the excess of the death benefit of a contract over its CSV (that is, to maintain a constant net amount at risk). A similar rule applies under a special version of the CVAT (discussed below).[28]

Under the first of the alternative death benefit rules, the GSP (like the NSP and the 7-pay premium) for a contract with an option 2 death benefit is calculated by assuming only a level death benefit,[29] while the GLP would be calculated assuming that the increase in the contract's death benefit would be prefunded to the extent permitted. In this case, the guideline premium limitation is equal to the greater of the GSP computed by assuming a nonincreasing death benefit or the sum of the GLPs assuming an increasing death benefit. According to the legislative history, this exception to the computational rules is generally intended to permit GLPs to be adequate to fund, on a guaranteed basis, a death benefit equal to the CSV plus a fixed amount of insurance benefit.[30]

Table 3.1 compares the resulting NSPs, guideline premiums and 7-pay premiums at various issue ages. The use of the section 7702(e)(2)(A) computational rule is not limited to an option 2 death benefit but may be applied to any increasing death benefit pattern. The statutory language provided two limits: the increase taken

---

[27] PLR 200910001 (Sept. 8, 2008).
[28] The third of the alternative death benefit rules, found in IRC § 7702(e)(2)(C) and applicable only to preneed or burial contracts, is discussed in Chapter 6.
[29] In computing the GSP, some insurers reflect the face or specified amount plus the initial premium (less any premium load) as the death benefit, while others use the face or specified amount only.
[30] DEFRA Senate Report, *supra* Chapter 1, note 11, at 577; DEFRA Blue Book, *supra* Chapter 1, note 20, at 652–53.

into account is provided in the contract and, as noted above, the increase may be recognized only to the extent necessary to prevent a decrease in the net amount at risk. Thus, any contractual increase in death benefit may be reflected, e.g., for a death benefit equal to a face amount plus a return of premiums paid (sometimes called an "option C" death benefit), so long as the increase is limited by the non-increasing net-amount-at-risk constraint.

| Table 3.1. Universal life options 1 and 2 premium limitations | | | | | | | |
|---|---|---|---|---|---|---|---|
| Age | 7-pay | NSP | GSP | GLP1 | % GSP | GLP2 | % GSP |
| 25 | 23.66 | 147.21 | 67.63 | 6.64 | 9.8 | 18.29 | 27.0 |
| 35 | 33.23 | 206.64 | 107.40 | 10.02 | 9.3 | 27.25 | 25.4 |
| 45 | 47.06 | 291.24 | 174.09 | 15.80 | 9.1 | 41.20 | 23.7 |
| 55 | 65.77 | 402.11 | 274.20 | 25.87 | 9.4 | 62.99 | 23.0 |
| 65 | 90.55 | 534.82 | 409.45 | 44.22 | 10.8 | 97.53 | 23.8 |

*Assumptions: $1,000 face amount, 2001 CSO male aggregate, ANB, 4% GLP and NSP, 6% GSP, curtate, no expenses*

## Net Level Reserve Test

The second alternative death benefit rule, the **net level reserve test** appearing in section 7702(e)(2)(B), allows for the death benefit increases described above to be reflected under the requirements of the CVAT if the contract satisfies the test using a net level premium reserve, rather than an NSP, as the basis for section 7702 compliance. Specifically, section 7702(e)(2)(B) permits an increase in the death benefit provided under a contract to be recognized in the CVAT calculations "assuming that the net level reserve (determined as if level annual premiums were paid for the contract over a period not ending before the insured attains age 95) is substituted for the net single premium," and so long as there is no increase in the net amount at risk.

As with the guideline premium test, the ability to reflect increasing death benefits under the CVAT is thus limited to a level premium test plan. The allowance provided for increasing benefit plans under the CVAT is significantly less than that for increasing benefit plans under the guideline premium test, especially in the early durations of a contract, as the CVAT when based on section 7702(e)(2)(B) does not permit CSVs up to the contract's NSP, i.e., there is no analog to the GSP. A footnote in the DEFRA Blue Book attributes this difference to a conscious tax policy choice related to the (then) availability of a deduction for policy loan interest on traditional life insurance contracts that were expected to use the CVAT.[31] The deduction for policy loan interest was eliminated in 1986 for individual taxpayers and in 1996 for most corporate taxpayers.[32]

The net level reserve test was the subject of a series of IRS private letter rulings in 1988.[33] Under the contract form involved in the rulings, the scheduled death benefit for the first contract year was $1,000 per unit of insurance, increasing each contract year by 6 percent of the prior year's death benefit. Using actuarial calculations submitted by the taxpayer demonstrating that CSVs were based on the standard nonforfeiture method (assuming the 1980 CSO and 7 percent interest), the IRS held in each ruling that the contract qualified as a life insurance contract under section 7702, reasoning that since the contract provided for increasing death benefits and the excess of the contract's death benefit over its CSV did not increase, the provisions of section 7702(e)(2)(B) governed the application of the CVAT to the contract. Accordingly, the increasing death benefit was taken into account and the net level reserve substituted for the NSP. In its ruling, the IRS applied a two-part test: the amount of the increase may be used only to the extent it is provided in the contract, and the amount to be recognized is limited to the amount necessary to prevent a decrease in the excess of the death benefit over the CSV. It should be noted that the IRS will no longer issue rulings holding that a contract in its entirety complies with section 7702 but will instead address in private letter rulings specific issues which arise in the interpretation of the statute.

---

[31] DEFRA Blue Book, *supra* Chapter 1, note 20, at 653, n. 55.
[32] *See* IRC §§ 163(h) and 264(a)(4).
[33] *See* PLRs 8839021, 8839022, 8839028, 8839030, 8839032 and 8839033 (all dated June 29, 1988).

Use of the net level reserve test may be problematic for contracts with adjustment events, as the net level reserve following an adjustment is not defined. In addition, there is no guidance as to whether the net level reserve test may be applied to a base plan, while, at the same time, the CVAT based on the NSP is applied to a paid-up addition resulting from a dividend (the contracts in the 1988 private rulings were described as non-participating). However, this treatment, if allowed, may be the only practical way to accommodate dividends applied to purchase paid-up additions under an increasing death benefit participating policy, and it does not appear to create any particular opportunity for abuse of the computational rules.

## Least Endowment Rule

The alternative death benefit rules provided by section 7702(e)(2)(A) and (B) override the computational rule under section 7702(e)(1)(A), which otherwise prevents the assumed death benefit from increasing based on the contract's guarantees. However, the section 7702(e)(2) rules do not provide relief from section 7702(e)(1)(D), which limits the deemed endowment benefit (including the CSV on the deemed maturity date) to the lowest death benefit payable under the contract.

The Tax Equity and Fiscal Responsibility Act of 1982 (TEFRA) legislative history, in commenting on the **least endowment** computational rule under section 101(f), states that "the amount of any endowment benefit (i.e., the benefit payable if the insured survives to the contract's maturity date) cannot exceed the smallest death benefit (determined without regard to any QABs) at any time under the contract."[34] The DEFRA legislative history, reflecting language added to the computational rule when section 7702 was enacted, observes that "[f]or these purposes, the term endowment benefits includes the cash surrender value at the maturity date."[35] In the context of the computational rules, the TEFRA Blue Book describes the cash value of the contract as "the cash value accumulated by using the same assumptions concerning interest rates, mortality charges, and other charges used to compute the guideline premiums."[36] Applying this concept, under the test plan concept discussed in Chapter 2, the endowment value assumed in the calculation is the value that results from the accumulation of the guideline premiums to the maturity date of the contract. Consistently with this approach, for purposes of the alternative benefit rules, the final maturity value is the amount that results from an accumulation of the option 2 GLPs.

Where a contract with an option 2 death benefit matures before the insured's age 100, such as an endowment at age 95, the least endowment rule limits the test plan values by restricting the endowment value under the contract to no more than the contract's face or specified amount (i.e., the risk amount) plus its initial net premium (but see the discussion of the initial premium below). This restriction results in CSVs and death benefits for the test plan that increase for a number of years but later decrease so that the maturity value can satisfy the section 7702(e)(1)(D) computational rule. However, where the definitional limitations are computed to age 100, and that corresponds with the end of the mortality table, as may be the case with a contract based on the 1958 or 1980 CSO tables, the final endowment benefit theoretically has no effect on the values of the NSPs or guideline premiums because the present value of the endowment benefit is zero (as all lives are assumed to have died). In addition, it was the stated intent of the framers of section 7702 to require that the CSV or benefit payable at maturity under the test plan, based on the accumulation of guideline premiums to the maturity date, not exceed the least death benefit under the contract. Note that for a CVAT plan, the least endowment is computed based on the current death benefit. Thus, an increasing benefit can be provided, so long as the CSV does not exceed the NSP for the (then) current death benefit.

## Treatment of the Initial Premium Under Option 2 Contracts

The option 2 death benefit design has historically generated more variations in the determination of the guideline premiums than most other contract designs, particularly with regard to the treatment of the initial premium paid. Because such a death benefit is defined in terms of the face amount of insurance plus the contract's

---

[34] TEFRA Blue Book, *supra* Chapter 1, note 95, at 370. *See also* S. REP. No. 97-494, VOL. I, at 354 (1982) (hereinafter TEFRA Senate Report). There was no House Ways and Mean Committee report for TEFRA.
[35] DEFRA House Report, *supra* Chapter 1, note 11, at 1447; DEFRA Senate Report, *supra* Chapter 1, note 11, at 576–77; DEFRA Blue Book, *supra* Chapter 1, note 20, at 652.
[36] TEFRA Senate Report, *supra* note 34, at 354; TEFRA Blue Book, *supra* Chapter 1, note 95, at 370.

cash value, some insurers have viewed the cash value resulting from the payment of the initial premium (net of premium loading) as part of the initial death benefit provided by the contract.

The section 101(f) legislative history (specifically, the TEFRA Blue Book) seems to suggest that for contracts with an option 2 death benefit, the calculation of the GSP should reflect the initial premium actually paid.[37] In fact, the calculation illustrated in the TEFRA Blue Book represents an interesting mixture of benefits. The GLP calculation takes into account the level amount at risk in the option 2 format, and an ending endowment benefit equal to the initial death benefit (risk amount plus first net premium). The endowment is then presumably equal to the least death benefit under the contract. The TEFRA Blue Book example is shown in Table 3.2.[38]

| Table 3.2. TEFRA Blue Book option 2 example |||||
|---|---|---|---|---|
| Specified amount | | 100,000 | | |
| Planned contract premium | | 20,000 | Premium less expense charge and initial cost of insurance ||
| Initial cash value | | 17,524 | | |
| | | | GSP | GLP |
| (1) | First-year expense | | 300.00 | 300.00 |
| (2) | Specified amount | | 100,000 | 100,000 |
| (3) | Present Value of $1 of death benefit | | 0.323638 | 0.650905 |
| (4) | (2) x (3) | | 32,360.80 | 68,090.50 |
| (5) | Endowment amount | | 117,524 | 117,524 |
| (6) | PV of $1 of endowment benefit | | 0.029212 | 0.089875 |
| (7) | (5) x (6) | | 3,433 | 10,562 |
| (8) | (1) + (4) + (7) | | 36,097 | 78,953 |
| (9) | Percent of premium load | | 10% | 10% |
| (10) | (8) ÷ (1 − (9)) | | 40,108 | 87,723 |
| (11) | Annuity factor | | 1.000000 | 22.299606 |
| (12) | (10) ÷ (11) | | 40,108 | 3,934 |

Care should be taken not to misinterpret the TEFRA Blue Book sample calculations. In particular, the blue book example does not suggest that the guideline premium is determined by computing a level premium for $1,000 amount at risk and then multiplying that premium by the sum of the number of thousands in the risk amount plus the initial net premium to obtain the level premium for a proposed issue (i.e., by substituting $117,524 on line (2) of Table 3.2). The error in that approach lies in confusing the death benefit with the real basis of computation for option 2, which is the amount at risk (often referred to as the face or specified amount). While recognition of the extra allowable endowment benefit can be justified based on the TEFRA Blue Book example, it is seldom followed in practice. Having guideline premiums depend on the first premium payment is felt to be too great an administrative burden and a potential source of calculation error.

## Computational Rules for the 7-Pay Premium

Section 7702A(c)(1)(B), which requires the 7-pay premium be computed assuming the death benefit provided for the first contract year continues to be provided until the maturity date of the contract disregarding any scheduled reduction after the first seven contract years, is somewhat elliptical in its phrasing. In particular, it leaves the reader wondering about the treatment of reductions *during* the first seven contract years. This gap arguably is closed, for all practical purposes, by the rule in section 7702A(c)(2)(A), which provides that if "benefits" under the contract are reduced during the first seven contract years, then section 7702A is applied

---

[37] TEFRA Blue Book, *supra* Chapter 1, note 95, at 373.
[38] *Id*. This example does not appear in the TEFRA Senate Report. *See also* Christian J. DesRochers, An Analysis of the Guidelines for Flexible Premium Life Insurance Under Section 101(f) of the Internal Revenue Code 22–23 (1983) (unpublished research paper, Milliman & Robertson Inc.).

as if the contract had originally been issued at the reduced benefit level. Thus, the section 7702A calculation rules seemingly anticipate scheduled (and unscheduled) benefit reductions in the first seven contract years and effectively require that the reduced benefits be incorporated into the determination of the at-issue 7-pay premium. Because of the retroactive treatment that section 7702A(c)(2)(A) applies to benefit reductions during the seven-year test period, reflecting anticipated benefit reductions in advance will prevent contracts from attaining unintended modified endowment contract (MEC) status as a result of a scheduled benefit reduction. In a 1995 private letter ruling, the IRS noted that, for purposes of determining a contract's 7-pay premium at issuance, "the rule in section 7702A(c)(2)(A) permits only the lowest amount of 'death benefits' (or the charges for the lowest amount of any 'qualified additional benefit') during the first 7 contract years to be taken into account under section 7702A(b)."[39]

## *Future Benefits Under Section 7702A*

As a general rule, section 7702A(e)(3) provides that the terms used in section 7702A have the same meaning as when used in section 7702, except as otherwise indicated in section 7702A itself. The "future benefits" referred to in section 7702A(b) are not defined in section 7702A and would therefore rely on the definition of the term in section 7702 for their meaning. As previously noted, section 7702(f)(4) defines the future benefits to mean "death benefits and endowment benefits." In turn, a death benefit is defined in section 7702(f)(3) as "the amount payable by reason of the death of the insured (determined without regard to any qualified additional benefits)." Complementing the parenthetical phrase in that definition, section 7702(f)(5)(B) provides that QABs are not treated as future benefits, but that the charges for them are treated as future benefits (as discussed later in this chapter).

## *Option 2 Death Benefits Under Section 7702A*

According to section 7702A(c)(1)(B), the 7-pay premium is computed "by applying the rules of section 7702(b)(2) and of section 7702(e) (other than paragraph (2)(C) thereof)." Section 7702(b)(2) defines the NSP computation under the CVAT, while section 7702(e)(1)(A)–(D) sets out the computational rules discussed earlier. However, the parenthetical phrase excludes section 7702(e)(2)(C), relating to preneed contracts, leaving open the question of the relationship, if any, of the net level reserve test under section 7702(e)(2)(B) to the computation of the 7-pay premium. This language could be cited as support for permitting certain increasing benefits to be recognized in the computation of the 7-pay premium. However, as section 7702(e)(2)(B) refers to a net level reserve, and not a premium, it is unclear how the 7-pay premium would be computed under a net level (annual premium) reserve method. Also, death benefit increases under the 7-pay test may result in material changes, as discussed in Chapter 4. Hence, the 7-pay premium usually is computed without taking increasing benefits into account.

Also, for a contract with an option 2 death benefit, the section 7702A(c)(1)(B) rule deeming the first-year death benefit to be provided to the maturity date may be interpreted to permit the recognition of the initial cash value of the contract in determining the death benefit to be used in the 7-pay premium calculation. In this case, the death benefit used to determine the 7-pay premium would be equal to the contract's face or specified amount plus the initial cash value (that is, based on the actual premium paid). Such an approach can be problematic, however, due to the potential application of the reduction-in-benefits rule resulting from a decrease in the cash value, and hence in the death benefit, from the at-issue value. As a result, the 7-pay premium is commonly computed based on the face or specified amount, as it would be in the case of an option 1 death benefit. The 1995 private letter ruling referenced above notes that "[p]resumably the reference to a 'reduction in benefits' in section 7702A(c)(2)(A) includes a reduction in any of the 'future benefits' taken into account under the 7-pay test."[40] If the death benefit used in computing the 7-pay premium includes the initial cash value, a subsequent reduction in that amount will reduce the future benefits under the contract, thus bringing the reduction-in-benefits rule into play. This may be a particular problem for a variable life insurance contract, given that its cash value can decrease.

---

[39] PLR 9519023 (Feb. 18, 1995).
[40] *Id.*, n. 25.

## Summary of Computational Rules Under Sections 7702 and 7702A

The computational rules under sections 7702 and 7702A are summarized in Table 3.3.

| Table 3.3. Sections 7702 and 7702A computational rules | |
|---|---|
| Section | Description |
| 7702(e)(1)(A) | Nonincreasing death benefit |
| 7702(e)(1)(B) | Maturity deemed between ages 95 and 100 |
| 7702(e)(1)(C) | Benefits "deemed" until the assumed maturity date |
| 7702(e)(1)(D) | Endowment cannot exceed the least death benefit |
| 7702(e)(2)(A) | Option 2 guideline level |
| 7702(e)(2)(B) | Option 2 net level reserve (CVAT) |
| 7702(e)(2)(C) | Preneed or burial insurance exception |
| 7702(f)(4) | Defines "future benefits" |
| 7702(f)(5)(B) | Treatment of "qualified additional benefits" |
| 7702A(c)(1)(B) | 7702(e) rules apply except (2)(C); benefit in 1st year deemed to be provided to maturity without regard to scheduled reductions after 1st 7 years |
| 7702A(c)(2)(A) | A reduction in benefits within the 1st 7 contract years is treated as if the contract had originally been issued at the reduced benefit level |

## Reinstatements

Life insurance contracts are required by state law to contain a provision allowing a policyholder to reinstate a lapsed contract within a stated timeframe following the lapse, typically three to five years, subject to meeting requirements such as the provision of sufficient evidence of insurability and the payment certain premium amounts. The nature of the lapse will differ as between a flexible premium contract and a fixed premium contract. In the flexible premium case, the contract generally will lapse when the policy value reduces to zero or when a policy loan equals the policy value. In the fixed premium contract case, a lapse may be occasioned simply by nonpayment of the required premium. In such a case, some amount of cash value may exist immediately after the lapse, and the death benefit may continue at the prelapse level for a period of time (i.e., extended term coverage) or in a reduced amount permanently (i.e., reduced paid-up coverage).

The treatment of a lapsed contract's reinstatement under the definitional limitations is unclear in a number of respects. This treatment and the issues involved, which entail application of the section 7702 and 7702A adjustment rules, are discussed in Chapter 4.

## Qualified Additional Benefits

Congress created the concept of QABs when it enacted section 101(f) in 1982 to address "other" benefits typically associated with life insurance contracts. Thus, like the term "modified endowment," the term "qualified additional benefit" has no particular meaning outside a few sections of the Code, namely, sections 101(f), 7702 and 7702A. Section 101(f)(3)(E) defines QABs to mean certain specified benefits, including guaranteed insurability, accidental death benefit, family term coverage and waiver of premium. Under section 101(f), the concept of a QAB applied only to the guideline premium limitation (not to the cash value test). In computing the guideline single and level premiums, a contract's future benefits (without regard to any QAB), plus the charges for any QABs, are reflected.

Section 7702 carried over treatment of QABs from section 101(f). Section 7702(f)(5)(A)'s list of QABs largely mirrors that under section 101(f)(3)(E). As noted in Chapter 2, the list is:

- Guaranteed insurability
- Accidental death or disability benefits

- Family term coverage
- Disability waiver benefit
- Other benefits prescribed under regulations (of which there are none)

However, unlike section 101(f), the value of future charges for QABs is reflected under both the CVAT and the guideline premium test. This is because sections 7702(f)(4) and 7702(f)(5)(B) define "future benefits" to mean death benefits, endowment benefits and the charges for QABs, and both the NSPs and the guideline premiums are computed by reference to a contract's future benefits. This extends as well to section 7702A, which relies on the same definition of future benefits.

A few comments on the items listed as QABs are in order. First, the "accidental death or disability benefits" QAB may have been intended to encompass only accidental death or dismemberment benefits, rather than any disability benefits. However, in writing the statute, Congress chose to use the term "disability," and thus it appears that QABs encompass at least some forms of disability insurance benefits. Second, the "family term coverage" QAB is defined in the TEFRA legislative history, albeit only by way of example, as being coverage "for the insured, a spouse or a child."[41] This description leaves open the precise scope of familial relationships that qualify as family for this purpose. For example, would coverage of the insured's sibling or grandchild qualify? In the absence of guidance, it seems such relationships should satisfy the definition based on the common meaning of the term "family" and historical industry practice with respect to term rider coverages. Consistently with published IRS guidance, the reference to spouse should be read to mean an individual legally married to the insured, including a same-sex spouse.[42] Finally, the "disability waiver benefit" QAB is generally interpreted to include a waiver of monthly deductions as well as a waiver of premiums and seemingly also should encompass riders that apply upon the disability of a payor of premiums, e.g., the owner or, in the case of juvenile coverage, the person controlling a contract on the juvenile's behalf.

As a general rule, when a QAB is present in a life insurance contract, the amounts of the definitional limitations are increased to reflect the charges imposed for the benefit. Specifically, characterization of a benefit as a QAB permits the NSPs, guideline single and level premiums, and 7-pay premiums for a contract to be increased, above the amounts reflecting only the contract's death and endowment benefits, by taking account of the (reasonable) charges for such a benefit. This, in turn, allows prefunding for the QAB in the contract's CSV. The concept of a QAB is another example of legislative line-drawing: Only those benefits deemed by Congress to be "qualified" are eligible to be incorporated into the section definitional limitations and, therefore, to be prefunded in the CSV.

The method of recognizing QABs was first discussed in the TEFRA Blue Book, which indicated that QABs are taken into account by reflecting the interaction of their cost in the base contract CSV. In computing the GSP, the TEFRA Blue Book noted:

> For example, under a universal life insurance policy with a death benefit equal to a specified amount (as opposed to a benefit equal to a level risk amount plus the cash value at death), the addition of a single premium for a qualified additional benefit will tend to increase the policy's cash value and thereby to reduce the "net amount at risk" with respect to the basic life coverage under the policy. In computing the guideline premiums, it would be appropriate to reflect this interaction in the computation.[43]

---

[41] TEFRA Senate Report, *supra* note 34, at 353; TEFRA Blue Book, *supra* Chapter 1, note 95, at 367. The DEFRA legislative history, while not repeating this definition, made clear that the QAB did not encompass "business term insurance," presumably referring to coverage of a business associate of the insured who was not a member of the insured's family. *See* DEFRA House Report, *supra* Chapter 1, note 11, at 1445; DEFRA Senate Report, *supra* Chapter 1, note 11, at 574; DEFRA Blue Book, *supra* Chapter 1, note 20, at 649. The IRS has applied this definition of the family term coverage QAB, developed in the enactment of IRC § 101(f), to the IRC § 7702(f)(5)(A)(iii) QAB. *See* PLR 9106050 (Nov. 16, 1990). Further to this point, see the discussion of "Term Insurance Riders on the Insured" later in this chapter.

[42] Prior to the decision of the U.S. Supreme Court in *United States v. Windsor*, 570 U.S. 12, 133 S. Ct. 2675 (2013), the IRS had interpreted section 3 of the Defense of Marriage Act of 1996 (DOMA), Pub. L. No. 104-199 (1996), codified at 1 USC § 7 (1997), as prohibiting it from recognizing same-sex marriages for purposes of IRC provisions referring to "spouse." In view of the court's ruling, the IRS issued Rev. Rul. 2013-17, 2013-38 IRB 201, stating that it would treat same-sex couples legally married in a jurisdiction that recognizes their marriages as married for federal tax purposes but would not extend this treatment to domestic partnerships or civil unions not recognized as marriages under state law.

[43] TEFRA Blue Book, *supra* Chapter 1, note 95, at 369.

For computational purposes, this means the effect a QAB has on guideline premiums differs for option 1 and option 2 death benefits. Under a basic principles approach to calculating guideline premiums, this "interaction" effectively means that charges for a QAB in a level death benefit (option 1) plan are discounted using both interest and mortality, while the charges under an increasing death benefit (option 2) plan are discounted using interest only.[44]

As noted earlier, in instances where a significant QAB is present, there is a need to reconcile the section 7702(e)(1)(A) computational rule requiring a nonincreasing death benefit with the role played by the section 7702(d) cash value corridor in view of the treatment of QAB charges as "future benefits." Specifically, a situation may arise in the calculation of guideline premiums under a prospective- or accumulation-based approach in which the projected CSV exceeds the death benefit, such that a negative amount at risk results, unless the cash value corridor is applied. Allowing the negative risk amount under the projection-based approach to enter the computation is a conservative approach that complies with the deeming of death benefits not to increase pursuant to the section 7702(e)(1)(A) computational rule. Further, it also is a necessary assumption for there to be equivalence with the basic principles approach to reflecting QABs in the determination of guideline premiums using the discounted charge approach described in the preceding paragraph.

The DEFRA legislative history also notes that just as the death benefit is deemed not to increase for purposes of the NSPs and guideline premiums, QABs are treated in the same way.[45] This comports with the statutory language of section 7702(e)(1)(A) and is generally interpreted to mean that the underlying benefits are assumed not to increase but that the charges may increase. For example, a level benefit term insurance rider to age 90 on a spouse, funded on an (increasing) annual renewable term basis, can be reflected in the definitional calculations.

Continuing with the contract characteristics developed for the sample calculations provided in Appendix 2.1, several additional calculations will be developed to illustrate the concepts discussed in this section relating to QABs. The contract characteristics are as follows:

- Sex: Male
- Age: 45
- Face amount: $100,000
- Mortality: 2001 CSO aggregate ANB
- Interest rate: 4.5 percent
- Expenses: 5 percent of premium load plus $60 annual administrative fee

The at-issue GSP and GLP (option 1) developed in Appendix 2.1 for our sample contract, exclusive of any QAB, are $19,790.19 and $1,644.60 respectively.

The first QAB example involves the addition of a spouse term rider at issue, where the QAB is funded with annually increasing charges to age 90.

**QAB example 1:** Spouse term rider to age 90

- Sex: Female
- Age: 45
- Benefit: $100,000
- Charges: 200% of 2001 CSO aggregate ANB
- Rider termination age: 90

---

[44] This result can be derived from the Fackler formula for successive cash values. The annual element for an option 1 plan is equal to $QAB \times (1 + i) \div p_{x+t}$ while the element option 2 value uses interest only. See Chapter 2 for the applicable formulas.

[45] DEFRA House Report, *supra* Chapter 1, note 11, at 1447; DEFRA Senate Report, *supra* Chapter 1, note 11, at 567; DEFRA Blue Book, *supra* Chapter 1, note 20, at 652.

The resulting GSP and GLP taking into consideration the spouse term rider are $46,025.16 and $3,755.42, respectively. Because of the increasing pattern of the charges, funding under both the GSP and GLP will create cash values in later policy durations that will exceed the base policy death benefit (i.e., a negative net amount at risk will emerge). Figure 3.1 illustrates the development of the cash values underlying the calculation of the GSP and GLP under an accumulation-based approach. As expected, the cash values following the expiry of the rider (i.e., durations 45 and later) will reduce to levels necessary to fund future benefits and expenses, without regard to the rider. For the GSP, the cash value exceeds the base policy death benefit in duration 22, five years earlier than under the GLP calculation. As noted above, it is necessary to incorporate the negative risk amounts under an accumulation-type approach to produce values consist with those developed using basic actuarial formulas.

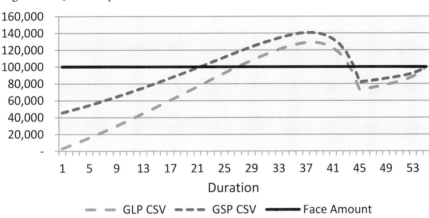

**Figure 3.1.** QAB example 1: cash surrender value

*Term rider assumptions: Female issue age 45, charges based on 200% of 2001 CSO ANB aggregate mortality, rider termination at age 90*

## *Reflecting QABs in the GLP*

In reflecting the charges for a QAB in the GLP, two approaches are possible: the QAB charges may be amortized over the term of the QAB or over that of the entire contract through the deemed maturity date. Both the TEFRA Blue Book and the DEFRA legislative history indicate the GLPs should reflect the charges over the period for which they are incurred (i.e., over the life of the QAB), thus avoiding **postfunding** of the benefits. Although this "bilevel" funding results in a higher initial guideline premium limitation, it eventually results in a lower overall guideline limit.

For example, assume the spouse term rider described in QAB example 1 is replaced with a 10-year level charge rider with the following characteristics.

**QAB example 2:** 10-year spouse term rider

- Sex: Female
- Age: 45
- Benefit: $100,000
- Charges: $300 annual charge
- Rider termination age: 55

In this example, the GLP can be computed in one of two ways to reflect the spouse term rider. If the GLP is calculated assuming the rider is funded over its term, it would result in a $300 increase in the GLP, with the increase expiring in 10 years (or age 55 of the spouse). In contrast, funding the spouse term rider to age 100 will result in an annual increment to the GLP of $148.80. As illustrated in Table 3.4, the guideline premium limitation based on a GLP that reflects the $300 charge only for years 1 through 10 would initially be higher but would eventually be lower, beginning in duration 21, compared to that under the level funding to maturity approach. Note that this difference in funding assumption does not occur in computation of the NSP, GSP or 7-pay premium.

Table 3.4. Reflecting QABs in the guideline level premium, QAB example 2

| Duration | GSP | Bilevel GLP | | | Level annual GLP | | | Difference |
| | | GLP | Cumulative GLP | Guideline premium limitation | GLP | Cumulative GLP | Guideline premium limitation | |
|---|---|---|---|---|---|---|---|---|
| 1 | 22,221.95 | 1,944.60 | 1,944.60 | 22,221.95 | 1,793.40 | 1,793.40 | 22,221.95 | — |
| 2 | 22,221.95 | 1,944.60 | 3,889.20 | 22,221.95 | 1,793.40 | 3,586.80 | 22,221.95 | — |
| 3 | 22,221.95 | 1,944.60 | 5,833.80 | 22,221.95 | 1,793.40 | 5,380.20 | 22,221.95 | — |
| 4 | 22,221.95 | 1,944.60 | 7,778.40 | 22,221.95 | 1,793.40 | 7,173.60 | 22,221.95 | — |
| 5 | 22,221.95 | 1,944.60 | 9,723.00 | 22,221.95 | 1,793.40 | 8,967.00 | 22,221.95 | — |
| 6 | 22,221.95 | 1,944.60 | 11,667.60 | 22,221.95 | 1,793.40 | 10,760.40 | 22,221.95 | — |
| 7 | 22,221.95 | 1,944.60 | 13,612.20 | 22,221.95 | 1,793.40 | 12,553.80 | 22,221.95 | — |
| 8 | 22,221.95 | 1,944.60 | 15,556.80 | 22,221.95 | 1,793.40 | 14,347.20 | 22,221.95 | — |
| 9 | 22,221.95 | 1,944.60 | 17,501.40 | 22,221.95 | 1,793.40 | 16,140.60 | 22,221.95 | — |
| 10 | 22,221.95 | 1,944.60 | 19,446.00 | 22,221.95 | 1,793.40 | 17,934.00 | 22,221.95 | — |
| 11 | 22,221.95 | 1,644.60 | 21,090.60 | 22,221.95 | 1,793.40 | 19,727.40 | 22,221.95 | — |
| 12 | 22,221.95 | 1,644.60 | 22,735.20 | 22,735.20 | 1,793.40 | 21,520.80 | 22,221.95 | 513.25 |
| 13 | 22,221.95 | 1,644.60 | 24,379.80 | 24,379.80 | 1,793.40 | 23,314.20 | 23,314.20 | 1,065.60 |
| 14 | 22,221.95 | 1,644.60 | 26,024.40 | 26,024.40 | 1,793.40 | 25,107.60 | 25,107.60 | 916.80 |
| 15 | 22,221.95 | 1,644.60 | 27,669.00 | 27,669.00 | 1,793.40 | 26,901.00 | 26,901.00 | 768.00 |
| 16 | 22,221.95 | 1,644.60 | 29,313.60 | 29,313.60 | 1,793.40 | 28,694.40 | 28,694.40 | 619.20 |
| 17 | 22,221.95 | 1,644.60 | 30,958.20 | 30,958.20 | 1,793.40 | 30,487.80 | 30,487.80 | 470.40 |
| 18 | 22,221.95 | 1,644.60 | 32,602.80 | 32,602.80 | 1,793.40 | 32,281.20 | 32,281.20 | 321.60 |
| 19 | 22,221.95 | 1,644.60 | 34,247.40 | 34,247.40 | 1,793.40 | 34,074.60 | 34,074.60 | 172.80 |
| 20 | 22,221.95 | 1,644.60 | 35,892.00 | 35,892.00 | 1,793.40 | 35,868.00 | 35,868.00 | 24.00 |
| 21 | 22,221.95 | 1,644.60 | 37,536.60 | 37,536.60 | 1,793.40 | 37,661.40 | 37,661.40 | −124.80 |
| 22 | 22,221.95 | 1,644.60 | 39,181.20 | 39,181.20 | 1,793.40 | 39,454.80 | 39,454.80 | −273.60 |
| 23 | 22,221.95 | 1,644.60 | 40,825.80 | 40,825.80 | 1,793.40 | 41,248.20 | 41,248.20 | −422.40 |
| 24 | 22,221.95 | 1,644.60 | 42,470.40 | 42,470.40 | 1,793.40 | 43,041.60 | 43,041.60 | −571.20 |
| 25 | 22,221.95 | 1,644.60 | 44,115.00 | 44,115.00 | 1,793.40 | 44,835.00 | 44,835.00 | −720.00 |

The notion of a bilevel GLP appears to be inconsistent with section 7702(c)(4), which defines the term GLP to mean "the level annual amount, payable over a period not ending before the insured attains age 95." This inconsistency between the statute and the legislative history has resulted in the use of both methods of reflecting QABs in the GLP, often depending on the capabilities of an insurer's testing system. Consistency would seem

## Deletion of QAB Coverage

Where the charges for a QAB are reflected in the definitional limitations, the deletion of the QAB, such as by the decision of the policyholder to drop the QAB coverage, gives rise to a change that is an adjustment event under section 7702 (and section 101(f)) and generally a reduction in benefits under section 7702A. It should be noted that in the case of the family term coverage QAB, the death of the insured covered by the QAB is treated in the same manner as the dropping of the coverage, on the theory that the funding permitted for the QAB under the definitional limitation is not thereafter needed. The TEFRA legislative history specifically comments that the death of the base contract insured's spouse who is covered under a QAB rider to the contract is treated as an adjustment event.[46]

## Treatment of Additional Benefits That Are Not QABs (non-QABs)

As noted in Chapter 2, a contract may also contain an additional benefit that is not a QAB, sometimes referred to as a non-QAB. Examples of non-QABs are term coverage on a nonfamily member, such as an unrelated business partner, or long-term care insurance provided by accelerating the base plan's death benefit. Section 7702(f)(5)(C)(ii) provides that in the case of "any additional benefit that is not a qualified additional benefit," the charge for the non-QAB is not included in the future benefits under the contract (i.e., it is not reflected in the calculation of the limitations). Hence, the definitional limitations are not increased to reflect the cost of the benefit, although the non-QAB is allowed to be associated with the contract (typically by rider).[47] Consistently with this treatment, a premium paid for the non-QAB is not considered a premium paid or an amount paid for purposes of section 7702 and section 7702A, respectively, provided the payment never enters into the CSV of the underlying contract. If the payment for the non-QAB is credited to the CSV, even for a brief period of time, this is considered "prefunding," and the rule disregarding the payment under the guideline premium test and 7-pay test does not apply. Stated otherwise, any amount that a policyholder pays prior to the period of coverage for a non-QAB, so that the payment resides in the CSV for some period of time after which the charges for the non-QAB are deducted from the CSV, is treated as a premium paid and an amount paid for purposes of the definitional limitations.

Conceptually, a contract with a non-QAB may be viewed as consisting of two elements for tax purposes: a life insurance contract and another contract. The definitional limitations apply to the life insurance contract only. Hence, the existence of the non-QAB contract will have no effect on the NSPs, guideline premiums or 7-pay premiums for the life insurance contract, and if a policyholder pays the charges for the non-QAB as they are incurred (and not beforehand), there will be no net effect on premiums paid or amounts paid. In this circumstance, one could view the payment for the non-QAB as being paid directly to the insurer for the nonlife insurance contract, separately from the life insurance contract, and so the payment never becomes part of the life insurance contract. However, if there is prefunding of the non-QAB, the payment ostensibly made for it will increase the premiums paid and amounts paid for the base contract and will be subject to the guideline premium limitation and the 7-pay test determined without regard for the non-QAB charges.

The inclusion in premiums paid of amounts that a policyholder pays prior to the period of coverage for a non-QAB apparently reflects a congressional concern over the fungible nature of money. That is, it is difficult to trace money paid into a multibenefit contract to the payment of a later charge for some particular benefit provided under the contract. To overcome this problem, section 7702(f)(5)(C)(ii) treats any amount a policyholder pays prior to the period of coverage for a non-QAB as a premium payment for the future benefits under the base contract. A subsequent payment of the non-QAB charges out of the contract's CSV may result in a

---

[46] TEFRA Blue Book, *supra* Chapter 1, note 95, at 371. There is no comparable statement in the TEFRA Senate Report.
[47] Under IRC § 101(f), in contrast, the mere presence of an additional benefit that was not a QAB could disqualify the contract from treatment under IRC § 101(f). In this connection, the TEFRA Blue Book commented that where a benefit rider providing term life insurance on a nonfamily member was added to a contract, the contract did not meet the definition of "flexible premium life insurance contract." TEFRA Blue Book, *supra* Chapter 1, note 95, at 367. The result, it was thought, was that the contract would be treated as a combination of term life insurance and either a taxable "side fund" or an annuity.

reduction of premiums paid at the time the charges for the non-QAB are assessed. Payment of the non-QAB charges in this manner is treated as a distribution from the contract, which generally reduces premium paid to the extent it is not taxable under section 72(e).[48]

The presence of non-QABs may also affect how compliance is measured under the CVAT. Compliance with the CVAT is based on the entire CSV of a contract, including any amounts attributable to the prefunding of the non-QAB that are reflected in the CSV. Hence, while the non-QAB is not used in determining the applicable limit (i.e., the NSP), any CSV resulting from the prefunding of the non-QAB is recognized in measuring compliance.

The treatment of non-QABs is well illustrated in a 1990 private letter ruling involving a universal life insurance contract that combined a five-year term insurance rider, a waiver of monthly deduction on total disability rider and a long-term care (LTC) rider.[49] Under the facts of the ruling, the cost of the term rider and the disability waiver rider increased with the policyholder's age and were deducted monthly from the contract's CSV. The cost of the LTC rider, however, was funded by a level monthly charge against the CSV. The IRS reached two principal conclusions in the ruling:

- The benefits provided under the LTC rider did not constitute QABs under section 7702(f)(5). As a consequence, neither the LTC rider benefits nor any charges for them were treated as future benefits under the contract for purposes of determining the contract's section 7702 definitional limits, and

- Additional premiums entering into the contract's CSV attributable to the LTC coverage and paid prior to the current month's coverage for the benefits under the LTC rider were included in and increased both the "premiums paid" under section 7702(f)(1)(A) and the "investment in the contract" under section 72(e)(6), even though those amounts may have been paid for the purpose of eventually paying charges for the LTC rider.

Under the ruling, amounts withdrawn from the underlying contract's CSV to pay for the LTC rider were treated for tax purposes as distributions to pay charges under a separate contract. These withdrawals could generate taxable income for the policyholder, particularly if the contract is a MEC.

It should be noted that for a benefit (other than a QAB) to be treated as a non-QAB, it must first be considered "additional." Questions can arise as to whether certain benefits are additional or instead are integral to the underlying contract. While it is clear the benefits in the list of QABs are additional, there is no similar brightline guidance in the case of non-QABs.

## *Treatment of Riders Under 7702A*

As previously said, QAB rider benefits, i.e., amounts payable upon the occurrence of the risk event insured against by the QAB, are not included in the future benefits taken into account under section 7702. However, the charges for QAB coverage are treated as future benefits in computing the NSPs or the guideline premiums.

While this rule generally applies under section 7702A as well, the legislative history of that statute discusses the status of a QAB rider, explaining that "riders" added to a base contract are not tested separately but are to be "considered part of the base insurance contract for purposes of the 7-pay test."[50] As a 1995 private letter ruling explained:

> This approach avoids any requirement that a policyholder allocate each premium payment between a base policy and any riders. Instead, the "future benefits" under the base policy and the "future benefits" under each rider are aggregated and a 7-pay premium is determined for the aggregate "future benefits" under the entire contract.[51]

This rule has created issues in the definitional calculations for contracts with term insurance riders on the life of the primary insured under the base contract. This is discussed next.

---

[48] *See* PLR 9106050 (Nov. 16, 1990).
[49] *See id.*
[50] *See* 134 Cong. Rec. S12,353 (daily ed. Sept. 12, 1988); TAMRA Conference Report, *supra* Chapter 2, note 64.
[51] PLR 9519023 (Feb. 8, 1995).

## Term Insurance Riders on the Insured: Death Benefit Versus QAB Treatment

In the 1990s, the IRS issued three private letter rulings addressing the treatment of term life insurance riders under sections 7702 and 7702A.[52] The rulings focused specifically on term insurance provided by a rider covering the life of the person insured by the underlying contract (**term coverage on the insured**). In the rulings, the IRS concluded that term coverage on the insured generally should be viewed as a QAB under section 7702. However, the IRS also held that the same term coverage constituted a death benefit (and not a QAB) for section 7702A(b) purposes. Specifically, the IRS determined that the term coverage on the insured constituted "benefits" and "death benefits" (not QABs) for purposes of applying certain section 7702A rules to the aggregate contract benefits. This dual treatment of term insurance riders on the insured prompted Adney and Griffin to comment:

> The IRS could logically conclude in the new rulings, true to the congressional purpose and after some struggle with the statutory wording, that term coverage on the primary insured must be imbued with a chameleon-like aspect, being classified as a death benefit in one context even if classified as a QAB in the other.[53]

It is important to comprehend the distinction in the treatment of term coverage on the insured as between section 7702 and section 7702A, both to assure that such coverage provided is properly incorporated into the definitional calculations and to obtain a better understanding of QABs generally.

### *Section 7702*

In general, term coverage on the insured falls within the scope of family term coverage and is therefore included in the list of QABs provided in section 7702(f)(5)(A) (and section 101(f)(3)(E)).[54] As such, subject to an exception discussed below, the charges for this coverage, but not the term death benefits themselves, are reflected in the section 7702 (and section 101(f)) calculations. Hence, the calculations may reflect prefunding for the QABs, but only for the charges expected to be paid, and only lasting as long as the period during which the charges would be assessed. In contrast, under the section 7702(e)(1)(C) computational rule, death benefits are assumed payable to the deemed maturity date (between age 95 and 100). In the case of term coverage on the insured with a limited benefit period (e.g., 10-year level term), extending death benefit treatment to the rider could, under an expansive reading of section 7702(e)(1)(C), incorporate death benefits into the calculation of the NSPs and the guideline premiums even though they are not provided by the contract. This prospect, in fact, was a principal concern of the IRS in determining in the private letter rulings that the term coverage on the insured constitutes a QAB, not a death benefit, for purposes of section 7702. Under the logic of these rulings, a term rider on the insured that provides a contractually varying amount of coverage could be seen as death benefit in part and a QAB in part. An element of rider coverage continuing to maturity would receive death benefit treatment, while temporary coverage would be treated as a QAB.

### *Section 7702A*

The private letter rulings also held that term coverage on the insured provides death benefits, and not a QAB, in the context of section 7702A. The logical question here relates to why the phrase "death benefit" in section 7702(f)(3), which by definition does not include the family term insurance QAB, does not carry over for purposes of applying section 7702A(b). If section 7702A were silent on this issue, the rules applicable to section 7702 would prevail, and term coverage on the insured generally would be considered a QAB, consistent with its treatment under section 7702. Importantly, however, section 7702A(e)(3) provides that if "otherwise provided" in section 7702A, terms can have a different meaning in section 7702A than in section 7702. In the rulings, the IRS noted that section 7702A(c)(1)(B), which generally deems the initial death benefit under a contract to continue until the deemed maturity date of the contract, recognized as "death benefits "amounts of coverage that

---

[52] These rulings are, in order of issuance, PLRs 9513015 (Dec. 30, 1994), 9519023 (Feb. 8, 1995), and 9741046 (July, 16, 1997). *See also* PLR 9441023 (July 8, 1994) (waiving errors pursuant to IRC § 7702(f)(8) for incorrect treatment of term life insurance riders).
[53] John T. Adney and Mark E. Griffin, *Commentary & Special Reports: Chameleon-Like Concepts in the Code's Insurance Definitions or When Is a QAB Not a QAB?*, 9 Ins. Tax Rev. 1013, 1022 (1995).
[54] TEFRA Senate Report, *supra* note 34, at 353; TEFRA Blue Book, *supra* Chapter 1, note 95, at 367.

could cease before contract maturity. On this basis, the IRS concluded that Congress intended the term "death benefit" as used in section 7702A to refer to more than life insurance coverage lasting until contract maturity or the earlier death of the insured, i.e., it included term coverage on the insured that continues through the end of the 7-pay period. Hence, according to these (non-precedential) rulings, term coverage on the insured can be viewed as death benefit for section 7702A purposes even though the same coverage retains its characterization as a QAB under section 7702.

### Both Statutes

The IRS reiterated its concern regarding the treatment of term coverage on the insured as a QAB in the third of the three private letter rulings, issued in 1997.[55] In that ruling, the insurance company sought to issue a life insurance contract consisting of a variable base contract and a rider providing term coverage on the insured that would remain in force without evidence of insurability so long as the base contract remained in force, potentially until age 100 of the insured or until the policyholder expressly canceled the rider. The total amount of coverage, or target death benefit under the contract, would equal the sum of the coverage under the base contract and the rider. The insurer asked the IRS if it could use the target death benefit as the contract's death benefit for purposes of both section 7702 and section 7702A. In response, the IRS ruled that the rider's coverage is includible in death benefits under both statutes since it is "scheduled" to continue until the insured attains age 95 and, thus, its inclusion would not afford the policyholder an opportunity to prefund on a tax-deferred basis insurance coverage that will never be provided. The IRS thus held that the insurer could use the sum of a contract's base death and the term coverage on the insured provided by rider as the death benefit for purposes of both section 7702 and section 7702A.

### Summary and Import of the Rulings

The foregoing rulings may be summarized in the following way. Term coverage on the insured is always treated as a death benefit under section 7702A, provided the coverage lasts throughout the 7-pay period, and is generally treated as a QAB under section 7702 except in the case where the coverage continues to the insured's age 95 or later. In the latter case, the coverage is treated as a death benefit under both sections. This difference in treatment is important for two reasons. First, a rider providing 10-year term coverage on the insured, by virtue of its treatment as a death benefit pursuant to section 7702A(c)(1)(B), can contribute substantially to the 7-pay premium limits of a contract. By contrast, QABs are not deemed to continue beyond their actual period of coverage and thus have a relatively smaller impact on the 7-pay premium limits. Second, mortality charges are subject to the safe harbor rules of Notices 88-128 and 2006-95, while QAB charges are subject to the reasonable expense charge standard of section 7702(c)(3)(B)(ii) (discussed below). While these rulings were well reasoned and appear to be sound under both statutes, one should not lose sight of the fact that they are private letter rulings and do not constitute precedential guidance.

## Mortality Rates Beyond Age 100

In 2004, with the adoption of the 2001 CSO tables by the NAIC, insurers were for the first time exposed to a CSO table that extended mortality rates past age 100. Accordingly, insurers started to develop life insurance products that matured at ages greater than age 100. These products presented certain challenges as to how to apply the computational rules in section 7702(e), which were developed at a time when products generally matured at or before age 100. As discussed below, the life insurance industry and the IRS worked together to resolve a number of the post-age 100 interpretive issues that emerged from the adoption of the 2001 CSO tables.

### Age 121 Terminal Values

Under the 2001 CSO tables, the terminal age is 121 as compared with age 100 under the 1980 CSO tables. Under section 7702(e)(1)(B), on the other hand, a life insurance contract's maturity date is deemed to be between the date the insured attains ages 95 and 100. This assumption is consistent with the limiting age of 100 under the 1958 and 1980 CSO tables, the mortality standards at the time sections 101(f) and 7702 were enacted. As

---

[55] See PLR 9741046 (July 16, 1997).

noted before, the upper age limit in the computational rule was included as an antiabuse measure, intended to discourage abuse of the statute by means of contractual charges (i.e., mortality or other charges that were unlikely to be imposed) applicable to insureds that attain age 100 and beyond, and to constrain the investment orientation of increasing benefit contracts.

Section 7702 does not require a life insurance contract to endow at age 100, nor does it preclude an insurer from charging for mortality beyond age 100 (although state law may in some circumstances). While a contract may mature at an age that exceeds 100, the premium or cash value limits under section 7702 must be based on a test plan that meets the statutory requirements.[56] There may, however, be a question as to whether and how the limits continue to apply beyond age 100, the latest "deemed" maturity age under the statute. For CVAT plans, which must satisfy section 7702 by their terms, the use of a maturity age greater than 100 may create interpretive issues under the statute. Starting with the observation that the NSP for an endowment at age 100 exceeds a whole life NSP (i.e., to age 121) under the 2001 CSO, it is possible to demonstrate compliance with the computational requirements of the CVAT for a 2001 CSO-based whole life plan through the statute's latest deemed maturity age of 100. More uncertain, however, is the method of demonstrating that such a plan meets the CVAT by its terms after that age (and thus qualifies under the CVAT from issue). While the DEFRA Blue Book noted that an actual maturity date later than age 100 could be provided, citing the example of a mortality table using an age setback for females, there was no guidance regarding how the calculations are to be made, in terms of the benefits to be assumed, after age 100.[57]

As a point of clarification, it should be noted that the NSPs and guideline premiums for an endowment at age 100 are generally greater than the corresponding values for a whole life plan to age 121 (the exception to this being the guideline level premium for an option 2 death benefit). Thus, from a computational viewpoint, the use of whole life to age 121 values should not present any particular problems. The "maturity problem" arises because precisely what happens under sections 7702 and 7702A after age 100 was not spelled out in the statutes or their legislative histories. In this connection, one possibility is that the requirements of the statutes cease after age 100 and no minimum net amount at risk is required. A variation of this possibility is that the mathematical tests of the definitional limitations simply continue to apply after the insured's attained age 100 is reached, but they may have no or limited effect. Under this view, arguably no net amount at risk would need to be provided under a contract subject to the cash value accumulation test after the insured's attained age 100 is reached (since the NSP per dollar of death benefit after this date could be presumed to be $1 due to the age 100 maturity assumption for the NSP under section 7702), and premiums paid would need to be limited to the guideline premium limitation that applies on the date the insured reaches attained age 100 for contracts subject to the guideline premium test (since the limitation, as written in the statute, does not appear to cease in its application after this date). Alternatively, as some have argued, in view of the apparent congressional intent (reflected in the legislative history) that the statutory limitation on age should be interpreted as referring to the end of the mortality table, age "100" in section 7702(e)(1)(B) should be read as "121" in the case of the 2001 CSO tables. While such an interpretation generally would not alter the definitional limitations materially, a notable exception would be for contracts with option 2 death benefits, which would see a significant increase in permissible values of the guideline level premiums. Moreover, this interpretation simply cannot be squared with the plain language of the statute.

### *Revenue Procedure 2010-28*
Fortunately, into this void of guidance stepped the IRS. Building on the work of the 2001 CSO Maturity Age Task Force of the Taxation Section of the Society of Actuaries (hereinafter the task force), the IRS published proposed safe harbor rules in 2009 followed by a final safe harbor in 2010 by way of a revenue procedure applicable to life insurance contracts with mortality guarantees based on the 2001 CSO tables that may continue in force after the day on which the insured attains age 100. In 2005, the SOA's Taxation Section had established the task force "to propose methodologies that would be actuarially acceptable under sections 7702 and 7702A of the Code for calculations under contracts that do not provide for actual maturity before age 100." The report

---

[56] Prior to the advent of 2001 CSO-based contracts with maturity dates up to age 121, the insurance industry dealt with the reality of insureds surviving to age 100 and beyond through the use of "extended maturity provisions," which allowed contracts to remain in force beyond age 100.

[57] DEFRA Blue Book, *supra* Chapter 1, note 20, at 652. The formal DEFRA legislative history does not address this point.

of the task force was published in 2006,[58] and the final IRS safe harbor closely followed the recommendations in the report. The revenue procedure expressly acknowledged these recommendations and cited to the publication of the report in the Taxation Section's newsletter, *Taxing Times*.

In introducing its safe harbor rules, section 3 of Rev. Proc. 2010-28[59] stated that the IRS "would not challenge" the qualification of a life insurance contract as meeting the requirements of section 7702 or "assert" that a contract is a MEC (by failing under section 7702A) if the contract satisfies the requirements of the statutes using *all* of the "Age 100 Safe Harbor Testing Methodologies," which the revenue procedure then listed. The IRS apparently took this safe harbor approach, rather than issuing a ruling prescribing precise rules, because the questions noted above were without exact answers, and also because the agency could take some comfort from the fact that it was following the recommendations of the task force, even though the task force was endeavoring to craft rules of practical application rather than a legal interpretation. Moreover, the life insurance industry asked the IRS to provide assurance the safe harbor would remain as such rather than begin to be read as a series of requirements, and the IRS obliged, specifically saying in section 3.03 of the revenue procedure that "[n]o adverse inference should be drawn" from a contract's failure to satisfy all of the requirements of section 3.

The testing methodologies listed in section 3.02 of Rev. Proc. 2010-28, applying the section 7702(e)(1)(B) computational rule and related rules, are summarized as follows:

a) All determinations under sections 7702 and 7702A (other than the cash value corridor) assume the contract will mature by the day on which the insured attains age 100, notwithstanding that the contract specifies a later maturity date (such as by reason of using the 2001 CSO mortality tables).

b) The NSPs under the CVAT and the "necessary premiums" under the material change rule of section 7702A(c)(3)(B)(i) (discussed in Chapter 4) assume an endowment on the day on which the insured attains age 100.

c) The GLP calculation assumes premium payments through the day on which the insured attains age 99.

d) In determining the guideline premium limitation, the GLPs accumulate through a date no earlier than the day on which the insured attains age 95 and no later than the day on which the insured attains age 99. Thereafter, premium payments may continue to be made, but the sum of all premiums paid is tested against the guideline premium limitation determined as if that limitation does not change after the day on which the insured attains age 100. (In other words, the limitation is frozen from that day forward.)

e) In the case of a contract issued or materially changed within fewer than seven years of the day on which the insured attains age 100, the 7-pay premium under section 7702A(b) is computed assuming level annual premium payments over the number of years between the date on which the contract is issued or materially changed and the date on which the insured attains age 100.

f) In the case of a contract issued or materially changed within fewer than seven years of the day on which the insured attains age 100, the sum of the 7-pay premiums increases until the day on which the insured attains age 100. Thereafter, it does not increase, but further premium payments (which are allowed to be made) are tested against this (frozen) limit for the remainder of the seven-year period.

g) In the case of a contract other than a last-to-die contract that is issued or materially changed within fewer than seven years of the day on which the insured attains age 100 and thereafter undergoes a reduction in benefits, the reduction-in-benefits rule of section 7702A(c)(2) applies for seven years from the date of issue or the date of the material change. In the case of a last-to-die contract, the special reduction-in-benefits rule for such contracts under section 7702A(c)(6) applies as long as

---

[58] 2001 CSO Maturity Age Task Force, *2001 CSO Implementation Under IRC Sections 7702 and 7702A*, 2 Taxing Times, no. 1, May 2006, at 23.
[59] 2010-34 I.R.B. 270.

the contract remains in force, whether or not the contract is issued or materially changed fewer than seven years before the day on which the insured attains age 100.

h) A change in benefits under (or in other terms of) a life insurance contract that occurs on or after the day on which the insured attains age 100 is not treated as a material change under section 7702A(c)(3) or as an adjustment event under section 7702(f)(7). Thus, necessary premium testing under the section 7702A material change rule ceases on the day on which the insured attains age 100.

The revenue procedure carries an effective date of August 23, 2010.

## *Some Observations on Revenue Procedure 2010-28*

The life insurance industry welcomed the publication of Rev. Proc. 2010-28, which it viewed as workable and beneficial. In particular, the industry was appreciative of the process followed in the construction of the safe harbor rules, which was initiated by the publication of Notice 2009-47.[60] That notice (as recited in the revenue procedure) proposed a series of safe harbor rules drawn from the recommendations of the task force, albeit with some modifications. Certain items contained in the notice (not sourced in the task force report) were not without controversy, e.g., the notice requested comments not only on the proposed safe harbor rules but also on such issues as the applicability of pre-1984 case law for purposes of defining a life insurance contract (discussed in Chapter 1) and the applicability of the doctrine of constructive receipt to a contract that matures (with a CSV equal to the death benefit) while the insured is still alive. These points essentially raised questions about the minimum net amount at risk, if any, that a contract must have to qualify as life insurance for tax purposes generally and to avoid having its inside buildup taxed if and when no material risk amount remains at a late age. In connection with such questions, the notice had proposed a requirement that, to qualify for the safe harbor, a contract must provide a death benefit equal to or greater than 105 percent of the contract's CSV—a requirement that no known contract met. The IRS, at the urging of the industry, dropped that requirement in the revenue procedure and declined to address other issues on which the notice had requested comments. The notice itself was "obsoleted" by the revenue procedure.

To illustrate the effect of the revenue procedure's safe harbor rules, Figure 3.2 considers the example of an ordinary whole life insurance contract with cash values based on the 2001 CSO tables and 4 percent interest. The graph below compares the development of the guaranteed tabular cash values of such a contract (which

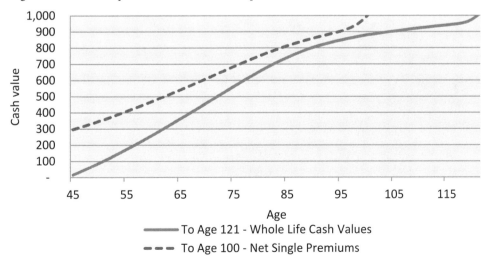

**Figure 3.2.** Cash value per $1,000 of face amount, option 1 death benefit

*Assumptions: 2001 CSO male aggregate, ANB, 4% interest, issue age 45*

---

[60] 2009-24 I.R.B. 1083.

reflect the termination of the 2001 CSO tables at age 121) with the NSPs under section 7702(b) (which reflect the deemed maximum maturity date of age 100).

As another illustration, Figure 3.3 considers the example of a universal life insurance contract with mortality charge guarantees based on the 2001 CSO tables and 4 percent interest that is funded with level annual premiums and provides an increasing death benefit (equal to face plus cash value). The graph below first shows the development of cash values based on level annual premiums (determined without regard to the guideline premium limitation) that are sufficient in amount to allow adequate funding to age 121, so that an endowment benefit equal to the face amount may be paid on that date. The graph then, however, shows the development of guaranteed cash values based on payment of guideline level premiums that are lower due to the requirement to reflect a maximum deemed maturity date of age 100. Thus, in this second illustration, the requirement to use a maturity date not exceeding age 100 in the calculation of the guideline level premium significantly reduces the funding levels, and thus investment orientation, relative to what would be allowed with a deemed maturity date at age 121.

Finally, while the revenue procedure's safe harbor rules technically apply only to contracts based on the 2001 CSO tables, it could be sound practice to use those rules for contracts subject to the 1980 CSO tables. Thus, for example, even though the 1980 CSO tables terminate at an insured's age 100, the safe harbor rules could be employed in the definitional calculations for universal life insurance contracts with maturity dates beyond age 100 or whole life insurance contracts that do not specify a maturity date.[61]

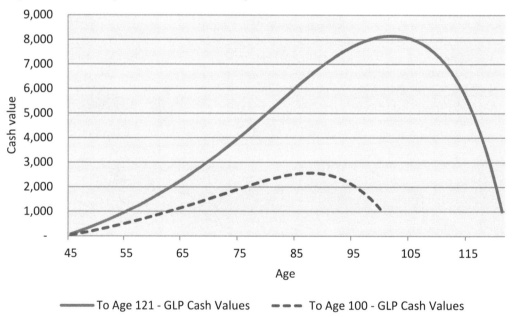

**Figure 3.3.** Cash value per $1,000 of face amount, option 2 death benefit

*Assumptions: 2001 CSO male aggregate, ANB, 4% interest, issue age 45*

---

[61] For additional information on Rev. Proc. 2010-28 and the predecessor notice, see John T. Adney, Craig R. Springfield, Brian G. King and Alison R. Peak, *IRS Issues Proposed Safe Harbor Prescribing "Age 100 Methodologies,"* 5 TAXING TIMES, no. 3, September 2009, at 19, and John T. Adney, Craig R. Springfield, Brian G. King and Alison R. Peak, *Life Beyond 100: Rev. Proc. 2010-28 Finalizes the "Age 100 Methodologies' Safe Harbor,"* 7 TAXING TIMES, no. 1, February 2011, at 10. The latter article included the following "Shorthand Guide to the New Age 100 Safe Harbor Methodologies":
   (a) All IRC § 7702 and 7702A calculations assume age 100 maturity.
   (b) NSP (CVAT) and "necessary premium" calculations assume endowment at age 100.
   (c) GLP is calculated assuming premiums through age 99.
   (d) GLPs accrue through date between ages 95 and 99, after which limit applies indefinitely.
   (e) 7-pay premiums are computed using remaining durations to age 100.
   (f) If 7-pay premiums accrue over fewer than seven years under (e), accrual ends at age 100, after which limit applies for the remainder of the 7-pay period.
   (g) Reduction-in-benefit rules apply regardless of attaining age 100.
   (h) Benefit change after age 100 is not material change or adjustment event.

## Substandard Mortality

After the reasonable mortality standards were enacted in 1988, a great deal of uncertainty arose regarding the treatment of substandard risks under sections 7702 and 7702A. The interim rule of section 5011(c)(2) of Technical and Miscellaneous Revenue Act of 1988 (TAMRA) (which remains the applicable legal standard) alludes to the need for the mortality assumptions in the definitional calculations to take "into account any relevant characteristic of the insured of which the company is aware." For substandard risks, this wording would seem to indicate a company generally must have some underwriting basis for expecting that its actual mortality experience will exceed standard mortality, leading to the need for mortality charges higher than those for standard risks. This is further discussed in the TAMRA Conference Report:

> For example, in determining whether it is appropriate to take into account mortality charges for any particular insured person as a substandard risk, a company should take into account relevant facts and circumstances such as the insured person's medical history and current medical condition. Other relevant factors include the applicability, if any, of State or local law prohibiting or limiting the company's inquiry into some or all aspects of the insured person's medical history or condition, increasing the potential unknown insurance risk with respect to insured persons in the jurisdiction.[62]

While guidance on reasonable mortality has been provided in the form of IRS notices as well as the 1991 proposed regulation previously discussed, little guidance has been directed toward the application of the reasonable mortality rules to substandard risk contracts, i.e., contracts in which substandard mortality rates are used. The IRS notices explicitly excluded any discussion relating to substandard risk contracts. The proposed regulation, for its part, provided special rules for substandard risk contracts and for nonparticipating contracts.[63] Those rules permitted the mortality charges assumed in the definitional calculations to exceed the charges set forth in the "prevailing" standard tables if the insurance company actually expected to impose those higher charges. By limiting the mortality charges to those actually expected to be imposed, the proposed regulation did not provide for an allowable mortality margin (e.g., the excess of the guaranteed maximum mortality charges over the current mortality charges) to be incorporated into the calculations. This result is generally inconsistent with the manner in which reasonable mortality applies to a standard risk contract and does not give adequate regard to the long-term nature of an insurer's obligations under the contract. Not surprisingly, the treatment of substandard mortality under the proposed regulation proved to be quite controversial and was universally opposed by the insurance industry. Accordingly, the proposed regulation, as previously noted, remains only in proposed form and is not effective. The interim rule under TAMRA section 5011(c)(2), with all of its ambiguity, remains the applicable rule governing the use of substandard mortality.

### *Methods of Computing Substandard Values*

The limited guidance on the reasonableness of mortality for substandard risk contracts has led to the use of different approaches to implementing the section 7702(c)(3)(B)(i) mortality charge restriction. The justification for a particular approach may lie in an insurance company's belief regarding how the reasonable mortality standards should be interpreted for substandard risk contracts under the TAMRA interim rule. It is also likely that the ability of a particular administrative system to support (or support with programming modification) one or more of the commonly used approaches for reflecting substandard mortality may influence a company's choice of one specific approach over another. In computing values for substandard risk contracts, factors other than mortality should be applied consistently for corresponding standard and substandard risk contracts.

For contracts issued after the effective date of the reasonable mortality rules, there are three approaches that typically are used to incorporate substandard mortality into the definitional calculations (others approaches may exist, but their use within the insurance industry is generally limited). These are referred to as the multiplicative (or ratio) method, the additive method and an approach using "current" substandard charges. For pur-

---

[62] TAMRA Conference Report, *supra* Chapter 2, note 64, at 108. The report's second sentence reflects concern, in particular, with the prohibition on insurers' testing for AIDS that was imposed under the laws of the District of Columbia.

[63] In the TAMRA Conference Report, the Treasury Department was specifically directed to include "standards with respect to substandard risks" in regulations defining "reasonable mortality." TAMRA Conference Report, *supra* Chapter 2, note 64, at 108.

poses of the following discussion, substandard mortality refers to percentage ratings applied to the mortality charges applicable to a standard risk contract (e.g., table rating or percentage extras, as opposed to flat extras). Each method will be discussed next in the context of the example in Table 3.5, which illustrates sample definitional limitations per $1,000 of level death benefit arising from the alternative approaches.

| Table 3.5. Standard premiums, male age 45 whole life, Table D (100%) | | | | | | |
|---|---|---|---|---|---|---|
| | NSP | % standard | GDP | % standard | GLP | % standard |
| Standard (100%) | 291.24 | — | 174.09 | — | 15.80 | — |
| Multiplicative (200%) | 368.67 | 126.6 | 242.91 | 139.5 | 22.46 | 142.2 |
| Additive (180%) | 356.04 | 122.2 | 231.25 | 132.8 | 21.26 | 134.6 |
| Current (160%) | 342.28 | 117.5 | 218.74 | 125.6 | 20.02 | 126.7 |
| Assumptions: 2001 CSO male aggregate, ANB, 4% GLP and NSP, 6% GSP, curtate | | | | | | |

In the example in Table 3.5, the standard risk is assumed to have a guaranteed maximum annual mortality charge of 100 percent of the 2001 CSO, and the substandard risk is assumed to have a 100 percent substandard rating (based on an appropriate underwriting record) above and beyond the rating that would apply to a standard risk. Hence, the guaranteed mortality specified in the contract for the substandard insured is two times the mortality for a standard risk, or 200 percent of 2001 CSO. (This would often be referred to as Table D.) At this rating, the insurer would expect to charge the substandard risk contract 200 percent of the mortality charges assessed against a standard risk contract. Assuming the current cost of insurance (COI) for standard contracts is 80 percent of the 2001 CSO, the current substandard COI charges will be 200 percent of 80 percent, or 160 percent of the 2001 CSO.

**Multiplicative method (or ratio method):** Under the multiplicative method, the mortality assumption is set equal to the substandard rating applied to the reasonable mortality applicable to a standard risk contract. Thus, an insurer using the multiplicative method would assume 200 percent of the 2001 CSO in computing substandard values. Where margin is defined as the difference between the guaranteed and current COI rates, this method gives the substandard risk contract twice the margin afforded the standard risk contract, i.e., a margin of 40 percent of 2001 CSO (since 200 percent of 2001 CSO exceeds 160 percent of 2001 CSO by this amount) as compared with a 20 percent of 2001 CSO margin for the standard risk case (100 percent of 2001 CSO less 80 percent of 2001 CSO). This has the benefit of maintaining a constant percentage margin in the substandard case relative to the risk assumed in the standard case.

**Additive method:** Under the additive approach, the assumed mortality for substandard risk contracts equals the amount necessary to maintain the same margin between guaranteed and current mortality charges as that applicable for a standard risk contract. Mathematically, this would be solved for by adding the "reasonable" mortality for a standard risk contract (100 percent of 2001 CSO) and the excess of (a) over (b), where (a) and (b) are defined as follows:

   a) the actual mortality charge for the substandard risk contract (i.e., 160 percent of the 2001 CSO)

   b) the actual mortality charge for an otherwise similar standard risk contract (i.e., 80 percent of the 2001 CSO)

In Table 3.5, the mortality assumed under the additive approach in computing the definitional limitations is 180 percent of the 2001 CSO, thus preserving the same margin inherent in use of the 2001 CSO tables for standard risk cases.[64]

---

[64] The additive approach also can be thought of as the sum of the current COI charges for the substandard contract (i.e., 160 percent of the 2001 CSO) and the margin that applies between guaranteed and current mortality charges for a standard risk contract (i.e., 20 percent of the 2001 CSO), for a total of 180 percent of the 2001 CSO.

**Current substandard charges:** The current substandard charge approach is based on the methodology outlined in the proposed regulation, allowing an insurance company to use mortality charges that exceed reasonable mortality charges applicable to an otherwise similar standard risk contract, but only to the extent the company actually expects to impose those higher charges. Under this approach, the definitional calculations are made using 160 percent of the 2001 CSO, the current mortality charges for this contract. Here, there is no margin provided, as only the current substandard charges are recognized in the calculations. For those seeking certainty, the use of current substandard charges (i.e., those the company expects to impose) clearly satisfies the interim rule in this example. However, that fact does not preclude the other methods from also meeting the interim rule's requirements.

It should be noted that for traditional CVAT products, substandard risk charges are often reflected as an increase in premiums, with CSVs limited to NSPs reflecting the safe harbors in the IRS notices on reasonable mortality charges. In such cases, the substandard risk issue is limited to the section 7702A calculations.

## Temporary or Flat Extras

Substandard mortality may also be expressed in terms of a temporary extra premium (i.e., an additional premium or COI charge payable for a number of years) or a flat extra (i.e., an extra premium or COI charge per $1,000 that does not vary by age). Although no guidance has been issued with respect to ratings of this type, one method used is to treat the extras as analogous to charges for QABs and reflect the present value of the charges in the definitional calculations. Under this method, for the GLPs, charges could be reflected over the period for which they are incurred as an increase in the GLP. To maintain the analogy to expense charges or QABs, the actual amount of the charges should be reflected. Note that where the value of temporary or flat extras has been reflected in the calculations, the removal of a rating prior to its expiry date would require an adjustment.

## Age Adjustments

A less common practice for reflecting substandard mortality in the section 7702 and section 7702A calculations involves age adjustment or age set-forwards. Under this approach, values for the substandard risk contract are computed using reasonable mortality for a standard risk contract, but instead of performing the calculation based on the attained age of the insured, the age is set-forward (i.e., increased). Therefore, the values in the definitional limitations for a substandard risk contract are set equal to the values for a standard risk contract based on an older insured, as a way of estimating the substandard mortality. Using the Table 3.4 examples, the current NSP at 160 percent ($342.28) could be approximated by assuming a standard male age 50 ($342.97). Thus, an alternative way of reflecting the higher expected substandard mortality would be to treat the insured as age 50 at issue, rather than age 45.

An age set-forward approach raises several issues, however, and probably should not be used. Not only does this approach appear to run afoul of the deemed maturity age/date rule in the computational rules of section 7702(e)(1), but it also seems to be in conflict with the principles of the attained-age regulations (even though those regulations do not purport to address reasonable mortality). In this connection, the DEFRA legislative history limits the insurance age to an age within 12 months of the insured's actual age in computing the definitional limitations.[65] As noted earlier, that legislative history seems to allow an age set-back, although the values computed using an age set-back could be viewed as conservative (i.e., by providing lower net single and guideline premiums than those computed at the actual age), while an age set-forward is not.

## Terminal Age of Substandard Tables

A potential issue that arises on highly substandard risk contracts is the possibility that the assumed mortality rates will be 100 percent (i.e., $q_x = 1.0$) at an earlier age than the terminal age of the mortality table. When this occurs, it can result in a deemed maturity age under age 95, thus potentially conflicting with the section 7702(e)(1)(B) computational rule. The most straightforward way of dealing with the potential problem is to impose

---

[65] DEFRA House Report, *supra* Chapter 1, note 11, at 1447; DEFRA Senate Report, *supra* Chapter 1, note 11, at 576; DEFRA Blue Book, *supra* Chapter 1, note 20, at 651.

limits on the assumed mortality charge, maintaining the rate at less than 1.0 until age 95 to avoid a conflict with the maturity age rule.[66]

## Simplified Underwriting

This discussion of substandard risks leaves unclear whether the expected mortality characteristics of a group as a whole can be reflected. For example, higher expected mortality typically occurs in simplified underwriting or guaranteed issue cases. In such instances, it is unclear whether some degree of higher expected mortality can be reflected. Rather than being based on "relevant characteristics" of each insured, in these cases the mortality expectation is based on an overall lack of specific knowledge. In general, the IRS has not been receptive to higher mortality assumptions in simplified issue products, as many of the single premium products that gave rise to the enactment of the reasonable mortality rules were issued on a simplified underwriting basis. While the use of the actual mortality charges (even when they exceed the 1980 or 2001 CSO) may be justifiable under the interim rule (although that is not clear), the use of a multiplicative method for simplified issue plans is generally not advisable, as the IRS is unlikely to consider such charges as being reasonable. The facts and circumstances may, however, provide a better case for such an approach, for example, where coverage is of individuals involved in a high risk occupation.

## Application of Reasonable Expense Charge Limitations to QABs

Section 7702 arguably is unclear whether charges for the family term coverage QAB on a contract entered into on or after October 21, 1988, are subject to the reasonable mortality rule of section 7702(c)(3)(B)(i) or the reasonable expense rule of section 7702(c)(3)(B)(ii) in determining the guideline premiums for the contract. If the former rule applies, then in computing the guideline premiums, the amounts of the charges that can be taken into account may be as high as the safe harbor mortality charges permitted under Notices 88-128 and 2006-95 (or under the TAMRA interim rule, in the case of substandard risk charges), even though the amounts actually expected to be charged are lower. In contrast, if the expense charge rule applies, the family term QAB charges taken into account are limited to those "reasonably expected to be actually paid," which will typically correlate to a company's actual charges.

In Rev. Rul. 2005-6,[67] following its decision in a series of private letter rulings waiving noncompliance with section 7702,[68] the IRS addressed which of the two rules imposed by TAMRA applies to QAB charges. The IRS held that the reasonable expense rule applies, thereby limiting the charges allowed to be used in the definitional calculations—including the NSPs and the 7-pay premiums as well as the guideline premiums—to ones reasonably expected to be actually paid. In reaching this conclusion, the IRS pointed out that pursuant to section 7702(b), the NSPs are computed based in part on QABs, and in this connection section 7702(b) expressly references section 7702(c)(3)(B)(ii), the reasonable expense rule. The agency also pointed out that since the 7-pay premiums are computed based on the same rules as the NSPs, those premiums, too, reflect the section 7702(c)(3)(B)(ii) reasonable expense rule. In addition, the IRS noted that under the reasonable mortality rule:

> There is no requirement that the charges taken into account be charges that are expected to be paid. In contrast, under the expense charge rule of § 7702(c)(3)(B)(ii), reasonable charges other than mortality charges are taken into account only if they are reasonably expected to be actually paid. For this reason, accounting for charges for the Rider under the mortality charge rule, rather than the expense charge rule, would in some cases produce a higher net single premium and higher guideline level premiums for purposes of testing a contract's compliance with § 7702.

The IRS acknowledged in the ruling that section 7702 does not indicate which of the two rules is to be used in computing guideline premiums. In light of the above considerations, however, the IRS concluded that it should rely on the apparent congressional intent with respect to the TAMRA rules. Thus, the IRS observed:

---

[66] A further consideration for highly rated contracts involves the point at which no material risk shifting may be involved with the contract. *See Helvering v. Le Gierse*, 312 U.S. 531 (1941), which was discussed in Chapter 1.
[67] 2005-6, 2005-1 C.B. 471.
[68] In chronological order, these are PLRs 200150014 (Sept. 12, 2001), 200150018 (Sept. 13, 2001), 200227036 (Apr. 9, 2002), and 200320020 (Feb. 6, 2003).

There is no indication that Congress intended charges for QABs to be accounted for under one rule for purposes of the cash value accumulation test of § 7702(b) and the 7-pay test of § 7702A(b), and under a different rule for purposes of the guideline premium requirements of § 7702(c). Moreover, there is no indication that Congress intended to take into account charges with respect to QABs that exceed amounts reasonably expected to be actually paid.

Accordingly, the IRS decided to extend the treatment of QABs under the reasonable expense rule to the calculation of guideline premiums, and the ruling therefore held that charges for QABs should be taken into account under the reasonable expense rule for all purposes of the definitional limitations.

Rev. Rul. 2005-6 carried an effective date of February 7, 2005, or just over 20 years after the general effective date of section 7702, and more than 15 years after the enactment of TAMRA. During those time periods, no guidance emerged from the IRS on the subject of the ruling. In view of this, as well as the acknowledged silence of section 7702 with respect to the guideline premium test in this context, the IRS went on in the ruling to provide relief to the insurance companies that had relied on the reasonable mortality rules rather than the reasonable expense rule. Specifically, and in a departure from requirements typically accompanying the correction of noncompliance with section 7702 (see Chapter 8), the ruling provided that if an insurer's compliance system did not take account of QAB charges (for family term coverage or otherwise) using the reasonable expense rule and, as a result, some of its contracts did not comply with section 7702 or 7702A, the issuer was allowed to request a closing agreement on or before February 7, 2006, identifying all contracts administered on the system involved, and pay only a limited "toll charge" based on the number of contracts administered by the system. Further, no corrective action was required to be taken with respect to either the compliance system or the contracts identified in the closing agreement. Moreover, this relief extended to the treatment of future QAB charges resulting from an increase in an existing QAB or the addition of a new QAB pursuant to the exercise of a right that existed in the contract before April 8, 2005. According to the ruling, a closing agreement also could be requested after the 2006 date, but in such a case the closing agreement must identify the contracts that fail to meet the requirements of section 7702 or 7702A, and the insurer must correct its compliance system and bring the identified contracts into compliance with the definitional limitations.

Today, the correction of the error dealt with in Rev. Rul. 2005-6 is addressed in Rev. Proc. 2008-38, as detailed in Chapter 8.

**Chapter 4**

# ADJUSTING THE LIMITATIONS UNDER SECTIONS 7702 AND 7702A

## Chapter Overview

Changes made to a life insurance contract after it is issued are commonplace. Contract changes include increases or decreases in coverage and the addition or deletion of a benefit added by rider. They may also include changes to the structure of a contract, including a change in underwriting class (e.g., from a smoker to a nonsmoker) and, in unusual cases, a change in interest or expense factors. Broadly defined, contractual changes can also include an exchange of contracts (perhaps a tax-free exchange under section 1035[1]), in which one life insurance contract is replaced by another.

Such changes have two potential effects with respect to the definitional limitations. First, they can subject a contract to the adjustment rules described in this chapter, presenting some of the most complex computational issues under sections 7702 and 7702A. This chapter addresses adjustments in the net single premiums (NSPs) and guideline premiums under section 7702 (and its predecessor, section 101(f)) and in the 7-pay premiums under section 7702A that occur when contracts are changed after they are issued. As the definitional limitations are first determined for a contract based on its future benefits (as permitted) and the prescribed actuarial assumptions at the time of the contract's issuance, some procedures are necessary to alter these limitations to reflect contract changes. Failure to adjust the limits for increases in death benefit could lead to situations in which the policyholder could not adequately fund the future death benefits under a contract, while the failure to reflect decreases could permit substantial overfunding. Beginning with section 101(f) and continuing under section 7702, the adjustment rules have accommodated the flexibility and nonstatic nature typical of many contracts—such as contractual rights allowing for increases and decreases in death benefits—while maintaining the integrity of the definitional limitations. Section 7702A provides additional rules under which events defined as "material changes" are reflected by restarting the statute's 7-pay test and under which benefit reductions within the first seven years of a contract (or at any time, in the case of a second-to-die contract) will cause the 7-pay premium to be recomputed retroactively to the beginning of the test period, often leading to modified endowment contract (MEC) status for the contract.

Second, it is possible a post-issuance change in a contract can result in the loss of "grandfathered" status, causing the contract to be newly subject to the section 7702 and 7702A limitations established after the issue date of the contract and before the contractual change. This topic is the subject of Chapter 5.

## Adjustments Under Section 7702

The adjustment rule of section 7702, which governs contracts under both the cash value accumulation test (CVAT) and the guideline premium test, is simply stated in the statute. Pursuant to section 7702(f)(7)(A), "[i]f there is a change in the benefits under (or in the terms of) the contract which was not reflected in any previous determination or adjustment made under this section, there shall be proper adjustments in future determinations made under this section." That is where the simplicity ends. The "proper" adjustments referenced in the statute are described in the legislative histories of three separate enactments and in rulings of the IRS, one of which is a published revenue ruling.

Before detailing the nature of the changes in contracts that give rise to adjustments and the manner in which those adjustments are made—details that differ depending upon which of the two section 7702 tests apply—it is important to recognize a threshold requirement of the section 7702 adjustment rule. Section 7702(f)

---

[1] Unless otherwise indicated, references in this book to "section" are to the provisions of the Internal Revenue Code of 1986, as amended (also referred to as "IRC" or the "Code").

(7)(A) does not require, and does not permit, adjustment of the definitional limitations due to a contractual change unless the changed benefits or terms were "not reflected in any previous determination or adjustment made under" section 7702. Hence, if a contract's benefits or terms as changed had no effect on the section 7702 calculations for the contract in the first instance, no adjustment is to be made in such calculations.[2] In addition, if the change that alters benefits or terms has previously been reflected in those calculations, as in a circumstance where a scheduled change in terms after issue is reflected in the at-issue calculations, no adjustment is to be made.[3] This same concept applies in the case of the section 7702A adjustment rules; illustrations of this concept appear later in this chapter.

## CVAT Adjustments

Under the CVAT, unlike the case with the guideline premium test (as discussed below), *all* changes in future benefits are required to be taken into account under the section 7702(f)(7)(A) adjustment rule, again assuming the change "was not reflected in any previous determination or adjustment made under" section 7702. This is accomplished by recalculating the NSPs in their entirety from the time of the change forward based on the attained age of the insured and the altered future benefits at that time. As provided in the Deficit Reduction Act of 1984 (DEFRA) legislative history:

> In the event of an increase in current or future benefits, the limitations under the cash value accumulation test must be computed treating the date of the change, in effect, as a new date of issue for determining whether the changed contract continues to qualify as life insurance under the definition prescribed in the Act. Thus, if a future benefit is increased because of a scheduled change in death benefit or because of the purchase of a paid-up addition (or its equivalent), the change will require an adjustment and new computation of the net single premium definitional limitation.[4]

Since a change in future benefits is dealt with under the CVAT by treating the date of the change as a new issue date for the entire contract, the CVAT is continuously applied using an attained-age NSP for the contract's future benefits. Therefore, changes are handled automatically. For this reason, as mentioned in Chapter 2, the test has been described as "self-adjusting," i.e., for a contract that complies with the CVAT "by its terms" (as it must), the NSPs will automatically adjust as benefit amounts change.[5] As only future benefits are considered in calculating NSPs, adjustments under the CVAT are considerably simpler than those under the guideline premium test. The simplicity of adjustments is one reason the CVAT has at times been applied to universal life and similar plans, even though the guideline premium test was designed to accommodate them.

Treating the date of the change in future benefits under a contract as "in effect" a new issue date for the contract, as provided in the legislative history quoted above, means the computation under the CVAT disregards the benefits as they existed under the contract before the change (contrary to the case with the guideline premium test). As discussed in Chapter 2, the new-issue-date concept, together with the language of section 7702(b)(2)(C), enables adjustments under the CVAT to be reconciled with the deemed-not-to-increase rule of section 7702(e)(1)(A), as well as the limitation on the final endowment value under section 7702(e)(1)(D).

This interpretation is borne out in the discussion in an IRS nondocketed service advice review (NSAR), a nonprecedential memorandum prepared by IRS attorneys for advice to revenue agents. The memorandum addressed the treatment of adjustments under the CVAT, and specifically the application of the "least endowment rule" under section 7702(e)(1)(D).[6] In addition, the NSAR considered whether the computational assumption in section 7702(e)(1)(A) continued to apply without change unless the death benefit increase results from one of the occurrences specifically listed in the legislative history passage quoted above. If so, a scheduled increase

---

[2] *See* PLR 201045019 (Aug. 5, 2010) (addition of an investment option to an equity-indexed universal life insurance contract qualifying under the CVAT or guideline premium test that did not alter the contract's minimum interest guarantee does not require an adjustment under IRC § 7702(f)(7)(A)). However, for a discussion of contractual changes sufficiently fundamental to be treated as exchanges to which IRC § 1001 applies, see Chapter 5.

[3] *See* PLR 200906001 (Oct. 17, 2008) (nonguaranteed, discretionary reductions in the cost of insurance charges under a universal life insurance contract (qualifying under the CVAT or guideline premium test) due to credits under a "wellness" rider do not require an adjustment under IRC § 7702(f)(7)(A)).

[4] DEFRA Blue Book, *supra* Chapter 1, note 20, at 653. *See also* DEFRA House Report, *supra* Chapter 1, note 11, at 1448; DEFRA Senate Report, *supra* Chapter 1, note 11, at 577.

[5] This implies, of course, the contract's CSV (*i.e.*, its cash surrender value as defined in section 7702(f)(2)) must not at any time exceed the adjusted NSP that will apply at such time based on the changed benefits and terms.

[6] NSAR 09594, Vaughn # 9594 (Nov. 27, 1991).

in death benefit or the purchase of paid-up additions would constitute an adjustment event under section 7702(f)(7), but other types of increases would not. Accordingly, the reason for the increase would determine whether the death benefit limit on endowment benefits under section 7702(e)(1)(D) would relate back to the initial death benefit or to the newly increased death benefit instead.

The analysis in the NSAR concluded that section 7702(f)(7)(A), by its terms, as supported by the legislative history, applies to all changes in terms or benefits that affect computations under section 7702. According to the analysis, the broad reach of this provision includes all increases in death benefits without regard to the mechanism causing the increase:

> The plain meaning of the statute, as supported by the legislative history, indicates that an increase in death benefit is an adjustment event, however caused. All increases in death benefits, even those that are scheduled or anticipated, are disregarded in the initial computations of allowable values under section 7702 of the Code, by reason of the computational rule of section 7702(e)(1)(A). Accordingly, any increase in death benefits is a change in benefits that was not reflected in any previous determination or adjustment and is an adjustment event under section 7702(f)(7)(A). If the contract is subject to the cash value accumulation test of section 7702(b), the entire contract is treated as newly issued at the time of the change, and the computational rules of section 7702(e)(1) are applied using the death benefit then in effect as the assumed level death benefit. Accordingly, if the trigger in the contract causes an increase in death benefits, the increase causes a deemed reissuance of the entire contract and a determination of compliance with section 7702 using the new death benefit as the assumed future death benefit under section 7702(e)(1)(A).[7]

On the other hand, the concept that the date of the change is effectively treated as a new date of issue does not appear to require short-term interest guarantees made after the original issue date to be reflected in the calculation of the NSP by virtue of the adjustment rule.[8] However, as noted in Chapter 3, the treatment of a short-term interest guarantee, as it relates to the adjustment computations following a policyholder-initiated change, has not been the subject of any guidance.

As a final matter, the application of the adjustment rule under the CVAT to a contract that has lapsed and been reinstated merits consideration. This topic is discussed below in connection with guideline premium test adjustments.

## Guideline Premium Test Adjustments

### *Background: Section 101(f) Adjustment Events and Methods*

As was the case with the discussion of the computational rules in Chapter 3, a review of the guideline premium test adjustment rules under the predecessor statute provides background helpful to understanding the comparable rules applicable under section 7702. Section 101(f)(2)(E) provides that guideline premiums for a contract are to be adjusted in the event of a change in the contract's future benefits or any of its qualified additional benefits (QABs), assuming the change was not reflected in any guideline single or level premium previously determined.[9] In discussing the adjustment rule, the legislative history of section 101(f) explains:

> At the start of the contract the guideline premiums are based on the future benefits specified in the contract as of such date. If future contract benefits are changed at a subsequent date, the guideline premiums will be adjusted (upward or downward) to reflect the change.[10]

---

[7] *Id.* In contrast, in the context of the guideline premium test, the changes that give rise to adjustments are more limited, as described below.
[8] *See* PLR 199929028 (April 27, 1999).
[9] The IRC § 101(f) adjustment rule, unlike the rule in IRC § 7702(f)(7)(A), does not reference changes in "other terms" of a contract, but limits itself to changes in a contract's future benefits. The inclusion of the "other terms" reference in the IRC § 7702 adjustment rule presumably was intended to encompass such changes as ones made in an interest or mortality charge rate guarantee.
[10] TEFRA Senate Report, *supra* Chapter 3, note 33, at 354. *See also* H.R. Conf. Rep. No. 97-760, at 648 (1982) (hereinafter TEFRA Conference Report).

Further on this point, the *Congressional Record* includes the Dole-Bentsen colloquy, a discussion on the Senate floor between Sens. Dole and Bentsen providing an explanation of the circumstances under which guideline premiums are to be adjusted:

> *Mr. Bentsen*: [I]f the death benefits or rider benefits are changed after issue of these policies, adjustments will need to be made. ... I understand that such adjustments are only to be made in two situations: First, if the change represents a previously scheduled benefit increase that was not reflected in the guideline premiums because of the so-called computational rules; or second, if the change is initiated by the policy [owner] to alter the amount or pattern of the benefits. Is this correct?
>
> *Mr. Dole*: That is my understanding.[11]

The colloquy is echoed in the text of the Tax Equity and Fiscal Responsibility Act of 1982 (TEFRA) Blue Book, which noted that adjustments can occur:

- if the amount or pattern of a policy's benefits (including qualified additional benefits) is changed by the policyholder, or
- upon the occurrence of a change in benefits previously scheduled under the contract that could not be taken into account earlier because of the computational rules.[12]

Hence, unlike the case with the CVAT, under which all changes are treated as adjustment events, adjustments under the guideline premium test of section 101(f)—as carried over to section 7702 (see below)—generally are restricted to the two categories of change described in the colloquy. The reason for restricting the guideline premium adjustment events to policyholder-initiated changes and the advent of a prescheduled benefit change that could not previously be accounted for in the guideline premiums (due to the computational rules) is that the treatment of changes beyond these as adjustment events would undermine the integrity of the test. Thus, by way of example, the crediting of excess interest to a universal life contract's cash value that results in an increase in its death benefit would result in a CVAT adjustment, a result that is sensible, and indeed necessary, under that test. However, if the same type of action resulted in a guideline premium test adjustment, then the test's limit would be increased, so that additional premium could be paid for the contract even though, all else being equal, there was no need for more premium to fund the contract beyond the guideline premium limitation already determined.

The TEFRA Blue Book expanded on Sen. Bentsen's statement in the colloquy, noting that "if a qualified additional benefit ceases for any reason, including the death of an individual (such as the insured's spouse) insured thereunder, this is considered a change in benefits requiring an adjustment of the guideline premium."[13] This expansion is arguably significant, in that a payment made by the insurer because the loss event insured against under the QAB was triggered could be thought of as carrying out the terms of the contract rather than as a change in the future benefits. It amounts to such a change, however, for the reason that because the loss event occurred, the full amount of funding for the contract previously calculated is no longer needed after the occurrence.

In the Dole-Bentsen colloquy, Sen. Dole's statement also provided guidance on the computation of the adjustments to the guideline level and single premiums. Specifically, it instructed that "adjustments may be computed in the same manner as the initial guideline premiums, but based on the change in the amount or pattern of benefits and the insured's attained age at the time of the change."[14] Consistently with this colloquy, in examples prepared for the TEFRA Blue Book, post-issue changes that increased benefits were reflected by calculating a guideline premium adjustment, which was then added to the original guideline premium to produce the new limitation. The TEFRA Blue Book then goes on to explain that "[t]he computational rules apply to the change in amount at the time of the change independently of their application at issue or for a previous

---

[11] Dole-Bentsen colloquy, *supra* Chapter 2, note 74.
[12] TEFRA Blue Book, *supra* Chapter 1, note 95, at 371.
[13] *Id.*
[14] Dole-Bentsen colloquy, *supra* Chapter 2, note 74.

change."[15] The examples of the calculation of guideline premiums, including the effect of adjustments, that were provided in the TEFRA Blue Book are summarized in Table 4.1.[16]

| Table 4.1. Guideline premium examples, TEFRA Blue Book, male age 35 ||||| 
|---|---|---|---|---|
| Contract duration | Death benefit | Guideline single premium | Sum of guideline level premiums | Guideline premium limitations |
| At issue | 100,000 | 17,219 | 1,590 | 17,219 |
| Year 10 | 100,000 | 17,219 | 15,901 | 17,219 |
| Year 20 | 100,000 | 17,219 | 31,801 | 31,801 |
| Year 30 | 100,000 | 17,219 | 47,702 | 47,702 |
| Incremental guidelines | 25,000 | 6,774 | 631 | — |
| Year 10 (before increase) | 100,000 | 17,219 | 15,901 | 17,219 |
| Year 11 | 125,000 | 23,993 | 18,122 | 23,993 |
| Year 20 | 125,000 | 23,993 | 38,110 | 38,110 |
| Year 30 | 125,000 | 23,993 | 60,320 | 60,320 |

Significantly, in the TEFRA Blue Book example, the guideline single premium (GSP) and the guideline level premium (GLP) components of the limitation were adjusted separately, and the new guideline premium limitation was based on the greater of the adjusted GSP or the sum of the GLPs, as follows:

- Guideline single premium = $\$17,219$ before adjustment and $\$23,993\,(\$17,219 + \$6,774)$ after
- Guideline level premium = $\$1,590$ before adjustment and $\$2,221\,(\$1,590 + \$631)$ after

Hence, the guideline premium limitation itself is not directly adjusted. Rather the GSP and GLP components are each adjusted and the limitation is merely reflective of these underlying changes in its components.

The Dole-Bentsen colloquy, as exemplified in the TEFRA Blue Book, thus introduced the concept of the **attained-age increment and decrement method** for adjusting guideline premiums in respect of increases and decreases in face amount. Since this method entails the modification of pre-existing guideline premiums by adding increments (or subtracting decrements), it is also referred to as a **layering** approach.

## Section 7702 Adjustment Events

Much of section 101(f) and its legislative history carried over to section 7702, and this was as true for the guideline premium test adjustment rule as for other rules in the statute. A comparison of the legislative history of section 7702(f)(7)(A), which is the adjustment rule under current law, with that of section 101(f)(2)(E) shows considerable similarity in the instructions (if not the language) regarding when and how to adjust the guideline premiums. In particular, following the approach taken in the Dole-Bentsen colloquy, and based on the same rationale, the DEFRA legislative history indicates that the guideline premiums under section 7702 generally are adjusted only in two instances: when the policyholder initiates the change, or when a scheduled change has not been reflected because of the computational rules. On the other hand, changes that do not trigger adjustments include changes initiated by the insurer and changes resulting from the growth of a contract's cash value, whether by the crediting of excess interest or the payment of premiums up to the level of the pre-existing guide-

---

[15] TEFRA Blue Book, *supra* Chapter 1, note 95, at 371.
[16] *Id.* at 371–74. The examples assumed mortality charges based on short-term (one year) guarantees of 75 percent of the 1958 CSO tables at contract issuance and at the time of the adjustment, a floor guarantee of 1958 CSO mortality, short-term (one year) interest guarantees of 10 percent and 8 percent, respectively, at contract issuance and at the time of the adjustment, and a floor interest rate guarantee of 4 percent. The insured in the examples was a male age 35 at contract issuance.

line premium limitation.[17] And, of course, by the terms of section 7702(f)(7)(A), no adjustment is required or permitted due to any other contractual change unless the changed benefits or terms were "not reflected in any previous determination or adjustment made under" section 7702.

The rule that declarations of excess interest, as well as of reductions in mortality or expense charges due to the use of "current" charges less than the contractual guarantees, are not adjustment events is consistent with the approach used in section 101(f). Under the guideline premium test, such a declaration or reduction is not an adjustment event, and any change in benefits resulting from the growth of cash value likewise is not an adjustment event. As described in Chapter 2, taking a broad view of the term "policyholder dividend" (i.e., as in section 808), benefit increases due to dividends do not give rise to adjustments under the guideline premium test, although changes in long-term guarantees may create a different result.[18] Similarly, increases in face amount resulting from the operation of the section 7702(d) cash value corridor do not create increases in the guideline premiums. An increase of the same amount elected in anticipation of (or subsequent to) an increase prompted by operation of the corridor generally should not call for an adjustment calculation, although there may be cases to the contrary.

Thus, by way of summary, guideline premium test adjustment events can include:

- An increase or decrease in death or endowment benefits made at the request of the policyholder. However, a special rule applies in the case of the election of a reduced paid-up insurance nonforfeiture option under a guideline premium-tested contract; this is discussed further below in connection with death benefit decreases.

- An increase in death or endowment benefits resulting from the operation of the contract and not previously reflected in the calculation of the guideline premiums, presumably because of the computational rules, but not including death benefit increases due to growth in cash value (e.g., death benefit increases required by the cash value corridor or under an option 2 (increasing) death benefit pattern).

- The addition or termination of a QAB, including by payment of a death benefit provided by a QAB but not including the termination of a QAB at a previously scheduled time.

- A change in death benefit pattern, e.g., a change from an option 1 (level) and an option 2 (increasing) death benefit pattern or vice versa.

- Long-term changes to basic interest and other guarantees generally, including a change in guaranteed mortality charges resulting from an insured's change from smoker to nonsmoker status and the termination or modification of a rating (e.g., the insured ceased piloting an airplane).

With respect to the last category, it is important to take account of the fact that the enactment of the "reasonable" mortality and expense charge rules by the Technical and Miscellaneous Revenue Act of 1988 (TAMRA), as discussed in Chapter 2, replaced the original section 7702 rules relating to such charges. For pre-TAMRA contracts, guideline premiums reflected the mortality and expense charges guaranteed in the contract. Hence, if such charges were altered, not through the mechanism of "current" charge reductions from time to time (in the nature of policyholder dividends) but through a change to the guaranteed charges, such a change would be one of the long-term changes referenced just above, and so it would constitute an adjustment event. One example of such a change, noted above, would be the replacement on a guaranteed basis of smoker-based mortality charges with nonsmoker mortality charges when an insured stopped using tobacco products. On the other hand, with the advent of the reasonable mortality and expense charge rules, it is less clear when a change in contract guarantees affecting mortality charges, or a change in the expense charges "expected to be actually paid," needs to be reflected in guideline premium adjustments for contracts subject to those rules, i.e., contracts entered into (or treated as entered into) post-TAMRA. In the case of such contracts:

---

[17] DEFRA House Report, *supra* Chapter 1, note 11, at 1448; DEFRA Senate Report, *supra* Chapter 1, note 11, at 577. *See also* TRA 1986 House Report, *supra* Chapter 3, note 26, at 966; TRA 1986 Senate Report, *supra* Chapter 3, note 26, at 987; Technical Corrections Blue Book, *supra* Chapter 3, note 21, at 106.

[18] *See* PLR 199929028 (April 27, 1999). Temporary guarantees for up to one year are dividends; longer guarantees may be dividends, but at some unspecified point the character of a temporary guarantee would change and an adjustment event or deemed exchange would occur. See the discussion in Chapter 2 on policyholder dividends under IRC § 808.

**1980 CSO mortality:** Under IRS Notice 88-128, as confirmed in IRS Notice 2006-95 (see Chapter 2 for details), 100 percent of the 1980 CSO tables is a safe harbor for contracts based on such tables, and so a change in a mortality charge that constituted a guarantee of less than 100 percent of the tables need not be treated as an adjustment event. However, if the contract's guaranteed mortality charges were based on smoker/nonsmoker distinct mortality under the 1980 CSO tables and these charges were reflected in the guideline premiums, then a change from smoker to nonsmoker status for the insured that resulted in a change (a reduction) in the guaranteed charges would be an adjustment event. Further, if a substandard rating existed at contract issuance such that guaranteed charges in excess of 100 percent of the tables were reflected in the guideline premiums, the dropping of such a rating would be an adjustment event. (These conclusions assume that the 1980 CSO tables continued to constitute the safe harbor for the contract after the changes were made; see the discussion of **grandfathering** in Chapter 5.)

**2001 CSO mortality:** The rules just discussed for contracts with guarantees based on the 1980 CSO tables also would apply to those with guarantees based on the 2001 CSO tables, with one significant exception. As explained in Chapter 2, Notice 2006-95 restricted the mortality charge safe harbor for 2001 CSO-based contracts to the lesser of 100 percent of the 2001 CSO tables and the mortality charge specified in the contract at issuance. Hence, if after issuance a change were made in a mortality charge that constituted a guarantee of less than 100 percent of the tables, it presumably would need to be treated as an adjustment event.

**Expense charges:** The reasonable expense charge rule, which is applied without the benefit of a safe harbor, by its terms requires expense charges reflected in guideline premiums to be both "reasonable" and "reasonably expected to be actually paid." The status of an expense charge as a guaranteed charge or as a lower, current charge is simply not relevant to this requirement. Assuming a charge is a reasonable one, the standard for its reflection in the guideline premiums is one of reasonable expectation as to the amount of its imposition, both at issuance of a contract and at future durations. If the amount of a charge were to change after contract issuance (relative to what was expected at issuance), this in and of itself would not seem to constitute a change that is inconsistent with that prior expectation, but merely an alteration in an insurer's current practice. On the other hand, were an adjustment event to occur for another reason, e.g., an increase in the contract's death benefit at the policyholder's request, it would be appropriate to reflect the changed amount of the charge in the future, assuming the new amount is reasonably expected to be actually paid thereafter.

Of course, as noted at the outset of the discussion of guideline premium test adjustments, no adjustment need be made if the benefit change already was reflected in the prechange guideline premiums. Hence, the mere existence of an adjustment "event" does not automatically translate into the need to apply the method discussed next to effect a change in the guideline premiums previously determined.

## *Section 7702 Adjustment Method: The Attained-Age Increment and Decrement Rule*

Under the guideline premium test, an increase or decrease in future benefits is treated separately from the existing guideline limits. That is, separate guideline premiums are computed to reflect the increase or decrease. Beginning with section 101(f), this has followed the method outlined in the Dole-Bentsen colloquy, which introduced the attained-age increment and decrement method. Equivalent "before and after" calculations based on the attained age of the insured at the time of the change can be used to implement this. Under this method, attained age layers of guideline premium values are added to the existing guideline single and level premiums. In symbols:

$$\textit{Incremental Guideline Single Premium}_{x+t} = GSP(\textit{After})_{x+t} - GSP(\textit{Before})_{x+t} \qquad (4.1)$$

$$\textit{Incremental Guideline Level Premium}_{x+t} = GLP(\textit{After})_{x+t} - GLP(\textit{Before})_{x+t} \qquad (4.2)$$

For an increase in death benefits, this method follows the example provided in the TEFRA Blue Book (see Table 4.1), with both the guideline single and level premiums adjusted by the corresponding guideline single or level premium for the change.

Note that the Dole-Bentsen colloquy discussed computation of an incremental guideline premium at the insured's attained age for the amount of the benefit change. The pattern shown here, computing guidelines at attained age for the entire "After" contract and subtracting the guidelines at attained age for the entire "Before" contract, has the same effect for benefit increases and decreases, and also the virtue of working for the GSP, and with modification for the GLP, where there is no change in a benefit itself. In addition, this approach may be easier from an administrative system perspective, e.g., when reasonable expense charges or initial guarantees vary depending on the face amount "band" of the contract. Figure 4.1[19] is intended to illustrate the general pattern of movement of the guideline premiums in the case of a face amount increase.

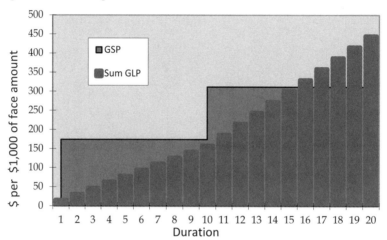

**Figure 4.1.** Guideline premium limitation

*Male age 45, 2001 CSO, aggregate ALB, 50% increase in face at age 55*

More specifically, the attained-age adjustment formulas (4.1 and 4.2) describe the incremental increase or decrease associated with the GSP and the GLP when future benefits are added to or removed from a contract. When changes occur to a contract other than those related to future benefits (e.g., when a substandard rating reflected in the guideline premiums is removed), modifications to the attained age layering formulas for the GLP may be needed.

Formula (4.1) can be expanded to solve for the "New" GSP following a contract change at attained age x+t, where each component of the formula is reflective of the present value of future benefits using actuarial assumptions appropriate for computing each GSP:

$$GSP(New)_{x+t} = GSP(Old)_x + GSP(After)_{x+t} - GSP(Before)_{x+t}$$

To account appropriately for the present value of future GLPs, an annuity factor is needed for each term:

$$GLP(New)_{x+t} \times \ddot{a}'_{x+t} = GLP(Old)_x \times \ddot{a}_{x+t} + GLP(After)_{x+t} \times \ddot{a}'_{x+t} - GLP(Before)_{x+t} \times \ddot{a}_{x+t}$$

The annuity factor underlying the present value of $GLP(New)_{x+t}$ and $GLP(After)_{x+t}$ would be reflective of the contract characteristics following the change ($\ddot{a}'_{x+t}$), while $GLP(Old)_x$ and $GLP(Before)_{x+t}$ would use an annuity factor based on the contract characteristics prior to the change ($\ddot{a}_{x+t}$). Solving for $GLP(New)_{x+t}$ yields the following attained-age adjustment formula:

$$GLP(New)_{x+t} = GLP(Old)_x \times \frac{\ddot{a}_{x+t}}{\ddot{a}'_{x+t}} + GLP(After)_{x+t} - GLP(Before)_{x+t} \times \frac{\ddot{a}_{x+t}}{\ddot{a}'_{x+t}}$$

---

[19] Age last birthday (ALB).

Because most contract changes involve adding and removing contract benefits, the annuity ratio ($\frac{\ddot{a}'_{x+t}}{\ddot{a}'_{x+t}}$) underlying the calculation of $GLP(New)_{x+t}$ reduces to 1 in most cases, causing the formula for $GLP(New)$ to parallel that for $GSP(New)$:

$$GLP(New)_{x+t} = GLP(Old)_x + GLP(After)_{x+t} - GLP(Before)_{x+t}$$

Other types of contract changes that can affect the assumptions used to calculate the annuity factors include changes in underwriting class (e.g., smoker to nonsmoker mortality charge guarantees) or a change in the death benefit pattern (e.g., option 1 to option 2). However, to simplify the administration and maintain consistency between the GSP and GLP adjustment formulas, some companies use an annuity ratio of 1 for all policy changes, including those that involve a basis change in the annuity.

As originally enacted, section 7702(f)(7)(B) provided that any change in the terms of a contract which reduced the future benefits under the contract was to be treated as an exchange of contracts (i.e., under section 1035), and so may have caused a distribution to be taxable to the policyholder on a gain-first basis. That is, money distributed in connection with a reduction in benefits would be treated as taxable "boot" under section 1031(b). However, the section 7702(f)(7)(B) rule was amended by the technical corrections title of the Tax Reform Act of 1986 (TRA 1986), prompting the legislative history of that enactment to discuss the use of the attained-age decrement method in the event of a reduction in benefits:[20]

> Under this [the attained-age decrement] method, when benefits under the contract are reduced, the guideline level and single premium limitations are each adjusted and redetermined by subtracting from the original guideline premium limitation a "negative guideline premium limitation" which is determined as of the date of the reduction in benefits and at the attained age of the insured on such date. The negative guideline premium limitation is the guideline premium limitation for an insurance contract that, when combined with the original insurance contract after the reduction in benefits, produces an insurance contract with the same benefit as the original contract before such reduction.

This discussion was intended to describe the Dole-Bentsen colloquy as applied to benefit decreases, but its use of terms not found elsewhere—e.g., the guideline single (or level) premium limitation—failed to shed additional light on the subject. In practice, the GSP and the GLP have continued to be adjusted separately, as described above. Oddly, the TRA 1986 legislative history discussion accompanied the amendment of section 7702(f)(7)(A) to remove the Treasury Department's authority to write regulations prescribing the adjustment method, which possibly could have supplanted the attained-age adjustment methodology. However, one effect of the change in 1986 was to apply a consistent method to both increases and decreases, to the exclusion of other possible methods. In this regard, the attained-age increment and decrement method has one overriding virtue not characteristic of other possible alternative methods: If an increase (or decrease) is made and adjusted for, and then immediately reversed, the result is the same limitation as before the change.

The application of the attained-age increment and decrement method in the case of death benefit option changes is discussed later in this chapter. Also, special considerations with respect to adjustments after payment of accelerated death benefits are discussed in Chapter 7.

### *Observations on the Attained-Age Increment and Decrement Method*

The attained-age increment and decrement method was first implemented under section 101(f) to preclude a "ratcheting" abuse of the guideline premium test,[21] and it was expected to be refined, if not replaced, by is-

---

[20] TRA 1986 House Report, *supra* Chapter 3, note 26, at 967–68; TRA 1986 Senate Report, *supra* Chapter 3, note 26, at 989; Technical Corrections Blue Book, *supra* Chapter 3, note 21, at 108.

[21] The ratcheting abuse, which focused on contracts fully funded by payment of the GSP, may be demonstrated by an example. Assume a contract was issued with a level death benefit of $100,000, and soon thereafter the death benefit was reduced to $50,000. If an issue-age adjustment were made to the GSP, the amount of the GSP would simply be cut in half. Further assume that some number of years later, the death benefit was increased to its original $100,000 amount. An issue-age replacement GSP (*i.e.*, a new GSP calculated at the attained age assuming the contract was newly issued for $100,000) would be greater than the original GSP, due to the insured's later age. This would have the effect of increasing the funding allowed for the previous, and already fully funded, $50,000 of the death benefit, a result deemed inappropriate. Note that this concern was identified in the early 1980s, at a time when interest credits at or above 6 percent were common.

suance of detailed regulations. However, with the 1986 amendment, as confirmed by Revenue Ruling 2003-95 (discussed at the end of this chapter), this method continues to govern the treatment of contract changes under the guideline premium test.

The application of the attained-age adjustment method when future benefits decrease can produce problematic results in some situations. As indicated above, when future benefits decrease, attained-age guideline premiums reflecting the amount of the decrease are deducted from the existing guideline premiums. Depending upon the size of the benefit decrease, the decrement in the GLP can be larger than the previous GLP, leading to a net negative annual addition to the sum of GLPs, which in turn can create a declining guideline premium limitation. This circumstance could require annual force-outs from the affected contract's cash value as the limitation continues to decline.[22] The legislative history of TRA 1986, reflecting statements in the DEFRA legislative history, anticipated the potential of a distribution from a contract to maintain compliance, noting "[i]f the contract fails to meet the limitation after proper adjustments have been made, a distribution of cash to the policyholder may be required to maintain qualification of the contract as life insurance."[23]

Further, if the decrease in benefits is large enough, the entire guideline premium limitation can become negative, throwing the operation of the test into question. In the case of a significant decrease, the GSP becomes negative immediately, but the contract can remain in force for some period of time with a positive guideline premium limitation, as the sum of GLPs to date declines more slowly through the annual addition of a negative amount. It is unclear precisely what may happen to a contract if and when the limitation becomes negative; the tax law arguably should not recognize the negative number, flooring the amount at zero. Alternatively, the rule in section 7702(f)(6), permitting premium payments in excess of the guideline premium limitation in certain conditions, might come into play. The issue of negative guidelines is discussed further in the examples, below.[24]

## *Timing of Adjustments to the Guideline Premiums*

Both the statute and the legislative history are silent when it comes to defining the details of adjusting guideline premiums when a contract change occurs. Thus, there is little in the way of guidance as to how the attained-age increment and decrement method should be applied to a contract change, particularly when the change occurs off-anniversary (i.e., at a date other than on the contract anniversary).

In discussing the differences between the new-date-of-issue approach applied to adjusting the NSPs under the CVAT and the approach used for guideline premium adjustments, the legislative history accompanying TRA 1986 provided only a brief reference to the date of the change:

> Thus, if a future benefit is increased because of a scheduled change in death benefit or because of the purchase of a paid-up addition (or its equivalent) the change will require an adjustment in the new computation of the net single premium limitation. Under the guideline premium limitation, an adjustment is required under similar circumstances, but the date of the change for increased benefits should be treated as a new issue date only with respect to the changed portion of the contract.[25]

A number of administrative decisions are needed to implement the attained-age adjustment method. Some commonly used approaches for dealing with off-anniversary adjustments are described below.

**Annual approach:** The annual approach to adjusting guideline premiums is based on an insurance age concept that assumes:

---

[22] *See* PLR 200838018 (June 10, 2008) (failure of insurer personnel to refund amounts as guideline premium limitation declined due to benefit reduction waived by IRS as reasonable error under IRC § 7702(f)(8)).

[23] TRA 1986 House Report, *supra* Chapter 3, note 26, at 966; TRA 1986 Senate Report, *supra* Chapter 3, note 26, at 987; *see also* Technical Corrections Blue Book, *supra* Chapter 3, note 21, at 106. The relevant DEFRA legislative history is found in: DEFRA House Report, *supra* Chapter 1, note 11, at 1448; DEFRA Senate Report, *supra* Chapter 1, note 11, at 577–78; DEFRA Blue Book, *supra* Chapter 1, note 20, at 654.

[24] For a discussion of issues associated with guideline premium test adjustments from the standpoint of a sales agent, *see* Ben G. Baldwin Jr., *GPT or CVAT: Which Choice Is in the Best Interests of the Policy Owner?*, 68 J. OF FIN. SERV. PROF., no. 4, July 2014, at 42.

[25] Technical Corrections Blue Book, *supra* Chapter 3, note 21, at 106. *See also* TRA 1986 House Report, *supra* Chapter 3, note 26, at 966; TRA 1986 Senate Report, *supra* Chapter 3, note 26, at 987. Similar language appears in the DEFRA legislative history. *See* DEFRA Senate Report, *supra* Chapter 1, note 11, at 577; DEFRA Blue Book, *supra* Chapter 1, note 20, at 653–54. The statement regarding the guideline premiums echoes the Dole-Bentsen colloquy.

- the attained age of the insured remains constant throughout the contract year, and
- off-anniversary changes occur on the prior contract anniversary.

Maintaining a constant attained age during the year is consistent with the definition of the insured's age provided in the regulations prescribing the age of the insured for section 7702 purposes (i.e., Treas. Reg. sec. 1.7702-2, described in Chapter 3) and earlier in the statute's legislative history.[26] Under the annual approach, adjustments to guideline premiums are conceptually equivalent to a change occurring on the contract anniversary prior to or coincident with the change. While the adjustment is computed as if it occurred on the previous anniversary, the change in the guideline premiums is not reflected until the change actually occurs. That is, if the change occurs during the contract year, the (adjusted) guideline premiums resulting from the change would be effective on the date of the change, and not from the prior anniversary date.

Implementing the annual approach for determining the GSP is relatively straightforward. Prior to the change, the "old" GSP would apply; the "new" GSP would apply for the remainder of the contract year following the change. Various practices have emerged, however, in determining the cumulative GLPs when an off-anniversary contract change occurs.

Consistently with its naming convention, the more common approach for defining the sum of the GLPs under the annual method involves the addition of the current year's new GLP to the sum of the GLPs as of the end of the prior contract year effective as of the date of the off-anniversary change. More particularly, when a contract change occurs off anniversary, the cumulative GLP is redetermined as of such date by subtracting the old GLP and replacing it with the new GLP. Subsequently, the new GLP would then be added to the sum of GLPs on contract anniversaries, barring any further adjustments.

**Pro rata approach:** A variant of the annual approach for determining the sum of the GLPs in the year of an off-anniversary contract change involves the use of a pro rata GLP. The pro rata approach assumes that, for the portion of the year prior to the change, the old GLP was in effect, followed by the new GLP for the remainder of the year. For example, for an increase $n$ months before a contract anniversary, allow $n/12$ times the increase in the GLP at the time of adjustment, and allow the full increment at each subsequent contract anniversary. The prorating is used to create a bridge to the next contract anniversary, at which point the entire enlarged GLP for the coming contract year is recognized. Subsequent annual increases are also made on the contract anniversary. In this fashion, increases are accommodated while still maintaining one contract anniversary, but with a somewhat lower sum of GLPs than is the case with the annual method.

**Layered approach:** While the annual and pro rata approaches process the entire contract as a single unit, adjustments have also been made by treating each "layer" as an independent entity, with its own anniversary date (following a literal interpretation of the language in the legislative history describing the date of the change as a new issue date). Using the layered method, the sum of the GLPs is changed on the anniversary of each contract change by the amount (positive or negative) of the GLP for the change. This approach may or may not be able to be used consistently with the regulation defining the insured's age, which (as explained in Chapter 3) does not permit off-anniversary changes to alter the insured's age for purposes of determining the level premium payment period, applying the corridor factors and making calculations in accordance with the section 7702(e) maturity date rules. If the layered approach retains the age of the insured as of the prior contract anniversary, then it arguably can be reconciled with the requirement of the regulation.

**Exact approach:** Another alternative approach to adjusting guideline premiums is an "exact" approach. Under the exact approach, while the age of the insured is assumed to increase on contract anniversaries, the calculation would take into account the remaining or fractional portion of the contract year from the date of the adjustment to the next contract anniversary. This approach would recognize the insured's age as of the beginning of the contract year, similarly to the annual approach, but unlike the annual approach, it would not assume the

---

[26] The DEFRA House Report, *supra* Chapter 1, note 11, at 1447; the DEFRA Senate Report, *supra* Chapter 1, note 11, at 576; and the DEFRA Blue Book, *supra* Chapter 1, note 20, at 651, each note that "[f]or purposes of applying the cash value corridor and the guideline premium limitation (as well as the computational rules described below), the attained age of the insured means the insured's age determined by reference to contract anniversaries (rather than the individual's actual birthday), so long as the age assumed under the contract is within 12 months of the actual age." The regulations follow this formulation (for single life contracts).

change occurred when the year began. For example, assume an adjustment occurs on a contract at the beginning of the 10$^{th}$ month of the contract year when the insured is age 40. The calculations underlying the exact approach would take into consideration that the insured has three months remaining at attained age 40, before the attained age would increment on the next contract anniversary date. The nature of the calculation under the exact approach would generally require the use of a monthly processing interval, which is needed to account for fractional portions of a contract year.

Formulas for one version of the exact approach can be developed for the face amount of insurance (i.e., disregarding QABs and loading) as follows:

- For q, the annual mortality rate of the year of increase, and i, the annual interest rate, monthly mortality and interest rates, $q^m$ and $i^m$, which equal $q^m = 1 - (1 - q)^{1/12}$ and $1 + i^m = (1 + i)^{1/12}$, respectively, are created. (Other methods of creating monthly mortality rates could also be used.)

- For an increase $n$ months prior to the anniversary at insuring age $x+t$, the curtate NSP (inclusive of the endowment benefit) at age $x+t$, $NSP_{x+t}$, is adjusted to a net single premium at the time of adjustment:

$$NSP_{x+t-n} = \frac{(1-q^m)^n}{(1+i^m)^n} \times NSP_{x+t} + \text{Face Amount} \times \frac{1-(1-q^m)^n}{(1+i^m)^n} \qquad (4.3)$$

- A "level" premium P is computed so that the future contract benefits are funded by the combination of (a) and (b), where

  a) equals $(n/12)$ times $P$, assumed to be paid at time of adjustment, and

  b) equals $P$, assumed to be paid at each subsequent anniversary.

P is then found by solving:

$$\left(\frac{n}{12}\right) \times P + \frac{(1-q^m)^n}{(1+i^m)^n} \times (P + \ddot{a}_{x+t}) = NSP_{x+t-n} \text{ (as defined above)} \qquad (4.4)$$

The resulting single and level net premiums are curtate values. As usual, multiplication of the insurance portion (not the endowment portion) of the premium by $(i \div \ln(1+i))$ will adjust to values appropriate for immediate payment of claims. Expense loading and QABs considerably complicate the exact approach.

## Sample Adjustment Calculations

The adjustment calculations presented in this section are based on the sample plan initially presented in Chapter 2 to illustrate the calculation of the section 7702 and 7702A limitations. The Chapter 2 at-issue calculations are based on an assumed endowment age of 100 (pursuant to Rev. Proc. 2010-28) with the following at-issue characteristics:

- Sex: Male
- Age: 45
- Face amount: $100,000
- Mortality: 2001 CSO aggregate ANB
- Interest rate: 4.5 percent
- Expenses: 5 percent of premium, plus $5 monthly administrative fee

The following examples illustrate the effect of both increases and decreases on the guideline premium and the NSP.

### Increase in Death Benefit Example

In the example shown in Table 4.2,[27] the face amount for the contract used to illustrate the at-issue calculations at the end of Chapter 2 is assumed to be increased by $100,000 to $200,000 at age 50 as of the fifth contract anniversary. The development of the revised limits is shown below. Calculations are annual curtate.

- Sex: Male
- Age: 50
- (New) face amount: $200,000
- Mortality: 2001 CSO aggregate ANB
- Interest rate: 4.5 percent
- Expenses: 5 percent of premium, plus $5 monthly administrative fee[28]

| Table 4.2. $100,000 on-anniversary increase at age 50 | | | | | |
|---|---|---|---|---|---|
| | Face amount | GSP | GLP-DBO1 | GLP-DBO2 | NSP |
| At-issue value | 100,000 | 19,246.67 | 1,610.13 | 3,928.08 | 25,444.35 |
| Attained age 50 "before" | 100,000 | 23,929.28 | 2,052.13 | 4,911.70 | — |
| Attained age 50 "after" | 200,000 | 46,987.19 | 4,041.10 | 9,760.24 | — |
| Increment | 100,000 | 23,057.91 | 1,988.97 | 4,848.54 | — |
| After increase value | 200,000 | 42,304.58 | 3,599.10 | 8,776.60 | 60,994.24 |

$$GSP(New)_{x+t} = GSP(Old)_x + GSP(After)_{x+t} - GSP(Before)_{x+t}$$

$$= 19,246.67 + (46,987.19 - 23,929.28) = 42,304.58$$

$$GLP^{DBO1}(New)_{x+t} = GLP^{DBO1}(Old)_x + GLP^{DBO1}(After)_{x+t} - GLP^{DBO1}(Before)_{x+t}$$

$$= 1,610.13 + (4,041.10 - 2,052.13) = 3,599.10$$

$$GLP^{DBO2}(New)_{x+t} = GLP^{DBO2}(Old)_x + GLP^{DBO2}(After)_{x+t} - GLP^{DBO2}(Before)_{x+t}$$

$$= 3,928.08 + (9,760.24 - 4,911.70) = 8,776.62$$

$$NSP(New)_{x+t} = Face\ Amount(New) \times NSP_{x+t} = \mathbf{60{,}994.24}$$

### Off-Anniversary Changes

As discussed above, if this contract change occurs during a contract year rather than on an anniversary, different approaches can be taken for determining the GLP in effect in the year of the change. Table 4.3 compares the effect of the annual, pro rata, layered and exact approaches on the GLP, described in detail below. In the example, the change in benefits and the adjustments are assumed to occur at in the middle of year six.

---

[27] Death benefit option 1 (DBO1); death benefit option 2 (DBO2).
[28] To accommodate the $5 monthly administrative fee under an annual curtate calculation, a $60 fee payable at the beginning of each policy year is assumed in the calculations.

### Table 4.3. Effect of off-anniversary increase in the sum of the guideline level premiums

| | | Adjustment approach | | | |
|---|---|---|---|---|---|
| | | Annual | Pro rata | Layered | Exact |
| Year 5 | Sum of GLP | 8,050.65 | 8,050.65 | 8,050.65 | 8,050.65 |
| Year 6 before increase | GLP | 1,610.13 | 1,610.13 | 1,610.13 | 1,610.13 |
| | Sum of GLP | 9,660.78 | 9,660.78 | 9,660.78 | 9,660.78 |
| Year 6 after increase | GLP | 3,599.10 | 2,604.62 | 3,599.10 | 3,652.11 |
| | Sum of GLP | **11,649.75** | **10,655.27** | **11,649.75** | **11,702.76** |
| Year 7 | GLP | 3,599.10 | 3,599.10 | 3,599.10 | 3,652.11 |
| Sum of GLP (beginning of year) | | 15,248.85 | 14,254.37 | 13,259.88 | 15,354.87 |
| Sum of GLP (midyear) | | 15,248.85 | 14,254.37 | 15,248.85 | 15,354.87 |

**Annual approach:** Under the annual approach, the cumulative GLP in any particular contract year would be based on the cumulative GLP for prior years plus the GLP in effect for the current year. Under this approach, at the time of a contract change, the new GLP simply replaces the old GLP at the time of the increase. The annual approach gives credit for the full amount of the GLP in the year of the change, as follows:

- In the above example, the cumulative GLP for the option 1 death benefit through the fifth contract year is $8,050.65 (five times the GLP of $1,610.13).

- Up until the change in the specified amount of insurance (midway through year six), the cumulative GLP would be $9,660.78 (six times the GLP of $1,610.13, or $8,050.65 + $1,610.13).

- When the increase in the specified amount of insurance occurs, the cumulative GLP for year six, effective from the date of the increase to the end of the contract year, would be $11,649.75 ($8,050.65 + $3,599.10, replacing the old GLP of $1,610.13 with the new GLP of $3,599.10).

**Pro rata approach:** Under the pro rata approach, the same cumulative GLP would be in effect in the sixth contract year up until the date of the increase in the specified amount of insurance ($9,660.78). A new GLP would be determined for year six based on the duration that the old GLP and the new GLP were in effect, as follows:

- Since the change occurred midway through the contract year, the GLP for that year would be $2,604.62, which equals (100% of $1,610.13) + [(100 − 50)% of ($3,599.10 − $1,610.13)].

- Therefore the cumulative GLP in the year of change (effective on the date of the increase) would be $10,655.27 (i.e., $8,050.65 + $2,604.62).

Note again that, compared to other approaches, the pro rata approach creates a permanently reduced guideline premium limitation for an increase. It also produces a slightly higher guideline premium limitation for a decrease.

**Layered approach:** Under the layered approach, the annual increment to the GLP occurs at two points during the year, at the anniversary and later on the "anniversary" of the increase.

**Exact approach:** Under the exact approach, both the NSP and the annuity factor used in the calculation of the GLP would be determined as of the contract anniversary following the change (i.e., based on attained age 51) and then adjusted for interest and mortality to take into account the period between the prior anniversary and the adjustment date.

- The first step in the calculation would be to determine the NSP based on formula (4.3), where $q^m = 1 - (1 - q_{50})^{1/12}$ and $i^m = (1.045)^{1/12}$.

$$NSP_{50.5} = \frac{(1-q^m)^6}{(1+i^m)^6} \times NSP_{51} + 100{,}000 \times \frac{1-(1-q^m)^6}{(1+i^m)^6}$$

$$NSP_{50.5} = \frac{.9981182295}{1.022252415} + 31{,}612.35407 + 100{,}000 \times \frac{.00188177053}{1.022252415}$$

$$NSP_{50.5} = 31{,}050.10$$

- The $GLP_{Inc}$ for the increased benefit would then be determined by rearranging the terms in formula (4.4) and solving for P.

$$GLP_{Inc} = \frac{NSP_{50.5} \times \frac{(1+i^m)^6}{(1-q^m)^6}}{0.95 \times \left[\left(0.5 \times \frac{(1+i^m)^6}{(1-q^m)^6}\right) + \ddot{a}_{51}\right]}$$

$$GLP_{Inc} = \frac{31{,}050.10 \times \frac{1.022252415}{.9981182295}}{0.95 \times \left[\left(0.5 \times \frac{1.022252415}{.9981182295}\right) + 15.88113111\right]}$$

$$GLP_{Inc} = 2{,}041.98$$

The new GLP under the exact approach would be the sum of $GLP_{Old}$ and the $GLP_{Inc}$ (1,610.13 + 2,041.98, or $3,652.11).

### Decrease in Death Benefit Example

As discussed above, the attained-age decrement method applies to decreases in future benefits under the guideline premium test. This method is similar to that applied for increases in death benefits, except that the "after" calculation reflects a reduction in benefits. As also previously noted, certain types of benefit reductions can have the unfortunate consequence of producing negative guideline single and/or level premiums. Although it may be difficult to conceptualize a premium limitation defined in terms of a negative value, negative guideline premiums do occur in practice and must be properly incorporated into the administration of contracts.

The challenge posed by negative GLPs is that they produce a sum of GLPs which declines over time. In particular, if a contract's cumulative GLPs dictate the amount of a contract's guideline premium limitation, that limitation will decline each contract anniversary because of the negative increment (i.e., the decrement) to the cumulative GLPs. To the extent that a decrease in benefits eventually reduces the guideline premium limitation below premiums paid, any "excess" premium will need to be "forced out" of the contract.

The example in Table 4.4 illustrates an attained decrement adjustment that results in a negative guideline premium limitation. It assumes a $100,000 face amount issued at age 45, which is decreased to $50,000 at age 70.

- Sex: Male
- Age: 70
- (New) face amount: $50,000

- Mortality: 2001 CSO aggregate ANB
- Interest rate: 4.5 percent
- Expenses: 5 percent of premium, plus $5 monthly administrative fee

| Table 4.4. $50,000 decrease at age 70 | | | | |
|---|---|---|---|---|
| | GSP | GLP-DBO1 | GLP-DBO2 | NSP |
| At-issue value | 19,246.67 | 1,610.13 | 3,928.08 | 25,444.35 |
| Attained age 70 "before" | 51,799.62 | 61,124.24 | 12,363.75 | — |
| Attained age 70 "after" | 26,186.20 | 3,088.70 | 6,213.45 | — |
| Decrement | −25,613.42 | −3,025.54 | −6,150.30 | — |
| After decrease value | **−6,366.75** | **−1,415.41** | **−2,222.22** | 28,586.14 |

$$GSP(New)_{x+t} = GSP(Old)_x + \left(GSP(After)_{x+t} - GSP(Before)_{x+t}\right)$$

$$= 19{,}246.67 + (26{,}186.20 - 51{,}799.62) = \mathbf{-6{,}366.75}$$

$$GLP^{DBO1}(New)_{x+t} = GLP^{DBO1}(Old)_x + \left(GLP^{DBO1}(After)_{x+t} - GLP^{DBO1}(Before)_{x+t}\right)$$

$$= 1{,}610.13 + (3{,}088.70 - 6{,}114.24) = \mathbf{-1{,}415.41}$$

$$GLP^{DBO2}(New)_{x+t} = GLP^{DBO2}(Old)_x + \left(GLP^{DBO2}(After)_{x+t} - GLP^{DBO2}(Before)_{x+t}\right)$$

$$= 3{,}928.08 + (6{,}213.45 - 12{,}363.75) = \mathbf{-2{,}222.22}$$

$$NSP(New)_{x+t} = Face\ Amount(New) \times NSP_{x+t} = \mathbf{28{,}586.14}$$

Note that under the example, the GSP element of the guideline premium limitation becomes negative immediately, while the sum-of-GLPs element does not become negative until attained age 98. Such a transaction will require that any "excess" premiums be refunded to maintain compliance with the guideline premium limitation. This is illustrated in Figure 4.2. While the figure illustrates a negative guideline premium limitation, it is unclear as to whether the guideline premium limitation would ever be negative, or simply be floored at zero.

As a practical matter, an insurer may impose administrative procedures that limit negative GLPs, or otherwise limit decreases that may result in a negative overall guideline premium limitation. One solution to this situation may be to attempt to engage in a section 1035 exchange, but that may result in other consequences to the policyholder, including the imposition of additional expense charges resulting from the newly issued contract, higher mortality charges due to deteriorating health of the insured or even a denial of coverage should the insured become uninsurable.

The challenge of benefit decreases under the attained-age decrement rule may also be addressed through the election of a reduced paid-up (RPU) insurance nonforfeiture option, which some guideline premium-tested contracts provide. If the attained-age decrement method is applied to adjust the guideline premiums upon such an election, the manner of making the adjustments, and the consequences arising from the adjustments, are essentially the same as those discussed above, including the potential for "force-outs." However, as discussed in connection with the "Choice of Tests" in Chapter 2, a special rule in the DEFRA Blue Book provides an exception to the general maxim that once a contract has been administered under one of section 7702's tests, it must continue to be administered under that test. The special rule permits contracts qualifying under the guideline premium test to switch to the CVAT upon election of a nonforfeiture option.[29] By changing the contract from

---

[29] DEFRA Blue Book, *supra* Chapter 1, note 20, at 646, n. 50. No comparable discussion appears in the formal DEFRA legislative history.

**Figure 4.2.** Decrease in face amount: attained-age decrement

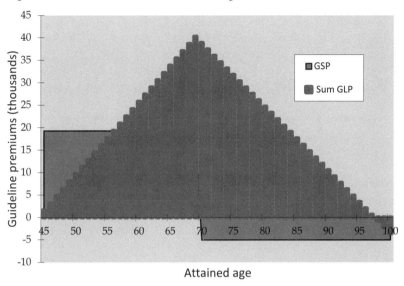

guideline premium testing to qualification under the CVAT when the RPU option is elected, the problem of a declining guideline premium limitation is avoided. That said, if this route is taken, it should be recognized that the RPU provisions of the contract must meet the requirements of the CVAT by their terms. In addition, other questions could arise upon the switch of tests, e.g., the switch could be viewed as tantamount to a new issuance of the contract, presenting potential grandfathering issues.[30] It should also be noted that in its discussion of the special rule, the DEFRA Blue Book stated that "any reinstatement of the original terms of such a contract would also reinstate the application of the original guideline premium test to the contract."[31] Precisely how that would be accomplished is unclear, as discussed further below.

## *Problems in Applying Guideline Premium Test Adjustments*

The attained-age adjustment rules under the guideline premium test have been the subject of a number of rulings issued by the IRS waiving noncompliance failures under section 7702(f)(8). The problems arose when the insurers involved failed to apply the attained-age increment and decrement method upon adjustment events, choosing to apply some other method instead. The waiver rulings demonstrate the logical attractiveness of alternative methods of adjusting the guideline premiums, at least as far as the insurers in the rulings were concerned, as well as the difficulty of the steps needed to be taken to remedy the problem in some cases.

One of the earliest examples of such a problem appeared in a 1992 private letter ruling granting a waiver under section 7702(f)(8).[32] The insurer involved had adjusted guideline premiums for contracts that underwent face amount decreases by using a "start all over" approach, as if there had been a full surrender and a new issuance. For decreases, this method produced guideline premiums higher than those resulting from the attained-age decrement method. The seeming logic of the insurer's approach (coupled, perhaps, with the rather disjointed legislative history on the subject) was apparently sufficient to convince the IRS that the error was reasonable, albeit an error, leading the IRS to grant the waiver.

---

[30] While viewing the election of an RPU benefit as a newly issued contract could provide a technical basis for test switching, such a construction of the statute is highly problematic. Insurers generally provide guarantees with respect to the mortality assumptions underlying RPU insurance features, and they cannot anticipate the mortality rates that may apply under CSO mortality tables that will only arise after a contract's actual issuance. Further, if election of RPU insurance were construed as a new contract issuance, the RPU insurance seemingly could fail to comply with the CVAT if there has been a change in the required mortality basis for newly issued contracts under IRC § 7702. If the DEFRA Blue Book reflects congressional intent and proper application of the statute for allowance of test switching when RPU insurance is elected, seemingly this avenue should not be construed to create a trap for the unwary.

[31] DEFRA Blue Book, *supra* Chapter 1, note 20, at 646, n. 50.

[32] PLR 9244010 (July 28, 1992).

In a similar vein, in waiver rulings in 1999,[33] the insurer had applied an adjustment method based on the original issue age of the insured, determining the guideline premium limitation that would apply had the contract originally been issued with the expectation that the benefits would increase or decrease on the date of the adjustment. The IRS noted that the insurer's "issue age" approach generally resulted in lower guideline premiums for an increase in benefits, and higher guideline premiums for a decrease, than would have been obtained by use of the attained-age adjustment method. (This method had the merit of avoiding the problem of a negative guideline premium limitation.) In its rulings waiving the errors, the IRS noted that "[c]onsiderable confusion has occurred in the application of the mechanics of the attained age decrement method.…"

A 2003 waiver ruling[34] addressed the application of the attained-age increment and decrement method to contracts designed to integrate traditional life insurance coverage with the flexibility of a universal life contract. Under the contracts, policyholders were accorded the ability to combine premium-paying whole life and term with paid-up life and paid-up deferred life insurance coverage. This was accomplished by using a policyholder account in connection with these coverages. During the life of the insured, the policyholder could modify, add or remove coverage elements. The plan sought to qualify under section 7702 using the guideline premium test.

According to the ruling, adjustments were made to the guideline premiums using an issue-age-based methodology in the cases of both increases and decreases in benefits. In reflecting adjustments, the insurer calculated a guideline premium for each element as of the date the element was issued, and then combined such guideline premiums for all of the elements to arrive at the new guideline premium. The IRS noted that, in the insurer's view, the attained-age decrement method "was designed for use in connection with universal policies, not policies such as the Contracts with fixed, traditional coverage elements and fixed charges therefore [sic]." Further, the insurer determined that the attained-age decrement method could not be applied in a manner that would allow gross premiums to be paid to maintain the contracts in force for the whole of life. Accordingly, the insurer determined that the issue-age methodology it employed was the only means by which it could make "proper" adjustments to the guideline premiums.

Ultimately, however, the insurer concluded that its issue-age adjustment method was inconsistent with the requirements of section 7702, and, as a result, a number of its contracts had premiums paid in excess of a properly computed guideline premium limitation. In concluding that the insurer's error was a reasonable one so that a waiver could be granted, the IRS noted the "legislative history is not clear as to the use of the attained-age increment-decrement method, nor is there a specific requirement for its use in section 7702(f)(7)(A)." In this connection, the IRS cited the lack of contemporaneous legislative history with respect to the attained-age decrement method in 1984 (see the discussion earlier in this chapter), although it noted that TRA 1986 contained technical corrections to the earlier legislation describing an attained-age decrement method to be used in making proper adjustments after a reduction in benefits.

Significantly, as the contracts involved in the ruling could not be successfully administered using the attained-age decrement rule, the insurer (with IRS approval) chose to amend all of its contracts so that they would be administered in the future under the CVAT. It did so by adding an endorsement to all in-force contracts (including failed contracts), effective retroactively to the original issue date. For those contracts where the current death benefit at the time of the endorsement was less than the new minimum death benefit under the endorsement, the insurer promised to increase the death benefit provided to meet the requirements of the CVAT.

## Reinstatements

As previously noted, the guideline premium test is most commonly applied to flexible premium universal life contracts, although it may apply to fixed premium universal life contracts as well. If a flexible premium contract lapses without value, the guideline premiums associated with the contract presumably cease to exist, as the contract is viewed as terminated for tax as well as for other purposes.[35] If, pursuant to the reinstatement rights that the contract provides to the policyholder, the contract is subsequently reinstated at its pre-existing death

---

[33] PLRs 200006030 and 200006032 (Nov. 10, 1999).
[34] PLR 200329040 (April 16, 2003).
[35] Recall that when a contract lapses with a policy loan outstanding, the tax law treats the payoff of the loan as a distribution from the contract, in the same manner as if the contract had been surrendered. See Appendix 1.1.

benefit amount, the question becomes whether the pre-existing guideline premiums are themselves reinstated or whether some other approach is indicated, perhaps using the attained-age adjustment methodologies. There may be some appeal to invoking the adjustment rule, since upon lapse the contract's death benefit decreased (to zero) and upon reinstatement that benefit increased back to where it was; this appears to be the view taken of the lapse and reinstatement situation under section 7702A (as discussed later) where the reinstatement occurs more than 90 days after the lapse. However, such guidance as exists on reinstatements of guideline premium-tested contracts counsels against using the adjustment rule in these circumstances. Rather, as previously noted, a special rule in the DEFRA Blue Book permitting such contracts to switch to the CVAT upon election of a nonforfeiture option, concluded by providing that "any reinstatement of the original terms of such a contract would also reinstate the application of the original guideline premium test to the contract."[36] Reawakening the pre-existing guideline premiums in the case of a reinstatement also adheres to the approach inherent in the state law treatment of a reinstatement, which generally resuscitates the contract in its prelapse form *nunc pro tunc*, albeit with a few exceptions. Consistently with that treatment, which essentially recognizes the reinstated contract as merely a continuation of the lapsed contract unchanged, the adjustment rule itself does not admit of its application unless there has been a change in a contract's future benefits (or other terms). Of course, following the blue book's instruction to "reinstate the application of the original guideline premium test" brings with it the need to use the premiums paid prior to the lapse in the testing going forward, a circumstance that can create a challenge for an underfunded contract as discussed above. That said, use of the pre-existing guideline premiums upon a reinstatement makes sense overall, avoiding a variety of puzzles that could arise in an attempt to apply the attained-age increment and decrement methodologies. It must be acknowledged, however, that the official guidance on this topic is thin, leaving the situation an uncertain one.

Where a flexible premium contract is reinstated with a change in its prelapse death benefit, it is of course not sufficient to use merely the pre-existing guideline premiums. Because the death benefit has changed at the time of the reinstatement, the pre-existing guideline premiums must be adjusted, employing the attained-age increment and decrement methodologies to account for the change. It is relatively easy to see how this may be accomplished in the case of a death benefit increase, where the attained-age layer added to the GSP and to each subsequent GLP enables additional funding for the reinstated contract. How a change to a reduced death benefit would be accomplished is far less certain insofar as the resulting decrements to the GSP and the subsequent GLPs may require force-outs from a contract that had previously lapsed without value. An insurer entertaining a request for reinstatement of a contract that had lapsed, e.g., due to the growth of a policy loan balance, would need to consider this situation.

A fixed premium contract subject to the guideline premium test also may lapse without value, but it could as well lapse due to nonpayment of its required premiums yet have a positive cash value. In the latter case, some amount of death benefit will remain, giving rise to two potential scenarios. In the first scenario, the continuing death benefit could be in a reduced amount, such as would be provided pursuant to the contract's RPU nonforfeiture option; this is the circumstance addressed by the DEFRA Blue Book's special rule mentioned above. If the special rule is availed of, the application of the guideline premium test to the contract yields to the application of the CVAT, assuming the RPU benefit complies with the CVAT by the contract's terms; upon reinstatement of the contract to its prelapse death benefit, the blue book's instruction to resume use of the pre-existing guideline premiums would then apply. If, on the other hand, the special rule is not (or cannot be) followed, then the adjustment rule applies to reduce the GSP and subsequent GLPs. In that unique setting, it would seem that upon reinstatement of the original death benefit, the adjustment rule should apply to increase the guideline premiums. In the second scenario, the amount of the death benefit remaining after the lapse could be unchanged from the prelapse benefit, pursuant to the contract's extended term insurance nonforfeiture option. In that case, the need or ability to apply the adjustment rule would not be apparent, and the pre-existing guideline premiums presumably would continue on as before. Of course, as was previously said, a reinstatement to a death benefit amount other than the prelapse amount would logically invoke application of the adjustment rule to the extent of the change from the prelapse amount. Again, though, it must be acknowledged that there is little official guidance on any of the foregoing.

---

[36] DEFRA Blue Book, *supra* Chapter 1, note 20, at 646, n. 50.

As the above discussion shows, there is complexity and some degree of uncertainty in the application of the guideline premium test to reinstated contracts. By and large, this is not the case with contracts subject to the CVAT. However, for both the CVAT and the guideline premium test, an issue has been raised by certain wording in Notice 2006-95, the latest guidance on "reasonable mortality," which was discussed at length in Chapter 2. One of the examples in section 5 of the notice, dealing with grandfathering of pre-2009 contracts from the need to use the 2001 CSO tables in the definitional calculations, intimated that such grandfathering would attach to a contract reinstated on or after January 1, 2009, only if the reinstatement occurred within 90 days of the lapse. Specifically, Notice 2006-95, after stating in section 5.02 that the grandfathering would attach to a changed contract if it was changed "pursuant to the terms of the contract" and continued on the same form (with no state law requirement to change to the 2001 CSO tables), provided in section 5.03 that the "changes, modifications, or exercises of contractual provisions referred to in section 5.02 include … reinstatement of a policy within 90 days after its lapse. …" It has been suggested that that item under section 5.03 of the notice constitutes a substantive limitation on the grandfathering relief otherwise extended by the notice. Such a view is difficult to reconcile with the private letter ruling the IRS issued in 2012, mentioned previously and discussed in detail in Chapter 5, declining to view the section 5.03 examples as having meaning independent of the section 5.02 rule.[37] For that matter, it is difficult to reconcile it with the wording of section 5.03 itself, which uses the term "include" to introduce the list of examples. If a limitation on the notice's grandfathering relief as to reinstated contracts—which typically are reinstated pursuant to a right granted to the policyholder in the lapsed contract—was intended by the reference in section 5.03, it was simply not expressed in a comprehensible manner. There also is little or no policy reason why the operative rule in section 5.02 should not exclusively control the consequences of a reinstatement for purposes of the notice.

## Adjustments Under Section 7702A

Two adjustment rules, both of which differ from the section 7702 adjustment rules, apply to the calculations under section 7702A—one for reductions in benefits that occur within the statute's 7-pay testing period and another for material changes. A special reduction-in-benefits rule applies to survivorship (i.e., second-to-die) products, requiring that the reduction-in-benefits treatment apply throughout the life of a contract. The treatment of survivorship contracts, including this special rule, is addressed in Chapter 6.

### *Reduction in Benefits*

Section 7702A(c)(2)(A) provides that if "benefits" under a contract are reduced during the first 7 contract years, then section 7702A is applied as if the contract had originally been issued at the reduced benefit level, and the new reduced limitation is applied to the cumulative amount paid under the contract for each of those first seven years. This includes the retroactive application of the reduced limitation to years within the 7-pay testing period that are prior to the occurrence of the benefit reduction. In this context, while the term "benefits" is not defined in the statute, it presumably refers to the contract's future benefits (death benefits, endowment benefits and those provided by a QAB[38]) previously reflected in the 7-pay premium calculation, paralleling the language of the section 7702(f)(7)(A) adjustment rule.

It should be noted that while this reduction-in-benefits rule applies by its terms only to reductions in the first seven contract years, a new 7-pay testing period begins at the time of a material change, which is treated as the issuance of a new contract. Absent a material change, reductions after the initial or currently applicable 7-pay testing period have no consequences unless the contract is a survivorship plan. (A discussion of the priority and relationship of the reduction-in-benefits rule and the material change rule appears at the con-

---

[37] PLR 201230009 (Jan. 30, 2012).
[38] Charges for a QAB that satisfy the reasonable expense charge rule are treated as "future benefits" under IRC § 7702(f)(5)(B), and such amounts, rather than the benefits provided by a QAB, are taken into account in calculating a contract's 7-pay premium. *See* IRC § 7702A(e)(3). While this treatment might imply that those charges similarly should be treated as "benefits" for purposes of the reduction in benefits rule of IRC § 7702A(c)(2) and otherwise under the statutes, there is no indication Congress intended such a result. Indeed, in the context of the computational rule of IRC § 7702(e)(1)(A), which generally precludes reflection of increasing benefits, the statute provides that "any qualified additional benefit … shall be deemed not to increase." This phrasing implies the benefits of a QAB itself that are taken into account, rather than its charges, must satisfy the computational rule. There is no reason the reference to "benefits" in IRC § 7702A(c)(2) should not be similarly construed, *i.e.*, as "benefits" as this term is ordinarily construed in the context of life insurance, and not as "future benefits" within the meaning of the statutes.

clusion of the material change rule below.) It may also be noted (perhaps stating the obvious) that a reduction in a benefit which was not reflected in the 7-pay premium calculations does not trigger application of the reduction-in-benefits rule, comparably to the case with the section 7702 adjustment rule and the section 7702A material change rule. Hence, since a short-term QAB (one lasting less than seven years) associated with a contract cannot be reflected in the 7-pay premium calculations, its expiration or removal is not subject to the reduction-in-benefits rule.

If, under the section 7702A(c)(2)(A) recomputation of the 7-pay premiums and retroactive application of the 7-pay test, a contract fails to satisfy the test for any prior contract year, the contract is considered a MEC. Further, according to section 7702A(d), the treatment of the contract as a MEC applies to:

- distributions that occur during the contract year in which "the failure takes effect" as well as in any subsequent contract year, and

- under regulations, distributions that occur "in anticipation" of a benefit reduction.

No such regulations have been issued, but a companion **look-back rule** in section 7702A(d) (in the flush language of this statute) treats distributions made within two years before the failure to meet the 7-pay test as having been made in anticipation of the failure. In the context of a benefit reduction and consequent failure to meet the 7-pay test due to the reduction-in-benefits rule, the date the "failure takes effect" is generally viewed as the date of the benefit reduction, although that is not completely clear. (And, to be completely clear, the section 7702A(d) rule applies to any 7-pay test failure, not solely to one occasioned by a benefit reduction.) Out of concern about the broad sweep of the reduction-in-benefits rule operating in combination with the two-year look-back rule, the TAMRA legislative history goes so far as to state that a full surrender of a contract is not a benefit reduction for purposes of these rules, thereby relieving the surrender situation—which inarguably does cause a reduction in benefits (down to zero)—from the worry that distributions made beforehand or at the time of surrender would be subjected to MEC treatment even though the contract was not a MEC prior to the surrender.[39]

An example of a benefit reduction causing a contract to become a MEC is shown in Table 4.5.

- Sex: Male
- Age: 45
- Face amount: $100,000, reduced to $80,000 after four years
- Mortality: 2001 CSO aggregate ANB
- Interest rate: 4.5 percent

| Table 4.5. Reduction in benefits under section 7702A | | | | | | |
|---|---|---|---|---|---|---|
| Year | Death benefit | Amount paid | Original limitation | | New limitation | |
| | | | Amount | Margin | Amount | Margin |
| 1 | 100,000 | 4,167.49 | 4,167.49 | 0.00 | 3,333.99 | −833.50 |
| 2 | 100,000 | 8,334.98 | 8,334.98 | 0.00 | 6,667.98 | −1,667.00 |
| 3 | 100,000 | 12,502.47 | 12,502.47 | 0.00 | 10,001.98 | −2,500.49 |
| 4 | 100,000 | 16,669.96 | 16,669.96 | 0.00 | 13,335.97 | −3,333.99 |
| 5 | 80,000 | 16,669.96 | — | — | 16,669.96 | 0.00 |

The example in Table 4.5 is interesting in that, in the absence of a premium payment in year five, the total amounts paid under the contract as of the fifth year are equal to the new 7-pay limit in that year. However, as the reduction-in-benefits rule applies the 7-pay test retroactively on a year-by-year basis, the contract becomes

---

[39] TAMRA Conference Report, *supra* Chapter 2, note 64, at 100, 102.

a MEC because the premiums paid in years one through four exceed the recomputed 7-pay premium limitation for those years.

At this juncture, one may ask why a rule like section 7702A(c)(2)(A), inflicting the maximum penalty under the statute (MEC status), is warranted merely because a policyholder asked for contractual benefits to be lowered during the 7-pay testing period. After all, section 7702 permits such reductions, merely treating them as requiring adjustments rather than as fatal violations of the statute. The need for a reduction-in-benefits rule in the section 7702A structure, however, is clear and compelling; without it, the statute would be devoid of integrity. This antiabuse rule prevents a policyholder from acquiring a policy with an inflated death benefit, paying the first of the 7-pay premiums for that benefit, and then reducing the death benefit to the amount that one premium would support as a single premium—ostensibly without having the contract incur MEC status. Since section 7702A(c)(2)(A) is an antiabuse rule, it will be construed, like other antiabuse measures in the tax law, broadly against the taxpayer so as to defeat any similar efforts to circumvent the 7-pay test. To the same end, the TAMRA legislative history cautions that the reduction-in-benefits rule applies "to any reduction in death benefits occurring during the first 7 contract years whether or not the reduction is considered an exchange of the original contract for a new contract."[40] Thus, according to the legislative history, an effort to escape the rule by employing an exchange of contracts during a 7-pay testing period (which otherwise would constitute a material change, giving rise to a contract treated as newly issued) will not be availing.

> **A Cautionary Note: The Double Meaning of "Material Change"**
>
> When a reader sees a term like "desert," one of two meanings come to mind: a verb connoting abandonment and a dry, sandy place that may contain cactus or camels. When an insurance tax practitioner sees the term "material change," two meanings also come to mind. The first is the one discussed in this chapter, i.e., the change that triggers the application of section 7702A(c)(3), leading to a new 7-pay testing period. The second is the one discussed in Chapter 5, invoking application of a broad doctrine of the federal tax law that can be fundamentally disruptive of the tax treatment of life insurance contracts.

The computational rules of section 7702A(c)(2) also address situations involving benefit reductions related to the nonpayment of premium, i.e., contract lapse. In particular, section 7702A(c)(2)(B) excuses the need to reflect a benefit reduction due to a lapse for nonpayment of premiums when benefits are reinstated within 90 days of the reduction/lapse. However, due to the limited nature of the relief provided by section 7702A(c)(2)(B), the lapse of a contract with no value during a 7-pay testing period can result in application of the 7-pay test with a 7-pay premium equal to zero if the contract's benefits are reinstated more than 90 days following the lapse. This, in turn, will most likely cause the contract to be a MEC.[41] For contracts reinstated from an RPU nonforfeiture option, the nonforfeiture benefits would represent the applicable benefits under the reduction-in-benefits rule. The potential application of the section 7702A(c)(3) material change rule upon the reinstatement of a contract more than 90 days after a lapse is discussed below.

## *Material Changes*

At contract issuance, the 7-pay test is applied to a contract based on the future benefits at that time. When changes occur to a contract, other than a reduction in benefits, the material change rule of section 7702A(c)(3) may apply. According to the statute, the rule generally will apply in the event of "a material change in the benefits under (or in other terms of) the contract which was not reflected in any previous determination under this section."[42] It is important to note that the material change rule applies throughout the life of a contract, i.e., it does not cease applying after a contract passes through a 7-pay testing period without becoming a MEC. The House Ways and Means Committee's report accompanying the TAMRA enactment notes:

---

[40] H.R. Rep. No. 100-795, at 479, n. 166 (1988) (hereinafter TAMRA House Report).
[41] This result is unfortunate. Since contracts typically permit reinstatements, subject to stated conditions, within three to five years after a lapse, the 90-day limit of the IRC § 7702A(c)(2)(B) relief rule represents a trap for the unwary, or at least for those not particularly speedy about curing a lapse.
[42] IRC § 7702A(c)(3)(A).

If there is a material change in the benefits or other terms of the contract *at any time that a life insurance contract is outstanding* that was not reflected in any previous determination under the 7-pay test, the contract is considered a new contract that is subject to the 7-pay test as of the date the material change takes effect.[43]

Section 7702A does not itself provide a comprehensive definition of what it calls a material change, but the wording of section 7702A(c)(3)(A) quoted above, echoed in the legislative history just referenced, indicates that *any* change in a contract's future benefits is potentially a material change, so long as that change was not previously taken into account in the calculation of the 7-pay premiums. Significantly, this reference to reflection in the previous calculation parallels a concept in the section 7702 adjustment rule, i.e., that if the purported change actually was already in the calculation of the definitional limitation, it does not count as a change.[44] The TAMRA legislative history adds two specific items to the list of changes that are material: a contract exchange, whether or not tax-free under section 1035, and a conversion of term coverage to whole life coverage. It also removes reductions in benefits from the list, for the reason that reductions are subject to their own, exclusive rule as discussed above.[45] As this shows, many changes in the benefits or terms under a contract that would be considered adjustment events under section 7702 would be treated as section 7702A material changes.[46]

But the foregoing does not exhaust all that the statute has to say about what is (or is not) a material change. Rather, section 7702A(c)(3)(B) steps in with a significant addition coupled with a significant (and highly complex) limitation. First, it provides that "any increase" in a contract's death benefit or any increase in, or addition of, a QAB under the contract is a material change. Given the sweep of this statement, without more, the purchase of any paid-up addition under a participating whole life contract, any corridor-driven death benefit increase under a universal life contract and any increase in cash value under a contract with an option 2 death benefit, would occasion a material change, with important consequences as discussed below. Then section 7702A(c)(3)(B) limits what it just said: Material change treatment does not apply if either of the following is true.

- The increase is attributable to the payment of premiums necessary to fund the lowest level of the death benefit and QABs payable during the 7-pay testing period (subject to certain increasing benefit rules) or to the crediting of interest or other earnings (including policyholder dividends) in respect of those **necessary premiums**. This rule, stated in 7702A(c)(3)(B)(i) and known colloquially as the necessary premium test (NPT), is the subject of detailed discussion later in this chapter.

- The increase is a cost-of-living increase, based on an established broad-based index, but only if, as specified in 7702A(c)(3)(B)(ii),
  - the increase is funded ratably over the required premium-paying period of the contract, and
  - it is so provided in regulations.
  - There are no such regulations, however, nor will there likely ever be.[47] Hence, there is no escape from material change treatment solely because an increase in future benefits is cost-of-living driven.

Upon the occurrence of a material change, section 7702A(c)(3)(A) provides that the contract is treated, for purposes of section 7702A, as a new contract entered into on the day on which the material change takes effect. That is, a material change to a life insurance contract causes the contract to be treated as if it were newly issued or, in section 7702A terms, "entered into," on the date of the change. Consequently, on that date new 7-pay premiums will be calculated, based on the (changed) future benefits and the attained age of the insured

---

[43] TAMRA House Report, *supra* note 40, at 480 (emphasis added).
[44] As noted at the outset of this chapter, it is possible a contractual exchange is sufficiently fundamental that it is treated as an exchange under IRC § 1001, which would imply that the change is an IRC § 7702A material change in any event. This is discussed in Chapter 5. On the other hand, it is clear that changes that can have no effect on the IRC § 7702A calculations, *e.g.*, a change in contract ownership or in the dividend option selected under a participating contract, do not amount to material changes.
[45] TAMRA House Report, *supra* note 40, at 480.
[46] This may include, *e.g.*, a correction in a contract's death benefit and/or its mortality guarantees due to a misstatement of age or sex.
[47] Not long after the enactment of IRC § 7702A, representatives of the life insurance industry learned this in informal discussions with the Treasury Department.

at that time, and the contract will be tested from that point forward, over the ensuing seven contract years, to determine whether it will meet a new 7-pay test. For a materially changed contract, however, the new 7-pay premiums will be computed reflecting the CSV (i.e., the cash surrender value as defined in section 7702(f)(2)) at the time of the change under the rollover rule (discussed below).

Where a non-MEC contract either has lapsed for nonpayment of premiums during a 7-pay testing period but is reinstated within 90 days of the lapse or has otherwise lapsed and then been reinstated pursuant to the terms of the contract, there is no guidance specifically addressing whether the reinstatement itself constitutes a material change under section 7702A(c)(3). In the former case, it seems material change treatment should not apply, partly because section 7702A(c)(2)(B) instructs that the temporary reduction in benefits (due to the lapse) is to be disregarded, and partly because the benefits on which the 7-pay premiums for the contract are calculated have not changed from what they were before the lapse (assuming the reinstated benefits actually equal the prelapse benefits). For other reinstatements, the answer is somewhat less clear. It may be that the increase in benefits from zero to their prelapse amount upon the reinstatement falls within the legislative history admonition that a change in benefits at any time can be a material change. If so, a new 7-pay testing period would attach to the contract, albeit with the benefit of new, attained-age 7-pay premiums. On the other hand, as was the response in the prior case, the benefits on which the 7-pay premiums for the reinstated contract are calculated have not changed from what they were before the lapse (again assuming the reinstated benefits actually equal the prelapse benefits). Under this view, there would be no material change, and thus no new testing period, since the reinstated benefits have in fact been "reflected in any previous determination" under the statute within the meaning of section 7702A(c)(3)(A).

With respect to the relationship of the reduction-in-benefits and material change rules, the TAMRA legislative history makes it clear, as already noted, that a reduction in benefits within the meaning of section 7702A(c)(2) is not a material change covered by section 7702A(c)(3).[48] Rather, the reduction-in-benefits rule governs contract changes to which it applies, to the exclusion of the material change rule. However, neither the statute nor its legislative history says much else about the relationship of the two rules, and yet their relationship, including the priority of application between the two, frequently warrants careful consideration. In this regard, several observations may be in order.

- As described earlier in this chapter, the reduction-in-benefits rule is an antiabuse rule, one necessary for integrity of the 7-pay test. Accordingly, where multiple contract changes occur simultaneously and both the reduction-in-benefits rule and the material change rule can apply—e.g., where a death benefit is increased and a QAB is removed during a 7-pay testing period—preference presumably should be given to application of the reduction rule, after which the material change rule may be applied.

- During a testing period, whether it be the first seven years of a contract or a 7-pay period begun thereafter, it is possible for multiple material changes to occur. This would be the case, for example, where a cost-of-living adjustment provision in the contract (or rider) increased the death benefit annually and the insurer chose not to apply the NPT to defer the material changes. In such a circumstance, it is also possible that a reduction in benefits could occur within the testing period, as by a decision to remove a QAB. This raises a question whether the reduction-in-benefits rule should be applied back to the most recent of the material changes or, alternatively, further back in the chain of changes. The TAMRA legislative history may be read to require the latter, at least in the case of a reduction within the actual first seven years of a contract,[49] although this is not clear. As a practical matter, insurers' administrative systems generally can be expected to relate the reduction back to the most recent material change.

- While the legislative history of section 7702A provides that the reduction-in-benefits rule will apply to benefit reductions within a 7-pay testing period even if the transaction otherwise constitutes an exchange,[50] insurers may not be able to apply this rule readily in the case of section 1035 exchanges

---

[48] TAMRA Conference Report, *supra* Chapter 2, note 64, at 101–02.
[49] *See* TAMRA House Report, *supra* note 40, at 479, n. 166 ("This rule applies to any reduction in death benefits occurring during the first 7 contract years whether or not the reduction is considered an exchange of the original contract for a new contract.").
[50] *Id.*

where the new life insurance contract is issued by a different insurer; however, insurers should exercise caution in connection with internal exchanges since they may have information available to them to ascertain whether the transaction would cause the prior contract to become a MEC based on the reduction rule.

## *The Rollover Rule*

In computing the 7-pay premium for a materially changed contract, as noted above, the calculations are based on the future benefits then provided by the contract and the insured's then attained age. While this computation is comparable to that for any newly issued contract having the benefits (and other terms) of the materially changed contract, "appropriate adjustments" are made to the computed 7-pay premium for the changed contract, as provided in section 7702A(c)(3)(A)(ii), to take into account the contract's existing CSV at the time of the change. This computation, using what is termed the **rollover rule**, thus differs from a guideline premium adjustment made pursuant to section 7702(f)(7), as the latter uses attained-age increments (and decrements) based on the change in coverage without regard to a contract's CSV.

The rollover rule is described in the conference report for TAMRA, which supersedes a slightly different calculation described in the prior House report.[51] According to the conference report, to compute the rollover rule adjustment to the 7-pay premium, the CSV as of the date of the material change is multiplied by a fraction, the numerator of which is the 7-pay premium computed for future benefits under the changed contract, and the denominator of which is the NSP for such benefits computed employing the same assumptions as used in determining that 7-pay premium. The result is then subtracted from the computed 7-pay premium to produce the adjusted 7-pay premium, a process illustrated in Table 4.6.

The section 7702A rollover rule may thus be thought of as analogous to the CVAT adjustment rule. Under the CVAT, the maximum premium that can be paid in connection with an adjustment is an amount that would generate a CSV equal to the portion of the new NSP that is not supported by the existing CSV. Under the rollover rule, the face amount that is not funded by the existing CSV serves as the basis for the new 7-pay premium calculation. A key difference, however, is that the CVAT is continually adjusted, while the 7-pay test is adjusted only in response to a material change.

Special considerations attendant to application of the rollover rule apply in the context of contract exchanges. While a contract issued in an exchange of contracts is treated as a new issue for tax purposes generally, including under section 7702A, a contract's status as a MEC cannot be eliminated by an exchange of contracts since a life insurance contract received in exchange for a MEC is itself a MEC.[52] Further, a material change under section 7702A includes the exchange of a life insurance contract for another life insurance contract, requiring the application of the rollover rule in determining the new 7-pay limitation. This rule is far more favorable than treatment of the transferred value as premium to be counted against the new 7-pay limit.[53] Presumably, a taxable exchange of contracts is just as entitled to the use of the rollover rule as is a tax-free exchange under section 1035, although the legislative history describing the rollover rule does not specifically discuss this point.

In describing the rollover calculation, section 7702A(c)(3)(A)(ii) uses the phrase "cash surrender value under the contract." Thus, the cash surrender value used in the calculation of the new 7-pay premium on an exchange of contracts is generally the CSV present at the time of the exchange. This leaves the question, however, regarding when such CSV should be measured, e.g., under the old or new contract and before or after the imposition of charges, explicit or implicit, then imposed. In 2000, section 7702A(3)(a)(ii) was amended to substitute the phrase "under the old contract" for "under the contract."[54] However, this change in statutory language was

---

[51] The House report would have used the greater of the CSV or the premiums paid to the date of the material change. *See* TAMRA House Report, *supra* note 40, at 480.

[52] The Community Renewal Tax Relief Act of 2000, Pub. L. No. 106-554, § 318(a)(1), amended IRC § 7702A(a)(2) to make clear that if a life insurance contract became a MEC, the MEC status could not be eliminated by exchanging the MEC for another contract. The concern was that IRC § 7702A(a)(2), as originally written, might be read to allow a policyholder to exchange a MEC for a contract that does not fail the 7-pay test of IRC § 7702A(b), then exchange the second contract for a third contract, which would not literally have been received in exchange for a contract that failed to meet the 7-pay test. The provision is effective as if enacted with TAMRA (generally, for contracts entered into on or after June 21, 1988).

[53] The general rule that an exchange gives rise to a newly issued contract for IRC §§ 7702 and 7702A purposes (among others) may not apply, it appears, where the new contract is issued in connection with a partition or division of the existing contract. See the discussion of PLR 200651023 (Sept. 21, 2006) in Chapter 5.

[54] Pub. L. No. 106-554, § 1(a)(7) [tit. III, § 318(a)(2)].

short-lived; it was repealed in 2002.[55] Although the 2000 amendment may have been intended to clarify the application of the rollover rule, the amendment was ambiguous, did not necessarily reflect funding provided for the materially changed contract and arguably led to adjustments in 7-pay premiums in amounts greater than were contemplated by Congress in its enactment of the original rule. Further, while the 2002 legislative history implies the reversal was undertaken because no clarification was needed,[56] that point remains debatable.

Because a contract's existing CSV is used to reduce the 7-pay premium for a materially changed contract, only premiums paid subsequently to the material change, and any "unnecessary" premium (as described later) at the time of the material change, are subjected to the new 7-pay test.[57] Note that, due to the rollover rule, it is possible for the adjusted 7-pay premium to be negative (where the CSV exceeds the NSP for the changed contract). When this happens (and the pre-existing contract was not a MEC), the materially changed contract is not considered a MEC, provided that no premium is paid during the ensuing 7 years and no unnecessary premiums need to be counted as amount paid for the new 7-pay test period.[58]

## Material Change Example

The example in Table 4.6 illustrates an increase in death benefits that is treated as a material change. This treatment results in the start of a new 7-year test period on the effective date of the death benefit increase. The new test period, in turn, requires the calculation of a new 7-pay premium, the amount of which is reduced based on the rollover rule.

Assume the following change in the facts of Table 4.5 five years after contract issuance:

- Sex: Male
- Age: 50
- Face amount: $200,000
- Mortality: 2001 CSO aggregate ANB
- Interest rate: 4.5 percent

Under the rollover rule, the newly computed 7-pay premium is adjusted by the ratio of the cash surrender value to the attained-age NSP, as follows:

$$7Pay(Adj) = 7Pay(New) - CV \times \frac{7Pay(New)}{NSP} \tag{4.5}$$

$$7Pay(Adj) = 7Pay(New) \times \left(1 - \frac{CV}{NSP}\right)$$

$$7Pay(Adj) = 10,028.54 \times \left(1 - \frac{12,000.00}{60,994.24}\right) = \mathbf{8,055.53}$$

---

[55] Pub. L. No. 107-147, tit. IV, § 416(f), provided, in part, that "clause (ii) of section 7702A(c)(3)(A) shall read and be applied as if the amendment made by such paragraph had not been enacted."

[56] Technical Explanation of 2002 Act, *supra* Chapter 3, note 15, at 45 (stating: "No reference is needed to the cash surrender under the 'old contract' ... because prior and present law provide a definition of cash surrender value for this purpose (by cross reference to section 7702(f)(2)(A))").

[57] TAMRA Conference Report, *supra* Chapter 2, note 64, at 105.

[58] H.R. Rep. No. 101-247, at 1439 (1989) (hereinafter OBRA (Omnibus Budget Reconciliation Act of 1989) House Report).

| Table 4.6. Section 7702A rollover calculation | |
|---|---|
| Current death benefit | 100,000 |
| Current cash surrender value | 12,000.00 |
| Age 50 7-pay per $1,000 | 50.143 |
| Age 50 NSP per $1,000 | 304.971 |
| New death benefit | 200,000 |
| 7-pay before rollover | 10,028.54 |
| NSP for death benefit | **60,994.24** |
| Ratio of cash value to NSP | 19.674% |
| Adjustment factor for 7-pay | 80.326% |
| New 7-pay | **8,055.53** |

Note that, as no unnecessary premium presumably has been paid under the contract in the example, the increase in face amount may be viewed as not creating a material change under the necessary premium exception discussed below.

## Necessary Premiums

Section 7702A(c)(3)(B), as noted above, defines the term **material change** to include "any increase in the death benefit under the contract, or any increase in, or addition of, a qualified additional benefit under the contract." However, the material change rules were intended to distinguish voluntary additions in coverage from those that result from the normal operation of the contract (e.g., increases resulting from the application of dividends to purchase paid-up additions, or from the operation of the section 7702(d) corridor). The necessary premium rule of section 7702A(c)(3)(B)(i) is designed to accomplish this, providing relief from the material change rules for these increases in coverage. In practice, though, the necessary premium rule has a broader application, as any increase in future benefits, regardless of the source of the increase, need not be treated as a material change unless premiums in excess of the necessary premium (i.e., "unnecessary premiums") have been contributed to the contract.

In concept, the necessary premium is the premium required under the contract's guarantees (subject to the reasonable mortality and expense limitations) to fund the lowest future benefits during the initial seven contract years (or for seven years following a material change). Technically speaking, section 7702A(c)(3)(B)(i) provides that the term "material change" does not include any benefit increase "which is attributable to the payment of premiums necessary to fund the lowest level of death benefit and [QABs] payable in the $1^{st}$ 7 contract years (determined after taking into account death benefit increases described in [section 7702(e)(2)(A) or (B)]) or to crediting of interest or other earnings (including policyholder dividends) in respect of such premiums."

The necessary premium rule effectively imposes an additional premium-based test on contracts. As will be discussed in more detail below, the necessary premium test requires tracking premium payments to determine whether a premium is a necessary premium. The standard for determining whether a premium is necessary (i.e., the necessary premium limitation) will vary based on the section 7702 qualification test a contract is designed to comply with. The basis for determining whether a premium payment is a necessary premium will parallel how the funding limitation is defined under section 7702.

For contracts designed to qualify under the guideline premium test, the necessary premium limitation is defined in terms of a "guideline premium limitation," which may be different from the guideline premium limitation used to establish compliance with section 7702. Thus, a premium would be necessary if it does not result in cumulative premiums exceeding the version of the guideline premium limitation used in applying the necessary premium rule.

For contracts designed to qualify under the CVAT, the necessary premium limitation is defined in terms of the contract's cash value determined based on certain assumptions (the **deemed cash surrender value**) at the time of the premium payment. More specifically, a premium is necessary if it does not cause the contract's deemed cash surrender value to exceed the contract's net single premium. As will be discussed in more detail below, both the deemed cash surrender value and net single premium used for defining a necessary premium have a specific definition that may differ from the CSV and the NSP used for determining compliance with the CVAT.

The operation of the necessary premium rule—or, again, the necessary premium test or NPT—is a creature[59] of the TAMRA legislative history. It was first described in that history in 1988, the details of which appear below under two separate headings relating to the guideline premium test and the CVAT, since the legislative history says that the NPT applies differently as between the two section 7702 tests. At this stage, however, it is important to understand a concept of the NPT that applies in both cases. Specifically, when section 7702A was revisited by Congress to make technical corrections in the statute the year after its enactment, the "broader application" of the NPT referenced above was the subject of congressional instruction. Thus, the legislative history of the Omnibus Budget Reconciliation Act of 1989 (OBRA)[60] provided:

> For this purpose, a death benefit increase *may* be considered as attributable to the payment of premiums necessary to fund the lowest death benefit payable in the first 7 contract years or the crediting of interest or other earnings with respect to such premiums if each premium paid prior to the death benefit increase is necessary to fund the lowest death benefit payable in the first 7 contract years. Any death benefit increase that is not considered a material change under the preceding sentence, however, is to be considered a material change as of the date that a premium is paid that is not necessary to fund the lowest death benefit payable in the first 7 contract years.[61]

Use of the word "may" in the quoted passage conveys a sense of choice, and, as noted in connection with Table 4.6 above, the statement is generally interpreted to mean that an insurer may treat a benefit increase as a material change, but if it chooses to defer recognition of a material change (presuming that no unnecessary premium has been paid), a material change must then be recognized no later than the first arrival of an unnecessary premium payment. Further, when a QAB is increased or added after issue, the statutory language of section 7702A(3)(B)(i) appears to allow the application of the necessary premium rule to the QAB, too, although the OBRA legislative history refers simply to "any death benefit increase." The use of "may," however, does not mean the NPT can simply be ignored, as the OBRA legislative history limits discretion (i.e., only to such time as an unnecessary premium is paid) and the statute is unequivocal. Thus, the NPT is central to determining whether and when a material change occurs. This conclusion is reinforced by a TAMRA legislative history rule requiring the testing of any unnecessary premium against the post-change 7-pay premium limitation,[62] in that such testing of that portion of a premium is premised upon the testing of each premium against the necessary premium limitation.

The optionality in the operation of the NPT may best be explained by an example. If a policyholder wishes to increase the death benefit or add a QAB after contract issuance, the necessary premium rule as construed in the OBRA legislative history would allow a choice: treat the increase as a material change, in which case a new 7-pay test period would apply, or defer recognition of the material change to the time that an unnecessary premium is paid under the contract. While life insurance companies commonly look to the NPT for deferring recognition of potential material changes that occur through the normal operation of the contract, such as option 2 death benefit increases, section 7702(d) corridor increases, and paid-up additions purchased with policyholder dividends, some companies are also applying the NPT to defer recognition of other increases. These include increases in death benefits resulting from underwritten face amount increases, non-underwritten increases for a cost-of-living feature or a guaranteed insurability option, and paid-up additions purchased with premium payments. Still other companies apply the NPT to defer recognition of certain types of increases (e.g., non-underwritten increases) while choosing to treat other increases as material changes when they occur (e.g.,

---

[59] See, for example, "Creature from the Black Lagoon" (1954). (As in "Not since the beginning of time has the world beheld terror like this!")
[60] Pub. L. No. 101-239.
[61] OBRA House Report, *supra* note 58, at 1438–39 (emphasis added).
[62] According to the TAMRA Conference Report, the unnecessary portion of the premium that gave rise to the material change is itself tested against the 7-pay limitation of the materially changed contract. This rule seeks to close an obvious loophole whereby a premium payment could otherwise escape from MEC testing. TAMRA Conference Report, *supra* Chapter 2, note 64, at 105.

underwritten increases). Given the optionality reflected in the 1989 OBRA legislative history, these practices all appear to be warranted.[63]

Use of the necessary premium exception to material change treatment will typically require the tracking of premium to determine whether unnecessary premium has been paid. It is important to note that the presence of unnecessary premium in a contract will result in retesting for any death benefit increase, even if resulting from paid-up additions purchased with policyholder dividends or from corridor increases required by section 7702(d), and whether the increase occurs within the first seven contract years or later. Further, in the case of a contract that is materially changed as a result of an increase in future benefits attributable (or attributed) to the payment of an unnecessary premium, the unnecessary portion of the premium is to be subject to the new 7-pay test, as previously noted, without regard to the timing of the premium payment. The NPT thus amounts to a fourth test imposed under the definitional limitations, joining the CVAT, the guideline premium test and the 7-pay test.

While the NPT's operation implies that an insurer has a choice of treating benefit increases (even including the purchase of paid-up additions with dividends) as material changes at the time they occur, or deferring the recognition of such increases until such time as unnecessary premiums are paid into the contract, the choice of methods may create different results for similarly situated policyholders. It may also result in a contract becoming a MEC under one method but not another. Thus, in some cases, treating the increase as a material change could significantly reduce the 7-pay premium due to application of the rollover rule, a result the policyholder may wish to avoid and that may be possible to accomplish by making use of the necessary premium rule.

The NPT is administratively complex and may be costly to implement. Notably, the application of the NPT with respect to a sequence of policy changes is subject to interpretation.[64] At the same time, however, continuous application of the material change rule due to death benefit increases (e.g., in the case of death benefits geared to cost-of-living adjustments) may result in a reduction of the 7-pay premium limitation over time as a result of the repeated use of the rollover rule or as a result of the attachment of the reduction-in-benefits rule beyond what would otherwise have been the end of the 7-pay testing period. This may potentially cause a contract to become a MEC in circumstances where use of the necessary premium exception to material change treatment would prevent it.

## *Necessary Premiums Under the Guideline Test*

As noted above, the standard for applying the NPT differs depending upon whether the contract is administered under the guideline premium test or the CVAT. For contracts that qualify as life insurance under the guideline premium test, a premium is considered necessary to fund the lowest death benefit (and any QABs) payable during the 7-pay testing period to the extent the premium paid does not exceed the excess, if any, of:

1) the greater of the GSP or the sum of the GLPs to date based on those lowest benefits, over

2) the sum of premiums previously paid under the contract.

According to the legislative history, these guideline single and level premiums are to be determined using the computational rules of section 7702(e) and the assumption that the "lowest" benefits payable during the 7-pay testing period is provided until the deemed maturity date of the contract, except the death benefit increases described in section 7702(e)(2)(A) may be taken into account.[65] Thus, under the guideline premium test, the necessary premium is defined in terms of the guideline premium limitation for the lowest death benefit (and any QABs) payable during the 7-pay testing period. To the extent the premiums actually paid under the contract do not exceed this version of the guideline premium limitation, any increase that occurs in the death benefit need not result in a material change.

In administering the NPT under the guideline premium test, it is important to note that the guideline premium limitation for a contract under section 7702 is not always equal to the version of that limitation applied under the NPT.

---

[63] Contract design and systems considerations often drive the manner in which insurers apply the NPT.
[64] See the discussions below in connection with the guideline premium test and the CVAT.
[65] *See* TAMRA Conference Report, *supra* Chapter 2, note 64, at 105.

- If there has been a benefit increase that was an adjustment event under section 7702 but was not recognized as a material change under section 7702A, or if a contract was issued with a short-term (less than seven-year) QAB that is reflected in the section 7702 guideline premium limitation but not in the version of it used in the NPT, the necessary premium limitation will not equal the section 7702 guideline premium limitation. On the other hand, a section 7702 adjustment event coincident with a section 7702A material change will have the beneficial effect of resetting the "lowest level" of benefits to take account of the increased benefits.

- Further, a benefit decrease may also cause these two limits to differ. One plausible reading of the operation of the NPT in the case of a benefit reduction during a 7-pay testing period is that a re-determination of the necessary premium is required by virtue of the reduction-in-benefits rule of section 7702A(c)(2).[66] Under this reading, the guideline single and level premiums, for purposes of the NPT, would be redetermined from issue (or a prior material change) based on the reduced benefits.[67] Carrying this line of reasoning forward, moreover, may require retesting for unnecessary premium from the contract's original issue date (or material change date) based on the lower necessary premium limits, paralleling the application of the 7-pay test for benefit reductions. One consequence of this approach is that it may create the need to recognize a material change prior to the effective date of the benefit reduction if unnecessary premium arises as a result of the reduced NPT limitation (and assuming there was an increase in benefits not previously recognized as a material change). Such treatment arguably is not needed, however, since the legislative history generally provides that a reduction in benefits subject to section 7702A(c)(2) should not be treated as a material change.[68] Another possibility, by way of simplifying administration, would be to assume an unnecessary premium has been paid whenever there is a benefit reduction, thereby triggering a material change upon the next benefit increase regardless of the source of the increase. How far this reasoning should be extended is not clear.

It is worth noting that contract administrative systems do not always separately track a necessary premium limitation for contracts administered under the guideline premium test, relying instead on the premise that the limitation under the NPT and the guideline premium limitation are identical. Under such an approach, it is assumed the payment of any unnecessary premium would result in noncompliance with section 7702 and therefore could not have been accepted in the first instance. While this premise may hold true for contracts that have not undergone any adjustments under section 7702(f)(7)(A), once contract changes occur and guideline premiums are altered as a result, the NPT limitation and the guideline premium limitation may diverge as just described.

Relying on the guideline premium limitation as the necessary premium limitation has several consequences that will affect how certain changes are administered under section 7702A, particularly with respect to material changes. Any section 7702(f)(7)(A) adjustment event that gives rise to a change in the guideline premiums arguably would need to be treated as a material change under section 7702A. Indeed, to maintain consistency between the measure of necessary premium and the guideline premium limitation, any death benefit increase or QAB addition or increase administered as a section 7702 adjustment must be administered as a material change. Further, a change in the death benefit option itself usually would need to be administered as a material change. Thus, relying on a contract's guideline premium limitation as the necessary premium limitation will greatly restrict the ability to avoid material changes via the necessary premium exception.

Even accepting such restrictions, the use of the guideline premium limitation as the measure of necessary premium can be problematic in certain instances. As indicated above, benefit reductions may create differences between the guideline premium limitation and the necessary premium limitation based on both the manner in which the reductions are reflected in the respective limitations (i.e., attained-age-based adjustments vs. issue-age-based reductions) and whether they are reflected in each of the respective limitations (e.g., in the case of

---

[66] Applying this rule, one could also conclude that a benefit reduction occurring after a 7-pay testing period has ended does not require an adjustment to the necessary premium, as that amount is, by definition, based on the lowest benefits during the 7-pay testing period.

[67] This approach creates a certain tension between the adjustment methodologies of the two statutes. The computational rules of IRC § 7702A(c)(2) require the contract to be viewed as originally issued at the reduced benefit level, suggesting an issue-age adjustment methodology is appropriate; such a methodology differs from the attained-age approach for adjusting guideline premiums for IRC § 7702 purposes.

[68] TAMRA House Report, *supra* note 40, at 480.

reductions outside a 7-pay testing period). Further, as discussed in Chapter 3, the definitional limitations may allow certain term insurance riders (e.g., a 10-year-term rider on the primary insured) to be viewed as providing "death benefit" for purposes of section 7702A but only as a QAB for purposes of section 7702. In addition, the rule limiting the necessary premium to the amount needed to fund the lowest level of benefits in the 7-pay testing period restricts the ability to incorporate short-term QABs into the necessary premium determination even though they are included in the guideline premium limitation.

In sum, certain changes to a contract may create a necessary premium limitation that is either higher or lower than the guideline premium limitation. Once differences begin to emerge between an appropriate measure of necessary premium and the guideline premium limitation, the guideline premium limitation may no longer serve as an appropriate (or even approximate) measure of the necessary premium limitation. Where an administrative system cannot track the guideline premium limitation separately for purposes of the NPT, an insurer may be limited in its ability to defer the recognition of material changes using the unnecessary premium exception, needing instead to treat each section 7702 adjustment and other death benefit increases as a section 7702A material change (or, where applicable, as subject to the reduction-in-benefits rule).

## *Necessary Premiums Under the CVAT*

For a CVAT product, a premium is "necessary" so long as the "net" amount of it does not exceed the difference between

- the attained age NSP for the lowest death benefit and any QABs during the 7-pay testing period, and
- the lesser of
  - the policy's "deemed cash surrender value," or
  - the actual CSV.

Said otherwise, and tracking the instructions given in the TAMRA legislative history, a premium is considered necessary to fund the lowest death benefit and any QABs payable during the testing period to the extent that the net amount of premium does not exceed the excess of

- the "attained-age net single premium for such benefits provided under contract immediately before the premium payment, over
- the deemed cash surrender value[69] of the contract (or its actual CSV value, if lower) immediately before the premium payment.[70]

For this purpose:

- **Net amount of premium:** The premium payment to be tested against the excess of (1) over (2) above is only its net amount, not its gross amount as is tested under the NPT for a guideline premium contract. The CVAT operates on a net premium basis, and so only the net amount of the premium payment must be tested under the CVAT-based NPT. What is this net premium? Or, in other words, by what amount (if any) is the gross premium payment reduced to yield this net premium? The TAMRA Conference Report instructs that the reduction amount equals "any expense charge."[71] While universal life-type contracts typically will disclose their guaranteed premium loading charges, and any lower charges actually imposed presumably can be determined from contract illustrations and annual reports, this is not usually the case with traditional whole life contracts (whether or not participating). For the latter, one sensible approach would be to treat the "net amount of premium" as the premium that "ties" successive terminal cash values, taking into account the interest, mortality and expense assumptions applicable to the contract, and adhering to the "reasonable" mortality charge and expense charge rules (and viewing the amount of expense charges as having been stated, based on the gross premiums and this methodol-

---

[69] TAMRA House Report, *supra* note 40, at 481.
[70] TAMRA Conference Report, *supra* Chapter 2, note 64, at 104–05.
[71] *Id.* at 104.

ogy). In the case of a traditional contract that provides cash values based on standard nonforfeiture law (SNFL) minimums, this net premium would be the SNFL-adjusted premium.

- **Attained-age NSP:** The attained-age net single premium for a contract is determined by applying the computational rules for the CVAT with the assumption that the lowest death benefit and any QABs during the 7-pay testing period are provided until the deemed maturity date of the contract (not before age 95 and not later than age 100), although death benefit increases described in section 7702(e)(2)(B) may be taken into account.

- **Deemed cash surrender value:** The deemed cash surrender value of a contract is the hypothetical CSV (determined without regard to any surrender charge or policy loan) that would have resulted if premiums paid under the contract had been credited with interest at the "policy rate" and had been reduced by the "applicable mortality and expense charges."[72] In this calculation, the policy rate is defined as the greater of 4 percent or the rate or rates guaranteed at contract issuance.[73] However, if the deemed cash surrender value exceeds the actual CSV of a contract (again, determined without regard to any surrender charge or policy loan), then the actual CSV is substituted for the deemed cash surrender value.[74] (Actual may be lower than deemed, for example, in a variable life contract.)

In regard to the mortality and expense charges used in the deemed cash surrender value calculation, the TAMRA House Report states that "[t]he applicable mortality and expense charges for any contract are those charges that were taken into account for prior periods under the cash value accumulation test or the guideline premium requirement, whichever is applicable."[75] This creates an interpretive question for CVAT-based contracts, as the CVAT does not recognize expense charges (apart from QABs) in the development of the NSPs. This could lead to the conclusion that expense loadings and charges are not to be recognized at all in the development of the deemed cash surrender value. On the other hand, the contractual CSV that is directly addressed by the CVAT is developed with full recognition of contract expenses, leading to the view that the deemed cash surrender value should be developed taking expense charges into account and measuring the premium paid net of any loading charge against the necessary premium determined as the excess of the NSP over that deemed cash surrender value. This view is the more sensible one, in that it is in better accord with the purpose of limiting contract funding to that which would be required, on a guaranteed basis, to fund the lowest level of benefits. It also conceptually accords with the legislative history's dictate that only the net amount of a premium is tested against the NPT. Fortunately, in the sole private letter ruling addressing the NPT to date, the IRS agreed with this construction of the rule.[76]

The deemed cash surrender value of a contract, accordingly, roughly equals the CSV that would appear in the test plan model at the inception of the contract. That said, the deemed cash surrender value concept is difficult to implement and often it is approximated at issuance for traditional participating whole life contracts by the CSV of the base contract along with that of any paid-up additional insurance purchased with a premium (CSVs of paid-up additions purchased with nonguaranteed dividends are excluded from this until a material change is recognized). The concept also involves some uncertainty, e.g., the legislative history is not clear as to whether guaranteed or "reasonable" mortality and expense charges should be used in the determination.[77]

Accordingly, assuming the loading element of a gross premium is properly deducted from that premium in performing necessary premium testing, one can then say that the necessary premium limitation for a CVAT contract generally permits the payment of the gross premium needed at any time to fund the contract fully for its lowest level of benefits (death benefit and QABs), viewing the contract's then CSV as equal to what it would be based on the premiums paid for the contract, the contract's minimum interest rate guarantee, and the application of reasonable mortality and expense charges. Stated formulaically, for a contract with no QABs, the

---

[72] TAMRA House Report, *supra* note 40, at 481. See below for the legislative history's definition of the applicable mortality and expense charges.
[73] Id.
[74] TAMRA Conference Report, *supra* Chapter 2, note 64, at 105, n. 3.
[75] TAMRA House Report, *supra* note 40, at 481.
[76] PLR 201137008 (June 14, 2011) (involving a flexible premium universal life contract tested under the CVAT).
[77] The discussion above assumes that the reasonable charge rules are applied, since this may be implied from the TAMRA House Report's discussion of the "applicable mortality and expense charges," but this is not clearly provided in the legislative history. PLR 201137008 was premised on a representation by the insurer that the expense charges met the reasonableness standard of IRC § 7702(c)(3)(B)(ii).

maximum premium (net of loading expenses) that may be paid at duration $t$ without the payment of unnecessary premium is defined by the relationship:

$$\text{Necessary Premium}^{Max} = A_{x+t} - {}_tCV_x, \tag{4.6}$$

where $A_{x+t}$ is the attained age NSP for the lowest death benefit payable during the 7-pay testing period (or the most recent period), and where ${}_tCV_x$ is the lesser of the actual CSV (without regard to surrender charge or policy loan) or the deemed cash surrender value. The limited increases in death benefits described in section 7702(e)(2)(B) may be recognized by replacing the NSP with the net level reserve (NLR), although this rule is not of significant import and is rarely used. $A_{x+t}$ may be increased to fund the charges for the lowest amount of a QAB that persists throughout the 7-pay testing period. For traditional contracts, this means that unnecessary premiums generally will not be present unless premiums for a paid-up additional insurance rider are paid subsequent to issue.

If a CVAT contract undergoes a reduction in benefits or a material change, how should the necessary premium limitation be adjusted, if at all, following the change? The TAMRA legislative history, which is the source of the details on the NPT, does not comment on this question (apart from saying that any unnecessary premium must be tested against the new 7-pay limitation following a material change), and there is no other guidance regarding it. Drawing a parallel to the treatment of the necessary premium in the case of guideline premium test contracts (as discussed above), suitable approaches could include:

- Where the reduction-in-benefits rule applies, redetermine the necessary premium from issue (or from a prior material change) based on the reduced benefits. This in turn may require retesting for unnecessary premium from the contract's original issue date (or material change date) based on the lower necessary premium limits, although this is not clear. The deemed cash surrender value calculation, on the other hand, would not appear to be affected retrospectively by the section 7702A(c)(2)(A) reduction-in-benefits rule.

- Where a material change occurs, determine the necessary premium anew, consistently with the treatment of the materially changed contract as newly issued (per section 7702A(c)(3)(A)(i)), treating the benefits at the time of the change as the new "lowest" benefits (assuming they persist for the new 7-pay testing period). Further, reset the deemed cash surrender value by taking account of the contract's actual CSV at the time of the change, effectively applying the concept of the section 7702A(c)(3)(A)(ii) rollover rule. (The "truing up" of the deemed cash value clearly would be required in the event of an actual contract exchange, and the material change rule generally applies in such a case.)

Since guidance is lacking in these respects, however, the foregoing is not clearly required, and practice can be expected to vary among insurers.

## CVAT Necessary Premium Example

The computation of the necessary premium can be illustrated by the following example, which assumes a base contract that is purchased with level premiums and has a CSV equal to the net level reserve for the contract, and to which a premium-paying additions rider has been added at issuance.

- Sex: Male
- Age: 45
- Face amount (base): $125,000
- Face amount (paid-up addition, or PUA): $ 15,720
- Initial death benefit: $140,720
- Mortality: 2001 CSO male aggregate ANB
- Interest rate: 4.5 percent

In the example, a material change does not occur until the start of the eighth contract year, when the payment of an unnecessary premium occurs ($1,416 was necessary, but $4,000 plus the base contract premium of $1,800 was paid). It is at that point that the initial face amount of $140,720 (the base plan plus the initial rider (PUA) face amount) is fully funded by the deemed cash surrender value. As death benefit increases beyond the tested level have already occurred, payment of the premium in year eight causes a material change to be recognized and starts a new 7-pay test. This can be seen in Table 4.7.

| Table 4.7. CVAT necessary premium example | | | | | | | | |
|---|---|---|---|---|---|---|---|---|
| Contract year | 1 | 2 | 3 | 4 | 5 | 6 | 7 | 8 |
| Base policy premium | 1,800 | 1,800 | 1,800 | 1,800 | 1,800 | 1,800 | 1,800 | 1,800 |
| Base policy death benefit | 125,000 | 125,000 | 125,000 | 125,000 | 125,000 | 125,000 | 125,000 | 125,000 |
| Base policy cash value (BOY)[78] | — | 1,594 | 3,231 | 4,916 | 6,663 | 8,473 | 10,343 | 12,269 |
| PUA rider premium | 4,000 | 4,000 | 4,000 | 4,000 | 4,000 | 4,000 | 4,000 | 4,000 |
| PUA death benefit | 15,720 | 30,875 | 45,488 | 59,584 | 73,181 | 86,297 | 98,950 | 111,159 |
| PUA cash value (BOY) | — | 4,149 | 8,451 | 12,908 | 17,528 | 22,139 | 27,281 | 32,418 |
| Total death benefit | 140,720 | 155,875 | 170,488 | 184,584 | 198,181 | 211,297 | 223,950 | 236,159 |
| Deemed cash value (BOY) | — | 5,743 | 11,682 | 17,824 | 24,191 | 30,791 | 37,623 | 44,687 |
| NSP for initial death benefit | 35,806 | 37,143 | 38,518 | 39,932 | 41,397 | 42,917 | 44,486 | 46,103 |
| Necessary premium | 35,806 | 31,400 | 26,836 | 22,108 | 17,206 | 12,126 | 6,862 | 1,416 |
| NSP per $1,000 | 254.45 | 263.95 | 273.72 | 283.77 | 294.18 | 304.98 | 316.13 | 327.62 |

While there is no guidance on how to administer a contract following the receipt of an unnecessary premium, insurers will need to determine how the material change rule should apply in year eight (in this example). One common approach to applying the material change rule following the payment of an unnecessary premium involves the following assumptions:

- The necessary premium component of the payment ($1,416) is assumed to be paid prior to the material change, and the net portion of that necessary premium would be taken into account as part of the CSV that is applied under the rollover rule to reduce the new 7-pay premium upon the material change. Further, the unnecessary premium component of the payment ($4,384) is treated as an amount paid in the first year of the new 7-pay test period.

- The death benefit used in the determination of the new 7-pay premium includes both the base policy death benefit ($125,000) as well as the death benefit for the premium purchased addition in effect at the start of year eight, including the PUA purchased at that time ($111,159). (If there had been any dividend-purchased PUAs in effect at the time of the material change, those PUAs also would be taken into account in determining the new 7-pay premium.)

- The CSV used in the determination the new 7-pay premium (i.e., pursuant to the rollover rule) would include:
    - the CSV for the base contract immediately prior to the payment of the year eight premium ($12,269), plus
    - as noted, the net necessary portion of the premium received ($1,416), plus
    - the CSV for the premium purchased PUA immediately prior to the year eight premium payment ($32,418).

---

[78] Beginning of year (BOY).

- A new 7-pay test period would begin on the date of the unnecessary premium payment (i.e., the start of year eight).
- As noted above, the unnecessary premium component of the year eight premium payment ($4,384) would be included as an amount paid in the first year of the new 7-pay test period.

Applying these assumptions to the example in Table 4.7, the new 7-pay premium resulting from the application of the material change rule at the start of year eight would be:

$$7Pay(New) = \frac{\left[(Base\ Face + PUA\ Face) \times NSP_{52}\right] - (Base\ CSV + PUA\ CSV + Net\ Nec.\ Prem.)}{\ddot{a}_{52:\overline{7}|}}$$

$$7Pay(New) = \frac{\left[(125,000 + 111,159) \times .32762\right] - (12,269 + 32,418 + 1,416)}{6.06537}$$

$$7Pay(New) = 5,155.11$$

In applying the NPT following the material change at the start of year eight, the following is assumed:

- The deemed cash surrender value used in the determination of whether a future premium is necessary would continue to include the CSV of the base contract along with the CSV of the premium-purchased PUAs.[79]
- The attained-age NSP would include the death benefit of the base contract ($125,000) and the death benefit of the premium-purchased PUAs ($111,519).

Note that in the example, the contract will fail the 7-pay test based in year 10 based on the new 7-pay premium of $5,155.11 assuming the policyholder continues to pay $4,000 annually to purchase PUAs.

## Summary of Adjustment Rules Under Sections 7702 and 7702A

Table 4.8 provides a brief summary of the section 7702 and 7702A adjustment rules, including the statutory citation to each rule.

| Table 4.8. Sections 7702 and 7702A adjustment rules | |
|---|---|
| Section | Description |
| 7702(f)(7)(A) | "Proper adjustments" required for a change in benefits or contract terms |
| 7702(f)(7)(B)–(E) | Recapture ceiling (see later in this chapter) |
| 7702A(c)(2)(A) | Reduction in benefits in 1st 7 years treated as originally issued for reduced death benefit |
| 7702A(c)(2)(B) | Reinstatements within 90 days ignored in (A) |
| 7702A(c)(3)(A) | Material change rules |
| 7702A(c)(3)(A)(i) | Treated as a new contract as of material change date |
| 7702A(c)(3)(A)(ii) | Rollover rule |
| 7702A(c)(3)(B) | Material change is any increase in death benefit or QAB |
| 7702A(c)(3)(B)(i) | Necessary premium exception |
| 7702A(c)(3)(B)(ii) | Cost-of-living adjustment (COLA) exception (currently inapplicable) |
| 7702A(c)(6) | Permanent reduction rule for last survivor |

---

[79] If any dividend purchased PUAs had been present at the time of the material change, the CSV of such PUAs at such time also would be included in the deemed cash surrender value. As noted above, such PUAs would be reflected in determining the new 7-pay premium.

## Option 2 and Death Benefit Option Changes

Perhaps the most difficult of the adjustment calculations are triggered by death benefit option changes, as the application of the section 7702 adjustment rules and the section 7702A material change rules to option 2 universal life insurance plans often has led to divergent views as to the appropriate way to perform the calculations. To a great degree this can be attributed to the hybrid calculation that applies to an option 2 plan under section 7702, but it is also affected by differing contract provisions or administrative practices.[80]

The section 101(f) computational rules permit both the GSP and the GLP to reflect increases in death benefit under an option 2 plan, requiring only that the net amount at risk be deemed not to increase. The section 7702 computational rules eliminated single premium funding of an option 2 death benefit, but continued to allow funding for an option 2 death benefit pattern for the GLP under section 7702(e)(2)(A). Eliminating the option 2 GSP created a hybrid limitation, with the GSP based on a level death benefit and the GLP based on an increasing death benefit.

Under section 7702A, the computational rules provide that the death benefit in the first year is assumed to continue to maturity. As discussed earlier, this has led to varying practices in computing the 7-pay premium limitation for an option 2 death benefit, with some insurers setting the initial death benefit equal to the face or specified amount and some setting it equal to that amount plus the initial cash surrender value (either of these approaches would seem to be justifiable).

### *Treatment of the Guideline Single Premium Under Option 2 Plans*

Under the adjustment rules, an increase in the GSP might, in theory, be made for that portion of the option 2 death benefit increase attributable to the "guaranteed" cash value, as it was not previously recognized in calculations under the contract. However, as death benefit increases attributable to excess interest and to "nonguaranteed" reductions in mortality charges are properly viewed as arising from amounts in the nature of dividends, they are not eligible to be recognized as adjustment events. In practice, the GSP generally is not adjusted to take account of option 2 increases. Reasons for this include:

- the difficulty of identifying the appropriate increase amount,
- the difficulty of applying the decrease rule when the cash value is reduced for any reason, and
- a belief (not universally shared) that such an adjustment is barred by the language in legislative history regarding adjustments: "Likewise, no adjustment shall be made if the change occurs automatically due, for example, to the growth of the cash surrender value (whether by the crediting of excess interest or the payment of guideline premiums) or due to changes initiated by the company."[81]

If the GSP is not so adjusted, a partial withdrawal from the contract, decreasing the cash value and hence decreasing the death benefit, is not considered an adjustment to the GSP since the withdrawal does not disturb the assumptions on which the GSP was previously calculated.

Because of the different rules that apply to the GLP depending upon the death benefit option used, a change in the option is considered an adjustment event under section 7702. For a guideline premium test contract, the mechanics of the adjustment follow the familiar attained-age increment and decrement rules. However, the precise nature of the calculation depends upon the manner in which the option change is administered.

Under section 7702A, the effect of changing the death benefit option has been interpreted in a variety of ways, particularly for purposes of determining whether a section 7702A material change or reduction in benefits has occurred. Part of this variation results from the view that, in computing the 7-pay premium, the option 2 death benefit pattern is generally not incorporated into the calculation. This has led some to question whether a change in the death benefit option, of itself, can trigger a material change at all, or if it can, whether the option change can be "protected" by the necessary premium rule. Similarly, a question arises as to whether

---

[80] The adjustment calculations for a death benefit option change under a CVAT contract utilizing the special computational rule of section 7702(e)(2)(B) are not discussed here, as that rule is not commonly used. In the case of a CVAT contract based on the general computational rules that undergoes an option change, the NSP simply adjusts with the amount of the death benefit when it changes.

[81] DEFRA Senate Report, *supra* Chapter 1, note 11, at 577. *See also* DEFRA House Report, *supra* Chapter 1, note 11, at 1448; DEFRA Blue Book, *supra* Chapter 1, note 20, at 654.

an option change must be administered as a material change in order to change the measure of necessary premium (computed from the date of the material change) from an option 1 amount to an option 2 amount (or vice versa). This is of particular importance to companies that rely on the section 7702 guideline premium limitation as a proxy for the necessary premium limitation. How an insurer chooses to answer these questions may be influenced by the capabilities of its administrative system.

## Sample Option Change Calculations

Changes in death benefit options thus create significant administrative issues under the guideline premium and 7-pay tests. Although there is no standard for how a life insurance contract adjusts the death benefit when a change in the death benefit option occurs, contract provisions generally provide that the change maintains either a constant specified amount (or face amount) or a constant net amount at risk. Since contract provisions regarding option changes are not uniform throughout the life insurance industry, the calculation method used to adjust guideline and 7-pay premiums must take into consideration the specifics of such provisions.

In the discussion that follows, two general types of option changes are considered: one from an option 1 death benefit to an option 2 death benefit, and one running in the opposite direction (from option 2 to option 1). These examples explore the differing practices that have emerged in applying the adjustment rules under sections 7702 and 7702A for changes in death benefit options that seek to maintain either a constant specified amount or a constant net amount at risk. Further adding to the complexity of administering a change in the death benefit option under section 7702, as compared with section 101(f), is the fact that the GSP does not reflect an option 2 death benefit pattern, and thus an adjustment resulting from a change in death benefit option operates differently on the GSP and the GLP.

In the following examples, the GLP resulting from a change in the death benefit option is determined using the following adjustment formula:

$$GLP(New)_{x+t} = GLP(Old)_x \times \frac{\ddot{a}_{x+t}}{\ddot{a}'_{x+t}} + GLP(After)_{x+t} - GLP(Before)_{x+t} \times \frac{\ddot{a}_{x+t}}{\ddot{a}'_{x+t}}$$

As discussed earlier in the chapter, the attained-age adjustment formula for the GLP involves the use of "annuity factors" when there is a change in the death benefit option, where $\ddot{a}'_{x+t}$ is the annuity factor based on contract characteristics following the change, and $\ddot{a}_{x+t}$ is the annuity factor based on the contract characteristics prior to the change.

### Death Benefit Option Change Example 1: Level (Option 1) to Increasing (Option 2)

When the specified amount remains constant in the course of a death benefit option change from a level death benefit pattern to an increasing pattern, the death benefit will necessarily increase by the amount of the contract's cash value. If, on the other hand, the net amount at risk remains constant, the death benefit remains unchanged, resulting in a reduction in the specified amount by the contract's cash value. Table 4.9 summarizes the resulting contract values for each alternative.

| Table 4.9. Death benefit option change: option 1 to option 2 | | | |
|---|---|---|---|
| | Before | Constant specified amount (Table 4.10) | Constant net amount at risk (Table 4.11) |
| Option | 1 | 2 | 2 |
| Specified amount | 100,000 | 100,000 | 88,000 |
| Cash surrender value | 12,000 | 12,000 | 12,000 |
| Death benefit | 100,000 | 112,000 | 100,000 |
| Change in death benefit | — | 12,000 | 0 |
| Change in specified amount | — | 0 | −12,000 |
| Guideline single premium | — | No change | Decrease |
| Guideline level premium | 7702(e)(1) | 7702(e)(2)(A) for 100,000 | 7702(e)(2)(A) for 88,000 |
| 7-pay premium | — | Material change | Material change, decrease or no change |

The contract characteristics underlying the following two examples dealing with a change from a level (option 1) to increasing (option 2) death benefit option are as follows at the date of the change:

- Sex: Male
- Age: 50
- Specified amount: $100,000
- Cash value: $12,000
- Mortality: 2001 CSO male aggregate ANB
- Interest rate: 4.5 percent
- Expenses: 5 percent of premium, plus $5 monthly administrative fee

**Constant Specified Amount**

Table 4.10 illustrates how a year five change in death benefit option from option 1 to option 2 with a constant specified amount is accounted for under sections 7702 and 7702A.

| Table 4.10. Option change at 50, constant specified amount | | | | |
|---|---|---|---|---|
| | GSP | GLP-DBO1 | GLP-DBO2 | 7-pay |
| At-issue value | 19,246.67 | 1,610.13 | | 4,167.49 |
| Attained age 50 "before" | 23,929.28 | 2,052.13 | | |
| GLP annuity factor "before" | — | 16.140113 | | |
| Attained age 50 "after" | 23,929.28 | | 4,911.70 | |
| GLP annuity factor "after" | — | | 20.651298 | |
| Increment | 0.00 | | 2,956.12 | |
| Post-change value | 19,246.67 | | 4,566.25 | 3,041.26 |
| Increase | 0.00 | | 2,956.12 | −1,126.23 |

The premises underlying the calculations in Table 4.10 are as follows:

- GSP adjustment: As the specified amount has not changed, the GSP does not change. While some might be tempted to adjust the GSP for the increased death benefit, most insurers do not take the cash value into account as death benefit for purposes of this calculation, to avoid applying the attained-age adjustment rule should the cash value decline.

- GLP adjustment: The GLP is increased from that applicable to a $100,000 level death benefit under section 7702(e)(1) to that applicable to a $100,000 increasing death benefit under section 7702(e)(2)(A). The new GLP of 4,566.25 represents an increment of $2,956.12 over the original at-issue GLP of 1,610.13.

- Application of the section 7702A(c)(2) reduction-in-benefits rule: The reduction-in-benefits rule of section 7702A(c)(2) would not apply in this example. The death benefit did not decrease below the lowest amount of benefits assumed in the original 7-pay premium as a result of the change in death benefit option. Further, the death benefit cannot reduce below $100,000 absent some other future adjustment to the contract.

- Application of the section 7702A(c)(3) material change rule: What is less certain is whether there is a need to recognize a material change under section 7702A(c)(3) at the time of the option change. Although there has been an increase in death benefit, there is no unnecessary premium in the contract (an unnecessary premium could not have been paid without otherwise causing premiums paid to exceed the section 7702 guideline premium limitation), making recognition of the material change optional. Choosing not to recognize the material change would seemingly require the necessary premiums to continue to reflect the GLP for the option 1 death benefit. One reason to recognize a material change in this instance would be to endeavor to change the measure of necessary premium to that based on an option 2 death benefit, allowing the section 7702 guideline premiums to continue to serve as a measure for necessary premium (assuming the attained-age adjustment methodology is an appropriate methodology for adjusting necessary premiums when a section 7702A(c)(3) material change occurs).

- If the option change is treated as a material change under section 7702A(c)(3), either due to the increase in death benefit or the change in the death benefit option, the material change rules would be applied at attained age 50 with a death benefit of $100,000 and a rollover amount of $12,000. Note that it is possible to recognize a death benefit of $112,000, but as previously observed, the initial cash value is not generally taken into account.

### Constant Net Amount at Risk

Table 4.11 illustrates a similar change in death benefit option from option 1 to option 2 five years after issue, but with a constant risk amount. In Table 4.11, the following calculations are presented:

| Table 4.11. Option change at 50, constant net amount at risk | | | | |
|---|---|---|---|---|
| | GSP | GLP-DBO1 | GLP-DBO2 | 7-pay |
| At-issue value | 19,246.67 | 1,610.13 | | 4,167.49 |
| Attained age 50 "before" | 23,929.28 | 2,052.13 | | |
| GLP annuity factor "before" | — | 16.140113 | | |
| Attained age 50 "after" | 21,162.33 | | 4,329.88 | |
| GLP annuity factor "after" | — | | 20.651298 | |
| Increment | −2,766.95 | | 2,374.30 | |
| Post-change value | **16,479.72** | | **3,984.43** | **2,439.54** |
| Increase | −2,766.95 | | 2,374.30 | −1,727.94 |

The premises underlying the calculations in Table 4.11 are as follows:

- GSP adjustment: When the net amount at risk is held constant, the specified amount is reduced from $100,000 to $88,000. This causes a decrease in the GSP. Although it is possible to continue with the existing GSP based on the original, at-issue specified amount of $100,000, companies will more often recognize the decrease in specified amount, again to avoid the need to adjust the GSP if there is a decline in the cash value.

- GLP adjustment: The GLP is adjusted from that applicable to a $100,000 level death benefit under section 7702(e)(1) to that applicable to an $88,000 increasing death benefit under section 7702(e)(2)(A). While there may be some optionality with recognizing the lower specified amount in the "after" calculation of the GSP, the use of the option 2 death benefit pattern permitted by the section 7702(e)(2)(A) computational rule would require the use of the $88,000 specified amount (reflecting the level net amount at risk of $88,000) in the "after" calculation of the GLP.

- Application of the section 7702A(c)(2) reduction-in-benefits rule: The section 7702A(c)(2) reduction-in-benefits rule arguably need not apply in this example because the change in death benefit option did not reduce the death benefit below the amount assumed in the determination of the at-issue 7-pay premium. However, it is common practice to apply the reduction-in-benefit rule based on the lower specified amount, $88,000, to avoid needing to apply this rule in the future if the cash value declines.

- Application of the section 7702A(c)(3) material change rule: When the net amount at risk remains constant as a result of the death benefit option changing from option 1 to option 2, the death benefit remains unchanged. As such, the practice of some companies is not to recognize this type of change as a material change under section 7702A(c)(3). Similar to the commentary expressed above for an option change where the specified amount remains constant, choosing not to recognize the material change would seemingly require the necessary premiums to continue to reflect the GLP for the option 1 death benefit. This has prompted some companies to treat an option change per se as a material change. In that case, the 7-pay premium would be reduced to $2,439.54 by the operation of the rollover rule, taking into account a cash surrender value of $12,000 and the reduction in the specified amount to $88,000.[82]

## *Death Benefit Option Change Example 2: Increasing (Option 2) to Level (Option 1)*

Like example 1, an adjustment under section 7702 also occurs when an option 2 plan is changed to an option 1 plan. As was the case with the change from option 1 to option 2, the effect of the change will depend upon the manner in which the option change is administered, with either the specified (or face) amount or the net amount at risk held constant. This is illustrated in Table 4.12.

---

[82] It arguably is appropriate to treat the reduction in specified amount as a reduction in benefits under IRC § 7702A(c)(2) but then to treat the change in option as a material change under IRC § 7702A(c)(3) occurring immediately thereafter. Where an insurer bases the 7-pay premiums only on the specified amount, consistency suggests that the reduction in specified amount upon the option change should invoke the reduction-in-benefits rule. Also, following this with a material change accounts for the change in option and allows for use of the contract's adjusted guideline premium limitation in applying the NPT thereafter.

# Chapter 4 | Adjusting the Limitations Under Sections 7702 and 7702A

### Table 4.12. Death benefit option change: option 2 to option 1

|  | Before | Constant specified amount (Table 4.13) | Constant net amount at risk (Table 4.14) |
|---|---|---|---|
| Option | 2 | 1 | 1 |
| Specified amount | 100,000 | 100,000 | 112,000 |
| Cash surrender value | 12,000 | 12,000 | 12,000 |
| Death benefit | 100,000 | 100,000 | 112,000 |
| Change in death benefit | — | −12,000 | 0 |
| Change in specified amount | — | 0 | 12,000 |
| Guideline single premium | — | No change | Increase |
| Guideline level premium | 7702(e)(2)(A) for 100,000 | 7702(e)(1) for 100,000 | 7702(e)(1) for 112,000 |
| 7-pay premium |  | No material change, no decrease | Material change |

Similarly to the examples above, the next two examples deal with a change from an increasing (option 2) to level (option 1) death benefit option. The contract characteristics for these examples are as follows at the date of the change:

- Sex: Male
- Age: 50
- Specified amount: $100,000
- Cash value: $12,000
- Mortality: 2001 CSO male aggregate ANB
- Interest Rate: 4.5 percent
- Expenses: 5 percent of premium, plus $5 monthly administrative fee

**Constant Specified Amount**

Table 4.13 presents an example of an option 2 to option 1 change five years after issue with a constant specified amount.

### Table 4.13. Option change at 50, constant specified amount

|  | GSP | GLP-DBO1 | GLP-DBO2 | 7-pay |
|---|---|---|---|---|
| At-issue value | 19,246.67 |  | 3,928.08 | 4,167.49 |
| Attained age 50 "before" | 23,929.28 |  | 4,911.70 |  |
| GLP annuity factor "before" | — |  | 20.651298 |  |
| Attained age 50 "after" | 23,929.28 | 2,052.13 |  |  |
| GLP annuity factor "after" | — | 16.140113 |  |  |
| Increment | 0.00 | −3,134.49 |  |  |
| Post-change value | **19,246.67** | **793.59** |  | **3,041.26** |
| Increase | 0.00 | −3,134.49 |  | −1,126.23 |

Where the specified amount remains constant, a change from option 2 to option 1 results in the following:

- GSP adjustment: When the specified amount remains constant, there is no change in the GSP, similarly to the case with a change from option 1 to option 2. Although the death benefit actually deceases from $112,000 to $100,000 at the time of the option change, the future benefits reflected in the at-issue GSP were reflective of the $100,000 specified amount, thus eliminating the need to make any adjustment to the GSP.
- GLP adjustment: The GLP will require an adjustment to account for the change from an increasing death benefit for the specified amount of $100,000 under section 7702(e)(2)(A) to a level death benefit for the specified amount of $100,000 under section 7702(e)(1). The result is in a reduction in the GLP.
- Application of the section 7702A(c)(2) reduction-in-benefits rule: For section 7702A, the option change does not cause the death benefit to be reduced below the original specified amount, $100,000, assumed in the determination of the at-issue 7-pay premium. Thus, the benefit decrease rule in section 7702A(c)(2) presumably would not apply in this example.
- Application of the section 7702A(c)(3) material change rule: The death benefit does not increase as a result of the change from option 2 to option 1 when the specified amount is held constant. Prior to the option change, there were increases in death benefit (due to the growth in cash value) that were not recognized as material changes under section 7702A(c)(3)(A) (they were deferred pursuant to the section 7702A(c)(3)(B)(i) necessary premium rule). The fact that these prior death benefit increases no longer exist after the death benefit option change brings into question the need to reflect a section 7702A(c)(3) material change. As noted above, by not reflecting the option change as a section 7702A(c)(3) material change, the necessary premiums would continue to reflect the GLP for the option 2 death benefit pattern. This would seemingly result in the continued use of necessary premiums (still reflecting the option 2 death benefit) that would be at least as great as the section 7702 guideline premiums (adjusted to reflect the change to an option 1 death benefit pattern). The payment of an unnecessary premium may therefore not be possible without otherwise failing the guideline premium test. For those companies that rely on the section 7702 guideline premiums for determining a contract's necessary premium, the need to reflect a section 7702A(c)(3) material change would appear to be unwarranted in this example.
- Of course, reflecting the option change in this example as a material change would alter the basis of necessary (guideline) premiums to that of an option 1 death benefit pattern. The adjusted 7-pay premium would be determined based on a specified amount of $100,000, applying the rollover calculation with a CSV of $12,000. This is illustrated in Table 4.13.

**Constant Net Amount at Risk**

The situation where the net amount at risk remains constant under a death benefit option change from option 2 to option 1 is shown in Table 4.14.

| Table 4.14. Option change at 50, constant net amount at risk | | | | |
|---|---|---|---|---|
| | GSP | GLP-DBO1 | GLP-DBO2 | 7-pay |
| At-issue value | 19,246.67 | | 3,928.08 | 4,167.49 |
| Attained age 50 "before" | 23,929.28 | | 4,911.70 | |
| GLP annuity factor "before" | — | | 20.651298 | |
| Attained age 50 "after" | 26,696.23 | 2,290.81 | | |
| GLP annuity factor "after" | — | 16.140113 | | |
| Increment | 2,766.95 | −2,895.81 | | |
| Post-change value | **22,013.62** | **1,032.27** | | **3,642.97** |
| Increase | 2,766.95 | −2,895.81 | | −524.52 |

Where the net amount at risk remains constant, a change from option 2 to option 1 results in the following:

- GSP adjustment: The specified amount increases from $100,000 to $112,000, causing the GSP to increase accordingly.

- GLP adjustment: An adjustment to the GLP would be needed to reflect the change from an increasing death benefit based on a specified amount of $100,000 under section 7702(e)(2)(A) to a level death benefit for the increased specified amount of $112,000 under section 7702(e)(1)(A).

- Application of the section 7702A(c)(2) reduction-in-benefits rule: Changing the death benefit option from option 2 to option 1 while maintaining a constant net amount at risk does not result in a reduction in the death benefit below the original specified amount of $100,000 assumed in the determination of the at-issue 7-pay premium, and so the benefit decrease rule in section 7702A(c)(2) would not apply here.

- Application of the section 7702A(c)(3) material change rule: Under section 7702A, the death benefit at issue was $100,000 (if the effect of the initial premium on the at-issue death benefit was disregarded). Prior to the option change, as noted above, there were increases in death benefit as a result of increases in cash values due to the option 2 death benefit pattern. Any material changes related to these prior increases were deferred pursuant to the section 7702A(c)(3)(B)(i) necessary premium rule.

- To continue deferring those material changes following the change to an option 1 death benefit pattern, an insurer would need to continue to test premium payments against the necessary premium limitation reflective of a GSP based on the original $100,000 specified amount and the sum of the appropriate GLPs (presumably based on the original option 2 death benefit pattern). Thus, if an insurer relies on the guideline premium limitation as the necessary premium limitation, it must also treat the change to an option 1 death benefit pattern as a section 7702A(c)(3) material change in this example.

- As noted above, if a material change is recognized here, either because of the increase in death benefit or the change in death benefit option, the new 7-pay premium would be based on the rollover calculation using a specified amount of $112,000 and a cash surrender value of $12,000.

## Recapture Ceiling Rules Under Section 7702(f)(7)(B)–(E)

The general rule for taxation of a surrender or partial withdrawal under a life insurance contract is found in section 72(e), which provides that lifetime proceeds paid from a contract that is not a MEC are taxable only to the extent they exceed the "investment in the contract," i.e., usually the premiums paid. The provisions of section 7702(f)(7)(B)—known as the **recapture rules**—define a narrow set of circumstances in which the general rule does not apply, resulting in the taxation of some amounts distributed on an income-first basis. The section 7702(f)(7)(B) rules were added by the 1986 technical corrections to section 7702, replacing the exchange treatment of distributions accompanying benefit decreases in the original enactment. The recapture rules are intended to prevent abuse of the tax law's normal treatment of distributions resulting from post-issue reductions in benefits.

The impact of the recapture rules was significantly limited by the enactment of the section 7702A rules in 1988. While it is possible to trigger tax under the section 7702(f)(7)(B) rules applied to a non-MEC, it requires a contract exchange or unusual circumstances to create an example of this.[83] Arguably, these rules serve little or no tax policy purpose in light of the enactment of section 7702A, but regardless of whether they serve any purpose, they are still in the law, creating administrative challenges.

Under the section 7702(f)(7)(B) rules, taxable income to the policyholder may be recognized in connection with a section 7702(f)(7)(A) adjustment event if all of the following five conditions are met:

- The change reduces the future benefits under the contract

---

[83] However, a force-out transaction in the eighth contract year is documented in the *IRS v. C.M. Holdings Inc.* case at footnote 46. *IRS v. CM Holdings Inc.*, 254 B.R. 578, 618 (D. Del. 2000), *aff'd* 301 F. 3d 96 (3d Cir. 2002).

- The change occurs within 15 years of the contract's original issue date
- Cash is distributed from the contract as a part of or a consequence of the change
- The "recapture ceiling," as defined in the statute, is greater than zero
- There is a gain in the contract (the CSV exceeds the policyholder's investment in the contract)

The applicable recapture ceiling, as defined in section 7702(f)(7)(C) and (D), varies depending upon when the reduction in benefits occurs, and under section 7702(f)(7)(C) in particular, the applicable recapture ceiling additionally varies depending upon which of the two tests is used to qualify the contract as a life insurance contract for federal tax purposes. Taxable income is to be recognized on the cash distributed, up to the gain in the contract, to the extent of the recapture ceiling.

For purposes of determining the recapture ceiling, the statute looks at two distinct periods: contract years one through five, and contract years six through 15. In a rough manner, the recapture ceiling can be thought of as measuring "forced-out cash" due to the benefit reduction, at least in the first five contract years.

**Years one through five:** The recapture ceiling is equal to the distribution required under section 7702(f)(7)(A) to maintain the contract in compliance with section 7702. This will differ for contracts under the CVAT and those under the guideline premium test.

- During the first five contract years, if the contract qualifies as a life insurance contract by satisfying the CVAT, then section 7702(f)(7)(C)(i) provides that the applicable recapture ceiling equals the excess of:

    1) the CSV of the contract immediately before the reduction in benefits, over

    2) the NSP (determined under section 7702(b)) for the contract immediately after the reduction in benefits.

- If the contract qualifies as a life insurance contract under the guideline premium test, then section 7702(f)(7)(C)(ii) provides that the applicable recapture ceiling during the first five contract years is the greater of (A) or (B), where

    A) equals the excess of

    1) the aggregate premiums paid under the contract immediately before the reduction in the contract's benefits, over

    2) the adjusted guideline premium limitation immediately after the reduction in the contract's benefits; and

    B) equals the excess of

    1) the CSV of the contract immediately before the reduction in the contract's benefits, over

    2) the maximum CSV permitted under the cash value corridor of section 7702(d) immediately after the reduction of the contract's benefits.

**Years six through 15:** During contract years six through 15, a single rule applies to contracts under *both* tests: the recapture ceiling uses only the section 7702(d) cash value corridor as the measure of a "force-out." This is described in (B) above. It may seem odd to apply the corridor to CVAT contracts, but this may be viewed as a triumph of fairness over mindless consistency.[84] The application of the section 7702(d) corridor percentages during years six to 15 to contracts under the CVAT means that taxable income is less likely to result under a CVAT plan than under a guideline premium test plan.

Finally, section 7702(f)(7)(E) addresses the prospect that a distribution may be taken from a contract in anticipation of a benefit reduction rather than as a result of one. The section 7702(f)(7)(B) rule facially oper-

---

[84] Or not. As Ralph Waldo Emerson wrote, "A foolish consistency is the hobgoblin of little minds. … With consistency a great soul has simply nothing to do."

ates on the premise that the distribution to which it applies is made "as a result" of a benefit reduction, but one presumably could argue about which came first, the distribution or the reduction. To preclude any such contention, section 7702(f)(7)(E) provides:

> Under regulations prescribed by the Secretary, [section 7702(f)(7)(B)] shall apply also to any distribution made in anticipation of a reduction in benefits under the contract. For purposes of the preceding sentence, appropriate adjustments shall be made in the provisions of [section 7702(f)(7)(C) and (D)]; and any distribution which reduces the cash surrender value of a contract and which is made within 2 years before a reduction in benefits under the contract shall be treated as made in anticipation of such reduction.

While no regulations have been issued under this provision, none are needed to implement it; the "under regulations" wording, together with the prescribed two-year rule, means that the statute is self-executing, although regulations are allowed to expand upon it. Thus, its two-year look-back rule, similar to the section 7702A(d) rule governing distributions from a MEC, seems sufficient to define the anticipation period of potential concern.

## Rev. Rul. 2003-95

The first substantive ruling regarding the section 7702 rules ever published, Rev. Rul. 2003-95, describes the tax treatment of a cash distribution made in connection with a reduction in benefits under a life insurance contract.[85] The ruling provides three examples of a partial surrender of a contract, as follows:

- Situation 1 involves a distribution in the fourth contract year from a CVAT contract.
- Situation 2 addresses the same year four distribution, but from a guideline premium test contract.
- Situation 3 moves the distribution to the sixth contract year.

The facts of the ruling are based on a contract with a $350,000 face amount, premiums paid by the fourth contract year of $45,000, and a cash value of $60,000. In the fourth or sixth contract year (depending upon the situation involved), the contract is partially surrendered, resulting in a distribution of $36,000 and a death benefit of $140,000. This can be seen in Table 4.15.

| Table 4.15. Rev. Rul. 2003-95, assumptions | |
|---|---|
| Death benefit | 350,000 |
| Cash surrender value | 60,000 |
| Premiums paid (investment in the contract) | 45,000 |
| Income on the contract under section 72(e) | 15,000 |
| Reduced death benefit | 140,000 |
| Distribution (partial surrender) | 36,000 |

Tables 4.16, 4.17 and 4.18 summarize the numerical examples provided in Rev. Rul. 2003-95. In Situation 1, the recapture ceiling is $10,300, which equals the $60,000 CSV less the NSP for the $140,000 death benefit. The recapture ceiling treats the excess of the prior CSV over the revised NSP as potentially taxable income. Therefore, of the $36,000 distributed, $10,300 is taxable while $25,700 is treated as a (nontaxable) return of premium.

---

[85] Rev. Rul. 2003-95, 2003-2 C.B. 358.

### Table 4.16. Rev. Rul. 2003-95, Situation 1: CVAT 4 years after issue

| | |
|---|---|
| CSV before reduction | 60,000 |
| NSP for reduced death benefit (140,000 × 355/1,000) | 49,700 |
| Recapture ceiling (60,000 − 49,700) | 10,300 |
| **Included as income under 7702(f)(7)(B) equals least of** | |
| Recapture ceiling | 10,300 |
| Income on the contract | 15,000 |
| Amount distributed | 36,000 |

| Policy values | Cash surrender value | Investment in contract | Income on contract |
|---|---|---|---|
| Prior to partial surrender | 60,000 | 45,000 | 15,000 |
| Partial surrender | −36,000 | −25,700 | −10,300 |
| After partial surrender | 24,000 | 19,300 | 4,700 |

In Situation 2, the recapture ceiling is $20,150, which represents the excess of the premiums paid, $45,000, over the revised GSP, $24,850, where the revised GSP is computed using the attained-age decrement method. As a result, a greater amount—$15,000, all of the income on the contract—is taxable.

### Table 4.17. Rev. Rul. 2003-95, Situation 2: guideline 4 years after issue

| | |
|---|---|
| **Recapture ceiling equals greater of:** | |
| (A) (1) Premiums paid immediately before reduction, over | 45,000 |
| (2) adjusted guideline limitation | 24,850 |
| Difference | 20,150 |
| (B) (1) Cash surrender value before reduction, over | 60,000 |
| (2) Section 7702(d) corridor limitation after reduction | 75,676 |
| Difference, minimum 0 | 0 |
| **Included as income under 7702(f)(7)(B) equals least of** | |
| Recapture ceiling | 20,150 |
| Income on the contract | 15,000 |
| Amount distributed | 36,000 |

| Policy values | Cash surrender value | Investment in contract | Income on contract |
|---|---|---|---|
| Prior to partial surrender | 60,000 | 45,000 | 15,000 |
| Partial surrender | −36,000 | −21,000 | −15,000 |
| After partial surrender | 24,000 | 24,000 | — |

In Situation 3, the section 7702(d) cash value corridor does not limit the amount distributed, and so all of the distribution is treated as a return of premium. That is, there is no taxable income to the policyholder.

### Table 4.18. Rev. Rul. 2003-95, Situation 3: 4 years after issue

| Included as income under 7702(f)(7)(B) equals least of | | | |
|---|---|---|---|
| Recapture ceiling | | | 0 |
| Income on the contract | | | 15,000 |
| Amount distributed | | | 36,000 |

| Policy values | Cash surrender value | Investment in contract | Income on contract |
|---|---|---|---|
| Prior to partial surrender | 60,000 | 45,000 | 15,000 |
| Partial surrender | −36,000 | −36,000 | — |
| After partial surrender | 24,000 | 9,000 | 15,000 |

While the purpose of Rev. Rul. 2003-95 was to illustrate the application of the recapture rules, the facts of the ruling approximately follow those for a contract issued to a male age 46 based on 1980 CSO mortality and 4.5 percent interest. Assuming that to be the case, the (cumulative) 7-pay limitation for the contract after the partial surrender would be $28,984. As the amount paid during the first four contract years was $45,000, the policy would become a MEC regardless of the pattern of premium payments during the four previous years. (The actual premium pattern is not shown in the ruling, which merely indicates that the contract is not a MEC at issue).

Thus, while various amounts of taxable income are illustrated under the recapture rules, in reality, a contract with characteristics similar to those described in Rev. Rul. 2003-95 would typically be subject to the MEC distribution rules as well as the recapture rules, thus making the distribution taxable to the extent of the section 72(e) income, and likely also subject to the section 72(v) penalty tax. In that case, in Situations 1–3 described in the ruling, the full amount of the $15,000 income on the contract under section 72(e) would be taxable upon distribution. This would most dramatically affect Situation 3, where no taxable income is generated under the recapture rule, but the full amount of the gain is taxable under the MEC rules.

As noted above, it is difficult to construct realistic examples (at least in the first seven contract years) in which the section 7702(f)(7)(B) rules apply to a given contract, not the section 7702A(c)(2)(A) rule. Thus, while the examples in Rev. Rul. 2003-95 convey the effect of the recapture ceiling rules by examples, a contract with those characteristics is likely to become a MEC as a result of a partial surrender during the first seven contract years, rendering the recapture ceiling rules moot. Perhaps the real import of this ruling is its implicit confirmation that decrease adjustments for the guideline premium test are done by the attained-age decrement method.

# Chapter 5

# STATUTORY EFFECTIVE DATES AND THE IMPACT OF MATERIAL CHANGES

## Chapter Overview

While life insurers' efforts to assure the compliance of their life insurance contracts with the requirements of sections 7702 and 7702A[1] (and section 101(f) for earlier flexible premium contracts) rightly focus on the actuarial tests imposed by these provisions, one of the many complexities entailed in these efforts lies in the different tax rules that apply to contracts over time. Because, as detailed in the preceding chapters, different rules apply to a contract based on the date it is "issued" or "entered into," preservation of that date, or else knowing when a new date applies, is an important element in administering the definitional limitations. Such complexities have arisen not only because Congress has revised (and further restricted) the federal tax treatment of life insurance from time to time, but also because changes occur in state law requirements that are relevant under the tax law—particularly changes in the "prevailing" mortality tables.

Adding to this, a **material change** in a contract, in the broadest sense of the term,[2] can cause the contract to be treated as newly issued or newly entered into, so that it becomes subject to new tax rules or perhaps to the same rules reapplied. Colloquially, the former is spoken of as a loss of grandfathering, i.e., a forfeiture of the tax treatment that existed under the prior rule of law. While an exchange of one contract for another clearly constitutes such a material change, alterations of existing contracts—modifying their guarantees or benefits (by rider or otherwise)—can give rise to this treatment. This chapter explores the interplay between differing kinds of contractual changes and the various effective dates under the definitional limitations,[3] describing and commenting on guidance from the IRS on the subject and reflecting on the prospect that a change may be material in one context but not in another.[4] It also explores the circumstances and effects of reapplying the definitional limitations anew to contracts already subject to them. In addition, the chapter provides a framework for identifying which version of the definitional limitations applies to a contract that undergoes a material change at a particular time, offering some practical advice with the goal of enabling an insurer to administer the contract using the appropriate requirements of the tax law.

## Contract Changes and New-Issuance Treatment: An Introduction

Changes to a life insurance contract can raise a number of questions in the context of the definitional limitations. Chapter 4 describes the manner in which the adjustment mechanism set forth in section 7702(f)(7)(A) requires a change in the net single premiums (NSPs) or guideline premiums of a contract already subject to section 7702 due to a post-issuance change in the contract's terms or benefits. That chapter also discusses the application of the section 7702A adjustment rules to a change in a contract already subject to section 7702A. The adjustment rules, however, do not comprehensively speak to all circumstances in which a change is made to a contract. Such circumstances exist (or arguably exist) in four distinct cases:

---

[1] Unless otherwise indicated, references in this book to "section" are to the provisions of the Internal Revenue Code of 1986, as amended (also referred to as "IRC" or the "Code").
[2] See the sidebar on this term in Chapter 4.
[3] Material changes to a life insurance contract can have consequences under other code provisions as well, *e.g.*, under IRC §§ 264(f), 101(j), 807 and 848.
[4] Portions of this chapter are drawn from two articles written by this book's co-authors and published in Taxing Times, the newsletter of the Taxation Section of the Society of Actuaries. For further information on the subject of material changes, reference may be made to these articles. John T. Adney and Craig R. Springfield, *They Go Bump in the Night: Life Insurance Policies and the Law of Material Change*, Taxing Times supplement, 1–32 (May 2012); Christian DesRochers and Brian G. King, *Administration of the "Material Change" Rule: Meeting the Challenge*, Taxing Times supplement, 33–39 (May 2012).

- First, section 7702 generally applies to contracts "issued" after December 31, 1984 (the **section 7702 effective date rule**).[5] Hence, when a change is made to an earlier issued contract (including a section 101(f) contract), it is necessary to determine whether the change causes the contract to be treated as newly issued and thereby subject to section 7702 for the first time.

- Second, there may be a question whether a contract already subject to section 7702 should be treated as newly issued due to a change, giving rise to new NSPs or guideline premiums. In such a case, the question may be answered by determining if the section 7702(f)(7)(A) adjustment mechanism controls the change.

- Third, the TAMRA reasonable mortality and expense charge rules apply to contracts "entered into" on and after October 21, 1988 (the **reasonable charge effective date rule**),[6] rendering it necessary to determine whether a change will subject an earlier contract to these rules or even subject a post-TAMRA contract to a reapplication of these rules.[7]

- Fourth and finally, TAMRA added section 7702A to the Code, potentially imposing modified endowment contract (MEC) status on contracts "entered into" on or after June 21, 1988 (the **MEC effective date rule**).[8] This requires assessing whether a change to an earlier contract will cause it to be treated as newly entered into after this date so that it becomes subject to section 7702A.

The discussion that follows focuses on when changes should and should not be considered material, giving rise to a need to treat the changed contract as newly issued (potentially entailing a loss of grandfathering), in the context of each of these four circumstances. While a substantial portion of the discussion deals with changes to pre-1985 contracts that trigger application of the section 7702 effective date rule, the principles explained in this discussion have much broader application, i.e., they also are at play in determining whether a contract should be treated as newly issued (or entered into) such that sections 7702 and 7702A should be applied anew to the contract.

## Contract Exchanges

Since 1954, exchanges of life insurance contracts have been granted favorable income tax treatment by virtue of section 1035. Under the Code generally, a gain or loss is recognized on the disposition of property,[9] but under section 1035, gain or loss is not recognized when one contract of life insurance is exchanged for another contract of life insurance covering the same insured(s). The House Ways and Means Committee's report on the Internal Revenue Code of 1954 indicates that section 1035 was designed to eliminate the taxation of individuals in circumstances where they "have merely exchanged one insurance policy for another better suited to their needs and who have not actually realized gain."[10]

However, an exchange of contracts has implications under sections 7702 and 7702A. As noted above, section 7702 generally applies to contracts issued after December

> **What is a Material Change?**
>
> At this juncture, desiring to see a definition or at least a list of examples indicating the kind of change giving rise to tax concerns, the reader may ask, "What is a material change?" Unfortunately, there is no easy answer to this question. The answer itself changes with the context, so that, as discussed below, it will differ depending on the statutory effective date rule involved and, in some cases, on the guidance provided by the IRS. It may also differ depending on the view taken of the precedence, or not, of the adjustment rules described in Chapter 4, evoking debate among tax practitioners. And the answer may be none other than that common refrain under the tax law: "It is unclear." That presents a challenge for programming a computerized administration system, as discussed later in this chapter.

---

[5] Deficit Reduction Act of 1984 (DEFRA), Pub. L. No. 98-369, § 221(a). Section 7702 also applies to contracts issued after June 30, 1984, that provide for an increasing death benefit and have premium funding more rapid than 10-year level premiums, subject to certain exceptions.
[6] Technical and Miscellaneous Revenue Act of 1988 (TAMRA), Pub. L. No. 100-647, § 5011(a) and (b).
[7] Certain other effective date rules also apply under IRC § 7702. For example, IRC § 7702(e)(2)(C), relating to contracts purchased to cover burial expenses or in connection with prearranged funeral expenses, was added to IRC § 7702 by the Tax Reform Act of 1986, Pub. L. No. 99-514 (TRA 1986) and applies to contracts entered into after October 22, 1986. TRA 1986 § 1825(a)(4)(A)–(C); TAMRA § 1018(j). These contracts are discussed in Chapter 6.
[8] TAMRA § 5012(c) and (e)(1).
[9] IRC § 1001. There are, of course, many exceptions to this.
[10] H.R. Rep. No. 83-1337, at 81 (1954).

31, 1984. At the outset of its discussion of the section 7702 effective date rule, the legislative history of section 7702 states, "Contracts issued in exchange for existing contracts after December 31, 1984, are to be considered new contracts issued after that date."[11] It is clear that a contract issued after 1984 in exchange for a contract issued before 1985 is subject to section 7702 under this rule. Specifically, the contract received in the exchange is treated as newly issued as of the date of the exchange. It is likewise clear that when a pre-June 21, 1988, contract is exchanged for a new contract on or after that date, the new contract is treated as entered into on the date of the exchange, subjecting it to testing for MEC status under section 7702A. Early in the lives of the two statutes, the IRS issued private letter rulings to this effect.[12] In the course of the exchange, the cash surrender value carried over from the replaced contract to the new one is considered premium for purposes of applying the guideline premium limitation to the new contract, and it is dealt with under section 7702A by applying the section 7702A(c)(3)(A)(ii) rollover rule. Further, the investment in the contract for purposes of section 72, and the tax basis of the contract for purposes of section 1001 (applicable to sales of contracts), are carried over from the old contract to the new one. Thus, while an exchange is tax free under section 1035, the exchange causes a loss of grandfathering under both section 7702 and section 7702A.[13] Also, in the case of a contract already subject to the definitional limitations that is exchanged for a new contract, the exchange causes those limitations to apply anew, treating the cash surrender value as just described.

While an exchange of contracts gives rise to a new entered-into date under section 7702A, a replaced contract's status as a MEC cannot be eliminated by an exchange. Pursuant to section 7702A(a)(2), MEC treatment applies to any life insurance contract received in exchange for a MEC.[14] Further, as discussed in Chapter 4, a material change under section 7702A(c)(3) includes the exchange of a life insurance contract for another life insurance contract, invoking the application of the rollover rule in determining the new 7-pay premiums for the contract received in the exchange. This enables a benign treatment of the cash value carried over from the replaced contract, i.e., the cash value is not treated as a premium but the available funding provided by that cash value is reflected by reducing the future 7-pay premiums.

Two final points about exchanges are in order. First, the discussion in the preceding paragraphs repeatedly mentions an exchange governed by section 1035, which treats as income tax free (technically, as a "nonrecognition" event) the exchange of a life insurance contract for another life insurance contract under which the insured remains the same.[15] It is possible, however, for an exchange of life insurance contracts to be a taxable exchange, such as when a contract insuring a single life is exchanged for one covering joint lives.[16] A taxable exchange of contracts also gives rise to new-issue treatment of the contract received in the exchange, so that the new contract is subjected to the definitional limitations anew, and any grandfathering treatment applicable to the replaced contract is lost. Beyond that, it appears that the other aspects of the tax treatment of section 1035 exchanges outlined above remain applicable, although the investment in the contract and the contract's tax basis would be determined by taking into account all of the consideration given for the new contract, including the value of the contract given in the exchange. Second, as discussed in Appendix 1.1, a tax-free exchange in theory can involve only a portion of a contract, although the manner of applying the "partial exchange" concept to a life insurance contract (as opposed to an annuity contract) is not well defined. In such a case, it would be necessary to determine, for example, whether a post-2008 partial exchange of a contract based on 1980 CSO mortality into a second contract also based on 1980 CSO mortality would require the definitional limitations

---

[11] DEFRA House Report, *supra* Chapter 1, note 11, at 1449; DEFRA Senate Report, *supra* Chapter 1, note 11, at 579; DEFRA Blue Book *supra* Chapter 1, note 20, at 656; *see also* PLR 8816015 (Jan. 11, 1988).
[12] PLR 9044022 (July 31, 1990) (holding that for purposes of IRC §§ 7702 and 7702A, a contract will be treated as issued and entered into, respectively, on the date it is received in exchange for another contract); PLR 8816015 (Jan. 11, 1988) (same for purposes of IRC § 7702). PLR 8816015 is related to General Counsel Memorandum (GCM) 39728 (April 29, 1988), in which the IRS Office of the Chief Counsel concluded that, for purposes of a grandfather provision under IRC § 264(a)(3), the "purchase date" of a life insurance contract received in an IRC § 1035 exchange is the date of the exchange.
[13] Other issues arise from an IRC § 1035 exchange as well. As discussed in Chapter 4, the application of the recapture ceiling rules of IRC § 7702(f)(7)(B)–(E), otherwise dormant for a contract since the enactment of IRC § 7702A, is reawakened for the 15-year period following the exchange and may result in income inclusion due to a partial withdrawal from a non-MEC. *See* PLR 8816015, *supra* note 12. Also, in certain instances, the "DAC tax" (the acquisition expense capitalization requirement) imposed by IRC § 848 may apply anew with respect to the contract received in the exchange.
[14] As noted in Chapter 4, the Community Renewal Tax Relief Act of 2000, Pub. L. No. 106-554, § 318(a)(1), amended IRC § 7702A(a)(2) to make clear that if a life insurance contract became a MEC, the MEC status could not be eliminated by exchanging the MEC for another contract.
[15] *See* Treas. Reg. § 1.1035-1.
[16] An exception to this arises when a joint and last survivor contract is exchanged for a single life contract following the death of one of the joint insureds. In that case, the exchange may still be tax free under IRC § 1035. *See* PLRs 9330040 (May 6, 1993) and 9248013 (Aug. 28, 1992).

for the second contract to be based instead on 2001 CSO mortality following the exchange.[17] Some insurers do not believe a life insurance contract can be partially exchanged.

## The Issue Date of a Contract

The discussion just concluded, as well as the discussion below regarding changes in contracts that are considered material and cause the contracts to be treated as if they were newly issued when the changes occur, assume it is known when a contract was issued (or treated as issued). But what is the issue date of a contract for purposes of the section 7702 effective date rule or other purposes of the definitional limitations? (The date a contract is considered entered into is discussed subsequently in this chapter, although the next discussion is relevant to it as well.)

Life insurance contracts typically state as part of a contract's terms (usually in the schedule or specifications pages) one or more dates that have relevance to the operation of a contract. The insurance law treatise *Couch on Insurance*, in discussing the beginning of a contract's contestable period, states that the term date of issue "refers to the date of issue appearing on the face of the contract, and not to the time of actual execution or delivery."[18] Thus, a contract's issue date generally is the issue date assigned by the issuing insurance company, and in this respect it is somewhat within the discretion of the company. Contract anniversaries and the dates for the assessment of contract charges also may be measured from this date. The issue date, however, will not necessarily be the date a binding contract is entered into or the date coverage becomes effective. The term "issue date," while having fairly uniform usage in the life insurance industry, is subject to some variation in use because contracts typically include their own definitions of the term, and the import of the term is dictated by the particular provisions of a contract. Thus, contracts may use one term (e.g., issue date) for one purpose but another term (e.g., effective date) for another purpose, and so may provide for an issue date that differs from the date coverage becomes effective.[19] In addition, contracts commonly provide that they will become effective only once they are delivered and the first premium is paid, provided the insured is in good health on that date.[20] In practice, there is frequently a time lag between the issue date and the effective date.

The industry usage of the term "issue date" would appear to control the interpretation of the section 7702 effective date rule.[21] The DEFRA Blue Book reflects this, stating, "For purposes of applying the [section 7702 effective date rule] ... the issue date of a contract is generally the date on the policy assigned by the insurance company, which is on or after the date the application was signed."[22] A footnote to this sentence modifies the statement somewhat: "The use of the date on the policy would not be considered the date of issue if the period between the date of application and the date on which the policy is actually placed in force is substantially longer than under the company's usual business practices."[23] Thus, the DEFRA Blue Book generally defers to

---

[17] The general rule that an exchange gives rise to a newly issued contract for IRC §§ 7702 and 7702A purposes (among others) arguably does not apply where the new contract is issued in connection with a partition or division of the existing contract. In PLRs 200652043 and 200651023 (both Sept. 21, 2006), the IRS addressed a proposal to partition a group corporate-owned life insurance (COLI) contract and the certificates issued thereunder in a circumstance involving the reorganization of a bank holding company following certain acquisitions and mergers and then the spin-off of one of the banks to the parent organization's public shareholders. Since the spin-off bank held ownership interests in the group contract and certificates along with the other banks in the organization with which it was no longer affiliated, it was proposed to partition the group contract and certificates between the spun-off bank and the others in a pro rata manner. This meant that after the partition, the former would own a newly issued group contract and new certificates based on its proportionate interest in the prior contract and certificates, while the latter would own a new contract and certificates reflecting the remaining interest in the prior arrangement. The IRS held on these facts that for purposes of IRC §§ 7702 and 7702A, the new contracts and certificates would succeed to the original issue dates of the contract and certificates they replaced. The IRS further held that the partition would not give rise to an adjustment event or a material change within the meaning of, respectively, IRC §§ 7702(f)(7)(A) and 7702A(c)(3).

[18] *See* COUCH ON INSURANCE 3D § 240:34 (2011). *Compare* DAN M. MCGILL (*revised by* BURKE A. CHRISTENSEN), MCGILL'S LIFE INSURANCE 769 (Edward E. Graves, *et al.* eds. 1994), which states:
  The policy may bear the date on which it was issued, the date on which the coverage becomes effective, or the date on which it was applied for. The most common practice is to date the policy as of the date of issue unless there is a conditional receipt. In this event the policy will bear the date of the application or the medical examination, whichever is later.

[19] *See, e.g.*, COUCH ON INSURANCE 3D § 14:2 (2011).

[20] *See, e.g.*, MCGILL'S LIFE INSURANCE, *supra* note 18, at 759.

[21] From the standpoint of the federal tax law, the starting point for analysis is the language of the tax statute (*i.e.*, the provision in DEFRA encompassing the section 7702 effective date rule), and an accepted principle of statutory construction is that, where a statute addresses a particular subject matter, such as life insurance contracts, technical terms and phrases that pertain to that subject matter should be given their technical meaning when used in the statute. *See, e.g., Atlantic Mut. Ins. Co. v. Comm'r*, 523 U.S. 382 (1998); *Evans v. US*, 504 U.S. 255, 259–60 (1992); *Northwest Airlines v. Transport Workers Union*, 451 U.S. 77, 91 (1981).

[22] DEFRA Blue Book, *supra* Chapter 1, note 20, at 655. No comparable statement appears in the formal DEFRA legislative history.

[23] *Id.*, n. 57. It is noteworthy that regulations finalized in 1999 implementing a special rule treating certain long-term care insurance contracts issued before 1997 as "qualified long-term care insurance contracts" even though they did not meet the requirements of IRC § 7702B followed the above-described formulation for determining the contract's issue date. *See* Treas. Reg. § 1.7702B(b)(3).

the date assigned by the insurer as the issue date, as long as the company has not altered its normal business practices with the purpose of avoiding the section 7702 effective date rule. On the other hand, under this formulation of the rule, the backdating of a contract cannot create a grandfathered contract if the application was signed after 1984.

Deferring to the date assigned by the insurer does not answer all questions regarding a contract's issue date for tax purposes. By way of example, if a contract identifies an issue date in a typical manner and also provides for an effective date of coverage, should the insurer be able to use either date for purposes of applying the section 7702 effective date rule? Use of the stated issue date seems contemplated by the statutory rule and its legislative history, but since calculations under section 7702 are based on the coverage provided, use of the contract's stated effective date seemingly would be reasonable, too. Similarly, for purposes of identifying the date as of which calculations under section 7702 are made, it seems reasonable to allow use of either date, although there is no guidance on this point.

## Material Changes and the Section 7702 Effective Date Rule

While the issue date identified in a contract typically will be used for purposes of the section 7702 effective date rule, so that a contract with an issue date before 1985 generally will not be subject to the requirements of section 7702, the DEFRA legislative history indicates that a change made to such a contract, even if not in the form of an exchange, may cause the contract to be treated as newly issued on the date of the change. If so, where that change occurs after 1984, the altered contract can become subject to section 7702. In particular, in describing the section 7702 effective date rule, the Senate Finance Committee's report on DEFRA states:

> Contracts issued in exchange for existing contracts after December 31, 1984 are to be considered new contracts issued after that date. For these purposes a change in an existing contract will not be considered to result in an exchange, if the terms of the resulting contract (that is, the amount or pattern of death benefit, the premium pattern, the rate or rates guaranteed on issuance of the contract, or mortality and expense charges) are the same as the terms of the contract prior to the change. Thus, a change in minor administrative provisions or a loan rate generally will not be considered to result in an exchange.[24]

This statement is both interesting and somewhat curious, for after intimating that a change in a contract can be deemed to be an exchange (forfeiting grandfathering), it proceeds to say what will not be such a material change. Thus, according to the statement, a change after 1984 in a contract issued before 1985 that does not affect the material terms or economics of the contract—that is, it does not change the amount or pattern of the death benefit, the premium payment pattern, the rate or rates guaranteed on issuance of the contract (presumably meaning the interest rates), or the guaranteed mortality and expense charges—is not considered the issuance of a new contract for purposes of section 7702. Even so, the statement often is read as an affirmative instruction, namely, that any amendment to a pre-1985 contract which has the effect of changing the guaranteed values of the contract will constitute a **deemed exchange** of that contract for a new one, thereby subjecting the amended contract to the requirements of section 7702.[25] It further indicates, however, that changes not so described do not have such an effect, i.e., they do not amount to material changes. Hence, in private letter rulings issued by the IRS, a change in ownership of a contract,[26] the addition of investment media underlying a variable or indexed contract,[27] and even an alteration in the identity of the insurer due to an assumption rein-

---

[24] DEFRA Senate Report, *supra* Chapter 1, note 11, at 579. *See also* DEFRA Blue Book, *supra* Chapter 1, note 20, at 656.
[25] *See, e.g.*, TAM (technical advice memorandum) 9347005 (treating the addition of an endorsement to certain life insurance contracts, offered to and accepted by the policyholders, that changed the contracts' interest rate guarantee as resulting in an IRC § 1035 exchange). *See also* the discussion of CCA (chief counsel advice) 200805022 (Aug. 17, 2007) below.
[26] *See* PLR 9109018 (Nov. 29, 1990) (assignment of a life insurance contract to an employer's grantor trust did not constitute a material change); PLR 9033023 (May 18, 1990) (assignment of a life insurance contract to a trust and subsequent return of the contract to the taxpayer did not constitute material changes).
[27] *See* PLR 201045019 (Aug. 5, 2010) (amendment to add an investment option under an indexed life insurance contract did not constitute a material change for purposes of IRC §§ 7702 and 7702A); PLR 8648018 (Aug. 27, 1986) (amendment to a pre-DEFRA variable life insurance contract to allow additional investment options did not constitute a material change subjecting the contract to IRC § 7702).

surance transaction,[28] reorganization[29] or demutualization[30] were all held not to constitute material changes. In this connection, the Senate report's statement expressly includes in this more favorable category a change to an existing contract's loan rate[31] or other "minor" administrative provisions.[32]

Before inquiring into which contractual changes fall into the material category for purposes of the section 7702 effective date rule, a more fundamental question is: What constitutes a change that can be a material one? Some changes in death benefits, even though arguably described (in the negative) in the Senate report's discussion, clearly do not fall within the ambit of that rule. Examples of situations in which death benefit increases would not cause contracts to be treated as newly issued for this purpose include those mandated by the normal operation of the contract to assure compliance with the cash value accumulation test (CVAT) or the section 7702(d) cash value corridor, such as increases resulting from the use of policyholder dividends to purchase paid-up additions and from variable contract market performance.

Further to the same question, can the exercise of an option or right granted under a contract, whether to the policyholder or to the insurer, constitute such a change at all? As a general rule, the tax law does not treat the exercise of a pre-existing option or right as implementing a change that can be considered material. Rather, following the reasoning of the U.S. Supreme Court in *Cottage Savings Association v. Commissioner*, it is necessary that the legal entitlements of the parties to a transaction differ, in kind or extent, before and after a change in order for the change to be material for tax purposes.[33] Thus, in the context of section 7702, the exercise of a contractually based option or right generally should not give rise to a material change because it is not, in the first instance, really a change at all. It does not alter any existing legal entitlement, but merely carries out the terms of the original property.

This view is supported by the DEFRA Blue Book, which elaborates on the Senate report's statement (quoted above) in saying, "The exercise of an option or right granted under the contract as originally issued does not result in an exchange and thus does not constitute the issuance of a new contract for purposes of new section 7702 and any applicable transition rules if the option guaranteed terms that might not otherwise have been available when the option is exercised."[34] While the DEFRA Blue Book does not represent official legislative history,[35] it mirrors the tax law's material change principle as subsequently articulated by the Supreme Court in *Cottage Savings*, fleshing out the more abbreviated material change discussion of the Senate report.

Accordingly, if a change is made after 1984 to a contract issued before 1985 pursuant to an option or right granted under the contract, the exercise of that option or right usually[36] will not cause the contract to be viewed as materially changed and thus as newly issued for purposes of the section 7702 effective date rule. One ex-

---

[28] *See* PLRs 201443015 (July 15, 2014); 9407019 (Nov. 19, 1993); 9034022, 9034021, 9034018, 9034016, 9034015 and 9034014 (all May 23, 1990); and 8645008 (Aug. 4, 1986). In these rulings, the IRS emphasized that no change was made in the terms of the contracts other than the substitution of the assuming reinsurer as the contracts' primary obligor. *See also* PLR 200446001 (July 13, 2004) on the difference between assumption reinsurance and an exchange of policies.

[29] *See* PLR 200804010 (Oct. 11, 2007) (statutory merger of mutual companies); PLR 200303028 (Oct. 2, 2002) (liquidation); PLR 200249013 (Sept. 12, 2002) (mutual holding company liquidation); PLR 9601041 (Oct. 5, 1995) (IRC § 338 election).

[30] *See, e.g.,* PLRs 200002010 (Sept. 30, 1999) and 199916023 (Jan. 21, 1999).

[31] *See, e.g.,* PLR 9737007 (June 11, 1997) (modifications to a life insurance contract to provide that policy loan interest is payable in arrears, rather than in advance, do not constitute material changes). To the same effect are PLRs 9714029 (Jan. 7, 1997), 9412023 (Dec. 22, 1993), 9150045 (Sept. 17, 1991), 9203009 (Jan. 29, 1991) and 9117011 (May 18, 1990).

[32] *See also* DEFRA Blue Book, *supra* Chapter 1, note 20, at 656.

[33] 499 U.S. 554, 565 (1991). In *Cottage Savings*, the Supreme Court concluded that portfolios of participation interests in mortgages exchanged by savings and loan institutions were "different" in a sense that was material for tax purposes where the exchanged properties entailed legal entitlements which were different in kind or extent. Thus, even though a property interest may seem to continue from an economic perspective or in legal form—*e.g.,* where a life insurance contract continues on the same form with the same contract number—a material change in the legal entitlements associated with the property interest can cause the changed property to be viewed as a property that is different from the original, with the consequence that the first property is considered to have been exchanged for the second property for tax purposes.

In the aftermath of *Cottage Savings*, the IRS issued regulations providing that any "significant modification" to the terms of a debt instrument would be deemed an exchange. Treas. Reg. § 1.1001-3(b). In the context of debt instruments, the regulations define such a modification as "any alteration, including any deletion or addition, in whole or in part of a legal right or obligation of the issuer or a holder of a debt instrument." Treas. Reg. § 1.1001-3(c)(1)(i). The regulations further state a modification is significant "if based on all the facts and circumstances, the legal rights or obligations that are altered and the degree to which they are altered are economically significant." Treas. Reg. § 1.1001-3(e)(1). These regulations expressly did not address changes made to life insurance contracts, apart from making comments supporting the conclusion in Rev. Rul. 90-109, 1990-2 C.B. 191, discussed below.

[34] DEFRA Blue Book, *supra* Chapter 1, note 20, at 656. The quoted statement does not appear in the formal DEFRA legislative history. As described later in this chapter, Congress followed a different approach in crafting the effective date of IRC § 7702A. In that case, as directed by statute, some changes may cause a contract to become subject to IRC § 7702A even if the changes are made pursuant to an option under the terms of the contract.

[35] See the discussion in Appendix 1.2.

[36] To understand why the word "usually" appears here, see the discussion of "fundamental change" below.

ample of a change that falls in this category is the ability of the policyholder of a traditional whole life contract to change the premium mode of the contract (e.g., from monthly to annual or vice versa) or to change the use of policyholder dividends (e.g., from purchasing paid-up additions to reduction of future premiums or payments in cash), or the ability of a universal life policyholder to change the death benefit pattern from option 2 to option 1.

Of course, there can be a question whether a change is being made pursuant to a contractual option or right. As an illustration, a universal life contract may include an express right of the policyholder to obtain an increase in the contract's death benefit, but this right is subject to underwriting approval by the issuing insurer. This would still seem to constitute a right, as the insurer would need to employ reasonable underwriting guidelines and could not arbitrarily deny the requested increase. (As discussed later, the IRS has followed this view in connection with the application of the reasonable mortality rule of section 7702(c)(3)(B)(i).) As another example, insurers commonly permit a change in a contract's smoking status or in a rating if the insured satisfies the underwriting criteria for an improved status, even though there may not be an express contractual right to make the change. Seemingly, a policyholder would need to possess a contractually enforceable right to make the change in order to characterize it fairly as a right. In the absence of an express contractual provision, it is necessary to examine whether an enforceable right otherwise exists under state law. In the case of a change in a contract's smoking status or in a rating, this may well be the case.

A similar question can arise when the change is being made not by the policyholder, but by the insurer. In a 1997 private letter ruling[37] addressing the treatment of excess interest under a contract subject to section 101(f), the IRS noted a difference between discretionary interest credits that may vary from year to year and a change in legal entitlements resulting in the deemed issuance of a new contract:

> For example, if an insurance company, as a result of an excess interest declaration, is obligated to pay excess interest for several years, then the excess interest credits may not be economically equivalent to discretionary policyholder dividend distributions. Instead, the excess interest credits may be the minimum amounts fixed in the parties' new contract. *Cf. Cottage Savings Ass'n v. Commissioner*, 111 S. Ct. 1503 (1991), 1991-2 C.B. 34 (change of legal entitlements was an exchange). If there is a new contract, then the declared excess interest rate would be the initial guaranteed minimum rate for the guarantee period and the declared excess interest rate would be used to determine the new contract's guideline premium limitation under section 101(f).

Yet another category of contractual changes that do not rise to the material level are those that fit within the Senate report's reference to "minor administrative provisions." According to this legislative history, even if a change is not made pursuant to an option or right, it usually will not cause the contract involved to be viewed as newly issued if the change can be characterized as merely a minor administrative one, or if the change is in the interest rate charged on a policy loan. Apart from the reference to the loan interest rate, the precise scope of the exception for "minor administrative" changes is not spelled out. The legislative history simply contrasts such changes with those that generally would result in a material change, i.e., a change in the amount or pattern of death benefit, the premium pattern, or the interest rate(s) or mortality or expense charges guaranteed on issuance of the contract. Thus, if the change does not relate to one of these elements, and if the change otherwise is not relevant to the calculations under section 7702, arguably it is a minor one that should not trigger application of the section 7702 effective date rule.

On the other hand, changes may be made to grandfathered contracts, even apart from their guaranteed values, which are so significant that the altered contracts should be treated as newly issued for purposes of the section 7702 effective date rule. The legislative history of section 7702 does not directly address this circumstance, but some guidance can be gleaned from other tax authorities. First, if under state law a contract is treated as new, it usually will be necessary to treat it as new for federal tax purposes.[38] Thus, if a contract has a new issue date, new contract number, new contestability and suicide periods, and otherwise is accounted for

---

[37] PLR 9723040 (March 11, 1997).
[38] *See U.S. v. Nat'l Bank of Commerce*, 472 U.S. 713 (1985) ("In applying the Internal Revenue Code, state law controls in determining the nature of the legal interest which the taxpayer has in property. ... The question whether a state-law right constitutes 'property' or 'right to property' for federal tax-collection purposes is a matter of federal law.").

under state law as a new contract, that characterization usually will apply for federal tax purposes. This also generally follows from the fact that section 7702 attaches, in the first instance, to contracts that constitute life insurance under "applicable law."

Second, even if the altered contract is not considered new for state law purposes, a change that is considered fundamental may require the contract's treatment as newly issued for tax purposes.[39] That said, whether and when this is the case are difficult questions, in part due to a paucity of guidance and also because the adjustment rules under sections 7702 and 7702A are usually capable of accounting for significant changes. One possibility is presented in Rev. Rul. 90-109,[40] in which the IRS held that a taxable exchange occurred when a policyholder exercised its contractual right to change the insured under a key person life insurance contract. In analyzing the tax treatment of a change of insured, the IRS noted, "A change in contractual terms effected through an option provided in the original contract is treated as an exchange under section 1001 if there is a sufficiently fundamental or material change that the substance of the original contract is altered through the exercise of the option." The IRS went on to observe that a change in insured in the context of an actual exchange would be subject to tax under section 1001 (i.e., section 1035 would not apply, due to the requirement that the insured remain the same[41]) and that the change of insured "resulted in a change in the fundamental substance of the original contract because the essence of a life insurance contract is the life that is insured under the contract."

While Rev. Rul. 90-109 does not expressly address the effect of a change of insured under section 7702, it is possible the ruling's holding may apply more generally for tax purposes, including under section 7702, especially given the ruling's reasoning that the change is so significant that it is proper to view the pre-existing property as having been terminated and replaced by a different property. On the other hand, according to the DEFRA Blue Book, a substitution of insured issued under a binding contractual obligation is not a new contract, so the contract's grandfather treatment is not lost,[42] although an adjustment under section 7702(f)(7)(A) based on the attained age of the new insured at the time of the substitution presumably would follow. A similar sentiment was expressed in 1986 with respect to the changes then being made in section 264 (related to the deductibility of policy loan interest) in a floor colloquy between Sen. Dole and Sen. Packwood. In their colloquy, the senators expressed their understanding that the exercise of an option or right granted under a contract as originally issued, including the substitution of the insured, would not be treated as the purchase of a new contract for purposes of a change being made to section 264.[43] However, in extended remarks, Rep. Rostenkowski, chairman of the House Ways and Means Committee, noted his disagreement with statements "which seem to validate the ability to substitute insureds under a policy and qualify under the [section 264] grandfather provisions."[44] Consistently with these remarks, the holding and reasoning of Rev. Rul. 90-109 potentially place a cloud over the optimistic discussion in the Blue Book language above. In any event, the extension of this to section 7702 is far from clear, in that the adjustment rule of section 7702 is capable of accounting for a change of insured.[45] Hence, the section 7702 treatment of a substitution of insured is at best unsettled, and resolution of the "fundamental change" question under the section 7702 effective date rule (and for other purposes) must await further guidance.

The reader, at this stage, may come away with some principles and a few illustrations regarding what are (and are not) material changes, at least in the context of the section 7702 effective date rule, but nothing approaching a comprehensive list of such changes. No official guidance provides such a list for purposes of any of the definitional limitations. It is of interest, however, that regulations finalized in 1999 to implement a special rule treating certain long-term care insurance contracts issued before 1997 as "qualified long-term care insurance contracts" even though they did not meet the requirements of section 7702B provided a list of changes that, if made to contracts issued before 1997, would or would not forfeit this grandfathering treatment. According to these regulations, which could be helpful by analogy in determining the materiality of a life insurance contractual change,

---

[39] While state law identifies the existence of legal rights, federal tax law generally governs the import of those rights. *See id.*
[40] 1990-2 C.B. 191.
[41] Treas. Reg. § 1.1035-1.
[42] DEFRA Blue Book, *supra* Chapter 1, note 20, at 656. This statement does not appear in the formal DEFRA legislative history.
[43] 132 Cong. Rec. S13,898 (daily ed. Sept. 27, 1986) (statements of Sen. Dole and Sen. Packwood).
[44] 132 Cong. Rec. E3,389 (daily ed. Oct. 2, 1986) (statement of Rep. Rostenkowski).
[45] When a contract is newly issued, guideline premiums are calculated based on the then attained age of the insured. In contrast, under the IRC § 7702(f)(7)(A) adjustment rule for guideline premium contracts, changes generally reflect the attained age of the insured only in respect of the changed portion of a contract. New-issue treatment of the changed contract could well result in an increased guideline premium limitation for the contract relative to the effect of a change under the adjustment rule.

a pre-1997 contract would be treated as newly issued if a change in its terms altered the amount or timing of an item payable by the policyholder or the insurance company or if, in the case of an individual contract, there was a substitution of the insured. On the other hand, new-issuance treatment would not apply to:

- a change made due to a policyholder's exercise of a right provided under the terms of the contract as in effect on December 31, 1996, or a right required by applicable state law to be provided to the policyholder;

- a change in the mode of premium payment;

- a reduction in coverage (with a corresponding reduction in premiums) made at the request of a policyholder;

- the addition, without an increase in premiums, of alternative forms of benefits that may be selected by the policyholder; and

- the substitution of one insurer for another insurer in an assumption reinsurance transaction.[46]

It should be no surprise that this list tracks the Senate report on the section 7702 effective date rule and the upshot of Rev. Rul. 90-109, although it encompasses some liberality that has yet to be applied in the case of the definitional limitations.

## Reapplying Section 7702: New Issue Treatment of Contracts and the Role of the Adjustment Rules

The preceding discussion focused on circumstances in which a change to a pre-DEFRA contract may be viewed as a material change, causing the contract to be treated as newly issued for purposes of the section 7702 effective date rule. But what about a material change to a contract already subject to section 7702 or to its statutory predecessor, section 101(f)? On the one hand, the standard set out in the legislative history of the section 7702 effective date rule might view the contract as newly issued, so that section 7702 would apply anew to the contract. On the other hand, the adjustment rules of sections 7702(f)(7)(A) and 101(f)(2)(E), respectively, arguably control the treatment of a change to a contract insofar as it does not alter the contract's "issue date" under state law. The discussion below first considers the kinds of changes that potentially subject a contract to treatment as newly issued for purposes of the definitional limitations—changes made via a new, bilateral agreement between the policyholder and the insurer, in the absence of the unilateral option or right vested in the policyholder under the contract, and those, in the words of Rev. Rul. 90-109, that "resulted in a change in the fundamental substance of the original contract." It will then consider the scope of the role played by the adjustment rules in the case of such changes.

### *Absence of an Option or Right*

The treatment of a change made to a contract that was already subject to section 101(f) or section 7702, in the absence of an option or right of the policyholder to obtain the change, has been the subject of IRS guidance in several instances. In 2007, for example, the IRS issued a chief counsel advice memorandum dealing with a change in a contract's death benefit pattern and the addition of a qualified addition benefit (QAB) to the contract.[47] As discussed in the CCA, a life insurance company had requested rulings that a change from an increas-

---

[46] *See* Treas. Reg. § 1.7702B-2(b)(4). A somewhat similar listing of changes not treated as material changes appears in the legislative history of the Pension Protection Act of 2006 (PPA), Pub. L. No. 109-280, although it is not clear that all changes listed there would avoid new-issuance treatment under the section 7702 effective date rule. *See* STAFF OF JT. COMM. ON TAX'N, 109TH CONG., TECHNICAL EXPLANATION OF H.R. 4, THE "PENSION PROTECTION ACT OF 2006," AS PASSED BY THE HOUSE ON JULY 28, 2006, AND AS CONSIDERED BY THE SENATE ON AUGUST 3, 2006, at 211, n. 233 (Comm. Print 2006) (hereinafter PPA 2006 Blue Book). This "technical explanation" serves as the Pension Protection Act's legislative history, since, due to the unusual procedural circumstances in which the act passed Congress, the customary Ways and Means Committee, Finance Committee and conference reports on legislation were lacking. *See* 152 CONG. REC. H6,158 (July 28, 2006) (statement of Ways and Means Committee Chairman Thomas); 152 CONG. REC. S8,763 (August 3, 2006) (statement of Finance Committee Chairman Grassley).

[47] CCA 200805022 (Aug. 17, 2007). A CCA is written advice or instruction, under whatever name or designation, prepared by any National Office component of the IRS's Office of Chief Counsel that is issued to field or service center employees of the IRS (or regional or district employees of the Office of Chief Counsel) and conveys any legal interpretation of a revenue provision, any position or policy of the IRS or of the Office of Chief Counsel concerning a revenue provision, or any legal interpretation of federal, state or foreign law relating to the assessment or collection of any liability under a revenue provision. IRC § 6110(i). CCAs generally may not be used or cited as precedent. *See* IRC § 6110(k) and IRC § 6110(b)(1)(A).

ing death benefit pattern to a level pattern or the addition of a QAB by rider would not result in new-issuance treatment (i.e., a material change resulting in a loss of grandfathering) under the section 7702 effective date rule as well as under TAMRA's reasonable charge effective date rule (discussed in detail later in this chapter). The CCA recorded that the contracts as originally issued provided only for an increasing death benefit pattern, with no ability for the policyholders to obtain a level death benefit, and also that the express terms of the contracts did not address QAB riders, although the taxpayer had a practice of allowing policyholders to add such riders with evidence of insurability.

In rejecting the company's arguments supporting its requested rulings,[48] the CCA pointed to the double-negative statement in the legislative history of the section 7702 effective date rule that a change to a pre-1985 contract would *not* be treated as an exchange (and hence as a newly issued contract for purposes of the effective date) if it did *not* alter, among other things, the amount or pattern of the death benefit or the mortality and expense charges. The CCA reasoned that this statement established, by "negative inference," that a death benefit pattern change or the addition of a QAB rider, with no option or right under the contract for the policyholder to obtain it, would cause a loss of grandfathering under DEFRA. With regard to the TAMRA effective date, the CCA cited a statement in the House Ways and Means Committee report on TAMRA that referred to contracts issued or materially changed on or after July 13, 1988 (the then proposed effective date for the TAMRA changes), and the CCA concluded that this material change language "will cause a life insurance contract to be entered into anew (for purposes of [the reasonable charge effective date rule]) if there is an increase in future benefits." Perhaps demonstrating a significant concern of the IRS underlying these conclusions, the CCA added that to conclude otherwise "would virtually eliminate the ability to lose grandfathered status except in the clearest of circumstances (new contracts actually issued after the effective date or tax avoidance) and does not follow the intent of Congress."

The CCA's conclusion and reasoning are not beyond question. Its analysis omits consideration of the section 101(f) and 7702 adjustment rules and misapplies the legislative history of the TAMRA effective date. Thus, for example, the DEFRA legislative history says that the "provision that certain changes in future benefits be treated as exchanges was not intended to alter the application of the transition rules for life insurance contracts and only applies with respect to such changes in contracts issued after December 31, 1984."[49] This legislative history thus clarifies that the exchange treatment accorded to reductions in benefits under section 7702(f)(7)(B), prior to its amendment by TRA 1986, was intended for purposes of determining the effect of a reduction in benefits for a contract already subject to section 7702 (i.e., distributions accompanying a benefit reduction would be taxed on a gain-first basis under the boot rule), but that this special statutory rule was not intended to affect the application of the section 7702 effective date rule otherwise. The DEFRA grandfather rule, in other words, coordinated with the adjustment rule, and since the adjustment rule was available to address the change in the CCA case for post-DEFRA contracts, there was no reason to conclude that grandfathering should be forfeited for such contracts. (The role of the adjustment rules in this context is explored below.) Further, the TAMRA legislative history shows that Congress rejected a previously proposed material change rule as part of the reasonable charge effective date rule. Under the House version of TAMRA, the reasonable mortality and expense charge rules were to be effective for contracts issued on or after July 13, 1988, and a contract that was materially changed (within the meaning of then new section 7702A(c)(3)) on or after that date was to be treated as newly issued.[50] However, under TAMRA as enacted, the effective date rule was changed simply to

---

[48] The revenue procedure governing private letter ruling requests states, "If a taxpayer withdraws a letter ruling request …, the Associate office generally will notify, by memorandum, the appropriate Service official in the operating division that has examination jurisdiction of the taxpayer's tax return and may give its views on the issues in the request to the Service official to consider in any later examination of the return. … If the memorandum to the Service official … provides more than the fact that the request was withdrawn and the Associate office was tentatively adverse, or that the Associate office declines to issue a letter ruling, the memorandum may constitute Chief Counsel Advice." Rev. Proc. 2007-1, 2007-1 C.B. 1, § 7.07 (which applied at the time the CCA was issued).

[49] TRA 1986 House Report, *supra* Chapter 3, note 26, at 966; TRA 1986 Senate Report, *supra* Chapter 3, note 26, at 988; Technical Corrections Blue Book, *supra* Chapter 3, note 21, at 107. *See also* DEFRA Blue Book, *supra* Chapter 1, note 20, at 654 (stating that "section 7702 will not become applicable to a contract that was issued before January 1, 1985 [*e.g.*, an IRC § 101(f) contract], because a reduction of the contracts [sic] future benefits resulted in the application of [the] adjustment provision"); DEFRA House Report, *supra* Chapter 1, note 11, at 1448 (to the same effect); DEFRA Senate Report, *supra* Chapter 1, note 11, at 578 (to the same effect).

[50] H.R. 4333, 100TH CONG. (reported July 26, 1988). *See* TAMRA House Report *supra* Chapter 4, note 40, at 545–46 (describing the proposed rule).

"contracts entered into" on or after October 21, 1988; the rule that material changes would trigger a loss of grandfathering was dropped.[51]

The theme sounded by the 2007 CCA, focusing on material change treatment in the absence of a policyholder's right to obtain a contractual change, was echoed in a 2012 private letter ruling in which the IRS addressed whether an extracontractual reduction in death benefits gave rise to a deemed new issuance of the contract under the section 7702(c)(3)(B)(i) reasonable mortality rules.[52] According to the ruling letter, a life insurance company requested a ruling regarding the effect, under the reasonable mortality rules, of death benefit reductions in 2012 and thereafter—that is, after the January 1, 2009 effective date of the 2001 CSO tables[53]—in certain CVAT-tested contracts the company had issued based on the 1980 CSO tables. The insurer represented that the contracts were issued before 2009 and complied with the section 7702(c)(3)(B)(i) rules based on IRS Notices 88-128 and 2006-95; if death benefit changes under the contracts caused them to be treated as newly issued after 2008, they would not comply with the CVAT unless their values were based on the 2001 CSO tables. The IRS noted that the contracts "do not include a provision that explicitly contemplates the owner's ability to request a decrease in coverage," but also that it was the insurer's historical practice, upon policyholders' requests to implement death benefit decreases, to grant the requests.

The IRS held that, due to the absence of a right of the policyholders to request the death benefit decreases, the contracts would be treated as newly issued for purposes of the reasonable mortality rules when the death benefits were reduced, meaning the contracts would thereafter need to comply with section 7702 based on NSPs computed assuming 2001 CSO mortality. Technically, the issue in this ruling involved the application of the safe harbor rule of Notice 2006-95 (addressed further below). The significance of the ruling in the present context, however, is that the IRS required section 7702 to apply anew to contracts already subject to it, and the agency did so by invoking the legislative history of the section 7702 effective date rule (which served as the notice's material change standard). The issues raised by the reapplication of the reasonable mortality rule are discussed below.

A conclusion more favorable to the issuing life insurance company is found in a 1998 private letter ruling,[54] in which the company offered policyholders an endorsement allowing them to change from an increasing death benefit pattern originally provided under their universal life contracts to a level death benefit pattern. Significantly, and fortunately for the insurer, the endorsement was made available to all of the company's policyholders *before* the October 21, 1988, effective date of the reasonable mortality rule, although at least some of the policyholders apparently had not exercised their rights under the endorsement by that date. The IRS held that the actual exercise of the option to change to the level death benefit pattern *after* the rule's effective date did not cause the contracts to be treated as newly entered for purposes of applying the rule, as the right to make the change had been granted prior to that effective date.

## *Fundamental Change*

Unlike the case in which a policyholder has no right to obtain a contractual change, the section 7702 treatment of a change made to a contract already subject to the statute that is considered material because the change is **fundamental** has not been the subject of guidance, with one possible exception. As previously discussed, in Rev. Rul. 90-109, the IRS held that a taxable exchange occurred when a policyholder exercised its contractual right to change the insured under a key person life insurance contract, observing that the change of insured "resulted in a change in the fundamental substance of the original contract because the essence of a life insurance contract is the life that is insured under the contract." This ruling, as noted above, specifically addresses the treatment of the change of insured under sections 1001 and 1035, not section 7702. However, given the ruling's reasoning that the change is so significant it is proper to view the pre-existing property as having been terminated and replaced by a different property, it seems possible that the ruling's holding may apply for tax purposes more generally, including under section 7702, and may do so despite statements to the contrary in

---
[51] *See* TAMRA Conference Report *supra* Chapter 2, note 64, at 108. Under principles of statutory construction, where Congress includes limiting language in an earlier version of a bill but deletes it prior to enactment, it may be presumed that the limitation was not intended. *See Russello v. United States*, 464 U.S. 16, 23-24 (1983).
[52] PLR 201230009 (Jan. 30, 2012).
[53] This effective date applies for purposes of the safe harbor provided by IRS Notice 2006-95.
[54] PLR 9853033 (Sept. 30, 1998).

the DEFRA Blue Book. Indicative of this (and possibly of the exception noted above), in a 1994 private letter ruling, the IRS waived as reasonable error under section 7702(f)(8) the treatment of a substitution of insured as an "adjustment event in a continuing policy" rather than as a new contract.[55]

### Role of the Adjustment Rules

If one of the types of material changes is made to a contract already subject to section 101(f) or 7702, should new-issuance treatment pursuant to the legislative history of the section 7702 effective date rule apply to the contract, or should the adjustment rules control the contract's treatment, assuming that change does not alter the contract's issue date under state law? This question and its answer are potentially complex, but the inquiry clearly requires interpretation of the statutes involved. In this connection, an important tenet of statutory construction is that more specific statutory rules govern over more general rules.[56] This tenet provides a firm basis for concluding that the adjustment rules, rather than the DEFRA legislative history, govern the treatment of a contract change which they are capable of handling. Congress obviously intended for these rules to account for changes in the terms or benefits of contracts, and nothing in the statutes or their legislative histories purport to limit the kinds of changes the rules can reach. Antiabuse considerations likewise enter into the calculus here. For example, in the case of a death benefit increase not made pursuant to an option or right, the adjustment rules (if applied) would increase guideline premiums by the attained-age amounts attributable to the increase, but if the contract were viewed as newly issued, guideline premiums would be calculated entirely anew. In this way, the guideline single premium would reflect the insured's attained age at the time of the change for all benefits, not just the increase.[57]

Unfortunately, the proper treatment of contract changes under section 7702 (and section 101(f)), especially those not pursuant to an option or right granted in the contract, is not clear. In large part the uncertainty arises because of the ill-defined relationship between section 7702 and the general material change principle embodied in *Cottage Savings*. At minimum, the deficiencies in the 2007 CCA's analysis call into question the soundness of its conclusions, leaving open the possibility that other reasonable conclusions may be drawn. Unless the IRS issues more definitive guidance, grandfathering issues likely will continue to be the subject of debate.[58]

## TAMRA: Reasonable Charges, Section 7702A and the TAMRA Effective Date Rules

As previously noted, in 1988 TAMRA imposed the section 7702(c)(3)(B)(i) and (ii) reasonable mortality and expense charge rules effective for "contracts entered into on or after October 21, 1988[59] (again, the reasonable charge effective date rule) and also applied section 7702A to "contracts entered into on or after June 21, 1988[60] (the MEC effective date rule). Unlike the section 7702 effective date rule, which is based on the date a contract is issued, the latter two rules are based on the date a contract is entered into. The use of different terms raises an initial question about how they are different. Whereas "issue date" has a technical meaning under state insurance law and generally refers to the date identified in a contract as the issue date, an "entered into" date does not appear to have a meaning specific to the insurance context, nor is it defined in the statutory language. Under normal principles of statutory interpretation, then, the term should be construed in accordance with its

---

[55] PLR 9438015 (June 23, 1994). Since, to request a waiver under IRC § 7702(f)(8), a taxpayer must concede an action as an error, it is not clear adjustment treatment in this case is objectively wrong.

[56] *See, e.g., Fourco Glass Co. v. Transmirra Products Corp.*, 353 U.S. 222, 228 (1957) (citations omitted) ("However inclusive may be the general language of a statute, it will not be held to apply to a matter specifically dealt with in another part of the same enactment."); George Costello, *Statutory Interpretation: General Principles and Recent Trends*, CRS REPORT FOR CONGRESS, March 30, 2006, at CRS-10.

[57] The DEFRA legislative history appears to reflect a similar concern when, in discussing the IRC § 7702 adjustment rule for guideline premiums, it states, "No adjustment shall be made if the change occurs automatically, for example, a change due to the growth of the cash surrender value (whether by the crediting of excess interest or the payment of guideline premiums) or *changes initiated by the company*" (emphasis added). There apparently was concern that changes which could unilaterally be made by an insurer could be used to increase guideline premiums based on the higher attained age of the insured at the time of the change. A deemed new issuance of the contract would present the same concern.

[58] In this connection, it may be worth noting that even a change to a contract to bring it into compliance with IRC § 7702, pursuant to an IRC § 7702(f)(8) waiver proceeding (*see* Chapter 8), may give rise to material change and loss-of-grandfathering concerns. In PLRs 200901028 (Sept. 29, 2008) and 200841034 (March 28, 2008), apparently at the insurers' requests, the IRS ruled the remedial changes (via contract amendment) would not give rise to new-issuance treatment.

[59] TAMRA § 5011(d).

[60] TAMRA § 5012(e)(1).

ordinary, plain meaning.[61] It seems that the plain meaning of the date a life insurance contract (or any contract) is entered into is the date on which the parties to the contract first enter into a binding contractual agreement under state or other applicable law—in other words, the date when contract formation occurs.[62]

The legislative history of TAMRA indicates that Congress' decision to reference the date a contract is entered into rather than its issue date was a deliberate one. In particular, the House Ways and Means Committee's report on TAMRA, in commenting on the MEC effective date rule, states that a contract will be considered entered into no earlier than "the date that (1) the contract is endorsed by both the owner of the contract and the insurance company; or (2) an application is executed by both the applicant and the insurance company and a premium payment is made by the applicant to the insurance company."[63] The report goes on to say, "The backdating of an application or an insurance contract shall be disregarded for purposes of this effective date."[64]

Unlike the case with the section 7702 effective date rule, the legislative history accompanying the reasonable charge effective date rule does not directly address whether a change to a pre-TAMRA contract could cause it to become subject to the then new mortality and expense charge rules. In fact, as described above, an effort made in the House version of the bill that became TAMRA to subject pre-existing contracts to an explicit material change rule (one modeled on section 7702A(c)(3)) was deleted from the version ultimately enacted. On the other hand, Congress broke its silence on material changes when it included detailed rules for purposes of the MEC effective date rule. TAMRA section 5012(e) includes the following two rules for purposes of determining whether a change will cause a contract to become subject to section 7702A:

> (2)... If the death benefit under the contract increases by more than $150,000 over the death benefit under the contract in effect on October 20, 1988, the [material change] rules of section 7702A(c)(3) ... shall apply in determining whether such contract is issued on or after June 21, 1988. The preceding sentence shall not apply in the case of a contract which, as of June 21, 1988, required at least 7 level annual premium payments and under which the policyholder continues to make level annual premium payments over the life of the contract.[65]

> (3)... A contract entered into before June 21, 1988, shall be treated as entered into after such date if—
> (A) on or after June 21, 1988, the death benefit under the contract is increased (or a qualified additional benefit is increased or added) and before June 21, 1988, the owner of the contract did not have a unilateral right under the contract to obtain such increase or addition without providing additional evidence of insurability, or

> (B) the contract is converted after June 20, 1988, from a term life insurance contract to a life insurance contract providing coverage other than term life insurance coverage without regard to any right of the owner of the contract to such conversion.

In considering changes commonly made under life insurance contracts, perhaps the most significant of these rules is TAMRA section 5012(e)(3)(A), since under it any underwritten increase in death benefit or underwritten addition of or increase in a QAB will cause the contract to be newly entered into, losing its grandfathering under the MEC effective date rule. Beyond these changes, however, the transition rules for the MEC effective date rule expressly treat changes as resulting in a newly entered-into contract only in limited circumstances, i.e., term conversions and certain non-underwritten death benefit increases in excess of $150,000 that would give

---

[61] *See, e.g., Perrin v. United States*, 444 U.S. 37, 42 (1979); *Crane v. Comm'r*, 331 U.S. 1, 6 (1946) ("[T]he words of statutes—including revenue acts—should be interpreted where possible in their ordinary, everyday senses.").

[62] This is consistent with a definition of "enter" in BLACK'S LAW DICTIONARY, which includes the following definition of the term: "To become a party to <they entered into an agreement>." BLACK'S LAW DICTIONARY 611 (9th ed. 2009). It is also consistent with a definition of "enter into" in WEBSTER'S THIRD NEW INTERNATIONAL DICTIONARY, which is defined in part as "to make oneself a party to or in." WEBSTER'S THIRD NEW INTERNATIONAL DICTIONARY, UNABRIDGED 757 (1986). With respect to when an insurance contract comes into being, *see* COUCH ON INSURANCE 3d § 17:1 (2011).

[63] TAMRA House Report *supra* Chapter 4, note 40, at 482.

[64] *Id.* "Backdating is the practice by which an insurer calculates premiums under the policy based on an earlier age for the proposed insured. Premiums are thereby lower than they otherwise would be. Backdating beyond six months is sometimes prohibited by law." Black, Skipper and Black, *supra* Chapter 1, note 15, at 454. While backdating thus generally serves a purpose wholly unrelated to tax considerations, Congress clearly had concern about use of the practice to avoid TAMRA's requirements.

[65] TAMRA § 5012(e)(2). This rule as originally enacted was subsequently amended to read as quoted above by § 7815(a)(2) of the Omnibus Budget Reconciliation Act of 1989 (OBRA), Pub. L. No. 101-239.

rise to material changes under section 7702A(c)(3). The latter rule is beneficial in that it prevents automatic death benefit increases after June 20, 1988, such as those due merely to paid-up additions purchased with policyholder dividends or to the crediting of premiums[66] and earnings (as in the case of an option 2 death benefit), from causing a contract to become subject to section 7702A. Even so, it is noteworthy that the rules of TAMRA section 5012(e)(3)(A) and (B) represent modifications of the normal meaning of "entered into" since otherwise they would not have been needed to supplement the general effective date rule of TAMRA section 5012(e)(1).

Despite this, a question remains about what changes, if any, beyond those enumerated above may cause a contract to be treated as newly entered into for purposes of the TAMRA effective date rules. While a section 1035 exchange clearly gives rise to a new contract, modifications to an existing contract (such as through an amendment) are not normally thought of as changing the date of contract formation or of creating a new contract. Further, the rejection of an explicit statutory material change rule for the reasonable charge effective date rule and the listing of the specific provisions of TAMRA section 5012(e)(2) and (3) relating to the MEC effective date rule imply a much more limited scope for the changes that may cause a contract to be newly entered into for purposes of TAMRA. On the other hand, it is questionable whether Congress would have intended to apply a more generous effective date rule in connection with TAMRA than it applied with respect to the section 7702 effective date rule, the treatment of changes under which largely depends on the existence (or not) of a contractual right to effect the changes. As noted above, in CCA 200805022, the IRS addressed a change to a life insurance contract's death benefit pattern and the addition of QABs to the contract in the absence of contractual terms contemplating such changes. The CCA concluded that for contracts issued on and after January 1, 1985 but before October 21, 1988, such changes would cause the contracts to be newly entered into for purposes of the reasonable charge effective date rule. There was no discussion of any implications to be drawn from the differences between the DEFRA and TAMRA effective date rules.

The arguments supporting a more limited view of changes that can cause a contract to be newly entered into make the most sense in the context of a contract already subject to section 7702 (including the pre-TAMRA mortality and expense charge rule), since the section 7702 effective date rule arguably is inapplicable in such a case (and the section 7702 adjustment rules should address any changes). However, where there is a change on or after October 21, 1988, to a contract not subject to section 7702 that causes it to be treated as newly issued for purposes of the section 7702 effective date rule, section 7702 would attach to the contract at that time, including the mortality and expense charge rules as then in effect. Thus, for pre-DEFRA contracts, a change that causes the contract to be newly issued seemingly would cause it to become subject to the reasonable mortality and expense charge rules. Further, if there were a fundamental change to a contract, seemingly the changed contract would become subject to those rules regardless of when the prior contract was issued or entered into.

## Reapplication of Section 7702's Reasonable Mortality Rule

Yet another material change question regards whether, or in what circumstances, a change to a contract already subject to the reasonable mortality rule of section 7702(c)(3)(B)(i) will result in a reapplication of this rule. The reasonable mortality rule requires the definitional calculations to be based on (among other things) charges "which (except as provided in regulations) do not exceed the mortality charges specified in the prevailing commissioners' standard tables (as defined in section 807(d)(5)) as of the time the contract is issued." Ascertaining whether a change causes a contract to be newly issued for purposes of this rule often is an important consideration for purposes of assuring compliance with section 7702. For many contracts (such as ordinary whole life insurance), reapplying the reasonable mortality rule could result in a failure to comply with section 7702, since the contracts' cash surrender values may be based on a prior prevailing mortality table. Also, even in the case of other contracts (such as universal life), reapplying the rule may be problematic, e.g., because the insurer may not realize that a change to the contract has triggered reapplication of the rule or because the section 7702 calculations on the insurer's computer-based administration system for all contracts issued on a particular form may be based on the prior prevailing mortality table. As a general matter, new-issue treatment also may require reapplication of section 7702 in its entirety, since a contract treated as newly issued for purposes of the reasonable mortality rule seemingly would be newly issued for all purposes under the statute.

---

[66] Assuming that premiums are "necessary" within the meaning of IRC § 7702A(c)(3)(B)(i).

These considerations often cause insurers to restrict the changes permitted under a contract for which section 7702 calculations are based on a prior prevailing mortality table, even if the insurer routinely would permit particular changes absent the risk that the reasonable mortality rule might be reapplied. In this regard, as discussed in Chapter 2, the IRS has issued helpful guidance in the form of Notice 2006-95. This notice, as previously described, establishes safe harbor rules for the definitional calculations, permitting the use of mortality charges based on particular prevailing mortality tables, and in doing so the notice addresses when changes would and would not be considered to result in a newly issued contract for purposes of applying these safe harbors, borrowing heavily from the legislative history of the section 7702 effective date rule.

In particular, Notice 2006-95 includes two rules, meeting either of which will prevent a contract from being considered newly issued for purposes of the notice's safe harbors. The first of these rules appears in section 5.01 of the notice:

> The date on which a contract was issued generally is to be determined according to the standards that applied for purposes of the original effective date of [section] 7702. *See* H.R. Conf. Rep. No. 861, 98th Cong., 2d Sess. 1076 (1984), 1984-3 (Vol. 2) C.B. 330; *see also* 1 Staff of Senate Comm. On Finance, 98th Cong., 2d Sess., *Deficit Reduction Act of 1984, Explanation of Provisions Approved by the Committee on March 21, 1984*, at 579 (Comm. Print 1984). Thus, contracts received in exchange for existing contracts are to be considered new contracts issued on the date of the exchange. For these purposes, a change in an existing contract is not considered to result in an exchange if the terms of the resulting contract (that is, the amount and pattern of death benefit, the premium pattern, the rate or rates guaranteed on issuance of the contract, and mortality and expense charges) are the same as the terms of the contract prior to the change.

By cross-referencing the section 7702 effective date rule, this rule should produce the same result (i.e., give rise to a new issuance of a contract or not) as would apply under the section 7702 effective date rule for a pre-DEFRA contract.

The second rule, dealing specifically with contractual changes, is set forth in section 5.02 of the notice, which provides:

> Notwithstanding section 5.01, if a life insurance contract satisfied section 4.01 or 4.02 [of the notice] when originally issued, a change from previous tables to the 2001 CSO tables is not required if (1) the change, modification, or exercise of a right to modify, add or delete benefits is pursuant to the terms of the contract; (2) the state in which the contract is issued does not require use of the 2001 CSO tables for that contract under its standard valuation and minimum nonforfeiture laws; and (3) the contract continues upon the same policy form or blank.

Section 5.03 of the notice then goes on to identify examples of changes that fall within the scope of section 5.02, stating:

> The changes, modifications, or exercises of contractual provisions referred to in section 5.02 include (1) the addition or removal of a rider; (2) the addition or removal of a qualified additional benefit (QAB); (3) an increase or decrease in death benefit (whether or not the change is underwritten); (4) a change in death benefit option (such as a change from an option 1 to option 2 contract or vice versa); (5) reinstatement of a policy within 90 days after its lapse; and (6) reconsideration of ratings based on rated condition, lifestyle or activity (such as a change from smoker to nonsmoker status).

The rule set forth in section 5.02 of the notice is an alternative to the rule set forth in section 5.01, rendering it necessary to satisfy only one of the two rules to avoid new-issue treatment on account of a contractual change. That said, sections 5.01 and 5.02 of the notice largely overlap. Between the two sections of the notice, it seems clear that if a change either does not affect the fundamental economic characteristics of the contract (the death benefit amount, the guaranteed interest rate(s), or mortality or expense charges, etc.) or does affect them but the change is made pursuant to the terms of the contract—i.e., based on a right granted to the policyholder or the insurer under the contract—then new-issuance treatment does not apply and the grandfathering of the prior mortality table remains intact for purposes of the notice's safe harbors.

Some question has arisen in connection with section 5.03 of the notice, which as set forth above provides examples of changes, modifications and exercises of contractual provisions described in section 5.02 of the notice. In particular, the examples include some changes, such as "the addition ... of a rider" for which there commonly is no contractual right to make the change. In this circumstance, should one look to the operative rule (section 5.02 of the notice) and if its conditions are not met conclude the change would cause a contract to be newly issued for purposes of the notice? In a private letter ruling issued in 2012, discussed above in connection with both the section 7702 effective date rule and the reasonable charge effective date rule, the IRS answered affirmatively.[67] As previously noted, in that instance the insurer had requested a ruling regarding the effect, under the reasonable mortality rules, of death benefit reductions in 2012 and thereafter under certain CVAT-tested contracts issued based on the 1980 CSO tables. A central fact, as the IRS noted, was that the contracts "do not include a provision that explicitly contemplates the owner's ability to request a decrease in coverage." The IRS held that, because of the absence of such a right, the contracts would be treated as newly issued for purposes of Notice 2006-95 when the death benefits were reduced, meaning the contracts would thereafter need to comply with section 7702 based on NSPs computed assuming 2001 CSO mortality. In the course of the ruling, the insurer had argued that its action in reducing a death benefit at a policyholder's request fell within the reference in section 5.03 of the notice to "an increase or decrease in death benefit" as the kind of change that would not lose grandfathering. The IRS read its notice as requiring a right established under the contract for the policyholder to obtain the reduction, i.e., it was necessary to comply with section 5.01 or 5.02 of the notice to benefit from grandfathering.

This private letter ruling turned out to be quite controversial, attracting criticism from many in the life insurance industry (and particularly from issuers of traditional contracts). It was argued that a contract should not need to undergo transplantation of a new mortality table when the contractual benefits are being reduced, thereby lessening rather than increasing the amount of inside buildup and the concomitant investment orientation with which section 7702 is concerned. In discussion with industry representatives, IRS officials appeared to acknowledge that the result reached in the ruling was premised solely on a technical reading of Notice 2006-95 (and section 5.02 in particular).

Apart from this controversy, while Notice 2006-95 has helpfully resolved many questions about certain common changes, such as underwritten death benefit increases pursuant to a contractual right, other questions persist. As mentioned previously in this chapter, one common change that has raised questions is a change in smoking status. In some cases (perhaps most), the owner may have a right to make the change, e.g., either as a matter of contract law or because an insurer's denial of the change would violate state law nondiscrimination requirements. Where there is no such right, however, odd—and potentially very harsh—results arise from treating the contract as newly issued for purposes of the reasonable mortality rule.[68] In such a case, as under the 2012 private letter ruling just discussed, it is necessary to reapply section 7702 using a completely different mortality table, one unrelated to the contract's guarantees (e.g., 2001 CSO versus 1980 CSO). Where the calculations under section 7702 are required to be based on new mortality tables, it often would be necessary to disgorge monies from the contract to maintain compliance, even though those same monies may be necessary to keep the contract in force based on its guarantees. In addition, changing the section 7702 calculations for a subset of contracts often would be impractical for computer-based administrative systems. The reality is that, where such material change issues are presented, insurers will simply refuse to permit changes, even where they commonly would permit such changes absent the concern with loss of grandfathering. Resolution of such a conundrum may need to await further official guidance.

---

[67] PLR 201230009 (Jan. 30, 2012).

[68] At minimum, the modification of a contract's guaranteed mortality charges due to a change in an insured's status from smoker to nonsmoker generally would result in an adjustment event under IRC § 7702(f)(7)(A), which would reduce the NSPs and guideline premiums for the contract. In effect, insurers following this approach treat a change not pursuant to a contract's terms as giving rise to a newly issued contract for purposes of the safe harbors of Notice 2006-95 but not otherwise under the statute, which seems reasonable for ensuring continued application of the safe harbors. As noted, however, new-issue treatment, if correct for purposes of the mortality charge rule, implies more generally—as a matter of consistency—that this same treatment should apply for all tax purposes, including IRC § 7702.

## The Special Case of Insurance Company Rehabilitations

The rehabilitation of an insolvent or financially distressed life insurance company generally involves the transfer of business, often using assumption reinsurance, from that company to one or more other insurers. This often is accompanied, moreover, by significant modifications or restructuring of the contracts being transferred. Administrative relief from the treatment of such changes to the contracts as material changes, warranting a loss of grandfathering, is provided by Rev. Proc. 92-57.[69] This revenue procedure sets forth certain conditions that, if satisfied, permit contracts modified or restructured in a rehabilitation proceeding to maintain grandfathered status under sections 72, 101(f), 264, 7702 and 7702A. Further, such contracts are not required to be retested or to begin a new testing period under sections 264(c)(1), 7702(f)(7)(B)–(E) and 7702A(c). The conditions specified in the revenue procedure for the maintenance of grandfathered treatment are that the modification or restructuring must be an integral part of the rehabilitation, conservatorship or similar state proceeding and be approved by the state court, the state insurance commissioner or other responsible state official overseeing the proceeding.

According to the revenue procedure, assuming the stated conditions are met, the modification or restructuring protected from new-issuance or retesting treatment "may include, but is not limited to, reductions in benefits, adjustments to mortality or other expense charges, reductions in the rate of interest credited to the contract, and restrictions on the policy owner's ability to receive benefits under the affected contract." However, while a contract subject to the definitional limitations that is so modified or restructured will not lose grandfathering with respect to the applicable mortality and expense assumptions, a change in those values must be reflected as an adjustment event under section 7702(f)(7)(A) (or section 101(f)(2)(E)). Thus, for example, in a 1993 private letter ruling, the IRS held that an increase in a life insurance contract's mortality and expense charges in connection with a restructuring in rehabilitation is an adjustment event under section 7702(f)(7)(A).[70] The IRS also held that where the interest rate or rates guaranteed on issuance exceed the minimum interest rates required to be used in the determination of guideline premiums of section 7702(c), and the rate or rates guaranteed are decreased, then the decrease constitutes an adjustment event under section 7702(f)(7)(A).[71] A number of other private letter rulings have been issued applying the relief provided by the revenue procedure.[72]

## Administering the Effective Date and Material Change Rules

While the tax law may contain an inherent level of uncertainty regarding the treatment of contractual changes, by their very nature life insurance administration systems cannot deal with uncertainty; they are rules-based. They must be programmed with specific interpretations of the definitional limitations for each and every transaction affecting a life insurance contract—interpretations made and specified for programming during the development and implementation of a system with respect to compliance. Failure to interpret the rules of the tax law correctly can lead to errors that in turn may result in a contract inadvertently failing compliance with section 7702 or becoming an inadvertent MEC. Additionally, since these rules can and do change and have changed over time, administration systems, including the procedures and controls supporting administration, are required to decipher whether a particular contract should have an at-issue rule set applied to it in processing a change request or whether, on the contrary, a new set of tax rules based on the effective date of the change should be applied.

There is a dual aspect to compliance with the life insurance definitional limitations. The first is at-issue compliance, which generally falls to the product development staff to ensure that the section 7702 and 7702A (and in the past, section 101(f)) requirements are met for newly developed and issued products. The second aspect relates to in-force management, for which contract administration systems and business procedures are the gatekeeper to tax compliance. In-force management is the primary area where the responsibility for administration of the material change rules falls.

---

[69] 1992-2 C.B. 410.
[70] PLR 9338023 (June 24, 1993).
[71] Id.
[72] See PLRs 200814005 (Dec. 27, 2007), 200249013 (Sept. 12, 2002), 199908013 (Nov. 23, 1998), 199908016 (Nov. 23, 1998), 199912022 (Dec. 22, 1998), 9720038 (Feb. 13, 1997), 9548022 (Aug. 31, 1995), 9516056 (Jan. 26, 1995), 9445013 (Aug. 9, 1994), 9430043 (May 6, 1994), 9338023 (June 24, 1993), 9335054 (June 9, 1993), 9312023 (Dec. 28, 1992), 9305013 (Nov. 9, 1992) and 9239026 (June 29, 1992).

Rules or procedures can generally be incorporated into an administration system in one of two ways: They can be explicitly put there by the administrator, or they can be implicitly put there by the developer of the administration system. In some cases, the administration system or procedures may not have a particular rule set for dealing with a particular transaction, implying that the transaction does not require any modifications or adjustments in the definitional limitations. This may be a conscious decision, or it may be an oversight on the part of the administrator. Regardless of the reasoning, it should be recognized that even the lack of a particular rule or procedure for a transaction does in fact create an applicable rule set—that is, the transaction is ignored. While this may be a perfectly acceptable outcome for certain transactions (e.g., the repayment of a policy loan), it may have unintended consequences for others and jeopardize the qualification status of contracts.

As promised at the outset of this chapter, the discussion that follows provides a framework for identifying which version of the definitional limitations apply to a contract that is issued or undergoes a material change at a particular time, with the goal of enabling an insurer to administer the contract using the appropriate requirements of the tax law. In this connection, the development of the section 101(f), 7702 and 7702A rules can be thought of as creating "categories" of life insurance contracts, classified according to the statutory requirements in effect when a contract is issued or is treated as issued. In this discussion, these categories, which generally correspond with the enabling legislation creating the several Code provisions, are called **rule eras**. Further, the amendment of section 7702 by TAMRA to impose the reasonable mortality and expense charge assumptions created additional subcategories referred to below as **assumption eras**. The various rule and assumption eras establish a broad framework for tax compliance by establishing actuarially based limitations on the permissible funding of life insurance contracts. Each era has its own effective date provisions, providing administrators with guidance as to when a life insurance contract would become subject to its requirements.

## *Rule Eras and Assumption Eras*

As noted above, rules eras are associated with the statutory requirements governing the definitional limitations. One may therefore conceive of four distinct rule eras as applying to life insurance contracts: pre-DEFRA, Section 101(f), Section 7702 and Section 7702A.

- **Pre-DEFRA** contracts consist of all life insurance contracts, other than flexible premium contracts, issued on or before December 31, 1984. As discussed in Chapter 1, there were no definitional limitations on a pre-DEFRA contract for it to be treated as life insurance for federal tax purposes other than the familiar risk-shifting and risk-distribution rules articulated in case law and a definition peculiar to section 1035 exchanges.

- **Section 101(f)** provided for the first time a statutory definition of life insurance for federal income tax purposes, albeit for only a limited time and for a limited class of contracts referred to as flexible premium life insurance contracts. A flexible premium contract was defined as a contract under which one or more premium payments were not fixed by the insurer as to both timing and amount. Section 101(f), which applied to contracts issued before January 1, 1984 (later extended to January 1, 1985), was expressly made temporary and limited in its application pending the more permanent and comprehensive solution that emerged under section 7702.

- **Section 7702** generally applies to contracts issued after December 31, 1984, and to certain increasing benefit contracts issued during 1984.[73] Section 7702, like the section 101(f) rules it superseded, provided a statutory definition of life insurance. However, unlike section 101(f), section 7702 applies to all life insurance contracts, resulting in the elimination of some forms of contracts (such as short-term endowments) from the market.

- **Section 7702A** created a new class of life insurance contract called a modified endowment contract, or MEC. Section 7702A applies to all life insurance contracts that qualify as life insurance under section 7702 and that are entered into on or after June 21, 1988.

---

[73] *See* note 5.

The rule eras conform to the effective dates of the definitional limitations to which they relate. Further complicating matters for tax-compliance administration, however, modifications were made to section 7702 by TAMRA that altered the permissible actuarial assumptions used in computing the definitional limitations for contracts entered into after October 20, 1988. This created assumption eras within the existing section 7702 rule era. More specifically, the section 7702 era is subdivided into multiple distinct assumption eras:

- **Pre-TAMRA era:** Section 7702 did not explicitly impose a statutory limit on the mortality or expense assumptions to be used in the determination of NSPs or guideline premiums apart from the need to follow the contractual guarantees.[74]

- **Post-TAMRA eras:** Pursuant to the changes enacted by TAMRA for contracts entered into on or after October 21, 1988, the NSPs, guideline premiums and 7-pay premiums are to be determined using "reasonable" mortality charges as defined in section 7702(c)(3)(B)(i) and "reasonable" other (expense) charges as defined in section 7702(c)(3)(B)(ii).[75] Further, the actuarial assumptions permissible under the reasonable mortality requirement for a given contract depend in part on the prevailing commissioners' standard mortality table in effect at the date of the contract's issuance. Thus, there are multiple post-TAMRA eras, one for each applicable prevailing table. In this regard, as described in Chapter 2, the IRS has issued guidance in the form of notices (Notices 88-128 and 2006-95) that provide safe harbors insurers can rely on for meeting the reasonable mortality requirements, with each safe harbor providing its own effective date rules.

### Table 5.1. Life insurance contract rule and assumption eras

| Rule era | | | Effective date range | | Assumption era | |
|---|---|---|---|---|---|---|
| Era | Statutory requirements | Applicability | From | To | Era | Prevailing CSO table |
| Pre-DEFRA | None | Other than flexible premium contracts | Issued on or before Dec. 31, 1984 | | None | |
| Section 101(f) | Section 101(f) | Flexible premium contracts | | | Pre-TAMRA | |
| Section 7702 | Section 7702 | All contracts | Jan. 1, 1985 | June 20, 1988 | Pre-TAMRA | |
| Section 7702A | Section 7702 and Section 7702A | All contracts | June 21, 1988 | Oct. 20, 1988 | Pre-TAMRA | |
| | | | Oct. 21, 1988 | Dec. 31, 1988 | Post-TAMRA | 1958 CSO |
| | | | Oct. 21, 1988 | Dec. 31, 1988 | Post-TAMRA | 1980 CSO |
| | | | Varies based on state adoption | Current | Post-TAMRA | 2001 CSO |

## Material Changes, Effective Date Rules and Contract Adjustments

Contract changes can have any number of potential impacts on the definitional limitations, depending on the rule and assumption era governing the contract, the type of contract change and the provisions of the contract undergoing the change. Further, each of the definitional sections has both effective date rules and adjustment provisions for dealing with contract changes. As explained above, in many instances it is simply not clear whether a particular contract change results in the contract being treated as newly issued for purposes of the various statutory effective date rules or whether the adjustment methodology of the previously applicable stat-

---

[74] This pre-TAMRA assumption era that governs prior to the effective date of the reasonable charge rules also applies for purposes of IRC § 7702A in the case of contracts entered into on and after June 21, 1988, and prior to October 21, 1988.

[75] In the context of IRC § 7702A, such reasonable expense charges would encompass only those with respect to QABs that may be reflected under this statute.

ute governs the change. In this connection, as noted at the outset of this chapter, because different rules apply to a contract based on the date it is "issued" or "entered into," preservation of that date, or else knowing when a new date applies, is an important element in administering the definitional limitations.

Regardless of the uncertainty in the tax law requirements, to be effective in assuring tax compliance, an administration system needs to be able to identify contract changes first and foremost, before it can determine when a change will result in either an adjustment to the definitional limitations based on the existing rule era applicable to the contract or, in contrast, will require the contract to be treated as newly issued or entered into for purposes of a new rule or assumption era. It needs to do so, moreover, for all types of changes that can apply to a life insurance contract. Put differently, rules and procedures need to be defined within the administrative process that can:

- identify each and every type of contract change,
- determine the appropriate set of rules to apply to the change transaction,
- apply the rules to determine the appropriate definitional limitations, and
- identify the consequences of the definitional limitations as applied to the contract.

### Step 1: Identify the Contract Change

The first step in dealing with a contract change is to identify the type of change involved. In this regard, it is important to understand that contract changes can surface in a number of ways. While most changes arise from a request made by a policyholder, contract changes can also arise, as the DEFRA legislative history points out, at the behest of the insurance company or through the normal operation of the contract (e.g., death benefit increases resulting from the application of the section 7702(d) corridor). Having the proper procedures and oversight in place for identifying all types of changes in contracts is important in determining both the potential applicability of the adjustment rules under the contract's then existing rule era and the potential impact of the effective date rules of the current rule and assumption era at the time of the change.

*Insurance company-initiated changes:* The discussion earlier in this chapter highlighted a number of the considerations governing the treatment of a change initiated by an insurance company. The IRS has ruled on certain types of insurer-initiated changes, such as a change to a policy loan interest rate provision or the addition of an investment option to a variable life insurance contract, concluding that these types of changes do not subject the contract involved to a new rule or assumption era (and similarly do not require a section 7702(f)(7)(A) adjustment). Likewise, assumption reinsurance transactions, corporate reorganizations and rehabilitations of insolvent insurers generally do not result in new-issuance treatment. On the other hand, as previously noted, the IRS has held that an increase in a life insurance contract's mortality and expense charges in connection with a restructuring in rehabilitation is an adjustment event under section 7702(f)(7)(A). Given the broad spectrum of the types of insurer-initiated changes that can occur, administrative controls or procedures need to be in place for identifying them. Once identified, the proper analysis of the change can take place to determine the appropriate set of rules to apply to the transaction.

Further complications can exist with administering insurance company-initiated changes when the change does not generate a "transaction" within the administration system, as transactions are typically the trigger that prompts an administration system to take action. This can create additional complexity and the need for intervention from outside the administration system to give effect to these types of changes, should the transaction require modifications to contracts' existing definitional limitations. However, where an insurer-initiated change is applied to a particular class of contracts, as in the case of an assumption reinsurance transaction, there is an opportunity to address tax compliance as part of planning for the transaction.

*Policyholder-initiated changes:* In addition to insurer-initiated changes, changes initiated by policyholders are commonplace in life insurance contracts. Cash value life insurance contracts provide policyholders with the ability to borrow, alter the investment elections in the case of variable contracts, increase or decrease coverage, request a change in death benefit pattern, etc. Administration systems need to be able to identify these types of changes and apply the appropriate rules for administering the changes.

Further complicating the administration of policyholder-initiated changes is the potential effect of changes explicitly provided for in the contract and those permitted through administrative practice (e.g., permitting a change in smoking status based upon a showing of cessation of smoking, even if there is not an expressly stated right in the written terms of policies regarding the change). A typical administration system does not have the ability to determine whether a particular contract form provides a policyholder with an explicit right (or even an implicit right) to request a particular change, and it may be necessary to impose additional controls (generally manual) in the administrative process to restrict those changes not contractually permissible. Therefore, in a rules-based structure typically found within an administration system, administrative procedures would need to be developed to account for the potentially differing treatment of contract changes that may be expressly permitted under some contract forms and permitted only through administrative practice under other forms.

As previously noted, Notice 2006-95 discussed the potential impact certain changes would have on a contract's existing assumption era. More specifically, the notice provided guidance on changes that would not cause life insurance contracts issued under a plan of insurance based on either 1958 or 1980 CSO mortality to become subject to the reasonable mortality requirements based on the 2001 CSO tables for purposes of the notice's safe harbors, i.e., changes that would not require a shift in the applicable assumption era. To avoid an assumption era shift, the notice requires that:

- the change, modification or exercise of a right to modify, add or delete benefits be pursuant to the terms of the contract,
- the state in which the contract is issued does not require use of the 2001 CSO tables for that contract under its standard valuation and minimum nonforfeiture laws, and
- the contract continues upon the same policy form or blank.

As noted above, the notice provides these examples of such a change:

- Addition or removal of a rider
- Addition or removal of a qualified additional benefit (QAB)
- Increase or decrease in death benefit (whether or not the change is underwritten)
- Change in death benefit option (such as a change from an option 1 to an option 2 death benefit or vice versa)
- Reinstatement of a lapsed contract within 90 days after its lapse
- Reconsideration of ratings based on rated condition, lifestyle or activity (such as a change from smoker to nonsmoker status)

This guidance caused some concern among administrators, as not all life insurance contracts expressly provide for the changes listed above. In response, some insurance companies altered their administrative practices with regard to changes not expressly provided for by the terms of the contract. More specifically, as noted above, some companies no longer allow contract changes not expressly permitted by a contract's terms, and some others have endorsed existing contracts to provide for certain types of changes. (Of course, an endorsement usually cannot be added to a grandfathered contract after the effective date of a rule change because the addition of the endorsement itself may cause a material change that would forfeit grandfathering.)

***Changes occurring under the normal operation of a contract:*** Some contract changes are not initiated by either the policyholder or the insurer but instead result from the normal operation of the contract. Examples include:

- Death benefit increases required by the CVAT or the section 7702(d) corridor
- Death benefit increases resulting from the application of policyholder dividends used to purchase paid-up additions under traditional participating contracts

- For universal and variable universal life contracts with an option 2 death benefit pattern, death benefit increases resulting from an increase in the contracts' cash surrender values

While these types of changes occur within the confines of a contract administration system, they may not always create a necessary transaction for the administration system to recognize the change event. As such, additional programming or procedures external to the administration system may be needed to identify these changes, so that proper adjustments can be made, if any are needed, to the definitional limitations, taking into consideration the requirements of the then applicable rule and assumption eras. Fortunately, these types of contract changes generally would *not* cause a contract to be treated as newly issued or require adjustments to the existing definitional limits.

**Step 2: Determine the Appropriate Set of Rules to Apply to the Change Transaction**
As discussed above, contract changes can take on many different forms and can arise in a number of different ways, and so contract issue dates and transaction effective dates become important elements in determining how to administer contract changes. Contract issue dates define the rule and assumption eras underlying the calculation of the definitional limits upon issuance of a contract, and establish the adjustment rules that apply to future contract changes. Transaction effective dates, along with the type of transaction, contract provisions, and the rule and assumption era at contract issuance, will determine whether an adjustment should be made based on that era or whether a shift to a new rule or assumption era is required. Determining the appropriate response to contract changes creates challenges for administrative systems, particularly when the transaction is not accounted for using the adjustment rules for the pre-existing era.

Because compliance problems arise when existing products are issued after the effective date of new rules (e.g., issuing a 1958 CSO contract after December 31, 1988), administrative procedures external to the administration system may be necessary to limit both contract issuance and changes to ensure the proper rule and assumption eras are applied. These procedures are particularly important when dealing with the "sunset dates" for a particular era, including:

- Section 101(f): December 31, 1984

- Reasonable mortality era for 1958 CSO contracts: December 31, 1988

- Reasonable mortality era for 1980 CSO contracts: December 31, 2008 (note that to use this date it appears necessary to comply with a safe harbor set forth in Notice 2006-95, for otherwise, the sunset date is December 31, 2007, under the section 807(d)(5) 3-year transition rule that applies for purposes of section 7702(c)(3)(B)(i))

Administrators typically deal with these types of changes in the tax law by developing new products. This would typically coincide with the elimination of any new sales of existing products designed to comply with requirements of a prior era, with future sales based on the new product. Administration systems commonly account for the actuarial assumptions that apply to the calculation of the definitional limitations through a mapping scheme that links, or maps, a particular assumption set to the product. This mapping scheme tells the administration system the actuarial assumptions (i.e., mortality tables, interest rates, etc.) to use in calculating or adjusting the definitional limits for all contracts associated with the product and would be reflective of the then applicable assumption era requirements.

As noted above, contract changes can complicate the administration of the definitional limitations to the extent a change to an existing contract would subject the contract to the requirements of a new era. Tracking for a shift in an era will be a function of the effective date of the contract change. For example, under one of the TAMRA transition rules, certain types of section 7702A(c)(3)(A) material changes may result in a contract being treated as entered into on the date of the change for purposes of the effective date of section 7702A, provided the change occurs after June 20, 1988. Also, following the view expressed by the IRS in CCA 200805022, a common occurrence under a universal life insurance contract—the addition of a QAB rider that was not pursuant to the exercise of a right granted under the contract—will potentially result in a rule era shift (in the case of a pre-DEFRA contract) or in an assumption era shift. While not all contract changes will produce such results, properly administering the implications of all contract changes is a necessary element to an effective tax-compliance system.

## Step 3: Apply the Rules to Determine the Appropriate Definitional Limitations

Recognizing the rule era and assumption era applicable to a contract change will in turn identify the appropriate action needed for determining the post-change definitional limitations. As detailed above, in some cases the change may require the contract to be viewed as newly issued, while in other cases the statutory adjustment rules may apply.

As a default, most administration systems are designed to account for contract changes under the adjustment mechanisms provided for in sections 101(f), 7702 and 7702A. While certain changes that require new-issue treatment are readily handled by most administration systems, such as an exchange of contracts made pursuant to section 1035, applying new-issue treatment to other types of contract changes (say due to a change not explicitly provided for in the contract) are generally not supported.

Administration systems are generally designed to retain the contract characteristics (death benefits, insured characteristics, rider specifications, etc.) used in the adjustment calculations—as would be necessary for applying the section 7702(f)(7) attained-age adjustment formula for guideline premium test contracts discussed in Chapter 4. Those calculations involve computing the guideline premiums by taking into consideration the characteristics of the contract before and after the contract change. While the "before" and "after" components of the calculation take into account the benefits immediately before and after the change (e.g., an increase in face amount or a change in death benefit pattern), administration systems would generally look to a common product level mapping for both calculations.

However, when the change also results in an era shift, functionality needs to exist to account for this, particularly when the shift results in a need to reflect different assumptions in the definitional calculations. This may require that new or dual mapping schemes be developed for a subset of contracts. Put differently, in determining the guideline premiums in the case of such an adjustment, the administration system may need to apply one mapping scheme to the before component of the adjustment calculation (e.g., reflective of 1980 CSO mortality) and a different mapping scheme to the after component (e.g., reflective of 2001 CSO mortality).

For CVAT contracts, the test is prospective, based on the NSP for the future benefits provided after the change. Some administration systems may involve mapping schemes that assign NSP factors stored within the administration system. Alternatively, the mapping scheme may point to a particular mortality table and interest rate and use those assumptions to calculate NSPs "on the fly" or when needed. If a transaction causes a contract to shift rule or assumption eras, it may be necessary for a new mapping scheme to be developed that points to a new set of NSP factors (or a new mortality table and interest rate if the NSP factors are calculated as needed) based on the requirements of the newly applicable era. This may result in the need to use different NSP factors for otherwise similar contracts issued under the same product. Note that this may create additional challenges in satisfying the terms-of-the-contract requirement that applies to CVAT contracts, as contract terms may also need to be amended to reflect the change in assumptions.

A comparable challenge is presented by the 7-pay test of section 7702A. This statute has its own effective date rules as well as two adjustment rules, all of which differ from those under section 7702. The necessary premium rule under section 7702A adds a further complication to compliance, by making recalculations optional for some changes.

Most administration systems are simply not designed to accommodate a change that requires an assumption era shift or a change in the mapping scheme applicable to a particular class of contracts, and thus would require some level of manual intervention to maintain the definitional limits. Because of this, administrators will seek to avoid contract changes that cause an assumption era shift.

## Step 4: Determine the Consequences of a Change in the Definitional Limitations

Once the appropriate revision has been made to the definitional limitations applicable to the post-change contracts, an additional assessment may be necessary to ensure ongoing compliance with the tax law requirements. In many instances, such a revision will simply modify the applicable limitations. In other circumstances, however, it may result in MEC status for the contract or even a "failed" contract under section 7702, particularly if the effect of the change was not recognized appropriately at the time of the change. Thus, the revision in the definitional limitations could require a refund of "excess" premiums (and interest) or a change in the contract's NSP factors used in determining the contract's minimum death benefit to maintain compliance with the limitations.

In this regard, both sections 7702 and 7702A (like section 101(f) before them) contain provisions that allow for the removal of excess premium, provided the excess premium along with earnings associated with it is distributed from the contract within 60 days after the end of the contract year. As described in Chapter 2, for contracts designed to meet the guideline premium test requirements, section 7702(f)(1)(B) provides that if, in order to comply with those requirements, any portion of any premium paid during any contract year is returned by the insurance company (with interest) within 60 days after the end of a contract year, the amount so returned (excluding the interest) is deemed to reduce the sum of the premiums paid under the contract during such year. While only applicable to contracts designed to comply with the guideline premium test requirements, this provision recognizes that certain transactions may result in a downward adjustment to the guideline premiums, which in certain instances may reduce the guideline premium limitation below the sum of the premiums paid prior to the date of the transaction. When this occurs, a company is provided a "window" within which to return the excess premium (and interest) to the policyholder. In such circumstances, failure to return the excess premium (and interest) within the 60-day window provided by section 7702(f)(1)(B) would cause a violation of the section 7702 requirements, resulting in a failed life insurance contract. An effective tax-compliance system for guideline premium contracts must be able to address the need to generate a refund in these circumstances.

A companion refund provision exists in section 7702A(e)(1)(B), as also discussed in Chapter 2. No similar provision exists for contracts subject to the requirements of the CVAT, which is not a premium-based test; this renders a window for the return of excess premium (and interest) inapplicable. On the other hand, the CVAT is a test that must be satisfied at all times by the terms of the contract. Any excess funding in a CVAT contract resulting from a contract change (e.g., cash surrender value in excess of the NSP for the post-change future benefits) must be remedied immediately at the time of the change, consistently with the contract terms, to maintain compliance with the terms-of-the-contract requirement.

## *A Concluding Comment*

The complexity of the tax law's identification and treatment of contract changes creates challenges in the development of an effective overall tax-compliance monitoring process for life insurance products. Any administration system will need to perform continual assessment over the entire product life cycle, even including vigilance for potential material changes after the end of a 7-pay testing period for a contract that theretofore was not a MEC. The insurance company will constantly need to assess administrative processes and procedures to address:

- advancements in product features and designs and how they interact with existing tax law requirements,
- emerging guidance on the various existing rule and assumption eras, and
- potential changes in those rules in the future, as for example, new mortality tables become prevailing under section 807(d)(5).

Material changes, with their complex interpretive issues, present a particular challenge for contract administration. Whether by default or design, every administration system interprets the rules, and a system will need to react to and address the rules even when they are not clear. An effective system will need to have assigned to it accountability and ownership for tax compliance. And finally, an effective compliance system must safeguard and ensure that existing processes and procedures are being followed, as the consequences of getting it wrong can be substantial.

# Chapter 6

# PRODUCT-SPECIFIC ISSUES

## Chapter Overview

Chapter 6 addresses products and features of products that pose special issues under sections 7702 and 7702A.[1] Products included in the discussion below have specific rules that apply under the statutes or their legislative history, have been the subject of rulings by the IRS, or simply raise product-specific issues under the definitional limitations. The products discussed are, in order, variable life contracts, including minimum guaranteed elements thereunder; equity indexed contracts; multiple-life contracts, both joint life and last survivor; interest-sensitive whole life plans; group universal life; single premium "net rate" products; burial or preneed contracts; reversionary annuity plans; and church-related plans. The chapter concludes with commentary on such features of life insurance contracts as cash value bonuses, scheduled decreasing face amounts, combinations of life insurance with annuities and premium deposit funds, no-lapse guarantees and return of premium provisions.

## Variable Life

Variable life insurance, including variable universal life, is a form of permanent life insurance. As such, variable life provides both a death benefit and a cash surrender value, both of which generally can vary in value based upon the investment performance of assets in an underlying separate account of the issuing life insurer. The variable life contract permits the policyholder to allocate the contract values among various investment options available under the separate account, which can include portfolios or funds of equity and debt instruments. Subject to any guarantees provided by the insurer under the variable contract (some of which are described in this chapter), the investment risk lies with the policyholder; while the policyholder may benefit from favorable investment performance, the death benefit and cash surrender value also may decline due to poor performance. As a result, variable contracts are considered securities and are regulated under federal securities laws.

The tax rules generally applicable to life insurance contracts also apply to variable life insurance plans. However, for variable life insurance contracts as defined in section 817(d),[2] a special compliance rule is provided in section 7702(f)(9). Under this **variable life rule**, the determination of whether a variable life insurance contract falls within the requirements of section 7702(a) must be made whenever the death benefit changes rather than "at any time" (the generally applicable rule). Hence, a variable life contract is required to be tested for compliance with the cash value accumulation test (CVAT) or with the cash value corridor of the guideline premium test only when its death benefit changes. In any event, the determination must be made at least once in each 12-month period. In this connection, the Deficit Reduction Act of 1984 (DEFRA) legislative history indicates that if the contract is checked for compliance once per year, the determination must be made at the same time each year.[3] The purpose of the section 7702(f)(9) rule is to allow traditional forms of variable life, under which the cash surrender value can fluctuate daily but the death benefit adjusts only on contract anniversaries, to qualify under the CVAT, although the rule is not limited in application to traditional forms.

The assets underlying the separate account of a variable life insurance contract can represent a variety of different investments. However, the characterization of the income in the separate account (e.g., dividend in-

---

[1] Unless otherwise indicated, references in this book to "section" are to the provisions of the Internal Revenue Code of 1986, as amended (also referred to as "IRC" or the "Code").

[2] IRC § 817(d) defines a "variable contract" for purposes of the life insurance company tax rules, and both IRC § 7702(f)(9) and (as discussed below) IRC § 817(h) reference it. In the case of a life insurance contract, IRC § 817(d) provides that such a contract is a variable contract if it "provides for the allocation of all or part of the amounts received" under it "to an account which, pursuant to State law or regulation, is segregated from the general asset accounts of the company," and "under which … the amount of the death benefit (or the period of the coverage) is adjusted on the basis of the investment return and the market value of the segregated asset account. …" The statute goes on to say that the contract can provide a guarantee and that the company's obligations under the guarantee are accounted for as part of the company's general account.

[3] DEFRA House Report, *supra* Chapter 1, note 11, at 1443; DEFRA Senate Report, *supra* Chapter 1, note 11, at 572–73; DEFRA Blue Book, *supra* Chapter 1, note 20, at 646–47.

175

come or capital gains) is not relevant to the policyholder. As with other life insurance contracts, gain is taxed as ordinary income only when the cash surrender value is accessed, regardless of the source of income within the separate account. A loss upon surrender is generally not deductible.[4]

In the case of a variable life insurance contract that provides for no principal or interest rate guarantee, the statutory minimum interest rate of 4 percent is used in the definitional calculations (6 percent for the guideline single premium, or GSP). On the other hand, if a variable life contract contains a fixed or general account investment option with a guaranteed interest rate in excess of 4 percent (6 percent for the GSP), that higher rate guaranteed at issue must be used in the calculations for the period of the guarantee. This is consistent with the analogous rules for nonvariable life insurance assumed interest rates.

## *Diversification Rules*

In addition to meeting the section 7702 limitations, a variable life insurance contract that falls within the section 817(d) definition also must comply with certain investment diversification requirements specified in section 817(h) and Treas. Reg. section 1.817-5. Pursuant to these requirements, for a variable contract to be treated as a life insurance (or annuity) contract, the assets of the segregated asset account supporting the contract must be "adequately diversified."[5] Further, the contracts must be structured in a manner that does not permit excessive control of the underlying investments by the policyholders.[6]

In the event the diversification requirements are not met, all of the gain on the contract that has accumulated since issuance will be taxable to the policyholder in the year the violation occurred, and the contract will lose its status as a life insurance (or annuity) contract, even if the investments are adequately diversified for all subsequent periods.[7] However, if the failure to diversify is inadvertent, the insurer may use the approach outlined in Rev. Proc. 2008-41[8] to correct the failure by entering into a closing agreement with the IRS. Under such a closing agreement, the insurer pays the tax and deficiency interest owed by the policyholder for the period the contract failed to comply with the diversification requirements, and also corrects the asset diversification failure. In turn, the IRS agrees to treat the contract as if the diversification failure had never occurred.[9]

## *Offshore and Private Placement Products*

Variable life insurance contracts also are offered by non-U.S.-based insurance companies that do no business in the United States, principally to high-net-worth individual and corporate purchasers. Popular jurisdictions for these **offshore contracts** are countries with stable governments and established insurance regulatory frameworks, including Bermuda, the Cayman Islands, and the Channel Islands of Jersey and Guernsey. Many insurers offering these polices to U.S. persons seek to have them treated as life insurance under U.S. tax laws; if so, the contracts must qualify as life insurance under section 7702. The applicable law requirement under section 7702 encompasses foreign laws.[10] Thus, for an offshore contract to be treated as life insurance under the Code, it must be treated as an integrated life insurance contract in the jurisdiction in which it is issued as well as meet the section 7702 actuarial tests. If the contract is based on a segregated asset account within the definition in section 817(d), it also must satisfy the diversification requirements for variable contracts under section 817(h). There is some question whether an offshore account falls within that definition, since section 817(d) refers to an account segregated "pursuant to State law," but the IRS has ruled, in the case of foreign life insurers that have elected under section 953(d) to be treated as domestic corporations, that at least certain offshore accounts will

---

[4] *See* Appendix 1.1.
[5] *See* IRC § 817(h)(1); Treas. Reg. § 1.817-5(b).
[6] See the discussion of the diversification and investor control rules in Appendix 1.1. In a 2002 private letter ruling, in response to a taxpayer's argument that "the specificity of section 7702 precludes the application of the investor control theory to assets held under a life insurance contract that satisfies the requirements of section 7702," the IRS held that the application of the investor control rules was not pre-empted by section 7702. *See* PLR 200244001 (May 2, 2002). *See also Webber v. Comm'r*, 144 T.C. No. 17 (2015). Additional detail on the diversification and investor control rules can be found in John T. Adney and Joseph F. McKeever III, *Tax Treatment of Variable Contracts*, ch. 4, in VARIABLE ANNUITIES & VARIABLE LIFE INSURANCE REGULATION (Clifford Kirsch, ed., 2014) (hereinafter Adney and McKeever).
[7] *See* Treas. Reg. § 1.817-5(a)(1).
[8] 2008-2 C.B. 155.
[9] *See* Treas. Reg. § 1.817-5(a)(2); Rev. Proc. 2008-41, *supra* note 8.
[10] *See* DEFRA House Report, *supra* Chapter 1, note 11, at 1443; DEFRA Senate Report, *supra* Chapter 1, note 11, at 572; DEFRA Blue Book, *supra* Chapter 1, note 20, at 646.

be treated as if they were organized pursuant to state law.[11] In any event, offshore insurers seeking treatment of their contracts as U.S. tax-compliant usually will have their variable contract accounts comply with the section 817(h) (and investor control) requirements.

For a contract qualifying under section 7702, the federal tax treatment of the policyholder and beneficiary is the same whether the contract is issued onshore or offshore. It is the increased regulatory flexibility and the reduction in cost resulting from state premium tax and possible deferred acquisition cost (DAC) tax savings, and often lower sales loads and administrative charges, that render products issued by offshore carriers attractive relative to those of domestic carriers. Offshore jurisdictions have few limitations on investments underlying variable life, and products offered offshore typically allow for a wider selection of international investment options than are available with domestic products. For example, some investment strategies may not have sufficient liquidity to meet U.S. regulatory requirements. Further, offshore plans may not be subject to antidiscrimination requirements and therefore may be negotiated on an individual basis. The investor control doctrine should be kept in mind, of course, as an insurer establishes available investment strategies.

The sale of **private placement** variable life, when done onshore and in many situations where the sale is made to U.S. purchasers in the offshore market, is subject to special rules. As previously noted, variable contracts are securities, subject to the Securities Act of 1933 as amended (the 1933 act), and so, when issued as retail products in the United States, the contracts may be sold only after registration with the Securities and Exchange Commission and if accompanied by a prospectus. Private placement insurance products, however, are sold to wealthy U.S. individuals and U.S. corporate purchasers—investors considered to be financially sophisticated and, therefore, not in need of all of the 1933 act's protections—pursuant to the exemption from registration under section 4(2) of the 1933 act for any "transaction by an issuer not involving a public offering." As a result, the rules applicable to retail sales need not be followed; rather, special rules governing private placements must be followed.[12]

## *M&E and Asset-Based Expenses*

Variable life insurance contracts, as well as some general account products, may have mortality and expense charges expressed as a percentage of a contract's account value. For a contract qualifying under the guideline premium test, the effective interest rate at which the calculations are made can be reduced, in appropriate circumstances, by percentage-of-asset charges specified in the contract. To the extent these charges are actually expected to be imposed and otherwise reasonable, they may be reflected as expense charges in the calculation of the guideline single and level premiums, generally as a reduction in the assumed interest rate (e.g., a 25 basis point charge could effectively be reflected in the GSP by assuming a 5.75 percent interest rate). Particular care should be taken, however, in the recognition of asset-based expense charges in the definitional calculations in the following instances:

- Part of the charge is attributable to mortality risk, as it may be limited by the reasonable mortality charge rule and cannot be counted as effectively reducing the interest rate

- The charges are attributable to separate account expenses and are not contract expenses because the ability to reflect expenses is limited to charges actually specified in the contract and may not be extended to charges levied by separate accounts or unit investment trusts that are not specifically set by the contract[13]

- A varying level of charges is imposed depending on the allocation of funds in the contract, including allocations to any available general account investment option[14]

---

[11] *See* PLRs 201410012 (Oct. 25, 2013), PLR 201038008 (June 24, 2010), PLR 201027038 (Mar. 31, 2010), PLR 200919025 (Jan. 29, 2009) and PLR 200246022 (Aug. 13, 2002).

[12] *See* David N. Brown and Kerry Shannon Burke, *Private Placement Variable Life Insurance*, ch. 25, in VARIABLE ANNUITIES & VARIABLE LIFE INSURANCE REGULATION, (Clifford Kirsch, ed., 2014); *see also* Stephen E. Roth, *Federal and State Securities Regulation of Annuity Products*, ch. 5, in ANNUITIES ANSWER BOOK (John T. Adney et al., eds., 4th ed. 2005).

[13] *See* IRC § 7702(c)(3)(B)(ii) and (D)(i).

[14] The application of the reasonable expense charge rule in this circumstance is unclear. The rule requires identification of charges reasonably expected to be imposed, and this in turn may require an assessment of expected policyholder behavior regarding fund allocations. An alternative approach would be to assume policyholders would choose allocations to minimize charges. A further possibility would be to apply the adjustment rule to account for reallocations of contract values between funds with different levels of charges. To date, no published guidance has been issued on this subject.

In addition, it is important to remember that expense charges (other than for qualified additional benefits, or QABs) may not be recognized in the determination of the net single premium (NSP) under the CVAT or the 7-pay premium under section 7702A.

## *Guaranteed Minimum Withdrawal Benefits*

For a number of years, variable annuity contracts have offered optional guarantees that, despite the variable nature of their values, promise certain minimum amounts of income payments will be available in any event, subject to the payment of specified charges and certain other restrictions. Such income amounts, typically provided by rider and often styled **guaranteed minimum withdrawal benefits** or **guaranteed lifetime income benefits** (generalized via the acronym **GMxB**), are permitted to be taken as annual or more frequent withdrawals from the annuity contract's cash value. While deferred annuity contracts (fixed as well as variable) generally have allowed partial withdrawals, the optional guarantee enables the withdrawals, up to a predetermined amount, to continue to be taken even after a contract's cash value has been reduced to zero. This benefit, which has been a popular one in the annuity marketplace, effectively provides assurance of "downside" protection of an income stream in an otherwise variable contract.

The popularity of GMxB riders in annuities has prompted insurers to begin offering them in connection with variable life insurance. Issues presented under the definitional limitations by the offering of life insurance-based GMxBs involve the potential treatment of the benefit payments as cash surrender value (CSV) for section 7702 purposes, the possible triggering of an adjustment in the definitional calculations when the payments are made and the treatment of the GMxB rider charges. To date, the only guidance on this subject has come in the form of one private letter ruling, which was issued in 2010 and addressed the first two of these issues in the context of a specific rider design.[15] According to the ruling's statement of facts, the rider could be added at issuance to a variable universal life insurance contract that qualified under either the CVAT or the guideline premium test. If certain conditions are satisfied (e.g., premiums have been paid for the contract in a prescribed manner and no withdrawals or loans have been taken prior to a prescribed date), the rider makes a minimum annual withdrawal or policy loan amount available to the policyholder beginning at a stated date and continuing generally for a specified number of years, so long as the contract remains in force and irrespective of the exhaustion of the contract's net cash surrender value, i.e., its post-surrender charge contract value less any policy debt. In this connection, both the contract and the rider contain no-lapse guarantees; neither will lapse if the rider conditions are met.

Under the contract terms, according to the ruling letter, the total amount of the rider benefit cannot exceed a maximum dollar amount, and if the policyholder chooses to withdraw or borrow less than the annual benefit amount, the period over which the benefit is made available is extended. The taxpayer seeking the ruling represented that the rider and any benefits payable under it are part of the life insurance contract for state law purposes rather than being regulated or otherwise treated under state law as an annuity contract or as some other type of non-life insurance contract.

The private letter ruling recites that withdrawals from the contract decrease its net cash surrender value and policy loans add to the policy debt, also reducing that value. To address the circumstance where the net cash surrender value is insufficient to allow a withdrawal or loan amount to be paid during the rider benefit period, the rider provides that the insurer will increase the contract value by the excess of the amount requested (not more than the annual rider benefit) over the net cash surrender value. Related to this, because the contract value is relevant in determining the minimum amount of the death benefit for section 7702 compliance, the rider amends the contract's death benefit provision. While the contract generally provides that its minimum death benefit is calculated by multiplying (1) the applicable minimum death benefit factor (for the CVAT or the cash value corridor) by (2) the contract value, the rider alters the second item so that during the rider benefit period, the minimum death benefit is the product of (1) the applicable minimum death benefit factor and (2) the greater of (a) the contract value and (b) the annual rider benefit. Charges for the rider also are assessed against the contract value, but if the net cash surrender value is insufficient to pay them and the no-lapse guarantee is in effect, they are waived.

---

[15] PLR 201046008 (Aug. 13, 2010).

The taxpayer's first requested ruling dealt with the section 7702(f)(2)(A) definition of CSV. Because, again, the CSV is a necessary element for determining the minimum required death benefit under section 7702, it is important that it be properly defined in a contract. By defining the CSV of the contract for minimum death benefit purposes as the greater of the contract value and the annual rider benefit, the contract as amended by the rider took into account the greatest amount by which the rider could increase the contract value at any time. In ruling favorably, the IRS agreed that the increase in contract value pursuant to the rider can create CSV for purposes of section 7702(f)(2)(A) in certain instances. In so ruling, the IRS relied on the definition of CSV contained in Prop. Reg. section 1.7702-2(b), i.e., the 1992 proposed regulations that sought to define CSV for section 7702 and 7702A purposes.

The second requested ruling addressed the potential effect of the rider on the definitional calculations, presumably in the at-issue calculations as well as when the rider causes an increase in the contract value. In holding that the NSPs and guideline premiums for the contract "are unaffected by the presence" of the rider, the IRS focused on whether the rider's operation would trigger an adjustment event under section 7702(f)(7)(A). The analysis in the ruling noted that upon issuance of the contract, it is not known if and when the rider will ever operate to increase the contract value. The IRS also concluded that the "factual circumstances" underlying the rider's operation were not those described in the DEFRA legislative history regarding changes in future benefits which require an adjustment.

It must be emphasized that the foregoing discussion describes the IRS's conclusions in a single, nonprecedential private letter ruling addressing a specific GMxB rider design. Insurers other than the taxpayer requesting the ruling cannot rely on it, and there is no official guidance on the issues involved. Further, the ruling itself dealt in part with a topic undergoing review by the IRS and is proposed to be the subject of future official guidance, namely, the definition of CSV for section 7702 and 7702A purposes.

Finally, the 2010 private letter ruling did not discuss the tax treatment of the rider charges. Insofar as the guaranteed minimum payment stream under a GMxB rider (whether via withdrawals or policy loans) is part of the related life insurance contract under state law and seemingly is as integral to the contract as is any other cash value nonforfeiture benefit or settlement option that a life insurance contract typically provides, the charges assessed to fund the rider benefit likewise should be viewed as integral to the contract. Hence, the charges should not be viewed as being distributed from the contract to pay for an additional benefit, but rather as being assessed to provide basic contractual benefits. As such, the rider charges arguably may be reflected in calculating the guideline premiums for the contract, subject to the requirements of the reasonable expense charge rules, although again, there is no official guidance on this point.

## Equity-Indexed Contracts

Another product currently popular in the life insurance marketplace is the **equity-indexed universal life insurance (EIUL)** contract. The EIUL contract typically contains a minimum guaranteed interest rate, a fixed or guaranteed investment option, and one or more indexed account investment options that enable the policyholder to tie the contract's account value, within limits, to a stock market-based index. If the policyholder allocates some or all of the contract value to an indexed option, the performance of the index (if above a minimum benchmark) is translated into an interest credit to the allocated contract value, provided the contract remains in force and the contract value is still allocated to the indexed option on the last day of the option period. The length of that period (often one year) and other details of the index and the interest crediting formula will vary from one EIUL design to the next. In general, EIUL differs from variable life insurance in that the former follows (more or less) a stock market index whereas the latter permits policyholders to allocate contract values among a variety of investment options, including portfolios and funds of equity and debt-based instruments. EIUL contracts are marketed on the basis that, as compared with fixed or variable life insurance, they offer policyholders both the growth potential of a variable contract and greater security against stock market declines and also that they are less expensive than their variable counterparts.

Issues potentially presented by EIUL under the definitional limitations fall into two categories:

- The determination of the interest rate guarantee used in the definitional calculations

- The manner in which the section 7702 definition of CSV interacts with the contract's own definition of its contract value for purposes of calculating its minimum death benefit

While it is somewhat difficult to generalize, given the variations of EIUL designs in the marketplace, it appears that only the minimum guaranteed interest rate, applicable to the contract values generally as well as to any fixed or guaranteed investment option, is relevant to the at-issue definitional calculations. The amounts of the index-based interest credits, if any, are unknown at the time of contract issuance, and hence, like the post-issuance excess interest credits discussed in the DEFRA legislative history, they cannot be used in the calculations. In the event of a section 7702(f)(7)(A) adjustment, any interest guarantees then existing should be employed in the calculations, but again, in a typical product these would not include any amounts other than the minimum interest rate guarantee.

The potential concern relating to the CSV of an EIUL contract for purposes of the definitional limitations is the treatment of index-based options that are "in the money" but as to which interest has not yet been credited. In this regard, the CSV should be the contract value at any time, increased by interest credits, including index-based credits, at the time they are credited. Although an index option may be in the money from time to time, i.e., it would give rise to an index-based credit if the index period were then ending, where the end of the period has not been reached and the amount of the credit has not been fixed as of any particular date, this usually should not be considered part of the CSV. The fact is that the in-the-moneyness may decline or disappear before the end of the index period. Even under the broad definition of CSV in the 1992 proposed regulations, none of the tentative, in-the-money amount under the option meets that definition so long as it cannot be withdrawn in cash or borrowed under the contract.

As is often the case with newer products, there is no official guidance on the foregoing issues, and very limited guidance on EIUL generally. To date, only one private letter ruling has dealt with an EIUL contract, and its focus was on an issue of more general import, i.e., the use of expense charges in determining the deemed CSV under the section 7702A necessary premium test.[16]

## Multiple-Life Plans

There are two broad types of multiple-life plans: joint life, or first-to-die; and survivorship, or last-to-die. These products may be offered either as traditional whole life insurance plans or as interest-sensitive whole life or universal life plans. Within these plans, variations may occur as to whether the actuarial values are computed on an exact-age basis or on a joint equivalent-age basis. Survivorship plans also vary as to whether they are traditional three-status plans, with values based on whether one or both of the insureds are alive, or frasierized (one-status) plans, under which contract values and mortality charges do not change at the first death.[17] In practice, universal life and other accumulation-type plans are available only as frasierized contracts.

There is no restriction in section 7702 limiting the number of lives that may be covered under a contract. There also is little guidance on the manner in which the section 7702 calculations are performed in the case of a multiple life contract.[18] Congress, however, has dealt indirectly with issues involving survivorship plans since the enactment of section 7702, confirming congressional awareness of such plans,[19] and the IRS finalized regulations in 2006 addressing certain aspects of the definitional calculations relating to the insureds' ages for both joint-life and survivorship plans.

### *Joint Life*

Joint-life, or first-to-die, contracts provide a death benefit payable on the first death of the covered insureds. First-to-die contracts may cover two or more lives. On the first death, the death benefit is paid, and the contract terminates. In a first-to-die contract, the cost of insurance (COI) reflects the number and characteristics (such as age and gender) of lives insured. First-to-die contracts typically are structured as a fixed or flexible premium universal life plan, rather than as a traditional whole life contract, since a universal life design can more readily accommodate more than two insureds. Coverage for five, eight or 10 insureds is possible,[20] although guidance as to the treatment of such coverage under the definitional limitations is very limited, even as it might apply to two lives. In some respects, a first-to-die contract functions in a manner analogous to a substandard contract,

---

[16] *See* PLR 201137008 (June 14, 2011), discussed in Chapter 4.
[17] *See* Frasier, *supra* Chapter 3, note 18. This method is discussed further below.
[18] The proposed reasonable mortality regulation's safe harbors only pertain to single-life plans. *See* Prop. Treas. Reg. § 1.7702-1(c), discussed in Chapter 2.
[19] See the discussion below of the IRC § 7702A(c)(6) reduction-in-benefits rule applicable to survivorship plans.
[20] *See Multiple-Life Developments*, panel at Boston SOA Meeting, May 3–4, 1993, 19 SOCIETY OF ACTUARIES' RECORD, no. 2, at 1255, 1265 (1993).

where the increased mortality from the additional life or lives increases required premiums, but the cash surrender value is effectively "shared" with respect to all of the insureds.

Given a single-life mortality table, two-life first-to-die computations may be performed as follows:

$$_tp_{xy} = {_tp_x} \times {_tp_y} \tag{6.1}$$

$$q_{x+t:y+t} = q_{x+t} + q_{y+t} - q_{x+t} \times q_{y+t} \tag{6.2}$$

$$A_{xy} = \sum_{t=0}^{\omega} v^t \times {_{t-1}p_{xy}} \times q_{x+t-1:y+t-1} \tag{6.3}$$

## *Survivorship*

Unlike first-to-die contracts, survivorship or last-to-die contracts provide a death benefit on the last death among the insureds. As noted above, survivorship contracts may be classified as traditional,[21] where the actuarial values are based on the three-status method and cash surrender values are adjusted on the first death, or as frasierized, where the actuarial values are based on the one-status method and cash surrender values are not adjusted on the first death.

Under the traditional approach, the life insurance contract's charges and cash surrender value reflect the status of both insured lives at all durations. Thus, for any given contract year, the cash surrender values (and reserves) take into account whether one or both of the insureds remains alive. The three statuses used in the traditional approach are: both insureds alive, only the first insured alive and only the second insured alive. The traditional approach operates on the principle of offsetting values during the period when both insureds remain alive, i.e., the NSP at any duration during that period is computed as NSPs for single-life coverage on each insured less the NSP for a joint-life (i.e., first-death) coverage, as follows:

$$A_{xy}^{Survivor} = A_x + A_y - A_{xy} = A_{\overline{xy}} \tag{6.4}$$

After the first death, values are determined for the surviving insured using single-life functions (i.e., either $A_{x+t}$ or $A_{y+t}$) in the same manner as for a single-life contract. Consequently, there is an increase in cash surrender value (and reserves) upon the first death to reflect the (higher) single-life mortality; as a result, the pattern of cash surrender values is not smooth but jumps upon the first death. Because of the increase in cash surrender value on the first death, only traditional whole life contracts use the three-status method, as there is not a practical way to reflect the increase in a UL-type contract.

The **Frasier method** uses a single status of "at least one insured alive." This method came into use in the 1980s after the publication in 1978 of an article by William Frasier that described the single status approach for computing reserves and cash surrender values for last survivor products. In his article, Frasier observed that this method "results in a single cash value and reserve scale [that] produces values that are greater than the values calculated by [the three-status method] when both insureds are alive and less than the [three-status method] after the first death."[22] Fundamentally, whereas the three-status method uses an offsetting values approach, the Frasier method operates at the level of the mortality table.

Given a single-life mortality table, the corresponding frasierized second-to-die NSPs are computed as follows:

$$A_{\overline{xy}} = \sum_{t=1}^{\omega} v^t \times {_{t-1}p_{\overline{xy}}} \times q_{\overline{xy}+t-1} \tag{6.5}$$

Specifically, let:

$q_{\overline{xy}+t-1}$ = *the probability the second death occurs in year t, assuming at least one of the insureds survives to the start of that year;*

---

[21] See Jordan, *supra* Chapter 2, note 81, at 210–17.
[22] Frasier, *supra* Chapter 3, note 18, at 4.

$$_tp_x = \prod_{j=0}^{t-1}(1-q_{x+j}) = \text{the probability } x \text{ survives to the end of year } t;$$

$$_tp_y = \prod_{j=0}^{t-1}(1-q_{y+j}) = \text{the probability } y \text{ survives to the end of year } t;$$

$$_tp_{xy} = \prod_{j=0}^{t-1}(1-q_{x+j}) \times \prod_{j=0}^{t-1}(1-q_{y+j}) = \text{the probability both survive to the end of year } t;$$

and

$$_tp_{\overline{xy}} = {_tp_x} + {_tp_y} - {_tp_{xy}} = \text{the probability at least one survives to the end of year } t.$$

Then, $q_{\overline{xy}+t-1} = 1 - \frac{_tp_{\overline{xy}}}{_{t-1}p_{\overline{xy}}}$, (i.e., $_tp_{\overline{xy}} = {_{t-1}p_{\overline{xy}}} \times (1-q_{\overline{xy}+t-1})$), and Formula (6.5) follows.

Thus, under the Frasier method, a unique mortality table is created at contract issuance based on a single status of "at least one insured alive" but taking into account the characteristics of both insureds. This single-status treatment continues throughout the life of the contract (i.e., it does not change on the death of the first insured), and the contract values are computed using survivorship mortality. The Frasier method can be used either to determine cash surrender values, premiums and reserves for whole life contracts or to determine the COI charges and reserves for universal life contracts. As the mortality basis does not change over the life of the contract, the Frasier method is easily adapted for UL-type products and therefore came into widespread use with the introduction of universal life last survivor plans.

Table 6.1 illustrates the NSPs for single lives, for joint lives and for survivorship traditional (three-status) and Frasier (one-status) methods.

| Table 6.1. Single and multi-life NSPs | | | | | |
|---|---|---|---|---|---|
| Equal age | Single male | Single female | Joint | Survivorship | Frasier |
| 25 | 147.21 | 127.83 | 182.57 | 92.48 | 92.48 |
| 35 | 206.64 | 182.39 | 253.22 | 135.81 | 135.81 |
| 45 | 291.24 | 258.12 | 350.67 | 198.69 | 198.69 |
| 55 | 402.11 | 357.79 | 472.61 | 287.30 | 287.30 |
| 65 | 534.82 | 477.12 | 606.90 | 405.04 | 405.04 |
| Assumptions: 2001 CSO aggregate, ANB, 4%, curtate | | | | | |

Under a three-status survivorship contract, it is necessary to know if one insured has died, as it will affect the NSPs (and corresponding cash values).[23] For example, if one of the lives dies at age 65, the NSP will increase from $405.04 to $477.12 if the female life survived and $534.82 if the male life survived. Under a Frasier method contract, the NSP at a given attained age will remain unchanged regardless of whether one or both insureds are alive.

## Determining the Insureds' "Age"

For purposes of computing actuarial values (e.g., cash surrender values, reserves, cost of insurance, etc.), the ages of the insureds under a multiple-life plan may be determined on either an exact-age basis or using a joint equivalent-age approach. The major advantage of working with exact-age computations is the avoidance of a need to develop an appropriate joint equivalent-age formula. However, insurers will often elect to use joint equivalent ages as opposed to exact ages to limit the number of age and class combinations needed in the calculation of contract values. The appropriate joint equivalent ages are derived from a table of age adjustments. For

---

[23] The survivorship values included in Table 6.1 assume a contract status where both insureds are alive.

example, if the underlying rates are based on a male and a female of the same age, a table of deductions from the older age would be used to develop a joint equivalent age.[24]

The use of age adjustments, or uniform seniority tables, can result in a wider variation in practice in the determination of premium values under multiple life plans than is likely to occur under comparable single-life calculations. Further, as had been recognized prior to the issuance of the attained-age regulations under sections 7702 and 7702A (discussed in Chapter 3 and below), the use of age adjustments may have conflicted with the DEFRA legislative history's definition of attained age for purposes of the definitional calculations, i.e., as the age determined by reference to contract anniversaries (sometimes called the "insurance age") so long as the age is within 12 months of the actual age.[25] That legislative history left the definition of attained age unclear in cases where two or more insureds are involved. In particular, in applying the section 7702(d) corridor, the absence of guidance produced a divergence of practice among insurers: exact-age plans commonly used the younger age, while equivalent-age plans more often used the joint equivalent age.

As noted in Chapter 3, the regulations issued in 2006 concerning attained age under the definitional limitations (i.e., Treas. Reg. section 1.7702-2) provide that for three purposes— the section 7702(d) corridor, the minimum premium payment period used in calculating the guideline level premium (GLP) and the section 7702(e) maturity date rule—the attained age of the insured under a contract insuring multiple lives:

- on a last-to-die basis—survivorship contracts—is the attained age of the youngest insured; and
- on a first-to-die basis is the attained age of the oldest insured.

These two rules for multiple life contracts, as recognized by the government in the preamble to the regulations, are without legal precedent and may well run counter to the practices adopted by many insurers prior to the issuance of the regulations. In the case of survivorship contracts, some insurers had been following the first rule for a considerable period of time, while others had made use of a joint equivalent-age methodology. In the case of first-to-die contracts, it is doubtful any insurer had followed the second rule, although application of the rule may not present a problem as a practical matter. If the guideline published by the NAIC (Actuarial Guideline XX) for determining the joint equivalent age for such contracts is adhered to, it appears that only a very limited group of contracts (depending upon the gender and age relationship of the insureds) would fall on the wrong side of the second rule. These rules apply regardless of the gender of the insureds or the presence of any smoker or substandard rating applicable to one of them.

Interestingly, as previously noted, the preamble to the regulations disclaims any relationship between the new rules for multiple life contracts and the reasonable mortality charge requirements of section 7702(c)(3)(B)(i). Hence, while the regulations preclude the use of joint equivalent-age assumptions with respect to, for example, the deemed maturity date for purposes of section 7702(e), the government did not address in these rules the appropriateness of mortality charges based on such assumptions under section 7702(c)(3)(B)(i).

The practical effect of the attained-age regulations, as a general matter, may be to preclude any use of joint equivalent-age mortality in the definitional calculations for contracts to which the regulations apply. Consider, for example, a second-to-die life insurance contract under which the joint equivalent age of the insureds at issue is 60, but the age of the younger insured at that time is 53. In this case, the regulations require use of a deemed maturity date at the end of the 47th contract year. In contrast, the use of mortality based on a joint equivalent-age assumption would place the contract's deemed maturity date—when the joint equivalent age is 100 years—on the 40th contract anniversary, when the younger insured in the example is only 93 years of age. Thus, the use of joint equivalent-age mortality would seem to have the effect of assuming a maturity date prior to the time permitted by the regulations. It also is unclear what adjustments to a joint equivalent-age-based mortality assumption might be appropriate to eliminate this apparent problem. As a result of the regulations,

---

[24] For example, if a contract is issued to a male age 55 and a female age 45, and the age adjustment factor is three, then the "equivalent ages" will be a male and female both age 52. Tables showing the deduction to be made from the age of the older of two lives in order to obtain the joint equivalent ages for the 1980 CSO tables have been published by the National Association of Insurance Commissioners (NAIC) in Actuarial Guideline XX. *See* NATIONAL ASSOCIATION OF INSURANCE COMMISSIONERS, *Guideline Concerning Joint Life Functions for 1980 Commissioners' Standard Ordinary Mortality Table* (Dec. 1986).

[25] *See* DEFRA House Report, *supra* Chapter 1, note 11, at 1447; DEFRA Senate Report, *supra* Chapter 1, note 11, at 576; DEFRA Blue Book, *supra* Chapter 1, note 20, at 651.

insurers may find it difficult, or even impossible, to apply a joint equivalent-age mortality assumption (at least for certain combinations of insureds) for contracts that the regulations govern.

### *Reduction in Benefits Under Survivorship Contracts*

A special reduction-in-benefits rule is provided under section 7702A—by section 7702A(c)(6) in particular—for survivorship contracts. Unlike the general rule of section 7702A(c)(2)(A), which applies for a period of seven years from the date of contract issuance (or material change), the section 7702A(c)(6) reduction-in-benefits rule applies for the *life* of any survivorship contract entered into or materially changed on or after September 14, 1989.[26] Thus, according to the statute, "[i]f a contract provides a death benefit which is payable only upon the death of 1 insured following (or occurring simultaneously with) the death of another insured" and "there is a reduction in such death benefit below the lowest level of such death benefit provided under the contract during the 1st 7 contract years," the rules of section 7702A are applied as if the contract had originally been issued at the reduced benefit level.

Section 7702A(c)(6) was added to the Code in 1989 to thwart products that ostensibly were designed as single premium plans to avoid modified endowment contract (MEC) status, a result inconsistent with the intent of the drafters of section 7702A. Addressing the development of a "single premium II" (SPII) plan (in which a 7-year last survivor term rider was used to make the total 7-pay premium for the policy equal to the GSP), Rep. Kennelly, the sponsor of the amendment to section 7702A, stated:

> However, it has come to my attention that certain companies have recently developed and are marketing a new insurance policy which can be called single premium II. This policy, by using a type of insurance contract common in estate planning known as a last survivor policy, allows policyholders to withdraw tax-free accumulated interest through zero net-interest loans after policy year one, but still meet the seven-pay test of TAMRA [Technical and Miscellaneous Revenue Act of 1988]. In other words, it subverts the purpose of traditional last survivor insurance by converting it into purely an investment vehicle for investors who care little or nothing about the insurance component.[27]

The SPII product design was based on the difference in the treatment under sections 7702 and 7702A of a rider covering the primary insureds under the base contract (discussed in detail in Chapter 3). The initial death benefit under a contract, including that provided by a rider covering the primary insureds, is deemed to last to maturity of the contract in computing the 7-pay premium but not necessarily in computing the NSPs or guideline premiums. Under the general section 7702A rules, expiration of the rider after a term of years has no effect beyond seven years of contract issuance or of a material change. However, through the use of a seven-year survivorship term rider on a survivorship contract (with relatively low COI charges), the SPII plans described by Rep. Kennelly could be created with a 7-pay premium equal to the GSP or NSP, thus creating a non-MEC single-premium plan. The permanent extension of the look-back rule for survivorship plans under section 7702A(c)(6) effectively eliminated the SPII design. At the same time, it added significantly to the complexity of the administration of survivorship plans under the MEC rules.

It should be noted that the special relief rule under section 7702A(c)(2)(B) for reinstatements, excusing reductions in benefits due to contract lapse for nonpayment of premiums where a reinstatement occurs within 90 days of the lapse, is not included in section 7702A(c)(6).

## Paid-Up Additions Riders

Paid-up life insurance riders are often used in connection with a traditional (or an interest-sensitive) whole life base contract to provide flexibility to the purchaser with respect to the level of cash surrender value per $1,000 of death benefit. As noted in the DEFRA legislative history, a "contract that provides for the purchase of paid-up or deferred additions [will be] treated as a single life insurance contract."[28] This statement in the legislative history is appropriately read to include not only paid-up additions purchased with dividends, but also to

---

[26] *See* Omnibus Budget Reconciliation Act of 1989 (OBRA), Pub. L. No. 101-239, § 7647(a).
[27] 135 Cong. Rec. E2,940 (daily ed. Sept. 6, 1989) (statement of Rep. Kennelly).
[28] *See* DEFRA Senate Report, *supra* Chapter 1, note 11, at 572; DEFRA Blue Book, *supra* Chapter 1, note 20, at 647.

encompass paid-up additions riders, as the language of the legislative history does not limit this treatment only to paid-up additions purchased with dividends.

While the base plan may provide the minimum cash surrender value per $1,000 allowed under state law, a paid-up additions rider generally provides incremental units of death benefit containing the maximum cash surrender value per $1,000 permitted under section 7702. Varying the relationship of the base plan premium to the rider premium allows a purchaser to select any level of cash surrender value between the minimum allowed under the nonforfeiture law and the maximum permitted under section 7702. Paid-up additions riders often are used to provide traditional permanent or **fixed-premium universal life** insurance contracts with premium flexibility.[29] Many insurers have used these riders to allow fixed-premium plans to compete with the flexibility of a universal life plan.

Compliance of a paid-up additions rider with the CVAT is typically accomplished either through a rider death benefit and CSV relationship dictated by the NAIC's *Standard Nonforfeiture Law for Life Insurance* (SNFL) and using interest and mortality assumptions consistent with the CVAT, or through a death benefit under the rider that is defined as the product of a "death benefit factor" times the rider's CSV at the time of death. The death benefit factor for each of the relevant attained ages is greater than or equal to the reciprocal of the attained-age NSP for a death benefit of $1.00. So long as the interest and mortality assumptions used in determining the factors comport with the statutory requirements, this structure guarantees that the CSV of the rider is always less than or equal to the section 7702 NSP for the rider death benefit, and that the CVAT requirements with respect to the rider are thus met by the terms of the rider. The use of a minimum death benefit provision based on death benefit factors also is often employed to ensure CVAT compliance of the entire contract, including riders. As noted in Chapter 2, it is important in the design of these riders that CVAT-based factors have sufficient decimal places or are appropriately rounded to provide enough death benefit so that the requirements of the CVAT are met by the terms of the rider.

## Combination Plans

Life insurance plans may also be marketed as a combination of a permanent base contract and permanent or term rider covering the life of the primary insured under the base contract. For example, in an "economatic" plan, a traditional participating whole life contract may be combined with an increasing whole life (paid-up additions) rider and a decreasing term rider. Similarly, a universal life, variable life or interest-sensitive whole life plan may be issued in combination with paid-up additions and term riders. As discussed in Chapter 3, a 1997 private letter ruling dealt with two such components: a variable universal life base contract and a term rider on the primary insured.[30] The sum of the base plan and rider death benefits, called the **target death benefit**, was scheduled to continue to the insured's age 95. Under the plan design, the rider death benefit would vary inversely with the performance of the base plan investment experience. The IRS concluded that, for purposes of the definitional calculations, the target death benefit could be used as the death benefit under section 7702(f)(3) and section 7702A(c)(1)(B), since it would last at least to the insured's age 95.

As also noted in Chapter 3, in a 1995 private letter ruling[31] the IRS addressed the treatment of a nonparticipating, level-premium life insurance plan made up of three components: a whole life insurance contract, a paid-up additions rider and an annually renewable term rider covering the primary insured. In that ruling the IRS determined that for purposes of section 7702A(b), the "future benefits" under the contract consisted of the aggregate amount of insurance coverage under the three components of the plan.[32] This treatment was applied even though a term rider that was not scheduled to continue to the insured's age 95 constitutes a QAB for purposes of section 7702.

As paid-up additions riders are treated as a part of the base contract for purposes of the definitional limitations, a guideline premium-tested rider should not be attached to a CVAT base plan, or vice versa. That is, care should be taken not to mix the definitional tests within a single contract.

---

[29] This structure also provides flexibility in the overall commission levels, as commissions are generally lower on the paid-up additions rider than on the base contract.
[30] PLR 9741046 (July 16, 1997).
[31] PLR 9519023 (Feb. 8, 1995). See Chapter 3 for a full discussion of the facts and implications of this ruling and the ruling cited in the preceding footnote.
[32] This is consistent with the legislative history of the Senate amendment relating to section 7702A. *See* 134 Cong. Rec. S12,352–53 (daily ed. Sept. 12, 1988).

## Interest-Sensitive Whole Life and Fixed-Premium Universal Life: The Challenge of Dual Cash Surrender Values

Interest-sensitive whole life (ISWL) and fixed-premium universal life (FPUL) contracts typically have both a universal life-type accumulation value and a tabular cash surrender value, sometimes referred to as a dual cash surrender value or a secondary guarantee. Such secondary guarantees typically occur in fixed-premium contracts that have cash surrender value scales based on the greater of an accumulation value less a surrender charge and a tabular cash surrender value based on the minimum values permitted under the nonforfeiture law. Plans of this type may comply with section 7702 using either the CVAT or the guideline premium test. As noted above, such plans commonly are sold with paid-up additions riders.

Because of the existence of dual cash surrender values and the potentially alternative contractual guarantees underlying them, the treatment of these plans under section 7702 is complex and, at minimum, not clear on the face of the statute. One methodology for identifying the actuarial values to use in the definitional calculations for such plans is described in the DEFRA Blue Book.[33] The blue book notes that any secondary guarantees present in a contract should be considered in identifying the appropriate contract guarantees of interest, mortality and expense to be recognized in the determination of values under section 7702, as follows:

> Also, if the contract's nonforfeiture values for any duration are determined by a formula that uses the highest value produced by alternative combinations of guaranteed interest rate or rates and specified mortality (and other) charges, the combination of such factors used, on a guaranteed basis, in the highest cash surrender value for such duration should be used for such duration in determining either the net single premium or the guideline premium limitation.[34]

This passage from the blue book has been interpreted by some as meaning that for ISWL and FPUL plans seeking to qualify under the guideline premium test, the GLPs and the contractual gross premiums can be equal by definition, thus rendering the plans in compliance with the guideline premium limitation automatically. In reality, this is true in some circumstances and not others, and does not preclude section 7702 compliance issues from arising in these plans. In addition, care should be exercised in applying the logic of this blue book passage beyond the products that appear to have been its inspiration, i.e., ISWL and FPUL, since doing so can lead to anomalous results which are difficult (or impossible) to reconcile with the statute and its intent as reflected in the legislative history.

The introduction of the reasonable mortality and expense charge rules in TAMRA also casts some uncertainty on the viability of the method described in the blue book passage, or at the very least adds complexity to it. The blue book's method is based on a comparison of potentially differing guarantees within a contract. Before TAMRA, when the definitional calculations were based exclusively on contractual guarantees (subject to floors on the interest rate assumptions), this method involved the identification of the applicable contract guarantees for the calculations. Post-TAMRA, when the calculations are based on "reasonable mortality," the identification of an applicable set of contractual mortality charge guarantees is no longer determinative. Another potential issue with respect to ISWL and FPUL contracts seeking to qualify under the guideline premium test arises because of a fundamental inconsistency between the funding needs and mechanics of traditional contracts and the section 7702 adjustment rules for guideline premium-tested contracts. These and other issues for guideline premium-tested ISWL and FPUL contracts are examined further below.

### *Application of DEFRA Blue Book Footnote 53*

A specific calculation process for determining the section 7702 values for FPUL contracts is outlined in **footnote 53** of the DEFRA Blue Book's description of the life insurance taxation changes made by DEFRA, as follows:

> For example, under a so-called fixed premium universal life contract, if the cash surrender value on a guaranteed basis (ignoring nonguaranteed factors such as excess interest) is not determined

---

[33] See DEFRA Blue Book, *supra* Chapter 1, note 20, at 649. The blue book description was added subsequently to the enactment of section 7702 and does not appear in the House, Senate or conference reports for DEFRA. See the discussion of the status of blue books as authority in Appendix 1.2.
[34] DEFRA Blue Book, *supra* Chapter 1, note 20, at 649.

by the guaranteed interest rate and specified mortality and expense charges used to determine the policy value for some duration, but is instead determined by a secondary guarantee using the guaranteed interest rate and specified mortality and expense charges associated with an alternate State law minimum nonforfeiture value for such duration, the guaranteed interest rate and the mortality and expense charges for the secondary guarantee are to be used with respect to such duration in determining either the net single premium or the guideline premium limitation.[35]

To apply the footnote 53 logic in calculating a guideline premium for a contract, the contract's accumulation values (i.e., the accumulation of net premiums assuming interest credits and mortality and other charges) resulting from the payment of the gross premiums must be projected, using the contract's accumulation value guarantees. If the contract premiums are set at a level that is insufficient to mature the contract under the accumulation value guarantees, the tabular cash surrender values will become the contractual minimum values at some duration (the crossover duration) and will remain so to the assumed maturity date of the contract. In durations where the guaranteed accumulation values exceed the tabular cash surrender values—i.e., the guaranteed accumulation values are the higher or "prevailing" values—the accumulation value guarantees for interest, mortality and expenses are the appropriate actuarial assumptions to use for computing guideline premiums under the footnote 53 methodology. Once a contract reaches the crossover duration, however, the assumptions used to determine guideline premiums are based on those underlying the tabular cash surrender values. If, on the other hand, the contract premiums were set at a level that matured the contract and provided a guaranteed accumulation value which was the prevailing cash surrender value for all durations, the tabular values would be irrelevant to the calculation of the guideline premiums.

Identification of the contractual guarantees appropriate for use in the definitional calculations is thus at the heart of the footnote 53 process. This process may be illustrated by way of the following examples.

**Example 1: Universal life contract design.** This first example focuses on the derivation of the GLP for a flexible premium universal life (UL) contract. The sample contract underlying example 1 is modified in examples 2 and 3, changing the form of the contract to an FPUL design, i.e., with a fixed annual premium and a secondary cash surrender value guarantee in the form of tabular cash surrender values. The sample contracts all assume:

- Sex: Female
- Age: 35
- Face amount: $100,000
- Death benefit option: Level

Accumulation value guarantees:

- Mortality: 2001 CSO female age last birthday (ALB)
- Interest: 4 percent all years
- Expenses: $60 annual administrative fee

Using basic actuarial principles, the GLP for a UL contract can be determined by dividing the sum of the present value of future benefits and expenses (PVFB and PVFE) by a life annuity, where all calculations are based on the accumulation value guarantees. This results in a GLP of $936.33. A similar result could be obtained by solving for the level annual premium that would endow the contract for its $100,000 face amount, assuming successive cash surrender values projected using a 4 percent interest rate, 2001 CSO mortality and the assessment of a $60 expense charge each year. The resulting cash surrender value scale under the projection-based approach is illustrated in Figure 6.1.

As expected, the calculation of the GLP under both the basic actuarial principles approach and the projection method produces the same result.

---

[35] *Id.*, n. 53.

**Figure 6.1.** $936.33 fixed annual premium

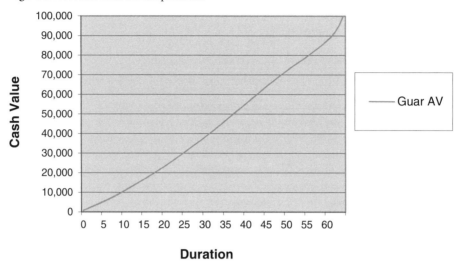

Assumptions: 2001 CSO ALB Female, Age 35, 4% interest and $60 annual administration fee

**Example 2: FPUL contract (fixed annual premium = $800).** If the form of the contract is FPUL instead of UL, several changes must be reflected in the calculation of the guideline premiums to account for the fact that the contract requires the payment of a fixed annual premium and provides a secondary guarantee in the form of tabular cash surrender values to comply with the requirements of the SNFL for fixed-premium contracts. In this example 2, the fixed annual premium is $800 per year and the tabular cash surrender values are based on the following assumptions:

- SNFL mortality: 2001 CSO female ALB
- SNFL interest: 6 percent all years
- SNFL adjusted premium: $687.44
- SNFL annual expense: $112.56 (excess of $800 over SNFL adjusted premium)[36]

The next step in the footnote 53 process is to identify the prevailing value in each duration based on the contract's guarantees, and from there to determine the appropriate contractual guarantees of interest, mortality and expense to be used in the definitional calculations. This process requires a projection of both the guaranteed accumulation value and the tabular cash surrender values. The assumptions with respect to interest, mortality and expense charges (applying the restrictions of section 7702 applicable to these assumptions) pertaining to the prevailing cash surrender value for each duration then need to be reflected in the calculation of the guideline premiums. Figure 6.2 illustrates the projection of both the guaranteed accumulation value and the tabular cash surrender values.

Figure 6.2 typifies the result of most FPUL designs in that the accumulation value dominates at the start but, by design, cannot mature the contract on its guarantees. The tabular cash surrender values eventually prevail and mature the contract on a guaranteed basis. Since the contract guarantees continuation of coverage as long as the fixed premiums are paid, the reduction of the fixed premium below the amount necessary to mature the contract under the accumulation value guarantees (i.e., the premium of $936.33 in example 1) effectively in-

---

[36] Tabular cash surrender values are typically defined on the basis of a net premium, adjusted premium or nonforfeiture factor. A nonforfeiture expense charge can be derived from the fixed premium and tabular cash surrender values (or nonforfeiture factor) stated on the contract specifications page. Recognition of this item as an expense charge in the development of guideline premiums is necessary to establish the intended equivalence between the GLP and the contractual gross premium. While a charge not specified in a contract generally cannot be taken into account in the guideline premium calculations pursuant to section 7702(c)(3)(D)(i), the use of this charge in the calculations is expressly contemplated in footnote 53.

**Figure 6.2.** $800 fixed annual premium

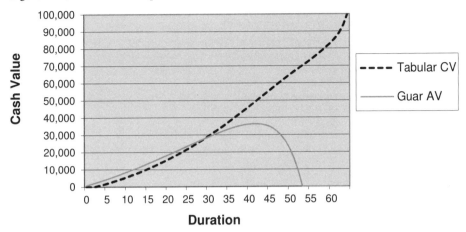

Tabular CV Assumptions: 2001 CSO ALB Female and 6% interest
Guar CV Assumptions: 2001 CSO ALB Female, 4% interest and $60 annual administration fee

creases the economic value of the death benefit provided by the contract to the policyholder, i.e., it is reflective of interest, mortality and expense guarantees provided by the tabular values that are more favorable in at least some durations. Again, identifying these guarantees, as well as those relating to the accumulation value when it is prevailing, is at the heart of the footnote 53 process.

In example 2, the accumulation value prevails for the first 31 years, with the tabular CSVs prevailing thereafter. Table 6.2 details the applicable guarantees for this contract.

| Table 6.2. Example 2 guaranteed assumptions under footnote 53 | | |
|---|---|---|
| **Prevailing CSV** | **Accumulation value** | **Tabular CSVs** |
| Durations | 1–31 | 32–65 |
| Mortality | 2001 CSO female ALB | 2001 CSO female ALB |
| Interest | 4% | 6% |
| Expense | $60 annually | $112.56 annually |

Footnote 53 thus provides the means for identifying the applicable guarantees for an FPUL contract. Once these are determined, the same principles would apply to the calculation of the GLP as illustrated in example 1. Put differently, if a UL contract were designed with the guarantees outlined in Table 6.2, the resulting GLP would be identical to the GLP for the contract defined in this example 2. Not surprisingly, this calculation, using basic actuarial principles and the assumptions defined in Table 6.2, produces a GLP of $800.

In applying the projection-based approach for determining the GLP, the process involves solving for the premium that will endow the contract for the original specified amount using the assumptions set forth in Table 6.2. For the first 31 contract years, the projection will be based on the accumulation value guarantees. For the remaining durations, the projection will be based on the tabular cash surrender values. Under this assumption set, the projected cash surrender values will exactly mirror the set of prevailing cash surrender values on the guarantees, and thus the GLP under the projection-based approach is also $800.

**Example 3: FPUL contract (fixed annual premium = $900).** Example 3 follows the contract design in example 2, except the gross premium is set at $900. Changing the premium will result in certain changes to the contract guarantees, as both the crossover duration and the "expense charges associated with an alternate State law minimum nonforfeiture value" (to quote from footnote 53) will be different.

The applicable guarantees in the determination of the GLP for example 3 are provided in Table 6.3.

190    Life Insurance and Modified Endowments

### Table 6.3. Example 3 guaranteed assumptions under footnote 53

| Prevailing CSV | Accumulation value | Tabular CSVs |
|---|---|---|
| Durations | 1–47 | 48–65 |
| Mortality | 2001 CSO female ALB | 2001 CSO female ALB |
| Interest | 4% | 6% |
| Expense | $60 annually | $212.56 annually |

Figure 6.3 illustrates the projection of both the accumulation value and the tabular cash surrender values for example 3. Because of the higher fixed premium in this example, the accumulation value will prevail for a longer period of time (47 years vs. 31 years). In addition, the higher fixed premium will necessarily result in higher expense charges associated with the SNFL, effectively serving as a balancing item in the process.

**Figure 6.3.** $900 fixed annual premium

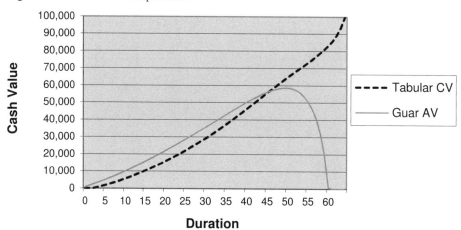

Tabular CV Assumptions: 2001 CSO ALB Female and 6% interest
Guar CV Assumptions: 2001 CSO ALB Female, 4% interest and $60 annual administration fee

As described above, applying basic actuarial principles to the determination of the GLP using the assumptions defined in Table 6.3 will return a GLP equal to $900 (the fixed premium for the contract). Similarly, under a projection-based approach, the accumulation of $900 annually using the Table 6.3 assumptions will exactly endow the contract for its original specified amount, resulting in a set of cash surrender values equal to the prevailing cash surrender values illustrated in Figure 6.3.

### *Observations On and Issues in Using the Footnote 53 Process*

As illustrated in examples 2 and 3, the footnote 53 process *generally* results in the equivalence of the GLP and the contractual gross premium. This equivalence will hold true, however, only if the contractual guarantees of interest, mortality and expenses as determined under the footnote 53 process are not in conflict with the restrictions on the allowable assumptions in computing guideline premiums. Assuming this to be the case, the upper limit on the allowable premium under the guideline premium test for a level premium FPUL (or ISWL) design is the GLP based on accumulation account guarantees ($936.33 in example 1). With such a premium, the accumulation value would constitute the prevailing cash surrender value for all durations in the above examples, and the tabular value thus would be irrelevant under footnote 53. Any higher level gross premium would overendow the contract on a guaranteed basis. Any gross premium below this amount arguably results in the equivalence between the GLP and the gross premium, the intended result of footnote 53.

The equivalence of the GLP and the contractual gross premium, however, does not necessarily guarantee compliance under the guideline premium test, a common misconception regarding FPUL and ISWL contracts. Monitoring the relationship between the premiums paid for a contract and its guideline premium limitation is still necessary, particularly for those product designs that apply premiums to the accumulation value immediately upon receipt by the insurer. The early payment of premiums, particularly those received (and applied) in one contract year that are otherwise due in the following contract year, can result in premiums exceeding the guideline premium limitation, even if for a short period of time. These early premium payments can create failures to comply with the guideline premium test if the guideline premium limitation is based on the sum of GLPs (i.e., where the cumulative GLP exceeds the guideline single premium).

Some of the difficulties and misconceptions surrounding the application of section 7702 to FPUL and ISWL plans may be illustrated by examining the various private letter rulings waiving (pursuant to section 7702(f)(8)) compliance errors in such plans.[37] A 2003 ruling[38] dealt with a FPUL plan that was designed to qualify under the guideline premium test but failed to do so. The contract's cash surrender values were based on a dual scale, equal to the greater of the contract's accumulation value less a surrender charge or its tabular cash surrender values. According to the ruling, the intention of the company's actuaries in designing the plan was that the tabular cash surrender value assumptions would control the determination of the guideline premiums for the contract, thus ensuring, in accordance with the footnote 53 process, that the gross single or level premiums would at all times equal the applicable guideline premiums. By design, the contractual guarantees underlying the accumulation value were insufficient to mature the contracts, causing the actuaries to look solely at the assumptions underlying the tabular values rather than the accumulation value assumptions in calculating guideline premiums. Unfortunately, at earlier durations of the contract, the cash surrender value was determined by the accumulation value less a surrender charge, not the tabular cash surrender values, and different guarantees applied under each. As a result, the company misapplied the footnote 53 methodology by failing to compare the accumulation value to the tabular cash surrender value, duration by duration, in order to identify the appropriate guarantees to use in the guideline premium calculations. The IRS concluded that the company's error was a reasonable one in the circumstances and waived the failure to comply with section 7702.[39]

As mentioned earlier, a conflict can exist between the operation of the guideline premium test's adjustment rules and the funding needs and mechanics of an ISWL or FPUL plan. Just such a conflict is illustrated in another 2003 waiver ruling.[40] That ruling addressed the application of the guideline premium test's attained-age decrement adjustment methodology in the context of "fixed traditional coverage elements and fixed charges therefore [sic]." While the contracts involved in the ruling were technically flexible premium adjustable life contracts rather than ISWL or FPUL in nature, they were said to be designed to integrate traditional life insurance coverage with the flexibility of a universal life contract by incorporating a UL-type accumulation account. According to the ruling, the insurer erroneously believed the attained-age adjustment method was designed for use only in connection with universal life contracts, as that method could not be applied for decreases in a manner which would allow sufficient gross premiums to be paid to maintain the contracts in force for the whole of life. The insurer therefore used an issue-age methodology to make what it believed to be "proper" adjustments to the guideline premiums in the event of a change to a contract. This approach caused a number of the contracts to fail to comply with the guideline premium limitation once recalculated using the prescribed attained-age adjustment method. The IRS also waived this error.[41]

This conflict, along with a second problem, also appeared in a 1998 private letter ruling waiving noncompliance with section 7702.[42] FPUL plans often were intended to be designed in a way that precludes the policyholder from taking any actions which could cause the contracts to violate the guideline premium requirements.

---

[37] See PLRs 200329040 (April 16, 2003), 200328027 (April 10, 2003), 200230037 (April 30, 2002), 199911010 (December 8, 1998) and 9601039 (October 5, 1995).

[38] PLR 200328027 (April 10, 2003).

[39] The error was corrected by adding an endorsement enabling the contract to comply with the CVAT, retroactively to the contract's original issue date. A 2002 private letter ruling granted a similar waiver, including use of a CVAT endorsement. See PLR 200230037 (April 30, 2002).

[40] PLR 200329040 (April 16, 2003).

[41] The solution, again, was to amend the contracts retroactively to issuance to comply under the CVAT, which has been the method typically applied to "cure" failures of ISWL and FPUL plans.

[42] See PLR 199911010 (Dec. 8, 1998).

The insurer involved in this ruling, expecting its product to operate in this fashion, did not implement a computer program or administrative procedure to monitor guideline premium test compliance. Under the plan addressed in the ruling, policyholders paid either an initial lump-sum premium to produce a paid-up contract or paid the contract's scheduled premiums. Two errors occurred in the section 7702 testing of the contracts. First, although the lump-sum amounts were appropriately limited to the then-current maximums allowed under the guideline premium test, subsequent scheduled premium payments caused the sum of the premiums paid for the contract to exceed the permitted amounts because of a product design error. Second, while the terms of the contracts did not permit decreases in the face amount, company personnel permitted extracontractual decreases. Upon processing these decreases, personnel reduced the contractual fixed premium in proportion to the amount of the face reduction rather than in accordance with the attained-age adjustment method, producing higher fixed premiums than would have been permitted under the properly adjusted guideline premium limitation. This enabled policyholders to make premium payments in excess of that limitation. The IRS waived both of these errors as reasonable ones.

Still other potential problems with guideline premium-tested ISWL and FPUL products may be identified. As noted before, to make the assertion that the GLP and the gross annual premium are equal, the accumulation value guarantees and the tabular cash surrender value assumptions used in the guideline premium calculations must meet the general requirements of section 7702, and with the introduction of the "reasonable" mortality limitations by TAMRA, that equivalence may no longer hold if mortality charge guarantees do not satisfy the reasonable mortality charge requirements. Further, the treatment of lump-sum payments and modal premiums must be reckoned with. Hence, if an insurer plans to make use of the guideline premium test for the section 7702 compliance of ISWL or FPUL contracts, care should be taken to follow the footnote 53 process and avoid the pitfalls that can produce noncompliance with the definitional limitations.

## Group Universal Life

Group universal life (GUL) insurance plans are those sold under a group master contract with individual employee coverage provided under a group certificate. GUL insurance contracts may take the form of corporate-owned contracts or may be used as part of an employee group life insurance program. Coverage is underwritten on a group basis and generally requires only limited evidence of insurability.

An important use of GUL is employer-sponsored payroll deduction coverage, potentially as a replacement of voluntary term insurance. Some of the more common features of this type of GUL follow:

- Certificates are funded on an employee-pay-all basis.

- Employers collect premiums for the insurer through payroll deductions and may provide other administrative services.

- Certificates provide for an option 2 death benefit (i.e., a death benefit defined as the face amount plus cash surrender value).

- Covered employees generally have all rights of ownership in their individual certificates, including access to certificate cash surrender values and their beneficiaries are entitled to all proceeds on death.

Although these are group contracts, the premiums, cash surrender values and face amounts are computed and reported for each individual certificate holder. In addition, the section 7702 and 7702A rules are applied at the level of the individual certificates, not the group contract in total. This "individual certificate" treatment is confirmed by the DEFRA legislative history's discussion of the effective date of section 7702. Specifically, for purposes of the effective date, "[w]ith respect to group or master contracts, the date taken into account for any insured is the first date on which the insured is covered under the contract and not the date of the master contract."[43] Thus, for measuring compliance with the definitional limitations, the premiums and the cash surrender value for each individual insured's certificate, based on the effective date of that individual's coverage, must be considered.

---

[43] See DEFRA Blue Book, supra Chapter 1, note 20, at 655. No comparable statement appears in the formal DEFRA legislative history. See also IRC § 264(f)(4) (similar master contract rule).

GUL provides some challenges in administration under the definitional limitations. Group master contracts are commonly designed with a group-level anniversary date that controls anniversary processing, including the date on which the insured's age increases. Such a common anniversary date simplifies the administration of the group contract. However, it has the potential to create certain administrative difficulties for section 7702 and 7702A compliance. For certificates issued off-anniversary, this can lead to a short first contract year (i.e., the duration between the certificate's issue date and the master contract anniversary date is less than 12 months). Because section 7702 and 7702A compliance is measured at the certificate level, incrementing either the sum of the GLPs or the 7-pay premiums on the group anniversary date rather than on the certificate anniversary date can lead to an overstatement of the applicable guideline premium limitation. Care also needs to be taken to abide by the restrictions on the assumed age of the insured under the attained-age regulations for sections 7702 and 7702A (as discussed in Chapter 3).

The master contract under many GUL plans is accompanied by a memorandum of understanding (MOU) that describes various aspects of the expected operation of the contract. In some cases, the MOU may limit the changes the insurer can make in the certificate cost factors, including changes in the COI rates. While it is not clear an MOU is part of the terms of the master contract or the certificates, so that any limits specified in the MOU translate into guarantees, the provisions of an MOU should be considered in identifying appropriate actuarial assumptions for use in the definitional calculations.

Also, because GUL contracts are commonly issued with little, if any, underwriting, mortality charge guarantees may exceed 100 percent of the applicable CSO rates. In such a case, care should be taken in the mortality assumptions used in the definitional calculations, as the use of mortality charges in excess of 100 percent of the applicable CSO tables may not satisfy the section 7702 and 7702A requirements relating to "reasonable mortality." The transition to a new mortality table may also create administrative issues for GUL plans, as the operative date for applying the reasonable mortality standards is based on the effective date of a certificate, not the group contract, absent relief from the IRS.

From time to time, at the insistence of its sponsoring employer, a GUL plan may be transferred from one insurer to another. A 2004 private letter ruling waiving noncompliance with section 7702 discussed the characterization of the transfer of GUL certificates to a new insurer, which that insurer treated as an assumption reinsurance transaction rather than as an exchange of contracts.[44] If the assumption reinsurance treatment had been correct, this arguably would have resulted in the carry-over of the certificates' issue dates and guideline premium limitations. Concluding later that this treatment was in error, the new insurer sought a waiver from the IRS. Noting that several terms of the original coverage, including the guaranteed and current COI charges and the maturity date for the coverage, were altered when the change in insurers occurred, the IRS held that the change in the arrangement's terms in the course of the transfer resulted in an exchange (i.e., the issuance of a new contract) rather than an assumption reinsurance transaction for federal income tax purposes. This in turn required the application of new definitional limitations at the time of the transfer, treating the cash surrender values of the certificates as new premium for section 7702 purposes and as rollover amounts under section 7702A.

## Single Premium Net Rate Products

Some single premium product designs do not provide for the explicit deduction of a COI charge. This is not to say insurers are not charging for the mortality risk inherent in this type of life insurance. Rather, the cost of insurance is implicitly assessed against the cash surrender value of the contract. In these designs, the cash surrender value equals the single premium accumulated at a **net rate** of interest (subject to reduction for any upfront load or surrender charge).[45] Such a design may prompt some uncertainty as to the interest and mortality assumptions appropriate for use in the definitional calculations. The treatment of these plans under section 7702 was anticipated during the development of the statute, leading to the **gross-up rule** in the DEFRA legislative history.[46] That rule was initially discussed in Chapter 2.

---

[44] PLR 200446001 (Nov. 12, 2004).
[45] From an actuarial perspective, the mortality cost for a net rate plan is covered by the spread between the earned rate and the credited rate. In its report on single premium contracts' mortality charges, the GAO identified 20% of its sample of single premium contracts as having no explicit mortality charge. *See* U.S. General Accounting Office, GAO/GGD-88-95, *Mortality Charges on Single Premium Life Insurance Should Be Restricted* (1988).
[46] DEFRA Senate Report, *supra* Chapter 1, note 11, at 573–74; DEFRA Blue Book, *supra* Chapter 1, note 20, at 648–49. *See also* DEFRA House Report, *supra* Chapter 1, note 11, at 1444.

The gross-up rule, as described in the DEFRA legislative history, was intended to address situations where a contract's cash surrender values are determined on a nonstandard basis, such as a plan under which the guaranteed values are a simple accumulation of premiums at interest. Its purpose was to preclude the possibility of a section 7702-compliant single-premium plan design that excessively funds the contract's future benefits on the contract's guarantees, based on the assumption that mortality charges would be reflected in the definitional calculations even though none are stated. In describing the rule, the legislative history provides that an insurer will not be considered to guarantee a lower interest rate by failing to state a mortality charge. In such a case, the mortality charges used for statutory reserves are to be assumed, and the interest rate or rates implicit in the guaranteed cash surrender values are to be used as the rate or rates guaranteed on issuance, for purposes of the definitional calculations.[47] The legislative history goes on to prescribe a procedure by which the interest rate is redetermined as the rate at which the cash surrender values would accumulate at each contract duration assuming that a mortality charge based on the statutory reserve mortality were actually applied.[48]

The application of the gross-up rule to net rate products has led to some confusion in the calculation of guideline premiums for these plans. Evidencing this, the rule's application was the focus of five private letter rulings in the late 1980s. Four of the rulings granted section 7702(f)(8) waivers to insurers that failed to adjust the interest guarantees for the implicit mortality charges in the definitional calculations.[49] The other ruling was a substantive one, wherein the company applied a single iteration gross-up (see below) on a product guaranteeing cash surrender values formed by accumulating the gross premium at 4 percent.[50]

Because there are no explicit mortality charges under a net rate contract, the gross premium for the contract (disregarding expense loads) often is simply the endowment amount discounted at whatever the interest rate guarantee happens to be. Table 6.4 illustrates the grossed-up interest rate implied by a guaranteed cash surrender value scale of a 6 percent net rate contract.

Table 6.4. Implicit interest rates under gross-up rule

| 6.00% | Guar CV | GSP | Qx | Implied rate |
| --- | --- | --- | --- | --- |
| 55 | 330.339 | 330.339 | — | — |
| 56 | 343.553 | 343.284 | 0.01047 | 6.08% |
| 57 | 357.295 | 356.506 | 0.01146 | 6.14% |
| 58 | 371.856 | 370.028 | 0.01249 | 6.20% |
| 59 | 386.450 | 383.856 | 0.01359 | 6.24% |
| 60 | 401.908 | 397.996 | 0.01477 | 6.29% |
| 61 | 417.984 | 412.428 | 0.01608 | 6.33% |
| 62 | 434.704 | 427.125 | 0.01754 | 6.37% |
| 63 | 452.092 | 442.046 | 0.01919 | 6.42% |
| 64 | 470.175 | 457.136 | 0.02106 | 6.47% |
| 65 | 488.982 | 472.354 | 0.02314 | 6.52% |
| 66 | 508.542 | 487.672 | 0.02542 | 6.55% |
| 67 | 528.883 | 503.093 | 0.02785 | 6.58% |
| 68 | 550.039 | 518.626 | 0.03044 | 6.59% |
| 69 | 572.040 | 534.286 | 0.03319 | 6.58% |
| 70 | 594.922 | 550.070 | 0.03617 | 6.56% |
| 71 | 618.719 | 565.923 | 0.03951 | 6.53% |
| 72 | 643.468 | 581.770 | 0.04330 | 6.50% |
| 73 | 669.206 | 597.496 | 0.04765 | 6.45% |
| 74 | 695.974 | 612.973 | 0.05264 | 6.39% |
| 75 | 723.813 | 628.111 | 0.05819 | 6.31% |

Assumptions: Male, age 55, 1980 CSO mortality, ANB

---

[47] DEFRA Blue Book, *supra* Chapter 1, note 20, at 649. No comparable statement appears in the formal legislative history of DEFRA.
[48] Id.
[49] *See* PLRs 8846018 (Aug. 19, 1988), 8843008 (July 26, 1988), 8816047 (Jan. 25, 1988) and 8751025 (Sept. 21, 1987).
[50] PLR 8827012 (March 31, 1988).

As in Table 6.4, where the formula $(CV_{n-1}(1 + i_n) - 1000q_n)/(1 - q_n)$ is used to find the implied interest rates, the gross-up rule can be applied by employing an iterative process. Specifically, since the contract's net amount at risk is based on the level of its cash value, and thus on the amount of the allowable premium, the process is arguably a circular one. The first iteration involves the calculation of a GSP based on the payment of the stipulated premium, imputed mortality rates applied to the contractual net amount at risk and the grossed-up interest rates (subject to the 6 percent statutory minimum rate applicable to the GSP). The resulting trial GSP is then used as the initial premium for the second iteration. The trial GSP will produce a new set of imputed interest rates and will produce a new trial GSP. At the prior iteration, the trial GSP could pay mortality costs and still endow the contract, so each successive trial GSP is smaller than the last. This increases the amount at risk, guaranteeing higher imputed interest rates at each iteration, causing a downward spiral of trial GSPs. Where an iterative process is used, it eventually converges to an arguably appropriate GSP when imputed interest rates in all durations are at least equal to the statutory minimum requirement of 6 percent.

The unfortunate result is that the use of an iterative process converges, slowly and painfully, to a point where the contract cannot comply with the requirements of the SNFL in the case of fixed-premium designs. The conclusion expressed in a 1998 private letter ruling is that a single premium net rate plan cannot meet both the requirements of section 7702 and the SNFL.[51] To resolve the problem, that ruling (another noncompliance waiver ruling) permitted the insurer to correct the problem by adding an endorsement to its contracts that gave the insurer the right to impose mortality charges, thus allowing what had been imputed costs of insurance to be actually charged. In this way, the GSP could be computed in a normal manner. Granting the insurer the ability to impose mortality charges eliminated the need to apply the gross-up rule in computing the guideline premiums for the contracts.

## Burial or Preneed Contracts

Burial or preneed contracts are generally small face amount contracts sold to older age policyholders. Preneed contracts are often sold in an arrangement set up by a funeral home to provide a death benefit that covers a predetermined cost of a funeral in the future for an individual insured. Typically, the funeral home guarantees this prearranged cost and is designated as the primary beneficiary or assignee under such a contract. The full amount of the premium, or a significant portion thereof, is often paid upfront. Further, the face amounts of such contracts generally are designed to increase by a guaranteed amount or percentage each year to cover the expected increase in burial costs.

As is the case with most traditional forms of life insurance, preneed contracts typically seek to qualify as life insurance using the CVAT. However, the generally increasing pattern of death benefits coupled with the limited pay design pose certain challenges in designing a product that satisfies both CVAT and the SNFL. As discussed in Chapter 2, the maximum permissible CSV under the CVAT is generally based on an NSP that reflects a nonincreasing death benefit pattern. This is in contrast with the SNFL, which generally requires that future guaranteed increases be taken into consideration in determining the nonforfeiture cash values. Absent any relief provided from the section 7702(e)(1)(A) computational rule requiring nonincreasing death benefits or the SNFL requirement that guaranteed future death benefits be taken into consideration in determining minimum nonforfeiture values, these types of products could not simultaneously satisfy both section 7702 and the SNFL. To resolve this conflict, special rules exist for preneed contracts.

Specifically, the Tax Reform Act of 1986[52] made technical corrections to DEFRA that granted some relief from the strict requirements of the CVAT for contracts "purchased to cover payment of burial expenses or in connection with prearranged funeral expenses." That act added section 7702(e)(2)(C) to the Code, establishing rules unique to these plans. Under section 7702(e)(2)(C), death benefit increases may be taken into account in applying the CVAT if the contract:

- has an initial death benefit of $5,000 or less and a maximum death benefit of $25,000 or less, and

- provides for a fixed predetermined annual increase not to exceed 10 percent of the initial death benefit or 8 percent of the death benefit at the end of the preceding year.

---

[51] PLR 9833033 (May 21, 1998).
[52] Pub. L. No. 99-514, § 1825(a)(4).

TAMRA clarified that the rule would be prospectively effective, applying to contracts entered into on or after October 22, 1986. The relief provision of section 7702(e)(2)(C) thus allows preneed contracts with future guaranteed increases in death benefits, subject to the limitations described above, to meet the SNFL requirements and still comply with the CVAT.

It should be noted that section 7702(e)(2)(C) contains an aggregation rule that requires the initial death benefit of a contract to be determined for its purposes by treating all contracts issued to the same owner as a single contract. This aggregation rule is designed to prevent an individual from buying two or more preneed contracts, each designed to qualify under section 7702(e)(2)(C), where the combined initial death benefit exceeds $5,000. This rule has raised some question as to whether a contract owner who holds other life insurance (e.g., a term or whole life insurance contract) would be eligible for the section 7702(e)(2)(C) relief. While there is no guidance directly clarifying the intent of this aggregation rule, it would seem reasonable to apply the rule narrowly, addressing only preneed contracts designed to meet the section 7702(e)(2)(C) requirements.

Given the complexity of the section 7702(e)(2)(C) rules, care needs to be exercised in the design and development of the contracts intended to fit within them, as the rules are very specific and narrowly targeted with regard to the contract characteristics to which they apply, and the consequences of non-compliance can be significant.

While the section 7702(e)(2)(C) relief targets preneed contracts that provide for future scheduled increases in death benefits, other preneed product designs can be constructed which do not fall within section 7702(e)(2)(C) but still meet the CVAT requirements. Common features of these products include limited early duration (or graded) death benefits or index-based death benefit increases (e.g., increases tied to the Consumer Price Index). Since index-based death benefit increases are not known in advance, they generally would not be eligible for the relief provided for in section 7702(e)(2)(C). These products therefore would need to qualify under CVAT using the section 7702(e)(1)(A) computation rule, i.e., reflecting level death benefits. In this regard, section 5c.C of the SNFL provides that "unscheduled changes in benefits" need not be taken into consideration in determining minimum nonforfeiture values. Actuarial Guideline XXV (AG25) was adopted in 1989, applicable to contracts issued on or after January 1, 1991, to interpret section 5c.C of the SNFL and clarify the application of the SNFL with regard to unscheduled changes in benefits. More specifically, AG25 provides that index-based increases in death benefits are "unscheduled" if they are contained in contracts having an initial face amount not greater than $10,000. Although not limited to preneed contracts, in practice AG25 primarily affects small face amount contracts sold to fund the costs of prearranged funerals. Treating index-based increases as unscheduled increases allows preneed contracts to qualify under the SNFL while meeting the CVAT using the section 7702(e)(1)(A) computational rule. AG 25 was modified in 2010 to apply an indexed threshold amount thereafter.[53]

**Mortality Assumptions**

In 2010, the NAIC adopted a model regulation establishing new minimum mortality standards for reserves and nonforfeiture values for burial or preneed life insurance.[54] The **preneed model** provides that "for preneed insurance contracts ... and similar policies and contracts, the minimum mortality standard for determining reserve liabilities and nonforfeiture values for both male and female insureds shall be the Ultimate 1980 CSO." The Ultimate 1980 CSO, in turn, means the 1980 CSO tables without 10-year selection factors. While the preneed model is generally effective for "policies and certificates" issued on or after January 1, 2009, it contains transition rules permitting continued use of the 2001 CSO tables for preneed contracts issued before January 1, 2012. The preneed model had been adopted by a majority of the states by the end of 2009.

As previously discussed, the definitional calculations post-TAMRA are made in part on the basis of reasonable mortality pursuant to section 7702(c)(3)(B)(i), which requires the calculations to be based on "reasonable mortality charges ... which (except as provided in regulations) do not exceed the mortality charges specified in the prevailing commissioners' standard tables (as defined in section 807(d)(5)) as of the time the contract

---

[53] *See* NATIONAL ASSOCIATION OF INSURANCE COMMISSIONERS, *Guidelines for Calculation of Minimum Reserves and Minimum Nonforfeiture Values for Policies with Guaranteed Increasing Death Benefits Based on an Index* (adopted 1989, modified Oct. 2010).

[54] NATIONAL ASSOCIATION OF INSURANCE COMMISSIONERS, *Preneed Life Insurance Minimum Standards for Determining Reserve Liabilities and Nonforfeiture Values Model Regulation*, NAIC MODEL LAWS, REGULATIONS AND GUIDELINES, Vol. 6, Model 817 (January 2010).

is issued." By cross-referencing section 807(d)(5), section 7702 generally permits use of the same mortality assumptions as permitted to be reflected in calculating the "federally prescribed reserves" with which section 807(d) is concerned (as relevant to life insurance company taxation). Thus, since the preneed model was adopted by at least 26 states in accordance with section 807(d)(5) as of 2009, the 1980 CSO tables today constitute the "prevailing commissioners' standard tables" for purposes of sections 7702 and 7702A for preneed contracts. From 2004 to 2009, the 2001 CSO tables were the prevailing commissioners' standard tables under section 807(d), and hence constituted the reasonable mortality standard for purposes of sections 7702 and 7702A, for preneed contracts. The adoption of the preneed model by the NAIC and a majority of the states had the effect of undoing the adoption of the 2001 CSO tables as of 2009—an unprecedented step as far as the federal tax law is concerned.

In considering the effect of the preneed model on calculations under sections 7702 and 7702A, it is necessary to take account of the effect, if any, of the various notices and other guidance the IRS has issued on the reasonable mortality rule, e.g., Notice 2006-95. These notices establish safe harbors, i.e., if the conditions for application of a safe harbor are satisfied, the assumption made with respect to mortality will be deemed to be reasonable, meeting the requirements of section 7702(c)(3)(B)(i). Significantly, none of the safe harbors described in the notices allow use of the 1980 CSO tables for a contract issued after December 31, 2008. Thus, if the 1980 CSO tables are desired to be used for such a contract's section 7702 and 7702A calculations, it generally will be necessary to rely on the statutory rule in section 7702(c)(3)(B)(i) as the sole governing authority. In light of that rule's reference to reasonable mortality and the life insurance industry's repeated requests for guidance as to what that term connotes, there is necessarily some uncertainty regarding the charges which would satisfy this requirement.

In defining the prevailing commissioners' standard tables, section 807(d)(5)(B) provides for transitional relief, allowing insurance companies to continue to treat a table as prevailing during the three-year period following the year in which a new table was approved by the 26$^{th}$ state. Thus, since the preneed model as prescribed by the NAIC was adopted by the 26$^{th}$ state during 2009, it arguably was permissible to continue to use the 2001 CSO tables in the definitional calculations for preneed contracts issued during 2010–12. On closer analysis, there may be some question about the interrelationship between the three-year transition rule of section 807(d)(5)(A) and that provision's basic rule, which states that "the term 'prevailing commissioners' standard tables' means, with respect to any contract, the *most recent* commissioners' standard tables prescribed by the [NAIC] which are permitted to be used in computing reserves for that type of contract under the insurance laws of at least 26 States when the contract was issued" (emphasis added). On the one hand, the three-year transition rule is permissive, since section 807(d)(5)(B) states that an insurance company "may" apply it and, conversely, seemingly could choose not to do so (i.e., a company could choose to apply the preneed model and the 1980 CSO tables for preneed contracts issued on and after the date of the approval of the model by the 26$^{th}$ state in 2009, consistently with the effective date of the model). On the other hand, one question that would need to be addressed is whether the transition rule set forth in the preneed model affects the identification of the "most recent" commissioners' standard mortality tables "permitted to be used in computing reserves for that type of contract" for purposes of section 807(d)(5)(A). If it does, then the 2001 CSO tables (being more recent than the 1980 CSO tables) may constitute the prevailing commissioners' standard tables during such transition period, and it therefore arguably would not be permissible to use 1980 CSO mortality in the definitional calculations during the model's transition period. This question has not arisen before, as there has not been a reversion to a prior mortality table since the enactment of sections 807(d) and 7702.

### Distributions

Under the distribution rules applicable to MECs, while the assignment or pledge of any portion of a MEC is generally treated as an amount received under the contract, that rule does not apply if the assignment or pledge is solely to cover the payment of burial expenses or prearranged funeral expenses, provided that the contract's maximum death benefit does not exceed $25,000.[55]

---

[55] *See* IRC § 72(e)(10)(B).

## Reversionary Annuity Plans

A reversionary annuity is a form of permanent life insurance that provides an annuitized payout of the death benefit, rather than a lump-sum payment, to the named beneficiary on the death of the insured. The continuance of the payout generally is contingent on the survival of the beneficiary, i.e., it is comparable to a life annuity without a period or amount certain. While a reversionary annuity is considered a life insurance contract under state law, it is not subject to the requirements of state nonforfeiture laws and, thus, need not provide a cash surrender value. In a 1997 private letter ruling,[56] the IRS held that a nonparticipating reversionary annuity which promised the payment of a monthly benefit on the death of an insured and provided no cash surrender value qualified as a life insurance contract under section 7702. The contract qualified for such treatment because of its characterization as life insurance under state law and because, in the absence of any cash surrender value, it necessarily complied with the CVAT. A deferred annuity contract containing a life-only payout option without a period certain would function similarly to a reversionary annuity, yet it would be subject to dramatically different federal income tax results. The difference in tax treatment stems from the fact the state law treats the former as an annuity but treats the latter as life insurance.

## Church-Related Death Benefit Plans

TAMRA added section 7702(j) to the Code, enabling certain church-based, self-funded death benefit plans to be treated as life insurance for federal tax purposes. A **church plan**, according to section 7702(j)(2)(B), is one provided by a church or a convention or association of churches for the benefit of its employees and their beneficiaries, either directly or through an organization described in section 414(e)(3)(A) or (B)(ii), i.e., a church-related organization (including a retirement or welfare benefit organization). The effect of this provision is to extend to the recipients of death benefits under such plans the section 101(a)(1) exclusion from gross income for life insurance proceeds payable at death. Specifically, section 7702(j) operates to provide an exception to the "applicable law" requirement of section 7702(a) (discussed in Chapter 1) for death benefits paid under a plan provided by a church or a church-related organization. Of course, where the coverage provides for cash values as well as death benefits, the definitional limitations still must be observed.

## Issues in Special Product Features

A number of special product features are addressed in the remainder of this chapter. Many of these features have been addressed in specific provisions of section 7702, in its legislative history or in private letter rulings. These features are presented alphabetically.

### Cash Value Bonuses

Some universal life contracts provide, on a guaranteed basis, additional credits to be made to the cash surrender values of the contracts if they remain in force at specified contract durations. Such "persistency" bonuses may be provided in the form of a higher credited interest rate, payment of an additional credit or a return of contract expense charges. The crediting of the bonus to the persisting contract's cash surrender value may be subject to certain contractual conditions, which may include the payment of specified (target) premiums. Where an interest bonus is involved, it may be limited to instances in which interest above the minimum guaranteed rate is being credited under the contract at the time the bonus is otherwise creditable. The crediting of a bonus may also be limited by the existence of policy loans.

It is generally appropriate to recognize bonus-based increases in a contract's cash surrender value in calculating the definitional limitations for the contract, provided the increases are fully guaranteed. As a general matter, the definitional calculations are made by using contract values and methods, subject to the statutory limits on actuarial assumptions and on benefits. Assuming a contract was structured consistently with the statutory requirements (e.g., the mortality and expense charge assumptions are reasonable, interest is guaranteed at the statutory minimum, etc.), it is anticipated that the NSP or guideline premiums at issue would be the amount required to mature the contract on its guarantees. Reflecting in the definitional calculations a provision increasing the contract's cash surrender value for persistency would reduce both the NSP and the guideline premiums so required,

---

[56] PLR 9717033 (Jan. 27, 1997).

as compared with those of a contract lacking such a provision. As a consequence, it can be argued that section 7702 requires the recognition of such a provision, in that it adheres to the tax policy objective of permitting the funding of contract benefits, while avoiding their overfunding, on a guaranteed basis. This view also is consistent with the notion that the contract mechanics generally are to be used in determining the definitional limitations.

In determining the need to recognize a cash value bonus in the definitional calculations, the discussion of the conceptual line between policyholder dividends and contract guarantees in Chapter 2 is relevant. A bonus would not need to be recognized in the calculations at all if it were provided on a nonguaranteed, fully discretionary basis. The contractual form of the bonus also is relevant in determining when the bonus is guaranteed, and therefore should be reflected in the calculations, versus when it is properly treated as a (broadly defined) dividend or excess interest credit. Where the crediting of a bonus is dependent on the payment of premiums, or is creditable at a specified contract duration, it is in all likelihood guaranteed. Where it is subject to the discretion of management, on the other hand, it may well be viewed as a dividend and not a contractual guarantee. In such a case, it would be treated in the same manner as any other dividend or excess interest credit.

A cash value bonus, where guaranteed and not discretionary, can be recognized in the definitional calculations in the amounts and at the durations in which it is to be applied to increase the contract's cash surrender value. For example, the credits could be incorporated into the calculations as an additional amount of interest or as a negative expense charge. If the cash value bonus is credited at contract issuance, such as for the purpose of reimbursing a policyholder engaging in a section 1035 exchange for surrender charges assessed against the replaced contract's cash surrender value, it presumably should be recognized as additional guaranteed interest credited at that time (rather than as a premium payment). Further, where a cash value bonus is reflected in a contract's guaranteed interest rate, that rate seemingly should be compared with the minimum statutory interest assumption to determine its effect on the calculations. Challenges exist, however, in identifying the rate equivalent for a lump-sum amount where the period in respect of which the lump sum is credited is unclear.

## *Decreasing Face Amount Plans*

While not common, a permanent life insurance contract may provide for a scheduled decrease in its death benefit. Section 7702 is unclear as to the recognition of scheduled decreases in coverage, except for the computational rule in section 7702(e)(1)(D). That rule provides that the amount of any endowment benefit under a contract cannot be assumed in the definitional calculations to be greater than the least amount payable as the contract's death benefit at any time.

As discussed in detail in Chapter 3, the four computational rules of section 7702(e)(1) constrain the future benefits under a contract that are "deemed" to apply in determining the NSPs and the guideline premiums. The first computational rule deems death benefits not to increase and is intended to prohibit reflection of either a pattern of increasing benefits or a pattern of decreasing and later increasing benefits in the definitional calculations. This rule, however, does not mandate that the assumed benefits be decreased to follow a scheduled decrease in contractual benefits; it requires only that, once benefits are decreased, future scheduled increases cannot be reflected in the calculations. The second and third computational rules literally permit the definitional calculations to assume an endowment at 95 for the least amount of death benefit even if the actual contract terminates prior to that time. Despite the wording of the third rule, it could be argued that a contractually guaranteed pattern of decreasing benefits should be reflected in the at-issue calculations, on the theory that the purpose of the rule, as amended in 1986, is only to permit partial endowments prior to age 95, and so the guaranteed death benefit structure of a contract otherwise should be followed in the calculations. But such an interpretation raises the question why it is appropriate to deem a level death benefit to exist where no benefits are provided but not where some coverage is provided (albeit at a lower level). Thus, for plans under which the face amount decreases subsequent to issue, it does not appear to be inconsistent with the section 7702 rules either to recognize the scheduled decreases at contract issuance or, alternatively, to assume a level death benefit pattern and recognize the decreases, as and when they occur, as adjustments under section 7702(f)(7)(A). In this regard, it is important to differentiate benefits provided under a base contract from those provided under a term rider on the primary insured, which may constitute a QAB if the benefit does not continue to maturity (see the discussion of this topic in Chapter 3).

## Intentionally Failed Contracts

There have been instances in which an insurer may wish to market, and a buyer may be willing to purchase, a contract that intentionally fails to meet the requirements of section 7702. Once a contract fails to comply with the definitional limitations (as discussed in detail in Chapter 8), taxable income, equal to the "income on the contract" (as uniquely defined under section 7702(g)), must be reported annually to the policyholder. A failed contract is treated as consisting of term life insurance, to the extent of the net amount at risk, in combination with a currently taxable fund. A buyer that is a tax-exempt entity or not subject to U.S. taxing jurisdiction may be interested in purchasing such a contract if the purchase is otherwise viewed as sound for nontax reasons.

Even though a contract by its terms may be designed to fail the CVAT (e.g., an endowment for the full face amount prior to age 95), it will not actually fail to comply with section 7702 until the premiums paid for it exceed the guideline premium limitation. Thus, absent a premium payment exceeding the GSP in its initial durations, a contract intentionally designed to fail section 7702 may nevertheless qualify under the statute as a compliant life insurance contract for some period of time before the contract achieves the intended failure. All the accrued income on the contract will be taxable at the point the contract actually fails the guideline premium limitation. Put differently, there is no provision in the Code for a policyholder or an issuer to choose to treat a contract as taxable by simply declaring that as their intention.

## Life Insurance and Annuity Combinations

Plans that combine life insurance and a single premium annuity would not appear to create issues under section 7702 or 7702A, so long as they are designed in such a way that they are not structured as a "combination" plan within the ambit of the *Le Gierse* case.[57] For example, an annuity issued in connection with an annual premium contract could be viewed as a premium payment mechanism and not a mortality "hedge." Where a single premium nonrefund life annuity is issued in connection with a life insurance contract, however, care should be taken that a material life insurance risk element remains in the arrangement.

A 1999 private letter ruling[58] held that the proceeds payable under a term life insurance rider on a deferred annuity contract would be excludable from the gross income of the death beneficiary as life insurance under section 101(a)(1). In the ruling, the IRS reasoned that, because the rider was a contract of life insurance under state law and economically separate from the annuity and because it satisfied the CVAT (it provided no cash surrender value), the rider qualified as life insurance under section 7702. The IRS also ruled that all charges for the rider assessed under the annuity contract are treated as distributions includible in the contract owner's gross income as provided in section 72(e).

## No-Lapse Guarantees

A number of universal and variable universal life insurance contracts contain a **no-lapse guarantee**, which provides that the contract will not go into default even if the account value is exhausted (or a policy loan plus accrued interest exceeds the cash surrender value) if certain no-lapse requirements are met. These requirements generally are of two types:

- **Minimum premium:** The no-lapse guarantee is met by satisfying a cumulative premium payment requirement over a specified period, often adjusted for partial withdrawals and policy loans. Longer no-lapse guarantee periods may require higher minimum premiums.

- **Shadow account:** The no-lapse guarantee is measured by the balance of an accumulation-type shadow account, which may reflect different interest, expense and COI assumptions than the underlying contract. The no-lapse provision is based on maintaining a positive shadow account value. The shadow account value is not available as a nonforfeiture or loan value.

At contract issuance, a no-lapse guarantee generally should not affect the calculation of the NSPs, guideline premiums or 7-pay premiums, as the test plan by definition would not lapse under the calculation assumptions. However, where an explicit charge is made for the no-lapse guarantee, an issue can arise as to whether

---

[57] 312 U.S. 531 (1941). See the discussion of this case in Chapter 1.
[58] PLR 200022003 (Dec. 9, 1999).

the charge can be reflected in the guideline premiums. The answer would appear to depend on whether the guarantee is properly viewed as a benefit integral to the contract or instead as an additional benefit (presumably a non-QAB). In that the no-lapse guarantee provides for the continuation of the most basic benefit under the contract, namely, life insurance coverage of the primary insured, it seems that a strong argument can be made that the guarantee is an integral one and thus the charge for the guarantee may be reflected in the guideline premiums, subject to the requirements of the reasonable expense charge rule. However, choosing to reflect the charge for a no-lapse guarantee in the at-issue guideline premiums may require an adjustment if the no-lapse guarantee terminates before its scheduled expiry.

Alternatively, in the absence of specific guidance, an insurer reasonably could view a no-lapse guarantee as an integral part of a life insurance contract but nonetheless conclude that it is proper to disregard the charges for such a feature in calculating guideline premiums. In that such a guarantee provides for continued coverage and thereby is associated with the mortality charges an insurer may collect over the life of a contract, it arguably is reasonable to distinguish such charges from those traditionally contemplated for reflection in a contract's guideline premiums.

Even under the broad definition of CSV under the 1992 proposed regulations (as discussed in Chapter 2), a shadow account for a no-lapse guarantee would not seem to constitute a section 7702 CSV, and, as such, it would have no effect on the definitional calculations.[59] After all, a shadow account's role is to lengthen the time death benefits are provided, and it typically has no effect on a contract's cash values, and hence on its investment orientation, other than to reduce them if charges are imposed. Similarly, premium payments to maintain a contract in force, while counted as premiums, would not seem to pose any special problem under the guideline premium test if they are within the limitations of that test.

As is often the case with sections 7702 and 7702A, there is no guidance specific to the application of the statutes to contracts containing no-lapse guarantees. One private letter ruling, discussed above in connection with guaranteed minimum withdrawal benefits under a variable life contract, did mention that the contract involved in the ruling included a no-lapse guarantee. The ruling focused on the section 7702 treatment of the rider's GMxB, however, and did not discuss the effect, if any, of the no-lapse guarantee's presence in the arrangement.[60]

## *Premium Deposit Funds*

Premium deposit funds have long been used in connection with life insurance contracts as a means of permitting the payment of advance premiums and their maintenance in interest-bearing accounts. In a 1995 private letter ruling,[61] the IRS held that a premium deposit fund rider which allowed a policyholder to prefund future planned periodic premiums was not part of a life insurance or endowment contract for purposes of section 7702. The rider provided an account, separately from the contract, that could be funded with a lump-sum single deposit. Premiums could then be paid periodically into the contract from the rider fund, preventing overfunding of the contract. Although the payments into the rider fund could vary in timing and amount at the option of the policyholder, the total paid was limited to an amount that would make the rider fund balance, including guaranteed interest, exactly sufficient to pay future premiums up to the guideline premium limitation of the contract. (Note that interest earned on a premium deposit fund is taxable to the policyholder as it is earned.)

## *Return of Premium Plans*

A popular feature of term life insurance contracts is a return of premium (ROP) benefit. The ROP benefit, which refunds all or a portion of the premiums paid for the contract, is provided if the insured survives and the contract remains in force to the end of the contract term, although the amount of the benefit may be reduced by amounts paid under the contract. A partial benefit may also be paid after a number of years. The ROP benefit may cover both a return of the base coverage premium and a return of rider premiums.

As discussed in Chapter 3, the 1992 proposed regulations, which have not been finalized, generally define cash value and cash surrender value for section 7702 and 7702A purposes as the greater of the maximum

---

[59] For this to be true, it is essential that the shadow account be a mere ghost, not accessible for cash (by withdrawal or loan) in any manner and not support any benefits apart from the death benefit on the primary insured.
[60] PLR 201046008 (Aug. 13, 2010), discussed in the text at note 15.
[61] PLR 9552016 (Sept. 27, 1995).

amount payable under the contract, without regard to any surrender charge or policy loan, and the maximum amount the policyholder can borrow under the contract. Further, as also discussed previously, the ruling position of the IRS, which tracks the proposed regulations, would appear to sweep virtually any ROP benefit under a term insurance plan into the CSV definition. Giving support to this view, Actuarial Guideline XLV[62] provides a methodology for computing minimum cash values for ROP products based on the period over which premiums are returned, even if the contract could continue in force for a longer period. The guideline is effective for all contract forms filed on or after January 1, 2009, and affects all contracts issued on or after January 1, 2010.

In view of this, in an effort to assure compliance with section 7702, some contracts incorporate a minimum floor on the amount of life insurance they provide in relation to their ROP benefit. In those cases, where an ROP benefit is provided, the contract (or an ROP rider) may provide that the base plan death benefit cannot be reduced below the amount needed to comply with the implied CVAT corridor or the section 7702(d) corridor, as applicable, treating the ROP benefit as CSV within the meaning of the statute.[63]

Where a contract's cash surrender values are equal to an ROP (or for that matter, any other nonformulaic alternative amount payable), treatment of the ROP as CSV may in turn make it necessary to take into account in the definitional calculations the interest rate or rates used in determining such ROP values or the rate or rates that may be inferred from such values. As previously discussed in connection with net rate products, where a contract provides a CSV and no express mortality charges are imposed in the determination of that value, the DEFRA legislative history contemplates imputation of an interest rate—using the gross-up rule—for purposes of the definitional calculations. The need for imputation in the case of ROP benefits is unclear, however, in that there is no indication in the legislative history that the gross-up rule's scope encompasses such benefits, especially where they are determined neither by reference to mortality charges nor by reference to interest and where they may apply only for limited durations. If the gross-up rule should be applied in the context of an ROP plan, however, it seemingly could be applied by taking into account cash surrender values at the beginning and end of each year and the mortality table, and then deriving the interest rate or rates as balancing items.[64]

For an ROP product issued to an insured age $x$, where the cash surrender values at the beginning of year $n$ are equal to $(n \times GP)$ and $GP$ is the contract gross premium (which may include rider premiums that are returned), this balancing item approach would calculate the implied interest rate in year $n$ of the ROP accumulation period as:

$$\frac{q_{x+n-1} \times \left[ \text{Face Amount} - (n \times GP) \right]}{n \times GP} \tag{6.6}$$

The numerator of Formula (6.6) parallels the general formula for determining the COI charge in a universal life insurance contract (e.g., COI × net amount at risk), where $n \times GP$ represent the cash value, and *Face Amount* − $(n \times GP)$ represent the net amount at risk. In this case, the interest amount for the year is equal to the mortality charge for the year, $q_{x+n-1} \times$ *[Face Amount* − $(n \times GP)]$, where the two values effectively net against one another as the cash value grows simply by the amount of each premium payment. Following the DEFRA Blue Book method, NSPs or guideline premiums could be computed for an ROP product using the interest rates so implied. Such rates, especially in the early years of a plan, can be rather high, particularly where a graded percentage of the premiums is returned at intermediate contract durations. (Such grading may be more akin to an implicit surrender charge mechanism than interest.)

For a guideline premium test level premium term life product, the interest rate shown above for year $n$ makes it clear that an increase in GP will lower the implied interest rates. (An increase in GP both lowers the amount at risk in the numerator and increases the denominator.) However, if the selected GP is too high, the 4

---

[62] NATIONAL ASSOCIATION OF INSURANCE COMMISSIONERS, *The Application of the Standard Nonforfeiture Law for Life Insurance to Certain Policies Having Intermediate Cash Benefits* (June 2014).
[63] When the form provides the section 7702(d) corridor, care should be taken that the premiums paid, including the premium for the ROP benefit, do not exceed the guideline premium limitation for the contract.
[64] There especially is a question whether any such interest imputation needs to be made with respect to an ROP benefit associated with a permanent life insurance contract, which otherwise will contain a cash surrender value (an accumulation value, a tabular cash surrender value or both). In the case of such a contract, the "normal" cash surrender value arguably provides the means of identifying the interest rate to be used in the definitional calculations and the ROP generally serves a more limited role as a stop-loss mechanism.

percent minimum will become effective at some duration or durations, which may cause the resulting GLP to be less than the selected GP, thus disqualifying the policy under section 7702 when the sum of the GPs exceeds the guideline premium limitation (which will occur when it first exceeds the GSP).

Note that the difficulty of applying the CVAT to these products is that the implied interest rate will vary with the ROP value. In effect, the CVAT will impose the same premium limitation as would the guideline premium test. (Of course, a corridor mechanism might be incorporated into a contract that reflects implied rates in excess of 4 percent and increases the death benefit accordingly.)

Finally, ROP provisions under a decreasing mortgage term plan may be problematic, as the amount of the premiums returned increases with duration, while the term coverage decreases with duration. In those instances, it may not be possible for the scheduled death benefit to meet the applicable CVAT or section 7702(d) corridor requirement. Further, decreasing coverage, or coverage that does not continue to age 95, arguably could result in a reduced guideline premium limitation for those products relying on the guideline premium test. (See the discussion above on decreasing face amount plans.) ◆

# Chapter 7

# LONG-TERM CARE INSURANCE RIDERS AND ACCELERATED DEATH BENEFITS

## Chapter Overview

This chapter principally focuses on riders to life insurance contracts that pay **accelerated death benefits (ADBs)** upon an insured's **chronic illness**. The chapter begins with a discussion of the origins and economic characteristics of ADB riders. It then introduces the dual regimes of the federal tax law for addressing the treatment of ADBs:

- under **section 7702B**,[1] which defines a **qualified long-term care insurance (QLTCI) contract**[2] and encompasses both ADBs and stand-alone long-term care insurance contracts that meet its qualification requirements, and

- under **section 101(g)**, which generally is exclusive to ADBs.

The chapter next provides a more detailed discussion regarding the tax treatment of QLTCI contracts and the qualification rules for such contracts, and this is followed by a similar discussion of section 101(g) benefits and requirements, including a summary of the differences between the two regimes. After this is a discussion of the tax reporting requirements for chronic illness benefits, followed by a discussion of the consequences of ADB payments under sections 7702, 7702A and 72. The chapter concludes with a discussion of grandfather considerations and section 1035 exchanges of contracts that include ADBs.

## Origin and Characteristics of Accelerated Death Benefits

Individuals face numerous financial risks throughout their lives, including the risk of premature death, of needing long-term care and of outliving one's assets. The severity of financial loss associated with these risks depends on an individual's circumstances and needs and typically varies over time. For example, an individual might purchase life insurance principally to cover the risk of premature death during his or her working life to provide protection for a surviving spouse and children; however, the financial consequences associated with the risk of death may become less severe over time for that purchaser, especially after retirement. In contrast, this individual's financial risk associated with the need for long-term care and medical care generally will rise with advancing age, especially in later retirement years. Recognizing the inverse timing relationship between the financial risks associated with premature death and of needing long-term care, insurers and purchasers increasingly have explored whether a single insurance product that covers both risks, such as life insurance contracts that include chronic illness accelerated death benefit riders, might best suit their needs. Similar to first-to-die life insurance, life insurance-ADB rider combination products are structured to pay benefits upon the first of two insured risks to occur. Thus, where chronic illness insurance benefits are provided as an ADB, the payment of such benefits reduces the life insurance proceeds payable upon the death of the insured. Further, to the extent ADBs do not fully accelerate a life insurance contract's death benefit, the unaccelerated portion of the death benefit remains payable upon the insured's death.

Both long-term care insurance, at least in its modern form, and ADBs are of relatively recent development. The beginning of the AIDS crisis during the 1980s saw many young insureds facing imminent death, which

---

[1] Unless otherwise indicated, references in this book to "section" are to the provisions of the Internal Revenue Code of 1986, as amended (also referred to as "IRC" or the "Code").

[2] In this chapter, references to a "QLTCI contract" and "QLTCI" include QLTCI riders to life insurance contracts. (They may also refer to QLTCI riders to annuity contracts.) In addition, references to long-term care insurance riders include such coverage provided as part of a life insurance contract even if not provided in the form of a rider.

typically produced high fair market values for their life insurance contracts relative to the contracts' nonforfeiture (cash) values. These high fair market values were driven by insureds' shortened life expectancies (and the corresponding expectation that death benefits would be payable much sooner on average than would otherwise be the case for insureds of similar ages) and gave rise to viatical[3] settlements, in which third parties purchased life insurance contracts from terminally ill individuals for more than the contracts' cash values.[4] Reflecting the higher fair market value that can arise for a contract from an insured's impending death, insurers also began developing ADB riders and features under life insurance contracts which provided policyholders a guaranteed, formal insurance benefit if the insured met a triggering event (such as the insured's terminal or chronic illness) that evidenced substantially reduced life expectancy.[5] Since the insurer already is obligated to pay the death benefit at the insured's death (given that life insurance generally is noncancellable), the economic cost to the insurer of providing the death benefit early as an ADB can be thought of as the time value of money cost of paying the death benefit—and most significantly the net amount at risk—a usually short period of time prior to the insured's expected death. ADB riders are priced on this basis, and thus there typically is only a modest cost for ADB coverage relative to the charge that would need to be assessed if the benefit were provided on a stand-alone, i.e., nonacceleration, basis.[6]

While the risk that serves as the trigger for payment of an ADB is the occurrence of a morbidity event (such as **terminal illness**, chronic illness or critical illness), the increase in a contract's value relative to its cash value is usually a function of the insured's expected mortality rather than incurred or expected future medical costs. This characteristic of ADBs—as involving principally mortality rather than morbidity risks—is reflected by the NAIC's *Accelerated Benefits Model Regulation* (ABMR),[7] which states: "Accelerated benefit riders and life insurance policies with accelerated benefit provisions are primarily mortality risks rather than morbidity risks. They are life insurance benefits. ..."[8] In effect, the insurance risk associated with ADBs is principally a timing risk for payment of the death benefit. Of course, the receipt of long-term care or other medical care services, which an ADB can facilitate, can itself affect an insured's expected mortality, as has long been recognized by the life insurance industry and care providers. Indeed, Lillian Wald, founder of the Visiting Nurse Service of New York and an advocate for public nursing, believed that the financial impact of life insurance death benefits to an insurer could be reduced if insureds had greater access to home health nursing services, and in 1909 she convinced the Metropolitan Life Insurance Co. to provide financial support for nurses to visit sick insureds.[9]

---

[3] In describing viatical settlements, the Fourth Circuit Court of Appeals has commented: "A 'viaticum' in ancient Rome was a purse containing money and provisions for a journey. A viatical settlement, by which a dying person is able to acquire provisions for the remainder of his life's journey by selling his life insurance policy, is thus thought to provide a viaticum. In the language of the industry, the insured is the 'viator,' who sells his policy at a discount to a 'provider' of the viaticum." *Life Partners Inc. v. Morrison*, 484 F.3d 284, 287 (4th Cir. 2007).

[4] While not a viatical settlement in the typical sense, an early sale of a life insurance contract by an ill insured was addressed by the U.S. Supreme Court in *Grigsby v. Russell*, 222 U.S. 149 (1911), in which Dr. Grigsby agreed to perform a surgical operation for a patient as consideration for the purchase of an existing life insurance contract on the patient's life. Justice Oliver Wendell Holmes Jr. delivered the court's opinion, stating: "So far as reasonable safety permits, it is desirable to give to life policies the ordinary characteristics of property. ... To deny the right to sell except to persons having [an insurable] interest is to diminish appreciably the value of the contract in the owner's hands." *Id.* at 156.

[5] In commenting on the market in the early years of long-term care insurance riders, Steve Lewis, president of First Penn-Pacific Life, also observed that the availability of riders appeared to be an important feature which helped drive life insurance sales for older purchasers. *Living Benefit Riders*, 16 SOCIETY OF ACTUARIES' RECORD, no. 3 (1990). For further information regarding the advent of ADB riders, *see* Ron Panko, *Two for One: Some People Won't Buy Long-Term-Care Insurance Because They May Never Need It. For Them, a Life Policy that Accelerates the Death Benefit for LTC Payments May be an Alternative*, BEST'S REVIEW, July 1, 2005 (quoting Tim Pfeifer who observed: "Combination products pay off at death and upon confinement. The coverages are complementary, and the pricing is efficient on both sides."); AMERICAN COUNCIL OF LIFE INSURANCE AND LIMRA INTERNATIONAL, ACCELERATED DEATH BENEFITS 1998 (1999); *Accelerated Benefits*, 17 SOCIETY OF ACTUARIES' RECORD, no. 2 (1991).

[6] ADB riders usually are funded through express charges or premiums, an actuarial discount (where the death benefit is reduced by an amount exceeding the ADB, often based on underwriting performed at the time of the insured's terminal or chronic illness for the purpose of ascertaining life expectancy) or through use of the **lien method** (where the ADB together with an interest charge offsets the death benefit payable on the insured's death). For more information regarding the design and pricing of ADBs, *see* Carl Friedrich and Teresa McNeela, *Chronic Illness Accelerated Benefit Riders*, MILLIMAN RESEARCH REPORT (April 2012) (available at http://us.milliman.com/uploadedFiles/insight/life-published/chronic-illness.pdf); and Linda Chow, Carl Friedrich and Dawn Helwig, *Quantification of the Natural Hedge Characteristics of Combination Life or Annuity Products Linked to Long-Term Care Insurance* (March 2012) (available at http://us.milliman.com/uploadedFiles/insight/life-published/quantification-of-natural-hedge-characteristics.pdf).

[7] NATIONAL ASSOCIATION OF INSURANCE COMMISSIONERS, *Accelerated Benefits Model Regulation*, NAIC MODEL LAWS, REGULATIONS AND GUIDELINES, Vol. 4, Model 620 (1991).

[8] ABMR § 3.

[9] Karen Buhler-Wilkerson, THE CALL TO THE NURSE: OUR HISTORY FROM 1893 TO 1943 (describing the history of the Visiting Nurse Service of New York) (hereinafter Buhler-Wilkerson). *See also* LILLIAN D. WALD PAPERS, 1889–1957, The New York Public Library, Humanities and Social Sciences Library, Manuscripts and Archives Division; Diane Hamilton, *Clinical Excellence, But Too High a Cost: The Metropolitan Life Insurance Company Visiting Nurse Service* (1909–1953), 5 PUBLIC HEALTH NURSING, no. 4, at 235 (1988); and METLIFE, *Helping and Healing People*, accessed Apr. 29, 2015 (available at https://www.metlife.com/about/corporate-profile/metlife-history/helping-healing-people/index.html).

By the close of 1916, more than 90 percent of the company's 10.5 million industrial life insureds had access to visiting nursing services.[10] An ADB's ability to facilitate an insured's access to needed long-term care and other medical care remains a strong public policy reason for encouraging the availability of such products.

While the mortality risk associated with chronic or terminal illness ADB coverage typically predominates over the morbidity risk associated with such coverage, it nonetheless is the case that ADBs are triggered by morbidity events and provide benefits which, as noted above, may address an insured's important lifetime needs, e.g., the financial costs of medical care. In the case of ADBs payable upon an insured's chronic illness, the dual nature of coverage—as involving both mortality and morbidity considerations—is reflected in both the NAIC's regulatory scheme and federal tax law. In particular, the NAIC's ABMR regulates "accelerated benefit provisions of individual and group life insurance policies" and applies "to all accelerated benefits provisions of individual and group life insurance policies except those subject to the Long-Term Care Insurance Model Act."[11] This regulation of ADBs as provisions of life insurance policies is consistent with the ABMR's characterization (as noted above) of ADBs as life insurance benefits. At the same time, where the triggering event for benefits is based upon the insured's chronic illness—involving either functional incapacity with **activities of daily living (ADLs)** or cognitive impairment (such as Alzheimer's disease)—the NAIC regime recognizes that ADBs alternatively may be provided in form as long-term care insurance benefits. In particular, the NAIC's *Long-Term Care Insurance Model Act* and *Long-Term Care Insurance Model Regulation* (the LTC Model Act and LTC Model Regulation respectively, and collectively, the LTC model rules[12]) contemplate that long-term care insurance can be provided as part of life insurance contracts, either as an ADB or as a nonacceleration long-term care insurance benefit.[13]

## Federal Tax Rules for ADBs: Introduction to Sections 101(g) and 7702B

### Chronic Illness ADBs

Similar to the NAIC regimes discussed above, the federal tax law also provides a dual structure for addressing ADBs payable upon an insured's chronic illness, allowing for tax treatment of ADBs either as accident and health (A&H) insurance benefits or as life insurance death benefits. As discussed below, however, the lines drawn between the two tax regimes are somewhat different than those of the NAIC and similar state laws. Indeed, from a tax perspective, it is possible for a single product covering chronic illness to satisfy the requirements of both the A&H insurance regime (section 7702B) and the life insurance regime (section 101(g)), whereas the NAIC regimes of the ABMR and LTC model rules are mutually exclusive.

Sections 101(g) and 7702B were both enacted as part of the Health Insurance Portability and Accountability Act of 1996 (HIPAA).[14] Section 7702B defines a **qualified long-term care insurance contract** for federal tax purposes and provides that such contracts will be treated as A&H insurance[15] and "amounts (other than policyholder dividends … or premium refunds) received under [such contracts] shall be treated as amounts received for personal injuries and sickness and … as reimbursement for expenses actually incurred for medical care (as defined in section 213(d))." As a result of this treatment, the insurance benefits received from a QLTCI contract generally are excludable from gross income under section 104(a)(3), subject to the **per diem**

---

[10] Buhler-Wilkerson, *supra* note 9. Other insurers also had visiting nurse and other home health benefits, including John Hancock Mutual Life Insurance Co., West Coast Life, Travelers and Aetna. GEORGE WEISZ, CHRONIC DISEASE IN THE TWENTIETH CENTURY: A HISTORY 19 (2014); Oscar Schisgall, *Insurance for Everybody*, XCVI THE ROTARIAN, no. 1, January 1960, at 34.
[11] ABMR § 1.
[12] As discussed below, various tax rules applicable to QLTCI are imposed by cross-reference to the January 1993 LTC model rules. In this chapter, references to "1993 LTC Model Act," "1993 LTC Model Regulation" and "1993 LTC model rules" are to the January 1993 version of these models. NATIONAL ASSOCIATION OF INSURANCE COMMISSIONERS, *Long-Term Care Insurance Model Act*, NAIC MODEL LAWS, REGULATIONS AND GUIDELINES, Vol. 4, Model 640 (January 1993); NATIONAL ASSOCIATION OF INSURANCE COMMISSIONERS, *Long-Term Care Insurance Model Regulation*, NAIC MODEL LAWS, REGULATIONS AND GUIDELINES, Vol. 4, Model 641 (January 1993).
[13] In PLR 9016050 (Nov. 16, 1990), the IRS addressed certain tax questions relating to a long-term care insurance rider to a life insurance contract that provided a nonacceleration benefit.
[14] PUB. L. NO. 104-191.
[15] IRC § 7702B(a)(1).

**limitation** of section 101(g)(3)(D) and 7702B(d) in the case of benefits provided on a non-reimbursement basis.[16] Section 7702B applies both to stand-alone QLTCI contracts and to QLTCI riders to life insurance contracts (including riders that accelerate death benefits and those that do not).

Section 7702B effectively creates a safe harbor for the tax treatment of QLTCI, confirming the A&H insurance status of such contracts and riders. HIPAA did not, however, address whether, or in what circumstances, other **nonqualified long-term care insurance** policies would be treated as A&H insurance for tax purposes or whether such policies would receive some different, less-favorable tax treatment. (See sidebar for a discussion of the tax treatment of nonqualified long-term care insurance.) While section 7702B does not speak to the treatment of nonqualified policies, it is fair to say that Congress' rules for QLTCI were largely intended to encompass the typical long-term care insurance contracts being issued at the time of HIPAA's enactment and that Congress did not intend that insurers would need to change the fundamental nature of such contracts in order to comply with section 7702B. Rather, Congress established safeguards, some of which were designed to protect the federal fisc (e.g., minimum standards for benefit triggers and restrictions on cash values, to ensure that A&H insurance tax status was not being conferred upon a contract that had insufficient A&H characteristics or provided an excessive investment orientation) while others were designed as consumer protections. Of course, the details of the qualification rules for QLTCI required some changes to contracts, e.g., new qualified contracts were required to state affirmatively that they were intended to be QLTCI, and thus insurers needed to redesign and refile their contracts in the aftermath of HIPAA's enactment.

> **Nonqualified Long-Term Care Insurance**
>
> The current federal income tax treatment of nonqualified long-term care insurance is unclear and likely depends upon the particular facts involved for a contract, such as the severity of the ADL or cognitive impairment that the insured must have in order to receive insurance benefits. The principal contexts in which the tax treatment is relevant consist of the treatment of premiums (e.g., whether they are considered as premiums for insurance coverage of "medical care" under sections 213 and 162(l), which allow a limited deduction for individuals and the self-employed) and the treatment of the insurance benefits received from a contract (e.g., whether they are considered A&H insurance benefits received by reason of personal injury or sickness that are excludable from income under section 104(a)(3)).
>
> A challenge faced in assessing the proper tax treatment of nonqualified long-term care insurance contracts derives from the fact that such contracts—like long-term care insurance generally—usually cover some costs that are medical in nature and other costs, such as room and board, that are personal in nature (which usually would be not deductible). Indeed, the line-drawing conundrum that arises when evaluating the proper tax treatment of a nonqualified contract is part of the reason Congress provided the safe harbor of section 7702B. See also section 213(d)(6), regarding contracts under which amounts are payable for other than medical care, and Treas. Reg. section 1.213-1(e)(1)(v)(a), which pre-dates HIPAA and states:
>
>> Where an individual is in an institution because his condition is such that the availability of medical care ... in such institution is a principal reason for his presence there, and meals and lodging are furnished as a necessary incident to such care, the entire cost of medical care and meals and lodging at the institution, which are furnished while the individual requires continual medical care, shall constitute an expense for medical care. For example, medical care includes the entire cost of institutional care for a person who is mentally ill and unsafe when left alone.
>
> Other questions arise where chronic illness benefits not designed to comply with section 7702B or 101(g) are included as part of a life insurance contract.

Section 101(g) applies only to chronic illness and terminal illness benefits provided under a life insurance contract. The benefit trigger that must be met as a condition for receiving beneficially taxed chronic illness benefits is the same as for QLTCI—the insured must be certified as a chronically ill individual by a **licensed**

---

[16] In this regard, the conference report for HIPAA states that "if the applicable requirements are met by the long-term care portion of the contract, amounts received under the contract as provided by the rider are treated in the same manner as long-term care insurance benefits, whether or not the payment of such amounts causes a reduction in the contract's death benefit or cash surrender value." H.R. REP. No. 104-736, at 298 (1996) (Conf. Rep.) (hereinafter HIPAA Conference Report). The concept of gross income is defined in IRC § 61.

**health care practitioner** (as discussed in detail below). Also, while QLTCI is accorded A&H insurance tax treatment, section 101(g) generally extends life insurance tax treatment to chronic illness ADBs, i.e., the benefits are treated as received by reason of the death of the insured and thus are excludable from gross income to the same extent as other death benefits under section 101(a), subject to the same per diem limitation that applies to QLTCI benefits provided on a non-reimbursement basis, and subject to certain other limitations. One structural difference between QLTCI and section 101(g) chronic illness riders is that section 7702B defines a type of insurance product—a QLTCI contract—whereas section 101(g) merely specifies the tax treatment of benefits payable from a life insurance contract where an insured is chronically ill and certain other requirements are met. As discussed below, however, some requirements for section 101(g) chronic illness riders must be satisfied by the terms of a rider or other provision of a life insurance contract, and thus in a sense section 101(g) defines a type of insurance product, too. At the same time, certain rules under sections 101(a) and (g) operate to limit the exclusion from income for chronic illness ADBs. These limiting rules include:

- the per diem limitation of section 101(g)(3)(D), which is based in part on reimbursements that a taxpayer receives from other sources;
- the rules of section 101(a)(2), which apply where a contract is acquired through a transfer for value; and
- section 101(g)(5), which denies the application of section 101(g) in certain business contexts.

Thus, a taxpayer's overall facts and circumstances must be assessed to determine the extent to which chronic illness ADBs under section 101(g) are excludable from income. As noted, the per diem limitation also applies in the context of QLTCI ADBs.

One can reasonably ask why Congress felt the need to enact two different (and overlapping) regimes for chronic illness ADBs payable from a life insurance contract. The legislative history of HIPAA does not shed much light on this question, although an explanation can be inferred from the larger context associated with the enactment of sections 7702B and 101(g).[17] The principal purpose underlying the enactment of section 7702B was to clarify the tax treatment of long-term care insurance, and the NAIC/state regulatory structure existing at the time of HIPAA's enactment clearly envisioned that this form of insurance could be provided under a life insurance contract, including through an ADB. Indeed, a number of the consumer protection rules adopted as part of the qualification rules for QLTCI are based on provisions of the January 1993 LTC model rules that apply specifically to life insurance riders which provide accelerated death benefits. For example, 1993 LTC Model Regulation section 4A defines long-term care insurance in part as "group and individual annuities and life insurance policies or riders which provide directly or which supplement long-term care insurance" and as "a policy or rider which provides for payment of benefits based upon cognitive impairment or the loss of functional capacity."[18] As another example, 1993 LTC Model Regulation sections 6I and 6J require disclosures to be provided both at the time of contract delivery and when benefits are being paid that describe aspects of a long-term care insurance ADB rider and the manner in which it interacts with the underlying life insurance contract, such as for the reduction in death benefit caused by an ADB.[19] Against this backdrop, it is not surprising that Congress, in enacting section 7702B, included specific rules—principally set forth in section 7702B(e)—which address riders to and provisions of life insurance contracts that provide long-term care insurance coverage. As explained further below, these rules allow long-term care insurance riders to qualify as QLTCI, and thus the beneficial tax clarifications provided by HIPAA for long-term care insurance generally extend to such riders.

---

[17] In commenting on the proposed addition of IRC § 101(g) to the Code and reflecting the legislation's new QLTCI rules, the House report for HIPAA stated: "The Committee believes that a single set of rules should apply to benefits received with respect to a chronically ill individual. To provide parity in treatment, the same definition of a chronically ill individual applies for purposes of the rules under this provision [i.e., section 101(g)] and the rules governing long-term care insurance contracts." H.R. Rep. No. 104-196, pt. 1, at 122 (1996) (hereinafter HIPAA House Report).

[18] A comment to 1993 LTC Model Act § 1 (which describes the purpose of the model act) states: "The Task Force recognizes the viability of a long-term care product funded through a life insurance vehicle, and this Act is not intended to prohibit approval of this product. Section 4 now specifically addresses this product."

[19] As discussed above, however, this definition excludes from the scope of "long-term care insurance" any riders governed by the ABMR. Note that if a rider states that it provides long-term care insurance coverage, the ABMR would not apply.

While section 7702B offered an avenue for clarified tax treatment of chronic illness ADBs, it alone would not have addressed similar ADBs governed by the ABMR and state laws modeled after the ABMR.[20] Given this, and Congress' desire to clarify the tax treatment of viatications and terminal illness ADBs, it also is not surprising that Congress enacted section 101(g) to address these circumstances. Confusion sometimes arises for chronic illness ADBs, however, in determining whether section 7702B or 101(g) applies to a particular product. As noted above, under the NAIC regimes, section 4A of the LTC Model Act (both in the 1993 version and as of the date of this writing in 2015) defines long-term care insurance, and it is clear that a product so treated will be subject to the LTC model rules and not to the ABMR. Congress could have adopted similar, mutually exclusive regimes for the tax treatment of ADBs, but it did not. Rather, both section 7702B and section 101(g) have their own independent requirements, and if a rider happens to satisfy the requirements of both statutes, then they both will apply. The good news is that no harm is occasioned by the applicability of both statutes. The further question is whether such dual qualification matters for tax purposes? The short answer is that it does not, as long as the requirements of *either* section 7702B or 101(g) are satisfied in their entirety. No added tax benefit results from qualification under both provisions because a dollar of income only needs to be excluded from gross income once to be non-taxable and that dollar cannot be excluded twice.

Later in this chapter, after discussing the qualification rules of sections 7702B and 101(g), some observations are offered regarding the advantages of one tax regime versus the other. For now, however, some key considerations regarding the applicability of (and overlap between) sections 7702B and 101(g) follow:

- First, a rider designed to be QLTCI under section 7702B must specifically state that it is intended to be qualified long-term care insurance.[21]

- Second, whether a chronic illness rider is intended to comply with section 101(g) is less easy to identify because of the breadth of rider designs that fall within its ambit. On the face of the statute, it is clear section 101(g) may apply both to riders that reimburse expenses for qualified long-term care (QLTC) services[22] and to riders that provide **per diem benefits**.[23] Also, section 101(g) does not require a rider to state that it is intended to comply with section 101(g), although many such riders do.

- Third, nothing in section 101(g) precludes long-term care insurance riders from receiving beneficial tax treatment under section 101(g). For example, none of the consumer protection requirements imposed by section 101(g)(3)(B) limits the scope of this provision to riders based on the ABMR and similar state laws. As a result, it is permissible for a rider that constitutes long-term care insurance under the LTC model rules and state law to qualify for favorable tax treatment solely under section 101(g).[24]

- Fourth, given the above points, and also the fact that the ABMR seemingly does not apply to riders that reimburse specific expenses,[25] chronic illness riders receiving beneficial tax treatment generally will fall into one of the following categories:

---

[20] ABMR § 2B describes various qualifying events that are permissible triggers for payment of an ADB, including the following trigger which is similar to long-term care insurance triggers: "(3) A condition that usually requires continuous confinement in an eligible institution as defined in the contract if the insured is expected to remain there for the rest of his or her life." IRC § 101(g) riders often require an insured to satisfy this criteria in addition to meeting the tax definition of a chronically ill individual as a condition for the payment of ADBs.

[21] IRC §§ 7702B(b)(1)(F), 7702B(g)(3) and 4980C(d), with the last of these stating: "The requirements of this subsection are met if the issuer of a long-term care insurance policy discloses in such policy and in the outline of coverage ... that the policy is intended to be a qualified long-term care insurance contract under section 7702B(b)."

[22] Qualified long-term care services are defined by IRC § 7702B(c)(1) and are discussed in more detail below.

[23] Contemplating the possibility of benefits that reimburse expenses incurred, IRC § 101(g)(3)(A)(i) provides as a general rule that IRC § 101(g) will apply to chronic illness benefits for a period only if "such payment is for costs incurred by the payee (not compensated for by insurance or otherwise) for qualified long-term care services provided for the insured for such period." Also, contemplating the possibility of per diem benefits, IRC § 101(g)(3)(C) states: "A payment shall not fail to be described in [IRC § 101(g)(3)(A)] by reason of being made on a per diem or other periodic basis without regard to the expenses incurred during the period to which the payment relates."

[24] Of course, if an ADB rider provides long-term care insurance under state law, it would be subject to the state's consumer protection requirements applicable to such insurance. Thus, while the consumer protection requirements of IRC §§ 7702B(g) and 4980C would not apply to such a rider, similar requirements usually would apply under state law. Also, there is little guidance from the IRS regarding ADBs, and the application of the tax requirements to such products is therefore unclear in a number of respects. For example, no guidance speaks to the effect, if any, under IRC § 101(g) of the separate contract rule of IRC § 7702B(e)(1) in the case of a nonqualified long-term care insurance rider providing ADBs. Seemingly, that rule should not limit the application of IRC § 101(g) since the latter provision on its face is directed at coverage of qualified long-term care services.

[25] The inapplicability of the ABMR to reimbursement designs seems implicit from ABMR § 5, which requires that "[c]ontract payment options shall include the option to take the benefit as a lump sum," and "no restrictions are permitted on the use of the proceeds."

- riders intended to meet the requirements of section 101(g) that do not purport to be long-term care insurance and instead are governed by state laws that may be modeled after the ABMR;

- riders intended to meet the requirements of section 101(g) that purport to be long-term care insurance but not QLTCI;[26]

- riders intended to constitute QLTCI under section 7702B and that also, by design or happenstance, meet the requirements of section 101(g); and

- riders intended to constitute QLTCI under section 7702B but which do not meet the requirements of section 101(g).[27]

Riders in the first of these categories usually provide only per diem benefits, and riders in the other three categories could provide either reimbursement or per diem benefits. Again, the beneficial tax treatment of insurance benefits does not depend upon which of the above four categories applies to a rider. Rather, in each case the tax treatment of those benefits is the same. Since for tax purposes it only is necessary for one exclusion provision to apply for benefits to be nontaxable—either the exclusion for A&H under section 104(a)(3) or that for life insurance under section 101—it does not matter which of the above four categories applies to a product; what matters is that the product must satisfy *all* of the requirements of either section 7702B or section 101(g). Where the requirements of one of these statutes are satisfied, ADBs are beneficially taxed, subject to the tax law's limits (such as the per diem limitation in the case of ADBs provided on a non-reimbursement basis).

## *Terminal Illness ADBs*

Section 101(g) provides that, for purposes of section 101, "[a]ny amount received under a life insurance contract on the life of an insured who is a terminally ill individual" shall be treated as "an amount paid by reason of the death of an insured." As a result, such payments generally are excludable from income under section 101(a) in the same manner as life insurance death benefits.[28] For this purpose, the term **terminally ill individual** "means an individual who has been certified by a physician as having an illness or physical condition which can reasonably be expected to result in death in 24 months or less after the date of the certification."[29] By limiting certifications to those made by physicians, the statute is somewhat more restrictive than for chronic illness ADBs, since in the latter case certifications can be performed by any licensed health care practitioner, which includes registered professional nurses and licensed social workers in addition to physicians. As used in section 101(g), the term **physician** "has the meaning given to such term by section 1861(r)(1) of the Social Security Act [SSA] (42 USC 1395x(r)(1))."[30] The definition of "physician" in SSA section 1861(r)(1), in turn, states: "The term 'physician', when used in connection with the performance of any function or action, means (1) a doctor of medicine or osteopathy legally authorized to practice medicine and surgery by the State in which he performs such function or action (including a physician within the meaning of [SSA section 1101(a)(7)]. ..." SSA section 1101(a)(7) states: "The terms 'physician' and 'medical care' and 'hospitalization' include osteopathic practitioners or the services of osteopathic practitioners and hospitals within the scope of their practice as defined by State law." SSA sections 1861(r)(1) and 1101(a)(7) both use the term "State" as part of their definitions, and this term, in turn, also is defined by the SSA. While the IRS has not issued guidance on this definition, it

---

[26] While riders described by this second category can accurately be called nonqualified long-term care insurance, in the sense that they are a form of long-term care insurance and are not QLTCI, they should be distinguished from the nonqualified contracts discussed in the sidebar because the tax treatment of benefits for such riders is clarified by IRC § 101(g).

[27] An example of this fourth category of rider would be a QLTCI rider issued in a business context that does not comply with IRC § 101(g) due to the proscription of IRC § 101(g)(5), discussed further below. If a rider complies with IRC § 7702B and thus constitutes QLTCI, the inapplicability of IRC § 101(g) has no adverse effect on the beneficial tax treatment of the rider under IRC § 7702B.

[28] The exclusion provided under IRC § 101(a)—for both terminal and chronic illness benefits—is subject to the limitations that otherwise apply with respect to the excludability of death benefits from income. For example, if a life insurance contract is purchased by a third party in a life settlement transaction, death benefits generally are excludable only to the extent of the consideration paid by the new owner for the contract, including premiums paid by the new owner after the life settlement transaction. *See* IRC § 101(a)(2), discussed in Appendix 1.1.

[29] IRC § 101(g)(4)(A).

[30] IRC § 101(g)(4)(D).

appears that the term "physician" generally excludes doctors who are not legally authorized to practice in one of the 50 states, the District of Columbia or certain territories.[31]

While terminal illness ADBs generally are excludable from gross income under section 101(a) by reason of section 101(g) in the same manner as life insurance death benefits, this beneficial tax treatment will not apply in the case of certain business-related policies. In particular, section 101(g)(5) states that section 101(g) will not apply "in the case of any amount paid to any taxpayer other than the insured if such taxpayer has an insurable interest with respect to the life of the insured by reason of the insured being a director, officer, or employee of the taxpayer or by reason of the insured being financially interested in any trade or business carried on by the taxpayer." (As noted, this limitation under section 101(g)(5) also applies to limit the applicability of section 101(g) for chronic illness benefits.)

If an insured is certified as terminally ill within the meaning of section 101(g) and no limiting provisions apply (such as section 101(g)(5) or the transfer for value rule of section 101(a)(2)), then section 101(g)(1)(A) provides that "[a]ny amount received under a life insurance contract on the life of an insured who is a terminally ill individual" "shall be treated as an amount paid by reason of the death of an insured." An interesting aspect of section 101(g) is that the statute does not appear to require any particular terms to be included in a contract or rider as a condition to such beneficial tax treatment. Thus, in the case of a life insurance contract that does not include a terminal illness rider, it appears that any payment from the contract will be excludable from income if the insured is certified as terminally ill, including an ADB the amount of which is agreed to by the insurer and the policyholder at the time of payment and even in a case where a policyholder simply exercises a right to partially or fully surrender the contract.[32] In the latter case, there would be no acceleration of the net amount at risk under a contract, and thus such a payment would not be an ADB in the usual sense. Section 101(g), however, is not limited in its application to ADBs.

As noted above, terminal illness is defined based on a life expectancy of 24 months or less, but what happens if the insured survives this period? Does section 101(g) continue to apply to amounts received from the contract? These questions would not, of course, arise if payment of the ADB resulted in the termination of the contract. However, where contracts continue and provide an available cash value or other amount that can be received, the applicability of section 101(g) must be ascertained in order to determine the tax treatment of distributions and the insurer's related tax reporting obligations. No guidance addresses this question, but it would seem reasonable for an insurer to require a new certification of terminal illness if the policyholder requests further ADBs or other predeath distributions from the contract after the 24-month period has elapsed.

## *Critical Illness and Other ADBs*

Neither section 101(g) nor section 7702B applies to ADBs payable upon a morbidity event other than an insured's chronic or terminal illness, as these terms are defined in the tax law. This is the case even though the ABMR contemplates ADBs payable upon other triggering events that evidence a substantially reduced life expectancy, such as an insured's critical illness, e.g., the occurrence of certain life-threatening illnesses such as heart attack, invasive cancer, coma, kidney failure, amyotrophic lateral sclerosis and the need of a major organ transplant. Also, the LTC model rules and similar state law rules govern nonqualified long-term care insurance ADBs that do not satisfy the requirements of either section 101(g) or section 7702B.

The tax treatment of insurance benefits payable from such nonqualifying riders generally would depend on the facts and circumstances of the particular coverage and whether benefits can properly be considered as "amounts received through accident or health insurance ... for personal injuries or sickness" within the meaning of section 104(a)(3). As noted in the sidebar above, the applicability of this rule to nonqualified long-term care insurance is unclear, and there is little authoritative IRS guidance regarding the treatment of critical illness and other types of nonqualifying riders, either. However, the IRS has issued a number of private letter rulings

---

[31] As relevant to the present discussion, SSA § 1101(a) (42 U.S.C. 1301(a)) provides that, "[w]hen used in this Act—(1) The term 'State', except where otherwise provided, includes the District of Columbia and the Commonwealth of Puerto Rico, and when used in titles IV, V, VII, XI, XIX, and XXI includes the Virgin Islands and Guam." SSA § 1861(r)(1) is in title XVIII of the SSA, and thus the term "State" as used in this part of the tax definition of "physician" appears to refer only to the U.S. states, the District of Columbia and Puerto Rico. SSA § 1101(a)(7) is in title XI of the SSA, and thus this part of the tax definition of "physician" appears to refer only to the U.S. states, the District of Columbia, Puerto Rico, the Virgin Islands and Guam.

[32] In the case of contracts covering more than one insured, one question regards the potential applicability of IRC § 101(g) upon the first insured's terminal illness. Seemingly, this should be permissible in the case of a first-to-die contract, and insurers generally will not provide ADBs upon the first insured's terminal illness under second-to-die policies.

in which it concluded that certain critical illness ADBs were excludable from income under section 104(a)(3), except where benefits were attributable to contributions of the taxpayer's employer that were excludable from the taxpayer's gross income.[33]

A further question is whether, or in what circumstances, critical illness and other types of ADB riders would affect the **cash surrender value** of a contract for purposes of section 7702, which defines "life insurance contract" for tax purposes. As discussed in Chapter 3, in proposed regulations issued in 1992, the IRS provided a comprehensive definition of "cash surrender value" for purposes of section 7702 and excluded benefits "payable solely upon the occurrence of a morbidity risk" if certain requirements are satisfied.[34] In Notice 93-37,[35] the IRS indicated that the effective date of the regulations would not be earlier than the date of publication of the final regulations in the *Federal Register*. More recently, the IRS has indicated that it intends to issue guidance regarding the definition of cash surrender value under section 7702.[36] Also, while not representing authority for purposes of section 7702, the IRS and Treasury Department issued helpful guidance with respect to morbidity risk benefits in the context of sections 1471–74 (i.e., the Foreign Account Tax Compliance Act, or FATCA, rules) clarifying that, for purposes of the definition of a "cash value insurance contract," cash value does not include an amount payable as "a personal injury or sickness benefit."[37]

## Qualified Long-Term Care Insurance: Tax Treatment of Premiums and Charges

### Premiums and Charges in General: Limited or No Deduction

As discussed later in this chapter, if a rider or other provision of a life insurance contract satisfies the requirements to be treated as QLTCI, it is treated for federal income tax purposes as a QLTCI contract that is separate from the related life insurance contract.[38] Where such a QLTCI rider is funded by premiums that are paid expressly and exclusively for the QLTCI rider and not through the assessment of charges against the life insurance contract's cash value (directly paid premiums), such premiums should be deductible to the same extent as premiums for a stand-alone QLTCI contract.[39] Subject to certain limitations, such premiums generally are deductible to the same extent as other premiums for insurance coverage of medical care.[40] For individual taxpayers who are not self-employed, this usually means that the taxpayer will be able to deduct those premiums to the extent that the premiums, together with all other medical care costs, exceed 10 percent of the taxpayer's adjusted gross income (or 7.5 percent of such income where the taxpayer or his or her spouse reaches age 65 prior to the end of calendar years 2013–16).[41] This treatment applies where the QLTCI contract covers the taxpayer, his or her spouse, or a dependent (within the meaning of section 152, but determined without regard to subsections (b)(1), (b)(2) and (d)(1)(B) thereof). In the case of a self-employed taxpayer, premiums for a QLTCI contract also are generally deductible, in this instance regardless of whether the taxpayer itemizes deductions.[42]

---

[33] *See* PLRs 200903001 (October 14, 2008), 200627014 (May 6, 2006), 200339016 (June 17, 2003) and 200339015 (June 17, 2003).

[34] 57 FED. REG. 59,319 (Dec. 15, 1992). Prop. Reg. 1.7702-2(f) specifies the following additional requirements: "(i) The benefit is payable solely upon the occurrence of a morbidity risk; (ii) The charges for the benefit are separately stated and currently imposed by the terms of the contract, and (iii) The charges for the benefit [must not be] included in premiums taken into account in the determination of the investment in the contract under section 72(c)(1) or 72(e)(6) and are not taken into account in the determination of premiums paid under section 7702(f)(1)." While the proposed regulations are not currently effective, it is noteworthy that the second and third requirements appear to be intended to ensure transparency and proper accounting between the life insurance contract and the ADB rider. Seemingly, these rules (and any subsequent guidance) should not be interpreted or applied to prohibit use of any of the financing options for funding ADBs described in ABMR § 10A as long as such financing mechanisms are applied in an actuarially appropriate manner.

[35] 1993-2 C.B. 331.

[36] *See, e.g.*, the Department of the Treasury's 2014–2015 PRIORITY GUIDANCE PLAN (April 28, 2015) which identifies the following as a subject for which guidance is intended: "Regulations under §7702 defining cash surrender value."

[37] Treas. Reg. § 1.1471-5(b)(3)(vii)(C)(2).

[38] IRC § 7702B(e)(1).

[39] In contrast, premiums for life insurance coverage generally are not tax deductible. IRC § 264(a)(1). It therefore is necessary that the premiums for the QLTCI rider be actuarially appropriate to be deductible. Other issues are presented where a QLTCI rider premium is paid through a waiver of premium benefit.

[40] IRC § 213(d)(1)(D).

[41] IRC § 213(a) and (f).

[42] IRC § 162(l). Other limitations apply under this provision. For example, IRC § 162(l)(2)(A) allows the deduction only to the extent of the taxpayer's earned income from the trade or business with respect to which the plan providing the medical care coverage is established and only if neither the taxpayer nor his or her spouse has access to employer-subsidized QLTCI coverage. Also, the deduction is not allowed for purposes of determining an individual's net earnings from self-employment, within the meaning of IRC § 1402(a), upon which the self-employment income tax of IRC § 1401 is assessed. IRC § 162(l)(4). A coordination rule precludes deducting a premium under both IRC § 213 and IRC § 162(l). IRC § 162(l)(3). This chapter does not otherwise discuss the provision of chronic illness ADBs in an employment context. Note, however, that the IRC § 106 exclusion from income for employer-provided coverage under an A&H plan may extend to directly paid QLTCI rider premiums in some circumstances, but that it would be necessary to consider the rules and restrictions which apply in that context, *e.g.*, on use of cafeteria plans and flexible spending arrangements to provide long-term care insurance benefits.

In each of these cases, however, QLTCI premiums are deductible only to the extent of **eligible long-term care premiums**, which vary by age and as indexed for inflation.[43] For 2015, the indexed eligible long-term care premiums are as follows in Table 7.1:[44]

| Table 7.1. Indexed eligible long-term care premiums | |
|---|---|
| Attained age before the close of the taxable year | Limitation on premiums |
| 40 or less | $380 |
| More than 40 but not more than 50 | $710 |
| More than 50 but not more than 60 | $1,430 |
| More than 60 but not more than 70 | $3,800 |
| More than 70 | $4,750 |

The ages identified in this table relate to the age of the insured prior to the close of the taxable year. As discussed later in this chapter, it should be permissible for a QLTCI contract to cover two joint insureds, such as spouses. It is unclear how this age-based limitation on the deduction of premiums should apply in such instances. In this regard, if an insurer separately identifies the portion of overall premiums that relates to each insured (allocated in an actuarially appropriate manner), such allocation seemingly should be respected for purposes of applying the limitation.

In contrast with the foregoing, in the case of QLTCI riders funded through charges assessed against the related life insurance contract's cash value, section 7702B(e)(2) denies a deduction for such charges.[45] Further, due to the treatment of QLTCI riders as separate contracts, such charges against the cash value are deemed to be distributions from the life insurance contract that are then used to fund the QLTCI rider. Distributions from life insurance contracts may be taxable; however, in this circumstance section 72(e)(11) provides relief from taxation. In particular, this provision states that such charges will reduce the **investment in the contract** of the life insurance contract (but not below zero) and such charges will not be includible in gross income. Section 72(e)(11) is discussed further below.

## *Health Savings Accounts*

Section 223 generally allows a deduction for certain amounts contributed to a health savings account (HSA) by individuals covered only by a high deductible health plan and if various other requirements are satisfied. For purposes of ascertaining whether an individual is covered by a high deductible health plan, coverage under a QLTCI contract is disregarded.[46] Also, any amount paid or distributed out of a HSA used exclusively to pay qualified medical expenses of any account beneficiary is not includible in gross income.[47] The term **qualified medical expenses** generally does not include any amounts paid for insurance,[48] but qualified medical expenses may include premiums paid for a QLTCI contract to the extent such premiums are paid by the account beneficiary for medical care within the meaning of section 213(d).[49]

In the case of a directly paid premium for a QLTCI rider, seemingly it should be permissible to use an HSA to fund the rider, since the rider is treated as a separate contract for federal tax purposes. It does not appear, however, that an HSA could be used for QLTCI riders funded through charges assessed against life insurance cash values. This is because the HSA monies generally first would need to be paid into the life insurance contract's cash value, and such a use of the HSA would not be for a qualified medical expense under section 223(d)(2), with the result that distributions from the HSA for this purpose would be taxable and subject to a penalty tax.[50]

---

[43] IRC § 213(d)(1) and (10) and IRC § 162(l)(2)(C). Indexing for inflation is based on the medical care component of the consumer price index. *See* IRC § 213(d)(10)(B).

[44] Rev. Proc. 2014-61, 2014-47 I.R.B. 860, 866.

[45] A similar deduction disallowance applies for QLTCI rider charges assessed against the cash value of a nonqualified annuity contract.

[46] IRC § 223(c)(1)(B)(ii).

[47] IRC § 223(f)(1).

[48] IRC § 223(d)(2)(B).

[49] IRC § 223(d)(2)(C)(ii).

[50] IRC § 223(f)(2) and (4). The penalty tax equals 20 percent of the amount includible in income. Exceptions to the penalty tax apply with respect to distributions after the death or disability of the account beneficiary or that are made after the age for which Medicare eligibility is attained (as specified in SSA § 1811).

## Charges for QLTCI Riders: Special Rule of Section 72(e)(11)

Section 72(e)(11), as amended by the Pension Protection Act of 2006 (PPA), states that "in the case of any charge against the cash value of an annuity contract or the cash surrender value of a life insurance contract made as payment for coverage under a [QLTCI] contract which is part of or a rider on such annuity or life insurance contract—(A) the investment in the contract shall be reduced (but not below zero) by such charge, and (B) such charge shall not be includible in gross income."[51] The premise of this provision is that charges assessed against the cash value of a life insurance contract to fund a QLTCI rider (e.g., monthly rider charges) generally are treated as distributions from the life insurance contract, which are then treated as having been paid for the QLTCI rider. This follows, in turn, from the treatment of QLTCI riders as separate contracts for federal tax purposes.[52]

Normally, deemed distributions would be subject to tax under section 72 in the same manner as other distributions from life insurance contracts. However, Congress concluded that an exclusion from income for charges which fund QLTCI was appropriate, likely in recognition of the fact that no actual cash distribution is associated with such charges and also to help facilitate more widespread long-term care insurance coverage.[53] Further, the reduction of investment in the contract by such charges (but not below zero) reflects Congress' decision to treat the deemed distributions as having been paid from the investment in the contract of the life insurance contract, to the extent any exists, before any gain is considered distributed for this purpose. And if any gain is distributed due to such charges, those amounts are similarly excluded from income.

## Qualified Long-Term Care Insurance: Tax Treatment of Benefits

### In General: A&H Tax Treatment of Benefits Under Section 7702B

Normally, income a taxpayer derives from any source is subject to federal income tax unless the Code provides an express exclusion from income for that amount or the Code allows a deduction which can offset the income.[54] One such exclusion, however, is provided by section 104(a)(3), which states: "Except in the case of amounts attributable to (and not in excess of) deductions allowed under section 213 (relating to medical, etc., expenses) for any prior taxable year, gross income does not include ... (3) amounts received through accident or health insurance ... for personal injuries or sickness. ..." Prior to the enactment of HIPAA, there was uncertainty in the law about whether long-term care insurance benefits satisfied the criteria of this provision. While accident and health insurance generally has a broad scope[55] and long-term care insurance policies clearly provide coverage of many medical and health-related costs, it was less clear whether insurance benefits from such policies were provided on account of "personal injuries or sickness," since benefits in part were for room and board costs and covered infirmities often related to advancing age rather than to a specific injury or sickness.[56]

---

[51] PPA, Pub. L. No. 109-280, § 844(a).
[52] IRC § 7702B(e)(1). In the context of life insurance contracts, long-term care insurance riders arguably already were recognized as separate contracts for tax purposes (i.e., as additional benefits that are not qualified additional benefits, or QABs) prior to HIPAA's enactment of IRC § 7702B. See, e.g., PLR 9106050 (Nov. 14, 1990). The premise that charges are distributions is reflected not only by the **separate contract rule** but also implicitly by the pre-PPA rules under IRC § 7702B(e)(2), which provided for an increase in the guideline premium limitation under IRC § 7702 generally to the extent charges did not otherwise reduce premiums paid (e.g., charges that gave rise to income under the rules for distributions from modified endowment contracts, or MECs), and under IRC § 7702B(e)(3), which denied a deduction for QLTCI charges except to the extent they were includible in income. The PPA repealed these rules for taxable years after 2009. The enactment of IRC § 72(e)(11) made the pre-PPA IRC § 7702B(e)(2) rule unnecessary since, due to the exclusion provided by IRC § 72(e)(11), charges reduce "premiums paid" under section 7702(f)(1) and eliminate the need for an upward adjustment to the guideline premium limitation. It should be noted that IRC § 72(e)(11) also applies to charges for a QLTCI rider under a nonqualified annuity contract.
[53] An economically similar tax-free result seemingly could be obtained through partial exchanges of a life insurance contract to fund QLTCI, including stand-alone QLTCI. No income would be recognized upon such partial exchanges due to IRC § 1035. However, some differences usually would exist between use of a charge structure and partial exchanges, e.g., the effect of the transactions on the life insurance contract's remaining benefits and tax basis.
[54] IRC § 61.
[55] Accident and health insurance generally is broader in scope than insurance coverage of medical care. Thus, in some instances, premiums may not be deductible under the medical care standard of IRC § 213(d) whereas benefits from the contract may be excludable under IRC § 104(a)(3).
[56] Indeed, in connection with the tax treatment of nonqualified long-term care insurance after HIPAA's enactment, a government official once informally commented: "The vicissitudes of old age is not a sickness." At the same time, it was clear under pre-HIPAA law that if the principal reason for an individual's stay in an institution was due to a need for medical care, the entirety of the costs for institutionalization, including normally nondeductible personal care costs such as room and board, would be treated as amounts incurred for medical care, and presumably insurance coverage of such costs similarly should be considered A&H insurance benefits for purposes of IRC § 104(a)(3). Treas. Reg. § 1.213-1(e)(1)(v) (quoted in the sidebar above). Seemingly, the standard of this regulation is inapplicable if expenditures are for QLTC services required by a chronically ill individual, since IRC §§ 213(d)(1)(C) and 7702B(a) specify the treatment of such expenditures. However, the regulation appears to remain applicable in other circumstances. See, e.g., IRS General Information Letter 2009-0010 (Dec. 18, 2008), which states that "medical care expenses include amounts paid for the treatment or mitigation of a mental illness and amounts paid for [QLTC] services ..." and then discusses the meaning of QLTC services and also the requirements of this regulation for purposes of evaluating whether meals provided with long-term care services were deductible as medical care expenses.

HIPAA, however, clarified that long-term care insurance which constitutes QLTCI is accorded accident or health insurance tax treatment.

In this regard, section 7702B(a), as enacted by HIPAA, states: "(1) a [QLTCI] contract shall be treated as an accident and health insurance contract, [and] (2) amounts (other than policyholder dividends, as defined in section 808, or premium refunds) received under a [QLTCI] contract shall be treated as amounts received for personal injuries and sickness and shall be treated as reimbursement for expenses actually incurred for medical care (as defined in section 213(d))." In effect, this provision creates a safe harbor for QLTCI insurance, confirming that insurance benefits received from the contract generally will be excludable from income in the same manner as other health insurance benefits, subject only to a special rule for per diem benefits which will be discussed later in this chapter. (HIPAA similarly prescribed A&H insurance tax treatment of QLTCI in the employment context,[57] although as discussed earlier in this chapter various limitations and restrictions apply to QLTCI riders to life insurance contracts. Such riders cannot be issued at all in connection with employer-purchased annuities and qualified retirement arrangements.[58])

ADBs paid from a QLTCI rider by reason of the insured's chronic illness generally are treated for tax purposes in the same manner as insurance benefits received under stand-alone QLTCI contracts. This treatment derives in part from the treatment under section 7702B(e)(1) of the QLTCI rider as a separate contract for federal tax purposes, which is discussed later in this chapter. Thus, chronic illness benefits from a QLTCI rider are treated as having been received "for personal injuries and sickness" from an "accident and health insurance contract" for purposes of the Code, and accordingly such benefits generally are excludable from income under section 104(a)(3), subject to the per diem limitation discussed below. The treatment of such ADB benefits as excludable from income applies regardless of the effect such benefit payments have on the related life insurance contract. In this respect, the legislative history of the PPA states:

> [I]f the applicable requirements are met by the long-term care portion of the contract, amounts received under the contract as provided by the rider are treated in the same manner as long-term care insurance benefits, whether or not the payment of such amounts causes a reduction in the life insurance contract's death benefit or cash surrender value or in the annuity contract's cash value.[59]

As evidenced by this legislative history, Congress was aware that life insurance-QLTCI combination products provided benefits partially funded through reductions in life insurance cash values and partially from net amounts at risk (NAR), including the same dollars of NAR provided with respect to the life insurance death benefit. From an economic perspective, excluding the entire QLTCI ADB from taxable income is similar to the tax treatment accorded to life insurance death benefits under contracts that provide a cash value. In particular, immediately prior to the insurable event that dictates entitlement to the benefit under a life insurance contract, i.e., the insured's death, the contract may have provided a cash value that would have been taxable if received before death as well as insurance coverage equal to the NAR. When the insurable event transpires, however, the life insurance benefit is respected in accordance with its form, so that it is excludable from income in its entirety as a death benefit (including the portion of such benefit paid from the predeath cash value) to the extent provided in section 101. Likewise, the above legislative history recognizes that a chronic illness ADB from a QLTCI rider should be respected in accordance with its form, as a chronic illness benefit in its entirety (including the

---

[57] In general, premiums for an A&H insurance contract paid by an employer are excludable from the employee's income under IRC § 106 (as discussed above), and insurance benefits received from the contract are excludable from income to the extent they reimburse expenses incurred by the employee for medical care. *See* IRC § 105(a) and (b).

[58] IRC § 7702B(e)(4).

[59] PPA 2006 Blue Book, *supra* Chapter 5, note 46. The PPA 2006 Blue Book is the only available legislative history on the PPA amendments to IRC § 7702B(e), and Congress intended it to serve as such. In that regard, in a floor debate relating to the PPA, Ways and Means Committee Chairman Thomas stated, "A detailed, plain-English explanation [of the PPA] is available from the Joint Committee on Taxation and will be a key resource in understanding the intent underlying the bill's provisions and, therefore, obviously of the legislative intent behind the bill." 152 CONG. REC. H6,158 (daily ed. July 28, 2006) (statement of House Ways and Means Committee Chairman Thomas). *See also* 152 CONG. REC. S8,763 (daily ed. Aug. 3, 2006) (statement of Finance Committee Chairman Grassley) (also indicating that the PPA 2006 Blue Book is reflective of legislative intent). A statement similar to that in the PPA 2006 Blue Book regarding the effect of long-term care insurance benefits provided through life insurance contracts was included in the legislative history of IRC § 7702B(e) as originally enacted in 1996. *See* HIPAA Conference Report, *supra* note 15, at 298–99; HIPAA House Report at 118 (1996). The IRS has reached the same conclusion in private letter rulings. *See* PLR 201213016 (Dec. 20, 2011) and PLR 200919011 (Feb. 2, 2009) (concluding that benefits paid pursuant to a QLTCI rider to an annuity contract were excludable from gross income in their entirety even though the payment of the benefits caused reductions to the annuity contract's cash value and other benefits).

portion of such benefit paid from the preinsurable event cash value) that will be excludable from income to the extent provided in section 104(a)(3).[60]

## Per Diem Benefits
### In General
Where a QLTCI contract reimburses expenses incurred for QLTC services, the insurance benefits received on account of the insured's chronic illness will be excludable from income under section 104(a)(3), as described above. However, if chronic illness insurance benefits under a QLTCI contract (and under section 101(g) riders) are provided on a periodic, lump-sum or other non-reimbursement basis (referred to in the statute as "periodic payments" and herein as **per diem benefits**),[61] such benefits are excludable from income only to the extent of the per diem limitation of section 7702B(d). More particularly, under section 7702B(d)(1):

> If the aggregate of—
>
> A) the periodic payments received for any period under all [QLTCI] contracts which are treated as made for [QLTC] services for an insured, and
>
> B) the periodic payments received for such period which are treated under section 101(g) as paid by reason of the death of such insured,
>
> exceeds the per diem limitation for such period, such excess shall be includible in gross income without regard to section 72.[62]

Section 7702B(d)(2) then defines the per diem limitation as follows:

> ... the per diem limitation for any period is an amount equal to the excess (if any) of—
>
> A) the greater of—
>
>   i) the dollar amount in effect for such period under [section 7702B(d)(4)], or
>
>   ii) the costs incurred for qualified long-term care services provided for the insured for such period,
>
>   over
>
> B) the aggregate payments received as reimbursements (through insurance or otherwise) for qualified long-term care services provided for the insured during such period.[63]

The dollar amount described in section 7702B(d)(4) is $175 per day, as adjusted for inflation since 1996 based on the medical care component of the consumer price index, or the equivalent amount in the case of payments on another periodic basis. This amount is announced annually by the IRS in a revenue procedure that lists a number of inflation-adjusted tax-related dollar amounts. For 2015, the inflation-adjusted dollar amount is $330 per day, or $120,450 in the case of payments made on an annual basis.[64] Also, policyholder(s) must apply an aggregation rule for purposes of the per diem limitation. In particular, section 7702B(d)(3) provides that all persons receiving periodic payments with respect to the same insured are treated as one person, and the per diem limitation is then allocated first to the insured and any remaining limitation is allocated among the other such persons in the manner prescribed by the Secretary of the Treasury.

---

[60] See the discussion below regarding the "separate contract" rule of IRC § 7702B(e). The legislative history for this rule clarifies that the form in which long-term care ADBs are cast, *i.e.*, as long-term care insurance benefits, controls their characterization for purposes of IRC § 104(a)(3), regardless of the effect of a benefit payment on the life insurance contract's death benefit and cash value. A practical limitation, however, derives from the requirement of IRC § 7702B(b)(1) (discussed below) that QLTCI constitute an "insurance contract" for tax purposes, meaning that there will need to be an expectation of meaningful provision for NAR as part of overall long-term care insurance benefits. Where ADBs proportionally reduce a life insurance contract's death benefit and cash values, this requirement should readily be met.

[61] IRC § 7702B(d)(6) defines "periodic payment" as "any payment (whether on a periodic basis or otherwise) made without regard to the extent of the costs incurred by the payee for qualified long-term care services."

[62] Under IRC § 7702B(d)(1), a payment is not counted against the per diem limitation if it is excludable from income under IRC § 101(g) by reason of the insured's terminal illness.

[63] In the case of contracts providing per diem benefits that were issued before July 31, 1996, a special rule is provided by HIPAA § 321(f)(5) under which the per diem limitation is not reduced by reimbursements of QLTC services from another contract issued before that date, as long as the contracts have not been exchanged and their benefits have not been increased.

[64] Rev. Proc. 2014-61, *supra* note 44.

In many cases, chronic illness ADBs received from QLTCI or section 101(g) riders will be equal to or less than the per diem limitation and thus generally will be excludable from gross income. This is because ADB riders often limit the amount of chronic illness benefits to the inflation-indexed dollar amount, insureds usually receive chronic illness benefits from only one contract or rider, and the per diem limitation usually is not reduced by other reimbursements.[65] However, an ADB rider may provide benefits that exceed the per diem limitation or an insured may receive benefits under other QLTCI contracts or section 101(g) riders, in which case such benefits would be taxable to the extent of such excess. Because of this and the other adjustments involved in calculating the per diem limitation, the insurance company usually will not be in a position to determine definitively the portion of benefits that are taxable, even if it sets the maximum benefits payable under a rider at or below the inflation-indexed component of the per diem limitation. Rather, only the policyholder and insured will have access to the information needed to make this determination. Benefits that count against the per diem limitation would include periodic or lump-sum chronic illness benefits used to satisfy a life insurance policy loan. Such benefits would be reportable on Form 1099-LTC together with other chronic illness benefits, even though they are not paid to the policyholder in cash. Having access to higher benefits (even if partially taxable) may be attractive to policyholders, especially since receiving benefits in excess of the per diem limitation does not adversely affect the excludability of benefits received up to the limitation. Also, having higher benefits may be needed due to the high costs that can arise in connection with an insured's chronic illness, e.g., upfront costs such as the installation of ramps in a home and other safety devices needed due to the insured's chronic illness and costs of relocating so there is greater availability of assistance from family members.

The discussion below explores additional aspects of the manner in which the per diem limitation may apply to chronic illness benefits provided on a non-reimbursement basis.

**"Period" for Which Benefits are Payable**

A key aspect of the per diem limitation relates to the "period" for which benefits are payable. As noted above, section 7702B(d)(1) generally provides that "periodic payments received for any *period*" in excess of the per diem limitation are taxable (emphasis added). Similarly, section 7702B(d)(2) defines the per diem limitation by reference to such period.[66] Through this mechanism, the per diem limitation applies based on the period for which the insurable event, i.e., the insured's chronic illness, occurs and the related contract conditions have been satisfied. Thus, while there is no official guidance on the point, it should follow that if payments are made by reason of an insured's chronic illness during a particular month, e.g., December 2014, that benefit generally would be subject to the per diem limitation that applies for that month, regardless of the actual date of payment of the chronic illness benefit. In contrast, tax reporting of chronic illness benefits by insurers on IRS Form 1099-LTC, and the reporting of those benefits by the recipient on IRS Form 8853 (an attachment to IRS Form 1040), generally is based on the date when benefits are paid, which seemingly is appropriate in recognition of the fact that individuals are cash-basis, calendar-year taxpayers.

Like other insurance, benefits are payable from QLTCI and section 101(g) chronic illness riders only upon an insurable event (again, the insured's chronic illness).[67] As discussed further below, an insured is considered to be a chronically ill individual as of the effective date of his or her written certification as such by a licensed health care practitioner.[68] Further, the chronically ill individual definition provides in part that: "Such term shall not include any individual otherwise meeting the requirements of the preceding sentence unless within the preceding 12-month period a licensed health care practitioner has certified that such individual meets such requirements." These rules implicitly define the beginning of the first period in respect of which benefits are paid, i.e., the effective date of the certification, and place an outer limit of 12 months on the period in respect of which the per diem limitation is calculated. Thus, if a single lump sum is payable as a result of an insured's

---

[65] It also is rare for other exceptions to beneficial tax treatment to apply, such as where the exclusion from income for chronic illness ADBs described in IRC § 101(g) is limited by IRC § 101(a)(2), which applies where a life insurance contract has been transferred for value.

[66] *See also* the instructions to IRS Form 8853, which refer to an "LTC period."

[67] Some contracts or riders provide insurance benefits due to the insured's chronic illness, but provide for payment periods that may be based on the date of approval of a claim instead of the effective date of the certification of the insured's chronic illness. These provisions typically serve an administrative function only, such as to reflect the time needed to process a claim, and thus application of the per diem limitation should be based on the period(s) for which the insurable event, *i.e.*, the insured's chronic illness, occurs and the related contract conditions have been satisfied, rather than being based on the administrative payment period(s).

[68] "Chronically ill individual" is defined in IRC § 7702B(c)(2), and "licensed health care practitioner" is defined in IRC § 7702B(c)(4).

certification as a chronically ill individual, the period seemingly should be the entire year, i.e., 365 days (366 for leap years) beginning with such effective date, since the insured is considered to be chronically ill for that period of time due to such certification. Similarly, if monthly benefits are payable, monthly periods (and correspondingly monthly per diem limitations) generally would apply, initially for the month beginning on the effective date of the certification and then subsequently for each succeeding month through the anniversary of the certification.[69] Again, however, there is no official guidance directly on point.

Since section 7702B(d)(4) describes the dollar amount of the per diem limitation (before indexing for inflation) as "$175 per day (or the equivalent amount in the case of payments on another periodic basis)," it appears that the per diem limitation applicable to per diem benefits received within a period, e.g., annual or monthly, should equal the product of the number of days within the period and the daily inflation-indexed amount ($330 for 2015), e.g., as noted above, $120,450 in the case of annual lump-sum benefits, and $10,230 in the case of monthly benefits for months with 31 days. Also, the reference to equivalent amounts in the case of payments on different period bases implies that the per diem limitation separately applies to each such period, so that the adjustments for higher QLTC service costs and reimbursements (as described in section 7702B(d)(2)(A)(ii) and (B)) would need to be made for each such period. In other words, the statute appears to require use of separate per diem limitations for each period associated with the mode of payment, and each such limitation then should be used to measure the extent to which benefits payable in respect of a period are excludable from income.[70] This notion generally accords with IRS Form 8853 and its instructions. In particular, the instructions state: "If you have more than one LTC period, you must separately calculate the taxable amount of the payments received during each LTC period."[71] Also, the instructions permit the LTC period to be defined in one of the following two ways:

- **Contract period method:** Under this method, the LTC period is the same period as that used by the insurance company under the contract to compute benefits. For example, if the insurance company computes benefits on a daily basis, the LTC period is one day. Similarly, if an ADB rider provides an annual benefit due to the insured's certification as a chronically ill individual, the LTC period should be for one year under this method. The instructions state: "If you choose this method for defining the LTC period(s) and different LTC insurance contracts for the same insured use different contract periods, then all such LTC contracts must be treated as computing benefits on a daily basis."[72]

- **Equal payment rate method:** Under this method, the LTC period is the period during which the insurer uses the same payment rate to compute benefits. The instructions provide the following example: "[The taxpayer has] two LTC periods if the insurance contract computes payments at a rate of $175 per day from March 1, 2013, through May 31, 2013, and then at a rate of $195 per day from June 1, 2013, through December 31, 2013. The first LTC period is 92 days (from March 1 through May 31) and the second LTC period is 214 days (from June 1 through December 31)." The instructions clarify that this method can be used even if the taxpayer has more than one QLTCI contract covering the same period. In this regard, the instructions provide the following example: "[The taxpayer has] one insurance contract that pays $100 per day from March 1, 2013, through December 31, 2013, and … a second insurance contract that pays $1,500 per month from March 1, 2013, through December 31, 2013. [The taxpayer has] one LTC period because each payment rate does not vary during the LTC period of March 1 through December 31. However, [the taxpayer has] two LTC periods if the facts are the same except that the second insurance contract did not begin making payments until May 1, 2013. …" It may be advantageous to use this method for determining the LTC period if costs for QLTC services are being reimbursed by other coverage or sources.

---

[69] As discussed below, in some instances, the instructions to Form 8853 may dictate use of a daily period even though a contract provides for monthly payments or some other mode of payment.

[70] Where a rider provides for monthly benefits, in some instances those benefits are capped at an amount equal to the per diem limitation that would apply for a 30-day month. In this circumstance, a question might be raised about whether the per diem limitation has been properly determined for the month of February. No guidance addresses this question; however, such riders generally pay benefits for each month in a year equal to the product of 30 and the daily per diem limitation (so that the annual benefit is 360 times the daily amount), and thus there seems little tax policy reason for treating the day or two of benefits for February in excess of the number of calendar days in such month as taxable.

[71] 2013 instructions to IRS Form 8853.

[72] Id.

According to these instructions, if multiple policyholders receive per diem benefits due to the insured's chronic illness during the same taxable year, a statement must be attached to the Form 8853 that shows the aggregate computation of the per diem limitation taking all per diem benefits and reimbursements into account. Each policyholder must use the same LTC period, and if they disagree the contract period method must be used. The per diem limitation is allocated first to the insured or to the insured and his or her spouse if a joint return is filed, and any remaining limitation is allocated among the other policyholders pro rata based on the payments they received.[73]

**Adjustments Made in Determining the Per Diem Limitation**
As stated above, the per diem limitation for any period equals the excess (if any) of (A) the greater of an inflation-indexed dollar amount (for 2015, $330/day or the equivalent amount in the case of payments on another basis) or the costs incurred for QLTC services, over (B) the aggregate payments received as reimbursements (through insurance or otherwise) for QLTC services provided for the insured during such period. This formula can be thought of as a tentative per diem limitation based on the inflation-indexed amount that must be adjusted upward by higher costs for QLTC services and downward by reimbursements of such costs. ADB riders that provide benefits solely on a per diem (i.e., non-reimbursement) basis generally do not require evidence of the particular expenses the insured has incurred due to his or her chronic illness.[74] Thus, insurers generally will not know whether a higher per diem limitation applies with respect to an insured based on costs incurred for QLTC services in excess of the inflation-indexed dollar amount. Of course, policyholders should take higher costs for QLTC services into account on their tax returns as appropriate to ensure that they receive the full benefit of the available exclusion from income for their chronic illness benefits. The meaning of QLTC services will be discussed later in this chapter.

As just indicated, it also is necessary to reduce the tentative per diem limitation by reimbursements (through insurance or otherwise) of costs for QLTC services provided for the insured during the applicable period. While this requirement on its face seems relatively straight-forward, in many situations it is difficult for a policyholder to apply. For example, because the tentative per diem limitation is reduced by "reimbursements ... for [QLTC] services provided for the insured during such period," it appears necessary to make the adjustment based on when QLTC services were provided rather than when the reimbursements for such services are received. More troubling is the scope of reimbursements encompassed by the rule. The statute states that such reimbursements may be through insurance or otherwise. Reimbursements through insurance typically will be through another QLTCI contract/rider or section 101(g) rider (for which benefits are reported on Form 1099-LTC), but that will not always be the case. While Medicare generally does not cover long-term care insurance costs, it could cover some costs after an insured has become chronically ill, and this raises the question of how policyholders should account for any such reimbursements, especially since it may be difficult to identify which reimbursements pertain to QLTC services.[75] "Reimbursements" as this term is used in the statute seemingly should not encompass benefits that do not actually reimburse specific expenses, e.g., disability benefits. There also is the practical consideration that the per diem limitation, as adjusted for higher actual costs for QLTC services and reimbursements of such costs, may be unknown at the time a chronic illness per diem benefit is paid, especially in the context of riders that provide a lump-sum benefit.

**Benefit Periods That Straddle Two Taxable Years**
Since the per diem limitation is based on the period for which benefits are payable due to the insured's chronic illness, one question regards the manner in which the limitation should be applied in circumstances where the

---

[73] *Id.*

[74] In some instances, insurers may want verification that at least some QLTC services are being incurred, such as in connection with verifying that the insured is receiving care in the type of facility that meets the requirements of the rider or as a further measure taken to ensure that the insured suffers from the ADL or cognitive impairment as contemplated by the rider.

[75] Medicare usually will only help pay for a short stay in a skilled nursing facility, for hospice care or for home health care if an individual recently had a hospital stay of at least three days and then is admitted to a Medicare-certified nursing facility within 30 days and meets certain other conditions. In these cases, Medicare will pay for some costs for up to 100 days. U.S. DEPARTMENT OF HEALTH AND HUMAN SERVICES, *Long-term Care Services — Skilled Nursing*, accessed Apr. 29, 2015 (available at http://longtermcare.gov/medicare-medicaid-more/medicare/). *See also* Howard Gleckman, *Medicare Settlement Does Not Expand Long-Term Care Benefits*, FORBES (Oct. 31, 2012) http://www.forbes.com/sites/howardgleckman/2012/10/31/medicare-settlement-does-not-expand-long-term-care-benefits/. While Medicaid covers long-term care insurance costs, an insured generally must have exhausted his or her assets as a condition to receipt of Medicaid benefits.

12-month period of chronic illness crosses the taxable year. For example, a rider may provide a lump-sum ADB for the full 12 months of an insured's chronic illness (as contemplated by section 5A of the ABMR) and the effective date of the certification of chronic illness by a licensed health care practitioner might be October 1, 2014. In such a case, the lump-sum ADB is provided for the 12-month period of chronic illness from October 1, 2014, through September 30, 2015, and if the amount of the payment is equal to or less than the per diem limitation for that period, it seems the full amount of the benefit should be excludable from income. This result is supported by the fact that the statute defines the per diem limitation based on the period for which benefits are paid (which in no event can exceed 12 months), and Congress would have been aware, of course, that an insured might become chronically ill at any time during a calendar year. Also, there is no indication in the statute or the legislative history of any proscription on providing benefits for a period that extends into the following calendar year. Even in the case of monthly benefits, certifications of chronic illness often will not be effective as of the first of a month, and thus the monthly per diem benefit payable for a benefit month that includes days in December and January raise the same question, albeit to a lesser degree.

The law regarding benefits that apply for a period which crosses taxable years is unclear in a number of respects. As a general matter, a taxpayer must ascertain whether, or the extent to which, amounts received within a taxable year are taxable.[76] Thus, if the policyholder in the above example received $140,000 in October 2014 as a lump-sum benefit for the 12-month period of chronic illness from October 1, 2014, to September 30, 2015, it seemingly is necessary to report the taxable portion of that benefit entirely in the year received, i.e., 2014,[77] but this raises the question of how the per diem limitation in respect of the portion of the 12-month period during 2015 should be calculated, since the inflation-indexed daily per diem amount for 2015 may not be known at the time of the benefit payment.[78] Also, the extent of higher actual costs for QLTC services and reimbursements for such period certainly will be unknown at year-end 2014.

The first of these considerations—i.e., next year's daily per diem amount—will be known by the time the 2014 tax return needs to be filed, and thus it should be reasonable to take this amount into account for the period of January 1, 2015, to September 30, 2015, for purposes of ascertaining the tax treatment of the annual per diem benefit received in 2014.[79] In the example above, since the $140,000 lump-sum benefit was provided due to the insured's chronic illness for the 12-month period beginning on October 1, 2014, it seems based on existing guidance that the tentative per diem limitation could appropriately be calculated (before reflecting any higher costs for QLTC services and reimbursements of costs for QLTC services) as the sum of the following two amounts:

- for the portion of such period in 2014, the product of the daily indexed per diem amount for 2014, $330, and 92 days, or $30,360, and

- for the portion of such period in 2015, the product of the daily indexed per diem amount for 2015, also $330, and 273 days, or $90,090.

This gives a total tentative per diem limitation of $120,450. Thus, before adjustments to the per diem limitation are taken into account, it appears on this basis that $120,450 of the $140,000 lump-sum benefit would be excludable from income, and the remaining $19,550 of such benefit would be taxable.

The proper manner for addressing the second of the above considerations—i.e., accounting for higher actual costs for QLTC services and reimbursements (through insurance or otherwise) of costs for QLTC services—also is unclear under the law. Where a per diem benefit is provided for a period that crosses calendar

---

[76] The annual accounting principle of federal tax law generally requires examination of a transaction or transactions on an annual basis "using the facts as they exist at the end of the year. That is, each taxable year is a separate unit for tax accounting purposes." Rev. Rul. 80-58, 1980-1 C.B. 1818, citing *Security Flour Mills Co. v. Comm'r*, 321 U.S. 281 (1944). *See also Burnet v. Sanford & Brooks Co.*, 282 U.S. 359 (1931).

[77] The cash basis method of accounting that governs individual taxpayers appears to compel this result, although no guidance directly addresses this question (apart from IRS Form 8853, which does not discuss benefit periods that cross taxable years but does require that the calculation of taxable income be made based on chronic illness benefits received in a taxable year). *See also* IRC § 446(c) and Treas. Reg. § 1.446-1, describing the cash receipts and disbursements method of accounting.

[78] Riders may limit benefits to the per diem limitation based solely on the inflation-indexed per diem amount of IRC § 7702B(d)(4) and (5), and thus uncertainty regarding the following year's limitation may make it difficult to apply this contractual restriction. Some riders address this issue by specifying that the maximum benefits will be based on the inflation-indexed per diem amount in effect on the effective date of the insured's certification as a chronically ill individual.

[79] No IRS guidance addresses this question, and other approaches also may be reasonable, such as basing the limitation on the indexed daily amount that applies for the year when the payment is made, 2014 in this example.

years, the necessary adjustments will not be known until after the period concludes, e.g., on September 30, 2015, in the above example. Thus, a threshold question is whether these adjustments should be made and accounted for solely in 2015 (since that is when knowledge of the needed adjustments will be known) or whether some other approach should be used, such as making adjustments for purposes of the 2014 tax return on the basis of QLTC service costs incurred and reimbursements thereof during 2014 and then doing likewise for purposes of the 2015 tax return with respect to such amounts incurred and received during 2015. Perhaps this question could otherwise be stated as whether a single 12-month period applies or whether there necessarily must be two periods in this example, one for October 1, 2014, through December 31, 2014, and another for January 1, 2015, through September 30, 2015.

In many cases, of course, these concerns are inapplicable, such as where policyholders receive chronic illness benefits from only one source, incur expenses for QLTC services in amounts less than the inflation-indexed per diem amount, and do not otherwise receive any reimbursements of those expenses. In these cases, the current tax reporting regime for insurers (on IRS Form 1099-LTC) and for policyholders (on IRS Form 8853) works well and is relatively straight-forward for taxpayers to apply. In order to avoid issues in connection with benefits for a period that straddles taxable years, some insurers contractually provide lump-sum benefits only for the period during which an insured is chronically ill that does not extend beyond the calendar year. Thus, in the above example, if the insurer would otherwise provide a $140,000 annual lump-sum benefit, the rider might be designed so that it would pay a benefit of $92/365^{th}$ of $140,000, i.e., $30,360, for the period of October 1, 2014, through December 31, 2014, and in January of 2015 a further lump-sum benefit would be provided of $273/365^{th}$ of $140,000, i.e., $92,820, for the period of January 1, 2015, through September 30, 2015, which is the remaining period for which the insured is considered chronically ill as a result of the October 1, 2014, certification. Due to this contractual mechanism, it appears that there would be separate periods and corresponding per diem limitations—one for the three-month period in 2014 and another for the nine-month period in 2015—for purposes of ascertaining the taxable portion of the two lump-sum benefit payments, in each case with adjustments made solely on the basis of costs for QLTC services and reimbursements of QLTC services as applicable to the respective periods. Of course, structuring a rider to pay two lump sums is cumbersome (especially if the effective date of the certification is near the end of the calendar year), and given that the period of chronic illness due to a certification is limited to 12 months, there is little or no tax policy reason why section 7702B(d) should be construed to require such an approach.

## Refunds from QLTCI Riders

As discussed below in connection with the definition of a QLTCI contract, Congress limited the investment orientation of QLTCI contracts in part by generally prohibiting the availability of cash and loan values.[80] However, an exception to this rule allows a refund of premium (ROP, sometimes called "return of premium") benefit to be provided upon the death of the insured or complete cancellation of the contract, as long as the amount of that refund does not exceed the aggregate premiums paid under the contract.[81] Such ROP benefits should be permissible in the context of QLTCI riders to life insurance contracts in the same manner as under a stand-alone QLTCI contract due to the separate contract rule of section 7702B(e)(1). Also, regarding the tax treatment of ROP benefits, section 7702B(b)(2)(C) states: "Any refund on a complete surrender or cancellation of the contract shall be includible in gross income to the extent that any deduction or exclusion was allowable with respect to the premiums."

When originally enacted as part of HIPAA, the tax treatment prescribed by section 7702B(b)(2)(C) for ROP benefits followed the tax benefit rule of federal tax law, in that if a taxpayer received a tax benefit from being able to deduct or exclude from income a premium in a prior taxable year and then recovered that previously paid premium in a subsequent taxable year, it was appropriate to tax the recovered amount.[82] In effect, the inherent inconsistency between the prior deduction or exclusion and treating the recovery as nontaxable compels a conclusion that the recovery is instead taxable. The close alignment between section 7702B(b)(2)(C)'s prescribed tax treatment of ROP benefits and the tax benefit rule faltered somewhat after the enactment

---

[80] IRC § 7702B(b)(1)(D) and (E). Assignments also are proscribed.
[81] IRC § 7702B(b)(2)(C).
[82] *See, e.g., United States v. Bliss Dairy Inc.,* 460 U.S. 370 (1983).

of the PPA in 2006 due to two changes made by that law: the allowance of tax-free exchanges of a life, annuity or QLTCI contract for a QLTCI contract, and the exclusion from income of charges assessed against the cash value of a life insurance or annuity contract to fund a QLTCI rider after all investment in the contract has been depleted. To illustrate the issue presented by the allowance of a tax-free exchange, consider a situation in which a life insurance contract (with a $50,000 cash value, $20,000 of which is gain) is exchanged for a whole life insurance-QLTCI rider combination product that requires payment of a $40,000 single premium for the whole life insurance portion of the contract and a $10,000 single premium for the QLTCI rider portion of the contract. Also assume that a ROP benefit is provided by the QLTCI rider, and the same individual is the insured and policyholder under both contracts. Such an exchange qualifies for tax-free treatment under section 1035, i.e., the transaction does not require the recognition of the $20,000 gain in the original contract upon the exchange. Upon a subsequent surrender of the QLTCI rider for its ROP benefit, if the tax basis of the original life insurance contract were allocated to the new whole life insurance contract and QLTCI rider on a pro rata basis according to the cash value of the original contract allocated to each upon the exchange,[83] $6,000 of basis would have been allocated to the QLTCI rider, and thus the $10,000 ROP benefit would exceed the rider's basis. However, in this instance, there has been no prior deduction or exclusion of any portion of the $10,000 premium paid for the QLTCI rider, and thus the reference to "any deduction or exclusion [that] was allowable" in section 7702B(b)(2)(C) appears inapplicable in this circumstance.[84] While income of $4,000 is realized—in an economic sense—upon the surrender of the QLTCI rider, reflecting part of the gain of the original contract given in the exchange, no guidance has addressed whether any of it must be recognized, whether under section 7702B(b)(2)(C), section 61 or otherwise.[85]

A further question regards whether ROP benefits payable upon the insured's death are taxed differently than ROP benefits provided upon surrender. Some have asked whether section 7702B(b)(2)(C) implies a different treatment, since it describes the treatment of "[a]ny refund on a complete surrender or cancellation of the contract" but is silent regarding the treatment of death proceeds. A general tenet of the tax law is that income is subject to tax unless there is an express exclusion from income or deduction to offset that income.[86] Here, some have argued that Congress contemplated that ROP benefits payable from a QLTCI contract (including under stand-alone contracts) upon the insured's death are excludable from income under section 101(a)(1) as "amounts received ... under a life insurance contract [that are] paid by reason of the death of the insured." A challenge facing this argument, however, is that a QLTCI contract (whether stand-alone or rider) is not a "life insurance contract" under section 7702, which defines this term for purposes of the Code.[87]

## Definition of a Qualified Long-Term Care Insurance Contract

### Introduction
Section 7702B defines a "qualified long-term care insurance contract" and prescribes the federal income tax treatment of such contracts. As noted above, the tax rules for QLTCI largely operate as a safe harbor, in that the

---

[83] *See* Rev. Rul. 2003-76, 2003-2 C.B. 355 (allocating "investment in the contract" upon a partial exchange of annuity contracts on a pro rata basis according to the allocation of the original contract's cash value); Treas. Reg. § 1.1031(j)-1(c) (describing the allocation of basis where multiple properties qualify for nonrecognition treatment in an exchange); Notice 2011-68, 2011-36 I.R.B. 205 (stating, "the Treasury and the IRS believe that, under § 1031(d), the adjusted basis of a [QLTCI] contract received in a tax-free exchange under § 1035(a) generally carries over from the life insurance, endowment, annuity, or [QLTCI] contract exchanged"). This example also assumes that no reduction in the adjusted basis for a life insurance contract or QLTCI contract/rider would arise due to cost of insurance charges, whether expressly or implicitly assessed.

[84] IRC § 1035 provided for the nonrecognition of income on the prior exchange; it did not operate to exclude income.

[85] It also is possible that the IRS would assert application of IRC § 1001, which generally requires the recognition of gain upon the sale or other disposition of property. IRC § 1001(c) generally limits the application of this provision where another provision of the Code, such as IRC § 7702B(b)(2)(C), prescribes the tax treatment of an item. Note that IRC § 72 does not govern the tax treatment of benefits from a QLTCI rider, and thus the concept of investment in the contract, within the meaning of IRC § 72(c)(1) and (e)(6), has no application to such a rider. It is unclear whether insurers have any tax reporting obligation with respect to ROP benefits under QLTCI contracts and riders. In addition, the prior deduction or exclusion referenced by IRC § 7702B(b)(2)(C) arguably should not encompass exclusions of income under IRC § 72(e)(11) which reduce investment in the contract, since in such circumstances such investment has effectively been transferred to the QLTCI rider.

[86] A taxpayer is entitled to an exclusion only if there is clear provision for the favorable tax treatment. *Templeton v. Comm'r*, 719 F.2d 1408, 1411 (7th Cir. 1983).

[87] As discussed earlier in this book, one of the requirements of IRC § 7702 is that the contract must constitute life insurance under applicable, *e.g.*, state, law. This requirement seemingly would not be met by a stand-alone QLTCI contract or by the QLTCI portion of a combination contract. Those arguing for exclusion treatment have pointed to Treas. Reg. § 1.101-1(a)(1), which indicates that the scope of IRC § 101(a) extends to death benefits paid under accident or health insurance contracts. This regulation as originally promulgated predates the enactment of IRC § 7702 and thus may be obsolete. It is fair to ask, however, whether Congress intended through the enactment of this statute to change the tax treatment of death benefits provided in connection with accident and health insurance contracts.

A&H insurance tax treatment of such contracts is confirmed by section 7702B whereas the tax law otherwise offers little specific guidance about if and when nonqualified long-term care insurance would be accorded such tax treatment. QLTCI can be offered as a stand-alone contract, as a life insurance rider or feature providing ADBs, as a life insurance rider or feature not providing ADBs, or as a combination annuity-QLTCI contract. Also, the tax rules for QLTCI are unusual in three key respects:

- First, some of the tax rules for QLTCI are intended to protect federal Treasury revenues by requiring that an insured reach a minimum threshold of functional or cognitive impairment as a condition for the receipt of insurance benefits and by limiting cash values and other investment-oriented elements, while other tax rules are intended to protect consumers.

- Second, some of these tax rules, especially those intended to protect consumers, are imposed by cross-reference to certain provisions from model state laws and regulations—specifically, certain provisions of the 1993 LTC model rules.

- Third, some of the tax rules for QLTCI are imposed as qualification requirements, i.e., the requirements must be met in order for the contract to qualify as QLTCI, while others are enforced through the imposition of a tax penalty. The qualification rules are generally set forth in section 7702B(b) and (g), whereas the rules enforced through the penalty tax generally are imposed by section 4980C.

## *Section 7702B(b)(1): Insurance Contract Requirement*

Section 7702B(b)(1) defines QLTCI as any "insurance contract" that meets the requirements of section 7702B(b)(1)(A)–(F). Neither section 7702B nor the regulations thereunder elaborate on the requirement that a contract must be an insurance contract, and the available legislative histories of the provision provide no further clarity on this point. Likewise, neither the Code nor the Income Tax Regulations provide a general definition of "insurance" or "insurance contract" for tax purposes.[88] As a result, whether an arrangement is an insurance contract for federal income tax purposes generally is determined under standards derived from federal case law.[89]

For stand-alone QLTCI contracts and QLTCI riders that provide ADBs consisting of a pro rata portion of a life insurance contract's NAR and cash values, the insurance contract requirement typically will be readily satisfied. This is because such insurance benefits consist either entirely of NAR or possess insurance characteristics that mirror those of the related life insurance contract. While QLTCI riders providing ADBs are commonly funded through direct premiums or charges assessed against life insurance cash values, it may be possible to fund such riders through an actuarial discount or using the lien method.[90] Under these alternative funding structures, a question might be raised about whether the arrangements constitute "retroactive insurance," since the consideration provided by the policyholder for receipt of insurance benefits, i.e., agreement to reduce the current and future death benefits, occurs simultaneously with the payment of such benefits—and thus after the insurable event (the fortuity of the insured's chronic illness) has occurred.[91] Despite this characteristic of such funding methods, long-term care insurance ADBs typically consist of significant NAR, and thus material risk shifting may take place prior to the payment of those ADBs. In general terms, where an actuarial discount or the lien method is employed, the economic funding of such ADBs typically consists of two principal elements:

---

[88] Of course, IRC § 7702 provides a definition of "life insurance contract" for purposes of the Code, but that definition is inapplicable here.

[89] *See, e.g., Haynes v. United States*, 353 U.S. 81, 83 (1957) (defining health insurance as "an undertaking by one person ... to indemnify another for losses caused by illness"); *Helvering v. Le Gierse*, 312 U.S. 531 (1941) (discussed in Chapter 1 and identifying the following four features that distinguish insurance from other arrangements: the form and registration of the contract, the existence of an insurance risk, the shift or transfer of that risk, and the pooling or distribution of the insurance risk by the party assuming it); *Epmeier v. United States*, 199 F.2d 508 (7th Cir. 1952) (stating that insurance "involves a contract, whereby, for an adequate consideration, one party undertakes to indemnify another against loss arising from certain specified contingencies or perils. Fundamentally and shortly, it is contractual security against possible anticipated loss. Risk is essential and, equally so, a shifting of its incidence from one to another."); *Allied Fidelity Corp. v. Comm'r*, 66 T.C. 1068, 1074 (1976) (stating, "In common understanding, an insurance contract is an agreement to protect the insured (or a third-party beneficiary) against a direct or indirect economic loss arising from a defined contingency" and "an essential feature of insurance is the assumption of another's risk of economic loss").

[90] No guidance from the IRS addresses such funding structures. Further, unlike the ABMR, the LTC model rules do not specifically address such structures. They do, however, require long-term care insurance to be guaranteed renewable, as discussed later in this chapter.

[91] *See* Rev. Rul. 89-96, 1989-2 C.B. 114 (concluding that risk transfer did not occur where the insurable event had already occurred and the arrangement only served to transfer an investment risk).

- imposition of life insurance cost of insurance charges prior to the onset of chronic illness that maintains NAR which is available to be paid upon the first of two insurable events, i.e., the insured's chronic illness or death; and

- the reduction or offset of future death benefits by the actuarial discount or lien method, which compensates the insurer for the time value of money cost of paying NAR prior to the insured's expected death as a chronic illness benefit.

The life insurance cost of insurance charges, by maintaining NAR which is available as a chronic illness ADB, distinguish such ADBs from retroactive insurance.[92]

## Section 7702B(b)(1)(A): Coverage of Only QLTC Services
### In General

One of the principal qualification rules imposed for the purpose of protecting federal Treasury revenues is the requirement that a QLTCI contract only provide coverage of "qualified long-term care services."[93] QLTC services, in turn, are defined as "necessary diagnostic, preventive, therapeutic, curing, treating, mitigating, and rehabilitative services, and maintenance or personal care services, which are (A) required by a chronically ill individual, and (B) provided pursuant to a plan of care prescribed by a licensed health care practitioner."[94] This requirement thus consists of two elements—one relating to the types of services provided and another relating to the insured's capacity. The various types of services listed in this definition are similar to those described in section 213(d)(1)(A), which is part of the general definition of "medical care" under the Code. The definition of QLTC services, however, also encompasses services—especially maintenance or personal care services—associated with the broader range of needs of chronically ill individuals due to their functional or cognitive incapacity rather than any specific disease or injury. The scope of QLTC services is largely dictated by the element of the definition relating to the insured's condition, i.e., his or her status as a chronically ill individual. Section 7702B(c)(2)(A) defines the term "chronically ill individual" as:

> [A]ny individual who has been certified by a licensed health care practitioner as—
>
> i) being unable to perform (without substantial assistance from another individual) at least 2 activities of daily living for a period of at least 90 days due to a loss of functional capacity,
>
> ii) having a level of disability similar (as determined under regulations prescribed by the [Secretary of the Treasury] in consultation with the Secretary of Health and Human Services) to the level of disability described in clause (i),[95] or
>
> iii) requiring substantial supervision to protect such individual from threats to health and safety due to severe cognitive impairment.
>
> Such term shall not include any individual otherwise meeting the requirements of the preceding sentence unless within the preceding 12-month period a licensed health care practitioner has certified that such individual meets such requirements.[96]

---

[92] The insurance contract question also arises in the context of annuity-QLTCI contracts. The question of whether a combination contract constitutes an insurance contract essentially is whether there is an expectation that material risk shifting and risk distribution are provided with respect to an insured's risk of chronic illness. In the absence of bright-line tests for purposes of assessing this question, especially in light of the variety of factual circumstances that may be present, the IRS has relied upon general case law and other analyses in reaching a conclusion that particular annuity-QLTCI arrangements satisfied the "insurance contract" criteria. See PLR 201213016 (Dec. 20, 2011), PLR 201105001 (Oct. 22, 2010) and PLR 200919011 (Feb. 2, 2009) (each concluding that adequate risk shifting and risk distribution were present under the facts and circumstances of the annuity-QLTCI contracts involved in the PLRs).

[93] IRC § 7702B(b)(1)(A). As discussed later, a special rule—set forth in IRC § 7702B(e)—allows QLTCI riders to be provided under life insurance and non-qualified annuity contracts, despite the insurance coverages otherwise provided under such contracts. As also discussed later, another special rule—set forth in IRC § 7702B(b)(2)(A)—allows for per diem benefits to be provided without running afoul of the requirement to cover only QLTC services.

[94] IRC § 7702B(c)(1).

[95] As of the date of publication (2015), the Secretary of the Treasury has not prescribed any similar level of disability that would allow an individual to meet the chronic illness definition. Thus, IRC § 7702B(c)(2)(A)(ii) is not currently operative.

[96] See also Notice 97-31, 1997-1 C.B. 417, which includes safe harbor definitions for the terms **substantial assistance**, **substantial supervision** and **severe cognitive impairment** for purposes of the definition of a chronically ill individual and also contains a safe harbor rule for continuation of certain pre-1997 interpretations used by an insurer.

The Code also provides definitions of terms that are components of the foregoing definitions of "qualified long-term care services" and "chronically ill individual."

**Activities of daily living (ADL)** means eating, toileting, transferring, bathing, dressing and continence.[97] A contract will not be treated as a QLTC insurance contract unless the determination of whether an individual is a chronically ill individual takes into account at least five of these ADLs.[98] The six ADLs identified by the statute are the only ones permitted to be taken into account for purposes of ascertaining whether the two-of-six-ADL requirement is satisfied. It is permissible, however, to prescribe a more stringent benefit trigger. Thus, a contract could provide benefits upon the insured's need of substantial assistance with two of five ADLs,[99] or with three of seven ADLs (where the seven ADLs consist of the six identified in the statute plus one other), since in that event the insured necessarily would have to need substantial assistance with at least two of the six ADLs referenced in the statute. In contrast, it would not be permissible under a QLTCI contract to provide benefits upon an insured's need of substantial assistance with two of seven ADLs.

**Maintenance or personal care services** means "any care the primary purpose of which is the provision of needed assistance with any of the disabilities as a result of which the individual is a chronically ill individual (including the protection from threats to health and safety due to severe cognitive impairment)."[100] A key aspect of this definition is that the care must have as its "primary purpose" the provision of needed assistance due to the insured's chronic illness. This limitation on the scope of "maintenance or personal care services" appears to have been intended to preclude use of contracts to reimburse costs not substantially related to the insured's needs resulting from his or her chronic illness. In other words, Congress did not want QLTCI to be used to reimburse personal expenses with little or no relationship to the insured's capacity.[101] At the same time, the scope of QLTCI services arguably should be construed broadly to the extent necessary to allow contracts and riders to address the full range of services required after the onset of chronic illness. For example, a key desire of many individuals is to stay in their home or another residential setting for as long as possible after the onset of chronic illness. Recognizing this setting for the provision of QLTC services, the legislative history of section 7702B states that such services "may include meal preparation, household cleaning, and other similar services which the chronically ill individual is unable to perform."[102] The legislative history anticipates that the scope of maintenance and personal care services would be defined in Treasury regulations.[103] To date, no such regulations have been issued.[104]

**Licensed health care practitioner (LHCP)** means "any physician (as defined in section 1861(r)(1) of the Social Security Act) and any registered professional nurse, licensed social worker, or other individual who meets such requirements as may be prescribed by the Secretary [of the Treasury]."[105] As noted earlier in connection with the discussion of terminal illness ADBs, the term "physician" for this purpose appears to exclude doctors who are not legally authorized to practice in one of the 50 states, the District of Columbia or certain territories.[106] Also, the HIPAA Blue Book clarifies that a licensed social worker includes "any social worker who has been issued a license, certificate, or similar authorization to act as a social worker by a State or a body authorized

---

[97] IRC § 7702B(c)(2)(B). The ADLs are not themselves defined in the statute or other IRS guidance, but their meaning as set forth in the LTC Model Regulation is indicative of the insurance industry's, and presumably Congress', understanding of these terms. *See also* NAIC Proceedings, 3rd Quarter 1994, 607, and 1st Quarter 1995, 580 (adopting and amending ADL definitions).

[98] IRC § 7702B(c)(2)(B).

[99] *See also* HIPAA House Report at 116, n. 7 (1996) (stating, "Nothing in the bill requires the contract to take into account all of the activities of daily living. For example, a contract could require that an individual be unable to perform (without substantial assistance) 2 out of any 5 such activities, or for another example, 3 out of the 6 activities").

[100] IRC § 7702B(c)(3).

[101] See, *e.g.*, IRC § 262(a), regarding the nondeductibility of personal living expenses.

[102] Staff of the J. Comm. on Tax'n, 104th Cong., General Explanation of Tax Legislation Enacted in the 104th Congress, at 338 (Comm. Print 1996) (hereinafter HIPAA Blue Book).

[103] *Id.*

[104] At the time of HIPAA's enactment, the question was sometimes raised whether long-term care insurance designs would cover situations where an individual has mild impairment and, for example, is no longer able to drive an automobile (*e.g.*, early scenes from the film *Driving Miss Daisy* (1989)). Any such concern is misplaced in the context of QLTCI since the "chronically ill individual" definition requires a substantial degree of impairment as a condition for benefits.

[105] IRC § 7702B(c)(4).

[106] It would be helpful if IRS guidance specified that foreign licensed physicians also will be treated as LHCPs. It seems clear that registered professional nurses and licensed social workers need not be U.S. licensed, *e.g.*, a Canadian registered nurse would appear to qualify as a LHCP. Given this, there seems to be little reason to exclude foreign-licensed physicians who have training comparable to that of U.S. physicians.

by a State to issue such authorizations."[107] The LHCP has two roles under section 7702B. First, an insured will be considered to be a chronically ill individual only if certified as such by a LHCP. It is permissible, however, for a QLTCI contract to limit the individuals who can perform certifications of chronic illness to a subset of LHCPs, e.g., to just physicians as defined by SSA section 1861(r)(1) or to LHCPs who are not the insured, the policyholder or a relative. It is important to recognize that the providers of QLTC services need not be LHCPs and, in fact, often will not be LHCPs, e.g., home health aides.

**Scope of QLTC Services**

Because a QLTCI contract is permitted to cover only QLTC services, it is necessary to design such contracts and riders so that no insurance coverage whatsoever is of non-QLTC services. In light of the definition of this term, and of its component "maintenance or personal care services," services that are substantially directed at providing assistance with an insured's needs resulting from an inability to perform ADLs or severe cognitive impairment should be considered QLTC services. Little guidance exists, however, regarding the line between QLTC services and other services, and the resulting uncertainty can present challenges in designing QLTCI contracts. In the aftermath of HIPAA's enactment, the insurance industry requested guidance on certain types of coverage that did not involve direct assistance or supervision of insureds, but where such coverages nonetheless were strongly focused on addressing the needs of insureds resulting from their chronic illness.

For example, the industry requested confirmation that it was permissible to provide a bed reservation benefit, which generally reimburses for costs incurred to reserve a room in a facility that provides long-term care (usually for a limited number of days) while the insured is temporarily absent from the facility, e.g., while receiving acute care in a hospital.[108] Here, one might argue that no "services" are even involved, but the benefit's clear purpose is to help ensure that the insured will be able to receive QLTC services upon returning to the facility. Similarly, QLTCI contracts often provide a caregiver training benefit, e.g., to help enable family members/friends who will be taking on the care-giving burden to perform tasks appropriately. While the services in this context are directly provided to the caregiver, again, the benefit's purpose is to help ensure that the insured will be able to receive QLTC services. Further examples are the various types of care coordination benefits that can be found in contracts. These benefits may facilitate the preparation of the plan of care[109] and provide information to insureds about options for receiving care. Such care coordination benefits may be provided directly by the insurer (where the insurer makes available the care coordinator or information source) or may provide for reimbursement of costs incurred by the insured. In the former case, the benefit arguably is merely part of the insurer's administration of the contract and not an insurance benefit at all; in the latter case, however, such benefits appear to constitute either an insurance coverage or a limited cash benefit, and thus it is necessary to consider whether the particular features of the benefit fall within the ambit of QLTC services.[110] In each of the above cases, there seems to be little or no tax policy reason for treating the benefits and features as being inconsistent with the requirement to cover only QLTC services.

A similar question was addressed by the IRS in private letter rulings that addressed riders to stand-alone QLTCI contracts which promoted wellness.[111] In particular, the riders provided policyholders with access to information pertaining to health wellness and long-term care that promoted and encouraged a healthy lifestyle. Policyholders also were provided access to a registered nurse or other health care professionals by telephone or through the Internet to answer questions on general wellness, long-term care and other health-related topics. The purpose of providing such information was either to facilitate the provision of long-term care services or to reduce the incidence or severity of any future need for long-term care. This information was provided regardless of the policyholder's health, i.e., no insurable event need have occurred. The rider provided that, if

---

[107] HIPAA Blue Book, *supra* note 102, at 339.
[108] *See, e.g.*, Letter from Bill Gradison, President, Health Insurance Association of America (HIAA), to the U.S. Department of the Treasury (March 5, 1997) (hereinafter Gradison letter).
[109] While a care coordinator may assist in the preparation of a plan of care, the definition of QLTC services requires such services be provided under a plan of care prescribed by a LHCP.
[110] Where reimbursement or per diem benefits are provided for care coordination, it is necessary at a minimum that the insured be chronically ill as a prerequisite to payment of such benefits, since QLTC services only consist of certain services required by a chronically ill individual. If such benefits were not provided as an insurance benefit, they seemingly would be contrary to the limitations on cash values under QLTCI contracts, which is discussed later in this chapter.
[111] PLRs 201105027 and 201105026 (both Nov. 5, 2010).

the policyholder participated in certain periodic health assessments to be offered by a third party, and satisfied certain medical criteria (e.g., a prescribed body mass index score) that evidenced healthy living, the policyholder would be entitled to incentive benefits declared by the insurer, such as premium discounts or increases in benefits. The IRS observed that the rider provided ancillary mechanisms aimed at minimizing long-term care needs and concluded that the rider would not cause the contract to be treated as providing insurance coverage other than of QLTC services. The IRS also explained that the information and incentives provided by the rider were not insurance benefits but rather constituted a loss prevention program consistent with the purpose of section 7702B, and it held that all premiums paid for contracts which include a rider were premiums for a QLTCI contract.

QLTCI contracts also typically include waiver of premium benefits that apply upon an insured's chronic illness and also possibly upon other events, e.g., the death of a payor of premiums. Here, the question is whether such benefits should be considered as an insurance coverage that possibly could run afoul of the requirement to cover only QLTC services or whether, for example, such provisions should merely be viewed as part of the pricing structure for a contract. While a risk event must have occurred for a waiver of premium to apply, this does not necessarily mean that the feature is more than part of the pricing mechanism of a contract. Again, the insurance industry asked for clarification of this point soon after HIPAA's enactment, but no guidance has addressed the question.[112]

**Plan of Care**

As noted above, for services to constitute QLTC services, they must be "required by a chronically ill individual [and] provided pursuant to a plan of care prescribed by a licensed health care practitioner." Neither the statute nor other guidance defines the term **plan of care**. However, since QLTC services are ones required by a chronically ill individual, it can be inferred that the plan of care should identify those services needed by the insured due to his or her chronic illness. Since the LHCP's prescription of needed care will typically identify all of the care required by an individual, it also usually will be the case that the plan of care may prescribe services not required due to the insured's chronic illness, e.g., services might be prescribed due to an acute condition. Being included in the plan of care does not cause the latter services to become QLTC services; however, neither does such inclusion invalidate the plan of care as applicable to those prescribed services needed by the insured due to his or her chronic illness.

Insurance contracts typically require that the plan of care be in writing, although this arguably is not required by the statute. For example, if the family physician verbally informs family members providing care at home that the insured needs assistance with particular ADLs, seemingly a LHCP has prescribed such services (although the certification of chronic illness itself must be in writing). Indeed, it usually will be the case that if a LHCP has certified that an insured is chronically ill, the LHCP would also have prescribed QLTC services. At the same time, if a QLTCI contract or rider provides reimbursements, it presumably will be necessary to include a contractual mechanism that limits reimbursements to costs for services prescribed by a LHCP under a plan of care, and to accomplish this it seemingly will be necessary for the insurer to require and obtain a written copy of the plan of care. Of course, insurance contracts generally cover only a subset of prescribed services, since daily or monthly maximums may apply and other requirements, such as receiving care in specified types of facilities, often must be satisfied.

**Additional Considerations Relating to the Definition of a Chronically Ill Individual**

Since the definition of "chronically ill individual" in section 7702B(c)(2)(A) establishes the minimum degree of impairment necessary for payment of insurance benefits under a QLTCI contract, it is permissible to impose

---

[112] *See, e.g.,* Gradison letter, *supra* note 108. Note that 1993 LTC Model Act § 6D(1)(c), which is a federal tax qualification requirement by reason of section 7702B(g)(2)(A)(ii)(II) (relating to prior hospitalization requirements), specifically refers to waiver of premium benefits, and thus it seems clear that Congress contemplated the permissibility of such benefits at least in some circumstances. Under QLTCI riders, waiver benefits may extend to charges or premiums required under the related life insurance contract. Again, the question is whether this is a pricing feature (in this instance also including the life insurance contract) or whether, for example, it is an insurance benefit that may count against the per diem limitation. A related question is whether such a feature, at least insofar as it waives life insurance charges or premiums, should be considered to be part of the QLTCI portion or the life insurance portion of the contract and, if the latter is correct, whether that feature should be considered to be a disability waiver benefit and thus a qualified additional benefit under section 7702. Chronic illness and disability are closely related and largely overlap, although there are differences, *e.g.,* disability often is associated with an inability to work in one's vocation.

additional requirements as conditions for the receipt of benefits, so that benefits are payable under a contract only to a subset of individuals who would satisfy that statutory definition. Also, state law cannot override the requirement that only QLTC services be covered by a contract, and thus state law cannot supplant the chronically ill individual definition with a benefit trigger of broader scope without disqualifying the contract. With this in mind, certain aspects of the definition of a chronically ill individual beyond those discussed above will be examined next.

**Functional incapacity benefit trigger:** As noted above, an individual will be a chronically ill individual if a LHCP has certified within the prior 12 months that such individual is "unable to perform (without substantial assistance from another individual) at least 2 activities of daily living for a period of at least 90 days due to a loss of functional capacity." For this purpose, IRS Notice 97-31 provides, as a safe harbor, that substantial assistance means "hands-on assistance and standby assistance"; in turn **hands-on assistance** means "physical assistance of another person without which the individual would be unable to perform the ADL," while **standby assistance** means "the presence of another person within arm's reach of the individual that is necessary to prevent, by physical intervention, injury to the individual while the individual is performing the ADL (such as being ready to catch the individual if the individual falls while getting into or out of the bathtub or shower as part of bathing, or being ready to remove food from the individual's throat if the individual chokes while eating)."[113] Since these definitions constitute a safe harbor, it is not necessary that they be used; however, using them avoids raising a question about whether the benefit trigger set forth in a contract allows for certifications where substantial assistance is not needed. It also may be advisable to set forth the definitions of these key terms (and also those associated with the cognitive impairment trigger) in the form an insurer supplies to the LHCP for purposes of the certification of chronic illness, to better inform the LHCP regarding the precise standard that must be met as a prerequisite to execution of the certification.

Another aspect of the functional capacity benefit trigger is that the ADL impairment must be "for a period of at least 90 days due to a loss of functional capacity." The purpose of this requirement is to distinguish chronic conditions from short-term ones. The legislative history of HIPAA reflects this by stating: "The 90-day period is not a waiting period. Thus, for example, an individual can be certified [as] chronically ill if the licensed health care practitioner certifies that the individual will be unable to perform at least 2 activities of daily living for at least 90 days."[114] The HIPAA Blue Book expands on this discussion, stating: "The certification of an insured as a chronically ill individual may occur at any time, and is intended to take into account the sum of continuous prior days when the insured was chronically ill and future days when the insured is expected to remain chronically ill."[115]

**Cognitive impairment benefit trigger:** As an alternative to the functional capacity benefit trigger, an individual also will be a chronically ill individual if a LHCP has certified within the prior 12 months that such individual requires "substantial supervision to protect such individual from threats to health and safety due to severe cognitive impairment." For this purpose, IRS Notice 97-31 provides, as a safe harbor, that "severe cognitive impairment" means "a loss or deterioration in intellectual capacity that is (a) comparable to (and includes) Alzheimer's disease and similar forms of irreversible dementia, and (b) measured by clinical evidence and standardized tests that reliably measure impairment in the individual's (i) short-term or long-term memory, (ii) orientation as to people, places, or time, and (iii) deductive or abstract reasoning."[116] The notice also provides, as another safe harbor, that substantial supervision means "continual supervision (which may include cuing by verbal prompting, gestures, or other demonstrations) by another person that is necessary to protect the severely cognitively impaired individual from threats to his or her health or safety (such as may result from wandering)."[117]

---

[113] *Supra* note 96.
[114] HIPAA Conference Report, *supra* note 16, at 297, n. 7.
[115] HIPAA Blue Book, *supra* note 102, at 338, n. 236.
[116] 1997-1 C.B. 417. *See also* HIPAA Conference Report, *supra* note 16, at 297; HIPAA Blue Book, *supra* note 102, at 339 (which mirrors this safe harbor and also states: "Because of the concern that eligibility for the medical expense deduction not be diagnosis driven, the provision requires the cognitive impairment to be severe. … In addition, it was intended that such deterioration or loss place the individual in jeopardy of harming self or others and therefore require substantial supervision by another individual.").
[117] 1997-1 C.B. 417.

Two aspects of these safe harbor definitions are noteworthy. First, while the word "severe" is subjective in nature, the reference to a condition "comparable to (and includes) Alzheimer's disease" provides an indication of the degree of impairment contemplated. The required degree of impairment arguably is also specified, implicitly, by the further element of the cognitive impairment trigger, i.e., that the individuals must require substantial supervision to protect himself or herself. Second, the requirement that the cognitive impairment be "measured by clinical evidence and standardized tests" indicates that objective evidence of the degree of impairment must be obtained for an individual to be considered severely cognitively impaired. Such objective evidence should be capable of being independently verified.

**The 12-month period of chronic illness:** Another aspect of the chronically ill individual definition that has raised questions is the rule providing that an individual will not be considered to be a chronically ill individual "unless within the preceding 12-month period a [LHCP] has certified that such individual meets" the two-of-six-ADL or severe cognitive impairment benefit trigger requirements. While there is little guidance regarding this 12-month rule, it appears to be a practical solution to the dual considerations of requiring objective periodic evidence of an insured's functional or cognitive incapacity and of not imposing overly burdensome re-examination requirements on insureds. Read in this light, and absent evidence to the contrary (e.g., of fraud), an insured generally should be considered to be a chronically ill individual from the effective date of the certification of chronic illness and for the ensuing 12 months.

When a chronic illness per diem benefit is provided under a QLTCI contract or rider, the benefit is provided in respect of a period (e.g., a month or year) for which the insured satisfied the insurable event condition for the payment of benefits, i.e., the insured's chronic illness.[118] In practice, it takes some time for policyholders to submit and insurers to process a claim and then pay benefits. Similar administrative delays in the payment of benefits typically also occur under life insurance and other types of insurance contracts. In some QLTCI contracts or riders (and similarly in section 101(g) riders), these administrative practices are formalized through use of a benefit period (or similar concept) which dictates the timing for the processing and payment of benefits. Use of such mechanisms make the claims process more understandable for policyholders and insureds. Such mechanisms do not, however, alter the period of coverage for which the insurable event has been satisfied and for which benefits are payable. Thus, where a benefit period feature of a contract serves solely an administrative function, benefits should be viewed as being payable for the period of chronic illness rather than for the benefit period.

More problematic issues can arise in the context of reimbursement designs. Since a QLTCI rider can only provide coverage of QLTC services and such services, in turn, only consist of services required by a chronically ill individual, seemingly the coverage must be of services actually rendered at a time when the insured was a chronically ill individual, i.e., within the 12-month period of chronic illness that begins on the effective date of certification by a LHCP. Thus, a service rendered prior to the effective date of such certification but paid by the insured within the 12-month period of chronic illness seemingly would not constitute a QLTC service and thus could not be reimbursed by a QLTCI contract or rider.

At the end of the 12-month period of chronic illness, the insured will no longer be considered a chronically ill individual unless he or she is recertified as chronically ill by a LHCP. This recertification requirement applies even if the original certification indicated that the LHCP expected the insured's chronic illness to be permanent. The criteria for recertification are the same as that applicable upon the initial certification. Also, it often is advisable for the effective date of the recertification either to be on the anniversary of the prior certification or a short period of time before such anniversary. This will ensure that no gap in time exists for which the insured would not be considered chronically ill (and for which chronic illness benefits therefore could not be paid). At the same time, if the recertification is prior to the anniversary of the previous certification, the recertification necessarily will extend the period of chronic illness for less than 12 months. Of course, if chronic illness is persistent, this simply means that the next recertification will be needed somewhat sooner than would otherwise apply if the first recertification were on the anniversary of the initial certification.

---

[118] As previously noted, if a QLTCI rider (or an IRC § 101(g) rider) provides for a lump-sum benefit payment due to the insured's chronic illness, that lump sum seemingly should be viewed as having been paid for the 12-month period of chronic illness, since the certification thereof is both the condition for the benefit payment that has been satisfied and such certification causes the insured to be a chronically ill individual for the 12-month period.

**Timing of a LHCP's certification and nature of the LHCP's evaluation:** As discussed above, in applying the 90-day requirement with respect to the certification of an insured's functional incapacity with ADLs, the legislative history of HIPAA indicates that it is permissible to take into account "the sum of continuous prior days when the insured was chronically ill and future days when the insured is expected to remain chronically ill."[119] This raises a question, more generally, regarding whether (and to what extent) it is permissible for a LHCP to certify that an insured was chronically ill effective as of a date prior to when the LHCP is physically putting pen to paper in rendering the certification. In other words, is such back-dating of certifications allowed? If the LHCP has sufficient evidence to verify that the insured satisfied the functional or cognitive impairment triggers as of a prior date and continuously thereafter, such as through prior personal examinations of the insured, it arguably should be permissible for the LHCP to specify an effective date for the certification as of that prior date. Also, since per diem benefits may be taxable based on the per diem limitation applicable to the period of chronic illness for which benefits are paid, there could be a substantial disconnect between such period and the date of payment where back-dating of a certification occurs.

Insurers may attempt to limit the use of back-dating through various means, including by expressly prohibiting the LHCP from specifying an effective date for the certification either preceding, or preceding by more than a set time period, the physical execution of the certification. In many instances, however, the insurer simply will not know whether there has been any back-dating, since a certification will only specify the effective date as of which the insured became chronically ill and will not include any indication of precisely when the LHCP executed the certification. (If only a single date is noted on the certification, it is reasonable to consider such date to be both the effective date of the certification and the date of physical execution thereof, absent an indication to the contrary.) However, insurers may address this issue in a practical manner by requiring the submission of a claim within a set period of time from the effective date of the certification. No IRS guidance has addressed the subject of back-dating in this context, and thus there is legal uncertainty regarding the use of back-dating for certifications of chronic illness.

**Joint insured contracts:** Section 7702B does not expressly refer to long-term care insurance coverage of more than one individual, but there seems to be little or no reason why such coverage could not qualify as QLTCI. While QLTCI can cover only QLTC services, seemingly it should be permissible to cover such services as provided to more than a single insured. Such a contract would still be one where "the only insurance protection provided ... is coverage of qualified long-term care services."[120] Spouses often purchase individual long-term care insurance contracts at the same time, and a discounted price may be available to reflect efficiencies of scale as well as the practical expectation that one spouse may be able to function as a caregiver when the other spouse becomes chronically ill. Joint coverage features can take a variety of forms, including riders or other provisions which allow for a sharing of a maximum pool of benefits, e.g., that pool is available, or available to a specified extent, to be used by either spouse. Such shared pools of benefits can help to ensure that adequate benefits are available for the first spouse to become chronically ill and can maximize overall benefits that will be received from the spouses' contracts.[121] As a further possibility, a single contract form could provide coverage of two or more individuals.

A further consideration for joint coverages relates to underwriting practices. For a life insurance contract, joint and last survivor coverage often can be written even if one of the two insureds otherwise might be uninsurable. However, if that same contract were to include a living benefit such as a QLTCI rider providing ADBs, it usually would be necessary to restrict chronic illness coverage to the insured who is insurable at issue.

**Terminology:** As discussed above, section 7702B uses various terms in connection with the definition of a QLTCI contract or rider, including qualified long-term care services, chronically ill individual, substantial assistance, substantial supervision, severe cognitive impairment and licensed health care practitioner. To satisfy the requirements of this statute, it generally is permissible to use alternative terminology in contracts, as long

---

[119] HIPAA Blue Book, *supra* note 102, at 338, n. 236.
[120] IRC § 7702B(b)(1)(A).
[121] Shared benefit features thus allow for flexibility but may operate to the detriment of the spouse (often the wife) who initially acts as a caregiver but later may become chronically ill herself. At the same time, such benefits may allow for the retention of family assets that otherwise would need to cover costs of the first spouse to become chronically ill. Prospective policyholders should be counseled to consider these aspects of shared benefit designs when evaluating the amount of coverage they need.

### Section 7702B(b)(1)(B): Coordination with Medicare

To constitute QLTCI, a contract or rider cannot "pay or reimburse expenses incurred for services or items to the extent that such expenses are reimbursable under title XVIII of the Social Security Act [i.e., Medicare] or would be so reimbursable but for the application of a deductible or coinsurance amount."[122] While Medicare generally pays only limited amounts for long-term care for a short time period, this rule requires QLTCI that reimburses expenses to coordinate with Medicare, so that an insured could not receive benefits under both Medicare and under a QLTCI contract as reimbursement for the same QLTC services. Also, the limitation on QLTCI benefits extends to circumstances where Medicare would pay for the services but for the application of a deductible or coinsurance requirement. This latter rule appears to have been intended to preclude QLTCI contracts from paying benefits that might be covered by Medicare supplement coverage or which otherwise reflect federal policy goals in connection with cost sharing that applies due to deductible and coinsurance requirements.[123]

### Section 7702B(b)(1)(C): Guaranteed Renewability

To constitute QLTCI, a contract or rider must be guaranteed renewable.[124] In fact, the requirement of guaranteed renewability is imposed twice under the Code—first by section 7702B(b)(1)(C), which simply states that QLTCI must be guaranteed renewable, and second by section 7702B(g)(2)(A)(i)(I), which incorporates by reference from the 1993 LTC Model Regulation a requirement that contracts be guaranteed renewable or noncancellable. While these rules appear redundant, they are not in that the former rule requires a contract to be guaranteed renewable as this term is generally understood under the tax law, whereas the latter rule requires a contract to be guaranteed renewable as this term is defined and understood in the context of the 1993 LTC Model Regulation.

Guidance issued in the context of life insurance company taxation offers some insight on the meaning of this term as used in section 7702B(b)(1)(C). In particular, the regulations state: "The term *guaranteed renewable life, health, and accident insurance policy* means a health and accident contract, or a health and accident contract combined with a life insurance or annuity contract, which is not cancellable by the company but under which the company reserves the right to adjust premium rates by classes in accordance with its experience under the type of policy involved, and with respect to which a reserve in addition to the unearned premiums ... must be carried to cover that obligation."[125] Noncancellable contracts also should satisfy the guaranteed renewability requirement of section 7702B(b)(1)(C) since such contracts guarantee renewal in the same manner as guaranteed renewable contracts and are principally distinguishable only in that the insurer is unable to alter guaranteed premiums, even on a class basis.[126] In this regard, "the term noncancellable life, health, or accident insurance policy means a health and accident contract, or a health and accident contract combined with a life insurance or annuity contract, which the insurance company is under an obligation to renew or continue at a specified premium and with respect to which a reserve in addition to the unearned premiums ... must be carried to cover that obligation."[127] The meaning of guaranteed renewability also is discussed later in this chapter together with the other consumer protection rules incorporated by reference from the 1993 LTC model rules.

---

[122] IRC § 7702B(b)(1)(B).
[123] As discussed later, IRC § 7702B(b)(2)(A) provides a special rule allowing for per diem benefits without running afoul of the Medicare coordination requirement.
[124] IRC § 7702B(b)(1)(C).
[125] Treas. Reg. § 1.801-3(d).
[126] *See also* 1993 LTC Model Act §§ 9A and 7A, which must be satisfied for a contract to be QLTCI under IRC § 7702B(g)(2)(A)(i)(I) and (VII) and require contracts to be either guaranteed renewable or noncancellable.
[127] Treas. Reg. § 1.801-3(c). This definition also provides that a health and accident contract is considered noncancellable even though it states a termination date at a stipulated age if, with respect to the health and accident contract, such age termination date is 60 or over.

## Section 7702B(b)(1)(D), (E) and (2)(C): Limitations on Cash and Loan Values and Allowance of Return of Premium Benefits

The definition of QLTCI also includes restrictions on the availability of cash and loan values. Like the requirement discussed above that QLTCI must only cover QLTC services, the purpose of this requirement is to limit the investment orientation of contracts and thereby protect federal Treasury revenues. Specifically, section 7702B(b)(1)(D) states that a QLTCI contract must "not provide for a cash surrender value or other money that can be—(i) paid, assigned, or pledged as collateral for a loan, or (ii) borrowed, other than as provided in [section 7702B(b)(1)(E) or section 7702B(b)(2)(C)]." Further, section 7702B(b)(1)(E) states that "all refunds of premiums, and all policyholder dividends or similar amounts, under such contract are to be applied as a reduction in future premiums or to increase future benefits."[128]

These two rules, taken together and before consideration of the special rule of section 7702B(b)(2)(C), generally would prohibit any payment of cash value from a QLTCI contract other than insurance benefits due to the insured's chronic illness. The special rule of section 7702B(b)(2)(C), however, allows for a return of premium (ROP) benefit to be provided upon the insured's death or termination of the contract or rider. Specifically, this rule states that section 7702B(b)(1)(E) "shall not apply to any refund on the death of the insured, or on a complete surrender or cancellation of the contract, which cannot exceed the aggregate premiums paid under the contract."[129]

This rule restricts both the timing of such refunds (they can be provided only "on the death of the insured, or on a complete surrender or cancellation of the contract") and the amount of such refunds (they "cannot exceed the aggregate premiums paid under the contract"). The permissibility of such benefits helps address a concern sometimes raised with respect to QLTCI that the policyholder may pay substantial premiums for the contract over time and then never need long-term care, thereby "losing" one's investment. While a prospective policyholder may prefer to purchase a QLTCI contract that includes a ROP benefit for this reason, such contracts are necessarily more expensive. Also, this sentiment somewhat ignores the fact that QLTCI is not intended to represent an investment in and of itself, but rather functions as insurance coverage to protect against the financial risk of need for long-term care that otherwise could substantially diminish a policyholder's other assets.[130]

As previously mentioned and discussed further below, a QLTCI rider is treated as a separate contract from the related life insurance or annuity contract for federal tax purposes. As a result, a ROP benefit provided by the QLTCI rider is not considered part of the life insurance contract's "cash surrender value" within the meaning of section 7702(f)(2)(A), and the life insurance contract's cash surrender value is not considered to be provided by the QLTCI rider. This separate contract rule thus allows for a combination life insurance contract-QLTCI rider to comply with both the cash surrender value (CSV)-related restrictions that apply under section 7702 and the restrictions on cash value which apply to QLTCI. Because of the rigidity of these dual restrictions, it is necessary to specify the charges for a QLTCI rider in an actuarially appropriate manner with respect to the benefits provided by the rider.[131] Also, while section 7702B(b)(2)(C) allows for ROP benefits under QLTCI riders, its interaction with other qualification rules should be carefully considered. For example, while cash values

---

[128] The use of dividends to reduce future premiums or increase future benefits arguably could be considered as a deemed distribution to the policyholder followed by a deemed re-contribution to the contract, since such treatment applies in other contexts. See, e.g., IRC § 808(e) (providing that any policyholder dividend which increases the cash surrender value of a contract or other benefits payable under the contract, or reduces the premium otherwise required to be paid, is treated as paid to the policyholder and returned by the policyholder to the company as a premium); IRC § 72(e)(4)(B) (regarding retained dividends and which is based upon the premise that dividends retained to pay annuity contract and life insurance premiums generally are deemed distributions and premium re-contributions). Since IRC § 7702B(b)(1)(E) expressly authorizes such uses of dividends, they would not violate the statute's restrictions on cash values.

[129] The tax treatment of ROP benefits was discussed earlier in this chapter.

[130] In this sense, long-term care insurance, including QLTCI, functions like other term insurance coverages. People do not complain about the lack of an investment return on term life insurance or home casualty coverage; in those contexts, having the good fortune of not needing the insurance is much preferred, and the same is true of long-term care insurance.

[131] Charges for QLTCI riders providing accelerated death benefits usually are set based on a rider's design and the incremental cost of providing the QLTCI benefits relative to the life insurance benefits otherwise provided by a contract, e.g., the time value of money cost associated with paying NAR with respect to the death benefit prior to the insured's death. In some instances the statute refers to "charges" and in other instances to "premiums" for a QLTCI rider. The former term should be considered a subset of the latter term, both because charges represent the consideration, or premium, paid for a rider, and by reason of the separate contract rule which treats amounts charged against a life insurance contract's cash value as having been distributed from that contract and then paid into a separate contract, i.e., the QLTCI rider, for tax purposes.

under life insurance usually are subject to borrowing or assignment, it appears to be impermissible to permit borrowing or assignment of the ROP benefit provided by a QLTCI rider.

One question sometimes raised with respect to ROP benefits under QLTCI riders concerns the timing for payment of the benefit. The statute allows a refund to be paid only "on the death of the insured, or on a complete surrender or cancellation of the contract," which usually is a readily ascertainable point in time. A QLTCI rider may, however, offer a noncash nonforfeiture benefit, such as extended term insurance or a shortened benefit period, if a policyholder ceases payment of rider premiums or charges (which may occur upon termination of the related life insurance contract). Often such noncash benefits may be small relative to the long-term care coverage previously provided, and insurers may prefer the flexibility to pay a ROP benefit once the contract is no longer in premium-paying status, especially given that policyholders may perceive their long-term care insurance coverage to have effectively terminated due to the relatively small size of nonforfeiture benefit coverage. No exception in the statute appears to permit payment of a ROP benefit in this circumstance, although there seems to be little tax policy reason for restricting such payment.

A further issue under section 7702B(b)(1)(D) and (E) regards the meaning of "cash surrender value" and "refund of premiums" as used in these provisions. As discussed elsewhere in this book in the context of life insurance contracts, the meaning of cash surrender value under section 7702 is uncertain in a number of respects. The IRS has issued proposed regulations defining this term under section 7702(f)(2)(A), but those regulations have not been finalized.[132] There similarly is uncertainty regarding the scope of a refund of premiums, especially in connection with payments that might be made prior to contract termination. Thus, for example, it is unclear whether a return of unearned premiums may be paid where an annual premium has been paid and a portion of that annual premium is waived due to the insured's chronic illness effective as of a date later during that contract year. Given that such returns of unearned premiums do not raise any tax policy concern with respect to investment orientation for which the restrictions on cash values were imposed, it would be helpful if IRS guidance clarified that such payments are permissible.

Finally, questions can arise in the context of QLTCI contracts and riders that provide, such as through a separate rider, for the sharing of benefits between two or more insureds. For example, if two QLTCI riders covering spouses each includes a shared benefit rider, should the premiums or charges for the shared benefit riders be attributed in their entirety to the respective QLTCI riders to which the shared benefit riders are attached, so that the premiums for a shared benefit rider could be returned upon termination of the underlying QLTCI rider even if the spouse's QLTCI rider continues to provide coverage?

### *Section 7702B(b)(2)(A): Special Rule for Per Diem Benefits*

Because a QLTCI contract or rider generally must cover only QLTC services, it usually is necessary to ensure that no expenses other than for QLTC services are reimbursed, since doing so would disqualify the contract or rider. It also is necessary, as discussed above, that QLTCI not reimbursement expenses covered by Medicare, including amounts which would be covered but for a deductible or coinsurance requirement. Because these requirements might be interpreted to preclude contract designs providing per diem benefits, section 7702B(b)(2)(A) states: "A contract shall not fail to [comply with section 7702B(b)(1)(A) or (B)] by reason of payments being made on a per diem or other periodic basis without regard to the expenses incurred during the period to which the payments relate."

While this special rule clearly is intended to allow for per diem designs, it seems apparent that the rule does not completely supplant the general requirement that only QLTC services be covered. In this regard, the requirement that an insured be a chronically ill individual as a condition for benefit payments is imposed through the requirement in section 7702B(b)(1)(A) that a contract only cover QLTC services. Clearly, the chronic illness requirement remains intact for QLTCI contracts and riders providing per diem benefits. This, in turn, implies that the special rule for per diem benefits should be construed as supplanting the requirements of sections 7702B(b)(1)(A) and (B) only to the extent reasonably necessary to allow for per diem designs, including the aspect of such designs that there should be no need to track specific expenses incurred by an insured as a condition for the receipt of benefits. Interpreted in this light, it seems that the chronic illness requirement, and

---

[132] Prop. Treas. Reg. § 1.7702-2.

perhaps the plan of care requirement, of section 7702(b)(1)(A) would continue to apply to per diem QLTCI designs. Even in this light, however, it appears that the Medicare coordination requirement of section 7702B(b)(1)(B) may be completely negated, since to coordinate it seemingly would be necessary to receive evidence of specific expenses incurred.

## Section 7702B(e): Special Rules for Long-Term Care Riders

As discussed above, the definition of QLTCI includes rules intended to limit investment orientation, including the requirement that such a contract provide only insurance coverage of QLTC services and limitations on cash values. To allow for compliance with these requirements and also in recognition of the non-QAB status of long-term care insurance riders, section 7702B(e) states:

> Except as otherwise provided in regulations prescribed by the [Secretary of the Treasury], in the case of any long-term care insurance coverage (whether or not qualified) provided by a rider on or as part of a life insurance contract or an annuity contract —(1) This title [i.e., the Code] shall apply as if the portion of the contract providing such coverage is a separate contract.

Because of this separate contract rule, the insurance coverage and cash values provided under a life insurance contract do not prevent a long-term care insurance rider from complying with the above noted qualification rules for QLTCI. Similarly, the benefits and features of the long-term care insurance rider generally do not have any effect on the application of sections 7702 or 7702A, except indirectly due, for example, to reductions in a life insurance contract's death benefit as a result of payment of ADBs. A key aspect of this separate contract rule is that it applies for purposes of the entire Code, not just for the limited purpose of defining a QLTCI rider. Also, the separate contract rule extends to long-term care insurance that is not QLTCI. This treatment accords with the general treatment of non-QABs for tax purposes and is consistent with the view expressed by the IRS prior to the enactment of HIPAA in PLR 9106050.[133]

For this purpose, as discussed earlier, the long-term care insurance "portion" of the contract is defined as "only the terms and benefits under a life insurance contract or annuity contract that are in addition to the terms and benefits under the contract without regard to long-term care insurance coverage."[134] This definition generally adopts an incremental approach to defining what is the life insurance versus the long-term care insurance portion of a contract. Such an incremental approach is necessary for the life insurance cash values and coverage of NAR not to create a qualification problem for a QLTCI rider. Further, the legislative history for this rule confirms that the form in which a contract casts life insurance and long-term care insurance benefits usually will control for purposes of ascertaining the respective portions of a contract.[135] Thus, if a long-term care insurance rider provides, in form, a long-term care insurance benefit, such benefit is treated in its entirety as an insurance benefit payment from the long-term care insurance portion of the contract, regardless of whether that benefit payment results in a reduction in the life insurance contract's death benefit or cash value.[136] As noted earlier, this treatment is akin to the treatment accorded to life insurance death benefits, i.e., the life insurance benefit in whole is treated as an amount received by reason of the death of the insured for purposes of section 101 regardless of the fact that a cash surrender value may have been available under the contract a moment before the insured's death.

Because a long-term care insurance rider (whether or not qualified) is treated as a separate contract for purposes of the Code, any charges assessed against the cash value of the life insurance contract (such as under a universal life insurance design) are treated as distributions from the contract for tax purposes, just as charges for other non-QABs generally result in deemed distributions.[137] As discussed earlier in this chapter, however,

---

[133] In PLR 9106050 (Nov. 16, 1990), the IRS concluded that long-term care insurance benefits provided under a "LTC rider do not constitute qualified additional benefits under section 7702(f)(5)" and that "the payment of any benefit under the LTC rider ... will not be an amount which is received under a life insurance contract ...; therefore, these benefit payments do not reduce either Taxpayer's 'investment in the contract' under section 72(e)(6) of the Code or the 'premiums paid' under section 7702(f)(1)(A). ..." The rider in this case did not provide for the acceleration of the life insurance contract's death benefit but rather was tantamount to a stand-alone long-term care insurance contract.

[134] IRC § 7702B(e)(3).

[135] See also the discussion of the tax treatment of ADB chronic illness benefits that affect a life insurance contract's values earlier in this chapter (under In General: A&H Tax Treatment of Benefits under Section 7702B).

[136] PPA 2006 Blue Book, supra Chapter 5, note 46, at 195; HIPAA Blue Book, supra note 102, at 341.

[137] See PLR 9106050 (issued pre-HIPAA and treating charges for a long-term care insurance rider assessed against the related life insurance contract's cash value as an "amount received" from the life insurance contract for purposes of IRC § 72(e)).

section 72(e)(11) as amended by the PPA provides that such charges will not result in income, although the investment in the contract is reduced (not below zero) by the amount of such charges. As also noted earlier, section 7702B(e)(2) denies a deduction under section 213(a) for any payment made or coverage under a QLTCI rider if such payment is made as a charge against the cash value of the underlying contract.

The separate contract rule applies to any combination of long-term care insurance with a life insurance contract or annuity contract. For this purpose, the treatment of a benefit as long-term care insurance under state law generally should control whether a benefit is considered this type of insurance in the first instance. Thus, for example, a benefit regulated by a state law modeled after the ABMR, rather than state laws that address long-term care insurance, should not be treated as long-term care insurance coverage for purposes of the separate contract rule.

Reflecting the separate contract rule, section 7702B(e) provided other special rules prior to the enactment of the PPA in 2006. For example, one such rule—in pre-PPA section 7702B(e)(2)—provided for an increase in a contract's guideline premium limitation by the sum of any charges (but not premium payments) against the life insurance contract's cash surrender value for such coverage, less any such charges the imposition of which reduces the premiums paid for the contract. The purpose of this rule was to allow for funding of a long-term care insurance rider on a non-prefunded basis without diminishing the otherwise permissible funding of the life insurance contract under the guideline premium test. In particular, in the case of a life insurance contract that was not a modified endowment contract, charges assessed against the contract's cash value to fund a long-term care insurance rider typically would be treated as nontaxable distributions that reduced "premiums paid" based on the general definition of this term in section 7702(f)(1). Thus, pre-PPA section 7702B(e)(2) generally would both increase and decrease premiums paid by the same amount, so that there would be no net effect of such charges on premiums paid. In contrast, in the case of a MEC, charges for the long-term care rider usually would not reduce premiums paid (since such charges typically would be taxable distributions), and, as a result, the net effect of pre-PPA section 7702B(e)(2) generally was to increase premiums paid by the amount of charges assessed.[138] With the enactment of section 72(e)(11), this special pre-PPA rule was no longer needed.

### *Sections 7702B(g) and 4980C: Consumer Protection Rules for QLTCI*

While the compliance rules for QLTCI discussed above principally are intended to limit investment orientation and thereby protect federal Treasury revenues, an additional set of rules is intended to protect consumers. These rules generally fall into two categories: one set of rules (imposed by sections 7702B(b)(1)(F) and 7702B(g)) that must be met for a contract or rider to qualify as QLTCI, and another set of rules (imposed by section 4980C) that must be met to avoid application of a penalty tax. The amount of the penalty tax is $100 per insured for each day any of certain requirements is not met with respect to each QLTCI contract.[139] Also, the IRS may waive all or part of the penalty tax where a failure is due to reasonable cause and not to willful neglect to the extent that payment of the penalty tax would be excessive relative to the failure involved.[140]

The consumer protection rules are mostly imposed by cross-reference to certain provisions of the NAIC's 1993 LTC model rules.[141] In some instances, HIPAA modified the 1993 LTC model rules in certain respects. Other consumer protection qualification requirements apply without reference to the 1993 LTC model rules, including a requirement that a contract disclose on its face that it is intended to be QLTCI[142] and a requirement to offer a nonforfeiture benefit in certain cases.[143] Recognizing that the consumer protection rules may differ from applicable state law requirements, a special coordination rule provides that if a state imposes any require-

---

[138] The legislative history of IRC § 7702B also states, "[It] is anticipated that Treasury regulations will provide for appropriate reduction in premiums paid (within the meaning of sec. 7702(f)(1)) to reflect the payment of benefits under the rider that reduce the cash surrender value of the life insurance contract. A similar rule should apply in the case of a contract governed by section 101(f) and in the case of the payments under a rider that are excludable under section 101(g) of the Code (as added by [HIPAA])." HIPAA Blue Book at 341. To date, no such regulations have been issued.

[139] IRC § 4980C(b)(1).

[140] IRC § 4980C(b)(2).

[141] HIPAA did not require contracts to meet all of the provisions of the 1993 LTC model rules. For example, the tax rules imposing consumer protections generally do not include provisions regulating the pricing of long-term care insurance contracts, *e.g.*, loss ratio standards under 1993 LTC Model Act § 6E. IRC § 7702B(g)(2)(B)(ii) provides, however, that "any provision of the [1993 LTC model rules imposed as qualification requirements] shall be treated as including any other provision of such [1993 LTC model rules] necessary to implement the provision." *See also* IRC § 4980C(c)(1)(C).

[142] IRC § 7702B(g)(3).

[143] IRC § 7702B(g)(4).

ment which is more stringent than the analogous requirement imposed by section 4980C or section 7702B(g), then the tax law's consumer protection requirements are treated as having been satisfied if the more stringent state requirement is met.[144] Also, Treas. Reg. section 1.7702B-1(b) implements this rule by imposing the following standards:

> (1) *Contracts issued in a State that imposes more stringent requirements.* If a State imposes a requirement that is more stringent than the analogous requirement imposed by section 7702B(g) or 4980C, then ... compliance with the more stringent requirement of State law is considered compliance with the parallel requirement of section 7702B(g) or 4980C. The principles of [Treas. Reg. section 1.7702B-1(b)(3), set forth below] apply to any case in which a State imposes a requirement that is more stringent than the analogous requirement imposed by section 7702B(g) or 4980C ..., but in which there has been a failure to comply with that State requirement.
>
> (2) *Contracts issued in a State that has adopted the model provisions.* If a State imposes a requirement that is the same as the parallel requirement imposed by section 7702B(g) or 4980C, compliance with that requirement of State law is considered compliance with the parallel requirement of section 7702B(g) or 4980C, and failure to comply with that requirement of State law is considered failure to comply with the parallel requirement of section 7702B(g) or 4980C.
>
> (3) *Contracts issued in a State that has not adopted the model provisions or more stringent requirements.* If a State has not adopted the [1993 LTC Model Act], the [1993 LTC Model Regulation], or a requirement that is the same as or more stringent than the analogous requirement imposed by section 7702B(g) or 4980C, then the language, caption, format, and content requirements imposed by sections 7702B(g) and 4980C with respect to contracts, applications, outlines of coverage, policy summaries, and notices will be considered satisfied for a contract subject to the law of that State if the language, caption, format, and content are substantially similar to those required under the parallel provision of the [1993 LTC model rules]. Only nonsubstantive deviations are permitted in order for language, caption, format, and content to be considered substantially similar to the requirements of the [1993 LTC model rules].[145]

In ascertaining whether a state has adopted "a requirement that is the same as or more stringent" than that imposed under the 1993 LTC model rules, an initial question regards the scope of the term requirement. For example, 1993 LTC Model Regulation section 8 (titled Unintentional Lapse) includes requirements regarding both lapses in coverage and reinstatement. Should the requirement be interpreted as section 8 as a whole, as each subsection (i.e., section 8A and 8B), as any subpart (e.g., section 8A(1)) or as any separately identifiable requirement contained within the regulation (e.g., the requirement of section 8A(1) that the insurer notify the insured of the right to change the written designation of a person to receive notice of lapse no less often than once every two years)? No guidance addresses this question, but the last of these views seems most reasonable, as long as the principles of Treas. Reg. section 1.7702B-1(b) can be reasonably applied to a separately identifiable requirement without conflicting with or undermining any companion requirements. Thus, if a state were to adopt 1993 Model Regulation section 8 exactly as set forth in 1993 LTC Model Regulation except that the right to change written designation must be provided more frequently than every two years,[146] then Treas. Reg. section 1.7702B-1(b)(1) (regarding more stringent requirements) arguably would apply to the timing of notices for designating another to receive notice of lapse, while Treas. Reg. section 1.7702B-1(b)(2) (regarding adoption of the same requirement as is in the model rules) arguably would apply for purposes of the remainder of 1993 Model Regulation section 8.

Another question regards what is meant by a more stringent requirement. In many cases, this may be obvious, but in others it will be less clear. For example, if a state prefers a different approach to an issue that is the

---

[144] IRC § 4980C(f).

[145] 63 Fed. Reg. 68,186–87 (December 10, 1998). These rules apply to contracts issued after December 10, 1999.

[146] This example is for illustration purposes only; it is not a comment on whether states should make a modification to the LTC Model Regulation in this regard. LTC Model Reg. § 7A(1), as in effect in 2014, retains the two-year rule from the 1993 LTC Model Regulation. NATIONAL ASSOCIATION OF INSURANCE COMMISSIONERS, *Long-Term Care Insurance Model Regulation*, NAIC MODEL LAWS, REGULATIONS AND GUIDELINES, Vol. 4, Model 641 (4th Quarter 2014) (hereinafter 2014 LTC Model Regulation).

subject of a 1993 LTC model rule and adopts requirements wholly different from the 1993 LTC model rule for purposes of addressing the issue, should those state law requirements be considered more stringent? How should the stringency of a requirement be measured in this circumstance? Given that Congress authorized states to adopt more stringent requirements with respect to the consumer protection rules as reflected by the coordination rule of section 4980C(f) and the historic role of the states in the regulation of long-term care insurance, arguably the phrase more stringent as used in Treas. Reg. section 1.7702B-1(b) should be broadly construed to encompass different rule regimes that a state may impose. At the same time, since noncompliance with the tax consumer protection rules can result in disqualification of a contract or imposition of a penalty, it is necessary to examine state rules carefully in reaching a determination that a particular requirement is more stringent than a 1993 LTC model rule in circumstances where this is not readily apparent.

A further question asks what is necessary to satisfy a state law requirement for purposes of Treas. Reg. section 1.7702B-1(b). This question may arise, for example, where there is an ambiguity under state law or it otherwise is unclear how a particular state requirement should apply to a design feature of a contract or rider. Again, no guidance has been issued on this point, but it seems a contract form, and the insurer's practices with respect to that form, should be viewed as satisfying the state's requirements as long as the insurer would not face adverse consequences under state law as a result of such form and practices. State insurance department approval of a contract form and other materials in many cases is helpful in establishing that state requirements have been met. To resolve ambiguities that may apply under state law, other steps may be appropriate to avoid raising a question under Treas. Reg. section 1.7702B-1(b)(1) and (2) about whether the tax law's consumer protection rules have been met. In contrast, if the regime of Treas. Reg. 1.7702-1(b)(3) applies, i.e., where a state has not adopted the same or a more stringent requirement, then state law and interpretations do not control the manner in which the 1993 LTC model rules apply. While section 4980C(f) and the Treasury regulations make state law relevant to whether a consumer protection requirement of sections 4980C and 7702B(g) has been satisfied, authority to determine whether a requirement has been met rests with the Secretary of the Treasury (and thus with the IRS) rather than with state insurance departments.[147]

These regulations apply to all of the consumer protection rules that apply by cross-reference to the 1993 LTC model rules. A summary of these consumer protection rules is included in Appendix 7.1.

As noted above, two consumer protection qualification requirements are imposed without reference to the 1993 LTC model rules: one regarding disclosure of intent to be tax-qualified and another requiring a nonforfeiture benefit to be offered.

**Disclosure requirement: Intent to be QLTCI:** To qualify as QLTCI, a contract or rider must disclose in the contract or rider and in the outline of coverage that the contract or rider "is intended to be a qualified long-term care insurance contract under section 7702B(b)."[148]

**Nonforfeiture benefit offer requirement:** If a contract is a level premium contract, to qualify as QLTCI the insurer must offer the proposed policyholder (including any group policyholder) a nonforfeiture benefit in the event of default in the payment of any premiums that is appropriately captioned and constitutes either a shorted benefit period, reduced paid-up insurance, extended term insurance or other similar offerings approved by the appropriate state regulatory agency.[149] Under a shortened benefit period, the same benefits (amounts and frequency in effect at the time of lapse but not increased thereafter) are provided, but the lifetime maximum dollars or days of benefits are reduced.[150] Under reduced paid-up coverage, both the periodic (e.g., monthly) and lifetime maximum benefits are reduced, usually by the same proportion. And under extended term insurance, the periodic and lifetime maximums are not reduced, but coverage applies for a finite period. In each case, the amount of the benefit may be adjusted subsequent to being initially granted only as necessary to reflect changes in claims, persistency and interest as reflected in changes in rates for premium paying contracts approved by the appropriate state regulatory agency for the same contract form.[151] In addition, while the non-

---
[147] IRC § 7702B(g)(2)(B)(iii).
[148] IRC §§ 7702B(g)(3) and 4980C(d).
[149] IRC § 7702B(g)(4).
[150] *See, e.g.*, 2014 LTC Model Regulation, *supra* note 146, § 28E(2).
[151] IRC § 7702B(g)(4).

forfeiture benefit, if elected, must be "available in the event of a default in the payment of any premiums," the HIPAA Blue Book clarifies that the requirement that insurers offer policyholders a nonforfeiture benefit "does not preclude the imposition of a reasonable delay period."[152] Unlike most of the consumer protection qualification requirements, the nonforfeiture benefit offer requirement is not imposed by cross-reference to the 1993 LTC model rules, even though such rules included requirements relating to nonforfeiture benefits.[153]

One question particularly pertinent to ADB riders regards the meaning of a "level premium contract," since it is only such contracts or riders that must offer a nonforfeiture benefit at the issuance of the contracts or riders. Resolution of this question for any particular rider design likely should take into account the general purpose of nonforfeiture benefits, i.e., to provide a policyholder with a portion of the value associated with reserves that have built up to fund future years' coverage of chronic illness due to prior years' premiums that exceeded the amounts needed to fund prior year's insurance coverage. On this basis, a single premium contract or rider would qualify as a "level premium contract." This being said, the mere presence of such a reserve accumulation arguably should not be dispositive of the question, especially since the premium or charge structure for riders to life insurance contracts may be facially nonlevel and the pattern of reserve accumulation may differ significantly from that typical of level premium, stand-alone long-term care insurance contracts. For example, long-term care insurance charges may be a function of current cost of insurance charges assessed for the related life insurance contract, and thus may increase per dollar of NAR as the insured's age advances but may decrease in absolute dollar terms if the NAR under the life insurance contract is declining. Here, any reserve build-up for the risk that the life insurance contract's NAR might be paid in future years, but earlier than death, due to chronic illness may be more a byproduct of simplifying assumptions in pricing. This raises a further question about how one should assess whether there are level premiums in the context of an ADB rider. For example, if a flat annual charge is assessed but it is expected that NAR will decline in amount, does this mean that there actually is an increasing rather than level premium for the rider, since the cost per dollar of NAR would be increasing? While not controlling, it is worth noting that the current versions of the LTC model rules exempt accelerated death benefits from the nonforfeiture benefit requirements.[154] For tax purposes, that exemption is unavailable; however, it may be that most long-term care insurance riders providing ADBs should not be considered to impose level premiums, in which case they would enjoy a similar exemption from having to offer nonforfeiture benefits under the QLTCI definition.

In addition to riders providing ADBs, life insurance contracts in some cases provide nonacceleration long-term care insurance benefits. For example, under an **extension rider**, long-term care insurance benefits continue after the death benefit has been fully accelerated. Such nonacceleration riders resemble stand-alone long-term care insurance, in that their pricing is not predicated upon the time value of money cost of paying the death benefit prior to the insured's death. Cost efficiencies are realized, however, due to the fact that ADBs usually must be utilized first in order for nonacceleration benefits to be payable and insureds may not survive through the close of the acceleration period. Given these attributes, extension riders typically provide for charges or premiums that are level annual or other periodic amounts, and thus such riders appear to be subject to the nonforfeiture benefit offer requirements of section 7702B(g)(4). In practice, however, application of the nonforfeiture benefit offer requirement in this context can be cumbersome. Since the extension rider is a rider to a life insurance contract that also includes an ADB rider, the nonforfeiture benefit for the extension rider usually will go into effect at a time when both the life insurance contract and that ADB rider lapse without value. Thus, the delay in benefits for an extension rider that otherwise would have been provided by the ADB rider must be accounted for through other means if the life insurance contract and ADB rider lapse without value, such as through a contractual delay mechanism that operates akin to a waiting period.

---

[152] HIPAA Blue Book, *supra* note 102, at 343.
[153] Later in 1993, the LTC model rules were amended to include a nonforfeiture benefit requirement. That rule mandated the inclusion of a nonforfeiture benefit in a contract. In prior proceedings of the NAIC, there had been considerable debate about whether nonforfeiture benefits should be mandatory or whether it should be sufficient to offer a nonforfeiture benefit. In enacting the nonforfeiture benefit requirement of IRC § 7702B(g)(4) in 1996, Congress decided that it was only necessary that an offer of a nonforfeiture benefit be made in order for a contract to qualify as QLTCI, and this explains why the requirement was not imposed by cross-reference to the LTC model rules.
[154] 2014 LTC Model Regulation, *supra* note 146, § 28A, Nonforfeiture Benefit Requirement, states that the section "does not apply to life insurance policies and riders containing accelerated long-term care benefits."

It also may be the case that the policyholder terminated his or her life insurance coverage not through failure to pay life insurance premiums but rather through a surrender of the life insurance contract. In this circumstance, should the lapse of long-term care insurance coverage under an extension rider be treated as being due to "a default in the payment of any premiums" so that a nonforfeiture benefit must be provided (if selected at issue)? Here, the policyholder's voluntary action in obtaining the life insurance contract's cash nonforfeiture value is the proximate cause of the extension rider's lapse; at the same time, the proceeds paid on surrender to that policyholder would not have included any value in respect of the reserves for the level premium extension rider. A further challenge in this circumstance is that the policyholder may have desired to terminate his or her relationship with the insurer (perhaps even by entering into a section 1035 exchange), but the nonforfeiture benefit requirements may operate so that it is necessary to maintain a relatively small nonforfeiture benefit with the insurer.

This raises the further question whether it is permissible to offer a cash nonforfeiture benefit under a level premium QLTCI rider instead of one of the three specifically identified types of nonforfeiture benefits. As previously noted, the requirement of section 7702B(g)(4) may be satisfied by offering "other similar offerings approved by the appropriate State regulatory agency." On the one hand, the reference to "similar offerings" may imply that some form of in-kind insurance benefit, rather than cash, must be offered as the nonforfeiture option. On the other hand, given the above considerations and the fact that life insurance contracts typically provide a cash nonforfeiture benefit, there seems little reason not to permit a cash nonforfeiture benefit, as long as use of such an option is approved by the relevant state insurance department.

Yet another challenge associated with QLTCI nonforfeiture benefits relates to reinstatement rights. In particular, the reinstatement requirements applicable to the base life insurance contract may differ from those applicable to the QLTCI rider. In designing products, careful consideration should be given to the interaction of these reinstatement rights together with the nonforfeiture benefits provided under the contract and rider.

Beyond the two consumer protection qualification requirements detailed above, section 4980C imposes certain requirements other than by cross-reference to the 1993 LTC model rules. One such requirement is that, if an application for QLTCI is approved, the insurer must deliver to the applicant or policyholder the contract of insurance not later than 30 days after the date of the approval.[155] Another requirement is that, if a claim under a QLTCI contract is denied, the insurer must within 60 days of the date of a written request by the policyholder provide a written explanation of the reasons for the denial and make available all information directly relating to the denial.[156] Finally, the issuer of a long-term care insurance contract must disclose in such contract and in the outline of coverage that the contract is intended to be QLTCI.[157]

## Section 101(g) Chronic Illness Riders

The discussion earlier in this chapter described the different federal tax and state regulatory regimes for chronic illness benefits (including ADBs) provided in connection with a life insurance contract. As discussed, for products designed to receive beneficial tax treatment under section 101(g), chronic illness benefits could reimburse specific expenses for QLTC services or provide per diem benefits on a lump-sum or periodic (e.g., monthly) basis. Further, section 101(g) could apply to riders regulated under state law as long-term care insurance or under state laws modeled after the NAIC's *Accelerated Benefits Model Regulation*. Given that the definition of "chronically ill individual" establishes the minimum standard of impairment for receipt of benefits under both QLTCI riders and section 101(g) riders, it is not surprising that there otherwise is substantial overlap in the requirements of sections 7702B and 101(g). Indeed, as noted earlier, in many instances, a rider designed to qualify as QLTCI may by happenstance also comply with section 101(g).

Since chronic illness ADBs principally involve mortality risks and are supplemental to a life insurance contract's primary benefits, it is understandable that Congress adopted a more simplified regime for chronic illness ADBs than that applicable to QLTCI. Thus, while an insurer can choose to design an ADB rider that constitutes QLTCI, a more efficient alternative is available under section 101(g), especially if the design provides per diem

---
[155] IRC § 4980C(c)(2).
[156] IRC § 4980C(c)(3).
[157] IRC § 4980C(d).

benefits and is regulated by state laws modeled after the ABMR. In the discussion below, we describe and offer commentary on the rules applicable to section 101(g) riders.[158]

## *Tax Treatment of Chronic Illness Benefits from Section 101(g) Riders*

Subject to certain limitations and restrictions, section 101(g)(1)(B) provides that "any amount received under a life insurance contract on the life of an insured who is a chronically ill individual" shall be treated for purposes of section 101 as an amount paid by reason of the death of the insured. In other words, such payments are treated as death benefits for purposes of section 101. Section 101(a), in turn, generally provides that "gross income does not include amounts received (whether in a single sum or otherwise) under a life insurance contract, if such amounts are paid by reason of the death of the insured." As a result of this treatment, payments received due to an insured's chronic illness are treated as death benefits excludable from the income of the policyholder, as long as the limitations and restrictions of section 101 are met. Thus, unlike chronic illness benefits governed by section 7702B—which receive A&H insurance tax treatment—chronic illness benefits governed by section 101(g) receive life insurance death benefit treatment.[159]

Where a section 101(g) rider reimburses expenses for QLTC services, those benefits usually will be fully excludable from income. Also, if benefits are provided on a non-reimbursement (i.e., per diem) basis, they usually are excludable from income to the extent of the per diem limitation. As discussed in detail earlier in this chapter, the per diem limitation applies to all chronic illness benefits received on a per diem basis—both those received under QLTCI contracts and riders and those received from section 101(g) riders.

## *Requirements for Chronic Illness Benefits Under Section 101(g)*

As noted above, section 101(g) generally provides beneficial tax treatment for "any amount received under a life insurance contract on the life of an insured who is a chronically ill individual." For this purpose, the term "chronically ill individual" has the meaning given to this term under section 7702B(c)(2),[160] which was discussed in detail above in connection with the definition of a QLTCI contract. In the usual case, section 101(g) riders provide ADBs, although the statute does not expressly limit its application to such payments.[161] Section 101(g)(3) also imposes the additional requirements discussed below that must be satisfied for section 101(g) to apply to chronic illness benefits.

### Costs Incurred by the Payee for QLTC Services

The treatment of a chronic illness benefit payment as a death benefit will not apply to any payment received for any period unless the "payment is for costs incurred by the payee (not compensated for by insurance or otherwise) for qualified long-term care services provided for the insured for such period."[162] This statement addresses a rider design under which specific expenses for QLTC services are reimbursed. (The exception for per diem benefits is discussed below.) Several aspects of this requirement are noteworthy. First, unlike QLTCI riders which can *only* cover QLTC services, section 101(g) appears to apply *to the extent* benefit payments satisfy the criteria of this section.[163] Second, since QLTC services are defined as certain services required by a chronically ill individual and "provided pursuant to a plan of care prescribed by a licensed health care practitioner," it is necessary that a reimbursement-design section 101(g) rider require a plan of care as a condition for the payment of benefits. (The meaning of a plan of care also was discussed above in connection with the

---

[158] This discussion focuses on IRC § 101(g) chronic illness riders. This Code provision also includes rules for addressing viatical settlement payments made on the life of a chronically ill insured. Those rules are beyond the scope of this chapter.
[159] As discussed earlier in this chapter, terminal illness benefits receive similar life insurance tax treatment under IRC § 101(g). Because chronic and terminal illness benefits are treated under IRC § 101(g) as life insurance death benefits, arguably this implies that such riders are viewed as part and parcel of the life insurance contract and not as "additional benefits" within the meaning of IRC § 7702(f)(5)(C). In any event, IRC § 101(g) riders would not be QABs.
[160] IRC § 101(g)(4)(B). A chronically ill individual does not, however, include a terminally ill individual. *Id.*
[161] Such a limitation may effectively apply, however, due to the consumer protection requirements applicable to a rider.
[162] IRC § 101(g)(3)(A)(i). For this purpose, QLTC services are defined by reference to IRC § 7702B(c)(1), which was discussed in detail above in connection with the definition of a QLTCI contract. IRC § 101(g)(4)(C).
[163] Thus, reimbursement of non-QLTC services will not "disqualify" an IRC § 101(g) rider but such reimbursement may be taxable, possibly as a distribution from the life insurance contract. The considerations discussed above in connection with QLTCI riders that reimburse expenses for QLTC services also generally would be applicable for reimbursement-design IRC § 101(g) riders. For example, if a service is rendered to an insured prior to the effective date of the insured's certification as a chronically ill individual, it appears that such service would not be a QLTC service, even if paid by the insured after the effective date of such certification. Where a rider reimburses non-QLTC services, it also would be important to consider whether doing so raises questions under IRC §§ 7702 and 72, *e.g.*, with respect to the amount of the contract's cash value.

definition of a QLTCI contract.) Third, limiting beneficial tax treatment to situations where the "payment is for costs incurred by the payee" appears to mean that the payee must have borne the entire cost of the expense being reimbursed. The exact application of this restriction seems unclear, however, especially in circumstances where costs may be borne by different family members. For example, if one of three children of a chronically ill insured is the policyholder of a life insurance contract that includes a reimbursement-design section 101(g) rider, the ongoing costs of long-term care, e.g., home health care, may be paid for in part by all three children as well as the insured, and those individuals might share the rider benefits for those costs among themselves as they best see fit. In this circumstance, there seems little tax policy reason for limiting the exclusion from income to just the policyholder's share of the costs, especially since the policyholder may be directing some of those proceeds to other family members, the burdens associated with care of a chronically ill relative cannot be measured purely on the basis of financial costs, and there may be implicit gifts among the parties. Given the costs-incurred-by-the-payee requirement, however, policyholders would be well advised to structure their arrangements to the extent possible so as to avoid raising questions in this regard.[164]

**Terms of the Contract Requirements**

Another prerequisite to beneficial tax treatment for chronic illness benefits under a section 101(g) rider is imposed by section 101(g)(3)(A)(ii), which requires that "the terms of the contract giving rise to [a chronic illness benefit payment must] satisfy—(I) the requirements of section 7702B(b)(1)(B) [relating to coordination with Medicare], and (II) the requirements (if any) applicable under section 101(g)(3)(B) [relating to consumer protections]." This rule appears to confirm the need for contractual terms providing for a chronic illness insurance benefit. Thus, unlike the case with terminal illness benefits, it appears that a contract or rider must provide for benefits upon an insured's chronic illness for section 101(g) to apply to those amounts. The first of these terms of the contract requirements—the need to satisfy the Medicare coordination rule of section 7702B(b)(1)(B)—is the same as that applicable to QLTCI contracts, discussed above. In brief, under this rule, a contract cannot "pay or reimburse expenses incurred for services or items to the extent that such expenses are reimbursable under title XVIII of the Social Security Act [i.e., Medicare] or would be so reimbursable but for the application of a deductible or coinsurance amount."[165] The second of these rules—relating to consumer protections—is discussed next, and this is followed by a discussion of special rules for the application of these requirements where a rider provides per diem benefits.

**Consumer Protection Requirements for Section 101(g) Riders**

Section 101(g)(3)(B) imposes the following consumer protection requirements that must be satisfied by the terms of a contract:

    i) those requirements of section 7702B(g) and section 4980C which the [Secretary of the Treasury] specifies as applying to such a purchase, assignment, or other arrangement,

    ii) standards adopted by the [NAIC] which specifically apply to chronically ill individuals (and, if such standards are adopted, the analogous requirements specified under clause (i) shall cease to apply), and

    iii) standards adopted by the State in which the policyholder resides (and if such standards are adopted, the analogous requirements specified under clause (i) and (subject to section 4980C(f) [relating to state standards that are more stringent than the consumer protection standards applicable under sections 4980C and 7702B(g)]) standards under clause (ii), shall cease to apply).

With respect to the first of these requirements, the Treasury Department has not as of the date of this writing (2015) specified any of the consumer protection requirements applicable to QLTCI as being applicable to section 101(g) chronic illness riders, and thus currently no such requirements apply to such riders. Also, a similar

---

[164] A more problematic situation may be where a life insurance contract is owned by a trust (perhaps with an estate planning purpose) and no portion of trust assets, including IRC § 101(g) rider benefits, may be used to cover costs for QLTC services rendered to the insured. Here, it may be that the costs-incurred-by-the-payee requirement would not be satisfied at all. Prospective purchasers of chronic illness riders (whether designed to comply as QLTCI or under IRC § 101(g)) also should consider whether such riders are suitable purchases if a life insurance contract is purchased for estate tax-planning purposes.

[165] IRC § 7702B(b)(1)(B). IRC § 101(g)(3)(A) also provides that, for this purpose, the rule of IRC § 7702B(b)(2)(B) will apply, so that it is permissible to reimburse amounts that Medicare covers only as a secondary payor.

circumstance arguably applies with respect to the second rule, at least where rider coverage is of a type that would be regulated by the NAIC's ABMR. In this regard, the ABMR does not specifically reference "chronically ill individual" or "chronic illness," and thus the ABMR appears not to include any requirement that would constitute a federal tax requirement under section 101(g)(3)(B)(ii).

If section 101(g)(3)(B)(ii) were interpreted so that the ABMR must be met, it would be necessary to reconcile its rules with those otherwise applicable under section 101(g).[166] For example, ABMR section 2B defines qualifying events for the triggering of benefits, but an insured's chronic illness is not specifically listed. The closest such event is probably the one described by ABMR section 2B(3): "A condition that usually requires continuous confinement in an eligible institution as defined in the contract if the insured is expected to remain there for the rest of his or her life." To fall within the ambit of state laws modeled after the ABMR, insurers often modify this provision to include a requirement that the insured be chronically ill in addition to being confined. Such a practice is consistent with the requirements of section 101(g), particularly since an insured's status as a chronically ill individual is clearly a prerequisite to beneficial tax treatment. Also, as noted above, from a federal tax standpoint, a rider's benefit trigger is not considered to be a consumer protection requirement in the first instance, but rather functions to protect federal tax revenues. ABMR section 2B(5) also allows for other qualifying events that the state insurance commissioner approves for a particular filing. Thus, it also should be acceptable for a section 101(g) rider simply to specify a benefit trigger that requires an insured to be a chronically ill individual as this term is defined in section 7702B(c)(2).

Another step often taken by insurers to reconcile the requirements of the ABMR with those of section 101(g) is to limit benefits to those permitted by the per diem limitation, since otherwise any higher benefits would be taxable. Thus, while ABMR section 5A requires a lump-sum benefit to be offered, e.g., as an alternative to monthly per diem benefits, it is reasonable to recognize that an insured's status as a chronically ill individual applies only for a 12-month period and to limit any such lump-sum offer to the per diem limitation that would apply for such 12-month period, i.e., the lump-sum benefit would be payable in respect of the 12-month period beginning on the effective date of an insured's certification as a chronically ill individual.

The final consumer protection rule—set forth in section 101(g)(3)(B)(iii)—requires compliance with standards of state law. Insurers will, of course, want to ensure compliance with those standards apart from tax considerations. One noteworthy aspect of the rule is that compliance with a state standard eliminates or modifies the requirements of any analogous NAIC requirement under section 101(g)(3)(B)(ii). Thus, for example, if a state required an insured to be a chronically ill individual and be confined in an eligible facility or at home to receive benefits,[167] that should be consistent with the ABMR, either under the catch-all rule of ABMR section 2B(5) or by reason of the rule in section 101(g)(3)(B)(iii) that places precedence on state requirements over those of applicable NAIC model rules.

**Special Rule for Per Diem Benefits**
Similar to section 7702B, section 101(g) includes a special rule that permits chronic illness benefit payments to be provided on a per diem basis, even though this form of benefit would otherwise be inconsistent with certain requirements of the statute. Under this special rule, a benefit payment will not fail to be described in section 101(g)(3)(A) "by reason of being made on a per diem or other periodic basis without regard to the expenses incurred during the period to which the payment relates."[168] Due to this rule, it appears that a rider providing only per diem benefits need not coordinate with Medicare. The interaction of this rule with other requirements of section 101(g)(3)(A) is less clear, however. For example, while it is implicit that a rider providing per diem benefits would not require receipts to validate expenses for QLTC services which had been incurred, it is unclear whether the special rule for per diem benefits supplants other aspects of the requirement under section 101(g)(3)(A)(i) that benefits be "for costs incurred by the payee ... for [QLTC] services provided for

---

[166] Under this interpretation of IRC § 101(g)(3)(B)(ii), the NAIC standards arguably would be the current rules (rather than the 1993 rules) governing the insurance coverage of chronic illness in question.
[167] *See, e.g.*, 11 NYCRR 41.2(a)(3) (defining accelerated death benefit under New York law in part as "proceeds payable in part or in full under a life insurance policy to a policyowner or certificateholder during the lifetime of the insured ... upon certification by a licensed health care practitioner of any condition which requires continuous care for the remainder of the insured's life in an eligible facility or at home when the insured is chronically ill, provided the accelerated payments qualify under section 101(g)(3) of the Internal Revenue Code and all other applicable sections of federal law in order to maintain favorable tax treatment").
[168] IRC § 101(g)(3)(C).

the insured…." For example, since QLTC services are ones provided pursuant to a plan of care prescribed by a LHCP, it may be that a plan of care must be in place for beneficial tax treatment to apply. Further, since section 101(g)(3)(A)(i) does not appear to impose a terms-of-the-contract rule, it may be acceptable for a plan of care merely to be in place for the policyholder to receive beneficial tax treatment, although this is not clear. As noted earlier, as a practical matter it usually will be the case that a chronically ill individual will in fact have been prescribed QLTC services by a LHCP due to the nature of his or her condition.

**Rule for Business-Related Coverage and Other Limitations on Beneficial Tax Treatment**
Section 101(g)(5) provides that section 101(g) does not apply "in the case of any amount paid to any taxpayer other than the insured if such taxpayer has an insurable interest with respect to the life of the insured by reason of the insured being a director, officer, or employee of the taxpayer or by reason of the insured being financially interested in any trade or business carried on by the taxpayer." Other provisions in the Code that otherwise limit or restrict beneficial tax treatment of life insurance death benefits also may cause section 101(g) rider benefits to be taxable. For example, where the "transfer for value" rules apply, any limitation those rules would impose on the excludability of an actual death benefit also would apply in the case of a section 101(g) benefit.[169]

**Other Questions**
Little guidance has been issued by the IRS regarding the application of section 101(g), and in some respects the law is unclear. For example, the exclusion provided by section 101(g) applies in respect of a person who receives a payment, and this would typically be the policyholder, i.e., the person entitled to exercise ownership rights under a contract. However, the statute does not appear to limit the person(s) who can be named to receive ADBs. Section 101(g) also does not specifically speak to the manner in which the statute applies in the context of joint and survivor life insurance contracts. Seemingly there is flexibility to provide ADBs upon the chronic or terminal illness of either of the insureds, even where the underlying coverage is on a joint and last-survivor basis.

## *Comparison of QLTCI Riders with Section 101(g) Riders That Are Not QLTCI*
As the discussion in this chapter shows, there is considerable overlap between the chronic illness rules of section 7702B and those of section 101(g), and as noted, in many instances a QLTCI rider may by happenstance also comply with section 101(g). A number of differences between the provisions typically affect design choices, however. One of the most significant considerations is the state regulatory regime that will apply to a rider. QLTCI riders will constitute long-term care insurance under state law and thus will be subject to the substantial regulatory regimes that apply under state law for this type of insurance. Given the supplemental nature of chronic illness ADBs, many insurers may opt for more simplified state law regimes based on the ABMR. This design consideration also is pertinent to the form of benefit payment. For example, the ABMR applies only to non-reimbursement (i.e., per diem) benefits whereas the long-term care insurance regimes apply both to reimbursement and per diem benefit structures. Also, the ABMR expressly authorizes three alternative manners for funding ADBs, i.e., use of express charges or premiums, an actuarial discount or the lien method where there is an offset to death benefits and cash values.[170]

Other differences relate to the somewhat different requirements of section 7702B and 101(g). For example, in the case of section 101(g) riders that do not provide long-term care insurance, no limitations are directly or indirectly imposed on cash values or dividends, since any such values are viewed as provided by the related life insurance contract.[171] Also, if an insurer wanted to issue a participating whole life insurance contract with a participating nonqualified long-term care insurance rider that pays cash dividends, the product could be designed to meet the requirements of section 101(g) but could not readily qualify as QLTCI. In the case of long-term care insurance riders (including nonqualified riders), the separate contract rule of section 7702B(e)(1) treats such riders as separate contracts from the related life insurance contract so that any cash values provided

---
[169] *See* IRC § 101(a)(2). Other examples include where insurable interest requirements were not met when a contract was issued and where a life insurance contract fails to comply with IRC § 7702.
[170] *See* ABMR § 10A.
[171] For such an IRC § 101(g) rider, it would be necessary to take into account any such cash value for purposes of applying IRC § 7702.

by the riders would not be considered part of the life insurance contract's CSV.[172] Also, section 101(g) does not require any offer of a nonforfeiture benefit. On the other hand, beneficial tax treatment for QLTCI riders is not limited by any costs-incurred-by-the-payee requirement, nor does section 7702B impose any restrictions for business-related coverage. In addition, the consumer protection regimes applicable as tax requirements differ between section 7702B and 101(g). It also is clear that charges assessed against a life insurance contract to fund a QLTCI rider would not be treated as taxable distributions by reason of section 72(e)(11); similar treatment arguably applies for charges that fund a section 101(g) rider which does not constitute long-term care insurance (since such riders arguably are integral parts of the life insurance contract and not additional benefits, as discussed above), but no guidance has been issued to confirm this treatment. A comparison of QLTCI riders and section 101(g) riders is set forth in Table 7.2.

| Table 7.2. Comparison of QLTCI riders and section 101(g) riders | | |
|---|---|---|
| | **Section 7702B: QLTCI contracts** | **Section 101(g) Chronic Illness Riders** |
| What trigger must be met for insurance benefits to be payable? | The insured must be chronically ill. | Same. |
| How is the benefit regulated under state law? | As long-term care insurance. | Either under the ABMR or as long-term care insurance. |
| Can the benefit be designed to reimburse expenses for QLTC services or provide per diem benefits? | Either is permissible. | If the product is long-term care insurance, then either is permissible. If the product is based on the ABMR, state law usually permits only per diem benefits. |
| Can expenses other than for QLTC services be reimbursed? | No. | For a reimbursement design, beneficial tax treatment applies only to the extent reimbursements are of QLTC services. If other costs are reimbursable, consideration would need to be given to the nature of those benefits. |
| Must the payee bear costs for QLTC services? | A QLTCI rider can reimburse QLTC service costs or provide per diem benefits without regard to whether the payee bears such costs. | For a reimbursement design, beneficial tax treatment may be limited to circumstances where the payee bears costs for QLTC services. For a per diem design, the payee also may need to bear some costs for QLTC services. |
| Are there restrictions on cash and loan values? | Apart from a return of premium benefit, QLTCI riders cannot have cash values or loan values. Also, any dividends must be used to reduce future QLTCI premiums or increase QLTCI benefits. | For a product based on the ABMR, any cash values would be part of the life insurance contract cash value. Also, for products based on the ABMR, dividends arising in respect of any cash or reserve value would be treated as a life insurance dividend and can be paid in cash. Further, the dividend restrictions applicable to QLTCI riders would not apply to a nonqualified LTC rider providing benefits under section 101(g). |

---

[172] The application of this treatment is most clear in the context of QLTCI riders since their cash values cannot exceed aggregate premiums and can only be provided on rider termination and IRC § 7702B(b)(2)(C) specifies the manner in which such ROP benefits would be taxed.

| Table 7.2. Continued | Section 7702B: QLTCI contracts | Section 101(g) Chronic Illness Riders |
|---|---|---|
| What is the treatment of return of premium benefits? | A ROP benefit can be provided on contract surrender or the insured's death. Such benefits generally are not part of the life insurance contract's cash value. | For a product based on the ABMR, any ROP benefit generally would be treated as part of the life insurance contract. |
| Must a nonforfeiture benefit be offered? | Yes, generally a shorted benefit period, reduced paid-up insurance or extended term insurance. | The tax law does not impose any requirement. |
| What other consumer protection rules apply as tax requirements? | The requirements include those applicable by cross-reference to the 1993 LTC model rules. | The consumer protection requirements for a section 101(g) rider generally include compliance with state law rules and certain other requirements applicable by cross-reference to NAIC rules. |
| Is beneficial tax treatment proscribed where a contract is purchased in a business context? | Generally no. | Yes, under section 101(g)(5). Also, the transfer for value rules of section 101(a)(2) may limit beneficial tax treatment. |
| What funding mechanisms are permitted? | QLTCI riders must be guaranteed renewable. Most commonly, funding is through imposition of one or more upfront charges assessed against a life contract's cash value or through directly paid premiums. Other mechanisms may be permissible. Charges do not give rise to income but do reduce investment in the contract. | Section 101(g) riders based on the ABMR can be funded through one or more upfront charges, through an actuarial discount or through use of the lien method. The tax treatment of charges for such riders is unclear. |
| Can benefits be provided as ADBs or as nonacceleration benefits? | Yes. | It is typical for section 101(g) chronic illness riders to provide benefits in the form of ADBs, and state law may require non-long-term care insurance benefits to take this form; however, this does not appear to be required by the statute. |

## Reporting Requirements for Chronic Illness Riders

A payor of chronic illness benefits must report those benefits on IRS Form 1099-LTC.[173] More specifically, the payor must file an information return with the IRS and provide a payee statement to the recipient using this form. This form is used to report both QLTCI contract and rider benefit payments and section 101(g) rider chronic illness and terminal illness benefit payments. The form requires identification of whether chronic illness benefits are provided on a per diem or reimbursement basis. Information (including taxpayer identification numbers) must be provided for both the policyholder and the insured. In optional boxes, the payor can identify whether benefits are provided on account of the insured's chronic illness or terminal illness and whether benefits are paid from QLTCI. It is unclear whether, or in what manner, a payor should report return of premium benefits from a QLTCI rider.

---

[173] These comments are based on the version of this form for the 2015 tax year.

As discussed earlier, under section 72(e)(11), charges assessed against the cash value of a life insurance contract to fund a QLTCI rider are excludable from income but reduce the investment in the contract for the life insurance contract.[174] Under section 6050U, insurers are required to tax report on Form 1099-R the amount of these charges that are excludable from income. For 2015, the instructions to Form 1099-R state that the amount of such charges should be identified in Box 1 (Gross Distribution), $0 should be entered in Box 2 (Taxable Amount), Code W should be used in Box 7 to identify the nature of these amounts, and the reduction in investment in the contract due to such charges should be identified in Box 8. This form must be filed with the IRS and provided to the payee. Penalties may apply for failures to comply with these information return and payee statement requirements.[175]

## Consequences of ADB Riders Under Sections 7702, 7702A and 72

When ADBs are paid, there typically is a reduction in a life insurance contract's death benefit and cash values, with cash values usually being reduced on a pro rata basis relative to the reduction in death benefit at the time of payment.[176] As discussed earlier in this book, sections 7702 and 7702A each include mechanisms for adjusting the definitional limitations of these statutes when there has been a change in benefits. The question therefore arises whether these rules should be applied in their normal fashion or whether some other methodology should apply in order to account for ADBs. In considering this point, it is necessary to evaluate the effect of an ADB on both elements of the definitional limitations—i.e., the limitation itself and the premiums or cash values measured against that limitation—as well as "next-day consequences," such as whether additional force-outs or adjustments will be required in ensuing years.

### *Section 7702: Accounting for ADB Riders*

As discussed earlier, if a QLTCI rider is funded with a charge assessed against the life insurance contract's cash value, those charges are treated as distributions from the contract that are not includible in income but which do reduce the investment in the contract, by reason of section 72(e)(11). Because rider charges are assessed against the life contract's cash value (that arose from prior premiums and enjoys inside buildup treatment), such charges are "prefunded" within the meaning of section 7702(f)(5)(C). Thus, the premiums that generated the cash value to fund such charges would count as premiums paid under section 7702(f)(1), and the charges subsequently imposed for the rider generally would reduce premiums paid under the life insurance contract (although not below zero) due to treatment of the charges as distributions. In contrast, in the case of a QLTCI rider to a whole life insurance contract that has its own stated premiums which never enter into the life insurance contract's cash value, the rider premiums are not prefunded and thus would not increase premiums paid.

Under section 7702, the key issues in accounting for ABDs principally relate to life insurance contracts designed to comply with the guideline premium limitation.[177] For such contracts, normally the adjustment rule of section 7702(f)(7)(A) would govern the treatment of contract changes that reduce the contract's death benefit, i.e., "proper adjustments in future determinations" are required, and premiums paid under section 7702(f)(1)(A) would need to be adjusted as well in applying the rules of this provision. The challenge, however, is that these rules were not designed with ADBs in mind. For example, the definition of premiums paid generally is reduced by "amounts (other than amounts includible in gross income) to which section 72(e) applies" and by certain force-out amounts.[178] However, the first category of amounts that reduce premiums paid—i.e., the section 72(e) amounts that are not income—seemingly would not apply since another provision of Subtitle A of the Code operates to exclude ADBs

---

[174] This rule also applies for charges that fund a QLTCI rider to a nonqualified annuity contract.
[175] *See* IRC §§ 6721, 6722 and 6724.
[176] An exception is where the lien method is used, since in this circumstance a contract's death benefit and cash values remain unchanged but are subject to an offset upon the insured's death or surrender. The use of such a mechanism is especially needed for whole life insurance contracts given the fixed nature of premiums and benefits under such contracts. Also, it is important to recognize that even for life insurance contracts which generally reduce cash and other values on a pro rata basis, the complexity of contract designs often will mean that some values will not be reduced precisely in a pro rata manner. For example, if a contract has multiple layers of death benefit with differing mortality guarantees with respect to each layer, an ADB rider might reduce each layer proportionately or it might apply an ordering rule.
[177] Where an ADB reduces a life insurance contract's death benefit and cash value on a pro rata basis, no issue usually is raised with respect to a contract's compliance with the CVAT.
[178] IRC § 7702(f)(1).

from income, namely either section 101(a) or section 104(a)(3).[179] This problem was indeed recognized by Congress in enacting sections 7702B and 101(g) by the following statement in the conference report for HIPAA:

> In addition, it is anticipated that Treasury regulations will provide for appropriate reduction in premiums paid (within the meaning of sec. 7702(f)(1)) to reflect the payment of benefits under the rider that reduce the cash surrender value of the life insurance contract. A similar rule should apply in the case of a contract governed by section 101(f) and in the case of the payments under a rider that are excludable under section 101(g) of the Code (as added by this bill).[180]

To date, no regulations or other guidance has been issued regarding the effect of ADBs on premiums paid. In the absence of guidance with respect to the definition of premiums paid and more generally regarding what constitutes a proper adjustment to guideline premiums when ADBs are paid, various practices have been adopted by insurers to account for chronic illness ADBs under the statute.[181] Two principal approaches (and likely a number of variations on them) have been used.

**Force-out approach:** As discussed earlier in this book, the legislative history of section 7702 prescribes the attained-age decrement method[182] as the adjustment methodology that normally should be applied upon a reduction in death benefits for a contract subject to the guideline premium test. Thus, applying this methodology to address a reduction in a contract's death benefit resulting from an ADB payment is well supported by existing law. Also, to provide for some corresponding reduction in premiums paid, this force-out approach utilizes the 60-day rule of section 7702(f)(1)(B), which provides that the definition of "premiums paid" for a contract year is reduced by "any portion of any premium paid during any contract year" if necessary to comply with the guideline premium limitation, but only if the forced-out premium is returned by the insurance company with interest within 60 days of the end of the contract year for which premiums paid is being measured. Under this approach, there would be no reduction in premiums paid unless a force-out is required as a result of the benefit reduction. As an example, assume that a contract prior to an ADB payment has a death benefit of $100,000, a guideline single premium of $10,000, a guideline level premium of $1,000, a sum of guideline level premiums of $30,000 (so that the guideline premium limitation is $30,000) and premiums paid of $28,000. An ADB that reduces the death benefit by $50,000 might reduce the sum of guideline level premiums to $26,500, which would necessitate a force-out of $1,500. Under this force-out approach, $1,500 of the ADB (or perhaps of the reduction in the life insurance contract's cash value resulting from the ADB) would be treated for purposes of section 7702(f)(1)[183] as a return of premiums that reduces premiums paid pursuant to the 60-day rule. Also, a portion of such ADB payment similarly would be viewed as returning interest (if any) on such excess premiums.[184]

Where this approach is used, the consequence will be that the guideline premium limitation and premiums paid will exactly equal one another immediately after payment of the ADB. Thus, while it is uncertain that this approach can be used, there should be little or no tax policy objection to it. One concern about this approach is that it may eliminate a policyholder's ability to continue funding a contract, which could be especially important if premiums are required or needed to keep the contract in force. Another concern is that it does not readily apply to force-outs which may be required in subsequent years. To illustrate, in the above example, there was a net decrement to the sum of guideline level premiums of $3,500 as a result of the initial ADB payment, and an additional consequence is that the sum of guideline level premiums generally will reduce by this amount

---

[179] See IRC § 72(e)(1)(A), describing the scope of IRC § 72(e).
[180] HIPAA Conference Report, *supra* note 16, at 299.
[181] See also Prop. Treas. Reg. § 1.7702-2(g) stating: "If a life insurance contract is not terminated upon the payment of a qualified accelerated death benefit or a [morbidity risk benefit described in Prop. Treas. Reg. § 1.7702-2(f)], any change in the benefits under (or in other terms of) the contract is a change not reflected in any previous determination or adjustment under section 7702 and is an adjustment event under section 7702(f)(7)." As noted earlier, these proposed regulations have not been finalized and are not currently effective. See Notice 93-37, *supra* note 35.
[182] This methodology is discussed in detail in Chapter 4.
[183] This treatment is at odds with the fact that the ADB, if paid from a QLTCI rider, is treated for all tax purposes as having been paid from the rider rather than from the life insurance contract. However, in light of the purpose of IRC § 7702 to permit appropriate (but not excessive) funding for a life insurance contract, some adjustment to premiums paid seems warranted. Note also that if an ADB otherwise reduces the investment in the contract as defined in IRC § 72(e)(6), some further reduction in premiums paid under IRC § 7702 (f)(1)(A) may be justified. See *infra* note 189 regarding IRS consideration of the issue in connection with long-term care insurance riders under annuity contracts.
[184] Since no excess premiums would arise until the ADB is paid and that ADB simultaneously is paid to the policyholder, there usually will be no interest that needs to be returned. This is akin to receipt of an actual excess premium that an insurer immediately returns to the policyholder.

in each ensuing year, e.g., from $26,500 to $23,000 in the year following initial ADB payment, or by an even greater amount if there is another reduction in death benefit due to an ADB payment. Of course, if the insured remains chronically ill and continues to receive ADBs, this approach usually will be able to address those force-outs as well as the further force-out required by the subsequent ADB payment.

**Partial extinguishment approach:** While the adjustment rule of section 7702(f)(7)(A) generally governs all changes to the terms or benefits of a contract, it is fair to characterize an ADB as a payment of an insurance benefit (i.e., as an A&H insurance benefit in the case of QLTCI ADBs or as a life insurance benefit in the case of section 101(g) ADBs) rather than as a reduction in benefits, especially where the payment reduces contract values on a pro rata basis. Reflecting this characterization, it arguably is appropriate to treat the life insurance contract as having been partially extinguished by the ADB. Stated differently, the life insurance contract arguably can be viewed as having been divided into two separate contracts immediately prior to the ADB payment, and then in turn, the ADB payment can be viewed as having extinguished one of those separate contracts in full. This treatment is little different than if a partial section 1035 transaction were entered into immediately prior to payment of the ADB that accomplished the same division of the life insurance contract. Also, other authorities of more general application arguably support this treatment.[185] To illustrate, the ADB in the above example reduced the $100,000 death benefit by 50 percent, and thus under this approach the guideline single premium, guideline level premium, sum of guideline level premiums and premiums paid each would also be reduced by 50 percent. One advantage of this approach is that an ADB should never, in and of itself, require any further force-out of premiums paid, either at the time the ADB is paid or in later years. Also, while no IRS guidance has authorized use of the partial extinguishment approach, there seems little or no tax policy reason why it shouldn't be available, at least where ADBs reduce values on a pro rata basis, since the same relative degree of investment orientation is maintained as existed immediately prior to the ADB payment.[186]

One variation on the above approaches would be to use a proportional adjustment methodology for guideline premiums—since arguably such an adjustment is "proper" in order to account for ADBs[187]—and then to apply the definition of "premiums paid" as described under the force-out approach. In the absence of guidance, insurers necessarily have had to adopt methodologies (either those described above or other methodologies) for the administration of their contracts. And given that ADBs predate the promulgation of proposed regulations in 1992 under section 7702 that in part addressed ADBs, these methodologies are now well ensconced in company administration systems. Thus, any IRS guidance on this subject that may be forthcoming should allow for flexibility, as long as the insurer consistently applies a reasonable methodology with respect to a contract. The onset of chronic illness is not a circumstance where policyholders have any incentive to increase the investment orientation of their contracts, and in the case of an ADB that proportionally reduces contract values, there is no reason an insured's chronic illness should give rise to any force-outs (beyond that which may be paid as part of the ADB) or for any adverse tax treatment to apply on account of the ADB (such as under the recapture rules of section 7702(f)(7)(B)–(E)).

In the case of whole life insurance contracts, it is more common for the lien method to be used to provide for ADBs, i.e., a lien, or offset, is established with respect to the death benefit and contract cash values. Under this method, the death benefit is not formally reduced, but a security interest applies and offsets future death benefit or surrender proceeds in reflection of the prior ADBs provided.[188]

---

[185] *See, e.g., United States v. Davis*, 370 U.S. 65 (1962) (wherein the Supreme Court concluded that the partition of property between two co-owners is a nontaxable event); PLRs 200651023 and 200652043 (both Sept. 21, 2006) (each addressing a division of a life insurance contract and the effect thereof under IRC §§ 7702 and 7702A and for certain other purposes). These rulings are noted in Chapter 5.

[186] The partial extinguishment approach effectively results in a proportional, rather than attained-age based, reduction in guideline premiums. While the attained-age adjustment method was adopted (as described in the legislative history of IRC § 7702(f)(7)(A)) to preclude a ratcheting abuse (i.e., where reductions in benefits would be accounted for through a proportional reduction in guideline premiums but the restoration of those benefits would be accounted for using an attained-age methodology), that concern does not apply in the case of ADBs that result from an insured's chronic illness.

[187] While the attained-age adjustment method is generally dictated by the legislative history of IRC § 7702(f)(7)(A), that legislative history is silent on the meaning of "proper adjustments" in the context of chronic or terminal illness ADBs. Thus, other methodologies arguably may provide for proper adjustments in these circumstances.

[188] As previously noted, the lien method is described in ABMR § 10A(3) as one of the three approaches that may be used for financing an ADB, the other two being use of upfront charge(s) or an actuarially determined discount assessed against the ADB proceeds. While IRC § 101(g) does not itself directly refer to the lien method, the ABMR predates the enactment of IRC § 101(g) and use of the lien method was common at the time of such enactment. Congress also emphasized the role of the NAIC's regulatory scheme for chronic illness ADBs through enactment of the special rule of IRC § 101(g)(3)(B)(ii), which authorizes rules specifically directed at chronic illness benefits.

## Section 7702A: Accounting for ADB Riders

The considerations under section 7702A for the treatment of ADBs are similar to those under section 7702, although the statutory rules for addressing contract changes differ. If an insurer adopts the partial extinguishment approach for applying section 7702, then for consistency and based on the same rationale, it also would be reasonable to apply that approach under section 7702A. Thus, for ADBs that reduce contract values on a pro rata basis relative to the reduction in death benefit, this approach would involve reducing the 7-pay premium, the sum of 7-pay premiums and "amount paid" under section 7702A(e)(1) on a proportional basis if the contract is still within a 7-pay testing period. Under this approach, the ADB would not, of itself, result in a reduction in benefits under section 7702A(c)(2) or a material change under section 7702A(c)(3).

If neither the partial extinguishment approach nor the lien method is used, then it would seem necessary to ascertain whether an ADB should be accounted for under the reduction-in-benefits rule or the material change rule. Use of the former rule would be reasonable in that the ADB does, in fact, result in a reduction in a contract's death benefit (where the lien method is not being utilized). Also, insurers may prefer this approach for contracts covering a single life since most ADBs likely arise at a time when a contract typically would not be within a 7-pay testing period. At the same time, the reduction-in-benefits rule generally serves to preclude abuse, and none is occasioned by the payment of ADBs upon an insured's chronic illness. Further, ADBs reasonably may be characterized as payments of benefits rather than reductions in benefits.[189] Given that benefits have, in fact, changed relative to those previously reflected in 7-pay premium calculations and under this view there has been no reduction in benefits within the meaning of the reduction-in-benefits rule, material change treatment of ADBs arguably is justified. Again, in the absence of guidance, other approaches may be reasonable, too. Similar uncertainty extends to application of the necessary premium test, but seemingly use of the partial extinguishment approach would involve pro rata reduction in a contract's lowest benefits (and guideline premiums and net single premiums based on such benefits), premiums and deemed cash value, and use of the reduction-in-benefits or material change rules would have consequences for the necessary premium test that follow those normally arising under such rules. Finally, regardless of the methodology applied for applying section 7702A, if an ADB causes a contract to become a MEC, there seems to be little or no tax policy reason for applying the two-year look-back rule of section 7702A(d) to recharacterize distributions and loans made within the prior two-year period as having been made from a MEC. IRS guidance to confirm this point would be appropriate.

## Section 72: Accounting for ADB Riders

As noted above, where a QLTCI rider is funded with a charge assessed against the life insurance contract's cash value, the rider is treated as a separate contract for tax purposes (i.e., it is a non-QAB), and by reason of section 72(e)(11), the charges are treated as distributions from the contract that are not includible in income but that do reduce the "investment in the contract." Prior to the assessment of the charge, the premiums paid for the contract, which created cash value that would be used to fund the charge, would have increased investment in the contract under section 72(e)(6).[190]

The proper treatment of an ADB payment is unclear for purposes of the definition of "investment in the contract" under section 72(c)(1) and (e)(6). In the case of a life insurance-QLTCI product, the QLTCI rider is treated as a separate contract for tax purposes, and thus an ADB arguably should be treated as paid from that QLTCI rider and not from the related life insurance contract, meaning there would be no reduction in investment in the contract. This treatment would be consistent with the legislative history of both HIPAA and the PPA describing the tax treatment of ADB payments, i.e., such payments are considered long-term care insurance benefits in their entirety regardless of the effect of those payments on the related life insurance or annuity contract's cash value and death benefit. At present, however, the law is unclear, and the IRS has indicated that

---

[189] The IRS could disagree with this characterization based, for example, on the treatment of QAB benefit payments as an adjustment event under IRC § 7702(f)(7)(A), *e.g.*, term insurance benefit payments upon the death of a family member.

[190] *See also* Notice 2011-68, *supra* note 84, stating that "the Treasury Department and the IRS believe that all premiums paid for a combination contract that is an annuity and also provides long-term care insurance are generally included in investment in the contract under IRC § 72 if (i) the premiums are credited to the contract's cash value (rather than directly to the long-term care insurance contract that is part of or a rider to the contract), and (ii) coverage under the long-term care insurance contract is paid for by charges against the cash value of the contract." The underlying rules for defining investment in the contract generally are the same for annuities and life insurance contracts.

guidance may be forthcoming on this question.[191] The treatment of section 101(g) rider ADBs not considered long-term care insurance—and thus not subject to the separate contract rule of section 7702B(e)—is even less clear. The question of the effect of chronic illness benefits upon a contract's investment in the contract often will not matter since life insurance death benefits paid upon the insured's death generally are excludable from income. In contrast, the issue has substantially greater significance in the context of annuity-QLTCI combination products since annuity death benefits are taxable to the extent of gain in a contract. (In the annuity case, if ADBs were to reduce the investment in the contract, there often would be a mere deferral of taxes rather than a permanent exclusion.)

## Grandfather Considerations

Long-term care insurance contracts and riders issued before January 1, 1997, generally are treated as QLTCI if they met the long-term care insurance requirements of the state in which the contract or rider was sitused at the time the contract was issued.[192] However, a material change to the terms or benefits of such a contract or rider on or after this date may cause the contract to be treated as newly issued, in which case it would constitute QLTCI only if it satisfied the qualification standards of section 7702B(b).[193] In addition to these grandfather rules that generally apply to long-term care insurance, two other rules address the effect of adding a chronic illness rider or provision to a life insurance contract. In particular, HIPAA section 321(f)(4) states, "For purposes of applying sections 101(f), 7702, and 7702A ... to any contract—(A) the issuance of a rider which is treated as [QLTCI], and (B) the addition of any provision required to conform any other long-term care rider to be so treated, shall not be treated as a modification or material change of such contract." Similarly, HIPAA section 322(b)(2) states, "For purposes of applying sections 101(f), 7702, and 7702A ... to any contract—(A) the issuance of a qualified accelerated death benefit rider (as defined in section 818(g) ...), and (B) the addition of any provision required to conform an accelerated death benefit rider to the requirements of such section 818(g), shall not be treated as a modification or material change of such contract." For this purpose, a qualified accelerated death benefit rider means "any rider on a life insurance contract if the only payments under the rider are payments meeting the requirements of section 101(g)."[194]

## Section 1035 Exchanges Involving ADB Riders

Section 1035 provides for the nonrecognition of gain or loss upon certain types of exchanges of insurance contracts, including the exchange of a life insurance contract for another life insurance contract and the exchange of a QLTCI contract for another QLTCI contract. Where a life insurance contract is exchanged for another life insurance contract, it is necessary that the insured under the contract given in the exchange be the same as the insured under the contract received in the exchange.[195] Also, the definition of the term "contract of life insurance" in section 1035(b)(3) provides the following special rule: "[A] contract shall not fail to be treated as a life insurance contract solely because a qualified long-term care insurance contract is a part of or a rider on such contract."

For many types of exchanges involving life insurance contracts, there would not seem to be a need for the above special rule. For example, if the original life insurance contract with a QLTCI rider (but no ROP benefit) is assigned to an insurance company in exchange for a new life insurance contract, no value would be derived by the insurance company from the original contract's QLTCI rider. Thus, when the insurance company immediately surrenders the assigned life insurance contract for its cash value (which will be applied as a premium under the new contract), no part of that cash value will relate to the QLTCI rider to the first contract. In other words, that QLTCI rider will expire without value upon such surrender, and for all practical purposes the trans-

---

[191] Department of the Treasury's 2014–2015 PRIORITY GUIDANCE PLAN, *supra* note 36, identifies the following project for which IRS guidance is expected: "Guidance on annuity contracts with a long-term care insurance rider under §§72 and 7702B."
[192] HIPAA § 321(f)(2).
[193] *See* Treas. Reg. § 1.7702B-2 for rules regarding the particular changes that will cause a contract or rider to be treated as newly issued and exceptions to such treatment. *See also* Notice 97-31, *supra* note 96.
[194] IRC § 818(g)(2). Payments meeting the requirements of IRC § 101(g) generally should include any ADB received due to the insured's chronic or terminal illness, but it is unclear whether a taxable payment (such as an amount in excess of the per diem limitation) is contemplated.
[195] Treas. Reg. § 1.1035-1. Upon an exchange of one annuity contract for another, the regulation provides that the obligee under the two contracts must be the same.

action is simply the exchange of one life insurance contract for another. Similarly, if a life insurance contract with no QLTCI rider is exchanged for a new life insurance contract that includes a QLTCI rider, and that rider in turn is funded through periodic charges assessed against the new contract's cash value, no part of the value of the first contract seemingly will have been exchanged for the QLTCI rider. Rather, that rider is funded through the subsequent charges which are independent of the exchange transaction.[196]

In contrast, if the original contract's QLTCI rider had included a ROP benefit, the above special rule provides tax-free treatment for the exchange, even though the value the insurance company receives in the exchange is partially attributable to the QLTCI rider. Similarly, if an existing life insurance contract with a cash value of $50,000 were exchanged for a whole life insurance contract and QLTCI rider that required single premiums of $40,000 and $10,000, respectively, the special rule again would operate so that the transaction would be treated for purposes of section 1035 as simply the exchange of a life insurance contract for another life insurance contract. No regulations have been issued under section 1035 to reflect the amendments made by the PPA, e.g., to address the "same-insured" and/or "same-obligee" requirements that may apply for life insurance and annuity contract exchanges which involve either stand-alone QLTCI or QLTCI riders. ◆

## Appendix 7.1. Consumer Protection Rules Imposed by Cross-Reference to 1993 LTC Model Rules

This appendix summarizes and offers comments on the key consumer protection rules of sections 4980C and 7702B(g) that are imposed by cross-reference to the 1993 LTC model rules. Again, references to model sections below are to the versions of the LTC Model Act and Regulation adopted as of January 1993 because sections 4980C and 7702B(g) generally reference these versions.[197]

### Summary of Consumer Protection Qualification Rules

The key consumer protection rules of section 7702B(g) that apply as qualification requirements and are imposed by cross-reference to the 1993 LTC model rules are as follows.

**Renewal, waiting periods and coverage of less than skilled care, 1993 LTC Model Act section 6B:** To qualify as QLTCI, a contract[198] must satisfy 1993 LTC Model Regulation section 7A (relating to guaranteed renewal and noncancellability) and the requirements of 1993 LTC Model Act section 6B "relating to such section 7A."[199] Section 6B(1) of the 1993 LTC Model Act prohibits the cancellation, nonrenewal or other termination of a contract on the grounds of age or the deterioration of the mental or physical health of the insured. Section 6B(2) of that act prohibits the establishment of a new waiting period if coverage is converted to or replaced by a new or other form within the same insurer, except with respect to increases in benefits. Section 6B(3) of the act prohibits the provision of coverage only for skilled nursing care and the provision of significantly more coverage for skilled care in a facility than coverage for lower levels of care. No IRS guidance addresses the scope of requirements of 1993 LTC Model Act section 6B that should be considered as "relating to such section 7A."

**Pre-existing condition limitations, 1993 LTC Model Act section 6C:**[200] This provision generally limits the ability of a contract to exclude coverage for a loss or confinement that is the result of a pre-existing condition. It prohibits use of a definition of pre-existing condition that is more restrictive than the following: "Preexisting condition means a condition for which medical advice or treatment was recommended by, or received from[,] a provider of health care services, within six (6) months preceding the effective date of coverage of an insured

---

[196] If a charge for the rider assessed on the first monthly deduction date coincides with the effective date of the exchange, it might be argued that part of the value of the prior life insurance contract has been exchanged for the QLTCI rider, i.e., to the extent of the amount of that charge. However, since in form the rider's funding is through assessment of a charge against the new contract's cash value, on these facts it seems that IRC § 72(e)(11) should govern the treatment of the charge rather than IRC § 1035. See to the same effect the analysis in PLR 200022003 (Dec. 9, 1999).

[197] IRC § 7702B(g)(2)(B)(i).

[198] The 1993 LTC model rules contain numerous special rules applicable to group coverage. This chapter generally does not discuss these rules in detail since they only infrequently arise in the context of life insurance-QLTCI combination products. It should be noted, however, that references to "contract" generally include certificates to group contracts. Also, the definition of QLTCI generally applies at the certificate level.

[199] IRC § 7702B(g)(2)(A)(i)(I).

[200] IRC § 7702B(g)(2)(A)(ii)(I) provides that a contract must satisfy 1993 LTC Model Act § 6C to qualify as QLTCI.

person." Also, a contract generally must not exclude coverage for a loss or confinement which is the result of a pre-existing condition unless such loss or confinement begins within six months following the effective date of coverage of an insured. Other restrictions on exclusions from coverage also apply.

**Prior hospitalization and institutionalization requirements, 1993 LTC Model Act section 6D:**[201] Under 1993 LTC Model Act section 6D(1), a contract must not condition eligibility for:

- any benefits on a prior hospitalization requirement,

- benefits provided in an institutional care setting on the receipt of a higher level of institutional care, or

- any benefits, other than waiver of premium, post-confinement, post-acute care or recuperative benefits, on a prior institutionalization requirement.

Section 6D(2) of the 1993 LTC Model Act requires that, if any contract contains limitations or conditions on post-confinement, post-acute care or post recuperative benefits, the contract must clearly label such limitations or conditions in a separate paragraph—"Limitations or Conditions on Eligibility for Benefits"—and include any required number of days of confinement. Section 6D(2) further requires that, if a contract conditions eligibility of noninstitutional benefits on the prior receipt of institutional care, the contract cannot require a prior institutional stay of more than 30 days.[202]

**Guaranteed renewability, 1993 LTC Model Regulation section 7A:**[203] This provision limits the use of the terms **guaranteed renewable** and **noncancellable**. In particular, the term "guaranteed renewable" may only be used when "the insured has the right to continue the long-term care insurance in force by the timely payment of premiums and when the insurer has no unilateral right to make any change in any provision of the policy or rider while the insurance is in force, and cannot decline to renew, except that rates may be revised by the insurer on a class basis."[204] Also, the term "noncancellable" may be used only when "the insured has the right to continue the long-term care insurance in force by the timely payment of premiums during which period the insurer has no right to unilaterally make any change in any provision of the insurance or in the premium rate."[205] QLTCI riders to life insurance contracts (especially universal life) often are funded through assessment of charges against the contracts' cash values. Similar to a universal life insurance contract's cost of insurance structure, these riders often specify a guaranteed charge structure but then lower, current charges may be assessed by the insurer in its discretion. Such structures generally are considered noncancellable, and thus also guaranteed renewable, in that the policyholder has a contractual guarantee to continue coverage at the guaranteed rates. The same treatment should extend to situations where guaranteed charges are ascertainable by reference to other contract provisions, such as the life insurance contract's guaranteed cost of insurance charges. (See also the discussion regarding 1993 LTC Model Regulation section 9A below, which requires contracts to include a renewability provision.)

Section 7A of the 1993 LTC Model Regulation speaks in terms of the right of the "insured" to continue coverage with timely payment of premiums. Of course, it is the policyholder of a contract who possess the legal entitlements and obligations under the contract, including the obligation to pay premiums. Use of the term "insured" appears to reflect the fact that the insured and policyholder of most individual long-term care insurance contracts historically have been a single individual, and thus there has been little need to distinguish between an insured and owner in contracts or in the regulatory structure applicable to contracts.

**Permitted limitations and exclusions, 1993 LTC Model Regulation section 7B:**[206] This provision prohibits limitations and exclusions from coverage by type of illness, treatment, medical condition or accident, except generally in the following cases:

---

[201] IRC § 7702B(g)(2)(A)(ii)(II) provides that a contract must satisfy 1993 LTC Model Act § 6D to qualify as QLTCI.
[202] A QLTCI contract also must meet 1993 LTC Model Act § 6D(3), which provides that no contract which provides benefits only following institutionalization shall condition such benefits upon admission to a facility for the same or related conditions within a period of less than 30 days after discharge from the institution. An editor's note in the NAIC's Model Regulation Service observes that 1993 LTC Model Act § 6D(3) does not reflect changes to the model act which prohibited a prior institutionalization requirement.
[203] IRC § 7702B(g)(2)(A)(i)(I) provides that a contract must satisfy 1993 LTC Model Reg. § 7A to qualify as QLTCI.
[204] 1993 LTC Model Reg. § 7A(2).
[205] 1993 LTC Model Reg. § 7A(3).
[206] IRC § 7702B(g)(2)(A)(i)(III) provides that a contract must satisfy 1993 LTC Model Reg. § 7C to qualify as QLTCI.

- Pre-existing conditions or diseases
- Mental or nervous disorders other than Alzheimer's disease
- Alcoholism and drug addiction
- Illness, treatment or medical condition arising out of war or act of war, participation in a felony, riot or insurrection, service in the armed forces or units auxiliary thereto, suicide, attempted suicide or self-inflicted injury, or aviation
- Treatment provided in a government facility, services for which benefits are available under Medicare or other government program (except Medicaid), and state or federal workers' compensation, employer's liability or occupational disease law, or any motor vehicle no-fault law
- Services provided by a member of the covered person's immediate family[207] and services for which no charge is normally made in the absence of insurance

Section 7B(6) of the 1993 LTC Model Regulation also clarifies that 1993 LTC Model Regulation section 7B is not intended to prohibit exclusions and limitations by type of provider or territorial limitations. There is uncertainty regarding the scope of exclusions from coverage that would be viewed as applying by type of illness, treatment, medical condition or accident.

**Extension of benefits, 1993 LTC Model Regulation section 7C:**[208] This provision requires that benefits be extended if the long-term care insurance would otherwise terminate for institutionalization if such institutionalization began while the insurance was in force and continues without interruption after termination. Such extension of benefits beyond the period the long-term care insurance was in force can be limited, however, to "the duration of the benefit period, if any, or to payment of the maximum benefits and may be subject to any policy waiting period, and all other applicable provisions of the policy." Section 7C of the 1993 LTC Model Regulation effectively operates as a required waiver of premium feature for institutionalization, subject to a contract's maximum benefits. The 1993 Model Regulation does not define institutionalization for this purpose. Seemingly, it should encompass nursing homes and assisted living facilities;[209] it should not encompass home care or adult day care. Whether other chronic illness benefits involve institutionalization, such as in a hospice context, likely depends on the nature of and conditions applicable to such benefits.

**Group policy requirements, 1993 LTC Model Regulation sections 7D and 7E:**[210] Under 1993 LTC Model Regulation section 7D, group long-term care insurance contracts must provide insureds with a basis for continuation or conversion of coverage when coverage would otherwise terminate. For this purpose, 1993 LTC Model Regulation section 7D(2)–(3) defines "a basis for continuation of coverage" and "a basis for conversion of coverage." Also, under 1993 LTC Model Regulation section 7E, if a group long-term care insurance contract is replaced by another group long-term care insurance contract issued to the same policyholder, the succeeding insurer must offer coverage to all persons covered under the previous group contract on its date of termination.

**Protection against unintentional lapse, 1993 LTC Model Regulation section 8:**[211] 1993 LTC Model Regulation section 8A(1) provides that a long-term care insurance contract may not be issued until the insurer has received from the applicant either a written designation of at least one person in addition to the applicant who

---

[207] The 1993 LTC model rules do not define immediate family for this purpose. BLACK'S LAW DICTIONARY (9th ed.) defines immediate family in part as a "person's parents, spouse, children, and siblings, as well as those of the person's spouse." In contrast, Dictionary.com defines immediate family as "one's parents, step-parents, siblings, spouse, children, step-children, foster children, in-laws, sibling in-laws, grandparents, great grandparents, step-great grandparents, grandchildren, aunts, uncles, nieces, and nephews." See http://dictionary.reference.com/browse/immediate+family (accessed December 2014). Given the exclusion's purpose of preventing fraud, there seems to be little or no public policy reason for adopting a restrictive meaning of the term.

[208] IRC § 7702B(g)(2)(A)(i)(II) provides that a contract must satisfy 1993 LTC Model Reg. § 7B to qualify as QLTCI.

[209] See Marc A. Cohen and Jessica Miller, *The Use of Nursing Home and Assisted Living Facilities Among Privately Insured and Non-Privately Insured Disabled Elders*, U.S. DEPARTMENT OF HEALTH AND HUMAN SERVICES REPORT (April 2000) (available at http://aspe.hhs.gov/daltcp/reports/2000/nhalfuse.pdf) (citations omitted), which describes nursing home and assisted living facility care as forms of institutionalization and observes that the term assisted living refers to care which "combines housing and services in a homelike environment that strives to maximize the individual functioning and autonomy of the frail elderly and other dependent populations."

[210] IRC § 7702B(g)(2)(A)(i)(IV) and (V) provide that a group contract must satisfy 1993 LTC Model Reg. §§ 7D and 7E to qualify as QLTCI.

[211] IRC § 7702B(g)(2)(A)(i)(VI) provides that a contract must satisfy 1993 LTC Model Reg. § 8 to qualify as QLTCI.

is to receive notice of lapse or termination of the contract for nonpayment of premiums or a written waiver of the right to so designate another person. Also, the insurer must notify the insured of the right to change this written designation no less than once every two years. In addition, 1993 LTC Model Regulation section 8A(3) provides that no individual long-term care insurance contract shall lapse or be terminated for nonpayment of premium unless the insurer has given notice to the insured and to those persons designated to receive notice at least 30 days before the effective date of the lapse or termination. Further, such notice cannot be given until 30 days after a premium is due and unpaid, and for this purpose notice is deemed to have been given as of five days after the date of mailing. In effect, there is a minimum 65-day grace period after a premium is due before a long-term care insurance contract may lapse or terminate due to nonpayment of premiums.

Under 1993 LTC Model Regulation section 8B, a long-term care insurance contract must include a provision that allows for reinstatement of coverage in the event of lapse if the insurer is provided proof of cognitive impairment or the loss of functional capacity.[212] This option for reinstatement must be available to the insured if requested within five months after termination and may allow for the collection of past due premiums, where appropriate. The standard of proof of cognitive impairment or loss of functional capacity must not be more stringent than the benefit eligibility criteria on cognitive impairment or the loss of functional capacity contained in the contract. Thus, the benefit trigger standards contained in the contract generally must be used for purposes of establishing the reinstatement right.

For QLTCI riders to life insurance contracts, there usually will be multiple sets of grace period and reinstatement rules with which to contend—those applicable to the long-term care insurance rider and those applicable to the life insurance contract. The rule for QLTCI riders should not be imposed indirectly to the life insurance contract if it is capable of applying solely to the rider. In some circumstances, however, it may be necessary for the overall contract to satisfy the most restrictive of the respective rules.

**Renewability and certain disclosures, 1993 LTC Model Regulation sections 9A–E:**[213] 1993 LTC Model Regulation section 9A provides that individual long-term care insurance contracts must contain a renewability provision and specifies that such provision must be appropriately captioned, must appear on the first page of the contract and must clearly state the duration, where limited, of renewability and the duration of the term of coverage for which the contract is issued and for which it may be renewed.[214] Section 9B of the 1993 LTC Model Regulation imposes various requirements with respect to riders and endorsements, including rules for post-issuance changes and disclosure requirements with respect to premiums required for riders. Sections 9C, 9D and 9E of the 1993 LTC Model Regulation require certain disclosure provisions to be included in a long-term care insurance contract, including provisions defining the terms "usual and customary" and "reasonable and customary" if used with respect to the description of benefits, and provisions, if applicable, regarding pre-existing condition limitations and limitations or conditions on eligibility for benefits.

**Prohibition on post-claims underwriting, 1993 LTC Model Regulation section 10:**[215] This provision imposes certain requirements relating to the application for a QLTCI contract (including requests for information designed to evaluate the insured's health), the insurer's practices in issuing such contracts and contract rescissions. For example, 1993 LTC Model Regulation section 10C(1) provides that the following language must be set out conspicuously and in close conjunction with the applicant's signature block on an application for a long-term care insurance contract: "Caution: If your answers on this application are incorrect or untrue, [company] has the right to deny benefits or rescind your policy." Also, 1993 LTC Model Regulation section 10C(2) requires the following language, or language substantially similar to the following, to be set out conspicuously on the long-term care insurance contract at the time of delivery: "Caution: The issuance of this long-term care

---

[212] While 1993 LTC Model Reg. § 8B does not speak to the identity of the individual who must be cognitively impaired or functionally incapacitated or to the timing of the measurement of such condition, the 2014 LTC Model Regulation, *supra* note 146, § 7B (which generally mirrors 1993 LTC Model Reg. § 8B) provides that the reinstatement right must be provided where "the policyholder or certificateholder was cognitively impaired or had a loss of functionally capacity before the grace period contained in the policy expired."
[213] IRC § 7702B(g)(2)(A)(i)(VII) provides that a contract must satisfy 1993 LTC Model Reg. § 9A–E to qualify as QLTCI.
[214] 1993 LTC Model Reg. § 9A clarifies that these requirements do not apply to policies which do not contain a renewability provision and under which the right to non-renew is reserved solely to the policyholder. A drafting note indicates this clarification is intended to apply to long-term care insurance that is part of or combined with life insurance contracts, since life insurance contracts "generally do not contain renewability provisions."
[215] IRC § 7702B(g)(2)(A)(i)(VIII) provides that a contract must satisfy 1993 LTC Model Reg. § 10 to qualify as QLTCI.

insurance [policy][certificate] is based upon your responses to the questions on your application. A copy of your [application][enrollment form] [is enclosed][was retained by you when you applied]. If your answers are incorrect or untrue, the company has the right to deny benefits or rescind your policy. The best time to clear up any questions is now, before a claim arises! If, for any reason, any of your answers are incorrect, contact the company at this address: [insert address]." Under 1993 LTC Model Regulation section 10C(3), certain special rules also apply where the applicant is 80 or older at issue. Also, 1993 LTC Model Regulation section 10E requires that every insurer or other entity selling or issuing long-term care insurance benefits must maintain a record of all contract or certificate rescissions, both state and countrywide, except those voluntarily effectuated by the insured, and must annually furnish this information to the insurance commissioner in the format prescribed by the NAIC in Appendix A to the 1993 LTC Model Regulation.[216]

**Home and community care coverage, 1993 LTC Model Regulation section 11:**[217] This provision specifies minimum standards for QLTCI that provides benefits for home health care or community care services. In particular, 1993 LTC Model Regulation section 11A states that a contract may not limit or exclude benefits by:

- requiring that the insured/claimant would need care in a skilled nursing facility if home health care services were not provided;
- requiring that the insured/claimant first or simultaneously receive nursing and/or therapeutic services in a home, community or institutional setting before home health care services are covered;
- limiting eligible services to services provided by registered nurses or licensed practical nurses;
- requiring that a nurse or therapist provide services covered by the contract that can be provided by a home health aide or other licensed or certified home care worker acting within the scope of his or her licensure or certification;
- excluding coverage for personal care services provided by a home health aide;
- requiring that the provision of home health care services be at a level of certification or licensure greater than that required by the eligible service;
- requiring that the insured/claimant have an acute condition before home health care services are covered;
- limiting benefits to services provided by Medicare-certified agencies or providers; or
- excluding coverage for adult day care services.

Sections 11B and 11C of the 1993 LTC Model Regulation impose requirements regarding the level of home health and community care coverage provided relative to the level of coverage for nursing home benefits, i.e., generally speaking, home health and community care coverage must be provided at levels at least half of that for nursing home benefits.

**Inflation protection, 1993 LTC Model Regulation section 12:**[218] This provision generally requires the offer of compound inflation protection. However, a special rule—contained in 1993 LTC Model Regulation section 12C—provides that the normally required offer of inflation protection need not be made for life insurance contracts or riders containing accelerated long-term care benefits. Where long-term care insurance coverage is not provided in the form of an ADB, e.g., coverage that continues after ADBs have been exhausted, it appears that the special rule would not apply with respect to the nonacceleration long-term care coverage. Section 12 of the 1993 LTC Model Regulation specifies a number of requirements for the offer of inflation protection, e.g., generally, increases in long-term care insurance benefits (both daily and maximum) must be at a rate of 5 percent compounded annually; the insurer must offer a premium for such increases that is expected to remain

---

[216] Despite the title of 1993 LTC Model Reg. § 10 (i.e., Prohibition on Post-Claims Underwriting), it is unclear whether this consumer protection rule would proscribe use of an actuarial discount provided for under a rider's terms.
[217] IRC § 7702B(g)(2)(A)(i)(IX) provides that a contract must satisfy 1993 LTC Model Reg. § 11 to qualify as QLTCI.
[218] IRC § 7702B(g)(2)(A)(i)(X) provides that a contract must satisfy 1993 LTC Model Reg. § 12 to qualify as QLTCI.

constant; increases in benefits must continue without regard to the insured's age, claim status or claim history, or the length of time the person has been insured; and such inflation protection must be provided unless the policyholder rejects it in writing.[219]

**Prohibition against pre-existing conditions and probationary periods in replacement policies, 1993 LTC Model Regulation section 23:**[220] Under this provision, if a long-term care insurance contract replaces another contract, the replacing insurer must waive any time periods applicable to pre-existing conditions and probationary periods in the new contract for similar benefits to the extent that similar exclusions have been satisfied under the original contract.

## Summary of Consumer Protection Rules Enforced Through a Penalty Tax

As noted above, section 4980C imposes further consumer protection requirements with respect to QLTCI through a penalty tax on the insurer if the requirements are not met. The Treasury regulations' framework for interpretation of 1993 LTC model rules, as discussed above, also applies to the requirements that relate to this penalty tax. The following is a summary of the key consumer protection requirements that apply by cross-reference to the 1993 LTC model rules and are imposed through the penalty tax.

**Right to return premium, 1993 LTC Model Act section 6F:**[221] This provision requires long-term care insurance contracts to print a notice prominently on the first page of the contract stating that the applicant has the right to return the contract within 30 days of its delivery and to have the premiums refunded if, after examination of the contract, the applicant is not satisfied for any reason. This requirement also applies to denials of applications, and any refund must be made within 30 days of the return or denial.[222] In the case of a long-term care insurance rider to a life insurance contract, this requirement should apply to charges or premiums imposed for the rider but should not apply to the life insurance contract premiums, by virtue of the separate contract rule. In the case of a universal life insurance contract where a long-term care insurance rider is funded through assessment of charges against the life insurance contract's cash value, seemingly it should be adequate to restore rider charges to the contract's cash value if the policyholder decides to drop the rider but retain the life insurance (rather than having to distribute those rider charges from the contract).

**Outline of coverage, 1993 LTC Model Act section 6G:**[223] This provision requires delivery of an outline of coverage to prospective applicants and provides a description of the specific items that must be included in the outline of coverage.

**Group policy requirements, 1993 LTC Model Act section 6H:**[224] This provision requires that certificates issued pursuant to a group contract must include:

- a description of the principal benefits and coverage provided by the contract,
- a statement of the principal exclusions, reductions and limitations contained in the contract, and
- a statement that the group master contract determines governing contractual provisions.

**Policy summary for long-term care benefits provided by a life insurance contract, 1993 LTC Model Act section 6I:**[225] This rule requires a policy summary to be delivered to prospective applicants and provides a description of the specific items that must be included in the summary. This requirement specifically applies to individual life insurance contracts that provide long-term care insurance benefits either within the contract or by rider. The policy summary must include, for example, an explanation of how long-term care benefits interact with other components of the contract, including the manner in which such benefits reduce the life

---

[219] IRC § 7702B(g)(2)(A)(i)(X) modifies the requirement of 1993 LTC Model Reg. § 12 by providing that "any requirement for a signature on a rejection of inflation protection shall permit the signature to be on an application or on a separate form."
[220] IRC § 7702B(g)(2)(A)(i)(XI) provides that a contract must satisfy 1993 LTC Model Reg. § 23 to qualify as QLTCI.
[221] IRC § 4980C(c)(1)(B)(i) provides that 1993 LTC Model Act § 6F must be met for the penalty tax not to apply.
[222] IRC § 4980C(c)(1)(B)(i).
[223] IRC § 4980C(c)(1)(B)(ii) provides that 1993 LTC Model Act § 6G must be met for the penalty tax not to apply.
[224] IRC § 4980C(c)(1)(B)(iii) provides that 1993 LTC Model Act § 6H must be met for the penalty tax not to apply.
[225] IRC § 4980C(c)(1)(B)(iv) provides that 1993 LTC Model Act § 6I must be met for the penalty tax not to apply.

insurance contract's death benefit. Other required content includes an illustration of the amount of benefits, the length of the benefit and the guaranteed lifetime benefits (if any); a summary of any exclusions, reductions and limitations on benefits for long-term care; and, if applicable, a disclosure of the effects of exercising other rights under the contract, disclosure of guarantees related to long-term care cost of insurance charges, and a summary of current and projected maximum lifetime benefits.

**Monthly reports for accelerated death benefits, 1993 LTC Model Act section 6J:**[226] This provision requires a monthly report to be provided to policyholders any time a long-term care benefit funded through acceleration of a life insurance contract's death benefit is in benefit payment status. The report must identify any long-term care benefits paid out during the month, explain any changes in the contract, e.g., to death benefits or cash values, due to long-term care benefits being paid out, and identify the amount of long-term care benefits existing or remaining.

**Incontestability period, 1993 LTC Model Act section 7:**[227] This provision restricts the circumstances in which an insurer can contest a contract. In particular, during the first six months after issuance, a contract may be rescinded by the insurer or an otherwise valid claim may be denied only upon a showing of misrepresentation material to the acceptance for coverage. After the first six months after issuance and prior to two years after issuance, a contract may be rescinded by the insurer or an otherwise valid claim may be denied only upon a showing of misrepresentation that is both material to the acceptance of coverage and which pertains to the condition for which benefits are sought. Also, after a contract has been in force for two years, it may be rescinded only upon a showing that the insured knowingly and intentionally misrepresented relevant facts relating to the insured's health. In the case of a long-term care insurance rider to a life insurance contract, these requirements should apply only to the rider; the life insurance contract should separately be subject to its own contestability provisions. Section 7 of the 1993 LTC Model Act also prohibits the field issuance of a contract and the recovery of benefits paid on rescissions.[228] For this purpose, "field issued" means that a contract has been issued by an agent or a third-party administrator pursuant to the underwriting authority granted to the agent or third-party administrator by an insurer.[229]

**Application forms and replacement coverage, 1993 LTC Model Regulation section 13:**[230] This provision imposes requirements for application forms and replacement coverage. For example, certain questions must be asked in the application that are designed to elicit information as to whether the applicant has another long-term care insurance contract in force or whether a long-term care contract is intended to replace any other accident and sickness[231] or long-term care contract presently in force. Certain requirements also are imposed on agents, such as to list information regarding other accident or health insurance policies sold by the agent to the applicant, and a notice must be provided to the applicant where a contract is replacing other coverage.[232] In addition, where a replacement is intended, the replacing insurer must notify, in writing, the existing insurer of the proposed replacement and identify the existing contract, name of the insured, and the policy number or address including ZIP code.[233] Such notice must be made within five working days from the date the application is received by the insurer or the date the contract is issued, whichever is sooner.[234]

**Reporting requirements, 1993 LTC Model Regulation section 14:**[235] This provision imposes record keeping and reporting requirements of specific items with respect to replacement sales by agents and lapse rates. For example, every insurer must maintain records for each agent of that agent's replacement sales as a percent of

---

[226] IRC § 4980C(c)(1)(B)(v) provides that 1993 LTC Model Act § 6J must be met for the penalty tax not to apply.
[227] IRC § 4980C(c)(1)(B)(vi) provides that 1993 LTC Model Act § 7 must be met for the penalty tax not to apply.
[228] The restriction on recoveries seemingly was not intended to apply where benefit payments were due to fraud.
[229] 1993 LTC Model Act § 7D(2).
[230] IRC § 4980C(c)(1)(A)(i) provides that 1993 LTC Model Reg. § 13 must be met for the penalty tax not to apply.
[231] *Compare* IRC § 4980C(c)(1)(A)(iv), relating to 1993 LTC Model Reg. § 21 (discussed below), which states that "no such requirements [under 1993 LTC Model Reg. § 21] shall include a requirement to inquire or identify whether a prospective applicant or enrollee for long-term care insurance has accident and sickness insurance."
[232] 1993 LTC Model Reg. § 13C.
[233] 1993 LTC Model Reg. § 13E.
[234] *Id.*
[235] IRC § 4980C(c)(1)(A)(ii) provides that 1993 LTC Model Reg. § 14 must be met for the penalty tax not to apply.

the agent's total annual sales and the lapses of long-term care insurance contracts sold by the agent as a percent of the agent's total annual sales. Also, each insurer must report annually by June 30:

- the 10 percent of its agents with the greatest percentages of lapses and replacements,
- the number of lapsed contracts as a percent of the insurer's total annual sales and as a percent of its total number of contracts in force as of the end of the preceding calendar year, and
- the number of replacement contracts sold as a percent of the insurer's total annual sales and as a percent of its total number of contracts in force as of the preceding calendar year.

Section 14F of the 1993 LTC Model Regulation states that for this purpose, policy means only long-term care insurance. Section 4980C(c)(1)(A)(ii) modifies these provisions so that an issuer also must report at least annually the number of claims denied during the reporting period for each class of business (expressed as a percentage of claims denied), other than claims denied for failure to meet the waiting period or because of any applicable pre-existing condition.

The 1993 LTC Model Regulation does not directly speak to the application of this provision in the context of long-term care insurance riders to life insurance contracts. Also, while these reporting requirements apply as federal tax requirements, the 1993 LTC Model Regulation contemplates that such reporting would be to the applicable state insurance department. A state may impose reporting requirements that are the same or more stringent than the requirements of 1993 LTC Model Regulation section 14. Where a state's rules are less stringent, however, it seemingly would be necessary to report the information required by 1993 LTC Model Regulation section 14, by virtue of the rules of Treas. Reg. section 1.7702B-1(b) discussed above.

**Filing requirements for marketing, 1993 LTC Model Regulation section 20:**[236] This provision imposes filing requirements for advertising of long-term care insurance. Under this provision, every insurer providing long-term care insurance or benefits must provide a copy of any long-term care insurance advertisement intended for use in a state (whether through written, radio or television medium) to the state insurance commissioner for review or approval to the extent it may be required under state law. Seemingly, this requirement only applies as a tax requirement to the extent state law imposes such a requirement. In addition, all advertisements must be retained by the insurer for at least three years from the date the advertisement was first used.

**Standards for marketing, 1993 LTC Model Regulation section 21 (other than 1993 LTC Model Regulation section 21C(1) and 21C(6)):**[237] This provision imposes requirements and standards related to the marketing of long-term care insurance. Under this provision, every insurer marketing long-term care insurance coverage, directly or through its producers, must:

- establish marketing procedures to assure that any comparison of contracts by its agents or other producers will be fair and accurate,
- establish marketing procedures to assure excessive insurance is not sold or issued,
- display prominently by type, stamp or other appropriate means, on the first page of the outline of coverage and contract the following: "Notice to buyer: This policy may not cover all of the costs associated with long-term care incurred by the buyer during the period of coverage. The buyer is advised to review carefully all policy limitations," and
- inquire and otherwise make every reasonable effort to identify whether a prospective applicant or enrollee for long-term care insurance already has long-term care insurance and amounts of any such insurance.[238]

---

[236] IRC § 4980C(c)(1)(A)(iii) provides that 1993 LTC Model Reg. § 20 must be met for the penalty tax not to apply.
[237] IRC § 4980C(c)(1)(A)(iv) provides that 1993 LTC Model Reg. § 21 (other than 1993 LTC Model Reg. § 21C(1) and 21C(6)) must be met for the penalty tax not to apply.
[238] *See* IRC § 4980C(c)(1)(A)(iv)(II), which indicates that this rule does not include any requirement to inquire or identify whether a prospective applicant or enrollee for long-term care insurance has accident and sickness insurance.

Also, no person may, in selling or offering to sell QLTCI, misrepresent a material fact.[239]

**Appropriateness of recommended purchase, 1993 LTC Model Regulation section 22:**[240] This provision requires that, in recommending the purchase or replacement of any long-term care insurance contract, an agent must make reasonable efforts to determine the appropriateness of a recommended purchase or replacement.

**Outline of coverage, 1993 LTC Model Regulation section 24:**[241] This rule provides a standard format for the outline of coverage that insurers must use.

**Delivery of shopper's guide, 1993 LTC Model Regulation section 25:**[242] This provision requires that a long-term care insurance shopper's guide be provided to all prospective applicants.

---

[239] IRC § 4980C(c)(1)(A)(iv)(I). Various unfair trade practices also are proscribed. See 1993 LTC Model Reg. § 21B. In addition, certain requirements are imposed where long-term care insurance is sold or endorsed by an association. See 1993 LTC Model Reg. § 21C (other than paragraphs (1) and (6) thereof, which are not tax requirements). IRC § 4980C(c)(1)(A)(iv).
[240] IRC § 4980C(c)(1)(A)(v) provides that 1993 LTC Model Reg. § 22 must be met for the penalty tax not to apply.
[241] IRC § 4980C(c)(1)(A)(vi) provides that 1993 LTC Model Reg. § 24 must be met for the penalty tax not to apply.
[242] IRC § 4980C(c)(1)(A)(vii) provides that 1993 LTC Model Reg. § 25 must be met for the penalty tax not to apply.

Chapter 8

# FAILED CONTRACTS AND INADVERTENT MODIFIED ENDOWMENT CONTRACTS: CORRECTIONS OF ERRORS, WAIVERS AND CLOSING AGREEMENTS

## Chapter Overview

Someone once described an insurer's likelihood of at least some noncompliance with the limitations under sections 101(f), 7702 and 7702A[1] as akin to riding a motorcycle—it is not so much a question of if you will fall, it is simply a matter of when. To this point, this book has addressed issues related to compliance with these limitations. Chapter 8 addresses the challenges involved with contracts that either fail to meet the limits under section 101(f) or 7702 (**failed contracts**) or inadvertently have become modified endowment contracts (MECs) under section 7702A (**inadvertent MECs**). Given the complexity of the rules, Congress expected that some failures would occur. Sections 101(f) and 7702 contain provisions authorizing the IRS to waive compliance failures where the failure results from **reasonable error** (waivable errors). Also, administrative procedures have been established by the IRS to deal with both nonwaivable errors under the definitional limitations and the correction of inadvertent MECs. These processes are described in this chapter.

### *"Self-Help" Corrections*

Before beginning a discussion of IRS administrative procedure, it is important to note that correction of a potential error without IRS involvement (i.e., **self-help**) may be possible, even sensible, in cases where no clear error has occurred, although such a course of action will not be possible where the error is clear. As has been noted in previous chapters, there are instances where practice varies with respect to application of certain provisions of the statute. Choices also exist in the selection of calculation assumptions or methodology. While allowing a "margin for error" to avoid failures is always advisable in contract administration, an insurer may be well advised to follow a less restrictive (but defensible) interpretation of the statute when a contract is identified, or is about to be identified, as a failed contract or an inadvertent MEC under a particular set of test parameters.

*"It's funny how two intelligent people can have such opposite interpretations of the tax code!"*

---

[1] Unless otherwise indicated, references in this book to "section" are to the provisions of the Internal Revenue Code of 1986, as amended (also referred to as "IRC" or the "Code").

That said, self-help based on acceptable but varying interpretations of the definitional requirements, with due regard to consistency, needs to be distinguished from the purported self-correction of contract failures that arise from a clear misinterpretation or misapplication of the statutes. The IRS would undoubtedly caution against implementing such attempted self-help corrections, warning of severe penalties for willful failure to comply with the tax laws (including withholding and reporting requirements). Remedies, such as exchanges of noncompliant contracts for compliant ones, do not resolve the tax exposure, and they may well lead to policyholder or insurance regulator questions, then to IRS inquiries, then to more serious exposures and problems. An insurer should strongly avoid the temptation to sidestep addressing compliance failures. Insurers (and their employees) that engage in such practices even run the risk of prosecution, if the IRS were to conclude that the insurer willfully evaded its obligations, or abetted others in evading their obligations, with respect to contracts in clear violation of the statute.

## Section 101(f) and 7702 Failures

Contracts failing to meet the definitional limitations create consequences to both the policyholders and the issuing insurers. If a life insurance contract fails to satisfy the section 101(f) or 7702 requirements, the **inside buildup** of the contract is taxed currently and is subject to reporting and possibly withholding obligations. For the policyholder of a contract that fails to comply with section 101(f) or 7702, section 7702(g)(1)(A) treats the **income on the contract** (i.e., the inside buildup, as defined more technically below) as ordinary income received or accrued by the policyholder in the year in which the income arises. Section 7702(g)(1)(C) also requires any past income on the contract to be included in income in the year of failure. Income on the contract, as defined in section 7702(g), would therefore be includible in the policyholder's gross income and subject to tax. However, the "pure" death benefit element of the contract (i.e., the net amount at risk) retains its favorable tax treatment under section 101(a).[2] (Although section 7702(g) technically applies only to contracts that are subject to and fail to satisfy section 7702, in practice it also has been used to address the consequences of a section 101(f) failure.)

An insurer that issued a failed contract typically also has penalty and other potential exposure under the tax law. Rev. Rul. 91-17[3] and Notice 99-48[4] describe a rather impressive list of penalties that the IRS can assess against a company relating to its reporting, record-keeping and withholding obligations resulting from the treatment of the income on the contract as a "nonperiodic distribution" under section 3405(e)(3). The penalties for failure to withhold and report the income on the contract can be substantial, potentially greater than the cost of entering into a **closing agreement** with the IRS to remedy the failures. It should be noted, however, that the IRS generally waives these penalties for an insurer that voluntarily submits failed contracts to the IRS in a correction proceeding.[5]

Failed contracts may also adversely affect the issuing company's deduction for reserves under section 807, absent a waiver or closing agreement. The legislative history of the Deficit Reduction Act of 1984 (DEFRA) indicates that life insurance reserve status under sections 807(c)(1) and (d) is denied in the case of a failed contract. For such a contract, the "investment portion" of the contract would be allowable as a section 807(c)(4) reserve, but no more.[6] While the contracts are specifically considered by section 7702(g)(3) to be insurance contracts for purposes of subchapter L of the Internal Revenue Code (the life insurance company income tax

---

[2] See IRC § 7702(g)(2).
[3] 1991-1 C.B. 190, *superseded in part by* Rev. Proc. 2008-40, 2008-2 C.B. 151 (discussed below). The penalty for failure to report imposed by IRC § 6652(e) prior to its amendment in 1996 could be draconian, totaling as high as $30,000 for each failed contract (taking into account both the failure to report to the IRS and the failure to send the payee statement). Today this penalty, imposed under IRC §§ 6721–24, is much reduced, although it can become significant, especially in the case of intentional disregard of the rules.
[4] 1999-2 C.B. 429, *superseded by* Rev. Proc. 2008-40, *supra* note 3.
[5] See Rev. Rul. 91-17, *supra* note 3 (providing that the IRS will waive civil penalties for failure to satisfy the reporting, withholding and deposit requirements for income deemed received under IRC § 7702(g) if an insurance company requests and receives a waiver of the failure to meet the definition of a life insurance contract pursuant to IRC § 7702(f)(8); or if, prior to June 3, 1991, an insurance company requested and subsequently executed a closing agreement under which the company agreed to pay an amount based on the amount of tax that would have been owed by policyholders if they were treated as receiving the income on the contracts and any interest with regard to such tax). See also Notice 99-48, *supra* note 4 (stating that, since June 3, 1991, the IRS has exercised its authority under IRC § 7121 to enter into closing agreements that waive the penalties applicable to insurance companies which issue failed contracts). As noted above, Rev. Rul. 91-17 was superseded in part, and Notice 99-48 was superseded, by Rev. Proc. 2008-40. The 2008 revenue procedures discussed later in this chapter refer to the foregoing authorities and contain model closing agreements in which the IRS agrees to waive civil penalties.
[6] See DEFRA House Report, *supra* Chapter 1, note 11, at 1413, n. 10; DEFRA Senate Report, *supra* Chapter 1, note 11, at 539, n. 10; DEFRA Blue Book, *supra* Chapter 1, note 20, at 597, n. 19.

rules), even though they have failed the requirements of section 101(f) or 7702, they are not life insurance contracts under the Code and so the reserves are not life insurance reserves.

Finally, and most significantly, an insurer's liability exposure to the IRS for issuing a failed contract may be dwarfed by its potential liability to the affected policyholders. Its policyholder-level liability, which potentially consists of the tax on the income on the contract, plus any other damages suffered by the policyholder, may well drive an insurer's decision to pursue an IRS correction proceeding. Reputational risk also is a concern.

## *Calculation of the Income on the Contract*

An annual calculation of the income on the contract under section 7702(g) is required for a life insurance contract that does not meet the requirements of section 7702. The income on the contract is defined in section 7702(g)(1)(B) for each taxable year as the increase in the net surrender value (NSV), plus "the cost of life insurance protection," less any premiums paid for that year. The NSV of a contract is its section 7702 CSV reduced by surrender charges but not by policy loans.[7] This calculation is made on a year-by-year basis, following the tax year of the policyholder (in the case of an individual, this is a calendar year). For a contract year that is concurrent with a calendar year (which would be rare, of course), and assuming no surrender charges or expense (including qualified additional benefit, or QAB) charges and that the cost of life insurance protection equals the mortality charge actually imposed, the calculation of the income on the contract is as follows:

| (8.1) Derivation of section 7702(g) income[8] | | |
|---|---|---|
| (1) | Section 7702(g) income on the contract (IOC) | $7702(g)\ IOC = (_tCV - _{t-1}CV) + q_{x+t}(B_t - _tCV) - P$ |
| (2) | The relationship of successive cash values is given by the Fackler accumulation formula | $_tCV = (_{t-1}CV + P)(1 + i_t) - q_{x+t}(B_t - _tCV)$ |
| (3) | Substituting terms | $7702(g)\ IOC = (_{t-1}CV + P)(i_t)$ |

On the assumptions stated above, the derivation in Formula (8.1) shows that the section 7702(g) income of a contract is, in theory, equal to the interest earned on the cash value—the contract's inside buildup. In reality, however, the values used in the section 7702(g) income calculation, i.e., the NSVs, are reduced by expense, QAB and surrender charges when applicable. This reduction gives rise to several consequences. On the one hand, it follows that the inside buildup is allowed to cover expense and QAB charges without being included in section 7702(g) income. On the other hand, the wearing off of a surrender charge during a year will effectively create section 7702(g) income, i.e., the wear-off will appear to increase the NSV. As discussed later in Chapter 10, the income on the contract under section 7702(g) is, in concept, equal to the income that would result on life insurance inside buildup under a broad-based definition of income as proposed by those tax theorists who favor a comprehensive tax base.

When section 7702(g) was framed in the legislative process in 1983–84 (there was no counterpart in section 101(f)[9]), the life insurance industry paid little attention to its terms, focusing instead on what would be necessary to comply with the restrictions of the statute under construction. This resulted in the enactment of terms both vague and anomalous in certain respects. For example, section 7702(g)(1)(D) provides that the cost-of-life-insurance protection element of the statute's income formula for a given taxable year is based on the lesser of "the mortality charge (if any) stated in the contract" or a charge based on a table to be prescribed by regulations. To date, no regulations have been prescribed addressing cost-of-insurance charges under section 7702(g), leaving the mortality charge "stated" in the contract (if there is one) to be used in the income formula. This circumstance warrants several comments. First, the stated mortality charge for a taxable year could be viewed as being either the charge guaranteed in the contract or the charge actually imposed during

---

[7] *See* IRC § 7702(f)(2)(B) (defining net surrender value).
[8] Assuming the contract year does not follow a calendar year, the expressions for the beginning and ending cash values are with reference to the calendar year, as are the premium, interest and cost of insurance.
[9] The Tax Equity and Fiscal Responsibility Act of 1982 (TEFRA) legislative history simply notes, "If these guidelines are violated at any time over the duration of the contract, the contract will not be treated as providing life insurance for tax purposes." TEFRA Senate Report, *supra* Chapter 3, note 33, at 353; TEFRA Blue Book, *supra* Chapter 1, note 95, at 367. The TEFRA Blue Book added that "the contract may be treated as providing a combination of term life insurance with an annuity or a deposit fund (depending upon the terms of the policy)." TEFRA Blue Book, *supra* Chapter 1, note 95, at 367.

the year. Using the latter in the income formula would make sense, in that it more closely captures the inside buildup actually credited to the contract. For universal life and other "unbundled" contracts, the exact amount of the charge actually imposed is known, although the amount of the guaranteed charge can be derived from the terms of the contract. For a contract with no stated mortality charge, such as a traditional whole life contract, the charge would need to be imputed, presumably by looking to the contract's nonforfeiture values.[10] Second, in the case of a contract with dual cash values (discussed in Chapter 6), the manner of determining the mortality charge to be used for a given year is uncertain, there being no official guidance on the point. Third, in no event is the charge for a QAB counted as a mortality charge, as official guidance provides that a QAB charge is an expense change subject to the **reasonable expense** rule.[11] As a final comment, it should be noted that the section 7702(g) rule was not updated when the **reasonable mortality** requirement was enacted by the Technical and Miscellaneous Revenue Act of 1988 (TAMRA), and hence the rule's coordination with that requirement (if any) is undefined.

Another area of uncertainty in the section 7702(g) income calculation relates to instances of **negative income** on the contract for a given year.[12] The annual calculations under section 7702(g) produce a negative number when, for example, first-year contract expenses (or surrender charges) result in a cash value that is less than the premiums paid in that year, and they also can produce a negative number in the year that a contract is fully surrendered. Negative income may also result from a loss of variable contract cash value caused by a decline in market values of the underlying separate accounts. The IRS has taken the position in executing closing agreements covering section 101(f) and 7702 failures that the income on the contract for any given year cannot be less than zero. In fact, the year-by-year calculation method of section 7702(g) can create tax on more than the amount of a contract's section 72(e) gain. This largely occurs as a consequence of the section 7702(g) income formula, which treats mortality charges as an additive element to the income formula for a failed life insurance contract. Also, section 7702(g) defines income for each year, with no provision for the carry-forward of a negative result to offset income in another year.[13] To the extent that an offset of negative and positive income is not allowed, the section 7702(g) income formula can distort the **toll charge** calculation for an IRS closing agreement based on section 7702(g) that covers a failed variable contract (the toll charge calculation is discussed in detail later in this chapter).

A sample calculation of the section 7702(g) income on the contract is illustrated in Table 8.1, below.

### Table 8.1. Sample section 7702(g) income on the contract calculation

| Policy number: | ABC12345 | | | Year of failure: | 1995 | |
|---|---|---|---|---|---|---|
| Issue date: | 5/24/95 | | | Death benefit: | 69,912 | |
| Tax year | Beginning of year NSV | End of year NSV | Change in NSV | Premiums paid | Cost of insurance | Section 7702(g) income on the contract |
| 1995 | 0 | 11,420 | 11,420 | 13,021 | 53 | 0 |
| 1996 | 11,420 | 12,500 | 1,080 | 0 | 60 | 1,140 |
| 1997 | 12,500 | 13,553 | 1,053 | 0 | 64 | 1,117 |
| 1998 | 13,553 | 14,683 | 1,130 | 0 | 68 | 1,198 |
| 1999 | 14,683 | 15,845 | 1,162 | 0 | 73 | 1,235 |
| 2000 | 15,845 | 17,122 | 1,277 | 0 | 78 | 1,355 |
| 2001 | 17,122 | 18,396 | 1,274 | 0 | 91 | 1,365 |

---

[10] In the case of a net rate product (described in Chapter 6), this charge presumably would be zero.

[11] See the discussion of Rev. Rul. 2005-6 in Chapter 3 and later in this chapter.

[12] In this regard, the practice of defining income on a year-by-year basis differs from the income calculation under IRC § 72(e)(3)(A), which defines income on a cumulative basis. Contra IRC § 72(u)(1)(B) and (2)(A) (relating to annuity contracts owned by non-natural persons and defining income on the contract on a year-by-year basis).

[13] In the case of a high first-year surrender charge, the failure to carry over "negatives" may create phantom income as the surrender charge wears off.

| Table 8.1. Continued | | | | | | |
|---|---|---|---|---|---|---|
| Policy number: ABC12345 | | | | Year of failure: 1995 | | |
| Issue date: 5/24/95 | | | | Death benefit: 69,912 | | |
| Tax year | Beginning of year NSV | End of year NSV | Change in NSV | Premiums paid | Cost of insurance | Section 7702(g) income on the contract |
| 2002 | 18,396 | 19,527 | 1,131 | 0 | 181 | 1,312 |
| 2003 | 19,527 | 20,427 | 900 | 0 | 223 | 1,123 |
| 2004 | 20,427 | 21,240 | 813 | 0 | 238 | 1,051 |
| 2005 | 21,240 | 22,034 | 794 | 0 | 249 | 1,043 |
| 2006 | 22,034 | 22,773 | 739 | 0 | 262 | 1,001 |
| 2007 | 22,773 | 23,069 | 296 | −379 | 278 | 953 |
| 2008 | 23,069 | 23,957 | 888 | 0 | 290 | 1,178 |
| 2009 | 23,957 | 24,734 | 777 | 0 | 387 | 1,164 |
| 2010 | 24,734 | 25,447 | 713 | 0 | 497 | 1,210 |
| 2011 | 25,447 | 26,032 | 585 | 0 | 625 | 1,210 |
| 2012 | 26,032 | 26,577 | 545 | 0 | 684 | 1,229 |
| 2013 | 26,577 | 26,184 | 237 | 0 | 236 | 473 |
| Total | — | — | — | — | — | 20,357 |

Table 8.1 also illustrates the problem of "negative income" under section 7702(g). In computing the section 7702(g) income in the first policy year, the increase in cash value is $11,420, and the cost of insurance is $53. As the initial premium paid is $13,021, the income in the first year is negative and is set to zero. In the second year, the income is $1,140 ($1,080 plus $60). Note that if the first two years were aggregated, no income would result. Under section 72(e), where the income is in the aggregate, there is no taxable gain, as the $12,500 cash value at the end of the second year is less than the premium paid ($13,021).

## Introduction to Remediation Processes

Because life insurance contracts sometimes fail to comply with section 7702 or its predecessor section 101(f) or inadvertently become MECs, procedures have been put in place to remedy the errors, enabling policyholders and insurers to be in compliance with the definitional limitations. In addition to the IRS waiver process and a general closing agreement process described next below, which have been in place since the earliest years of the statutes, a series of revenue procedures issued by the IRS in 2008 rewrote and systematized the approach to remedying definitional noncompliance. These revenue procedures, which have eclipsed the earlier processes, are described subsequently in this chapter. Before describing the currently applicable revenue procedures, this chapter preserves and expands upon the discussion of those earlier processes that appeared in the original edition of *Life Insurance & Modified Endowments*, principally for three reasons. First, the waiver process is provided for in sections 101(f) and 7702 themselves, and hence that process remains available even if it generally is less needed or desirable in light of the improvements brought about by the 2008 revenue procedures. Second, the waiver rulings, which are publicly disclosed although not precedential (they are private letter rulings), provide insight into some of the compliance errors that have occurred and, as discussed in the earlier chapters of this book, some detail on the statutes' interpretation by insurers as well as the IRS. (As an important caution in this regard, a number of the waiver rulings reviewed below are quite dated, and there is no assurance that current IRS personnel would reach the same conclusions were they to be asked.) Third, the general closing agreement process described next can apply to remedy errors where the improved procedures of 2008 turn out to be unavailable.

## Waiver and Closing Agreement Processes

In section 101(f)(3)(H) and continuing in section 7702(f)(8),[14] Congress provided an extraordinary power to the IRS to waive noncompliance with the requirements of the statutes. It is fair to say that inadvertent failures to comply were expected to occur from time to time. Problems can arise as a result of errors in administration, in the construction of compliance systems or in statutory interpretation, all of which can lead to the necessity for the IRS to be asked to waive noncompliance. A section 7702(f)(8) "waiver" of noncompliance can be granted by the National Office of the IRS where the admitted problem arises from "reasonable error" and where "reasonable steps" are being taken to correct it.

In framing the waiver process, Congress prescribed very general, common law-type conditions under which a waiver may be granted. The legislative history of TEFRA simply notes that "the Secretary [of the Treasury has] discretion to allow corrections of excessive premium payments [under the guideline premium test],"[15] indicating that "if it is established to the satisfaction of the Secretary that the [guideline premium requirements of section 101(f)(1)(A)(i) and (2)(A) were] not met due to reasonable error and reasonable steps are being taken to remedy the error, the Secretary may waive the [error]."[16] A similar statement is included in the DEFRA legislative history, providing "if it is established to the satisfaction of the Secretary that the requirements of the definitional tests were not met due to reasonable error and reasonable steps are being taken to remedy the error, the Secretary may waive the failure to satisfy the requirements."[17]

As just noted, the first standard for an error to be waivable by the IRS is that it must be reasonable. There are three broad conditions that apply in making this determination. First, for the IRS to view an error as reasonable, the error must first be shown to be inadvertent.[18] Second, the IRS generally takes the position that the error must not be a direct violation of a clear rule (e.g., computing a guideline single premium taking increasing death benefits into account, as prohibited by section 7702(e)(1)(A)). Third, in assessing the reasonableness of the situation, the IRS looks to the overall reasonableness of the circumstances in which the error arose. Thus, as a condition to the issuance of a waiver, the IRS has required that the insurer generally have an adequate compliance system in place.[19] The other statutory requirement for the issuance of a waiver is that reasonable steps must be taken to correct the error which resulted in the compliance failure.

The form that a waiver request to the IRS takes is relatively straightforward. The request is made in the form of a submission to the IRS for a private letter ruling. The request identifies the problem (i.e., the cause of the contract failures) and explains how the error(s) resulted in the failure of the contract, thereby informing the IRS of the nature of the failure. This explanation typically contains considerable historical detail, rendering the ruling request both time-consuming and expensive to prepare. If the waiver is granted, the insurer will need to correct the contract, but no penalties will be assessed, and no tax (or deficiency interest) will be due on the section 7702(g) income on the contract. There will, therefore, be no amount paid to the IRS by either the insurer or the policyholder, except for the usual filing fee for a private letter ruling.

The alternative to seeking a waiver prior to the issuance of the 2008 revenue procedures was for the insurer to offer to enter into a **closing agreement** with the IRS. A closing agreement, which is one of the means used by the 2008 revenue procedures to remedy noncompliance, is in essence a contract between a taxpayer and the IRS that specifies future conduct by both parties as it eliminates the taxpayer's liability. Such an agreement, which the IRS enters into pursuant to the authority granted under section 7121, is broadly used to settle out tax liabilities, not simply in cases of noncompliance with the definitional limitations.

---

[14] IRC §§ 101(f)(3)(H) and 7702(f)(8) provide essentially the same rule for the waiver of errors that result in contracts failing to qualify as life insurance under the tax law.
[15] TEFRA Conference Report at 648.
[16] TEFRA Senate Report at 353; TEFRA Blue Book, *supra* Chapter 1, note 95, at 368.
[17] DEFRA Blue Book, *supra* Chapter 1, note 20, at 654, n. 56.
[18] While it is a safe assumption that few, if any, insurers have confessed to a willful error, only a closing agreement can deal with such an error. Whether an error is inadvertent is sometimes a complex factual question. By way of example, an error might be considered inadvertent on the part of an insurer, even though one of its employees took the erroneous action and did so knowingly, where the insurer had rules and processes in place to the contrary.
[19] *See, e.g.*, the discussion of PLR 200150018 (Sept. 13, 2001) under the heading "Programming or Systems Errors" below.

Prior to the issuance of the 2008 revenue procedures, a closing agreement typically was used to address a contract's failure to comply with section 101(f) or 7702 where a reasonable error waiver was unavailable, either because the IRS denied the application for the waiver or because the insurer chose not to seek a waiver. Like a waiver, a closing agreement is sought by the insurer through the same procedural mechanisms that apply to requests for private letter rulings, and in practice it often was sought through amendment of a waiver submission following an IRS denial of a waiver request. The conditions of a section 7702 (or section 101(f)) closing agreement were rather straightforward, and they continue to apply under the 2008 procedures with modifications (as discussed further below). As described in Rev. Rul. 91-17,[20] the insurer that issued the failed contracts must agree to pay the tax and deficiency interest on the section 7702(g) income on the contract—see the discussion of the "toll charge" below—and to correct the contracts, in return for which the IRS agrees to waive the error and not pursue penalties against the insurer.[21] The process presupposes that the insurer has corrected the compliance system deficiencies which gave rise to the failure. In most respects, the waiver and closing agreement processes are similar, with the notable exceptions that the burden on the insurer of adducing the facts in support of a waiver request is much greater than in the case of a closing agreement offer, and that toll charges are not imposed when a waiver is granted but are paid under a closing agreement.

In the past, a number of factors have tended to influence an insurer's decision, in the first instance, to seek a section 7702(f)(8) (or section 101(f)(3)(H)) waiver or instead to offer to enter into a closing agreement to address contract failures. (It was not a prerequisite for an insurer to file a waiver request before offering to enter into a closing agreement.) The waiver process is typically time-consuming and expensive. In the past, it was not uncommon for the processing time of a waiver request within the IRS to exceed four months and to generate $100,000 or more in internal and external legal and actuarial costs, all in addition to the IRS filing fee required for either a waiver request or closing agreement offer. Depending on the number of contracts involved, the potential toll charge at stake and the nature of the error(s) committed, an insurer may have decided prior to the 2008 revenue procedures that it was more economical to offer to enter directly into a closing agreement. With the improvements attendant to the issuance of the 2008 procedures, today the decision is typically to pursue the closing agreement unless an **automatic waiver** is available under Rev. Proc. 2008-42 (discussed below).

A key consideration in an insurer's decision to seek a waiver rather than to offer to enter into a closing agreement has been the likelihood that the IRS would grant a waiver given the cause(s) of failure. This amounted to a judgment call, usually based on the experience to date under the waiver ruling process. In this connection, a statutory precondition to the granting of a waiver with respect to any failed contract requires the IRS to determine not only that the error giving rise to the failure is reasonable but also that "reasonable steps are being taken to remedy the error." In making the latter determination, the IRS considers, *inter alia*, whether the error was brought to its attention within a reasonable period of time after the error was discovered. If there is evidence that the responsible personnel of an insurer discovered the existence of the error at a prior time but chose to take no action to address it, the IRS may deny the insurer's later-filed waiver request on the ground that reasonable steps were not taken in a timely manner, a condition sometimes referred to as laches. In this connection, determining who knew what, and when they knew it, can be a complex undertaking.

Another consideration was the amount of the toll charge the company would pay under the terms of a closing agreement, an amount based in principle on the tax the IRS would have collected (along with deficiency interest) had the insurer reported the section 7702(g) income on the contract and the policyholder paid the tax involved (as detailed below). Where the cost of investigation of the causes of error to argue for the waiver promised to exceed this toll charge, pursuing the closing agreement proved to be the practical expedient.

Under the waiver and closing agreement process, the responsibility and financial burden to identify and correct the error generally fall on the issuing company as a practical matter, but the affected policyholders may incur tax on interest on excess premiums paid that are returned to them as a result of the correction process.

---

[20] *Supra* note 3.
[21] In administering closing agreements related to failed contracts, the IRS typically has not sought penalties against the insurer. *See* note 5.

Because of the potential for non-tax liability on the insurer, it would be a highly unusual situation (e.g., a bankruptcy or insolvency) in which an issuing company would even consider the possibility of reporting the income on failed contracts to policyholders.

## Correction of Failed Contracts

Regardless of whether a company receives a waiver or enters into a closing agreement to remedy a section 101(f) or 7702 failure, the failed contract must be corrected. The standard remedies for correcting failed contracts are:

- to increase the contract's death benefit to an amount necessary to ensure compliance with section 101(f) or 7702,
- to return excess premiums with interest, or
- some combination of the two.

Correction of a terms-of-the-contract failure of a cash value accumulation test (CVAT) contract may also require a contract restructuring to remedy the cause of failure.[26] As noted in Chapter 6, the amendment of a guideline premium-tested contract to one tested under the CVAT has also occurred with respect to certain failures, particularly those involving excess interest whole life or fixed premium universal life plans. Similarly, the correction of a single premium net rate plan (i.e., one that imposed no mortality charge) was also accomplished by amending the contracts to permit the imposition of a mortality charge.

> **A Better Penalty?**
>
> One might wonder whether the life insurance industry would have been better served by the adoption of the Senate proposal in 1984 to apply an excise tax directly to companies with respect to any failed contracts that they may have issued.[22] The imposition of such a tax on the issuing company was "intended to make the issuer of the life insurance contract as well as the policyholder bear the responsibility for meeting the statutory definition or [incur] some economic burden for failure to do so."[23] The legislative history of the House provision, which was ultimately adopted, indicated that the income on the contract, because of its treatment as received by the policyholder, "would be a distribution subject to the recordkeeping, reporting, and withholding rules under present law relating to commercial annuities (including life insurance)."[24] It went on to say, "It is hoped this will provide the policyholder with adequate notice that disqualification has occurred, thus giving some protection against underpayment of estimated taxes."[25]

The correction of contracts is generally required to occur within 90 days of the date the waiver or closing agreement is granted (i.e., signed by the IRS). The correction process may not be quite as simple as it appears from the neatly phrased remedies, particularly if the number of contracts affected is large. The nature of the death benefit increase and/or the refund of excess premiums (and interest) may require special administrative processing. Under the guideline premium test, the intent of the contract correction is to bring into alignment the relationship between premiums paid and the corresponding guideline premium limitation. If, at the time the IRS grants a waiver or enters into a closing agreement, the premiums paid for a failed contract exceed the respective premium limitation, the insurer must either return the excess premiums (and interest) or increase the death benefit. While the intent of such a death benefit increase is simply to increase the premium limitation to support the premiums paid to date, implementing such an increase raises questions as to how the increase in death benefit should be accounted for in determining the definitional limitations. In particular, what should be the effective date of the additional death benefit for purposes of determining the definitional limitations? Further, an insurer may decide that it does not want to pay commissions, assess a cost of insurance charge or impose a surrender charge on the increase in death benefit, all of which may prove difficult to administer without some type of modification to its existing administrative system.

Similarly, administrative systems may have difficulty processing the removal of excess premiums and earnings. System overrides may be necessary so that the removal of the excess premiums is not administered as a

---

[22] Under the Senate provision, contracts that failed were to be treated as a combination of term life insurance and an annuity as of the date of failure; upon failure, an excise tax of 10 percent of the net surrender value of the contract would have been imposed on the company. See DEFRA Senate Report, *supra* Chapter 1, note 11, at 578–79.
[23] DEFRA Senate Report, *supra* Chapter 1, note 11, at 579.
[24] DEFRA House Report, *supra* Chapter 1, note 11, at 1449.
[25] *Id.*
[26] *See, e.g.*, PLR 200841034 (March 28, 2008).

partial surrender, which otherwise may result in a corresponding reduction in the contract's specified amount of insurance resulting in an adjustment calculation (and further complicating the calculation of the refund).

Timing may also be a problem where a contract amendment is required, as in the case of the correction of a failure under the CVAT.[27] To meet the deadline for completion of the correction, it may be advisable to submit a contract amendment to state insurance regulators for approval in advance of the finalization of the remedial action by the IRS. This requires that the remedy be determined earlier in the process rather than later, which may itself be problematic, in that the IRS could ultimately object to the proposed corrective action. An alternative approach may be to request a time period for correction that differs from the standard one (i.e., correction within 90 days of IRS signature of the waiver or closing agreement) where there are unique circumstances, such as the need to obtain state regulators' approval of a corrective endorsement or rider. Another problematic situation is where an insurer is still issuing life insurance contracts that contain a flaw and no approved contract forms exist that can be used to ensure continuity of business.

Other issues may also arise in the process of correcting failed life insurance contracts. Policyholder contact, policyholder consent and insurance department contact or approval may be necessary. A potentially large liability under a closing agreement may create financial disclosure issues. Further, policyholder reactions, particularly in connection with corrective payments or contract changes and possibly in the form of legal actions, may need to be dealt with. All of this will likely require a substantial commitment of insurance company time and resources.

## Waivable Errors and the Causes of Noncompliance

Failures under sections 101(f) and 7702 can occur for a variety of reasons including the complexity of both the actuarial limitations themselves and the products to which the limitations are applied. Ambiguity and the lack of published guidance are often cited as reasons for noncompliance, as is inattention to compliance on the part of insurance companies. In addition, some products are designed to take maximum advantage of the definitional limitations and on occasion overstep the boundaries. A review of the waiver rulings issued by the IRS (which are disclosed to the public in redacted form) indicates that many errors result from compliance systems with a significant manual component. Also, as the waiver process has amply documented, some errors occur simply as a result of a variety of human errors in administration of the limitations. In either case, compliance errors are discovered in a number of ways, including internal compliance reviews, system changes and due diligence by a distributor, by a prospective purchaser of the insurer or a block of its business, or by a financial auditor of the insurer. Potentially, the IRS could discover errors by auditing, but such activity has been limited.

As discussed below, most of the waivers granted by the IRS have dealt with failures under the guideline premium test. The retrospective nature of the guideline premium test makes administration of the limitation reliant on the availability (and accuracy) of transaction history. Shortcomings in contract administrative systems or insurance company practices can and do lead to guideline premium test failures, as is documented below. In this regard, historical data often is lost in the process of converting systems or archiving transaction data, either as a part of ongoing administration or in connection with an acquisition or sale. Prudence would suggest that, if historical transaction data is not carried by an administrative system, it be archived in a format that makes it accessible for historical testing should the need arise.[28] While the CVAT is a prospective test based on future benefits that must be met by the terms of the contract (and consequently is not reliant on transaction history to the same extent), the IRS has on occasion waived "administrative" errors where the taxpayer has misapplied the net single premium (NSP) limitation. Accurate historical contract data is needed to compute the toll charge for a section 101(f) or 7702 closing agreement (or, as detailed later, the **overage earnings** in a closing agreement to correct inadvertent MECs) regardless of whether the contracts have been tested under the CVAT or the guideline premium test.

Errors that have been waived under section 7702(f)(8) or section 101(f)(3)(H) may be thought of as falling into five principal categories:

---

[27] *See* PLR 200901028 (Sept. 29, 2008).
[28] Rendering archived data accessible implies that the insurer maintains (in working order) the hardware and software needed to access the data. Remember mag tapes?

- Interpretive errors, or errors made in applying the various rules of sections 101(f) and 7702
- Product design errors
- Programming or systems errors
- Contract administration errors
- Manual calculation and input errors[29]

Interpretive and design errors that have been the subject of waiver rulings were described or cited in Chapters 2 through 6 in the context of the statutory provisions to which they relate. Programming, administration, and manual calculation and input errors are discussed below. (Many of these same errors have been cited by insurers as reasons contracts inadvertently became MECs.)

Two additional comments are in order at this point. First, it should be noted that errors judged by the IRS not to be reasonable generally do not appear in ruling letters made public, as they are addressed in closing agreements that are not publicly disclosed. Hence, the determinations made in the closing agreements are not presented below. Second, it is again worth noting that a number of the waiver rulings reviewed below are quite dated. As said before, there is no assurance that current IRS personnel would reach the same conclusions were they to be asked.

## *Programming or Systems Errors*

The first category of errors discussed here, programming or systems errors, deals with a variety of systems-related errors, including system conversion and maintenance and rounding errors.

With respect to these types of errors, under the waiver rulings issued, the IRS has generally taken the position that if the fundamental design of a compliance program is wrong, it will not waive the error. Thus, the IRS has been fairly unbending in holding insurers to a standard of absolute liability in the construction of the basic compliance system. In a 1991 private letter ruling,[30] the IRS (in a rare ruling letter documenting a refusal to waive an error) held that errors resulting from an "inherent structural flaw" in a compliance system were unreasonable and not waivable. Similarly, in a footnote to a 2001 private letter ruling granting a waiver for other reasons, the IRS noted an insurer's contention that its error was a reasonable one because the insurer "should have been able to rely on the accuracy and correct analysis contained in the programming for off-the-shelf compliance software marketed to the insurance industry."[31] In response, the IRS restated its longstanding view that "[t]axpayers [i.e., insurers] are required to independently analyze, test, and verify all assumptions and methodology contained in … software."[32] The IRS went on to say that the obligation to comply with the requirements of section 7702 belongs to the taxpayer (the insurer) and responsibility for failure to comply may not be delegated.

On the other hand, waivers have been granted in instances where the instructions of an insurer's actuaries and attorneys were inadvertently not followed in implementing its compliance system. In 1997, the IRS granted a waiver in a case where the insurer's actuaries and attorneys had correctly interpreted the requirements of the definitional limitations and created instructions for programmers to follow. However, certain inadvertent errors were made in manually programming the compliance tests into the insurer's computer system, causing contracts to fail.[33] Similarly, in granting a waiver in 2009, the IRS noted that an insurer's instructions to programmers were based on proper interpretations of the definitional limitations, but inadvertent errors were made in programming the insurer's system.[34] Another waiver ruling described how an insurer's computerized compliance system failed to account properly for a change in death benefit option. More specifically, instruc-

---

[29] Many of the waiver rulings bear an issue date in 1991. This stems from the fact that, as discussed in note 5, Rev. Rul. 91-17 contained an offer by the IRS not to assert penalties for compliance failures to the extent a taxpayer sought a waiver or offered to enter into a closing agreement by June 3, 1991.
[30] PLR 9202008 (Oct. 31, 1991).
[31] PLR 200150018 (Sept. 13, 2001).
[32] Id.
[33] PLR 9801042 (Oct. 2, 1997).
[34] PLR 200917002 (Jan. 15, 2009). *See also* PLR 199941024 (July 14, 1999).

tions as to how the attained-age decrement method should have been incorporated into the computer software were not followed due to a programming error.[35]

Errors in programming or systems can occur in a variety of ways, including errors made in converting and updating systems, differences in rounding between systems, and improper accounting for premiums.

**System Conversion and Maintenance Errors**
This category of errors arises in connection with the conversion from one system to another, or as a result of improper system maintenance. A 2007 waiver ruling described how mathematical errors in an insurer's prior manual compliance system were carried over on conversion to a computerized system.[36] Also, a 1990 waiver ruling described, in connection with a conversion to a more sophisticated computer system, how insurance company personnel failed to correctly insert new data relating to existing contracts or to recalculate the guideline premiums as necessary when contract changes or exchanges were made.[37] Another conversion error occurred when, in a system conversion, the date of conversion was used in place of the actual issue date of contracts, resulting in compliance errors that were waived.[38] In a fourth waiver ruling in this category, a programmer failed to ensure that the records for all contracts contained guideline premium limitations after conversion.[39]

Apart from conversions, the IRS has waived inadvertent programming errors that led to compliance failures. This was the case in a 1997 private letter ruling in which an insolvent insurer's administration system was programmed to bypass, indefinitely, the guideline premium monitoring mechanism of the system to allow the administration system to continue administering the contracts after the system had "crashed."[40] This programming error, which caused guideline premium monitoring to be suspended for nearly two years, was waived. Similarly, the IRS has waived a programming error that led to the failure of the guideline premium testing system to access stored premium data in determining the premiums paid for purposes of comparing them with the guideline premium limitation.[41] A waiver also was granted in an instance where an insurer's contract administration system billed policyholders for planned premiums even though the premiums, when paid, would cause the guideline premium limitation to be exceeded; the insurer's guideline premium testing system failed to address these premium payments.[42] However, it appears the IRS has not always been consistent in granting waivers for inadvertent programming errors.

**Rounding Errors**
As discussed in Appendix 2.2, the DEFRA legislative history[43] provides for reasonable approximations and rounding, generally limited to rounding up to the nearest dollar of premium per $1,000 of death benefit, in the calculation of NSP and guideline premium values. Even so, insurers have encountered compliance errors due to problems in rounding. Rounding-related errors often occur when an insurer's proposal (i.e., illustration) system and its administrative system produce slightly different results. Also, rounding differences between systems have been waived in a number of rulings.[44]

*Errors in Contract Administration*
Errors can occur both in the process used to assure compliance, particularly where there is a significant manual component, and in the manner in which the limits are administered. Errors in administration include: procedural errors, where the failure occurred as a result of a breakdown in the administrative process; assumption and calculation errors; and system overrides, where a system-generated limit was incorrectly overridden by administrative staff.[45]

---

[35] PLR 200150018 (Sept. 13, 2001).
[36] PLR 200819003 (Dec. 27, 2007).
[37] PLR 9042039 (July 23, 1990).
[38] PLR 9621016 (Feb. 21, 1996).
[39] PLR 9723040 (Mar. 11, 1997).
[40] Id.
[41] PLR 200227036 (Apr. 9, 2002).
[42] PLR 9203049 (Oct. 23, 1991).
[43] DEFRA Blue Book, *supra* Chapter 1, note 20, at 653.
[44] PLRs 200143008 (July 17, 2001), 9436037 (June 13, 1994), 9144020 (July 31, 1991) and 9144009 (July 26, 1991).
[45] *See* PLR 9625046 (March 21, 1996) (waiving an error in the administration of the CVAT).

### Procedural Errors

Procedural errors often result from a failure to act or to communicate among various departments of an insurance company charged with administering the definitional limitations. They may also result from testing procedures that are partly computerized and partly manual. In one waiver ruling, the insurer's contract administration system did not contain any programming for monitoring tax compliance, so criteria were developed for selecting those contracts that would be manually tested to assure such compliance. However, the selection criteria failed to identify all contracts that needed to be manually tested.[46]

Waivers of procedural errors also have been granted for various failures of administrative personnel to act on computer-generated notices indicating that the definitional limitations were being violated. In a 2007 waiver ruling, an insurer's computer system correctly generated violation notices, but due to a miscommunication between the insurer's employees in two different locations, no action was taken to address the notices.[47] Likewise, in a 1991 waiver ruling, an insurer's employees failed to forward system-generated violation notices to the work units responsible for responding to the notices.[48] A 1994 waiver ruling involved flexible premium contracts issued prior to the effective date of section 101(f), for which notices to policyholders proposing to change the death benefits to bring the contracts into compliance with section 101(f) were not followed up.[49] In another instance, customer service representatives inadvertently accepted payments in excess of the guideline premium limitation notwithstanding a violation warning message generated by the monitoring system at the time the payments were processed.[50] Finally, according to a 2002 ruling, an insurer's computer system generated an initial report of excess premium payments, but the employee responsible for processing the report did not realize the report needed to be processed in the same manner as other violation notices. The IRS waived the error.[51]

A number of procedural error waivers involved a failure of employees to take preplanned, required actions. For example, in one 1994 waiver ruling, scheduled decreases in premium after the first year were not processed, and the failure to reduce the planned premiums eventually resulted in violation of the guideline premium limitations.[52] Likewise, in a 2007 waiver ruling, an insurer's personnel failed to refund amounts from contracts following death benefit reductions despite instructions to do so from the insurer's computerized compliance system.[53] In a 1996 waiver ruling, an employee responsible for manually recomputing the guideline premium limitation upon a contract change failed to make the required computation.[54] In another waiver ruling that year, the failure of the actuarial department to retest contracts for possible guideline premium limitation violations after a change in premium payments or other contract terms was waived, as was the failure of the policyholder service department to refer a contract to the actuarial department when a change was made in the contract's premiums or other terms.[55] In a 1997 ruling, the IRS waived a failure to compare premiums paid under a contract to a diskette-generated policy illustration that set forth the guideline premium limitation.[56] In a 1998 waiver ruling, in which manual procedures were used to ensure compliance with the guideline premium test, the actuarial department failed to retest contracts for continued compliance after changes in the amount of scheduled premiums to be paid by payroll deduction, requests to pay an unscheduled premium amount and decreases in coverage amounts.[57]

A variation of the foregoing, frequently encountered in the past, involves a failure to act in time. In a 2002 waiver ruling, a monthly violation report was sorted by contract number and did not include the contract anniversary date of each of the contracts identified as potentially having excess premiums. The failure of administrative staff to process those contracts on the monthly report that were closest to the deadline under the section

---

[46] PLR 9144009 (July 26, 1991), supplemented by PLR 9244010 (July 28, 1992). It is unclear whether the IRS would today consider a completely manual system to be a reasonable approach to compliance with the definitional limitations.
[47] PLR 200838018 (June 10, 2008).
[48] PLR 9146011 (Aug. 9, 1991).
[49] PLR 9416017 (Jan. 13, 1994).
[50] PLR 199949026 (Sept. 14, 1999). See also PLR 200143008 (July 17, 2001).
[51] PLR 200227036 (Apr. 9, 2002).
[52] PLR 9416017 (Jan. 13, 1994).
[53] PLR 200819003 (Dec. 27, 2007).
[54] PLR 9623068 (Mar. 15, 1996).
[55] PLR 9712006 (Dec. 17, 1996).
[56] PLR 9723040 (Mar. 11, 1997).
[57] PLR 9843028 (July 24, 1998).

# Chapter 8 | Failed Contracts and Inadvertent Modified Endowment Contracts 273

101(f)(3)(B) and section 7702(f)(1)(B) 60-day rules ahead of those which were further from the deadline was waived.[58]

In a 2003 waiver ruling, excess premiums were received under section 1035 exchanges when the initial calculation of the death benefit to be applied under the new contract did not anticipate the increase in premium resulting from interest applied to the old contract's cash value before the amounts were transferred from the previous issuer. In processing the premiums, the new insurer's administrative staff "was under the erroneous belief that they could neither increase the death benefit nor refund the excess premiums received."[59]

A final category of procedural errors that have been waived involves the breakdown of communications between the actuarial and administrative areas. In a 2001 ruling, although an insurer required its clerical personnel processing unscheduled premium payments to refer the premium to the actuarial department to ensure compliance with the guideline premium limitation, the personnel processing the payments in some cases failed to do so. Their failure to report contracts to the actuarial department upon learning of changes in contracts, and their failure to record new guideline premium limitations for the contracts in the administration system upon the occurrence of such changes, were waived by the IRS.[60] Occasionally, the lack of communication is in the other direction. In another ruling that year, the failure of an insurer's actuarial department to notify its policy change department that a face reduction would cause a contract to violate the guideline premium limitation was waived.[61]

**Assumption and Calculation Errors**

Assumption and calculation errors deal with the use of incorrect assumptions in the computation of the guideline premium limitation. These errors, all of which were waived, fall into several categories, including:

- The use of incorrect expense charges[62]

- The entry of the incorrect age of the insured into an administrative system[63]

- The use of an incorrect mortality table[64] (e.g., the guideline premiums were erroneously recomputed assuming that the insured was a smoker)[65]

- Errors due to changes in underwriting class from smoker to nonsmoker status, substandard to standard risk class and the use of incorrect gender factors[66]

- Errors in the application of the effective date rules of section 7702 to contracts issued under section 101(f)[67]

- The use of the premium due date rather than the date of receipt of the premiums to test compliance[68]

- The failure to input, manually in this case, the correct amount of premiums paid into the guideline premium testing system[69]

- The computation of a death benefit that was not sufficiently high to allow a contract to receive in the entirety of rollover cash value as well as the scheduled premiums[70]

---

[58] PLR 200227036 (Apr. 9, 2002).
[59] PLR 200350001 (Sept. 3, 2003).
[60] PLR 200150014 (Sept. 12, 2001).
[61] PLR 200150018 (Sept. 13, 2001).
[62] PLRs 200917002 (Jan. 15, 2009), 200143008 (July 17, 2001) and 9801042 (Oct. 2, 1997).
[63] PLRs 9723040 (Mar. 11, 1997) and 9517042 (Jan. 31, 1995).
[64] PLRs 200027030 (Apr. 10, 2000), 199924027 (Mar. 19, 1999) and 9517042.
[65] PLR 9623068 (Mar. 15, 1996).
[66] PLR 199924027 (March 19, 1999).
[67] PLR 9723040 (Mar. 11, 1997). See also PLR 200143008 (July 17, 2001).
[68] PLR 200143008 (July 17, 2001).
[69] PLR 9801042 (Oct. 2, 1997). Similarly, the IRS has granted waivers for other types of input errors. See for example, PLRs 200143008, 9805010 (Oct. 28, 1997) and 9436037 (June 13, 1994).
[70] PLR 9843028 (July 24, 1998).

### System Reporting and Overrides

Unlike waivers resulting from a failure to communicate or act on potential errors, the waiver rulings next discussed deal with customer service errors, where system-generated notices were overridden or otherwise disregarded, resulting in compliance failures. For example, in a 2000 waiver ruling, an insurer's customer service representatives made improper manual overrides to the guideline premium testing system, and they also did not act on error reports automatically generated by the system, thereby allowing premium payments for contracts to exceed the contracts' guideline premium limitations.[71] In a similar 1995 waiver ruling, an insurer's computerized compliance system rejected a premium payment that exceeded the guideline premium limitation, but the employee investigating the rejection overrode the system, so that the premium payment was erroneously accepted.[72] In another 1995 waiver ruling, an insurer's administrative personnel sometimes accepted and credited scheduled or unscheduled premiums that exceeded the guideline premium limitation by manually disabling the computer system feature that tested newly received premiums for compliance with the guideline premium limitation.[73]

### *Manual Calculation and Input Errors*

The final category of previously waived errors, manual calculation and input errors, are just that—clerical errors that result in an improper or erroneous calculation of the guideline premiums or the sum of the premiums paid-to-date. For example, in a 1991 waiver ruling, the IRS waived noncompliance resulting from errors made by an insurer's clerks in calculating the guideline premiums.[74] The IRS has also waived:

- Failures resulting from errors in manual computations made in the monitoring of premiums paid under the guideline premium test[75]

- Errors made in manual retesting of contracts identified by a computer monitoring program as having premiums in excess of the guideline premium limitation[76]

- Mathematical errors resulting in the failure to calculate the guideline premiums properly after an adjustment within the meaning of section 7702(f)(7)(A)[77]

- The inadvertent deletion of a year-end record of a contract's guideline premium limitation that caused the limitation to be exceeded[78]

- Errors in manual recalculations that incorrectly indicated the guideline premium limitation had not been exceeded[79]

- Errors resulting from the failure of personnel to input correctly the contract information necessary to calculate the correct amount of a refund to ensure compliance[80]

## The Remediation Revolution (Part 1): Failed Contracts

Not long after the enactment of section 7702 in 1984, the IRS began receiving submissions from life insurance companies seeking waivers and offering to enter into closing agreements to correct instances of inadvertent noncompliance with the statute and its section 101(f) predecessor. The enactment of section 7702A generated similar problems of inadvertent noncompliance and requests from insurers, beginning in the mid-1990s, that they be allowed to remedy the noncompliance through closing agreements, the benefit of a waiver procedure not being available under that provision. By the end of that decade, the IRS had accumulated considerable experience dealing with section 101(f) and 7702 waivers and closing agreements, had published Rev. Rul. 91-

---

[71] PLR 200045029 (Aug. 17, 2000). Typically in the "override" rulings, it was evident the employees' actions were not consistent with the insurers' procedures.
[72] PLR 9524021 (Mar. 21, 1995).
[73] PLR 9601039 (Oct. 5, 1995). In granting the waiver, the IRS noted, "These individuals are no longer employed by Taxpayer."
[74] PLR 9144009 (July 26, 1991), supplemented by PLR 9244010 (July 28, 1992). *See also* PLR 9202008 (Oct. 31, 1991).
[75] PLR 9144020 (July 31, 1991).
[76] PLR 9214039 (Dec. 31, 1991).
[77] PLR 9723040 (Mar. 11, 1997). *See also* PLR 199924027 (Mar. 19, 1999).
[78] PLR 9801042 (Oct. 2, 1997).
[79] PLR 199911010 (Dec. 8, 1998).
[80] PLR 200227036 (Apr. 9, 2002).

17[81] and Notice 99-48[82] addressing section 101(f) and 7702 waivers and closing agreements, and had taken an initial step in grappling with inadvertent MECs, publishing Rev. Proc. 99-27[83] to enable the submission of closing agreement offers to correct MEC problems for a limited period of time. The MEC correction procedure resulted in filings from many insurers by the time of the procedure's filing deadline in 2001, prompting the IRS to extend and somewhat simplify the program via the issuance of Rev. Proc. 2001-42.[84] The new decade also brought with it a series of waiver requests that ended with the publication of the first substantive revenue ruling (Rev. Rul. 2005-6)[85] interpreting an aspect of the definitional limitations relating to QABs and offering a remedy for noncompliance other than a standard waiver or closing agreement. By mid-decade, it had become clear to the government and the life insurance industry that more was needed to enable insurers to remedy problems of noncompliance and, in particular, remove certain disincentives that had discouraged some from pursuing corrective measures.

In Notice 2007-15,[86] the Treasury Department and the IRS requested comments on how to improve the procedures then available to correct

- life insurance contracts that failed to satisfy the requirements of section 101(f) or 7702, as applicable,

- contracts that inadvertently failed the 7-pay test of section 7702A(b) and became MECs, and

- failures to diversify the investments of variable contract separate accounts as required under section 817(h).

In response to comments received from the industry, and as part of an effort to streamline tax compliance procedures from the standpoint of both insurers and the government, five new revenue procedures were issued in June 2008:

- Rev. Proc. 2008-38,[87] elaborating on the "Alternative C" QAB error correction procedure under Rev. Rul. 2005-6

- Rev. Proc. 2008-39,[88] revising the pre-existing correction process for inadvertent MECs

- Rev. Proc. 2008-40,[89] addressing closing agreements for contracts failing to comply with section 101(f) or 7702

- Rev. Proc. 2008-41,[90] revising a previous closing agreement procedure for section 817(h) diversification failures

- Rev. Proc. 2008-42,[91] providing an automatic procedure for obtaining a waiver of clerical-type errors under sections 101(f)(3)(H) and 7702(f)(8)

The publication of these revenue procedures represented a virtual revolution in the government's approach to the correction of contract errors, emphasizing simplification, cost reduction and, more generally, a pro-compliance attitude. The new procedures also entailed a shifting of audit-type responsibility from the IRS's National Office to its field auditors (namely, in many cases, the Large Business and International Division (LB&I)).

Each of the four new procedures dealing with compliance problems under the definitional limitations is discussed in detail below, and they also appear in the appendix materials later in this book.[92] The procedures

---

[81] *Supra* note 3.
[82] *Supra* note 4.
[83] 1999-1 C.B. 1186.
[84] 2001-2 C.B. 212.
[85] 2005-1 C.B. 471.
[86] 2007-1 C.B. 503.
[87] 2008-2 C.B. 139.
[88] 2008-2 C.B. 143.
[89] *Supra* note 3.
[90] 2008-2 C.B. 155.
[91] 2008-2 C.B. 160.
[92] Rev. Proc. 2008-41, revising Rev. Proc. 92-25, 1992-1 C.B. 741, deals with the diversification requirements for separate account assets, not the definitional limitations, and is therefore not included in the discussion below. For additional information on this procedure, *see* Adney and McKeever, *supra* Chapter 6, note 6.

addressing the correction of failed contracts under sections 101(f) and 7702 are described first, followed by a discussion of the MEC correction procedure. It should be noted that each of these revenue procedures applies by its terms not only to the original issuer of contracts but also to a "company that insures a contract holder under a contract originally issued by another company." In this manner, the procedures allow their use by a reinsurer of failed contracts or inadvertent MECs, whether via assumption reinsurance or coinsurance, as well as by the issuer of such contracts. Hence, in the discussions below, references to "issuer" include such a reinsurer.

## *Rev. Proc. 2008-38: Correcting the QAB Error*

As mentioned above and discussed in Chapter 3, Rev. Rul. 2005-6 held that the reasonable expense charge rule of section 7702(c)(3)(B)(ii) applies to charges for QABs, including the family term QAB. Further, because the IRS was aware in publishing the ruling that a number of insurance companies were not following the rule in their definitional calculations (the QAB error), and because it recognized that the normally applicable procedures for addressing errors under sections 7702 and 7702A would not produce an equitable result in the case of the QAB error, the ruling provided a new form of remedy for the noncompliance involved. The remedy provided came in the form of special rules and procedures for entering into a closing agreement with the IRS. To this end, the ruling deviated from the normal remediation procedures in two significant respects.

First, Rev. Rul. 2005-6 did not require the issuer to take corrective action with respect to the QABs accounted for using the reasonable mortality charge rule rather than the reasonable expense charge rule (as required under the ruling) if the issuer requested "Alternative B" relief through a closing agreement by February 7, 2006.[93] This was done in recognition of the fact that, in many instances, the QAB error was embedded in older computerized compliance systems that would be difficult and expensive to correct, and yet the magnitude of the excess inside buildup the error allowed was usually relatively small. On the other hand, under "Alternative C" of the revenue ruling, which applies to the filing of a closing agreement request after February 7, 2006, the contracts and the compliance system affected by the QAB error need to be corrected.

Second, a special toll charge structure was adopted, imposing costs significantly below those of a closing agreement based on the section 7702(g) income on the contract or the toll charge to correct inadvertent MECs. This special structure, which applied to Alternatives B and C and did so regardless of whether the failure was under section 7702 or section 7702A (or both), called for a charge determined using a sliding scale based upon the aggregate number of contracts for which relief was requested. This structure is described further below.

Rev. Proc. 2008-38 continues the relief provided under Alternative C of Rev. Rul. 2005-6 for post-February 7, 2006, closing agreement requests and amplifies the corrective action that must be taken to bring failed contracts, inadvertent MECs and the system(s) on which they are administered into compliance with the applicable statutes.[94] The request for a closing agreement under the revenue procedure, as was the case under Rev. Rul. 2005-6, is required to be submitted following the usual procedures governing requests for private letter rulings, including payment of the IRS filing fee. In addition, the request must include a representation by the taxpayer that it is within the scope of section 3 of the revenue procedure, i.e., that the taxpayer is an "issuer" of one or more contracts that became failed contracts or inadvertent MECs as a result of the QAB error. As noted above, the definition of an issuer in this revenue procedure and its companion 2008 procedures is broad enough to encompass reinsurers of affected contracts as well as the contracts' original issuers. The revenue procedure, like Rev. Rul. 2005-6, is silent as to the effect of its issuance on the section 7702(f)(8) waiver request process, but it is likely the revenue procedure is now the sole remedy for correcting the QAB error.

Under Rev. Proc. 2008-38, as under Rev. Rul. 2005-6, the closing agreement request must identify the contracts that are failed contracts or inadvertent MECs. Specifically, according to section 4.01 of the revenue procedure, the request must include an exhibit setting forth the policy number of each contract for which relief is

---

[93] This relief also extended to future QAB charges resulting from an increase in an existing QAB or the addition of a new QAB pursuant to the exercise of a right that existed in the contract before April 8, 2005. Alternative A in the revenue ruling provided that where an issuer's compliance system improperly accounted for QAB charges but no contracts failed under IRC § 7702, the issuer could correct its system to account for charges using the reasonable expense charge rule without any need to contact the IRS. This simply restated the actions insurers may take under existing law, with the statement in the ruling perhaps serving as a reminder that insurers do not need to involve the IRS in circumstances where no contracts have failed to comply with the definitional limitations.

[94] If a contract is affected by the QAB error but also fails due to a separate error, the revenue procedure does not provide for remediation of that other error. To remedy that other error, resort must be had to Rev. Procs. 2008-40 or 2008-42 (or perhaps to a waiver ruling request).

sought. The IRS followed up Rev. Rul. 2005-6 with Notice 2005-35,[95] which provided procedures under which a list identifying the contracts subject to a closing agreement under that ruling could be submitted in electronic format. Under Alternatives B and C of the ruling, a request for a closing agreement was required to include a list identifying the contracts for which relief is requested, since this provided the IRS with information on the contracts affected by the QAB error as well as the basis for determining the amount of the toll charge. Under Alternative B, this list typically would be voluminous (and it could be sizeable under Alternative C as well). Accordingly, the notice allowed this list to be submitted electronically, in read-only format, on either a CD-ROM or diskette.[96] In this event, a total of three CD-ROMs or diskettes, one for each of the three copies of the closing agreement, needed to be submitted. The revenue procedure (in section 4.07) continues this practice.

**Model Closing Agreement**
Like its companion 2008 procedures, Rev. Proc. 2008-38 provides a model closing agreement to be used under Alternative C of Rev. Rul. 2005-6. Section 4.02 of the revenue procedure requires the closing agreement request to include an executed proposed closing agreement that is in the same form as the model closing agreement in section 5 of the procedure. The terms of the model closing agreement require the issuer to take the following actions:

- The issuer must pay the applicable toll charge to the IRS within 60 calendar days of the date that the IRS executes the closing agreement.

- If the sum of the premiums paid for a contract as of the effective date of the closing agreement exceeds "the amount necessary to keep the Contracts in compliance with the requirements of § 7702 *[and § 7702A, if applicable]*," the issuer must either "[i]ncrease the death benefit to not less than an amount that will ensure compliance with § 7702 *[and § 7702A, if applicable]*," or "[r]efund to the Contract holder the amount of such excess with interest."[97] If there are no such excess premiums for a contract as of the effective date of the closing agreement, then the issuer is not required to take corrective action with respect to the contract. The model closing agreement also provides that if a contract terminated due to the death of the insured prior to the effective date of the closing agreement and at a time when the premiums paid exceeded the guideline premium limitation for the contract, the issuer must pay the policyholder or the policyholder's estate the amount of the excess with interest.

- The issuer must correct its compliance system(s) to account properly for QAB charges as provided in Rev. Rul. 2005-6. Further, and significantly, this and other corrective actions must be completed no later than 90 calendar days from the date the IRS executes the closing agreement. As a practical matter, if a taxpayer anticipates it will take more than 90 days in which to make the corrections, that work should be undertaken prior to the submission of the request.

In exchange for a taxpayer's actions, the IRS agrees under the terms of the closing agreement to treat the contracts that are in force on the effective date of the closing agreement as having satisfied the requirements of sections 7702 and 7702A (as applicable) with respect to the QAB error during the period from the date of issuance of the contracts through and including the latest of:

- the effective date of the closing agreement,
- the date of any corrective action required with respect to in-force contracts, or
- the date of any corrective action required with respect to the taxpayer's compliance system.

Further, contracts that terminated prior to the effective date of the closing agreement are treated as complying with the definitional limitations during the period from date of issuance of such contracts through and including the date of the contracts' termination.

---

[95] 2005-1 C.B. 1087.
[96] Adobe portable document format (PDF) also was listed as a suitable format. According to the notice, other formats could be arranged on a case-by-case basis.
[97] Rev. Proc. 2008-38 § 5(1)(D) (the model closing agreement) (brackets and bolded text in the original). *See also* Rev. Proc. 2008-38 § 4.05. For additional considerations in determining the amounts of the excess premiums and the interest to be refunded, *see* the discussion under Rev. Proc. 2008-40 below.

**Toll Charge**

Under Rev. Proc. 2008-38 as under Rev. Rul. 2005-6, in lieu of the potentially more onerous toll charge imposed by Rev. Procs. 2008-39 and 2008-40 to correct inadvertent MECs and failed contracts, respectively, the amount due from an issuer under the special toll charge structure is based on a schedule contained in the revenue procedure (repeating the schedule that appeared in the revenue ruling). The schedule sets forth a sliding scale of charges keyed to the "number of contracts for which relief is requested." According to the chart set forth in section 4.03 of the revenue procedure (and reproduced in Table 8.2 below), this scale ranges from $1,500 for 20 contracts or fewer, to $50,000 for over 10,000 contracts.

| Table 8.2. Toll charges under Rev. Rul. 2005-6 | |
|---|---|
| Number of contracts | Amount due |
| 20 or fewer | $1,500 |
| 21 to 50 | $2,000 |
| 51 to 100 | $5,000 |
| 101 to 500 | $10,000 |
| 501 to 1,000 | $16,000 |
| 1,001 to 5,000 | $30,000 |
| 5,000 to 10,000 | $40,000 |
| Over 10,000 | $50,000 |

For relief requested on or before February 7, 2006, under Alternative B of the revenue ruling, the "number of contracts" typically equaled all contracts administered under the compliance system that contained the QAB error. After that date and continuing today, where the ruling's Alternative C applies, this number equals the number of contracts actually failing the definitional limitations due to the QAB error. According to section 4.06 of the revenue procedure, the closing agreement request must include a representation that the required toll charge is computed correctly under section 4.03 of the procedure.

## *Rev. Proc. 2008-40: Correcting Failed Contracts Generally*

The general revenue procedure for correcting failed contracts is Rev. Proc. 2008-40.[98] In publishing this procedure, the IRS took a major step in addressing the fact that under the prior closing agreement procedure for failed contracts, innocent mistakes by an insurer, often involving an immaterial amount of excess premium or CSV, in many cases led to the imposition of very high toll charges as a condition for remediation of contracts. The closing agreement process set forth in Rev. Proc. 2008-40 is similar to the one described in Rev. Rul. 91-17, although the 2008 procedure institutes a number of changes to streamline the process and to make the toll charge assessed as a condition to remediation generally more equitable.

More specifically, sections 4.01 and 4.02 of Rev. Proc. 2008-40 require that a request for a closing agreement to correct failed contracts be made in accordance with the process for requesting a private letter ruling, including payment of the IRS filing fee. Further, the request must include:

- The policy number of each failed contract to be covered by the closing agreement
- A description of the defects that caused the contracts to fail to comply with section 101(f) or 7702, as applicable, and an explanation of how and why the defects arose
- A description of the administrative procedures the issuer has implemented to prevent additional failures in the future (again, the issuer is defined to include reinsurers of affected contracts)

---

[98] The effective date of Rev. Proc. 2008-40 is July 21, 2008. As previously noted, it supersedes Rev. Rul. 91-17 in part and it supersedes Notice 99-48.

- A proposed closing agreement, executed by the issuer in triplicate, that follows the model closing agreement appearing in section 5 of the revenue procedure and in which the issuer agrees to pay the appropriate toll charge

The model closing agreement and the toll charge imposed under the revenue procedure are discussed in detail below.

To streamline the process further, the revenue procedure (again, like its companion 2008 procedures) permits the information required to be submitted with the closing agreement request to be provided by the issuer electronically, in read-only format on a CD-ROM, in triplicate.[99]

**Required Representations**

Rev. Proc. 2008-40 (in section 4.06) requires a request for a closing agreement covering failed contracts to include representations to the effect that the issuer of the contracts:

- is within the revenue procedure's scope (i.e., it issued or reinsured the failed contracts),
- properly computed the toll charge, and
- has brought the contracts into compliance with the definitional limitations or will do so within the time period specified in the model closing agreement.

These representations must be made under penalties of perjury, and the issuer must retain documentation available for audit to support the representations. The revenue procedure does not specify how long such documentation must be retained. Given the long-term nature of contracts and the fact that a failure (or inadequate correction) can only be remediated through a proceeding with the IRS, it would be prudent for an issuer to retain documentation for as long as each contract in question remains in force and for some reasonable period of time thereafter (perhaps reflecting the three-year statute of limitations that typically would apply to policyholders and the issuer's otherwise applicable document retention policies).

**Correction of Failed Contracts**

Section 4.05 of Rev. Proc. 2008-40 requires, for each failed contract in force on the effective date of the closing agreement, that the issuer take certain corrective action as necessary to bring the contract into compliance with section 101(f) or 7702, as applicable. Like the case with an Alternative C closing agreement under Rev. Proc. 2008-38, this corrective action must be made not later than 90 days after the date of execution of the closing agreement by the IRS, a fact that, again, requires advance planning (if not advance action) by the issuer.

According to section 4.05 of Rev. Proc. 2008-40, the corrective action must be:

- to increase the death benefit to not less than an amount that will ensure compliance with section 101(f) or 7702, as applicable, or
- to refund to the policyholder the excess of the sum of the premiums paid as of the effective date of the closing agreement (i.e., when the IRS executes the agreement) over the guideline premium limitation as of that date, with interest at the contract's interest crediting rate.

If, however, the sum of the premiums paid does not exceed the guideline premium limitation on the closing agreement's effective date, no corrective action is necessary. Further, the model closing agreement provides that in the case of a contract which terminated by reason of the death of the insured prior to the closing agreement's effective date and at a time when the premiums paid exceeded the guideline premium limitation for the contract, the issuer must pay the policyholder (or the policyholder's estate) the amount of such excess premiums with interest thereon.[100] The revenue procedure does not specify how such interest should be determined, although insurers often use the contract's current interest crediting rate for this purpose. This could be, for in-

---

[99] The fact that three CD-ROM copies are required to be filed—one for each of the three copies of the closing agreements—indicates that the IRS intended for the policy number list to be submitted in this way, rather than the description of the error or the corrective action.

[100] If all rights under a contract have vested with the beneficiary of the death benefit, it would seem reasonable to treat such person as the policyholder for this purpose.

stance, the current rate(s) that applied with respect to the excess premiums while the contract was in force, the rate as of the date of termination or perhaps the rate(s) applicable since that date.

As should be obvious from the wording of section 4.05 of the revenue procedure and its model closing agreement just referenced, and as is also apparent in the procedure's "excess earnings" toll charge described below, the revenue procedure was crafted with guideline premium test failures in mind. Thus, section 4.02 of the revenue procedure states, "In the case of a failure to meet the guideline premium [test], the issuer must submit a proposed closing agreement, in triplicate, executed by the issuer, in the same form as the model closing agreement in section 5 of this revenue procedure." The revenue procedure, however, clearly does not exclude from its scope a contract that sought, but failed, to comply with the CVAT. To this end, section 4.02 goes on to state, "In the case of *any other failure*, the issuer may propose amendments to the proposed closing agreement set forth in section 5 of this revenue procedure, including the amount required to be paid, as appropriate on a case-by-case basis" (emphasis added). Aside from potentially increasing a failed CVAT contract's death benefit to correct it in accordance with the first option in section 4.05, special considerations apply to achieve such a contract's compliance with the CVAT. A discussion of this and related issues under the revenue procedure for failed CVAT contracts appears below under the heading "Contracts That Fail to Satisfy the CVAT."

**Toll Charge**

Section 4.03 of Rev. Proc. 2008-40 allows an issuer to calculate the toll charge required to be paid in connection with a closing agreement covering failed contracts using, for a given contract, one of three alternative methodologies:

- A section 7702(g) approach (referred to in the revenue procedure as the "amount determined based on income on the contract")

- An "excess earnings" approach, provided that the excess earnings do not exceed $5,000 (referred to as the "amount determined based on excess earnings")

- A "100 percent of error" approach (referred to as the "amount determined based on excess premiums")

Under the **section 7702(g) approach**, a toll charge determined in accordance with Rev. Rul. 91-17 as supplemented by Notice 99-48, may apply for contracts with excess earnings (described below) greater than $5,000.[101] This toll charge equals the tax the policyholder would have had to pay each year if he or she were treated as receiving the section 7702(g) income on the contract, along with deficiency interest on that tax amount.[102] (The calculation of the section 7702(g) income on the contract was discussed above in connection with the consequences of failure to comply with section 101(f) or 7702.) Before 1999, the IRS had required use of a 28 percent tax rate in determining closing agreement toll charges. In that year, to conform the failed contract closing agreement tax rates with those used in the first MEC correction revenue procedure (Rev. Proc. 99-27), the IRS issued Notice 99-48,[103] which introduced the use of a three-tiered tax rate structure in determining the amounts due under closing agreements on failed life insurance contracts. Under this structure, which is adopted for use in Rev. Proc. 2008-40 closing agreements by virtue of a cross reference in section 4.03 of that procedure to section 3.11 of the new MEC correction procedure (Rev. Proc. 2008-39, discussed below), the tax rates used to determine the toll charge are:

- 15 percent for contracts with death benefits under $50,000,

- 28 percent for contracts with death benefits equal to or exceeding $50,000 but less than $180,000, and

- 36 percent for contracts with death benefits equal to or exceeding $180,000.[104]

---

[101] The IRC § 7702(g)-based toll charge under the revenue procedure generally mirrors the toll charge required under the prior correction procedure for failed contracts. One difference, however, appears to relate to prior reported amounts. In the past, the IRS often had allowed an offset to tax for income amounts that were reported to policyholders due to distributions from contracts. The model closing agreement set forth in Rev. Proc. 2008-40 § 5 does not, however, provide for any such offset.

[102] The deficiency interest is determined under IRC § 6621(a)(2) as if the amounts treated as received by the policyholder as income on the contract caused underpayments of tax in the appropriate years.

[103] *Supra* note 4.

[104] Because life insurance ownership is positively correlated with income, the three-tier structure more closely approximates the tax rates of policyholders.

For this purpose, section 3.11(2) of Rev. Proc. 2008-39, echoing Notice 99-48, provides that a contract's death benefit is its death benefit (as defined in section 7702(f)(3)) as of any date within 120 days of the date of the request for a closing agreement, or the last day the contract is in force. Based on experience with submissions under both Rev. Rul. 91-17 and Rev. Proc. 2008-40, the toll charge to be paid for a failed contract closing agreement is generally expected to be current as of the date the IRS executes the closing agreement. Effectively, this means that issuers must calculate the toll charge through a date that is beyond the date on which the executed closing agreement is submitted to the IRS with the request for the closing agreement, e.g., perhaps to a date that is 60 to 90 days beyond the date the request is filed. Since the issuer will have actual data relating to the contract only through a current date (that usually must be close in time to the date of the submission of the executed closing agreement), the issuer will need to adopt certain assumptions (and disclose them to the IRS) to calculate the income accruing from this current date through the future date, i.e., for the estimation period. For example, one might assume that no premiums are paid and no withdrawals are taken after that current date.

The major innovation wrought by Rev. Proc. 2008-40, the **excess earnings approach**, permits an issuer to calculate the toll charge by reference to the excess earnings that accrue under the failed contract, provided the excess earnings do not exceed $5,000. This approach essentially adopts a methodology for calculating the toll charge based on the tax benefit a policyholder received from funding a contract at levels higher than permitted by section 101(f) or 7702. The concept of excess earnings is intended to reflect the earnings accruing under a contract on such higher funding, and the toll charge based on such excess earnings is narrowly tailored to "take away" the tax benefit arising from the excess funding. In limiting use of this approach to contracts with excess earnings not exceeding $5,000, the IRS appears to have made a policy judgment that larger contracts should not be eligible for such a narrowly tailored toll charge out of concern that they tend to be more investment oriented.

Under the excess earnings approach, modeled on the toll charge used under the earlier MEC correction revenue procedure, a failed contract's excess earnings generally equal the product of "the sum of a contract's excess premiums for a contract year and its cumulative excess earnings for all prior contract years," and "the applicable earnings rate as set forth in section 3.07 of Rev. Proc. 2008-39."[105] For this purpose, the excess premiums are defined as the amount by which the premiums paid for the contract, as defined in section 7702(f)(1), exceeds its guideline premium limitation. Rev. Proc. 2008-40 does not specify a methodology for identifying "excess premiums for a contract year," and thus it should be permissible, for example, to measure excess premiums on each day of a contract year and to accrue excess earnings using the applicable earnings rate based on this methodology.[106] The "applicable earnings rate" for the years 1988 through 2007 and the related formulas are set forth in Rev. Proc. 2008-39 as described later in this chapter. For contract years prior to 1988, the earnings rates are to be determined in a manner consistent with the formulas in section 3.07 of that procedure for calculating earnings rates for contract years after 2007.

The toll charge under the excess earnings approach equals the tax on the excess earnings and the deficiency interest on that amount, determined using the tax rates described above. Again, based on experience with prior submissions, the amount of this toll charge is generally expected to be current as of the date the IRS executes the closing agreement, and so, as discussed above, issuers must calculate the toll charge through a date that is beyond the date on which the executed closing agreement is submitted to the IRS, such as 60 to 90 days after the date of the submission.

The other toll charge methodology introduced by Rev. Proc. 2008-40, the **100 percent of error approach**, bases the toll charge exclusively on the amount paid for a failed contract that section 101(f) or 7702 did not permit to be paid for a comparable compliant contract. Thus, as the name of the approach indicates, the toll charge under this approach equals 100 percent of the "excess premiums" paid for a contract, i.e., "the highest amount by which the total premiums paid under the contract exceed the guideline premium limitations under section 7702(c) at any time the contract is in force." This effectively amounts to a toll charge equal to 100 per-

---

[105] Rev. Proc. 2008-40 § 4.03(5)(b)(i)–(ii).
[106] The IRS has allowed this approach for the calculation of overage earnings under both the MEC correction procedures and under Rev. Proc. 2008-40. While Rev. Proc. 2008-40 § 4.03(5)(c) sets forth a definition of excess premiums that looks to the highest amount by which premiums paid exceeded the guideline premium limitation at any time under a contract, this definition applies only for purposes of the "100 percent of error" toll charge calculation (discussed below) and not for the calculation of excess earnings. The use of such a definition in the excess earnings case would frustrate the purpose of capturing the inside buildup associated with the excess premiums, the amount of which changes over the life of a contract.

cent of the error. No tax rate or excess earnings (or other) calculation, and no deficiency interest, is employed in determining the amount of the toll charge.

As in the case of the companion 2008 procedures, Rev. Proc. 2008-40 does not require an issuer to submit the details of the toll charge calculations to the IRS, although, as noted above, it is required to represent that the calculations are correct and to retain documentation supporting them.

**Model Closing Agreement**

As noted above, section 4.02 of the revenue procedure requires the submission (with the closing agreement request) of "a proposed closing agreement, in triplicate, executed by the issuer" based on the model closing agreement contained in section 5 of the procedure. This model closing agreement generally follows the principal terms of closing agreements entered into under the prior correction procedure. In particular, in return for the issuer's agreement to pay the toll charge (within 60 calendar days of the date the IRS executes the closing agreement) and take corrective action as described above, the IRS agrees to treat the contracts involved as retroactively complying with section 101(f) or 7702, as applicable. As result, no income is deemed to arise under section 7702(g) and death benefits paid prior to the effective date of the closing agreement are treated as paid by reason of the death of the insured for purposes of the section 101(a)(1) exclusion from gross income.

Under the terms of the model closing agreement, the issuer must agree not to deduct or seek refund of the toll charge paid, or to increase the policyholder's investment in the contract under section 72 or the premiums paid for the contract by any portion of the toll charge (or by any portion of the income on the contract). The IRS, for its part, agrees to waive civil penalties for failures of the issuer to satisfy reporting, withholding and deposit requirements with respect to the section 7702(g) income, and also to forbear treating any portion of the toll charge as income to the policyholders. In addition, the IRS agrees to treat the compliance failures and any required corrective action as having no effect on the date that a contract covered by the closing agreement was issued, entered into or purchased for purposes of the tax law, since a change in that date could have other consequences under the definitional limitations as well as other tax rules (e.g., section 7702A or section 264(a) or (f)).

The model closing agreement contained in section 5 of Rev. Proc. 2008-40 is by its terms addressed to failures to comply with the guideline premium test. As previously noted, however, section 4.02 of the revenue procedure states, "In the case of any other failure [i.e., one not involving the guideline premium test], the issuer may propose amendments to the proposed closing agreement set forth in section 5 of this revenue procedure, including the amount required to be paid, as appropriate on a case-by-case basis." This refers to CVAT failures, which are discussed next.

**Contracts That Fail to Satisfy the CVAT**

The sentence in section 4.02 of Rev. Proc. 2008-40 just quoted seemingly indicates a willingness on the part of the IRS to enter into closing agreements to address CVAT failures, along with a recognition that doing so would require modifications to the model closing agreement. The IRS did not amplify in the revenue procedure what modifications to the toll charge or the required corrective actions might (or might not) be appropriate. In this regard, a key consideration is that the statute requires that a contract seeking to comply with the CVAT do so by its terms; also, of the many waiver rulings the IRS issued between 1988 and 2008, very few related to CVAT failures. The revenue procedure contemplates, however, that closing agreements to correct CVAT errors are available, but the appropriate toll charge and corrective action generally would need to reflect that the error is under the CVAT. The revenue procedure essentially indicates that a taxpayer should make a reasonable offer to the IRS to address such an error, and it should be borne in mind that the IRS possesses considerable discretion with respect to whether and on what terms it will enter into closing agreements. Also, while CVAT errors often involve a contract design flaw, the considerations that led the IRS to modify the toll charge for guideline premium test failures ought to be allowed in the case of CVAT failures. Thus, for example, it would be reasonable for a toll charge to be based on the gains arising from cash values exceeding those permitted under the CVAT, paralleling the toll charge under the excess earnings approach.

Because the CVAT must be satisfied by the terms of a contract, failures under this test often involve an error in a contract's terms. As a result, corrective action for CVAT contract failures often will require that a modification to such terms be made, such as through the addition of an endorsement to increase a contract's death benefit. Of course, if the error affects values only during an initial time period under a contract (e.g., during the first year) and the contract is now past that time period, it seemingly should not be necessary to amend the contract, since any such amendment would be inconsequential.

In some instances, a contract may fail to comply with the CVAT but by happenstance comply with the guideline premium test. Where a contract is intended to satisfy the requirements of the CVAT, there should be no obligation placed on an issuer seeking a closing agreement under Rev. Proc. 2008-40 to verify whether the contract inadvertently complies with the guideline premium test, and the IRS's closing agreement procedure should allow the contract to be corrected so that it complies with the CVAT. At the same time, if the issuer is aware that certain failed CVAT contracts inadvertently comply with the guideline premium test, this arguably should be an important consideration in determining the amount of the toll charge. In such a case, there has not been any harm to the government, i.e., no section 7702(g) income has ever accrued, and in fact it would be permissible for the policyholder to exchange the contract in question for a new, complying CVAT contract in a section 1035 exchange. Similarly, if an issuer of failed CVAT contracts is able to test them under the guideline premium test and can identify the toll charge that would apply to such contracts under section 4.03 of Rev. Proc. 2008-40 using the excess earnings approach or the excess premium approach, it seemingly should be permissible for a closing agreement to make use of that toll charge while allowing correction of the contracts so that they comply with the CVAT. There has been, however, little experience in applying Rev. Proc. 2008-40 to CVAT failures.

## *Rev. Proc. 2008-42: Automatic Waivers*

In a dramatic departure from the IRS's prior practice, Rev. Proc. 2008-42 permits certain errors leading to section 101(f) or 7702 compliance failures to be waived under section 101(f)(3)(H) or 7702(f)(8) on an automatic basis. Specifically, an issuer[107] seeking relief under this revenue procedure for such **automatic waivers** is required to file an Automatic Waiver Request Under Rev. Proc. 2008-42 statement (**waiver statement**) with the IRS's National Office and to attach a separate statement to its federal income tax return (**return attachment**). These filings are in lieu of requesting a waiver ruling or a closing agreement through the private letter ruling process.

- The waiver statement must provide a "brief description" of the error(s), the steps taken to remedy the error(s), the policy numbers of the failed contracts and the representations set forth in section 4.04 of the revenue procedure (described below).[108] Further, it must be signed, dated and filed (in duplicate) with the IRS National Office no later than the date the tax return is filed for the taxable year during which the insurer relies upon the revenue procedure for the waiver(s). The waiver statement may be filed electronically as provided in section 4.05 of the revenue procedure, but unlike other submissions filed with the IRS National Office, it is not governed by the private letter ruling process, thereby eliminating the requirement to pay a user fee to the IRS.

- The return attachment must include the following statement: "Issuer has submitted an Automatic Waiver Request under section 4.02 of Rev. Proc. 2008-42 for certain errors that caused one or more life insurance contracts it issued to fail to comply with §7702(f)(8) or §101(f) of the Internal Revenue Code."[109] According to section 4.03 of the revenue procedure, an issuer filing its return electronically should include the return attachment as a PDF file named "Rev. Proc. 2008-42."

Rev. Proc. 2008-42 provides that an issuer is eligible for an automatic waiver for a failed contract if it can represent in its waiver statement that:

- it had compliance procedures in place with specific, clearly articulated provisions that, if followed, would have prevented the contract involved from failing to comply with the definitional limitations;

---

[107] Again, as with the other 2008 revenue procedures, the issuer is defined to include reinsurers of affected contracts as well as the contracts' original issuers.

[108] The brief description of the error(s) called for in the revenue procedure is to be contrasted with the substantial, and even exhaustive, error description and associated explanation needed in the case of waiver requests made under the prior procedures.

[109] The reference in the quoted language to "fail to comply with §7702(f)(8)" is curious. By definition, since a waiver is being sought and presumably (automatically) granted, the error is a reasonable one, and thus it does not fail to comply with IRC § 7702(f)(8).

- an employee or independent contractor of the issuer acted, or failed to act, in accordance with those compliance procedures; and

- the act or failure to act was inadvertent and was the sole reason for the compliance failure.

The revenue procedure goes on to identify examples of the types of errors eligible for an automatic waiver, such as the input of an incorrect age or sex for an insured, and the input of incorrect information regarding the amount or time of a premium payment, into the issuer's compliance system. On the other hand, the revenue procedure excludes from its purview computer programming errors and defective legal interpretation errors, e.g., errors in interpreting the statutory requirements.

In its waiver statement, the issuer also must represent that it is within the scope of section 3 of Rev. Proc. 2008-42 and is otherwise entitled to the automatic waiver(s). The required representations must be executed under penalties of perjury, and the revenue procedure states, "The issuer must retain documentation available for audit to support the representations." While the quoted language is not unique to Rev. Proc. 2008-42 and the responsibility for auditing compliance with waiver rulings and closing agreement undertakings has always rested with the IRS field rather than the National Office, the revenue procedure's heavy reliance on the issuer's representations as to the overall sufficiency of its compliance system seemingly underscores the shifting of review responsibility from Washington to the field offices of the IRS.

Finally, to be eligible for an automatic waiver under Rev. Proc. 2008-42, the issuer must take "reasonable steps" to remedy the failed contracts; this accords with the reasonable steps language of the statutory waiver provisions. Specifically, the issuer must refund excess premium with interest, increase the death benefit under the contract, or some combination of these no later than the date on which the issuer files the federal income tax return to which the return attachment is affixed. The revenue procedure points out that a reasonable step to remedy the error does not include changes to the issuer's compliance procedures, for the reason that, to be eligible for the automatic waiver, the issuer must have represented that it already had specific, clearly articulated procedures that, if followed, would have prevented the error. It points out as well that if errors are reasonable albeit excluded from the revenue procedure's purview, the issuer still may request a waiver of the error by filing a private letter ruling request under section 101(f)(3)(H) or 7702(f)(8),[110] and for other errors, the revenue procedure refers taxpayers to Rev. Proc. 2008-40.

## The Remediation Revolution (Part 2): Inadvertent MECs

As described in the earlier chapters of this book, section 7702A has proven to be very complex and quite difficult to administer, with the result that many life insurance contracts have inadvertently become MECs. Inadvertent MECs[111] can arise for a variety of reasons, such as the early payment of a premium, errors in administering section 1035 exchanges, or incorrect processing of material changes or death benefit reductions. An insurer's failure to identify a MEC as such can lead to withholding and reporting errors on distributions, which carry a number of penalties for failing to report properly amounts that should be includible as income to the policyholder.

Unlike sections 101(f) and 7702, section 7702A contains no provision enabling the IRS to waive errors in its interpretation or administration. Apart from the statutory provision allowing the return of excess premium and interest within 60 days after the contract anniversary,[112] insurers possessed no means to "un-MEC" an inadvertent MEC. To address this problem, the insurance industry asked the IRS to make use of its general authority under section 7121 to enter into closing agreements to reverse a contract's inadvertent MEC status. This led to the publication of Rev. Proc. 99-27[113] in May 1999, in which the IRS provided a uniform closing agreement under which insurers could cure inadvertent, "non-egregious" overfunding errors that caused contracts to become MECs. This revenue procedure was effective as of May 18, 1999,[114] but was limited to relief requests received by the IRS on or before May 31, 2001.[115] Soon after the expiration of the filing period under that revenue pro-

---

[110] This is the sole written indication that the IRS will continue to entertain waiver requests. To the authors' knowledge, no waiver ruling has been issued since January 15, 2009.
[111] With apologies to Apple Inc., one insurer of which the authors are aware took to referring to an inadvertent MEC as an "iMEC."
[112] IRC § 7702A(e)(1)(B).
[113] *Supra* note 83.
[114] Rev. Proc. 99-27 § 7.
[115] Rev. Proc. 99-27 § 8.

cedure, the IRS issued Rev. Proc. 2001-42,[116] establishing a permanent avenue for the correction of inadvertent MECs. The principal substantive difference between the temporary program under Rev. Proc. 99-27 and the permanent program under Rev. Proc. 2001-42 lay in the scope of the products and errors covered (e.g., most corporate-owned life insurance (COLI) contracts were not eligible for correction under the earlier procedure but were allowed to be corrected under the later one). The information that issuers of inadvertent MECs were required to provide with respect to those contracts was unchanged.[117]

After almost a decade of experience with the correction of inadvertent MECs, the IRS published Rev. Proc. 2008-39 to continue and improve on the permanent program established by the predecessor revenue procedure.[118] Like its predecessor and the companion 2008 procedure dealing with failed contracts, Rev. Proc. 2008-39 requires that a request for a closing agreement to correct inadvertent MECs be filed with the IRS National Office and that it conform to the process for requesting a private letter ruling (which includes payment of the IRS filing fee), and that the filing include:

- The policy number of each inadvertent MEC to be covered by the closing agreement
- A description of the defects that caused the contracts to become inadvertent MECs along with an explanation of how and why the defects arose
- A description of the administrative procedures the issuer has implemented to prevent additional inadvertent MECs in the future (once again, the issuer includes reinsurers of affected contracts)
- A proposed closing agreement, executed by the issuer in triplicate, that follows the model closing agreement appearing in section 6 of the revenue procedure and in which the issuer agrees to pay the appropriate toll charge

Further, as under its companion 2008 procedures, the revenue procedure permits the information required to be submitted with the closing agreement request to be provided by the issuer electronically, in read-only format on a CD-ROM, in triplicate. It is noteworthy that the revenue procedure, in imposing the above requirements and requiring the two representations discussed next, dispensed with most of the other information required to be submitted in a filing under the predecessor procedure.[119]

**Required Representations**

Unlike its predecessor, Rev. Proc. 2008-39 requires (in section 5.06) that issuers seeking relief for their inadvertent MECs make two specific representations. First, an issuer must represent that it is within the scope of section 4 of the revenue procedure. While this may appear to be comparable to the closing agreement requirements under the failed contract revenue procedures, this representation is of enhanced significance because it implements limits that Rev. Proc. 2008-39 places on the relief it affords. Specifically, section 4.01 of the revenue procedure addresses the issuers that may seek a closing agreement under it, stating that except as provided in section 4.02 thereof, the revenue procedure applies:

> to any issuer of one or more life insurance contracts that desires to remedy the inadvertent non-egregious failure of contracts to comply with the requirements of § 7702A. For this purpose, the term "issuer" means any company that issues a contract that is intended to satisfy the definition of a life insurance contract under § 7702 and comply with the MEC rules under § 7702A. The term also includes a company that insures a contract holder under a contract originally issued by another company.

---

[116] *Supra* note 84.
[117] The IRS made some additional modifications to the MEC correction procedure when it issued Rev. Proc. 2007-19, 2007-1 C.B. 515, in January 2007. These modifications to Rev. Proc. 2001-42 further improved the MEC correction process by, for example, allowing taxpayers to submit to the IRS electronically the information required by the revenue procedure.
[118] Rev. Proc. 2008-39 was made effective on July 21, 2008, superseding Rev. Procs. 2001-42 and 2007-19.
[119] The predecessor procedure required two reports, or templates, to be filed with the closing agreement request. The first template detailed all historical premium transactions and 7-pay premiums related to the inadvertent MEC. The second template detailed the CSV of the contract at the end of each contract year, which changes with each material change, along with all historical distributions (loans and withdrawals), including any amounts reported to the policyholder as taxable.

Section 4.02 of the revenue procedure then addresses the types of inadvertent MECs that the IRS may choose not to correct under the revenue procedure's terms. In particular, the IRS may exclude from correction under the revenue procedure an inadvertent MEC that

(1) is attributable to one or more defective interpretations or positions that the [IRS] determines to be a significant feature of a program to sell investment oriented contracts, or

(2) arises where the controlling statutory provision, as supplemented by any legislative history or guidance published by the [IRS], is clear on its face and the [IRS] determines that failure to follow the provision results in a significant increase in the investment orientation of a contract.

These potential exclusions from the scope of the revenue procedure carry forward corresponding limitations of the predecessor procedure. Presumably, if the IRS determines that a MEC falls into these exclusions of "egregious" failures to comply with the 7-pay test, the issuer might still offer to enter into a closing agreement with the IRS, although it is unclear whether or on what terms the IRS would entertain such an offer.

Second, an issuer must represent that it has correctly computed the toll charge to be paid for the inadvertent MECs under the closing agreement. (The details of this toll charge calculation are presented below.) This is a significant change from, and an improvement on, the predecessor procedure, which had required submission of the toll charge detail as part of the filing. The prior requirement, now eliminated, contributed to the substantial volume of material in MEC correction filings made under the predecessor procedure.

These two representations must be provided under penalties of perjury, and the issuer must retain documentation to support the representations if they were to be examined on audit, similarly to the document retention requirement imposed under the companion 2008 procedures. Rev. Proc. 2008-39 does not provide any additional detail regarding the nature of the documentation that must be retained or the period for which it must be retained. As previously noted, however, it seems prudent for an issuer to retain documentation setting forth, e.g., how the toll charge was determined and, given the long-term nature of life insurance contracts, to retain that documentation for as long as the contract in question is in force as well as for some reasonable period of time thereafter.

## Correction of Inadvertent MECs

Continuing the practice under the predecessor revenue procedure, under the model closing agreement in section 6 of Rev. Proc. 2008-39 the issuer agrees to "bring Contract[s] for which the testing period (as defined in section 3.01 of Rev. Proc. 2008-39) will not have expired on or before the date 90 days after the execution of this Agreement into compliance with § 7702A, either by an increase in death benefit[s] or the return of excess premiums and earnings thereon to the Contract holder[s]" (brackets in the original). Thus, whether an inadvertent MEC requires corrective action under the closing agreement depends upon whether the contract is in a 7-pay testing period at the end of 90 days after the IRS executes the closing agreement. If by that date, an inadvertent MEC's 7-pay testing period has expired, the issuer need not take any corrective action with regard to that contract, but if the testing period has not expired, the issuer is required to bring the contract into compliance with the 7-pay test either by increasing the contract's death benefit or returning the contract's excess premiums and earnings thereon to the policyholder.

Rev. Proc. 2008-39, like its companion 2008 procedures, does not provide guidance on the meaning of the terms "excess premiums" and "earnings thereon" as used in the correction requirement. Issuers requesting closing agreements have taken the position, under the revenue procedure and its predecessor, that to the extent the amounts paid, within the meaning of section 7702A(e)(1), under an inadvertent MEC were in compliance with the 7-pay test as of a closing agreement's effective date, corrective action was not required. The IRS appears to have accepted this approach, which is consistent with the approach taken under Rev. Proc. 2008-40. Issuers have also taken the position that if the amounts paid under an inadvertent MEC were greater than permitted by the 7-pay test as of an agreement's effective date, the excess amount would need to be refunded (with earnings thereon), or the death benefit of the contract would need to be increased, to bring the contract into compliance with the 7-pay test. For this purpose, issuers have often determined the "earnings thereon" in differing ways. Such earnings have been determined, for example, by reference to the contract's cumulative **overage earnings** within the meaning of that term in the toll charge calculation (see below) or by looking to contract crediting rates.

It should be noted that correcting an inadvertent MEC by refunding excess premiums and the earnings on them can be problematic, as the issuer's administrative system, if currently characterizing the contract as a MEC, may not allow for the removal of premium, albeit excess premium, until all gain is first distributed from the contract. Removal of earnings on the excess premium can also prove to be problematic, as certain administrative systems may not have the capability of removing earnings from a contract's cash value without causing a corresponding reduction to premiums paid or a reduction in benefits. While the closing agreement under Rev. Proc. 2008-39 may provide up to 90 days after its execution by the IRS to effect the correction of contracts, this is likely not enough time absent much advance planning, particularly planning to address the administrative issues that may arise.

**Toll Charge**

Rev. Proc. 2008-39 allows the issuer of an inadvertent MEC to calculate the toll charge for correcting the contract using either of two alternative methodologies:

- An overage earnings approach, which is largely a continuation of the complex approach previously in use (referred to in the revenue procedure as the "amount determined based on overage earnings"); or

- A "100 percent of overage" approach that is new with the 2008 revenue procedure (referred to as "amount determined based on overage").

The manner in which the toll charge is calculated under the **overage earnings approach** depends upon the amount of overage earnings that accrue under an inadvertent MEC during the 7-pay testing period(s). If the overage earnings *exceed $100* at any time during the testing period, the toll charge equals the sum of the following three amounts:

- **Tax and penalty tax, if applicable, on unreported distributions.** Under section 5.03(1)(a)(i) of the revenue procedure, this amount equals the income tax, and, if applicable, the penalty tax, on unreported amounts[120] received (or deemed received) under the inadvertent MEC during the period starting with the date two years before the contract first failed the 7-pay test and ending on the effective date of the closing agreement. The income tax rate used for this purpose and for the tax on the overage earnings (below) is determined on the same basis as under Rev. Proc. 2008-40 for failed contracts; in section 3.11 of Rev. Proc. 2008-39, it is referred to as the "applicable percentage." The penalty tax rate is 10 percent.

- **Deficiency interest on the above amount.** The deficiency interest, according to section 5.03(1)(a)(ii) of the revenue procedure, is determined pursuant to section 6621(a)(2) as if the income tax and penalty tax on the unreported amounts are underpayments by the policyholders for the tax years in which the amounts are received (or deemed received).

- **Tax on overage earnings.** Under section 5.03(1)(a)(iii) of the revenue procedure, this amount (not less than zero) equals: (a) the excess, if any, of the inadvertent MEC's "cumulative overage earnings over the proportionate share of overage earnings allocable to taxable distributions" from the contract, multiplied by (b) the applicable percentage for the contract (i.e., the tax rate keyed to the death benefit), and further multiplied by (c) the "distribution frequency factor" for the contract.

The concepts employed in the third element of this version of the toll charge bear some explanation. First, the cumulative overage earnings of an inadvertent MEC are the sum of its overage earnings for all contract years. For this purpose, the overage earnings for a given contract year are defined as the "applicable earnings rate" (described in detail below under the heading Derivation of the Earnings Rates) multiplied by the sum of the overage for that year and the cumulative overage earnings for all prior contract years.[121] The overage for a particular contract year is simply the excess, if any, of the sum of the section 7702A(e)(1) amounts paid to that date during the 7-pay test period over the 7-pay limit applicable to the contract year.[122] In determining such

---

[120] While an unreported amount, as such, is not defined in the revenue procedure, the term "reported amount" is defined as the amount that either the issuer reports on a timely filed information return as includible in the policyholder's gross income, or the policyholder includes in gross income on a timely filed income tax return. *See* Rev. Proc. 2008-39 § 3.12.
[121] Rev. Proc. 2008-39 § 3.06.
[122] Rev. Proc. 2008-39 § 3.05.

overage, as in determining excess premiums under Rev. Proc. 2008-40, it should be permissible to measure the excess of the amounts paid over the 7-pay limit on each day of a contract year, and to accrue the overage earnings using the applicable earnings rate based on this methodology.[123] Further, unlike the case with the section 7702(g) income on the contract, negative overage earnings in a particular contract year arising from a negative applicable earnings rate can be used to offset positive overage earnings in prior contract years.

Second, the "proportionate share of overage earnings allocable to taxable distributions" is defined as the product of:

- the total amount of taxable distributions under the inadvertent MEC, and
- a fraction, defined as -
  - the contract's cumulative overage earnings, divided by
  - the total income on the contract, defined as the contract's cash surrender value less the premiums paid for it, which in turn are reduced by prior distributions that were excludable from the gross income.[124]

Third, the "distribution frequency factor" is either 0.8 or 0.5 depending upon the loan interest rate and withdrawal provisions of a particular contract. For most flexible premium universal life insurance contracts, the distribution frequency factor will be 0.8. Most traditional participating whole life contracts also will have a 0.8 distribution frequency factor because of the possibility of surrender of paid-up additions. Other contract forms, such as indeterminate premium contracts, may qualify for the 0.5 factor.[125]

If the overage earnings that accrue under an inadvertent MEC *do not exceed $100* at all times during the 7-pay testing period (the *de minimis* **overage earnings rule**), then the toll charge to correct the contract under the overage earnings approach is determined more simply, without including the income tax and any applicable penalty tax on unreported distributions and without the related deficiency interest.[126] This treatment apparently stems from the observation that the inadvertent MEC that falls within the *de minimis* overage earnings rule will have very little inside buildup associated with overage and, thus, the policyholder will not have received a significant tax benefit from owning such a contract.

While Rev. Proc. 2008-39 (like its predecessor and like Rev. Proc. 2008-40) requires the filing of an executed closing agreement with the issuer's request, the toll charge identified in the agreement is generally expected (based on experience with prior submissions) to be current as of the date the IRS executes it. Hence, once again, an issuer requesting a closing agreement should calculate this toll charge through a date that is beyond the date on which the executed closing agreement is submitted to the IRS.

By now it should be apparent that computing the toll charge using the overage earnings approach is not a simple undertaking, particularly in the case of a filing involving a large number of contracts. To make this computation, the issuer requesting the closing agreement must be able to access significant amounts of historical contract-level information, a task that may prove difficult. Fortunately, under a new alternative provided by Rev. Proc. 2008-39, the 100 percent of overage approach, that computation need not be attempted. Rather, under this new alternative, the toll charge simply equals (as the name suggests) the entire overage under an inadvertent MEC. The toll charge under this approach, following the 100 percent of error approach under Rev. Proc. 2008-40, involves neither the application of a tax rate nor the payment of deficiency interest.

As noted above, overage for a particular contract year is defined in the revenue procedure as the excess, if any, of the sum of the section 7702A(e)(1) amounts paid to that date during the 7-pay test period over the 7-pay limit applicable to the contract year.[127] To be able to determine the amount of this overage for purposes of calculating the toll charge, an issuer must know as of what date that determination is to be made. The revenue procedure does not expressly identify this date, although examples appearing in the procedure do address this issue for an inadvertent MEC that is no longer in a 7-pay testing period. For such a contract, the examples indicate that the toll charge is to be determined by reference to the overage that existed in the contract at the

---

[123] As previously noted, the IRS has allowed this approach for the calculation of overage earnings.
[124] Rev. Proc. 2008-39 § 3.08–.09.
[125] Rev. Proc. 2001-42 § 3.10(1).
[126] Rev. Proc. 2008-39 § 5.03(1)(b). Under the predecessor procedure, the limit for the *de minimis* overage earnings rule was $75.
[127] Rev. Proc. 2008-39 § 3.05.

end of its 7-pay testing period.[128] While the examples do not specifically address the date the overage is to be determined in the case of an inadvertent MEC still in a 7-pay testing period, it is reasonable to calculate the toll charge by reference to the overage that existed on the date as of which the issuer obtained the data necessary to perform the toll charge calculation. The IRS has accepted this approach in filings under Rev. Proc. 2008-39.

**Derivation of the Earnings Rates**

Both Rev. Proc. 2008-39 and its counterpart for correcting failed contracts, Rev. Proc. 2008-40, provide for toll charge calculations based in whole or in part on the earnings that accrue on amounts in excess of the respective premium limitations. While both revenue procedures define "earnings" using different terminology (overage earnings vs. excess earnings), both are determined using the same set of earnings rates. In defining the earnings that underlie the development of the toll charge, the revenue procedures do not look to the actual earnings accruing inside the contract undergoing correction, but instead base the earnings calculation on proxy earnings rates. These earnings rates are defined in section 3.07 of Rev. Proc. 2008-39, vary based on whether the contract qualifies as a variable contract under section 817(d) or not, and apply on a contract year basis according to the calendar year in which the contract year begins.

For contract years beginning in calendar years 1988 through 2007, the earnings rates are specified in section 3.07(2)(a) and (3)(a) of Rev. Proc. 2008-39, while section 3.07(2)(b) and (3)(b) provides the formulas to be used to determine the earnings rates for contract years after 2007.[129] The **general account total return rate** defines the earnings rate applicable to contracts other than variable life insurance contracts, and the **variable contract earnings rate** defines the rates applicable to variable life insurance contracts.

The general account total return equals:

- 50 percent of the Moody's Seasoned Corporate Aaa Bond Yield,[130] frequency annual, or any successor thereto, plus
- 50 percent of the Moody's Seasoned Corporate Baa Bond Yield, frequency annual, or any successor thereto.

The variable contract earnings rate is equal to the sum of:

- 10 percent of the general account total return, and
- 90 percent of the **separate account total return** for the calendar year in which the contract year begins.

The separate account total return equals:

- 75 percent of the **equity fund total return**, plus
- 25 percent of the **bond fund total return**, less
- 1.1 percentage point.

The equity fund total return equals:

- the calendar year percentage return[131] represented by the end-of-year values of the Standard and Poor's (S&P) 500 Total Return Index, with daily dividend reinvestment, or any successor thereto, less
- 1.5 percentage point.

The bond fund total return equals:

---

[128] *See* the examples set forth in Rev. Proc. 2008-39 § 5.03(3)(a) and (b).
[129] Rev. Proc. 2008-39 § 3.07(2)(a) and (3)(a) provides earnings rates only back to 1988 because IRC § 7702A was enacted in that year. However, IRC §§ 101(f) and 7702 were enacted earlier, and, as a result, earnings rates prior to 1988 are needed to calculate excess earnings under Rev. Proc. 2008-40 for contracts failing to comply with those sections prior to 1988. In this regard, Rev. Proc. 2008-40 § 4.03(5)(b)(ii) provides that the applicable earnings rate for contract years beginning prior to 1988 is determined using the formulas set forth in Rev. Proc. 2008-39 § 3.07 for contract years after 2007.
[130] Moody's Seasoned Corporate Aaa and Baa Bond Yields are publicly available at https://research.stlouisfed.org/.
[131] The calendar year percentage return is calculated by dividing the end-of-year value of the index for the calendar year by the end-of-year value of the index for the immediately preceding calendar year, and subtracting one from the result. The rates involved can be found using the link in note 130.

- the calendar year percentage return represented by the end-of-year values of the Merrill Lynch U.S. Corporate Master Index (C0A0),[132] or any successor thereto, less
- 1.0 percentage point.

To compute the earnings rate for calendar year 2008 and later, the calendar year-end values for the various indices must be available. If the general account total return or the separate account total return for a calendar year cannot be determined because the calendar year in which the contract year begins has not ended, the earnings rate for the contract year (or portion thereof) is determined by taking the average of the rates (general account total return or variable contract earnings rates) for the prior three years. For example, the general account total return for 2015 (assuming the year-end indices are not available) would be based on the average of the general account total return rates for 2012, 2013 and 2014 ((4.3% + 4.7% + 4.5%)/3 = 4.5%).

Table 8.3 contains the earnings rates for years 1982 to 2015. The earnings rates for years 1982–87 and 2008–14 are based on the application of the formulas contained in Rev. Proc. 2008-39, while the earnings rate for 2015 is based on the arithmetic average of the earnings rates for the prior three years (i.e., years 2012–14).

### Table 8.3. Earnings rates to be used to calculate either excess earnings or overage earnings

| Year | Contracts other than variable contracts | Variable contracts | Source |
|---|---|---|---|
| 1982 | 15.0% | 21.8% | Application of Rev. Proc. 2008-39 section 3.07 formulas |
| 1983 | 12.8% | 16.4% | |
| 1984 | 13.5% | 7.0% | |
| 1985 | 12.0% | 26.1% | |
| 1986 | 9.7% | 15.0% | |
| 1987 | 10.0% | 2.7% | |
| 1988 | 10.2% | 13.5% | Rev. Proc. 2008-39 |
| 1989 | 9.7% | 17.4% | |
| 1990 | 9.8% | 1.4% | |
| 1991 | 9.2% | 25.4% | |
| 1992 | 8.6% | 5.9% | |
| 1993 | 7.5% | 13.9% | |
| 1994 | 8.3% | −1.0% | |
| 1995 | 7.8% | 23.0% | |
| 1996 | 7.7% | 14.3% | |
| 1997 | 7.6% | 17.8% | |
| 1998 | 6.9% | 19.7% | |
| 1999 | 7.4% | 12.8% | |
| 2000 | 8.0% | −5.5% | |
| 2001 | 7.5% | −7.1% | |
| 2002 | 7.2% | −14.1% | |
| 2003 | 6.2% | 19.6% | |
| 2004 | 6.1% | 6.9% | |
| 2005 | 5.6% | 2.1% | |
| 2006 | 6.0% | 10.0% | |
| 2007 | 6.0% | 3.6% | |

---

[132] The Merrill Lynch U.S. Corporate Master Index (C0A0) is publicly available at www.mlindex.ml.com.

## Table 8.3. Continued

| Year | Contracts other than variable contracts | Variable contracts | Source |
|------|------|------|------|
| 2008 | 6.5% | −28.1% | |
| 2009 | 6.3% | 20.7% | |
| 2010 | 5.5% | 10.6% | |
| 2011 | 5.2% | 1.4% | Application of Rev. Proc. 2008-39 section 3.07 formulas |
| 2012 | 4.3% | 11.3% | |
| 2013 | 4.7% | 19.8% | |
| 2014 | 4.5% | 9.2% | |
| 2015 | 4.5% | 13.4% | Average of prior 3 years |

Employing these rates, Table 8.4 illustrates the calculation of overage earnings. The example details the calculation of the overage earnings through the end of the 7-pay test period, which expired on December 31, 2004.

## Table 8.4. Sample calculations of overage earnings, Rev. Proc. 2008-39 closing agreement

| Policy number: | ABC123 | | | Death benefit: | | 10,000.00 | | |
|---|---|---|---|---|---|---|---|---|
| Original issue date: | 1/1/1998 | | | Reason for MEC failure: | | Early premium | | |

| Beginning of contract year | 7-pay year | Transaction date | Transaction amount | Cumulative amounts paid | Cumulative 7-pay premium | Overage | Earnings rate | Overage earnings |
|---|---|---|---|---|---|---|---|---|
| 1/1/1998 | 1 | 1/1/1998 | 1,142.00 | 1,142.00 | 1,142.00 | 0.00 | 6.9% | 0.00 |
| 1/1/1998 | 1 | 12/26/1998 | 1,142.00 | 2,284.00 | 1,142.00 | 1,142.00 | 6.9% | 1.25 |
| 1/1/1999 | 2 | 1/1/1999 | 0.00 | 2,284.00 | 2,284.00 | 0.00 | 7.4% | 0.09 |
| 1/1/2000 | 3 | 1/1/2000 | 1,142.00 | 3,426.00 | 3,426.00 | 0.00 | 8.0% | 0.11 |
| 1/1/2000 | 3 | 12/25/2000 | 1,142.00 | 4,568.00 | 3,426.00 | 1,142.00 | 8.0% | 1.69 |
| 1/1/2001 | 4 | 1/1/2001 | 0.00 | 4,568.00 | 4,568.00 | 0.00 | 7.5% | 0.24 |
| 1/1/2002 | 5 | 1/1/2002 | 1,142.00 | 5,710.00 | 5,710.00 | 0.00 | 7.2% | 0.24 |
| 1/1/2002 | 5 | 12/30/2002 | 1,142.00 | 6,852.00 | 5,710.00 | 1,142.00 | 7.2% | 0.44 |
| 1/1/2003 | 6 | 1/1/2003 | 0.00 | 6,852.00 | 6,582.00 | 0.00 | 6.2% | 0.25 |
| 1/1/2004 | 7 | 1/1/2004 | 1,142.00 | 7,724.00 | 7,724.00 | 0.00 | 6.1% | 0.26 |

| | | | | | | | | |
|---|---|---|---|---|---|---|---|---|
| Income on the contract: | | | | 0.00 | Income tax: | | | 0.00 |
| Total taxable distributions: | | | | 0.00 | Penalty tax: | | | 0.00 |
| Overage earnings allocated to prior distribution: | | | | 0.00 | Deficiency interest: | | | 0.00 |
| Distribution frequency factor: | | | | 0.80 | | | | |
| Applicable percentage: | | | | 15% | Total overage earnings: | | | 4.57 |

**Model Closing Agreement**

As previously noted, section 5.02 of Rev. Proc. 2008-39 requires an issuer seeking a closing agreement to submit a proposed closing agreement that is executed in triplicate by the issuer in the same form as the model closing agreement set forth in section 6 of the revenue procedure. This model is for the most part the same as the model closing agreement provided under the predecessor revenue procedure. Thus, under the model closing agreement, the issuer agrees to pay the toll charge (within 60 calendar days of the date the IRS executes the closing agreement), take corrective action as required, and neither deduct nor seek refund of the toll charge paid nor increase the policyholder's investment in the contract under section 72 or the premiums paid for the contract under section 7702 by any portion of the toll charge (or by any portion of the income on the contract). In return, the IRS agrees to treat the contracts involved as retroactively complying with the 7-pay test, to waive civil penalties for failures of the issuer to satisfy reporting, withholding and deposit requirements with respect to any actual or deemed distributions, and to forbear treating any portion of the toll charge as income to the policyholders. In addition, the IRS agrees to treat the compliance failures and any required corrective action as having no effect on the date that a contract covered by the closing agreement was issued, entered into or purchased for purposes of the tax law.

## Treatment of Failed Contracts or Inadvertent MECs in an Acquisition

A key manner in which failed contracts and inadvertent MECs are often uncovered is as a result of the transfer of business between insurers through the acquisition of a company or a block of business. Discovery of potential failed contracts or inadvertent MECs may result from preclosing due diligence by a potential buyer or as the result of a post-closing system conversion. The remainder of this chapter discusses acquisition-related issues, including the identification and correction of failed contracts and inadvertent MECs in the context of a sale or acquisition.

### *Presale Due Diligence*

Due diligence is the process of examining the books and records of a potential acquisition candidate to uncover any issues that may affect the buyer's willingness to proceed with the transaction or the sales price. With respect to the definitional limitations, items typically covered by presale due diligence examination include, but are not limited to, the following broad categories of documents and other information:

- Contract forms and related product information

- Information covering internal or external product-related tax or audit issues, as well as known failed contracts or inadvertent MECs

- Information on product-related letter rulings, closing agreements or technical advice memoranda directed toward or entered into by the acquisition candidate

- Compliance-system-related information, including the use of vendor-based systems or third parties to monitor compliance, disclosure of system conversions and the availability of contract transaction data from issue[133]

- Information related to compliance with the "applicable law" requirements of section 7702, including the state or offshore filing status of contracts

- Documentation of calculation methodologies for guideline premiums, NSPs and 7-pay premiums (This may vary by system; often, multiple systems are involved.)

- Documentation on administrative practices, including the treatment of premiums in excess of the guideline premium limitation, and the procedures for contract adjustments

### *Product and Contract Review*

Presale due diligence, by its nature, generally takes the form of a simplified **product review**, which involves reviewing contract forms and sample calculations to identify systematic errors in computing the definitional

---

[133] As noted earlier, one common result of a system conversion, or the sale or acquisition of a block of contracts, is the loss of transaction history data. In these instances, the guideline single premium (GSP) and the sum of the guideline level premiums (GLPs) are typically transferred to the new administration system as of the conversion date. Backup history at the time of the conversion or the acquisition may or may not be available. Where an error in the computations is subsequently discovered, this may necessitate a major effort to bring the contracts into compliance. Note that for MEC testing, a benefit decrease causes the 7-pay limitation to be recomputed and reapplied during the first seven years (or for seven years from a material change) for most contracts, and from issue for a survivorship contract.

limitations. A product review is intended to uncover systematic errors that could result in a significant liability under a closing agreement, costs related to the filing of a waiver request or closing agreement offer, and the costs of correcting the affected contracts and the compliance system. Such a review typically will not identify errors made in policy administration that have resulted from clerical or nonsystematic administrative errors (unless such an exercise has been previously undertaken by the selling company and can be documented as a part of due diligence). A product review is thus based on a limited data set of policy-level information. These include, but are not limited to, contract forms, product descriptions and sales materials. The following describes the steps in a typical product review:

1) An inventory of plan codes and related contract forms and actuarial memoranda is prepared relative to the business being purchased.

2) Using this information, the actuarial assumptions applicable for each plan code are documented.

3) Sample contracts are individually selected from the in-force block to stress-test the guideline premium and 7-pay calculations over a cross-section of products.

4) Values for the sample contracts are independently computed.

5) System-generated values are compared, at issue and after adjustments, to the values determined in step 4.

6) The differences in the values are documented and researched to determine the cause of any discrepancies.

Note that simply identifying a potential issue does not lead to the conclusion that a contract has necessarily failed the requirements of section 101(f) or 7702 or is an inadvertent MEC. For example, a contract tested under the guideline premium test will not fail until the premiums paid actually exceed the guideline premium limitation. As part of this process, while not undertaking a contract-by-contract review of compliance, it is possible to use in-force data to screen for contracts that were reported by the administrative system as having been funded at or near the guideline premium limitation or the 7-pay limit. Such data can also be used to identify characteristics of contracts that do not meet the CVAT "by their terms." Thus, some estimate of potential liability for failed contracts or inadvertent MECs can be developed even where a product review is all that has been completed.

In contrast, a more detailed **contract review**, involving recomputing guideline and 7-pay premiums for each contract in a block of in-force contracts, is needed to uncover contract-level errors (in addition to systematic errors) and to provide an accurate estimate of the potential liability. For guideline premium-tested products, the only accurate way to assess the potential liability is to recompute guideline premiums for the entire in-force block and then compare the resulting guideline premium limitation against the premiums paid for each contract. While the product review screening process described above can identify a number of potential errors, it is at best a rough approximation and is likely to change when a more thorough analysis is completed. The filing of a closing agreement offer (or a waiver request) with the IRS would be based on a contract review, since in making the filing the contract issuer must assert under penalties of perjury (to the best of its knowledge) that one or more errors exist resulting in compliance failures and that it has calculated the toll charge correctly. In fact, a contract review is a necessary initial step in the process of identifying and correcting potential errors. Because of the data required as well as the limited time offered to an acquiring company to evaluate the compliance of a book of business, a contract-level review is all but impossible during normal presale due diligence, however. If the need to undertake a contract review is identified in due diligence, it will, in all likelihood, not occur until after closing (or will have previously been completed by the seller).

## *Remediation Plan*

Some purchase and sale agreements specifically address product tax matters (and all probably should). One approach is to include a provision in such an agreement that commits both buyer and seller to the terms of a remediation plan. Among other things, a remediation plan outlines the responsibilities of the parties for sharing the costs of identification of errors as well as any toll charges that may be due as a consequence of a filing with the IRS. Note that the party having control of the contracts is responsible for tax compliance. Under an assumption reinsurance transaction or an outright sale of a company, this will be the acquiring company; under a coinsurance agreement, it will be the ceding company.

One key to a successful remediation plan is to have an agreement in advance on how to manage the process. The expectation at the outset is that the remediation process is likely to take a year or more. Thus, it is generally not possible to have all of the issues outlined and contracts identified before closing. In effect, a remediation plan is an agreement on the "rules of engagement" as to how the buyer and seller will proceed through the process.

An important part of the analysis is agreement on the list of potential issues that will be considered to create failed contracts or inadvertent MECs. The findings of presale due diligence are a starting point for discussions as to which issues will be considered to create potential compliance failures and which will not. In approaching the IRS, an insurer must confess error, and there often is room for interpretation. In reviewing the issues, one approach may be to request an opinion of counsel for issues where there is a disagreement or uncertainty.

As noted above, identification of all the failed contracts or inadvertent MECs is based on a contract-level review. The principal problem in connection with a contract-level review is the development of quality contract-level data. While historical data (from issue) is necessary for accurate testing, there have been many instances in which data has needed to be re-created where actual data is not available or where the cost of acquiring the data is prohibitive. However, this process may produce results that are adverse to the seller, as the IRS will need to accept the approach used in testing if the results are to be used in a filing, and the IRS will likely insist on conservative (i.e., pro-government) assumptions where data has been imputed.

Once a transaction data set of the contracts to be tested has been developed, compliance-testing programs are run for each individual contract, developing period-by-period limitations. From this testing, a database of failed contracts and inadvertent MECs is constructed. (This can also be used for the procedure known as **re-clocking**, or replacing incorrect system-generated limits with correct limits.) Based on the information developed from the testing process, the contracts are classified into categories, a process sometimes known as "slicing and dicing." In addition to identifying the contracts that do not comply with the definitional limitations, this process may identify contracts that would meet those limitations under more aggressive but nonetheless reasonable assumptions.

Using the database of compliance failures, the amount of the potential liability can be computed using the available toll charge approaches under the remediation revenue procedures (or, where possible, the automatic waiver approach under Rev. Proc. 2008-42). Once the liability is computed, a grid of the potential liability by cause of failure can be developed. Among other things, this serves as a resource for decision-making.

From this database, potential corrections to the contracts can also be identified. Generally, the solution is to return excess premium, with interest, although an increase in death benefit is also possible. As a return of premium is often a lower cost solution, it may be addressed in initially developing the procedure for correcting failed contracts and inadvertent MECs.

Finally, a strategy is needed for implementing the corrections. This may include the development of a communication strategy for notification of policyholders. As the system fixes are likely to be done in the context of a system conversion, the timing of the conversion becomes a financial issue that is tied into the allocation of the closing agreement toll charge. An element of the remediation plan may be the allocation procedure for the toll charge (i.e., the seller will pay toll charges attributable to failures occurring through a particular date; after that the buyer pays charges). The time frame should recognize that issues may arise in developing the data, and no one can control the length of time the remediation process takes at the IRS. ◆

Chapter 9

# THE DEVELOPMENT OF THE TAX LAW'S LIMITATIONS ON LIFE INSURANCE: HISTORY AND PRECEDENTS

## Chapter Overview

Chapter 9 explores the developments in the history of the federal income tax system that have defined and constrained the design and financing of life insurance. It traces the key precedents leading to the development of the current section 7702 and 7702A[1] limitations. Since the beginning of an income tax in the United States, life insurance death proceeds generally have been free of such taxation. The Civil War and subsequent reconstruction were financed in part by a tax on income in effect from 1862 until 1872. However, rulings from the Treasury Department's Office of Internal Revenue in 1866 and 1867 declared life insurance death proceeds to be exempt from the Civil War-era income taxes.[2]

Although the tax treatment of life insurance death proceeds has largely remained unchanged for nearly a century and a half, life insurance products and their tax treatment have evolved significantly during that time. Beginning with the enactment of the modern federal income tax in 1913 and the federal estate tax in 1918, tax considerations have played a significant role in the thinking of designers, marketers and purchasers of life insurance products. An appreciation of the lessons of history is important in understanding the current tax treatment of life insurance contracts. In many respects, the tax treatment applied to life insurance products, and the changes in their tax treatment at various times, are reflective of the products offered at such times.

This chapter traces four significant developments, from the inception of the modern income tax to today, which helped shape the trends and issues in the taxation of life insurance products. These are:

- The emergence of a savings element in life insurance contracts through the development of cash surrender values. During the mid- to late 19th century, life insurance surrender values were in their infancy, and early life insurance contracts did not contain a savings element by today's definition. By the dawn of the modern income tax in 1913, however, cash surrender values generally were available, though frequently reflecting little or no gain.[3] The 1913 income tax law exempted death proceeds and a portion of surrender proceeds from taxation, laying the foundation for the income tax treatment of permanent life insurance that continues today. The view of a permanent life insurance contract as an inherent combination of savings and insurance protection, which is found both in case law and tax policy analysis, is fundamental to the tax treatment of life insurance products today.

- The emergence of an economic definition of life insurance in *Helvering v. Le Gierse*[4] and related cases, spurred by the development of life insurance and annuity "hedges" that allowed uninsurable lives to secure the benefit of a then-available exemption from the estate tax. The economic or actuarial definition of insurance set forth in *Le Gierse* was the precursor to the definitional limitations established in

---

[1] Unless otherwise indicated, references in this book to "section" are to the provisions of the Internal Revenue Code of 1986, as amended (also referred to as "IRC" or the "Code").
[2] *Sums Paid to Life Insurance Companies not Liable to Legacy or Income Tax*, III THE INTERNAL REVENUE RECORD & CUSTOMS JOURNAL, no. 18, whole no. 70, May 5, 1866, at 140; *Instructions to United States Assessors, Concerning the Assessment of Income and Special Taxes for the Year 1867*, V THE INTERNAL REVENUE RECORD & CUSTOMS JOURNAL, no. 14, whole no. 118, April 6, 1867, at 109.
[3] An analysis of the rate book for nonparticipating contracts of a major carrier in the early 1900s indicates that some small gain (i.e., the excess of cash surrender values over premiums paid) was present for endowment contracts on the endowment date, but the cash surrender values of level premium permanent life insurance contracts often were substantially less than the sum of the premiums paid. *See also* NATHAN WILLEY, A TREATISE ON THE PRINCIPLES AND PRACTICE OF LIFE INSURANCE: BEING AN ARITHMETICAL EXPLANATION ON THE COMPUTATION INVOLVED IN THE SCIENCE OF LIFE CONTINGENCIES Table LX, 155 (2nd ed., revised and corrected by R.G. Hann, 1876) (hereinafter Willey).
[4] 312 U.S. 531 (1941).

sections 7702 and 7702A. *Le Gierse* and related cases established the precedent that life insurance can be defined under federal tax law using economic principles.

- The long-standing controversy over financed life insurance (i.e., life insurance purchased either with funds borrowed from an insurer through policy loans or from a bank using a contract's cash surrender value as security), which generated legislation and litigation beginning in 1942. Through various legislative enactments over many years, Congress limited the terms under which policyholders could finance the purchase of life insurance with debt and deduct the interest paid, culminating with an end to the deductibility of policy loan interest for individuals (along with other "personal" interest) in the Tax Reform Act of 1986 and significant constraints on deductibility by businesses. In this connection, the section 264 rules established in 1954 and 1963 and revised in 1986,[5] disallowing or conditioning the policy loan interest deduction, illustrate the practice of congressional line-drawing in determining the tax treatment of life insurance—in this instance, relative to debt-financed insurance. Still other limitations, specific to life insurance contracts or transactions involving these contracts, exist that are not discussed here (e.g., the section 101(a)(2) transfer for value rules).[6]

- The "product revolution" that spanned the 1970s and early 1980s and led to the introduction of many contemporary life insurance products, including variable life and universal life. The availability of these new products prompted the development of a statutory definition of life insurance in the Internal Revenue Code. Ultimately, it was the congressional desire to constrain, and the life insurance industry's desire to preserve, the income tax treatment of these modern products as life insurance that produced the enactment of section 101(f) and, later, sections 7702 and 7702A.

## Development of Cash Surrender Values and Their Tax Treatment

The contemporary economic view of a permanent life insurance contract is that it provides a form of savings through the cash surrender value together with pure insurance protection as represented by the net amount at risk. As noted in Chapter 1, a key purpose of the definitional limitations is to regulate the relationship of the savings and risk elements of a life insurance contract, so that the contract's "inside buildup" is properly supporting its death benefit. The economic view of the savings component (as well as the income tax treatment of that component) is grounded in the minimum cash surrender values mandated by a uniform provision of state laws, i.e., the **Standard Nonforfeiture Law for Life Insurance**. Indeed, under modern nonforfeiture principles, the cash surrender value represents the policyholder's equity in a life insurance contract, that is, it effectively belongs to the policyholder upon cessation of the insurance coverage. This was not always the case, however, and the issue of the ownership of the policy values was the subject of controversy throughout the period of development of modern cash surrender values. The mandate imposed by state law (and the consequent practice adopted by life insurers) in resolution of this controversy has played an important role in establishing the income tax treatment of life insurance.

### *The Insurance Value Concept*

The view of cash surrender values[7] as representing an equity interest in the contract is consistent with and may be traced to the "insurance value concept" as attributed to Elizur Wright in the late 1800s. One commentator has described Wright's view in the following way:

> According to Wright, a death benefit to a policyholder was composed of two parts: (a) the amount at risk ... and (b) the accumulations under his policy, which resulted from overpayments in the early years of the policy as a part of the level premium scheme.[8]

---

[5] As discussed in note 93 *infra*, these rules were revised again in 1996.
[6] These rules, which apply an important exception to the exemption of life insurance death proceeds from income taxation, are summarized in Appendix 1.1.
[7] Early discussions of nonforfeiture and cash surrender values focus on the policy reserve as the measure of policy value to the insured. Nonforfeiture benefits are natural corollaries of the reserve system necessary in level premium insurance. *See* Alfred Guertin et al., *Report of the Committee to Study Non-forfeiture Benefits and Related Matters*, National Association of Insurance Commissioners report, September 10, 1941, at 43 (hereinafter Guertin report).
[8] J. David Cummins, Development of Life Insurance Surrender Values in the United States 19 (1973) (hereinafter Cummins).

Wright's view of the reserve as representing the equity of the policyholder can be found in life insurance literature of the time. An 1876 publication described the reserve in the following way:

> The reserve on a policy when compared with the amount at risk is called by Hon. Elizur Wright "self insurance," since it is the unearned and unexpended part of the premiums which the policyholder has on deposit in the company to provide for the future payment of his claim. For this reason Hon. Gustavus W. Smith, Insurance Commissioner of Kentucky, calls it the "trust fund deposit."[9]

The author went on to state, "No subject in life insurance is more thoroughly discussed at the present day [i.e., 1876] than the proper rule for determining the surrender value of a policy. The common method of computing the surrender value is to deduct from the reserve 25 to 50 per cent, as a surrender charge, and pay the remainder as an equitable surrender value."[10]

The first nonforfeiture law, enacted by Massachusetts in 1861 when Wright was commissioner of insurance, did not mandate cash surrender rights but did tie the policyholder's interest in the policy to the reserve.[11] The Massachusetts law required single premium term insurance for as long a period as provided by the "value" of the policy.[12] (During his time as Massachusetts commissioner, Wright maintained a register where policyholders could come to the department and find the value of in-force contracts.) Although Wright thus established the economic principle underlying the availability of cash surrender values, additional time passed before the payment of such values upon surrender was widespread. According to another life insurance historian, "Guaranteed values payable in cash, which in modern times have been credited to, and as often blamed upon, Elizur Wright, were not required, in fact, until long after he had been ousted from his post as Massachusetts Commissioner."[13]

Contrary to Wright's view was that of many actuaries of that era, who believed that reserves did not represent ownership equity but instead belonged to the insurance company and not to individual policyholders. Under this view, upon surrender, reserves simply reverted to the insurer, consistently with the view that premium was similar to a gambling bet that some parties would win and others lose, but which created no ownership equity for surviving policyholders. The proper "ownership" of life insurance cash surrender values (which generally were based on the reserve less a surrender charge) continued to be debated through the early 20th century.

In a 1911 paper, Moir noted that 50 years earlier (in the 1860s) "[g]uaranteed surrender values were then practically unknown, anyone desiring to surrender being at the mercy of the company."[14] By 1911, Moir reported, "liberal [surrender] values are guaranteed in various forms."[15] However, Moir went on to comment that "[t]he values now guaranteed [in 1911] seem to be on a basis which ignores … the principle which the older school of actuaries so strongly upheld, namely—that reserve values do not belong to individual policyholders. …"[16] In his 1912 discussion of Moir's paper, Rhodes expressed the opposite view, observing that a "great American actuary and lawyer [presumably a reference to Wright] several years ago stated that the truth was too clear to be disputed, that reserves are, mathematically, and in morals, the property of the person from whose premiums they have come."[17] Eventually, Wright's concept of the accumulated overpayments (as represented by the individual reserve) as a measure of the policyholder's equity in the contract prevailed, forming the economic underpinning for the cash surrender value as savings.

## *The Development of Cash Surrender Values*

Thus, during the mid- to late 19th century, policy loans, premium notes and surrender values were provided at times, although the lapse or surrender of a contract often led to a loss or substantial forfeiture of the policy

---

[9] Willey, *supra* note 3, at 47.
[10] *Id.* at 64.
[11] Cummins, *supra* note 8, at 14–15.
[12] J. Owen Stalson, Marketing Life Insurance: Its History in America 318 (1969) (hereinafter Stalson).
[13] E. J. Moorehead, Our Yesterdays: the History of the Actuarial Profession in North America 1809–1979, at 23 (1989).
[14] Henry Moir, *Liberality of Modern Policies*, 12 ACTUARIAL SOC'Y OF AM. TRANSACTIONS 175, 177 (1911).
[15] *Id.* at 177.
[16] *Id.* at 184.
[17] E. E. Rhodes, *Discussion of Liberality of Modern Policies*, 13 ACTUARIAL SOC'Y OF AM. TRANSACTIONS 107 (1912).

reserve. As a reaction to both regulatory and competitive pressures, cash surrender values in life insurance contracts developed during that period, despite the (then) ongoing actuarial debate about the nature of, and the wisdom of granting, cash surrender values. As early as April 1860, the New York Life Insurance Co. offered a policy with a contractual nonforfeiture guarantee. The New York Life plan provided paid-up insurance based on a single premium at the attained age of the insured. The first contractual cash surrender values appeared in 1866.[18] Stalson notes:

> We have seen that the very earliest companies in this country sometimes granted cash surrender values, but they did so gratuitously, not by contract obligation. The first instance of contractual obligation in the matter seems to have been that of the Universal Life [Insurance Co.], which in its second year (1866) treated the matter of cash value with definiteness in the contract itself [via] a clause which guaranteed the holder's equitable interest both in the life and endowment contracts, and the surrender value for every year was printed in the body of the policy.[19]

In 1879, New York enacted a nonforfeiture law based on the reserve underlying a contract less a surrender charge. The New York law also included the value of dividend additions.[20] By 1880, tables of nonforfeiture values began to appear in contracts, and were generally provided in all contracts by 1907.[21] Massachusetts also enacted a new nonforfeiture law in 1880, providing for statutory cash surrender values. Under the Massachusetts statute, "the value of the policyholder's equity was still to be measured in terms of the reserve," less a surrender charge.[22]

As noted above, opposition to the provision of cash surrender values did not end with the enactment of nonforfeiture statutes, but continued throughout the 1890s. Cummins notes the "actuarial debates of the 1890s [sparked by statutory recognition of the insurance value theory] provided many of the foundations of present-day surrender value theory." He goes on to cite two principal reasons that "changed the practices, if not the attitudes, of most companies"[23] and created the demand for cash surrender values. These were the decline of the tontine movement[24] and the favorable experience of insurance companies offering surrender values. For these companies, the fear that surrender rates would increase as a result of providing cash surrender values was not realized. The provisions of life insurance contracts were liberalized during the 1890s, including a widespread introduction of cash surrender values. A history of the Northwestern Mutual Life Insurance Co. relates that the "process of [policy] liberalization was greatly accelerated in 1896 when, for the first time, Northwestern adopted guaranteed cash, loan, and paid-up policy values which were incorporated in the policy contract in easily read, tabular form."[25]

Rotman-Zelizer notes that "the introduction of nonforfeiture values, which bequeathed the [life insurance] policy with monetary value, was largely instrumental in redefining its functions from purely protective to a form of savings and investment for the policyholder."[26] With the development of cash surrender values after the 1870s, "the investment features of a policy were advertised more loudly than its protective functions." In paying life insurance premiums, it was noted that a policyholder is "saving money and insurance is taking care of it for you."[27]

## *The Revenue Act of 1913*

In the early 20th century, at the same time that life insurance contracts began to provide a distinct savings component in the form of cash surrender values, Congress was faced with the issue of the appropriate treatment of these contracts under the income tax. Although the treatment of corporate-owned contracts was not without

---

[18] Cummins, *supra* note 8, at 21.
[19] Stalson, *supra* note 12, at 319.
[20] Cummins, *supra* note 8, at 24.
[21] Guertin report, *supra* note 7, at 31.
[22] Cummins, *supra* note 8, at 26.
[23] *Id.* at 29, 39.
[24] A tontine contract divided surplus among policyholders after a stated period for those who were available to receive it. In today's terms, tontines were an early version of a lapse-supported contract. To curb the abuse of tontine contracts, New York required an annual distribution of surplus.
[25] HAROLD F. WILLIAMSON AND ORANGE A. SMALLEY, NORTHWESTERN MUTUAL LIFE: A CENTURY OF TRUSTEESHIP 104 (1957).
[26] VIVIANA A. ROTMAN-ZELIZER, MORALS AND MARKETS, THE DEVELOPMENT OF LIFE INSURANCE IN THE UNITED STATES 106 (1979).
[27] *Id.* at 111, citing JAMES T. PHELPS, LIFE INSURANCE SAYINGS 11 (1895).

controversy (and was not ultimately resolved until the Revenue Act of 1921), life insurance death proceeds paid to individuals were exempted from tax from the inception of the modern income tax in 1913.[28]

The Revenue Act of 1913, enacted in October 1913, contained a statutory exclusion for life insurance, providing that "the proceeds of life insurance policies paid upon the death of the person insured or payments made by or credited to the insured, on life insurance, endowment, or annuity contracts, upon the return thereof to the insured at the maturity of the term mentioned in the contract, or upon surrender of [the] contract, shall not be included as income."[29] The treatment of the cash value upon surrender (or maturity) was addressed in the congressional debate surrounding the 1913 act, as is documented in a discussion between Rep. Barkley and Rep. Hull, the manager of the tax bill on the House floor:

> *Mr. Barkley:* Suppose that a policy is taken out and the premiums paid for a period, and then the policy has a certain cash-surrender value in tontines or endowment. The man may surrender his policy and take endowment. Now, is that cash-surrender value taxable as income?
>
> *Mr. Hull:* No part of the principal invested in [life] insurance which comes back to the insured during life is considered taxable income any more than the return of money which he might have loaned to another or a deposit that he might have made in the bank.[30]

Rep. Hull went on to note that the exclusion from income "includes the proceeds of life-insurance policies paid on the death of the person insured, and also includes the return of any and all sums which a person invests in insurance and receives back at one time or at periodical times during his life, as distinguished from any actual gains or profits which he derives out of the investment."[31]

In providing that no tax would be imposed on life insurance proceeds at death, and only upon maturity or surrender, the 1913 law implied the absence of tax on the year-by-year crediting of interest to the cash value, i.e., the inside buildup. As one commentator has noted, the "other principal tax benefit of life insurance, the tax free inside buildup of value, was also established in the 1913 legislation."[32] In the context of the 1913 enactment, this result made perfect sense: The tax approved that year fell almost exclusively on cash receipts, since the ability of Congress to reach unrealized appreciation was then in doubt.[33]

It is interesting to note that life insurers were politically active in 1913, not unlike today, leading Rep. Hull to complain at the time:

> Now, some of the companies have sent out alarming circulars to the stockholders, which are calculated to impress upon them that they are about to be outraged or in some other respect seriously injured by some of the provisions to be found somewhere in the pending measure. As a matter of fact, there is no tax, as I said, upon the proceeds of life insurance policies paid at the death of another. There is no tax imposed upon any individual with respect to the return of any sum or amount invested in insurance as a business proposition during his life.[34]

The 1913 act thus established the pattern of taxation that continues today. Namely, death proceeds are free of federal income tax to the beneficiary, and gains on surrender (i.e., the excess of the cash surrender value over the premiums paid) are taxable only upon receipt.

---

[28] The 16th Amendment, which empowered Congress to impose an income tax, was effective in February 1913. A constitutional amendment was necessary for Congress to be able to impose a federal income tax because of the Supreme Court's decision in *Pollock v. Farmers' Loan and Trust Co.*, 157 U.S. 429 (1895). The decision declared unconstitutional an income tax provision built into the 1894 Wilson-Gorman Tariff. The point was that the income tax was a "direct" tax that was not apportioned among the states in proportion to population as then required by the Constitution.

[29] Act of 1913, ch. 16, § I(.B), Pub. L. No. 363-16, 38 Stat. 167. *See also* E. E. Rhodes, *The Income Tax Law of the United States, as it Affects Life Insurance Companies*, 14 ACTUARIAL SOC'Y OF AM. TRANSACTIONS 201, 207 (1913). Kabele notes that Rhodes, chief actuary of the Mutual Benefit Life, served as a consultant on the 1913 act. *See* Thomas G. Kabele, *Universal Life and Indeterminate Premium Products and Policyholder Dividends*, 35 SOC'Y OF ACTUARIES TRANSACTIONS 153, 166 (1983).

[30] 50 CONG. REC., as reported in J. S. Seidman, SEIDMAN'S LEGISLATIVE HISTORY OF FEDERAL INCOME TAX LAWS, 1938–1861, 988–89 (1938) (hereinafter Seidman).

[31] *Id.*

[32] Wayne M. Gazur, *Death and Taxes: The Taxation of Accelerated Death Benefits for the Terminally Ill*. 11 VA. TAX REV. 263, 307 (1991) (hereinafter Gazur).

[33] *See Eisner v. Macomber*, 252 U.S. 189 (1920) (holding that a stock-split dividend did not give rise to income subject to tax).

[34] Gazur, *supra* note 32, at n. 142, citing 50 CONG. REC. 513 (1913).

## Developments After 1913

Section 4 of the Act of September 8, 1916, altered the language of the 1913 statute, exempting death proceeds from tax and clarifying that a return in excess of the amount paid is taxable on receipt:

> The following income shall be exempt from the provisions of this title: The proceeds of life insurance policies paid to individual beneficiaries upon the death of the insured; the amount received by the insured, as a return of premium or premiums paid by him under life insurance, endowment, or annuity contracts, either during the term or at the maturity of the term mentioned in the contract or upon the surrender of the contract. ....[35]

Similar language was included in section 213 of the Revenue Act of 1918. In the legislative history of the 1918 act, Rep. Hull remarked that "in any kind of insurance investment the profits are the amount received back from the investment in excess of the amount paid in."[36] However, the exemption continued to be provided for "proceeds of life insurance policies paid upon the death of the insured to individual beneficiaries or to the estate of the insured."[37]

In 1914, the Treasury Department ruled that the exclusion in section II(B) of the 1913 act exempting life insurance death proceeds from tax did not apply to corporations in "cases wherein corporations pay premiums on insurance policies insuring, in favor of the corporations, the lives of officers or others. ..."[38] The Treasury Department reasoned that, as premiums were deductible, the proceeds were taxable when received. The 1916 act, cited above, provided an exception for proceeds payable to individual beneficiaries. In August 1917, the Treasury Department modified its position, ruling that premiums paid on corporate policies would no longer be deductible from gross income in the year paid but would be permitted to be deducted from the gross proceeds when received.[39]

In the congressional debate over the 1918 act, an attempt was made to exempt from tax the death proceeds "of life insurance carried in favor of corporations." However, no change was made at that time, as Rep. Hull complained of the "evil" of aggressive tax planning by corporations which, according to Hull, also led to elimination of the corporate deduction for life insurance premiums in the 1916 act with respect to corporate-owned contracts:

> We found a number of large corporations, at the instance of big stockholders, had dropped into the habit of taking out policies for such individuals and paying the premium in a way which would enable the individual to escape his proper income-tax liability and probably later on to escape his estate-tax liability.[40]

The opposition of Hull and other Democrats in the House of Representatives defeated the effort, at least temporarily maintaining the phrase "to individual beneficiaries or the estate of the insured" in the language of the statute. Ultimately, the phrase was not carried forward into the Revenue Act of 1921,[41] thus removing the distinction between individuals and corporations. The legislative history of the 1921 act notes that the change "would leave no doubt as to the right of a partnership to exclude from gross income the proceeds of any life insurance policy in which the partnership is named as beneficiary and would extend to corporations a similar right."[42]

Prior to the Revenue Act of 1926, the income tax statutes provided that "a return of premiums paid under a life insurance, endowment or annuity contract are exempt only when returned to the insured."[43] As a clarification, the 1926 act granted "to the various persons to whom the payments are made an exemption of an amount

---

[35] Act of September 8, 1916, ch. 463, Pub. L. No. 64-271, § 4, 39 Stat. 756, 758.
[36] 56 Cong. Rec., as cited in Seidman, *supra* note 30, at 920.
[37] Revenue Act of 1918, ch. 18, Pub. L. No. 65-254, § 213(b)(1), 40 Stat. 1065.
[38] T.D. 2090, 16 Treas. Dec. Int. Rev. 269, 281 (1914).
[39] T.D. 2519, 19 Treas. Dec. Int. Rev. 150 (1917).
[40] 56 Cong. Rec. 10,371 (September 16, 1918).
[41] Revenue Act of 1921, ch. 136, Pub. L. No. 67-98, § 213(b)(1), 42 Stat. 227, 238.
[42] H.R. Rep. No. 67-350, at 10 (1921).
[43] S. Rep. No. 69-52, as reported in Seidman, *supra* note 30, at 594.

equal to their proportionate share of the premiums paid."[44] The predecessor to the current statutory language is found in sections 213(b)(1) and (2) of the Revenue Act of 1926,[45] which excluded from gross income:

> (1) Amounts received under a life insurance contract paid by reason of the death of the insured, whether in a single sum or in installments (but if such amounts are held by the insurer under an agreement to pay interest thereon, the interest payments shall be included in gross income); [and]

> (2) Amounts received (other than amounts paid by reason of the death of the insured and interest payments on such amounts) under a life insurance, endowment, or annuity contract, but if such amounts (when added to amounts received before the taxable year under such contract) exceed the aggregate premiums or consideration paid (whether or not paid during the taxable year) then the excess shall be included in gross income. ...[46]

Thus, in addition to providing an exception for death proceeds, the 1926 act clarified the treatment of gain in surrender, now found in section 72(e). With the changes made in the 1926 Revenue Act, the basic pattern of life insurance taxation was established for both individual and corporate taxpayers. However, the path followed for corporate policyholders was slightly different, as is discussed below.

## *Supplee-Biddle Hardware*

In addition to generating a debate in the Congress, the early treatment of the death benefit on corporate-owned contracts led a corporate taxpayer to challenge the income tax treatment of death proceeds under the 1918 act. Litigation began in the U.S. Court of Claims and was appealed to the U.S. Supreme Court, where the taxpayer, the Supplee-Biddle Hardware Co., argued successfully that life insurance proceeds payable to corporate beneficiaries were properly excludable from income. In 1917, Supplee-Biddle had taken out life insurance contracts on its president "to make secure the financial position of the company" in the event of his death, which occurred as a result of the influenza epidemic of 1918.[47] In filing its tax return for 1918, Supplee-Biddle Hardware did not include the "amount of the policy, less the premiums paid" in income, although it subsequently paid the tax in 1921, filing suit in the Court of Claims for a refund. The Court of Claims noted that if "these proceeds [are] to be regarded as indemnity for the loss incurred ... then the company should have not been required to pay the tax."[48] The court went on to say "we do not think that the Congress intended to tax the proceeds of life insurance policies as income, because such proceeds are not income in the accepted meaning of that word."[49] (The position of the Court of Claims is interesting in light of the legislative history indicating that it was precisely the intent of Congress to tax life insurance proceeds paid to corporations.) In upholding the Court of Claims decision, the Supreme Court stated that "it is reasonable that the purpose of section 213 to exclude entirely the proceeds of life insurance policies from taxation in the case of individuals should be given the same effect in adapting its application to corporations. ..."[50] The Court went on to say, in response to the contention that "the proceeds of life insurance paid on the death of the insured are in fact capital and cannot be taxed as income under the Sixteenth Amendment"[51] that it "is enough to sustain our construction of the act to say that proceeds of a life insurance policy paid on the death of the insured are not usually classed as income."[52] After

---

[44] *Id.*
[45] Beginning with section II(B) of the Income Tax Act of 1913, the income tax exclusion for death proceeds of life insurance policies has been provided in each succeeding revenue act or Internal Revenue Code provision, with only a few minor modifications. *See* Act of September 8, 1916, *supra* note 35; Act of October 3, 1917, ch. 63, Pub. L. No. 65-50, § 1200, 40 Stat. 300, 329; Revenue Act of 1918, *supra* note 37, at 1057, 1065; Revenue Act of 1921, *supra* note 41; Revenue Act of 1924, ch. 234, Pub. L. No. 68-176, § 213(b)(1), 43 Stat. 253, 267; Revenue Act of 1926, Pub. L. No. 69-20, ch. 27, § 213(b)(1), 44 Stat. 9, 24; Revenue Act of 1928, ch. 852, Pub. L. No. 70-562, § 22(b)(1), 45 Stat. 791, 797; Revenue Act of 1932, ch. 209, Pub. L. No. 72-154, § 22(b)(1), 47 Stat. 169, 178; Revenue Act of 1934, ch. 277, Pub. L. No. 73-216, § 22(b)(1), 48 Stat. 680, 687; Revenue Act of 1936, ch. 690, Pub. L. No. 74-740, § 22(b)(1), 49 Stat. 1648, 1657; Revenue Act of 1938, ch. 289, Pub. L. No. 75-554, § 22(b)(1), 52 Stat. 447, 458; Internal Revenue Code of 1939, ch. 1, Pub. L. No. 76-1, § 22(b)(1), 53 Stat. 1, 10; Internal Revenue Code of 1954, ch. 736, § 101(a), 68A Stat. 1, 26.
[46] Revenue Act of 1926, *supra* note 45, at 9, 17.
[47] *Supplee-Biddle Hardware Co. v. United States*, 58 Ct. Cl. 343, 344 (1923).
[48] *Id.* at 347.
[49] *Id.* at 349.
[50] *United States v. Supplee-Biddle Hardware Co.*, 265 U.S. 189, 194 (1924).
[51] Citing *Eisner v. Macomber*, 232 U.S. 189, 207.
[52] *United States v. Supplee-Biddle Hardware Co., supra* note 50, at 194–95.

the enactment of the Revenue Act of 1921, the Bureau of Internal Revenue conceded that life insurance proceeds received by corporate beneficiaries were exempt from income tax.

### Early Cases and the Treatment of Cash Surrender Values

The treatment of life insurance as combining protection and savings in the form of cash surrender values also emerged in federal income tax cases in the early 20th century. A view of life insurance as savings was expressed in 1920 by the U.S. Supreme Court in *Penn Mutual Life Insurance Co. v. Lederer,* where the Court noted that "in level premium life insurance, while the motive for taking it may be mainly protection, the business is largely that of savings investment. The premium is in the nature of a savings deposit."[53] In the 1934 case of *Century Wood Preserving Co. v. Commissioner,* the 3rd Circuit Court of Appeals commented "the policies of insurance involved here have a double aspect. They provide the present protection of ordinary life insurance and also a means of investment."[54] Similarly, in the 1927 case of *Appeal of Standard Brewing Company*, the Board of Tax Appeals commented:

> To the extent that the premiums paid by the petitioner created in it a right to a surrender value, they constituted a capital investment. To the extent they exceeded the surrender value, they constituted payment for earned insurance and were current expenses [citing *Appeal of E. A. Armstrong*, 1 B.T.A. 296]. The surrender value of the policy was the measure of the investment. ...[55]

These cases also generally supported the principle that losses incurred under life insurance contracts are not deductible. In *London Shoe Co. v. Commissioner* the 2nd Circuit Court of Appeals stated:

> The subdivision [of the Revenue Act of 1928] dealing with the computation of taxable gains somewhat favors the taxpayer at the expense of the government, because it allows the deduction of the full amount of the premiums paid from the total amount received, though the premiums are in excess of what would normally be required for insurance protection, and thus lessens the amount of the taxable gain. It does not necessarily result that such statutory indulgence will be given the taxpayer in computing losses, especially where there is no statutory provision that contains language that will justify it.[56]

Thus, by the early 1930s the principle that life insurance combines savings and a pure risk element was well established in federal tax case law, thereby establishing the underpinnings of one key element of today's definitional limitation, namely, the cash surrender value represents the equity, or savings, of the policyholder in a life insurance contract.

## The Development of an Economic Definition of Life Insurance

As discussed in Chapter 1, beginning in the early 1940s an actuarial or economic definition of life insurance emerged for federal tax purposes, focusing on the shifting and distribution of risk. Before that time, the definition of what constituted a life insurance contract generally was based on contractual form and the presence of an insurable interest. In the landmark case of *Helvering v. Le Gierse*,[57] the U.S. Supreme Court established the principle that, although a contract (or a combination of contracts) is in the form of a standard commercial life insurance contract, it is not treated as a life insurance contract for purposes of federal tax law unless it provides for risk shifting and risk distributing (or pooling). As with other developments in the taxation of life insurance, it was a response to a life insurance product that was seen as abusive of provisions of the tax law related to advantages given to life insurance—in that case by endeavoring to enable access to the estate tax exemption for uninsurable lives by hedging the mortality risk with an annuity.

However, in requiring the presence of risk shifting and risk distribution, the Supreme Court in *Le Gierse* left open the question of how much risk is necessary for a life insurance contract to qualify for the customary tax

---

[53] 252 U.S. 523, 531 (1920).
[54] 69 F.2d 967, 968 (3d Cir. 1934).
[55] 6 B.T.A. 980, 984 (1927).
[56] 80 F.2d 230, 232 (2d Cir. 1935), cert. denied, 298 U.S. 663 (1936).
[57] *Supra* note 4.

treatment of life insurance, and over what period such risk was required. It was not until Congress established definitional limitations by devising the actuarial tests under sections 101(f), 7702 and 7702A that these questions were addressed.

## Le Gierse *and the Estate Tax Exemption*

The 1918 act provided an exemption from the federal estate tax for life insurance proceeds of up to $40,000.[58] To take advantage of the exclusion, some insurers marketed a combination of a single premium life insurance contract and a single premium, non-refund immediate life annuity to otherwise uninsurable clients. As described by Judge Clark in the Third Circuit's opinion in *Commissioner v. Keller's Estate*:

> No one knows better than insurance salesmen that only the "excess over $40,000" of life insurance proceeds receivable by beneficiaries other than the insured's executor are subject to the estate tax (26 USCA Int. Rev. Code, § 811(g)). This $40,000 exemption, a unique characteristic of their general stock in trade, is quite naturally stressed to the customer. Sometimes, however, it is stressed to a paradoxical extreme. The paradox consists in applying a life insurance exemption to the estate of an uninsurable prospect.[59]

A footnote was added to this passage that reads:

> Salesmen are instructed: "If the prospect has a reasonable income and is insurable he unquestionably should be advised to purchase annual premium life insurance to take advantage of his full insurance exemption. If he is not insurable a single premium life or endowment policy combined with an annuity provides the prospect with income comparable with that received from high grade bonds, and at the same time secures him this additional tax saving."[60]

The marketing of such combination life insurance and annuity plans to elderly and otherwise uninsurable policyholders allowed them to qualify for the estate tax exemption, leading to the development of a federal common law definition of insurance in *Helvering v. Le Gierse* and related cases. The Revenue Act of 1942 eliminated the specific estate tax exemption for life insurance.[61]

## *Cecile Le Gierse and Anna Keller*

Two buyers of these combination plans were elderly women named Cecile Le Gierse and Anna Keller. Le Gierse died at age 80 on January 1, 1936. On December 6, 1935, she executed two contracts with the Connecticut General Life Insurance Co., a single premium non-refund immediate life annuity and a $25,000 face amount single premium life insurance contract. Almost a year earlier, on December 31, 1934, Keller, then age 75, executed similar contracts with the Equitable Life Assurance Society of the United States. On March 28, 1936, a few months after Le Gierse's death, Keller also died.

Both of Le Gierse's contracts were issued on standard contract forms. The insurer, Connecticut General Life, accounted separately for the two contracts on its books. As noted in Table 9.1, the premium for the life insurance was $22,946, while the annuity premium was $4,179, for a total of $27,125, an amount equal to the $25,000 death benefit plus an 8.5 percent load for agent compensation and premium tax. The annuity would provide an annual payment of $590, which represented an annual 2.2 percent return on Le Gierse's $27,125 investment (i.e., the rate of return is the annual annuity payment divided by the total premium). Note, however, that if Le Gierse's death occurred in the first three years, the transaction would have generated a loss to the policyholder resulting from the expense loading. Keller had purchased a life insurance contract with a $20,000 death benefit. The premium for the life insurance contract was $17,942 and the annuity premium was $3,258, or a total of $21,200, which was equal to the $20,000 death benefit and a 6 percent load.

---

[58] The specific life insurance exemption in the estate tax was eliminated in 1942. *See infra* note 61 and related text.
[59] *Comm'r v. Keller's Estate*, 113 F.2d 833, 833–34 and note 1 (3d Cir. 1940).
[60] *Id.*, citing J. BLAKE LOWE AND JOHN DOWNING WRIGHT, SELLING LIFE INSURANCE THROUGH A TAX APPROACH 80, 81 (1936).
[61] The Revenue Act of 1942 was passed to support the financing of World War II. It was not kind to life insurance products, eliminating both the $40,000 estate tax exemption and the deduction of interest for loans used to purchase single premium plans. Revenue Act of 1942, ch. 619, Pub. L. No. 77-753, § 404(g), 56 Stat. 798, 827 and 944–45.

### Table 9.1. Le Gierse contract values

**Values at time of purchase**

| | |
|---|---|
| Issue age | 80 |
| Life insurance premium: | 22,946 |
| Life insurance death benefit: | 25,000 |
| Annuity premium: | 4,179 |
| Annual annuity payment: | 590 |
| Total premium: | 27,125 |
| Expected annual rate of return: | 2.20% |

| Age | Surrender value | Annuity payment | Death benefit | Gain or loss on death |
|---|---|---|---|---|
| 81 | 19,550 | 590 | 25,000 | −1,535 |
| 82 | 20,400 | 590 | 25,000 | −945 |
| 83 | 21,550 | 590 | 25,000 | −355 |
| 84 | 21,775 | 590 | 25,000 | 235 |
| 85 | 22,000 | 590 | 25,000 | 825 |
| 86 | 22,225 | 590 | 25,000 | 1,415 |
| 87 | 22,425 | 590 | 25,000 | 2,005 |
| 88 | 22,625 | 590 | 25,000 | 2,595 |
| 89 | 22,800 | 590 | 25,000 | 3,185 |
| 90 | 22,975 | 590 | 25,000 | 3,775 |
| 91 | 23,150 | 590 | 25,000 | 4,365 |
| 92 | 23,300 | 590 | 25,000 | 4,955 |
| 93 | 23,425 | 590 | 25,000 | 5,545 |
| 94 | 23,550 | 590 | 25,000 | 6,135 |
| 95 | 24,275 | 590 | 25,000 | 6,725 |
| 96 | 25,000 | 590 | 25,000 | 7,315 |

The Board of Tax Appeals upheld the validity of the estate tax exclusions for both Le Gierse and Keller, noting, in the Keller case, that "[w]e think effect should be given to these policies in accordance with their plain terms. ..."[62] On appeal, the 2nd Circuit Court of Appeals, applying a contractual analysis, also found for Le Gierse, noting:

> In the life policy she took out insurance upon her life which is squarely within the exemption granted by the statute. The fact that she could not have gotten that policy unless she had also bought an annuity contract does not change the character of what she got.[63]

Conversely, in the Keller case, the 3rd Circuit Court of Appeals adopted an economic analysis, analyzing the transaction as a whole under actuarial principles. Recognizing that, regardless of the age of the insured, the total premium was (always) equal to the death benefit plus a load, the court characterized the transaction as a "loan" (with interest) to the insurance company that would be returned on death, as follows:

> By an actuarial tour de force (because the continuance of life is a matter of minutes, not probabilities), the amount of the loan advanced is split into the single premiums appropriate to each policy as if taken out by a normal person. In other words, the sure thing (loan) is artificially sepa-

---

[62] *Estate of Keller v. Comm'r*, 39 BTA 1047, 1060 (1939).
[63] *Comm'r v. Le Gierse*, 110 F.2d 734, 735 (2d Cir. 1940).

rated into doubtful bet (life insurance) and hedge (annuity). It is on this general principle that an uninsurable life becomes "insured."[64]

The court went on to express the view that, in providing the estate tax exclusion, Congress used the word "insurance" with the economic rather than the purely contractual aspects of the term in mind, thus overturning the Board of Tax Appeals and denying the tax benefits.

Presented with the different outcomes, the Supreme Court heard both the *Le Gierse* and *Keller* cases. Adopting an economic analysis, in 1941 the Court overturned the *Le Gierse* case, promulgating the now familiar risk-shifting and risk-distributing standard as an essential element of "insurance" for federal tax purposes. Under the *Le Gierse* standard, unless a transaction is insurance from both the client's perspective (risk shifting) and the underwriter's perspective (risk distribution), it is not insurance for purposes of the Code. In its decision, the Supreme Court expressed the standard in the following way:

> We think the fair import of [section 302(g), providing the estate tax exemption] is that the amounts must be received as the result of a transaction which involved actual "insurance risk" at the time the transaction was executed. Historically and commonly insurance involves risk-shifting and risk-distributing. That life insurance is desirable from an economic and social standpoint as a device to shift and distribute risk of loss from premature death is unquestionable. That these elements of risk-shifting and risk-distributing are essential to a life insurance contract is agreed by courts and commentators.[65]

The *Le Gierse* case established an economic definition of insurance under federal tax law, which, in the view of the IRS, continues to apply.[66] For example, in Rev. Rul. 65-57,[67] the IRS addressed the income tax treatment of an arrangement similar to that in *Le Gierse* (which related to the estate tax treatment of the arrangement there involved). Under the facts of the ruling, a life insurance contract purchased by a taxpayer could not have been acquired except in combination with a non-refund life annuity contract (for which the taxpayer paid a single premium equal to the face value of the insurance contract). The IRS held that the arrangement had no element of insurance, even though it had the usual form of an insurance contract and contained all the usual provisions, and that the proceeds of the contract, even though received by reason of the insured's death, were not excludable from gross income under section 101(a) but were subject to income tax to the extent they exceeded the net premiums paid for the contract. The IRS further ruled that the annual payments received under the annuity contract were subject to the provisions of section 72(b).

## *Developments after* Le Gierse

The standards that courts applied in cases subsequent to *Le Gierse* addressing whether arrangements constituted insurance for tax purposes included the characterization of the contract for state law purposes, the presence of insurance risk in terms of the relationship of the face amount to the cash value and the actuarial soundness of the fund from which death benefits were to be paid.[68] As discussed in Chapter 1, other cases determined that survivor benefit funds, including stock exchange death benefit payments, qualified as life insurance.[69] While the existence of an amount at risk was important, there was no quantification of how much was enough.

In a revenue ruling addressing the treatment of retirement income contracts, the IRS also considered the existence of an amount at risk. Rev. Rul. 66-322[70] held that a retirement income contract would be treated as providing life insurance even after net amount at risk disappeared (under a retirement income contract, the cash value eventually exceeds the death benefit) because the risk element had existed for many years. However,

---

[64] *Comm'r v. Keller's Estate, supra* note 59, at 834. If life insurance with amount (F) is to be bought along with an annuity equal to an annual interest return (i) on the net premium paid by the policyholder (NSP), the net premium is defined by the equation (NSP = F × $A_x$ + i × NSP × $a_x$). Using the relationship $A_x$ = 1 − d × $ä_x$, gives a result that NSP = F × (1 ÷ (1 + i)). The net premium depends on the amount and interest rate, but not the age of the insured. Thus, there is no life contingency.
[65] 312 U.S. at 539.
[66] *See, e.g.,* PLR 200022003 (December 9, 1999).
[67] 1965-1 C.B. 56.
[68] *See, e.g.,* Barnes v. United States, 801 F.2d 984 (7th Cir. 1986); *Davis v. United States,* 323 F. Supp. 858 (S.D. W. Va. 1971).
[69] See *Comm'r v. Treganowan,* 183 F.2d 288 (2d Cir. 1950).
[70] 1966-2 C.B. 123.

the Tax Court, in *Evans v. Commissioner*,[71] disagreed, holding that insurance only existed so long as the contract contained a risk element. Through *Le Gierse* and subsequent cases and rulings, the existence of insurance risk was established generally as a critical definitional element for a contract to be considered as a life insurance contract under federal tax law.

## The Limitations on Financed Life Insurance

The reason for discussing the Code's limitations on financed life insurance is to provide the reader a sense of the long-standing tension between the life insurance industry and the tax authorities over the deduction of policy loan interest used to finance the purchase of life insurance. More broadly, the tension is between the beneficial treatment of life insurance under the Code and the general norms of the tax law. This is relevant to the development of the section 101(f), 7702 and 7702A definitional limits in that it illustrates a willingness of Congress to draw lines relative to the tax treatment of life insurance, in this case the ability to finance the purchase of a life insurance contract with interest-deductible debt, and on a recurring basis with ever-increasing impact. Congressional line-drawing, together with the concepts of cash surrender value as savings and risk transfer discussed earlier, are key precedents in the evolution of the definitional limitations.

The perception that Congress would act to restrict the use of policy loans where it perceived "abuse" was noted by Victor E. Henningsen in his presidential address to the Society of Actuaries in October 1965. In addressing the (then) recently enacted limitations regarding policy loans (i.e., the changes in section 264 in the 1964 legislation), Henningsen commented that "we know full well that abuse of financed [life] insurance led to a change in the federal income tax law. ... Schemes for circumventing the intent of the present law, when viewed in the light of tax history, seemingly invite more restrictive legislation."[72] Limits on debt-financed life insurance and annuities appeared first in 1942, again in 1954 and 1963, and again in 1986 when interest paid for debt-financed life insurance for individual taxpayers was no longer deductible. (By 1996, interest deductions for business taxpayers purchasing life insurance were largely eliminated.)

As early as 1917–18, Congress disallowed interest deductions where indebtedness was used to purchase tax-exempt obligations or securities.[73] However, in the first few decades of the modern income tax, there was no specific limitation on the deduction of interest on loans used to purchase life insurance and annuities, leading to the development of financed insurance programs, where the funds to acquire life insurance contracts were made available through bank loans. (Where the financing was provided by a policy loan and not a bank loan, the term "minimum deposit" has been applied. The term "minimum deposit plan" refers to the method of financing the premium, and not to the contracts themselves.)

The operation of these programs was described as follows:

> Under a financed policy program, each year the insured borrows an amount equal to the increase in cash value, either under a policy loan or from a commercial lender. The insured pays an amount equal to the premium, plus interest on the loan, less the dividend, less the increase in cash value.[74]

And,

> Bank loan and minimum deposit (or minimum outlay) plans for purchasing permanent life insurance are simply methods of financing premium payments by systematically using the yearly increases in the cash value of a policy as collateral for loans to pay all or a substantial portion of the yearly premiums.[75]

---

[71] 56 T.C. 1142 (1971).
[72] Victor E. Henningsen, *Address of the President*, 17 Soc'y of Actuaries Transactions, part I, 227, 234 (1965). Henningsen, FSA, managed Northwestern Mutual Life's actuarial department from 1953 to 1968. *See* John Gurda, The Quiet Company: A Modern History of Northwestern Mutual Life 155 (1983).
[73] Melvin C. Teske, *Bank Loan Insurance and Minimum Deposit Plans; Using Life Insurance to Fund Buy-Sell Agreements*, 481, in Proceedings of NYU Eighteenth Annual Institute on Fed. Tax'n (1960).
[74] Thurston P. Farmer Jr., *Financed Policies*, 65, in XIV Proceedings 1964–1965, Conf. of Actuaries in Public Practice.
[75] Teske, *supra* note 73, at 479.

The key to any financed insurance plan is the idea that, where interest is deductible, by borrowing against the cash values and applying the money so borrowed to pay premiums, insurance protection may be purchased at a very low net cost or outlay because the cost of insurance and the after-tax interest charged on the indebtedness may be almost wholly offset by the interest earned on the increase in the cash surrender values. Five conditions must be met for the policyholder to achieve a net gain from financed insurance using policy loans:

- The inside buildup must not be taxed.
- Policy loans must not be treated as taxable distributions.
- The interest credited to the policy must exceed the after-tax policy loan interest.[76]
- Life insurance reserves must be deductible by the insurance company.[77]
- The policy expenses must be such that the tax benefit is not offset by transaction costs.

Table 9.2 illustrates that it is possible to achieve an after-tax gain from the financed purchase of a life insurance contract, assuming loan interest is deductible and the inside buildup is not taxed. In this case, both the individual taxpayer and the insurer face an income tax rate of 50 percent.

### Table 9.2. Financed insurance economics

|  | Taxpayer gain | Insurer gain | Total gain |
|---|---|---|---|
| Policy loan interest | −100 | 100 | 0 |
| Tax on loan interest at 50% | −50 | 50 | 0 |
| Net after-tax interest | −50 | 50 | 0 |
| Interest earnings on cash value | 90 | −90 | 0 |
| Tax on cash value interest at 50% | 0 | −45 | −45 |
| Net interest earnings | 90 | −45 | 45 |
| Net after-tax gain from inside buildup | 40 | 5 | 45 |

Note that it is the interest credit, and not solely the tax benefit of the interest deduction, that creates the gain in a financed policy. In a financed life insurance sale, so long as the net after-tax gain from the inside buildup is greater than the cost of insurance, the life insurance is "free" to the policyholder on an after-tax basis. Thus, the greater the inside buildup relative to the cost of insurance (i.e., the greater the investment orientation), the lower the after-tax cost of a financed policy.[78] The "flaw" in financed insurance is that if a policyholder surrenders the policy, a tax on the gain in the policy may be due without policy funds (which have been used to repay the policy loan) available to pay the tax.[79] Thus, a critical assumption from the policyholder's perspective is that the contracts are held until the death of the insured, when the proceeds are received free of federal income tax.

Until 1942, single premium contracts financed with bank loans[80] were widely sold on the basis that interest on the borrowed funds would be tax-deductible and the interest added to policy cash values could be received

---

[76] This implies, but does not mandate, that the policy loan interest is deductible. In the absence of a deduction for loan interest, there are (and have been) circumstances in which the interest credited to the cash surrender value of a contract will exceed the cost of funds.

[77] In the absence of a deduction for reserves, the insurance company would be unable to credit a competitive rate of interest on the cash surrender value.

[78] In describing his use of minimum deposit, a famed economist commented, "Under reasonable assumptions, the present value of the cost of the policy, is negative." Fisher Black, How I Got Free Insurance from TIAA 1 (unpublished paper, Graduate School of Business, University of Chicago, 1974). Minimum deposit "works" so long as the cost of insurance inside the contract does not exceed the tax benefit on the inside buildup and the policyholder maintains the policy until death. On surrender of a fully borrowed contract, there are no funds available to pay the tax on gain, as the cash value must be used to repay the loan. This fact has brought misery to many.

[79] At this point, to place the matter in perspective, it is important to note the economics of the purchase of life insurance are the same whether a contract is acquired using debt financing (leveraged) or simply using the policyholder's own funds (unleveraged). For an unleveraged purchase, the net after-tax loan interest would simply be replaced in the analysis by the after-tax cost of funds. It should also be noted that it is possible to achieve a net gain under a financed insurance program in the absence of a deduction for policy loan interest. This occurs where the amounts credited to loaned cash surrender values are greater than the pretax loan interest, as occurred under some whole life contracts in the late 1970s. A gain can also result from actual mortality that exceeds that reflected in the pricing of the life insurance contract.

[80] From the 1930s until the mid-1950s, the rate charged on policy loans generally exceeded market interest rates. As a result, most financed insurance sales were through banks. As interest rates rose in the mid-1950s, policy loans were increasingly used in minimum deposit plans.

as part of a tax-free death benefit. The Revenue Act of 1942 disallowed the deduction of interest paid on indebtedness used to purchase single premium life insurance or endowment contracts.[81] Under this provision, a contract was considered to be purchased for a single premium if "substantially all" of the premiums were paid within a period of four years from the date the contract was purchased. The House Report for the Revenue Act of 1942 notes:

> Under the present law, a considerable loophole exists through which persons who borrow money to purchase single premium or fully paid-up life insurance or endowment contracts secure substantial tax advantages.[82]

After enactment of the interest deduction disallowance for single premium plans in the Revenue Act of 1942, a "battle of wits" continued between the proponents of the bank loan plans and the taxing authorities.[83] From that point until the enactment of the Internal Revenue Code of 1954, the "bank loaners" adopted different strategies, including the prepayment of premiums on life insurance contracts or the use of borrowing on annuities.[84] One commentator has noted:

> Congress had barred interest deductions on indebtedness incurred to carry single-premium policies, but insurance companies were not so easily daunted in their quest to convert the tax-exempt status of insurance policy accumulations into an attractive tax-saving option for policyholders. The new medium of avoidance consisted of an insurance contract enabling the holder systematically to borrow against the policy's incremental cash value in order to pay his insurance premiums—the logical next step from the now useless (for tax avoidance) single-premium plan. For higher-bracket taxpayers, this resulted in extremely low-cost (and sometimes cost-free) insurance coverage.[85]

In 1954, noting the use of single premium annuities and the use of premium deposit funds where "the purchaser borrows an amount approximating the single-premium cost of the policy but, instead of purchasing the policy outright, deposits the borrowed funds with the insurance company for payment of future premiums on the policy,"[86] Congress eliminated the interest deduction for loans related to annuities and prepaid premiums on single premium plans.

### *High Early Cash Value Contracts and Minimum Deposit Life Insurance Plans*

With the 1954 changes in what today is section 264 that eliminated the deduction of loan interest on single premium plans, the financed insurance market turned to high early cash value contracts. At the same time, because of changes in interest rates generally, the preferred source of borrowing became policy loans rather than bank loans.

High early cash value policies were initially developed for use in the split dollar market, in the wake of Rev. Rul. 55-713,[87] which attempted to tax split dollar plans as interest-free loans. Guertin,[88] an actuary with the American Life Convention, described high early cash value contracts as being "tremendously attractive" to

---

[81] Revenue Act of 1942, *supra* note 61, § 129, 56 Stat. 798, 827. Another ban on interest deductibility appeared in the Revenue Act of 1932, affecting indebtedness incurred in connection with the purchasing or carrying of an annuity, but Congress repealed this provision in 1934. *See* Revenue Act of 1932, *supra* note 45, at 169, 179 (imposing limitation); Revenue Act of 1934, *supra* note 45, at 680, 688 (repealing limitation). *See also* Robert W. Smith Jr., *Minimum Deposit Plans: A Primer for Life Ins. Counsel,* paper read before the Ass'n of Life Ins. Counsel 575, 589 (May 26, 1959) (on file with authors).

[82] H.R. Rep. No. 77-2333, at 47 (1942).

[83] Smith, *supra* note 81, at 590.

[84] The use of annuity "bonds" in bank loan programs led to the Supreme Court holding in *Knetsch v. United States*, 364 U.S. 361 (1960), in which the Court applied a sham transaction theory to the purchase of a single premium annuity with borrowed funds. The story of Knetsch and the annuity cases cannot be told without mentioning the notable "entrepreneurs" Rufus C. Salley and Beulah S. Salley, husband and wife, who were officers and directors of Sam Houston Life Insurance Co., the principal promoter of the annuity product that led to the *Knetsch* case. The Salleys themselves lost two policy loan cases, one involving a *Knetsch*-type annuity (*Salley v. Comm'r*, 319 F. 2d 847 (5th Cir. 1963)) and another involving life insurance (*Salley v. Comm'r*, 464 F.2d 479 (5th Cir. 1972)). In the latter case, the 5th Circuit Court of Appeals commented, "In sum, taxpayers have produced and directed a choreography of some stylistic contrivance and ingenuity. It appears that taxpayers' dance with Houston National was not an arms-length cha-cha after all, but rather a clinched two-step. Like the Tax Court, we conclude that taxpayers' performance at its outset should have been declared a turkey and trotted off the stage of tax deductibility." 464 F.2d at 486.

[85] Curtis Jay Berger, *Simple Interest and Complex Taxes*, 81 Colum. L. Rev., no. 2, at 217, 227 (1981) (hereinafter Berger).

[86] H.R. Rep. No. 83-1337, at 31 (1954).

[87] 1955-2 C.B. 23.

[88] Guertin, who was the actuary of the New Jersey Insurance Department at the time, headed the efforts to modernize reserve and cash value legislation in the late 1930s and early 1940s. His name is enshrined in the Guertin report, *supra* note 7.

those who "look upon a policy of life insurance as an asset of financial value in the same sense that they look upon a stock or a bond." He went on to say:

> They have been planned with unusually high cash values in the early years. The difference between the actual deposit of premiums and the increase in the cash value becomes relatively small even in the early years, and the premium paid for protection becomes very low. These policies look extremely attractive in a ledger statement. They do, therefore, have attractive facets for people who are investment conscious and, from a competitive standpoint, establish cost patterns which are somewhat new in this business.[89]

Insurance purchased using a minimum deposit strategy with the high early cash value plans became extremely popular with the insurance-buying public. In some companies, the high cash value plans represented a significant portion of new life insurance sales in the late 1950s.[90]

One such product, later the subject of litigation related to the deduction of policy loan interest, was a nonparticipating increasing benefit whole life policy,[91] providing for the prepayment of premiums through an advance premium deposit fund. In the years in which such policies were issued, interest on advance premium deposits was not treated as income to the policyholder. Consequently, the premium deposit funds were treated in the same manner as policy cash values, with tax-free inside buildup.[92] As a result, policyholders were able to borrow amounts in excess of the premiums due during the initial policy years and receive the same income tax treatment as policy loans. Under these plans, the policyholders generally borrowed the full cash value (including the deposit funds) in the first and all subsequent years.

In response to the widespread use of policy loans to finance the purchase of life insurance, the section 264(c)(1) four-out-of-seven rule (now found in section 264(d)(1)) was applied to policy loan interest paid or accrued after December 31, 1963. Under that rule, policy loan interest is deductible only if no part of four of the annual premiums due during the seven-year period starting with the first premium is paid by means of indebtedness. While not limiting the design of the policies, these limitations under section 264 restricted the treatment of policy loans. Even with the enactment of the four-out-of-seven rule, however, minimum deposit continued to be a popular method of financing the purchase of permanent life insurance contracts until the elimination of the deduction for personal interest for individuals in the Tax Reform Act of 1986, which made policy loan interest deductions unavailable for individuals.[93]

## Universal Life and the Product Revolution: The Rise of a Statutory Definition of Life Insurance

Driven by the advent of high interest rates and inflation, in the late 1960s and early 1970s the life insurance industry began to develop a new generation of life insurance products that were more flexible and attractive to consumers than the then traditional product offerings. The new plans introduced during this period included:

- Extraordinary Life, introduced by Northwestern Mutual in 1968, an "economatic" plan combining whole life, term insurance and dividend additions as a self-contained whole.

- Adjustable Whole Life, introduced by Minnesota Mutual (now Minnesota Life) and Bankers Life of Iowa (now Principal Life) in the early 1970s, incorporating increased product flexibility in premium and benefit level.

---

[89] Alfred N. Guertin, *Price Competition in the Life Insurance Business*, XXV THE JOURNAL OF INSURANCE, no. 1, July 1958, at 8–9.

[90] David G. Scott, *Our Changing Product*, Part of Panel Discussion Titled *The Latest Word—Some Thoughts About Our Business*, 61, 65, in PROCEEDINGS OF THE 1959 ANNUAL CONFERENCE OF THE LIFE OFFICE MANAGEMENT ASSOCIATION. *See also* 13 SOC'Y OF ACTUARIES TRANSACTIONS D47 (1961).

[91] Under the contract design, the death benefit increased annually during the first 20 policy years and was level thereafter. The gross annual premiums were approximately equal to whole life premiums plus $50 per $1,000 per year in the first 20 contract years.

[92] *See* I.T. 3513, 1941-2 C.B. 75; Rev. Rul. 65-24, 1965-1 C.B. 31. Rev. Rul. 65-24 was later revoked by Rev. Rul. 65-199, 1965-2 C.B. 20. Under Rev. Rul. 65-199, "[a]ny increment in value of so-called 'advance premiums,' 'prepaid premiums,' or 'premium deposit funds' which is applied to the payment of premiums due on annuity and life insurance policies, or made available for withdrawal by the policyholder, will result in taxable income to the policyholder at that time."

[93] The Tax Reform Act of 1986 left in place the deduction of policy loan interest for corporations up to a loan of $50,000 per covered employee. The deduction for policy loan interest by corporations, with some exceptions for key employees, was phased out by the Health Insurance Portability and Accountability Act of 1996 (HIPAA). *See* Pub. L. No. 104-191, § 501. However, policy loan interest remains deductible to corporations for contracts purchased on or before June 20, 1986, subject to certain limitations.

- Variable life insurance, first marketed by The Equitable (now AXA) in the mid-1970s, in which the death benefits and contract values were tied to the performance of a segregated asset account.

- Term insurance and annuity combinations, including Split Life, marketed as substitutes for whole life (and which formed the basis of Jim Anderson's famous prediction of a "Cannibal Life" product[94]).

- Indeterminate or nonguaranteed premium whole life plans, introduced by the Aetna and others in the early 1970s, which provided current and guaranteed premiums in a nominally nonparticipating whole life plan.

- Universal life, technically known as flexible premium adjustable life, a product introduced by E.F. Hutton Life in 1979 that opened the "black box" of traditional life insurance and rather clearly revealed the insurance and savings components of a life insurance contract.

- Executive Life's Irreplaceable Life and similar products introduced beginning in 1980, which were interest sensitive whole life plans (also known as fixed premium universal life) that combined universal life-type accumulation accounts with traditional cash values.

Faced with this new generation of products, the IRS responded with a series of public and private rulings holding generally that their federal income tax treatment would be the same as the more traditional permanent contracts, provided risk shifting was present and the products were insurance under state law, consistently with the IRS position on insurance products after *Le Gierse*.

## *Variable Life*

In Rev. Rul. 79-87,[95] the IRS held that the entire amount of the death benefit paid under two variable life insurance contracts was excludable from tax under section 101(a). The contracts were level annual premium plans providing benefits that would increase or decrease (but not below a guaranteed minimum) using paid-up whole life elements. When the returns under the contract exceeded an assumed rate of return, additional paid-up elements would be added. Similarly, when the investment returns were less than the assumed return, prior additional paid-up elements would, in effect, be cancelled. Thus, under the contract described in the ruling, the relationship of the cash surrender value and the death benefit would always be maintained within a traditional relationship, based on a combination of annual and net single premiums (NSPs). A private letter ruling issued by the IRS in 1981 elaborated on the 1979 published ruling, noting that "insurance risk, as described in *Le Gierse*, is present with respect to both the guaranteed and variable components of the death benefit," and concluding that the death benefits payable would be excludable from the gross income of the beneficiary and that the owner would not be deemed to be in constructive receipt of the cash surrender value, including increments therein, prior to actual surrender of the contract.[96]

## *Universal Life*

The most significant of these new products was universal life insurance and its variable counterpart, variable universal life. The most notable proponent of universal life was by James C.H. Anderson, whose paper *The Universal Life Insurance Policy* was published in November 1975. In that paper, Anderson described universal life as "a flexible premium annuity with a monthly renewable term insurance rider."[97]

Some early universal life-type arrangements, based on Anderson's design, were structured as a combination of a term life insurance contract and a deferred annuity. In August 1980, the IRS considered a term and annuity combination similar in concept to Anderson's original universal life design. The IRS was presented with a combination term and annuity plan, where the premiums for the life insurance coverage were deducted from the net cash value of the annuity on a quarterly basis, and the death benefit of the term insurance, under one of the options available to the policyholder, was reduced each year relative to the increases in the annuity cash

---

[94] *See infra* note 98.
[95] 1979-1 C.B. 73.
[96] PLR 8120023 (February 17, 1981).
[97] James C.H. Anderson, *The Universal Life Insurance Policy*, 203, at 211, in THE PAPERS OF JAMES C.H. ANDERSON (1997).

value. Citing Rev. Rul. 65-57 (which had applied the principles of *Le Gierse* in determining the excludability of death proceeds under section 101(a)), the IRS concluded that the life insurance death benefit was excludable from gross income. However, the IRS also concluded that, even though the product was sold as a single contract under which all premiums were credited to the annuity and the term insurance premiums were deducted as partial withdrawals, the life insurance and annuity elements could not be treated together as an endowment policy for tax purposes because they were "clearly set up as a separate annuity contract and insurance policy" under state law.[98] As the death proceeds paid out of the annuity contract were taxed on the gain in the contract, creating a less favorable federal income tax result for the beneficiary than under a life insurance contract, this design fell out of favor.[99]

## *The Hutton Life Rulings*

With the introduction of a "true" universal life insurance contract by E.F. Hutton Life in 1979, and later variable universal life, the consumer could purchase a contract with premium and death benefit flexibility and providing a cash surrender value to which premiums paid and interest were credited and from which expenses and the cost of insurance were deducted. A number of life insurance companies entered the market with universal life designs in 1980–81. In January and February of 1981, the IRS issued private letter rulings to E.F. Hutton Life (the Hutton Life rulings), granting favorable income tax treatment to the death proceeds of the universal life plan, holding that the product was to be treated for tax purposes in the same manner as the traditional permanent life insurance contract.[100] The Hutton Life rulings specifically reached conclusions on three separate issues on which the taxpayer requested rulings.

The first ruling request dealt with the exclusion from tax of the death benefit under section 101(a)(1). The IRS noted that "if the cash value is, in fact, the equivalent to the cash value or reserve under a more traditional life insurance policy, then the total death benefit can be compared with the death benefit equal to the face amount plus the cash value under such traditional life insurance policy."[101] On this basis, the IRS concluded that the basic reserves under the policy were life insurance reserves and, thus, the total death benefit was "an amount paid by reason of the death of the Insured under a life insurance contract"[102] and thereby excludable from the gross income of the beneficiary under section 101(a).

The second ruling request related to rider death benefits (on a spouse or child). As the riders "provide[d] for pure term insurance," the IRS concluded that the death benefit payable was an amount "paid by reason of the death of a covered insured,"[103] and thus were excludable from the gross income of the beneficiary under section 101(a).

The third ruling request addressed the treatment of the inside buildup of the contract, asking that the insured not be deemed to be in constructive receipt of the contract's cash surrender value, including increments thereof. The IRS responded that "a specific answer to [the third ruling] request would be dependent upon a determination as to what the reserve increments are,"[104] suggesting two possible interpretations, neither of which would result in current taxation of the inside buildup:

- "(1) The policy is considered to be a nonparticipating contract. The assumed rates of interest and the cost of mortality are stated in the policy. An increase in the assumed rate of interest and/or a reduction of the cost or mortality is possible only by changing the basis under [then] section 806(b) of the Code."[105] Under this interpretation, the IRS concluded that an increase in reserves due to a change in basis would not result in constructive receipt.

- "(2) The policy is, in fact, a participating contract and the assumed rates of interest and the cost of mortality, as stated in the policy, are subject to change at the sole discretion of the management of the Insurer.

---

[98] PLR 8047051 (August 27, 1980).
[99] *See* Black, Skipper and Black, *supra* chapter 1, note 15, at 59–60.
[100] PLR 8116073 (January 23, 1981); PLR 8121074 (February 26, 1981) (clarifying PLR 8116073).
[101] PLR 8116073, *supra* note 100.
[102] *Id.*
[103] *Id.*
[104] PLR 8121074, *supra* note 100.
[105] PLR 8116073, *supra* note 100.

In this situation, any excess interest credited or any reduction in the cost of mortality is a dividend."[106] Under this approach, policyholder dividends would not be considered to be income to the policyholder until the sum of all dividends received exceeds the sum of all premiums paid under section 72(e)(1)(B). This was clarified in PLR 8121074 to note, "Any such dividends, since they must be applied to purchase paid-up insurance under the policy, would be considered as premiums paid for such paid-up insurance."

In May 1981, a similar result was reached on an interest-sensitive whole life plan with a "corridor" equal to the lesser of 5 percent of the contract's cash surrender value or $50,000.[107]

## GCM 38934

By the summer of 1981, however, the ruling position of the IRS on universal life came under attack, with critics in the life insurance industry focusing on the degree of risk required under universal life and similar plans. Under the products then available in the marketplace, a large amount of cash surrender value could accumulate with a relatively small amount of risk. If the Hutton Life rulings were followed, it was argued, these plans would qualify for the favorable treatment under sections 101(a) and 72(e) with only minimal required risk amounts. Since the *Le Gierse* life insurance test required only that there be an insurance risk element (without explicitly requiring a minimum necessary level for such risk), dissatisfaction with these rulings developed within the government, too. Although ruling requests for several universal life plans were pending, after the Hutton Life rulings the IRS issued no further rulings and began a review of its prior position.

After a year-long review, General Counsel Memorandum (GCM) 38934, issued in July 1982 but not released to the public until December of that year—after section 101(f) had been enacted—recommended that the IRS treat a universal life contract as term insurance and a savings element, not as an integrated contract of life insurance.[108] Although noting that the required "elements of risk-shifting and risk-distributing are present," the GCM argued that this, in itself, would not preclude a finding that the universal life contracts were in reality a combination of term insurance and savings (either a taxable fund or deferred annuity). While not providing a standard, the GCM noted "authority exists for considering the relationship between premiums and death benefits when determining whether a contract is a life insurance contract." It went on to comment that allowing life insurance tax treatment to any arrangement providing a death benefit that exceeds the reserve would, carried to its logical extreme, allow life insurance tax treatment for a contract "providing for a death benefit one dollar more than the reserve." The GCM concluded that only the pure amount at risk would qualify as life insurance proceeds and that the cash surrender value would be treated in the same manner as that of a deferred annuity. It went on to recommend that the position expressed by the IRS in the Hutton Life rulings, as well as in the May 1981 ruling on excess interest whole life, be "reconsidered in light of this memorandum." This position raised, but did not resolve, what some commentators believed was the principal issue: quantification of the risk element necessary to qualify the entire contract as life insurance.

## Section 101(f)

The recommendations of the 1982 GCM were never translated by the IRS into a ruling on universal life. The prospect that universal life insurance would not receive the same federal income tax treatment as traditional permanent life insurance spurred those companies that had tied their fortunes to universal life to seek congressional recognition of the product as an integrated life insurance contract. Recognizing the possibility that the Hutton Life rulings (and thereby the viability of universal life) were threatened, a group of life insurance companies issuing universal life lobbied Congress for the addition of section 101(f) to the Code by the Tax Equity and Fiscal Responsibility Act of 1982 (TEFRA).

By that time, the key tax precedents that led to the enactment of a statutory definition of life insurance were present. Life insurance was seen as economically divisible into savings and risk components. Further, under *Le Gierse* and later cases, the presence of insurance risk was a necessary element for treatment as life insurance

---
[106] *Id.*
[107] PLR 8132119 (May 18, 1981).
[108] The commentary in the legislative history of IRC § 101(f) that any flexible premium contract that is treated as a single integrated contract under state law be treated in the same manner for federal tax purposes was a response to the IRS position in the GCM. *See* TEFRA Conference Report, *supra* Chapter 4, note 10, at 649 (1982); TEFRA Blue Book, *supra* Chapter 1, note 95, at 368.

under federal tax law. Finally, in response to abuses associated with financed insurance, Congress had demonstrated a willingness to draw lines to limit the access of taxpayers to life insurance tax benefits.

Section 101(f) provided statutory rules for the taxation of the proceeds of flexible premium contracts—the first definition of life insurance to appear in the Code. Compliance with the section 101(f) rules provided a full exclusion for death benefit proceeds of contracts written prior to January 1, 1984, and this treatment was made retroactive as a response to the cloud over the Hutton Life rulings created by IRS reconsideration of its ruling position. Section 101(f) was adopted as a temporary measure to resolve the immediate problem of universal life, and its application was limited to flexible premium products, defined as plans that:

- had one or more premiums not fixed by the insurer as to both timing and amount; and
- were treated as integrated contracts of life insurance under state law.

As a result, section 101(f) applied principally to universal life plans and certain adjustable life products. As a part of the "stopgap" provisions of TEFRA, section 101(f) covered only those plans issued on or before December 31, 1983. Under the transition rules later adopted as a part of Deficit Reduction Act of 1984 (DEFRA), the section 101(f) rules were retroactively extended to contracts issued through December 31, 1984.[109]

Two alternative tests were provided under section 101(f). The first test was a guideline premium and cash value corridor test designed to legitimize and regulate universal life contracts. The second was a cash value test, establishing a limit on cash surrender values based on an attained-age NSP for the death benefit in order to accommodate adjustable whole life contract designs. These tests were similar in concept to the tests currently found in section 7702 but were more limited in their application. Section 101(f) was a pragmatic, political solution that gave the IRS legislative guidance and resolved life insurance industry concerns over the IRS's reconsideration of its ruling position. Although a temporary expedient, section 101(f) also served as a model for future legislation. William B. Harman, Jr., commented, "In return for clarifying that flexible premium policies would be treated as integrated contracts of life insurance for tax purposes, not as term insurance with a taxable side fund, section 101(f) required that a minimum amount of insurance risk be present in each contract's death benefit."[110]

## *GCM 39022*

Despite the passage of section 101(f), tax policy concerns at the Treasury Department and the IRS about products other than universal life were not answered, and some concerns with universal life remained. In GCM 39022, dated March 31, 1983, the IRS considered whether the death benefits of a guaranteed increasing face amount single premium contract were excludable under section 101(a). By virtue of its design, the contract involved contained little pure insurance risk relative to its cash surrender value.

Noting that, were the contract a flexible premium plan, it would not have met the cash value corridor test under section 101(f), the IRS concluded in GCM 39022 that "the insurance company assumes a risk under the policy that is insufficient to warrant characterization of the policy as a life insurance policy in its entirety." The IRS went on to say that, in enacting section 101(f), Congress "indicated a disapproval of policies that fail to demonstrate a relationship between the size of the death benefit and the cash value of the contract that is comparable to that of traditional contracts." In the 1983 GCM, the IRS Chief Counsel effectively served notice that the principles espoused in GCM 38934 were still applicable to contracts other than flexible premium contracts (whose treatment was governed by section 101(f)). In addition to requiring that the *Le Gierse* economic standard be met, the IRS attempted to impose an additional standard, based on traditional relationships of death benefit to cash surrender value, for a contract to receive life insurance tax treatment.

In April 1983, the IRS issued a private letter ruling granting life insurance status to a single premium increasing whole life plan. The ruling concluded that favorable income tax treatment of the death benefit was indicated due to the presence of risk shifting and risk distributing as well as "an amount of pure insurance which

---

[109] *See* Pub. L. No. 98-369, § 221(b)(3).
[110] Harman, *supra* Chapter 1, note 13, at 1085, 1090.

is substantially comparable to that which could be obtained under a level-premium whole life insurance policy." A short time later, in June, the ruling was revoked and a "no ruling" position was adopted.[111]

## Section 7702

Section 101(f), like most of the life insurance taxation rules adopted in TEFRA, was viewed as only a stopgap measure along the road to broader insurance product tax reform. Hence, in the period leading up to the enactment of DEFRA, there was considerable debate regarding the proper definition of life insurance contracts.

Within a year after the enactment of section 101(f), the Treasury Department noted in testimony before the Ways and Means Committee that the investment features of insurance products were increasingly emphasized in the marketing of those products. The Treasury suggested that Congress consider whether single premium life insurance policies, and life insurance policies that endowed at an early age, should be treated as life insurance for federal tax purposes.[112] The Treasury also suggested that it would be appropriate to examine whether the inside buildup of life insurance contracts generally should continue to be exempt from current tax (an idea that had already attracted the attention of some members of Congress). Harman noted:

> At this time, some in both the government and academia argued that the inside buildup in life insurance contracts should be included in a broadened income tax base. Unfortunately, to a degree their argument was bolstered by some elements within the insurance industry that aggressively developed overly investment-oriented life insurance products and marketed them by stressing the beneficial tax treatment available.[113]

As a part of industrywide discussions in 1983 concerning the comprehensive revision of the federal income taxation of life insurance companies, the need for a permanent statute defining life insurance was agreed to by both the insurance industry and the government. The principal policy concerns were:

- The expiration of section 101(f) at the end of 1983

- The continued need to deal with forms of life insurance other than universal life, most notably single premium plans

- The absence of rules for variable life

- The perception by some of the need to strengthen the section 101(f) rules

### *Stark-Moore Proposal*

As a result, in the lead-up to DEFRA, a provision defining life insurance was incorporated into the Stark-Moore proposal of July 14, 1983, to revise life insurance company and product taxation. The proposal was named for Rep. Stark and Rep. Moore, the chair and ranking member, respectively, of the Select Revenue Measures Subcommittee of the House Ways and Means Committee, charged with proposing the life insurance tax rules in what became DEFRA.

The proposed new provision employed a two-test format quite similar to that of section 101(f). The first alternative test, a cash value accumulation test, limited a contract's cash surrender values to those of a level 10-payment contract maturing at age 95, with an exception for "reasonable" paid-up additions. The second test, a guideline premium and cash value corridor test, limited premiums to the greater of the sum of the premiums for a level 10-payment contract or the sum of the premiums for a level annual premium contract. The new provision also significantly expanded the applicability of the tests from section 101(f), which applied only to flexible premium plans. The new provision provided a definition of life insurance contract for all purposes of the Code, as a result of which the provision was accorded a new section number, 7702, befitting its Code-wide definitional status. As initially proposed, the definition would have virtually eliminated life insurance tax treat-

---

[111] The original ruling was published as PLR 8332021 (April 29, 1983). *See also* Rev. Proc. 83-45, 1983-1 C.B. 780 (adding the following to the list of issues on which the IRS would not issue advance rulings: "Whether the death benefit payable under a single premium increasing death benefit life insurance policy will be excludable from the gross income of the beneficiary thereof pursuant to section 101(a).").

[112] *Tax Treatment of Life Insurance: Hearings Before the Subcomm. on Select Revenue Measures of the H. Comm. on Ways & Means,* 98th Cong., 1st Sess. 36 (1983) (statement of John E. Chapoton, Assistant Sec'y for Tax Policy, Department of the Treasury) (hereinafter 1983 Hearings).

[113] Harman, *supra* Chapter 1, note 13, at 1090 (citations omitted).

ment for all single premium plans. It also would have limited the calculation of allowable values for all plans to a level death benefit basis by eliminating the prefunding of increasing death benefits. Limited payment plans with fewer than 10 annual premiums and endowments maturing prior to age 95 for the full face amount also would have been disqualified.

## DEFRA

After additional consideration and discussion between congressional tax writers and life insurance industry representatives over the summer and fall of 1983, a final version of section 7702 was incorporated into DEFRA, with several important changes from the initial proposal. Specifically, the 10-payment tests were removed and single premium tests were substituted; the corridor requirements were adjusted to a level higher than the levels in section 101(f); the treatment of qualified additional benefits was liberalized; and specific rules were included for variable life insurance. A provision permitting the level premium funding of an increasing death benefit plan also was included. In July 1984, section 7702 was enacted into law as a part of DEFRA.

## Section 7702A

Although some forms of the single premium life insurance contract (e.g., the guaranteed increasing face plan) were ended with the enactment of section 7702, Congress expressly declined to eliminate the single premium contract from the definition of a life insurance contract in drafting section 7702. The result was that, along the spectrum of life insurance contracts, the single premium contract became the most investment-oriented type of life insurance contract recognized as life insurance under the Code. In the years following the introduction of the definition of life insurance under section 101(f) in 1982 and section 7702 in 1984, various life insurance products were designed to maximize their investment orientation,[114] providing minimum levels of pure insurance in relation to their cash surrender values within the context of the section 7702 limitations.

The investment orientation of the single premium contract came into sharper focus after the enactment of the Tax Reform Act of 1986. With the broad simplification of the Code that occurred in 1986, some in the life insurance industry began aggressively marketing the single premium life insurance contract as the "last remaining tax shelter." Full-page ads, like the one seen here, appeared in numerous newspapers and other publications portraying the single premium life insurance contract as an investment "too good to be true," combining tax deferral or exemption on investment earnings with tax-free loans for access to the untaxed inside buildup. These ads naturally attracted the attention of the tax authorities,[115] and so it followed the path of all other "too good to be true" schemes.

---

[114] For a technical discussion of investment orientation, see Chapter 10.
[115] The advertisement shown here was included in a press release from the House Ways and Means Committee, dated January 21, 1987, announcing that the Subcommittee on Select Revenue Measures would review "whether the 1984 Act provisions regarding the definition of a life insurance contract have achieved the goals of that Act." The release, which attached the advertisement, went on to note that some insurance companies may be issuing contracts that "appear to be designed to generate tax-free earnings and have the provision of insurance coverage only as a secondary purpose."

In response to this activity, Congress again revised the life insurance product tax rules in the Technical and Miscellaneous Revenue Act of 1988 (TAMRA), adding section 7702A to the Code. Before discussing this outcome, a detour to look briefly at proposals considered to address the problem in 1987–88 is in order, so that the reader may have the necessary perspective on the highly complex solution that followed in the form of section 7702A. At base, two different approaches to the single premium/tax shelter "problem" were considered during that time. The first was a distributional approach, wherein the limitations of section 7702 would remain unchanged but predeath distributions would be taxed in the same manner as annuity distributions. The second was a definitional approach, which would not have changed the distribution rules but would have narrowed the actuarial limitations under section 7702. As discussed below, section 7702A effectively combines elements of these two approaches.

## *The Stark-Gradison Bill*

On October 7, 1987, Rep. Stark, mentioned above, and Rep. Gradison introduced H.R. 3441 (the Stark-Gradison bill). Rep. Stark, with his background in section 7702's enactment, explained that he and Rep. Gradison introduced the bill because life insurance was "attract[ing] investors who have no intention of holding life insurance to provide death benefits to dependents. Rather, these investors are using life insurance as a means to shelter investment earning from current taxation."[116] The problem, specifically, was that creative use of policy loan and withdrawal provisions allowed policyholders to access their money without any tax being imposed. That is, the problem was thought to be the then-current law's treatment of loans and distributions. The Stark-Gradison bill thus took what may be termed a distributional approach to the problem of investment-oriented life insurance products.

Under the Stark-Gradison bill, a predeath distribution from any life insurance contract would have been taxed on an income-first or last-in, first-out (LIFO) basis in the same manner as a distribution from an annuity contract (as previously modified by TEFRA). Technically, the amount of the distribution would be includible in gross income to the extent of any "income on the contract," as defined in section 72(e)(3). For this purpose, a loan provided under, or secured by, a life insurance contract would have been treated as a distribution, and also, as in the case of annuities, distributions would have been subject to a 10 percent penalty tax, with specified exceptions. These new rules would have applied to distributions (including loans) made after October 6, 1987, but not to distributions from a contract entered into on or before October 6, 1987, to the extent that the distribution was attributable to premiums or other consideration paid for the contract on or before such date. This proposal attracted intense lobbying activity, and eventually arrived in the graveyard of legislative proposals.

## *The NALU-AALU Proposal*

Concern over the broad scope of the Stark-Gradison proposal led the National Association of Life Underwriters (NALU), the Association for Advanced Life Underwriting (AALU) and several life insurance companies to propose an alternative to the bill. By comparison to the Stark-Gradison distributional approach, this group saw the problem as one of excessive inside buildup. Thus, in contrast to the Stark-Gradison bill, the NALU-AALU proposal took a definitional approach. Instead of changing the tax treatment of distributions under a life insurance contract, the NALU-AALU proposal would have narrowed section 7702 to exclude single premium and similar contracts from the tax definition of a life insurance contract while maintaining the traditional distribution rules.

Under the NALU-AALU proposal, any life insurance contract under which premiums were paid more rapidly than would be necessary to pay up the contract's benefits with five level annual premiums (a five-pay rule) would fail to qualify as a life insurance contract for federal tax purposes. In applying the five-pay rule, the five level annual premiums were to be computed using the section 7702 computational rules and the 4 percent minimum interest rate from the cash value accumulation test. In addition, the proposal required the use of deemed expense charges (expressed as a percentage of the net premium) and limited the mortality charges that could be assumed to those used in the statutory reserves for the contract. Under an antiabuse look-back provision, if the contract's death benefits were reduced at any time during the first five contract years, the five-pay

---

[116] 133 CONG. REC. H8,289 (Oct. 7, 1987) (floor statement of Rep. Stark on introduction of H.R. 3441).

rule would be reapplied as if the contract had been originally issued with the lower benefits. In contrast with the Stark-Gradison bill, the NALU-AALU proposal would not have applied to life insurance contracts issued on or before its date of enactment.

## *The ACLI Proposal*

Under the combination approach developed by the American Council of Life Insurance (ACLI), policy loans and other distributions from a contract that failed to meet the five-pay rule of the NALU-AALU proposal would be taxed under a LIFO rule as in the case of annuity contracts. However, loans and distributions would not be subject to a penalty tax, and application of the LIFO treatment would be limited to loans and distributions during the first five contract years (the durational limit). The ACLI believed that the imposition of a five-year durational limit would adequately balance the objective of addressing investment uses of life insurance with the need for policyholders to have access to their contract values in order to meet legitimate financial needs, including the provision of retirement income.

Unlike the NALU-AALU proposal, the ACLI did not propose to amend section 7702. However, computation of the five-pay premiums in the ACLI proposal drew upon the NALU-AALU proposal and on rules from section 7702. Under the ACLI proposal, the five-pay premiums were determined using the contractual interest rate (though not less than 4 percent), no expenses, the mortality charges specified in the contract and the section 7702 computational rules.

The ACLI proposal also introduced into the statutory framework the notion of a material change,[117] under which a contract that was materially changed would be treated as a new contract issued on the date of the change, triggering a new application of the five-pay rule. A materially changed contract would include an exchange of contracts, a conversion from term to permanent insurance, or an increase in death benefits beyond amounts that the policyholder already possessed a unilateral right to obtain. To address the problem of how to deal with the existing cash surrender value under the material change provision, the ACLI proposal contained a rollover rule. Under the rollover rule, the pre-existing cash surrender value would not be counted as a new premium but would ratably reduce the five-pay limit applicable in each subsequent year. This rule was intended both to allow contract exchanges and benefit increases and to deal equitably with reapplications of the five-pay rule.

Extending the rules applicable to distributions from annuities, the ACLI proposal provided that certain amounts retained by the insurer would not be treated as distributions from a contract that failed the proposal's five-pay limit. These amounts retained included:

- dividends and excess interest either credited to a contract's cash surrender value or used to reduce premiums for the contract,
- dividends used to buy paid-up additions or term insurance,
- surrenders of paid-up additions to pay premiums,
- charges to a contract's cash value to provide QABs,
- policy loans used to pay premiums, and
- policy loans used to cover interest on existing policy loans.

The ACLI proposal would have applied prospectively, governing contracts issued or materially changed (subject to the rollover rule) after its enactment.

## *The Joint Industry Proposal*

The differences among the various industry groups prompted them to attempt to reach a unified industry approach. These efforts led to an agreement between the ACLI Tax Steering Committee and NALU-AALU on a joint industry proposal. This proposal generally followed the ACLI proposal, with three principal exceptions. First, section 7702 would be amended to define a special class of life insurance contracts that failed a five-pay

---

[117] As discussed earlier in this book and discussed at length in Chapter 5, the term material change as used in IRC § 7702A is specific to that section and differs from the broad concept of a material change in federal tax law.

rule. These failed contracts would be termed modified endowment contracts (MECs).[118] Second, section 7702 would be further amended to provide that all life insurance contracts and MECs would be treated as life insurance for tax purposes, but that loans and distributions under MECs would be taxed on a LIFO basis under section 72. Third, the durational limit of the ACLI proposal would be extended to 10 years.

## *TAMRA*

As ultimately enacted by TAMRA, section 7702A created a new class of life insurance contracts called MECs, based largely on the joint industry proposal although substituting a 7-pay rule. As previously discussed, a MEC is not accorded the favorable tax treatment that otherwise applies to predeath distributions and policy loans under life insurance contracts. Instead, predeath distributions and policy loans are subject, without any durational limits, to the withdrawal and distribution rules applicable to deferred annuities. This treatment generally includes, contrary to the joint industry proposal, surrenders of paid-up additions to pay premiums. Congress also rejected the joint industry proposal's suggested treatment of policy loans used to pay premiums and policy loans used to cover interest on existing policy loans. Simply put, for MECs, policy loans and other predeath distributions are taxed under a LIFO rule, and a penalty tax may apply. For life insurance contracts that are not MECs, loans are not treated as distributions at all and distributions are taxed under a basis-first or first-in, first-out (FIFO) rule.

During the process of enactment of the MEC legislation, one enterprising life insurance agent somewhat prematurely advertised a way to limit the LIFO rule and penalty tax: rather than paying a $1 million premium into a single MEC, the purchaser would buy (say) 10 contracts, each for a $100,000 premium. At 10 percent interest, each of these individual contracts would have income of $10,000 instead of one large contract having income of $100,000 after one year. Should the contract holder want to withdraw $100,000, he could simply surrender one of the contracts and recognize income of only $10,000 for tax purposes, rather than being deemed to realize income of $100,000 under the single contract alternative. This would have effectively converted the section 7702A distributional rules to a proportional method of taxing distributions, rather than the income-first approach anticipated by Congress. Clearly, this would undermine the effectiveness of the MEC distribution rules and penalty tax.[119] Equally clearly, the remedy was to put together that which was broken apart, and thus, the aggregation rule of section 72(e)(12) was enacted as part of the TAMRA legislation. Under that rule, in determining the amount includible in income, all MECs issued by the same insurance company to the same policyholder in the same calendar year are required to be treated as one contract. It is likely this rule has generated more administrative expense for issuers of contracts than tax for the government, especially since insurers often administer contracts on distinct administrative systems. The rule works, as it was designed to work, through its deterrent effect.[120]

As discussed in Chapter 2, TAMRA also changed section 7702 to address yet another problem that emerged after DEFRA. Some of the pre-TAMRA single premium plans took advantage of the fact that, under DEFRA, both the NSPs and the guideline premiums were calculated using the mortality charges and, in the case of guideline premiums, expense charges specified in the contract instead of those actually imposed in the administration of the contract. Unlike the case with the interest rates to be assumed, as originally enacted section 7702 did not explicitly limit the mortality or expense charges that may be applied in the determination of guideline premiums or NSPs.[121] The greater the mortality or expense charges, the higher the allowable values. After 1984, it became clear that it was possible to make very conservative actuarial assumptions and, in turn, increase the permissible investment potential of a contract.

---

[118] The reader should not assume that this term has any meaning in the U.S. insurance market beyond that given by the definition in IRC § 7702A. A name was needed, and one duly came forth. A MEC is not necessarily an endowment contract, single premium whole life being a prime example.

[119] This was also an issue for deferred annuities, where one insurer reportedly sent a flip-top box of small annuity contracts to owners in an effort to finesse the LIFO rules.

[120] The aggregation rule may create issues for forms of corporate-owned life insurance (COLI), particularly bank-owned life insurance, where a large number of contracts are purchased under a single premium plan (resulting in classification as MECs). Under the aggregation rules, if a single contract or small group of the contracts is surrendered, all of the distribution could be classified as gain, subject both to tax and penalty. A related, but as yet unanswered, question relates to the manner in which the policyholder's investment in (i.e., basis of) the surrendered contracts is to be allocated among the remaining contracts.

[121] The statute's framers expected that market forces would limit the size of the charges so specified and, hence, the amount of the increase in the guideline premiums (or NSPs) attributable to their conservatism. *See* Jeffrey P. Hahn & John T. Adney, *The New Federal Tax Definition of "Life Insurance Contract,"* 38 J. of the Am. Soc'y of CLU, no. 6, November 1984, at 40.

In response to the perceived abuse of mortality and expense assumptions, in TAMRA Congress required that mortality and expense assumptions used in the tests be reasonable. This means, according to section 7702(c)(3)(B)(i) as amended by TAMRA, that the mortality charges used in computing guideline premiums or NSPs for a contract covering a standard risk insured must be reasonable ones that meet the requirements (if any) prescribed by regulations and which, except as provided in regulations, do not exceed the mortality charges specified in the prevailing commissioners' standard tables (as defined in section 807(d)(5)) as of the time the contract is issued (in 2015, the 2001 CSO tables). Given section 7702A's use of section 7702's structure and assumptions to calculate its limits, section 7702A also imports the mortality charge limitation into the calculation of its 7-pay rule. Further, according to section 7702(c)(3)(B)(ii) as amended by TAMRA, the expense charges assumed in the section 7702 computations may not exceed "reasonable charges ... which (on the basis of the company's experience, if any, with respect to similar contracts) are reasonably expected to be actually paid." ◆

# Chapter 10

# TAX POLICY AND THE TAXATION OF LIFE INSURANCE CONTRACTS

## Chapter Overview

Chapter 10 addresses tax policy considerations underlying the federal income tax treatment of life insurance contracts. While the focus of earlier chapters has been on the specifics of sections 101(f), 7702 and 7702A,[1] this chapter provides a more general discussion of the reasons that life insurance contracts, and particularly permanent life insurance contracts, are accorded the treatment they are under the federal tax law, including the evolution of the definitional limitations that are the subject of this book. To some extent, this discussion supplements the historical context provided by Chapter 9, but it delves more deeply into some of the theoretical underpinnings of life insurance taxation.

In this regard, Chapter 10 first provides background on the basic concepts of economic income upon which the current system of federal income taxation in the United States is based, however imperfectly, along with a review of the tax treatment currently and historically provided to life insurance purchasers and beneficiaries. Following this, the tax policy issues associated with the tax treatment of the inside buildup of permanent life insurance contracts are discussed, leading then to a description of the evolution of the related definitional limitations. The chapter next focuses on the relationship between the requirements of sections 7702 and 7702A, on the one hand, and those of state nonforfeiture law on the other, exploring both the tension and the synergism in that relationship. Finally, the chapter speculates about the potential for future changes in the rules governing the tax treatment of life insurance contracts.

By way of background, this discussion briefly describes the general concept of economic income along with the related ideal of a comprehensive income tax that reaches all economic income regardless of its source. As discussed below, this notion is the theoretical base upon which the U.S. federal income tax system rests, although the realities of tax administration and public policy determinations routinely cause the system to diverge from this ideal. Indeed, U.S. tax law is replete with examples of deviation from the concept of a truly comprehensive income tax base.

### Tax Policy and the Ideal of a Comprehensive Income Tax

Any system of taxation that aims to impose a tax upon the population's income necessarily must endeavor to identify what, in fact, constitutes income. Ironically, the Code does not comprehensively define the term,[2] leaving it to academics and tax practitioners alike to divine the meaning of income. From an academic perspective, the concept of income can be considered a question of economics, and the concept of economic income is generally regarded as the broad foundation upon which the federal income tax rests.

To this end, the ideas developed by economists Haig and Simons are widely accepted as providing a comprehensive definition of economic income. Writing in 1921, Haig defined income as "the money value of the net accretion to one's economic power between two points of time."[3] In 1938, Simons wrote, "Personal income may be defined as the algebraic sum of (1) the market value of rights exercised in consumption and (2) the change in the store of property rights between the beginning and end of the period in question."[4] Thus, Haig-

---

[1] Unless otherwise indicated, references in this book to "section" are to the provisions of the Internal Revenue Code of 1986, as amended (also referred to as "IRC" or the "Code").
[2] MICHAEL J. GRAETZ AND DEBORAH H. SCHENK, FEDERAL INCOME TAXATION PRINCIPLES AND PRACTICES 106 (3d ed. 1995) (hereinafter Graetz and Schenk).
[3] ROBERT HAIG, THE FEDERAL INCOME TAX 1, 7 (1921), *as quoted in* Graetz and Schenk, *supra* note 2, at 106.
[4] HENRY C. SIMONS, PERSONAL INCOME TAXATION 50 (1938), *as quoted in* Graetz and Schenk, *supra* note 2, at 107.

Simons income, as the concept has become known, can be defined as the sum of an individual's consumption plus change in wealth over a given time period.

Of course, the foregoing definition of income provides only a theoretical ideal upon which to base a system of taxation. Social needs and goals, as well as the practicalities of administering an income tax system, cause the law to deviate from the ideal of a comprehensive income tax on economic income. As noted by law professor Ginsburg in a 1997 essay:

> You should not be misled into thinking, even for a moment, that any country's income tax law tightly embraces the Haig-Simons definition of personal income as consumption plus savings. U.S. tax law certainly does not.[5]

In other words, while the federal income tax may be based upon a broad concept of economic income, the law is tempered with rules of convenience and peppered with exceptions aimed at achieving important public policy goals. The appropriateness of such exceptions has long been debated, as exemplified in the following statement by law professor Bittker:

> [Since] World War II, our ablest commentators on federal income taxation have repeatedly attacked the "exceptions," "preferences," "loopholes," and "leakages" in the income tax provisions of the Internal Revenue Code and have called upon Congress to reverse the "erosion of the income tax base" caused by these "special provisions." It is no exaggeration to say that a "comprehensive tax base"... has come to be the major organizing concept in most serious discussions of our federal income tax structure.... The aim, in short, is a reformed Internal Revenue Code with a "correct" tax base, to which all men of good will can and will rally when it is threatened by "exceptions," "special provisions," "preferences," "loopholes," and "leakages."[6]

Despite these lofty aspirations, the Code continues to house a collection of exceptions to the concept of a comprehensive federal income tax, some of which Congress has enacted to encourage specific economic behaviors. For example, deductions or exclusions from income are allowed for contributions to various types of retirement arrangements in order to encourage Americans to save for their retirement. Likewise, the tax law deviates from the Haig-Simons ideal to encourage the purchase of a home, health insurance or capital assets, savings for educational expenses and for countless other reasons. Such deviations often are considered entirely appropriate under the federal income tax system as a surrogate for direct governmental funding of items on the social agenda. Hence, the myriad exclusions, deductions and other special rules of the tax law have been termed tax expenditures,[7] embracing the notion (not universally acclaimed) that they represent tax revenue the government otherwise is entitled to receive but which the government instead re-directs to the beneficiaries of those special rules.[8]

## *Tax Treatment of Life Insurance*

As discussed throughout this book, policyholders and beneficiaries of life insurance contracts are, and historically have been, accorded a unique treatment under the federal income tax law, at least in comparison with certain other types of financial instruments. By way of review, a life insurance contract is treated differently from, e.g., demand deposits or certificates of deposit, in the following three respects:[9]

- **Exclusion of death proceeds:** Amounts paid by reason of the death of the insured are excluded from the gross income of the beneficiary under section 101(a). (There are exceptions to this rule relating to

---

[5] Martin D. Ginsburg, *Taxing the Components of Income: A U.S. Perspective*, 86 Geo. L.J. 123, 127 (1997).
[6] Boris I. Bittker, *A "Comprehensive Tax Base" as a Goal of Income Tax Reform*, 80 Harv. L. Rev. 925, 925–26 (1967) (hereinafter Bittker).
[7] "Tax expenditures," which first became part of the federal government's official budget process in 1974, are defined as "revenue losses attributable to provisions of the Federal tax laws which allow a special exclusion, exemption, or deduction from gross income or which provide a special credit, a preferential rate of tax, or a deferral of tax liability." Congressional Budget and Impoundment Control Act of 1974, Pub. L. No. 93-344 § 3(a)(3), 88 Stat. 297, 328 (1974).
[8] *See* Stanley S. Surrey and Paul R. McDaniel, Tax Expenditures 3 (1985); Stanley S. Surrey, *Tax Incentives as a Device for Implementing Government Policy: A Comparison with Direct Government Expenditures*, 83 Harv. L. Rev. 705 (1970).
[9] For further discussion of these differences, see Staff of the J. Comm. on Tax'n, Major Issues in the Taxation of Life Insurance Products, Policyholders, and Companies (J. Comm. Print 1983) (hereinafter Major Issues).

interest on deferred benefit payments, contracts that have been transferred for value, etc., as discussed in Appendix 1.1.)

- **Deferral of tax on cash surrender value increments:** Interest or earnings credited on life insurance cash surrender values (i.e., the inside buildup) are not taxed currently to the policyholder and, as stated above, are not taxed at all if paid by reason of the insured's death. A life insurance contract's inside buildup is taxed only upon a lifetime distribution from the contract, and thus remains tax-deferred until such time. In addition, for a non-MEC, amounts may be withdrawn from the contract on an investment-first or first-in, first-out (FIFO) basis, with taxation resulting only after the owner has withdrawn all prior premiums from the contract,[10] and policy loans are not treated as distributions.

- **Treatment of certain charges:** If a contract is surrendered, income to the policyholder is measured in a way that effectively reduces taxable gain by the amount of mortality, expense and qualified additional benefit (QAB) charges. The taxable gain is equal to the (a) cash surrender value (unreduced by any loans outstanding at surrender) minus (b) premiums paid, net of dividends received in cash and partial withdrawals to the extent these were not subject to tax.[11]

By virtue of the foregoing, the owners and beneficiaries of life insurance contracts arguably are recipients of some of the many tax preferences or "tax expenditures" that Congress has enacted in the Code, although that is debatable (and frequently debated). As discussed in Chapter 9, these basic rules, and most prominently the income tax exclusion for death benefits, have remained largely unchanged since the beginning of the modern income tax era, dating to the 16th Amendment to the Constitution and the Revenue Act of 1913. Elements of such treatment have even earlier roots, which can be traced to the original income tax enacted during the Civil War. Hence, it is clear that Congress has never strayed from its recognition of the social needs that life insurance serves, from providing support for widows and orphans following the loss of a family breadwinner, to providing solutions to various liquidity needs of the business taxpayer. The congressional determination that death benefits should be excluded from gross income also has an intensely practical side: Since premiums are largely nondeductible, much of the death benefit is merely a post-tax transfer payment,[12] and if the benefit were subjected to tax, still more life insurance would need to be purchased to cover it.

This congressional tax policy determination, however, has not been free from controversy, especially with regard to the tax deferral benefit that historically has been associated with the inside buildup of permanent life insurance. This aspect of the federal income tax treatment of life insurance, and the tax policy issues that surround it, are discussed next.

## Inside Buildup of Permanent Life Insurance Contracts

During hearings before the House Ways and Means Committee's Subcommittee on Select Revenue Measures, leading up to the 1984 enactment of section 7702, Assistant Secretary for Tax Policy Chapoton, of the Treasury Department, testified, "Perhaps the most significant tax benefit afforded cash-value life insurance is that the investment income earned on the policyholder's savings account is not subject to current income taxation."[13] This notion was not novel at the time section 7702 was being considered by Congress, but rather had been a frequent topic of academic and political discussion. The remainder of this part discusses the economic income that arises by virtue of increments in a permanent life insurance contract's cash surrender value, and the reasons traditionally offered in support of tax deferral for such amounts.

### Economic Income Associated with the Inside Buildup

As noted by Bittker, the appropriateness of congressional "tax expenditures" in general has long been debated, and the case of life insurance is no different. Such debate has focused principally on the tax deferral benefit provided to the increments in cash value of permanent life insurance contracts. For example, consistently with

---

[10] Taxation of the inside buildup also may remain deferred following an exchange under IRC § 1035.
[11] *See* IRC § 72(e)(2)(B), (3)(A) and (6). *See also* Appendix 1.1.
[12] In effect, representing a transfer of funds from all the surviving members of an insurance pool to the beneficiaries of those members who die in a particular period.
[13] 1983 Hearings, *supra* Chapter 9, note 112, at 30.

his view that the federal income tax should strive toward the ideal of a comprehensive tax base, one tax theorist has noted, "The exclusion of interest on life insurance savings from taxable income is clearly inconsistent with using a comprehensive definition of economic income for tax purposes."[14] Such theorists have sought to demonstrate this by comparing permanent life insurance with term life insurance that is combined with a separate, taxable fund.[15] To the same end, they have conceptualized a whole life insurance contract as "a combination of insurance plus an option to buy further insurance," so that the annual economic income associated with the inside buildup under a whole life insurance contract equals "the increase in its cash surrender value plus the value of the term insurance for that year (the term insurance premium) less the whole life premium, net of dividend."[16] This diverges sharply from the legal view of such a contract, which treats it as an integrated instrument, as well as from the actuarial view of the contract, which looks to the contract's inside buildup to support its continuation despite the inadequacy of the net premiums in later contract durations.

## *Reasons for Tax Deferral on the Inside Buildup*

The tax theorists just noted do not address whether the deferral of tax on the inside buildup of life insurance is appropriate—other than through their general assertion that such deferral is inconsistent with the notion of a comprehensive income tax base. Of course, the easy answer to this question is simply that Congress says the tax deferral benefit is appropriate, and so it is.[17] Quite apart from this reason, however, the tax deferral benefit afforded inside buildup shares an important characteristic with other types of tax preferences that generally are viewed as appropriate—even by theoretical purists. As noted in the testimony of representatives of the Stock Company Information Group, during the 1983 hearing before the House Select Revenue Measures Subcommittee mentioned above:

> Even Henry Simons, one of the original proponents of a "comprehensive" income tax, recognized that an ideally comprehensive tax base could never be achieved. He concluded that necessary imperfections well might be regarded as tolerable from a distributional standpoint, if those imperfections were distributed in a roughly equal way across income classes. Indeed, one of the principal criticisms of income tax "incentives" or tax "expenditures" is that they are disproportionately beneficial to those in the upper income brackets to the disadvantage of the lower and middle classes.[18]

When measured against this criticism, the tax benefit accorded to the inside buildup fares well. In other words, because permanent life insurance contracts are widely held by an economically diverse population, the tax deferral benefit provided by such contracts falls within a range of "tolerable imperfections."

In addition, the tax deferral benefit afforded permanent life insurance has been said to be consistent with a fundamental concept of federal income taxation—namely, the notion of realization. Under federal tax law, gains and losses relating to property generally are reflected in taxable income—"recognized," in tax parlance—only at the time they are "realized" by a taxpayer. Thus, for example, increases in the value of a capital asset such as corporate stock are not taken into account as income until the taxpayer sells or otherwise uses the asset to realize an economic benefit. The fact that such unrealized appreciation generally is not taken into account under the federal income tax law represents a key, and universally accepted, deviation from the Haig-Simons ideal of economic income and a comprehensive income tax.

---

[14] Charles E. McClure Jr., *The Income Tax Treatment of Interest Earned on Savings in Life Insurance*, 371, *in* THE ECONOMICS OF FEDERAL SUBSIDY PROGRAMS, A COMPENDIUM OF PAPERS SUBMITTED TO THE JOINT ECONOMIC COMMITTEE (Comm. Print 1972) (hereinafter McClure). IRC § 7702(g) incorporates the concept of economic income in this subsection, which governs the taxation of life insurance contracts that fail to meet the requirements of IRC § 7702(a) (as discussed in Chapter 8). In general terms, IRC § 7702(g) imposes tax on the annual interest or earnings credits to the contract's cash value, less contract expenses and QAB charges.

[15] For example, see McClure, *supra* note 14.

[16] DAVID H. BRADFORD AND U.S. TREASURY TAX POLICY STAFF, BLUEPRINTS FOR BASIC TAX REFORM 55–56 (rev. 2d ed. 1994). Bradford describes the cash surrender value as the value at which the company's actuaries have determined they will buy back from the insured the option to continue his insurance. Hence, the contract's cash surrender value equals the value of the option. *Id.* at 55.

[17] One commentator has noted that "speculation as to why Congress has not eliminated this preference requires an inquiry into the metaphysical forces behind congressional action and inaction, which is beyond the scope of this paper." Todd Kreig, *Tax Arbitrage and Life Insurance: A Tax Policy Critique of Section 264*, 42 TAX LAW., no. 3, at 747, 753, n. 38 (1989).

[18] 1983 Hearings, *supra* Chapter 9, note 112, at 346 (statement of Hartzel Z. Lebed, Samuel H. Turner and Raymond H. Kiefer on behalf of the Stock Company Information Group) (footnote omitted).

In this regard, some commentators consider the increase in life insurance cash values to constitute a form of unrealized appreciation that should not be taxable until received by the taxpayer upon surrender. Treatment of cash values in this manner has been codified in the rules under section 72, governing the tax treatment of distributions from life insurance contracts that qualify as such for federal tax purposes. This view also was noted in the congressional debates underlying the Revenue Act of 1913, in which the treatment of inside buildup was compared to the appreciation in value of a building:

> Now, in the case of a life insurance policy, it is the same as an investment in a house. The [insurance company], instead of the insured person, will be taxed on its net profits during the period the insurance runs, and at the termination of the period the insured will not pay a tax on his capital, but will pay a tax on the return of his profits, just as the man would pay a tax on the increased value of his storehouse in the case I cited.[19]

Many years later, Bittker, commenting on the possibility of taxing the inside buildup, concluded that such a tax would amount to a tax on unrealized appreciation and asked, "If the exclusion of this type of unrealized appreciation erodes the tax base, what is the rationale for excluding other readily measurable appreciation?"[20] In other words, the tax deferral benefit afforded to the inside buildup of permanent life insurance contracts is consistent with the broader federal income tax concept and treatment of unrealized appreciation.

In addition to the view that inside buildup represents unrealized appreciation, the deferral of tax on inside buildup has been justified by the courts and the IRS as consistent with the tax law doctrine of constructive receipt. Under that doctrine, codified in section 451 and the regulations thereunder, a taxpayer must include in income not only amounts that he or she actually receives, but also amounts that are unreservedly subject to his or her demand. In other words, if the taxpayer could have received an amount (such as interest on a bank account) but chose not to do so, then the amount is regarded as **constructively received** and taxable as if it actually had been received. However, the amount is not constructively received if the taxpayer's control of its receipt is subject to "substantial limitations or restrictions."[21] In this regard, the courts generally have held that there is no constructive receipt of income where a taxpayer must surrender a valuable right to realize that income.[22] With regard to life insurance contracts, the IRS and the courts have held that the full or partial surrender of such a contract, which the owner must undertake to access the contract's inside buildup, constitutes the surrender of a valuable right, presumably on the theory that the surrender would result in a loss of insurance coverage and other rights granted in the contracts.[23] Thus, the constructive receipt doctrine has been viewed as operating to preclude inclusion of inside buildup in income.

Whether speaking of the concept of realization or the doctrine of constructive receipt, the common underlying thread is the need for cash with which to pay tax. If tax deferral on the inside buildup were eliminated, the absence of cash with which to pay the tax due on account of that buildup would make permanent life insurance a difficult asset for taxpayers to hold. It would be as difficult to hold as a house or a share of stock if that asset's appreciation, still unrealized, were subjected to current taxation. On this account, one wonders why life insurance buildup is categorized as a tax expenditure, a concept supposedly limited to a tax relief provision that deviates from the norm.[24]

Although a comprehensive income tax base is the focus of a great deal of tax theory, not everyone strives for that result as an ideal outcome. Some favor consumption taxation instead, and so would be comfortable with inside buildup tax deferral for that reason alone. Treasury's treatment of life insurance during the development

---

[19] Gazur, *supra* Chapter 9, note 32, at n. 148, quoting 50 Cong. Rec. 1,259 (1913) (statement of Rep. Underwood). *See also* Seidman, *supra* Chapter 9, note 30, at 990.
[20] Bittker, *supra* note 6, at 969.
[21] Treas. Reg. § 1.451-2(a).
[22] See, for example, *Edwards v. Comm'r*, 37 T.C. 1107 (1962), *acq.* 1963-2 C.B. 4; *Griffith v. Comm'r*, 35 T.C. 882 (1961).
[23] See *Cohen v. Comm'r*, 39 T.C. 1055 (1963), *acq.* 1964-1 C.B. 4 (cash surrender value not constructively received where taxpayer could reach it only by surrendering the contract); *Nesbitt v. Comm'r*, 43 T.C. 629 (1965) (cash surrender value of paid-up additions not constructively received). See also *Griffith v. Comm'r*, *supra* note 22 (finding no constructive receipt where a policyholder must divest herself of her entire interest in a life insurance contract to receive its cash surrender value and dividends).
[24] Seemingly, the norms of the tax law associated with either the treatment of unrealized appreciation or the constructive receipt doctrine amply and independently justify a conclusion that the tax deferral accorded to inside buildup is not a tax expenditure. The fact that both norms apply presents a clear policy rationale for concluding that such treatment is not a tax expenditure.

of the definitional limitations in the 1982–84 period can be attributed, in some degree, to the pro-consumption tax views held by some policymakers at the time.

## The Limitations on Inside Buildup

As discussed in detail in Chapter 9, in the 1970s the life insurance industry began developing a new generation of life insurance products designed to be more flexible and attractive to consumers than the traditional products offered at that time. Some of these new products were viewed as highly investment-oriented compared to traditional whole life plans, which caused Congress to focus more sharply on the tax treatment of such products—particularly the benefit of tax-deferred inside buildup. As observed in the Report of the House Ways and Means Committee on the legislation that ultimately added section 7702 to the Code:

> [I]n recent years, companies have begun emphasizing investment-oriented products that maximize the advantages of the deferral provided in the Code. When compared to traditional products, these products offer greater initial investments or higher investment returns, or both. In response, the committee adopted a definition of life insurance that treats as currently taxable investments, those life insurance policies that provide for much larger investments or buildups of cash value than traditional products.[25]

Hence, in the context of the high-interest-rate environment of the early 1980s, and in the face of significant innovation within the industry, Congress was faced with the tax policy question of whether, or how much, tax deferral is appropriate in the case of permanent life insurance. Congress ultimately answered this question with the enactment of section 7702 in 1984 and section 7702A in 1988. As previously discussed, the limitations defined in these two Code provisions were intended, respectively, to impose (for the first time) a comprehensive statutory definition of "life insurance contract" for federal income tax purposes and to classify contracts falling within that definition into more-favored and less-favored groupings. It was thought that this would, among other things, address concerns regarding the investment orientation of life insurance products and the quantitative sufficiency of the risk element thereunder.

Interestingly, Congress could have chosen a different route to address this tax policy concern, but it decided upon the limitations set forth in sections 7702 and 7702A. The additional options Congress considered, but did not take, are discussed briefly in the remainder of this part, followed by a discussion of the limitations ultimately enacted in sections 7702 and 7702A and the relationship between those limitations and state nonforfeiture law.

### *The Roads Not Taken*[26]

In a 1983 study, the staffs of the Joint Committee on Taxation and the Senate Finance Committee suggested five possible answers to the question of the extent to which the owners of permanent life insurance contracts should be allowed to defer tax on the inside buildup of their contracts:

- Allow unlimited deferral
- Impose current taxation on the inside buildup
- Limit the amount of tax deferral by allowing tax-preferred earnings up to a predetermined interest rate
- Limit the amount of investment in a life insurance product that earns tax-deferred investment income
- Allow deferral for only certain defined insurance products[27]

Congress was thus faced with a decision of which of the multiple approaches it would take to address the tax policy concerns raised over the investment orientation of the new life insurance products being developed at the time.

---

[25] Deficit Reduction Act of 1984 (DEFRA) House Report, *supra* Chapter 1, note 11, at 1399. *See also* DEFRA Senate Report, *supra* Chapter 1, note 11, at 572.
[26] With apologies to poet Robert Frost.
[27] Major Issues, *supra* note 9, at 18.

Yogi Berra once said "When you come to a fork in the road, take it."[28] Congress did. The option of allowing unlimited deferral would not have addressed the tax policy question at issue and, thus, Congress rejected that option in favor of a more active approach. On the other extreme, the choice of subjecting inside buildup to current taxation also was eschewed by Congress, despite early support for such an approach by some members of Congress. The fork in the road taken by Congress in section 101(f), and ultimately followed in sections 7702 and 7702A, was to pursue first a definitional approach based on the relationship of the premiums, death benefits and cash surrender values of a contract, and then a distributional approach embodied in the rules of section 7702A.

## *Sections 7702 and 7702A*

Having decided upon a definitional approach to the tax policy question regarding the extent to which inside buildup should remain tax deferred, Congress was faced with the dilemma of how to craft the appropriate definitions. In the previously mentioned hearings before the House Select Revenue Measures Subcommittee during the consideration of this issue, Assistant Secretary Chapoton testified:

> The treatment of investment income bears an important relationship to the definition of life insurance. To the extent the definition of life insurance is tightened, thereby placing narrower limits on the investment orientation of a life insurance policy, there is more reason for allowing favorable tax treatment to the investment income under policies that fall within the definition. Conversely, if a looser definition is adopted, it seems appropriate to place some limits on the tax-free accrual of investment income in order to prevent savings through life insurance from obtaining an unfair advantage over other forms of savings.[29]

Hence, the definitional limitations to be created by Congress would need to be sufficiently "tight" to prevent the perceived abuse of investment-oriented life insurance contract designs and to justify the tax treatment of other, more favorably viewed products. In this regard, consistently with the view of the cash surrender value as the savings element in a life insurance contract, the **investment orientation** of a contract can be thought of as the relationship of, or the balance between, the contract's cash surrender value and its net amount at risk (or "pure" insurance benefit).

From an actuarial perspective, the investment component of a life insurance contract can be derived from the classical Fackler accumulation formula.[30] Where the benefit paid under the contract at the end of year $t+1$ (for death in that year) is given by $B_{t+1}$, the cash value at the end of contract year $t+1$ equals the cash value at the end of contract year $t$ plus the net premium for the year $t+1$ ($P_{t+1}$) accumulated with interest for one year at the rate for year $t+1$ ($i_{t+1}$) less the mortality cost ($B_{t+1} \times q_{x+t}$), all accumulated with the benefit of survivorship. The Fackler accumulation formula generates successive end-of-year cash values as follows:

$$_{t+1}CV = \frac{\left[\left(_tCV + P_{t+1}\right) \times \left(1 + i_{t+1}\right) - B_{t+1} \times q_{x+t}\right]}{p_{x+t}} \qquad (10.1)$$

By rearranging terms in the formula, it can be shown that:

$$_{t+1}CV = \left[\left(_tCV + P_{t+1}\right) \times \left(1 + i_{t+1}\right)\right] - \left(B_{t+1} - {_{t+1}}CV\right) \times q_{x+t} \qquad (10.2)$$

Formula (10.2) translates to an expression for the annual increase in cash value:

$$_{t+1}CV - {_tCV} = P_{t+1} + \left[\left(_tCV + P_{t+1}\right) \times i_{t+1}\right] - \left(B_{t+1} - {_{t+1}}CV\right) \times q_{x+t} \qquad (10.3)$$

As Formula (10.3) illustrates, the annual increase in cash value can be shown to equal:

---

[28] Lawrence Peter "Yogi" Berra, autographed baseball from the collection of Christian DesRochers, No. 125/500, LTD Enterprises, 2003.
[29] 1983 Hearings, *supra* Chapter 9, note 113, at 37.
[30] Jordan, *supra* Chapter 2, note 81, at 115.

- the premium paid at the start of the year ($P_{t+1}$), plus
- interest on the beginning of the year cash value (($_tCV + P_{t+1}) \times i_{t+1}$), less
- the cost of insurance assessed on the year-end amount at risk ($q_{x+t} \times (B_{t+1} - {_{t+1}}CV)$).

The investment orientation of life insurance can be quantified by examining the relationship of the inside buildup (i.e., ($_tCV + P_{t+1}) \times i_{t+1}$) with the cost of the insurance for the net amount at risk (i.e., ($q_{x+t} \times (B_{t+1} - {_{t+1}}CV)$). The greater the ratio of the inside buildup to the cost of insurance, the higher the investment orientation of the life insurance contract (i.e., the more investment orientation a life insurance contract is said to have). It is the control of investment orientation, and, thereby, the tax-deferred inside buildup in relation to the death benefit provided that lies at the heart of the section 7702 limitations. Using Formula (10.3), it can be demonstrated that the income tax that would be payable on a taxable deposit fund equal to the cash value in year $t+1$ equals (($_tCV + P_{t+1}) \times i_{t+1}$) $\times$ *tax rate*. This quantity represents the tax benefit of the inside buildup.

The adoption of definitional limitations necessarily creates complexity, of course, and any attempt to incorporate actuarial principles into such limits adds greatly to such complexity. In describing this process, one commentator noted:

> After deciding in principle to move the Code into a realm previously unmapped, Congress must decide exactly where to place the new boundary. Whether the measure confers a benefit upon an activity newly graced or presses a burden upon an activity newly disfavored, the Legislature must carve that activity away from those just beyond the measure's reach. This is rarely a simple matter.[31]

The complexity of the limitations enacted in section 7702 was appreciated in hindsight by the Treasury Department in a 1990 report:

> Since the actuarial limitations in the [section 7702] definition may create opportunities for employing actuarial strategies to avoid the investment limitations in the definition, the definition also includes a series of specific and complicated rules intended to prevent such avoidance.[32]

One commentator noted that "an author examining the income taxation of life insurance products ... realizes that, to even the most learned general practitioner, the language of the Internal Revenue Code sometimes appears to have been co-authored by James Joyce and Casey Stengel."[33] In a similar vein, referring to section 7702A, William B. Harman, Jr., commented:

> The mesmerizing array of conceptual entanglements, legal and actuarial, that comprise section 7702A must cause all to question strongly whether the perceived abuse could not have been controlled by a more simple and straight-forward method.[34]

Despite the admonitions regarding the complexity of sections 7702 and 7702A, the limitations set forth therein generally have operated since their inception in the manner intended by Congress. As discussed in

---

[31] Berger, *supra* Chapter 9, note 85, at 254.
[32] U.S. Dept. of Treasury, *Report to the Congress on the Taxation of Life Insurance Products* 20 (March 1990).
[33] See Theodore P. Manno, *The Federal Income Taxation of Life Insurance Annuities and Individual Retirement Accounts After the Tax Reform Act of 1986*, 60 St. John's L. Rev. 674, 674 (1986). The authors believe Casey Stengel would have made a great tax practitioner. As evidence, consider the following excerpt from an exchange with Sen. Kefauver in Stengel's 1958 testimony during the Senate Anti-Trust and Monopoly Subcommittee hearings:
*Sen. Kefauver:* Mr. Stengel, I am not sure that I made my question clear.
*Mr. Stengel:* Yes, sir. Well that is all right. I am not sure I am going to answer yours perfectly either.
*Sen. Kefauver:* I was asking you, sir, why it is that baseball wants this bill passed.
*Mr. Stengel:* I would say I would not know.
After dismissing Mr. Stengel, Mickey Mantle entered.
*Sen. Kefauver:* Mr. Mantle, do you have any observations with reference to the applicability of the antitrust laws to baseball?
*Mr. Mantle:* My views are about the same as Casey's.
Like Mickey Mantle, our views are about the same as Casey's.
[34] Harman, *supra* Chapter 1, note 13, at 1085, 1090. Further evidence of the complexity of IRC §§ 7702 and 7702A, apart from a simple glance at their provisions, is found in a comment made in a 1981 article by Berger, who noted, "Writing its first income tax statute after passage of the sixteenth amendment, Congress needed only six printed pages...." Berger, *supra* note 31, at 217. This total is far surpassed by IRC §§ 7702 and 7702A, which are the subject of more than 4,000 words of statute and even more legislative history. By comparison, President Abraham Lincoln's Gettysburg Address contains only 267 words.

previous chapters in this book, sections 7702 and 7702A were intended to impose limitations on the amount of tax-deferred inside buildup, while at the same time allowing for adjustments in future benefits and minimizing potential abuse. To this end, sections 7702 and 7702A impose maximum premium and minimum risk requirements. As also previously discussed, the definitional limitations generally are based upon actuarial principles, and were intended to allow many, but not all, of the products that existed at the time of enactment to continue to qualify as life insurance for federal income tax purposes. As law professor Pike, one of the framers of section 7702, noted in his seminal paper on the statute, "Because section 7702 codified most existing life insurance policy designs, it is necessarily based on actuarial principles."[35] In addition, a two-test definition was included in order to facilitate parity of treatment between traditional products (generally under the cash value accumulation test or CVAT) and universal life and other accumulation-based products (generally relying on the guideline premium test).

As described in Chapter 2, the actuarial limitations in sections 7702 and 7702A are based on the concept of a premium, and operate by restricting the key elements used in the calculation of a premium—namely, the assumptions that may be used for interest rates, mortality, QAB charges, policy expenses and maturity age, as well as the pattern of premiums, death benefits and cash surrender values. These requirements are designed to ensure the presence of at least a minimum amount of pure insurance risk, thereby eliminating the tax benefits normally associated with life insurance for contracts that are too heavily investment oriented. Thus, the provisions address the specific abuse that Congress perceived was in need of redress. In addition, the enactment of sections 7702 and 7702A can be thought of as a "backstop" approach that addresses the concerns of those who advocate a comprehensive income tax base. That is, in their view, if it is not possible to tax the economic income currently as a part of a comprehensive income tax base, a limitation is a second-best alternative, as a way to "ration" the life insurance tax preference and restrict the use of life insurance as purely an investment vehicle. Under this view, the requirement of minimum net amounts at risk help ensure that life insurance has a substantial purpose of providing insurance protection, and the costs for such protection necessarily reduce the investment return of a contract's savings element and ability to serve purely as an investment. Also, it can be argued that the key purpose of sections 7702 and 7702A is to separate life insurance contract earnings into three classes:

- **The good:** Earnings in a contract that meets the requirements of section 7702 and is not a modified endowment contract

- **The bad:** MEC earnings subject to deferred annuity predeath distribution rules

- **The ugly:** Currently taxable earnings in a contract that fails to meet the requirements of section 7702[36]

In fact, it might be said that section 7702 has worked even better, from the government's standpoint, than the Treasury Department designers of the statute anticipated. The gradual decline of interest rates over the period from 1982 (when section 101(f) was framed) through the date of this writing, when rates hover around historic lows, has had the effect of constraining the growth of inside buildup both directly and via the rates' interaction with the statutory limits on premium funding. Under the 1980 amendments to the **Standard Nonforfeiture Law for Life Insurance** (SNFL), the maximum rate of interest that may be assumed in the calculation of minimum nonforfeiture values is indexed.[37] This maximum rate applies based on the issue date of the contract and the duration of the interest guarantee. As Table 10.1 indicates, the minimum interest rates mandated under sections 7702 and 7702A have not changed, while the maximum nonforfeiture rates have declined. The difference between the maximum permissible nonforfeiture rate and the minimum section 7702 rate has been reduced and in fact has become negative with respect to the guideline single premium (GSP).

---

[35] Pike, *supra* Chapter 2, note 2, at 491, 539. Professor Pike served in the Treasury's Office of Tax Legislative Counsel during the framing of DEFRA.
[36] This is an illustration of the "outside theory of inside buildup" that Congress adopted in successive enactments in the 1980s, under which monies that are either outside of a contract, e.g., due to a distribution or loan, or which are not needed for funding a contract's benefits (at least on some set of assumptions) would be currently taxed. *See* Adney and Griffin, parts 1–3, *supra* Chapter 1, note 75. For the reference to the good, the bad and the ugly, our apologies also to Sergio Leone, Clint Eastwood, Lee Van Cleef and Eli Wallach.
[37] The 1980 amendments to the standard valuation and nonforfeiture laws provide that the interest rate to be used in defining the minimum valuation and nonforfeiture values is to be calculated annually as a function of Moody's Corporate Bond Yield Averages. The nonforfeiture rates in Table 10.1 are applicable to guarantee durations of more than 20 years.

### Table 10.1. Maximum nonforfeiture interest rates

| Years | Nonforfeiture rates | GSP | GLP, NSP and 7-pay |
|---|---|---|---|
| 1982 | 7.00% | 6.00% | 4.00% |
| 1983–1986 | 7.50% | 6.00% | 4.00% |
| 1987–1992 | 7.00% | 6.00% | 4.00% |
| 1993–1994 | 6.25% | 6.00% | 4.00% |
| 1995–2005 | 5.75% | 6.00% | 4.00% |
| 2006–2012 | 5.00% | 6.00% | 4.00% |
| 2013–2014 | 4.50% | 6.00% | 4.00% |

Figure 10.1 compares the section 7702 and 7702A minimum interest rate restrictions with maximum rates permitted under the SNFL (for life insurance contracts of durations of 20 or more years) as well as the average of the Moody's Aaa and Baa rates (which is used as a proxy for the general account earnings rate under Rev. Proc. 2008-39).

As a final note to any discussion of the limitations imposed by sections 7702 and 7702A, it is important to understand that, in many respects, such limitations are arbitrary. That is, Congress engaged in legislative line drawing which reflects a mixture of tax policy, actuarial mathematics and political compromise. In commenting on section 101(f), the immediate predecessor of section 7702, Harman noted:

> While the statute's specification of a minimum amount of insurance risk involved drawing a somewhat arbitrary line, this was necessary to ensure that flexible premium contracts did not permit too great an investment orientation. The willingness of Congress to draw lines with this purpose in mind began a pattern which would manifest itself in 1984 and again in 1988.[38]

**Figure 10.1.** Selected interest rates 1982–2014

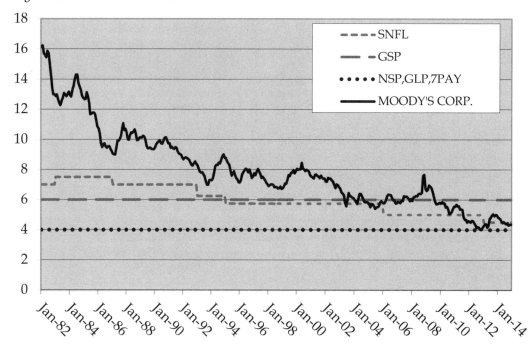

---
[38] Harman, *supra* Chapter 1, note 13, at 1090.

The significance of this point is that Congress could determine at some future time that the lines it drew in 1984 and 1988 are no longer sufficient to prevent the use of life insurance contracts for purposes which are inconsistent with the tax policy reasons for affording such products favorable treatment under the income tax laws. This potential for additional change is discussed in the last section of this chapter. But first, a discussion of the relationship between section 7702 and state nonforfeiture law follows.

## *Relationship Between Section 7702 and State Nonforfeiture Law for Life Insurance*

In addition to satisfying the actuarially based limitations in section 7702, a life insurance contract must qualify as such under "applicable law" in order to satisfy the requirements of that provision. This reference to applicable law generally is understood to mean state law, or the law of the jurisdiction controlling the issuance and interpretation of the contract.[39] This interpretation makes intuitive sense, as life insurance contracts sold in the United States are subject to a system of dual regulation. On the one hand, state laws, modeled after and typically incorporating the provisions of the SNFL, regulate the minimum cash surrender values that may be provided under a life insurance contract. On the other hand, the federal tax law limits the maximum permissible cash surrender value a contract may provide and still qualify for tax treatment as a life insurance contract.

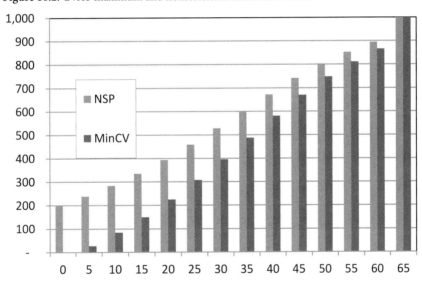

**Figure 10.2.** CVAT maximum and nonforfeiture minimum values

*Assumptions: Male 35, 2001 CSO ANB, 4% interest, endowment at 100*

The actuarial limitations under sections 7702 and 7702A interact with the minimum nonforfeiture requirements of state law.[40] As the limitations were intended, in part, to accommodate many then-existing life insurance products (and to deny life insurance treatment for others), this interaction is quite natural and, in fact, necessary.

This interaction occurs in two ways. First, both current tax law and nonforfeiture requirements apply to products, in this case life insurance, on a stand-alone basis. That is, both the tax treatment and the nonforfeiture requirements for life insurance are different from those for other products (e.g., a deferred annuity). Second, the section 7702 tests are in some respects a mirror image of state nonforfeiture requirements. By creating a

---

[39] See the discussion of the applicable law requirement in Chapter 1.
[40] *See* DEFRA Senate Report, *supra* Chapter 1, note 11, at 573–74 (stating that, for purposes of IRC § 7702, "rate or rates guaranteed on the issuance of the contract" means "the interest rate or rates reflected in the contract's nonforfeiture values assuming the use of the method in the Standard Nonforfeiture Law."). *See also* DEFRA House Report, *supra* Chapter 1, note 11, at 1444; DEFRA Blue Book, *supra* Chapter 1, note 20, at 649.

limitation that mirrors the nonforfeiture law, the actuarial standards in section 7702 codified many (although not all) contract designs which existed at the time section 7702 was enacted. Figure 10.2 illustrates the nonforfeiture minimum values and the CVAT maximum values for a contract based on 2001 CSO mortality and 4 percent interest.

Minimum cash surrender value requirements under the SNFL are computed using:

- the pattern of guaranteed future benefits under the contract;
- the contract nonforfeiture rate, subject to statutory maximum interest rates; and
- nonforfeiture mortality assumptions.

In contrast, but also somewhat in parallel, the section 7702 calculations today are based on:

- generally nonincreasing future benefits;
- the contract nonforfeiture interest rate, subject to a statutory minimum assumption (4 percent or 6 percent); and
- reasonable mortality assumptions.

The nonforfeiture standards thus act as a floor, while the section 7702 limitations serve to create a ceiling, on permissible values. Table 10.2 provides a comparison of the two sets of requirements as of this writing.

### Table 10.2. Comparison of nonforfeiture minimum and section 7702 maximum requirements

| Assumption | Nonforfeiture minimum | IRC § 7702 ceiling |
|---|---|---|
| Mortality | 2001 CSO | 2001 CSO under IRS Notice 2006-95 |
| Interest | 4.5% maximum subject to lower contract guaranteed rate | 4% minimum for net single premiums (NSP), guideline level premiums (GLP); 6% minimum for GSP subject to higher contract guaranteed rate |
| Death and endowment benefits | Future guaranteed benefits provided by the policy | Generally nonincreasing under IRC § 7702(e)(1)(A); assumed to be provided to the deemed maturity date under IRC § 7702(e)(1)(C); endowment limited to least death benefit under IRC § 7702(e)(1)(D) |
| Maturity date | Contractual date | Deemed between 95 and 100 under IRC § 7702(e)(1)(B) |
| Premium | On the date of issue and each anniversary on which a required premium falls due | Single or level premium, as applicable |

In cases where the floor is above the ceiling, a contract design cannot meet both state law and federal tax requirements. For example, when section 7702 was implemented, certain products for which the nonforfeiture minimum values exceeded the maximum cash surrender value allowed by the definitional limitations (for example, full-face endowment contracts maturing before age 95) simply disappeared from the marketplace. While the section 7702 requirements provide a standard by which favorable tax treatment is obtained, they also eliminated from the market some types of life insurance contracts that were sold prior to the statute's enactment (and served a legitimate insurance need, as a 1990 report by the General Accounting Office (GAO) noted[41]) and create potential conflicts with state law-mandated minimum values.

---

[41] See U.S. Gen. Accounting Office, GGD-90-31, Tax Treatment of Life Insurance and Annuity Accrued Interest 45 (1990) (hereinafter GAO Report).

## *The Nonforfeiture Law for Life Insurance as a Safety Net*

The nonforfeiture law also plays other, and more subtle, roles with respect to the definitional limitations. First, for permanent life insurance (and particularly traditional whole life) products, the nonforfeiture law, by mandating a floor on the cash surrender values they provide, in turn effectively mandates the continuation of the tax treatment of the inside buildup if the products are to remain viable in the marketplace. As noted in the earlier discussion of the rationale for this treatment, if the inside buildup tax deferral were eliminated, the absence of cash with which to pay the tax due on account of that buildup would make permanent life insurance a difficult asset for taxpayers to hold. Insofar as the existence of cash surrender values are required by the nonforfeiture law and Congress does not see fit to make permanent products unavailable, the tax deferral benefit afforded to inside buildup must remain.

Second, in addition to acting as a floor on allowable cash surrender values, the nonforfeiture law provides a safety net of sorts for some existing product designs, particularly traditional whole life contracts, in their efforts to qualify under section 7702 by means of the CVAT. This results from the need to define the section 7702 limitations so that many existing life insurance products would continue to qualify as life insurance, consistently with the intent of Congress in enacting the limitations. For traditional whole life products, once the contract has become fully paid up, the standard nonforfeiture law appears to mandate a cash value not less than a net single premium computed on the basis of an allowed rate of interest and a prescribed mortality table (for current issues, the 2001 CSO tables for standard cases).

For these products, the dual requirements of section 7702 and the state nonforfeiture laws create the possibility of a conflict along the lines noted above. (This would be ironic, in that the CVAT was created as a natural test to apply to traditional products, enabling them to comply with the statute.) Section 7702 mandates that the net single premiums used in the CVAT be computed using "reasonable" mortality charges. However, to the extent that the nonforfeiture law provides a margin in the assumed mortality table, the same margin must be incorporated into the reasonable mortality component of the section 7702 limitations if traditional products that meet state nonforfeiture requirements are also to qualify under the CVAT.

In 1989, the IRS initiated a project to issue regulations on reasonable mortality that Congress had directed in Technical and Miscellaneous Revenue Act of 1988 (TAMRA) to be finalized by January 1, 1990. Starting with the knowledge that the cost of insurance actually charged in universal life-type contracts for standard lives was based on, perhaps, 80 percent of the 1980 CSO mortality rates at that time, with contractual maximums set at the full 1980 CSO level, there was keen interest within the IRS in setting the reasonable mortality assumption in the definitional calculations at something less than 1980 CSO, thereby reflecting average rather than maximum charges. If brought to fruition, this would have abolished the 1980 CSO safe harbor established by Notice 88-128. Years of discussion, not to say acrimonious debate, were needed to persuade the IRS that traditional contracts simply could not satisfy state law and also qualify under the CVAT with such a standard—that this vision of "reasonable" was, in fact, unreasonable. With reasonable mortality set at a level below 1980 CSO mortality, the maximum permissible NSP under the CVAT would be less than the state-required level of cash surrender value for any traditional contract that was paid-up and, as a practical matter, for many contracts not yet fully paid-up. Given that a life insurance contract intending to qualify under the CVAT must do so "by the terms of the contract," contracts would fail the test at issue because they inevitably would fail at some late duration. Since the IRS (and the Treasury) could not defend such a result, the proposed regulation allowed the 1980 CSO as a safe harbor. This conclusion, by which a safety net was extended to preclude the definitional failure of traditional products, likely would not have been achieved absent a significant industry education effort as to the interrelationship of the definitional limitations and the nonforfeiture law. (The proposed regulation was never finalized for other reasons, leaving the TAMRA mandate still unfulfilled.)

The replacement of the 1980 CSO tables with the 2001 CSO tables, and the required use of the updated mortality assumptions in the section 7702 and 7702A calculations, diminished the relative tax benefits of life insurance contracts by reducing the level of minimum nonforfeiture values. This can be illustrated using after-tax internal rates of return (IRR) computed for single premium life (SPL) and 7-pay contracts. The resulting rates of return can then be grossed-up to the corresponding pretax equivalent rates of return to compare to the crediting rate. The resulting differences in IRR for contracts based on 1980 CSO and 2001 CSO are summarized in Table 10.3.

- Sex: Male
- Issue age: 40
- Mortality: 1980 CSO male aggregate and 2001 CSO male ultimate composite for guaranteed mortality; 105 percent of 2001 CSO select male composite for actual mortality
- Assumed interest rates: 4 percent and 6 percent (for the CVAT and the guideline premium/cash value corridor test, respectively)
- Actual interest rates: 6.5 percent and 8 percent
- Expenses: 6 percent of premium
- Surrender: At age 65
- Tax rate: 28 percent

| Table 10.3. Pretax equivalent rates of return | | | |
|---|---|---|---|
| | 1980 CSO | 2001 CSO | Difference |
| **6.5% single premium** | | | |
| GPL | 6.35% | 5.80% | −0.55% |
| CVAT | 6.48% | 6.28% | −0.20% |
| GPL/CVAT difference | −0.13% | −0.48% | −0.35% |
| **8.0% single premium** | | | |
| GPL | 8.53% | 8.15% | −0.38% |
| CVAT | 8.39% | 8.19% | −0.20% |
| GPL/CVAT difference | 0.14% | −0.04% | −0.18% |
| **6.5% 7-pay** | | | |
| GPL | 6.27% | 5.81% | −0.46% |
| CVAT | 6.25% | 6.03% | −0.22% |
| GPL/CVAT difference | 0.02% | −0.22% | −0.24% |
| **8.0% 7-pay** | | | |
| GPL | 8.33% | 7.99% | −0.34% |
| CVAT | 8.14% | 7.91% | −0.23% |
| GPL/CVAT difference | 0.19% | 0.08% | −0.11% |

Generally, CVAT contracts lost .20 percent to .23 percent of pretax equivalent IRR in the change, with the higher losses in the 7-pay form. Guideline premium/cash value corridor contracts lost .34 percent to .55 percent of IRR, with the heaviest loss in the SPL form and the lower interest scenarios.[42] Future modifications to the assumptions used in the calculations under sections 7702 and 7702A, such as with the advent of the planned new CSO tables, promise to have a somewhat similar (if perhaps smaller) effect on the investment orientation of permanent life insurance contracts.

## Potential Future Limitations on the Inside Buildup

For the definitional limitations to remain in their current form, they must be effective in controlling the investment uses of life insurance, while at the same time promoting the social goal of life insurance ownership as

---

[42] It appears that this is due to the fact that guideline premium test contracts have the ability to "go into corridor"—that is, to generate death benefit/cash surrender value relationships prohibited by the CVAT. (CVAT contracts have the advantage of higher allowed initial funding.) It takes longer for guideline premium test contracts to get to the corridor with the 2001 CSO tables, especially in low credited interest illustrations.

protection against financial loss from premature death. Thus, the definitional limitations can be thought of as a main line of defense for the current tax treatment of the inside buildup.[43] As the General Accounting Office commented in its 1990 report to Congress on life insurance product taxation, "Congress has narrowed the tax definition of life insurance, but that definition is likely to remain an issue as long as preferential tax treatment is granted to life insurance products."[44] The GAO report further commented:

> Until now, Congress has chosen to deal with concerns about the potential misuse of the tax preference associated with inside buildup by narrowing the definition of what qualifies as life insurance. The definitional approach involves two dangers. First, the definition may not be narrow enough. Policies may qualify that are primarily oriented toward producing investment returns rather than insurance protection. Second, the definition could be too narrow. Products serving a legitimate life insurance need may be disqualified.[45]

The GAO report describes what might be characterized as the Goldilocks approach to the definitional limitation—not too hot, not too cold, but just right. The history of the taxation of life insurance products illustrates that, where life insurance products are perceived as "too hot," Congress will ultimately act to lower the temperature, either by limiting the products themselves or the methods by which the products are purchased. As noted by the authors of a 1997 article appearing in the *Insurance Tax Review*:

> [I]n the early 1980s, Congress gave life insurers the keys to drive flexible premium contracts through the back roads of sections 101(f) and 7702, only to take the T-bird away through section 7702A, when companies dared to utter the term "tax shelter" a bit too loudly in public.[46]

In other words, in light of the tax treatment of the owners and beneficiaries of permanent life insurance products, the government will continue to monitor the uses of such products and has shown a willingness to react to perceived abuses. Moreover, congressional and regulatory action are not the only forces acting upon the federal income tax treatment of life insurance, as judicial interpretations have and will continue to shape the parameters in which life insurance operates. For example, in his opinion in the *CM Holdings* case, Senior District Judge Schwartz described an "invisible line" that separates life insurance, which qualifies for favorable tax treatment, from tax-driven or tax-sheltering investments, as follows:

> One can readily appreciate that these tax advantages have invited talented actuaries to design life insurance policies which approach becoming tax driven investment vehicles and/or tax shelters, which were never intended by Congress to receive favorable life insurance tax benefits. Over the years, Congress has limited, but not eliminated, these tax advantages in an attempt to curb the use of life insurance policies as investment vehicles. … Thus, Congress and the courts have stepped in when life insurance policies have crossed the line separating insurance against an untimely death and tax driven or tax sheltering investments.[47]

As Judge Schwartz observed, designers of life insurance products seek to discover the invisible line in an effort to maximize the appeal of life insurance products to the public, but not invite an adverse reaction by Congress or the courts. ◉

---

[43] Arguably, the enactment of IRC § 7702 in 1984 was one consideration in Congress's decision not to enact a Reagan Administration proposal, in its 1985–86 tax reform plan, to impose a tax on inside buildup. Certainly, this was a prime point in the insurance industry's argument against the enactment of the proposal.
[44] GAO Report, *supra* note 41, at 3.
[45] *Id.* at 45.
[46] Howard Stecker et al., *The Insurance Product Continuum: Complexity of Tax Laws Feeds Demand for Proactive Management of Risk*, 12 Ins. Tax Rev. 1001, at 1001 (June 1997) (footnotes omitted). Citing The Beach Boys, *Fun, Fun, Fun*, on Shut Down Volume 2 (Capitol Records 1964). "And with the radio blasting, Goes cruising just as fast as she can now, And she'll have fun fun fun, Til her daddy takes the T-Bird away."
[47] *IRS v. CM Holdings Inc.*, 254 B.R. 578, 581 (D. Del 2000), *aff'd* 301 F.3d 96 (3d Cir. 2002). The case involved the deductibility of interest under a corporate-owned, leveraged life insurance plan. The taxpayer lost.

# GLOSSARY

From "accelerated death benefits" to "waiver ruling," sections 7702 and 7702A[1] and related tax rules have generated their share of jargon. This glossary presents a selection of terms with definitions.

**ACCELERATED DEATH BENEFITS (ADBs):** Insurance benefits that generally are payable due to the occurrence of a morbidity event or status (e.g., the insured's terminal, chronic or critical illness) from a rider or other provision of a life insurance contract which reduce the life insurance contract's death benefit.

**ACTIVITIES OF DAILY LIVING (ADLs):** A set of common, everyday tasks, the performance of which is required for personal self-care and independent living.[2] As used in the tax definition of a chronically ill individual, the ADLs are eating, toileting, transferring, bathing, dressing and continence.

**ACTUARIAL ASSUMPTIONS:** Sections 7702 and 7702A place limits on the actuarial assumptions, such as for interest, mortality and death benefits, that may be assumed in computing definitional values (NSP, GSP, GLP and 7-pay premium). Interest rates must be no lower than 4 percent (for the NSP, GLP and 7-pay premium) or 6 percent (for the GSP) and must reflect higher guaranteed rate(s). For contracts issued on or after October 21, 1988, the mortality assumed must be "reasonable" and generally not higher than mortality charges specified in the "prevailing commissioners' standard table" as defined in section 807(d)(5).

**ADJUSTMENT EVENT:** The legislative history of section 7702(f)(7) provides that, if there is a change in benefits under (or in the other terms of) the contract, "proper adjustments [are to] be made for any change in future benefits or any qualified additional benefit (or in any other terms) under the contract, which was not reflected in any previous determination made under the definitional section." *See* Chapter 4.

**ADJUSTMENT RULES:** These rules permit a degree of flexibility, allowing increases and decreases in death benefits while still maintaining the definitional limitations in the section 7702 and 7702A tests. Beginning with section 101(f), procedures were established to recompute the limitations in the event of a change in benefits provided by the contract.

**AGGREGATION RULE:** Pursuant to section 72(e)(12)(A)(i), all MECs issued by the same company to the same policyholder in the same calendar year are to be treated as one contract for purposes of applying the "LIFO" ordering rule to predeath distributions.

**ALTERNATE DEATH BENEFIT RULES:** In computing the guideline level premium, an increasing death benefit may be taken into account under section 7702(e)(2)(A), but only to the extent necessary to prevent a decrease in the excess of the death benefit over the cash surrender value (that is, to prevent a decrease in the net amount at risk).

**AMOUNTS PAID:** Generally, the sum of all premiums paid less any amount distributed from the contract that was not included in gross income for tax purposes.

**AMOUNTS RETAINED RULE:** Under this rule, any amount distributed from an annuity contract or a MEC that is a policy dividend or similar distribution is not included in gross income to the extent that it is retained by the insurer as premium for the contract. See section 72(e)(4)(B). Note that policy loans or partial surrenders applied to pay premiums are not excluded from income by this rule, as they are not dividends. Similarly, dividends applied other than as premium (e.g., to reduce a policy loan) are not protected from taxation by this rule.

**APPLICABLE LAW:** This section 7702(a) requirement delegates to state law the task of defining the four corners of the contract under consideration as a life insurance contract that must meet the numerical tests of section 7702. This is necessary because some contracts providing life insurance benefits are treated as bifurcated (e.g., an annuity with a term life insurance rider) while other contracts are treated as integrated life insurance contracts (e.g., universal life) under state law.

---

[1] Unless otherwise indicated, references to "section" are to the provisions of the Internal Revenue Code of 1986, as amended (also referred to as "IRC" or the "Code").

[2] *See* Joshua M. Wiener and Raymond J. Hanley, *Measuring the Activities of Daily Living Among the Elderly: A Guide to National Surveys*, Department of Health and Human Services and The Brookings Institution report (1989).

**ATTAINED AGE:** The **attained-age regulations** (see below), tracking the legislative history of section 7702, define "attained age" for section 7702 purposes as generally the age of the insured determined by reference to contract anniversaries, so long as the age assumed under the contract is within 12 months of the actual age.

**ATTAINED-AGE INCREMENT AND DECREMENT METHOD:** Under the guideline premium test, an increase or decrease in benefits is treated separately from the existing guideline limits. That is, separate guideline premiums are computed to reflect the increase or decrease in face amount. This is accomplished by using the attained-age increment and decrement approach of "before and after" calculations based on the attained age of the insured at the time of the change.

**ATTAINED-AGE REGULATIONS:** Section 1.7702-2 of the Income Tax Regulations establishes the general rules for determining an insured's attained age for purposes of calculating the guideline level premium under section 7702(c)(4), applying the cash value corridor of section 7702(d) and utilizing the computational rules of section 7702(e). The regulations contain special rules for multiple life contracts.

**BASIC ACTUARIAL PRINCIPLES:** This approach uses the techniques of actuarial mathematics for defining insurance premiums, relying on the fundamental relationship that equates the present value of future premiums with the present value of future benefits and expenses (and other charges). This method provides the greatest flexibility for accommodating unique product designs and contract features, particularly when it comes to adjustments under the attained-age increment and decrement method.

**BLUE BOOK:** The general explanation of a tax bill prepared by the staff of the Joint Committee on Taxation is often called a Blue Book because of the color of its cover. The TEFRA Blue Book is the general explanation of the revenue provisions of the Tax Equity and Fiscal Responsibility Act of 1982. Cited as: STAFF OF THE JT. COMM. ON TAX'N, 97TH CONG., GENERAL EXPLANATION OF THE REVENUE PROVISIONS OF THE TAX EQUITY AND FISCAL RESPONSIBILITY ACT OF 1982 (Comm. Print 1982).

The DEFRA Blue Book is the general explanation of the revenue provisions of the Deficit Reduction Act of 1984. Cited as: STAFF OF THE JT. COMM. ON TAX'N, 98TH CONG., GENERAL EXPLANATION OF THE REVENUE PROVISIONS OF THE DEFICIT REDUCTION ACT OF 1984 (Comm. Print 1984). Two Blue Books were prepared for the Tax Reform Act of 1986. The Blue Book covering most of the 1986 act is cited as: STAFF OF THE JT. COMM. ON TAX'N, 99TH CONG., GENERAL EXPLANATION OF THE TAX REFORM ACT OF 1986 (Comm. Print 1987). The Blue Book referred to as the Technical Corrections Blue Book, covering the technical corrections to prior legislation (including the enactment of section 7702) that were enacted as part of the 1986 act, is cited as: STAFF OF THE JT. COMM. ON TAX'N, 99TH CONG., EXPLANATION OF TECHNICAL CORRECTIONS TO THE TAX REFORM ACT OF 1984 AND OTHER RECENT LEGISLATION (Comm. Print 1987). The Blue Book is often used as legislative history although it is not a part of the official legislative history, as it is a post-enactment document.

**BURIAL INSURANCE:** Generally small face amount contracts sold to older policyholders. Section 7702(e)(2)(C) establishes special computational rules for these burial or preneed plans.

**CASH SURRENDER VALUE (CSV):** A contract's cash value determined without regard to any "surrender charge, policy loan, or reasonable termination dividends," as defined in section 7702(f)(2)(A).

**CASH VALUE:** This functions as the savings or investment element of the contract. The cash value is the basis of the amount payable upon surrender of a contract before death or maturity. Under a retrospective or accumulation approach, premiums increase the cash value, as does the interest or earnings credited, while contract charges and partial withdrawals reduce it. Term insurance contracts that provide coverage for a limited period of time generally do not have cash values. Permanent insurance contracts, which cover a longer period of time, make provision for a cash value.

**CASH VALUE ACCUMULATION TEST (CVAT):** The CVAT limits the relationship of the cash value and the death benefit under a contract. Under the CVAT, by the terms of the contract, the cash surrender value of the contract cannot exceed at any time the net single premium for the death benefit, the endowment benefit and charges for any QABs. The effective "risk corridor" provided by the CVAT can be expressed as the reciprocal of the net single premium for a death benefit of $1.00.

**CASH VALUE CORRIDOR:** Under the guideline premium test, the death benefit is also limited by the cash value corridor factors in section 7702(d). The cash value corridor is satisfied if the death benefit at any time is not less than the applicable percentage (as set forth in section 7702(d)(2)) of the cash surrender value at that time.

**CHRONIC ILLNESS:** An individual generally is treated as a "chronically ill individual," within the meaning of section 7702B(c)(2)(A), if he or she has been certified by a licensed health care practitioner within the preceding 12-month period as either being unable to perform (without substantial assistance from another individual) at least two activities of daily living (see above) for a period of at least 90 days due to a loss of functional capacity, or requiring substantial supervision to protect such individual from threats to health and safety due to severe cognitive impairment.

**CHURCH PLANS:** TAMRA added a new Code subsection, section 7702(j), which provided that certain church-based self-funded death benefit plans are treated as life insurance for federal tax purposes.

**CLOSING AGREEMENT:** This is a contract between a taxpayer and the IRS that liquidates the taxpayer's liability for past-due federal taxes. For a section 7702 failure case, a closing agreement between the issuing life insurer and the IRS historically was used where a reasonable error waiver under section 7702(f)(8) was unavailable. Under the 2008 revenue procedures (see Chapter 8), closing agreements are used to remediate failed contracts and inadvertent MECs. Closing agreements are not available for public inspection.

**CORPORATE-OWNED LIFE INSURANCE (COLI):** A corporation is the owner and beneficiary of the COLI contract. Leveraged COLI refers to corporate-owned life insurance financed with policy loans. Life insurance (often single premium) owned by a bank is known as bank-owned insurance (BOLI), while life insurance owned by a trust but benefitting a corporation or its employees is referred to as trust-owned life insurance (TOLI).

**COLLOQUY:** This is a discussion appearing in the *Congressional Record* intended to expand upon or clarify a particular issue. *See, e.g.,* **Dole-Bentsen colloquy** and **Packwood-Baucus colloquy**.

**COMMUTATION FUNCTIONS:** These are labor-saving devices that simplify the construction and manipulation of actuarial values. They have been used by actuaries for determining monetary values, but have declined somewhat in importance since the widespread use of computers.

**COMPUTATIONAL RULES:** Under the section 7702(e) computational rules for purposes of calculating the guideline premiums and net single premiums of any contract, limitations are imposed on the pattern of future death benefits, the assumed maturity value (i.e., the endowment value) and the assumed maturity date. Similar computational rules are imposed by section 7702A(c)(1) for purposes of calculating 7-pay premiums.

**CONSTRUCTIVE RECEIPT DOCTRINE:** The doctrine of constructive receipt, found in regulations under section 451, requires the inclusion in income of amounts that, although not within the physical possession of the taxpayer, were actually available to the taxpayer. Conversely, amounts not actually or constructively received generally are not subject to taxation. Treas. Reg. section 1.451-2 provides that income is not constructively received if the taxpayer's control or enjoyment of the amount in question is "subject to substantial limitations or restrictions." This doctrine generally applies to taxpayers on the cash receipts and disbursements, as opposed to the accrual, method of accounting.

**CONTRACT YEAR:** Section 7702A(e)(2) defines "contract year" as "the 12-month period beginning with the 1$^{st}$ month for which the contract is in effect, and 12-month period beginning with the corresponding month in subsequent calendar years." See also section 7702A(c)(3), which treats a contract as newly entered into after a material change.

**COST OF INSURANCE (COI):** The charge assessed under a contract for the pure insurance risk.

In a universal life-type contract, the current cost of insurance is deducted from the cash value.

**CURTATE:** In connection with mortality, the assumption that death claims for a policy year are paid at the end of that year.

**DEATH BENEFIT DISCOUNT RATE:** The interest rate used in a universal life insurance contract to discount the death benefit in determining a contract's net amount at risk.

**DEEMED CASH SURRENDER VALUE:** The hypothetical cash surrender value (determined without regard to any surrender charge or policy loan) that would have resulted if premiums paid under the contract had been credited with interest at the policy rate and had been reduced by certain mortality and expense charges, for purposes of the necessary premium test of section 7702A(c)(3)(B)(i) and as described by the legislative history of section 7702A.

**DEEMED EXCHANGE:** A contract modification significant enough to cause the contract to be treated as having been exchanged for a new contract for federal tax purposes.

**DEEMED MATURITY DATE:** Section 7702(e)(1)(B) provides that the maturity date assumed in the guideline and net single premium calculations can be no earlier than the day on which the insured attains age 95 and no later than the day on which the insured attains age 100.

**DEFRA:** The Deficit Reduction Act of 1984; cited as: Pub. L. No. 98-369 (1984). Congress enacted section 7702 of the Code as part of DEFRA. *See* Pub. L. No. 98-369, section 221(a) (1984).

**DIVERSIFICATION RULES:** In addition to meeting the section 7702 and 7702A limitations, the separate account supporting a variable contract must meet certain investment diversification requirements specified in section 817(h) and in Treas. Reg. section 1.817-5.

**DIVIDEND:** Section 808(a) defines the term "policyholder dividend" as "any dividend or similar distribution to policyholders in their capacity as such." Section 808(b)(1) provides that this term includes "any amount paid or credited (including as an increase in benefits) where the amount is not fixed in the contract but depends on the experience of the company or the discretion of the management." In other words, under section 808, policyholder dividends generally encompass any amount that is not guaranteed under a contract but that is provided based on experience or management discretion.

**DOLE-BENTSEN COLLOQUY:** The *Congressional Record* includes a colloquy between Sen. Dole and Sen. Bentsen providing an explanation of the circumstances under which guideline premiums are to be adjusted and how they are to be adjusted. Cited as: 128 CONG. REC. S10,943 (daily ed. Aug. 19, 1982).

**EXCESS INTEREST:** A rate of interest credited to a contract in excess of the minimum guarantee or floor rate. Under section 808 of the Code, excess interest is treated as a policyholder dividend.

**EXPENSE CHARGES:** Expense charges in a life insurance contract can take a variety of forms, including (but not limited to) per policy, per $1,000 of face amount and percentage of premium charges. For contracts issued before October 21, 1988, use of the contractual expense charges was permitted in section 101(f) and later section 7702, which allowed "any other charges specified in the contract" to be used in determining the guideline premiums. For contracts issued on or after that date, *see* **reasonable expense charges**.

**FAILED CONTRACT:** A life insurance contract that fails to satisfy the section 101(f) or 7702 requirements. In the case of a failed contract, the **inside buildup** of the contract is taxed currently and is subject to reporting and withholding obligations by the issuing insurer. Income on the contract, as defined in section 7702(g)(1)(B), becomes taxable to the policyholder and would therefore be includible in gross income.

**FAIL-SAFE PROVISION:** A provision included in a contract designed to ensure compliance with a definitional limitation by cross-referencing that limitation, e.g., a provision enabling the insurance company to modify the contract to attempt to maintain qualification with the definitional limits. In some circumstances, a fail-safe provision in conjunction with other contract provisions can be helpful in ensuring compliance, but care should be exercised in use of such provisions, e.g., in the context of the CVAT in light of its terms-of-the-contract requirement.

**FIFO TAXATION:** Under the section 72 ordering or stacking rules for non-MEC life insurance contracts, a predeath distribution generally is treated first as a recovery of the policyholder's investment in the contract and is not includible in gross income except to the extent it exceeds the investment in the contract—the "FIFO" (first-in, first-out or basis recovery first) rule.

**FIXED PREMIUM UNIVERSAL LIFE (FPUL):** A universal life-type of contract that specifies a premium which must be paid to prevent the contract from lapsing; also known as a current assumption whole life insurance, or interest sensitive whole life, contract. See **footnote 53** below.

**FLOOR INTEREST RATE:** The TEFRA Blue Book at page 369 defined the term "minimum rate or rates of interest" as the "floor rate or rates of interest guaranteed at issue of [a] contract." It went on to note that, "although the company may guarantee a higher interest rate from time to time [after contract issuance], either by contractual declaration or by operation of a formula or index, the minimum rate still should be taken to be the floor rate, that is, the rate below which the interest credited to the contract [for the period] cannot fall."

**FOOTNOTE 53:** The DEFRA Blue Book at page 649 noted that any secondary guarantees present in a contract should be considered in selecting the appropriate guarantees of interest, mortality and expense to be recognized in the determination of values under section 7702. Footnote 53 on that page of the DEFRA Blue Book illustrates the application of the rule with respect to a fixed premium universal life insurance contract.

**FRASIER METHOD:** This method is used to compute survivorship or last-to-die mortality using a single status of "at least one insured alive." This method came into use in the 1980s after the publication in 1978 of an article by William Frasier that described the single status approach for computing reserves and cash values for last survivor products.

**FUTURE BENEFITS:** Sections 7702(f)(4) and 7702(f)(5)(B) define the term "future benefits" to mean death benefits (as defined in section 7702(f)(3)), endowment benefits and the charges for any qualified additional benefits under the contract. Future benefits, as used in section 7702A(b), is not defined in section 7702A. Section 7702A(e)(3) states, however, that except as otherwise provided in section 7702A, terms used in section 7702A are to have the same meaning as when used in section 7702.

**GROSS-UP RULE:** As described in the DEFRA Blue Book, the rate or rates guaranteed on issuance of a contract generally are the interest rates reflected in the contract's nonforfeiture values, assuming the use of the method in the standard nonforfeiture law. The gross-up rule was intended to address situations where the cash values are determined on a nonstandard basis, such as in a plan under which the guaranteed values are a simple accumulation of premiums at interest.

**GUARANTEED MORTALITY RATE:** The maximum cost of insurance rate that may be charged to the policyholder. A life insurance company generally charges a cost of insurance rate that is less than the guaranteed rate. This is sometimes known as the current mortality rate.

**GUIDELINE LEVEL PREMIUM (GLP):** The level annual amount, payable over a period that does not end before the insured attains age 95 or after age 100, which is necessary to fund the future benefits under the contract. *See* section 7702(c)(4).

**GUIDELINE PREMIUM LIMITATION (GPL):** The GPL at any time equals the greater of the **guideline single premium** or the sum of the **guideline level premiums** to that time (i.e., generally the guideline level premium multiplied by the contract duration).

**GUIDELINE PREMIUM TEST (GPT):** The GPT limits the premiums that may be paid for a contract and also limits the relationship between the contract cash value and its death benefit. For a contract to satisfy the guideline premium test, it must satisfy the guideline premium requirements of section 7702(a)(2)(A) and (c) and fall within the cash value corridor of section 7702(a)(2)(B) and (d). A contract satisfies the guideline premium requirements if the sum of the premiums paid under the contract does not at any time exceed the guideline premium limitation as of such time.

**GUIDELINE SINGLE PREMIUM (GSP):** The premium necessary at the date of issue to fund the future benefits under the contract. *See* section 7702(c)(3)(A).

**HAIG-SIMONS INCOME:** This concept is widely viewed as the foundation of a comprehensive definition of income for tax purposes. Haig-Simons income is generally defined as the sum of a taxpayer's consumption plus change in wealth over a given time period and is widely accepted by economists as a definition of economic income.

***HELVERING V. LE GIERSE*, 312 U.S. 531 (1941):** This Supreme Court case established the principle that although a contract (or a combination of contracts) was in the form of a standard commercial life insurance contract, it is not treated as a life insurance contract for purposes of federal tax law unless it provides for risk shifting and risk distributing. The case is discussed in Chapters 1 and 9.

**HIPAA:** The Health Insurance Portability and Accountability Act of 1996; cited as: Pub. L. No. 104-191 (1996). Congress enacted sections 101(g) and 7702B as part of HIPAA. *See* Pub. L. No. 104-191, sections 321, 325, and 331 (1996).

**HUTTON LIFE RULINGS:** In January and February of 1981, the E.F. Hutton Life private letter rulings were issued by the IRS, granting favorable tax treatment to the death proceeds of a universal life plan and holding that such products were to be treated for tax purposes in the same manner as the traditional cash value life insurance contract.

**ILLUSTRATION-BASED PROJECTION:** This approach simulates monthly contract mechanics in computing the applicable definitional limitations. Applying the **test plan** concept, the values of the guideline premiums or the net single premiums are the premiums that will mature the contract on the assumed maturity date under the actuarial assumptions and future benefits applied in computing the limitation.

**IMMEDIATE PAYMENT OF CLAIMS (IPC):** Another way of saying that death benefits are assumed to be paid promptly on death. *Contrast with* **curtate**.

**IMPLIED GUARANTEES:** For certain contract designs, the interest rate or rates guaranteed in the contract may not be explicitly stated in the contract. Instead, the guarantees may be implicitly stated by a guarantee of a particular cash surrender value (e.g., nonforfeiture cash value).

**INADVERTENT MEC:** For a contract that mistakenly (i.e., inadvertently or unintentionally) becomes a MEC, the treatment of the inside buildup and death benefit is unaffected, but distributions are generally taxed on a less favorable basis. Such a MEC may be correctable under Rev. Proc. 2008-39.

**INCOME ON THE CONTRACT (IOC):** In the context of section 72, this is the gain, or inside buildup, in the contract, i.e., generally the excess of the cash value over the investment in the contract. For the policyholder of a contract that ceases to meet the section 7702 definitional tests, the income on the contract is calculated in the manner described by section 7702(g)(1)(B) and is treated as ordinary income received or accrued by the policyholder in the year in which the income arises. This includes interest or earnings credits used to pay COI charges. Section 7702(g)(1)(C) also requires that past income on the contract be included in income in the year of failure.

**INITIAL GUARANTEES:** These guarantees are common on universal life insurance-type contracts, where the account value is generally credited with interest at a rate in excess of the contract's guaranteed minimum or floor rate. When the initial credited rate exceeds the guaranteed minimum rate and the credited rate is guaranteed for an initial period of time (e.g., 12 months), the initial credited rate is the rate guaranteed upon issuance for the duration of the initial guarantee period.

**INSIDE BUILDUP:** This is the portion of the growth in a contract's cash or accumulation value attributable to the crediting of tax-deferred interest or earnings.

**INSURABLE INTEREST:** In the context of life insurance, this represents the interest a purchaser of a contract has in the insured's continued life due to the relationship between the purchaser and the insured, such that there is a reasonable expectation of financial benefit to the purchaser in the continued life of the insured. Where no insurable interest exists, an insurance contract may be considered an illegal wagering or gambling contract.

**INTERIM MORTALITY RULES:** Section 5011(c)(2) of TAMRA provides an interim rule relating to the **reasonable mortality charge** requirement imposed by TAMRA for contracts entered into on or after October 21, 1988, but before the effective date of final regulations. Because, as of the date of this publication, regulations have yet to be issued on reasonable mortality, the interim rule is operative. The interim rule provides that mortality charges which do not differ materially from the charges actually expected to be imposed by the company (taking into account any relevant characteristics of the insured of which the company is aware) are treated as meeting the requirements of section 7702(c)(3)(B)(i). *See also* **Notice 2006-95**.

**INVESTMENT ORIENTATION:** Relationship of the cash value of a contract to its death benefit. Life insurance contracts with large amounts of cash value relative to the insurance risk are said to be highly investment oriented. Investment orientation is related to the amount and pattern of premium payments. A traditional annual premium whole life insurance contract has an increasing cash value and a decreasing pure insurance component, while a term insurance contract generally has only the pure insurance element, and so the former is said to be more investment oriented than the latter.

**JOINT LIFE:** A joint life contract provides insurance coverage for multiple insured lives. First-to-die life insurance contracts provide a death benefit payable on the first death of the covered insureds. First-to-die contracts may cover two or more lives. On the first death, the contract terminates. For last-to-die or survivorship contracts, *see* **survivorship contract**.

**LEAST ENDOWMENT RULE:** Section 7702(e)(1)(D) states that the amount of any endowment benefit (or sum of endowment benefits) taken into account cannot exceed the least amount payable as a death benefit at any time under the contract. The endowment benefit includes any cash surrender value on the deemed maturity date.

**LEGISLATIVE HISTORY:** Legislative history consists of House and Senate committee reports, including conference committee reports and floor statements in the *Congressional Record*. Materials prepared by the Joint Committee on Taxation are also useful as legislative history. These include background materials prepared as a part of the legislative process as well as general explanations, or Blue Books, which are prepared after the passage of major tax legislation. As a post-enactment writing, Blue Books usually are less significant as a tool of statutory construction relative to the official legislative history.

**LICENSED HEALTH CARE PRACTITIONER (LHCP):** Under section 7702B(c)(4), this term means any physician (as defined in section 1861(r)(1) of the Social Security Act), and any registered professional nurse, licensed social worker or other individual who meets such requirements as may be prescribed by the Secretary of the Treasury.

**LIFE INSURANCE:** For a contract that is life insurance under the Code, interest credited to its cash value is not taxed as current income, and its death proceeds are excluded from gross income of the beneficiary. A contract issued after December 31, 1984, is subject to the section 7702 rules to determine its tax status as a life insurance contract. A life insurance contract entered into after June 20, 1988, is subject to section 7702A to determine the applicable income tax rules with respect to dividends paid in cash, partial withdrawals and policy loans.

**LIFO TAXATION:** Distributions from a life insurance contract that is a MEC are accorded LIFO taxation treatment. If a predeath distribution is made from a MEC, the amount included in gross income is based on the income on the contract just prior to the distribution; the LIFO (last-in, first-out or income first) rule applies.

**LOOK-BACK RULES:** According to section 7702A(d), the treatment of the contract as a MEC applies, in addition to distributions that occur during and after the contract year in which the contract becomes a MEC, to any distributions that, "under regulations," occur "in anticipation" of MEC status. No such regulations have been issued, but a companion rule in section 7702A(d) treats distributions made within two years before the contract becomes a MEC as having been made "in anticipation." A similar look-back rule applies as part of the **recapture rules**.

**MATERIAL CHANGE:** The 7-pay test is applied when a contract is issued, based on the **future benefits** at that time. When changes occur to a contract other than a reduction in benefits, the material change rule of section 7702A(c)(3) may apply. In computing the 7-pay premium for a materially changed contract, the calculations are based on the future benefits then provided by the contract, the contract's cash value and the insured's then attained age. The term "material change" also has a broader meaning under federal tax law as discussed in Chapter 5.

**MINIMUM DEPOSIT:** The use of policy loans to finance the purchase of a life insurance contract.

**MINIMUM INTEREST RATE:** *See* **floor interest rate**.

**MODEL PLAN:** *See* **test plan**.

**MODIFIED ENDOWMENT CONTRACT (MEC):** A MEC is defined in section 7702A(a) as a contract entered into on or after June 21, 1988, that qualifies as a life insurance contract within the meaning of section 7702 but fails to meet the **7-pay test** prescribed in section 7702A(b), or is received in exchange for a MEC.

**MONTHLY MORTALITY ASSUMPTION:** Where monthly processing is done, definitional calculations may assume claim payment at the end of the month of death (monthly curtate). There are standard methods for converting annual mortality probabilities into monthly probabilities. The monthly mortality rate under an arithmetic approach is simply defined by dividing the annual rate by 12. Using an exponential conversion of annual mortality rates to monthly rates has the benefit of producing consistency between the annualized rates and the original annual rates. A monthly exponential rate is derived as follows: $q^{monthly} = (1 - (1-q)^{(1/12)})$.

**NECESSARY PREMIUMS:** The "necessary premium" rule of section 7702A(c)(3)(B)(i) provides an exception to the material change rule applicable to an increase in future benefits. Under the necessary premium exception, also referred to as the necessary premium test (NPT), an increase in future benefits will not result in a material change if the increase is attributable to the payment of premiums necessary to fund the lowest level of benefits payable in the first seven contract years or to the crediting of earnings in respect of such premiums. More detail on the definition of necessary premium is found in the legislative history of TAMRA and of the Omnibus Budget Reconciliation Act of 1989 (and in Chapter 4).

**NET AMOUNT AT RISK (NAR):** The pure insurance element inside a life insurance contract. The annual charge made to the cash value of a contract for this protection is the cost of insurance.

**NET LEVEL RESERVE TEST:** Section 7702(e)(2)(B) allows for option 2 death benefit increases to be reflected under the requirements of the CVAT if the contract satisfies the test using a net level premium reserve (rather than a net single premium) as the basis for qualification.

**NET PREMIUM:** This is the mechanism by which the relationship between the cash value and net amount at risk is controlled and the section 7702 and 7702A limitations are imposed. As expressed by the net premium formula, the cost of a life insurance contract is a function of assumed mortality, interest and expense.

**NET RATE PRODUCTS:** Some single premium product designs do not provide for the explicit deduction of a cost of insurance. Rather, the cost of insurance is expressed in terms of a spread or asset-based expense charge assessed against the earnings on the cash value. In these designs, the cash value is the premium paid accumulated at a net rate of interest. The treatment of certain of these plans under section 7702 was anticipated during the development of the statute.

**NET SINGLE PREMIUM (NSP):** The amount required to fund the future guaranteed death and endowment benefits and QAB charges under a contract. It is the premium that would be paid at issue to fully fund the future benefits (but not expenses) under section 7702.

**NET SURRENDER VALUE (NSV):** Section 7702(f)(2)(B) provides that the "net surrender value of any contract shall be determined with regard to surrender charges but without regard to any policy loan." The net surrender value is used in to compute the income on the contract under section 7702(g). It also plays a role in a life insurance company's reserve deduction.

**NONGUARANTEED ELEMENT:** An element within a life insurance contract that enables more favorable value to the policyholder than guaranteed at the time of issue of the contract. Examples of nonguaranteed elements include policyholder dividends, excess interest, and reductions in mortality or other charges from those guaranteed in the contract.

**NON-QAB:** An additional benefit that is not qualified. Section 7702(f)(5)(C)(ii) provides that, in the case of a nonqualified additional benefit, any charge for such benefit which is not "prefunded" is not treated as a premium.

**NONQUALIFIED LONG-TERM CARE INSURANCE:** A long-term care insurance policy or rider that does not satisfy the requirements of section 7702B(b).

**NOTICE 88-128:** This IRS notice applies to contracts issued on or after October 21, 1988, and before January 1, 2009. Notice 88-128 provides interim rules interpreting the reasonable mortality charge requirements, and defines the sex distinct 1980 CSO tables as a safe harbor under section 7702's reasonable standard. Cited as: Notice 88-128, 1988-2 C.B. 540.

**NOTICE 99-48:** This IRS notice introduced the use of a three-tiered tax rate structure in determining the amounts due under closing agreements on failed life insurance contracts. This structure was carried forward in the 2008 revenue procedures (see Chapter 8). Cited as: Notice 99-48, 1999-2 C.B. 429.

**NOTICE 2006-95:** Published specifically to provide guidance on reasonable mortality charges after the 2001 CSO tables became the prevailing tables for tax purposes, this IRS notice technically applies to contracts issued on or after October 21, 1988. The notice provides that charges guaranteed under a contract issued on or after January 1, 2009, that do not exceed 100 percent of the 2001 CSO tables satisfy section 7702's reasonable mortality standard. It also sets out rules governing the application of its safe harbor to pre-2001 CSO contracts that undergo changes. Cited as: Notice 2006-95, 2006-2 C.B. 848.

**NOTICE 2011-68:** This IRS notice provided interim guidance and requested public comment on certain tax issues involving qualified long-term care insurance contracts and riders. Cited as: Notice 2011-68, 2011-36 I.R.B. 205.

**OFF-ANNIVERSARY:** While it is generally understood that the attained-age increment and decrement approach is the appropriate method for adjusting guideline premiums, there is little in the way of guidance as to how it should be applied to contracts, particularly when the change occurs off-anniversary. As discussed in Chapter 4, some commonly used approaches for dealing with off-anniversary adjustments include an annual method, a pro-rata method and an exact method.

**OFFSHORE CONTRACT:** This usually refers to a life insurance contract offered by a non-U.S. life insurance company, which may be a subsidiary of a U.S. company.

**OPTION 1:** The option under which the death benefit is defined as a level amount.

**OPTION 2:** The option under which the death benefit is defined as a stipulated amount plus any cash value at time of death. The use of option 1 to denote a level death benefit and option 2 to denote a level net amount at risk is used by some, but not all, life insurance companies to describe death benefit options provided under a universal life insurance contract. Options 1 and 2 are used in this text consistently with the meanings ascribed above, but may have different meanings with respect to the products offered by a specific life insurance company.

**PACKWOOD-BAUCUS COLLOQUY:** When the reasonable expense requirements were introduced in 1988, it was expected that regulations would be issued defining the terms reasonable expenses and reasonably expected to be paid. A colloquy between Senators Packwood and Baucus indicated that regulations interpreting the expense charge limitation should permit the amendment or exchange of contracts, without prejudice to pre-existing contracts (so that they are not treated as failing to meet the requirements of section 7702), if that is necessary to comply with the regulations. Cited as: 134 CONG. REC. S17,208 (1988).

**PARTIAL WITHDRAWAL:** Withdrawal of a part of the cash value of a universal life insurance contract. The death benefit is typically reduced by the amount of the withdrawal.

**PENALTY TAX:** In addition to subjecting distributions from a MEC to a LIFO rule, section 72(v)(1) imposes on such distributions a penalty tax similar to the penalty tax applicable to annuities set forth in section 72(q)(1). The penalty tax is 10 percent of the portion of the distribution includible in gross income and applies even to amounts received on a full surrender. Importantly, however, there are several exceptions to the penalty tax, e.g., distributions made on or after the date the taxpayer attains age 59 ½. *See* section 72(v)(2).

**PER DIEM BENEFITS:** In the context of qualified long-term care insurance and section 101(g) chronic illness benefits, this term refers to insurance benefits paid in a lump sum or on a periodic basis that do not reimburse specific expenses for qualified long-term care services. The tax treatment of such benefits it addressed by section 7702B(d).

**PERMANENT MORTALITY RULE:** This refers directly to the statutory requirements specified in section 7702(c)(3)(B)(i). Although this provision requires that mortality charges used in section 7702 calculations be reasonable, it does not generally define "reasonable," leaving that task to regulations. It does, however, provide that reasonable mortality cannot exceed the rates in the prevailing commissioners' standard tables at the time the contract is issued, unless regulations provide otherwise. The 1980 CSO tables were the prevailing commissioners' standard tables at the time the reasonable mortality standards were added to section 7702(c)(3)(B)(i). Therefore, under the permanent rule, absent regulations, 100 percent of the 1980 CSO tables then provided an upper bound on reasonable mortality. Today, the 2001 CSO tables are the prevailing tables.

**PLAN OF CARE:** Usually, this is a written document that identifies the diagnosis for the insured, i.e., his or her functional or cognitive impairment, the care required to address such impairment, the objectives of such care and follow-up steps such as the timeline for future evaluations. In the context of qualified long-term care insurance and section 101(g) chronic illness benefits, the plan of care must be prescribed by a licensed health care practitioner in order for services provided thereunder to be considered qualified long-term care services.

**POLICY LOAN:** A loan made by a life insurance company to a policyholder secured by the cash surrender value of the contract. The policy loan is granted based on the end-of-year cash value, less accrued policy loan interest.

**POLICY VALUE:** A term sometimes used to describe an accumulation of premiums, interest and dividends credited, less the cost of insurance, expenses and withdrawals. The premiums, less expense charges, are added to the policy value. In universal life, each month, interest is credited to the policy value, generally on the same day that cost of insurance charges are deducted. Some contracts refer to this value as the accumulation value, accumulated value or simply the cash value.

**POSTFUNDING OF QABS:** In reflecting the charges for a QAB in the guideline level premium, two approaches are possible: The QAB charges may be amortized over the term of the QAB or over that of the contract. Both the TEFRA Blue Book and the congressional committee reports on section 7702 indicate that, in determining guideline level premiums, the guideline premiums should reflect the charges over the period for which they are incurred, thus avoiding postfunding of the benefits. The notion of a bilevel guideline level premium appears to be inconsistent with section 7702(c)(4), which defines the term guideline level premium to mean "the level annual amount, payable over a period not ending before the insurance attains age 95." This inconsistency between the statute and the legislative history has resulted in the use of both methods of reflecting QABs in the guideline level premium, often depending on the capabilities of the testing system.

**PREMIUMS PAID:** The determination of the premiums paid under a life insurance contract is important both in terms of measuring compliance with sections 7702 and 7702A and of determining the taxable gain on surrender or maturity under section 72. The term "premiums paid" may have different meanings, however, depending on the context in which it is used.

**PREVAILING TABLES:** The "prevailing commissioners' standard tables" are the mortality tables required for the calculation of tax reserves under section 807(d). The prevailing tables are the most recent Commissioners' Standard Ordinary tables prescribed by the National Association of Insurance Commissioners permitted to be used for valuing the reserves of a contract under the insurance laws of at least 26 states at the time a contract is issued. Under sections 7702 and 7702A, reasonable mortality charges for a contract generally cannot exceed the mortality charges specified in the prevailing tables at the time the contract is issued. Beginning in July 2004, the 2001 CSO replaced the 1980 CSO as the prevailing table, and transition rules address when that table must be used for tax purposes.

**PRIVATE LETTER RULING (PLR):** A PLR is the IRS response to a request by a taxpayer for guidance regarding the tax consequences of a particular proposed transaction. Officially, only the addressee can rely on a letter ruling, and then only for the specific transaction the ruling discusses. *See* section 6110(k)(3). Due to a lack of published guidance, life insurance companies are forced to rely on private letter rulings in some areas. These rulings indicate what the IRS National Office thought about a certain transaction or issue at the time of their issuance.

**PRIVATE PLACEMENT:** Private placement variable life insurance, both in the onshore and offshore markets, is sold under special rules of the securities law relating to private sales.

**PROCESSING FREQUENCY:** This term refers to the time interval over which discrete policy level events are assumed to occur in the calculation of actuarial premiums.

**PROJECTION-BASED METHOD:** *See* **illustration-based projection**.

**PROPOSED MORTALITY REGULATIONS:** In 1991, the IRS issued proposed regulations to define reasonable mortality charges under section 7702. Under the proposed regulations, reasonable mortality charges were defined to be "those amounts that an insurance company actually expects to impose as consideration for assuming the risk of the insured's death (regardless of the designation used for those charges), taking into account any relevant characteristics of the insured of which the company is aware." The proposed regulations also had a 1980 CSO safe harbor for single life contracts. The proposed regulations were never finalized.

**PROPOSED REGULATIONS DEFINING CASH VALUE:** In 1992, the IRS issued proposed regulations defining the term "cash value" (a component of the term "cash surrender value") as the greater of the "maximum amount payable" under a contract (determined without regard to any surrender charge or policy loan), or the maximum amount that the policyholder could borrow under the contract, subject to stated exceptions (such as the death benefit). The proposed regulations were never finalized.

**PROSPECTIVE CALCULATION:** A successive approximation technique for determining definitional limits. One finds the premium (single or level) that will fund the test plan contract's benefits, generally endowing for the death benefit at the maturity date assumed in the test plan.

**QUALIFIED ADDITIONAL BENEFIT (QAB):** As a general rule, when a QAB is present in a life insurance policy, the actuarial limitations under section 7702 or 7702A may be increased to reflect the charges imposed for the benefit. Thus, characterization of a benefit as a QAB permits the guideline single and level premiums, net single premium and 7-pay premium for a contract to be increased, above the amounts reflecting only the contract's death and endowment benefits, by taking account of the (reasonable) charges for such a benefit. This, in turn, allows prefunding for the QAB in the contract's cash value. The QABs are listed in section 7702(f)(5)(A).

**QUALIFIED LONG-TERM CARE INSURANCE (QLTCI) CONTRACT:** A long-term care insurance contract or rider that satisfies the requirements of section 7702B(b). Such contracts generally are accorded health insurance tax treatment under the Code.

**REASONABLE ERROR:** The first standard for an error to be waivable by the IRS is that it must be reasonable. There are three broad conditions that the IRS applies in making this determination. First, the error must first be shown to be inadvertent. Second, the IRS generally takes the position that the error must not be a direct violation of a clear rule (e.g., computing a guideline single premium taking increasing death benefits into account, as prohibited by section 7702(e)(1)(A)). Third, in assessing the reasonableness of the situation, the IRS looks to the overall reasonableness of the situation in which the error arose. Thus, as a condition to the issuance of a waiver, the IRS has required that a company generally have an adequate compliance system in place. The other statutory requirement for the issuance of a waiver is that reasonable steps must be taken to correct the error which resulted in the compliance failure.

**REASONABLE EXPENSE CHARGES:** In parallel with the limitations on reasonable mortality, TAMRA amended section 7702 to provide that, for contracts entered into on or after October 21, 1988, the guideline premiums must be computed assuming any "reasonable charges (other than mortality charges) which (on the basis of the company's experience, if any, with respect to similar contacts) are reasonably expected to be actually paid."

**REASONABLE MORTALITY CHARGES:** For contracts issued on or after October 21, 1988, net single premiums, guideline premiums and 7-pay premiums are to be determined using reasonable mortality charges as defined by section 7702(c)(3)(B)(i). The reasonable mortality requirements imposed on contracts under section 7702(c)(3)(B)(i) can be viewed as having both an interim rule and a permanent rule.

**RECLOCKING:** A procedure by which incorrect system-generated guideline premiums, net single premiums or 7-pay premiums are replaced with correct values.

**RECAPTURE RULES:** The general rule for taxation of a surrender or partial withdrawal under a life insurance contract is found in section 72(e), which provides that in the case of a non-MEC, predeath distributions are taxable only to the extent that they exceed the investment in the contract. The provisions of section 7702(f)(7)(B) define a narrow set of circumstances in which the normal FIFO rules of section 72(e) for a non-MEC do not apply, and the amounts distributed are taxed on an income-first or LIFO basis. Under the section 7702(f)(7)(B)–(E) recapture rules, taxable income to the policyholder may be recognized in connection with a change in contract benefits with an associated distribution. Taxable income is to be recognized on the cash distributed, up to the gain in the contract, but only to the extent of the "recapture ceiling" defined in the statute. See **Rev. Rul. 2003-95**.

**REDUCTION-IN-BENEFITS RULE:** Section 7702A(c)(2)(A) provides that if benefits under a contract are reduced during the first seven contract years, then section 7702A is applied as if the contract had originally been issued at the reduced benefit level and the new reduced limitation is applied to the cumulative amount paid under the contract for *each* of the first seven years. A special reduction-in-benefits rule is provided under section 7702A(c)(6) for survivorship contracts.

**REV. PROC. 92-57:** Sets forth the requirements which must be satisfied in order that a modification or restructuring of a contract in the case of an insolvent insurer will not upset the grandfathered status of the old contract under sections 72, 101(f), 264, 7702 and 7702A. Under the revenue procedure, the modification or restructuring must be an integral part of the rehabilitation, conservatorship or similar state proceeding and approved by the state court, the state insurance commissioner or other responsible state official. Cited as: Rev. Proc. 92-57, 1992-2 C.B. 410.

**REV. PROC. 99-27:** This revenue procedure was superseded by Rev. Proc. 2001-42 and subsequently by Rev. Proc. 2008-39 (*see below*).

**REV. PROC. 2001-42:** This revenue procedure was superseded by Rev. Proc. 2008-39 (*see below*).

**REV. PROC. 2008-38:** This revenue procedure continues the relief provided under Alternative C of Rev. Rul. 2005-6 (relating to the required use of the reasonable expense charge rule for QABs; *see below*) for post-February 7, 2006, closing agreement requests and amplifies the corrective action that must be taken to bring failed contracts, inadvertent MECs and the system(s) on which they are administered into compliance with the applicable statutes. Cited as: Rev. Proc. 2008-38, 2008-2 C.B. 139.

**REV. PROC. 2008-39:** This revenue procedure provides a uniform closing agreement process under which an insurance company may cure inadvertent overfunding errors that cause life insurance contracts to become MECs. Cited as: Rev. Proc. 2008-39, 2008-2 C.B. 143.

**REV. PROC. 2008-40:** This revenue procedure provides a uniform closing agreement process under which an insurance company may remediate a life insurance contract that fails to comply with sections 101(f) or 7702. Cited as: Rev. Proc. 2008-40, 2008-2 C.B. 151.

**REV. PROC. 2008-41:** This revenue procedure provides a uniform closing agreement process under which an insurance company may remedy a section 817(h) diversification failure in the investments of a separate account underlying a variable contract. Cited as: Rev. Proc. 2008-41, 2008-2 C.B. 155.

**REV. PROC. 2008-42:** This revenue procedure provides an automatic procedure for obtaining a waiver of clerical-type errors under sections 101(f)(3)(H) and 7702(f)(8). Cited as: Rev. Proc. 2008-42, 2008-2 C.B. 160.

**REV. PROC. 2010-28:** This revenue procedure provides that the IRS "would not challenge" the qualification of a life insurance contract as meeting the requirements of section 7702 or "assert" that a contract is a MEC (by failing under section 7702A) if the contract satisfies the requirements of the statutes using the "Age 100 Safe Harbor Testing Methodologies" listed in the revenue procedure. Cited as: Rev. Proc. 2010-28, 2010-34 I.R.B. 270.

**REV. RUL. 91-17:** This revenue ruling details penalties that the IRS can assess against a company relating to reporting, record-keeping and withholding obligations on the income on the contract for "failed" life insurance contracts. Cited as: Rev. Rul. 91-17, 1991-1 C.B. 190.

**REV. RUL. 2003-95:** This revenue ruling, the first substantive ruling regarding the section 7702 rules ever published, describes the tax treatment of a cash distribution made in connection with a reduction in the benefits under a life insurance contract. Cited as: Rev. Rul. 2003-95, 2003-2 C.B. 358.

**REV. RUL. 2005-6:** This revenue ruling, the second and last substantive ruling published regarding the section 7702 rules, held that the reasonable expense charge rule of section 7702(c)(3)(B)(ii) applies to charges for QABs, including the family term QAB, and provided a remedy for the noncompliance due to failure to use that rule in the form of special procedures for entering into a closing agreement with the IRS. The ruling was "amplified" by Rev. Proc. 2008-38 (*see above*). Cited as: Rev. Rul. 2005-6, 2005-1 C.B. 471.

**ROLLOVER RULE:** Unlike a newly issued contract, the computed 7-pay premium for a materially changed contract must be adjusted to take into account the existing cash surrender value at the time of the material change. To do this, multiply the 7-pay premium by *(1 – CSV/NSP)*.

**SECTION 72(e):** Governs the income tax treatment of a predeath distribution from a life insurance contract.

**SECTION 101(a):** Proceeds from a life insurance contract payable on the death of the insured are generally excluded from the gross income of the beneficiary.

**SECTION 101(f):** Provided for the first time a statutory definition of life insurance for federal income tax purposes, albeit for a limited class of contracts referred to as flexible premium life insurance contracts issued before January 1, 1985.

**SECTION 101(g):** Addresses the tax treatment of terminal illness and chronic illness benefits, usually in the form of accelerated death benefits, paid under a life insurance contract, and also addresses the treatment of certain viatical settlements. There is an overlap between this Code provision and section 7702B, in that both address chronic illness accelerated death benefits.

**SECTION 1035:** Allows the tax-free exchange of one life insurance contract for another life insurance contract, for an annuity contract, or for a qualified long-term care insurance contract. The Senate Finance Committee Report for DEFRA provides that life insurance "contracts issued in exchange for existing contracts after December 31, 1984 are to be considered new contracts issued after that date." While an exchange of contracts is treated as a new issue date under section 7702A, a contract's status as a MEC cannot be eliminated by an exchange of contracts.

**SECTION 7702:** Contains actuarial requirements that a life insurance contract must meet to qualify as life insurance under the Code. Section 7702 is generally effective for contracts issued after December 31, 1984. Section 7702 restricts favorable tax treatment to life insurance contracts that provide at least a certain amount of pure insurance protection in relation to the cash value.

**SECTION 7702A:** Defines a class of rapidly funded life insurance contracts to be MECs. These plans are considered life insurance under section 7702 but are subject to the distribution rules applicable to deferred annuities by virtue of section 72(e)(10). The section 7702A rules operate within the section 7702 limits.

**SECTION 7702B:** Defines the term "qualified long-term care insurance contract" and prescribes the tax treatment of such contracts. This provision effectively provides a safe harbor, generally according accident and health insurance tax treatment for long-term care insurance policies that satisfy this definition.

**SELF-HELP:** Correction of a possible section 7702 or 7702A error without IRS involvement, e.g., by terminating a contract and issuing an entirely new contract.

**7-PAY PREMIUM:** The net level premium required to pay for the future death benefits and qualified additional benefits under the contract with seven level annual payments.

**7-PAY TEST:** A contract fails to meet the 7-pay test if the accumulated amount paid under the contract at any time during the first seven contract years exceeds the amount that would have been paid on or before that time if the contract provided for paid-up future benefits after the payment of seven level annual premiums. The amount paid is generally defined as premiums paid less distributions received (not including amounts included in gross income).

**SHORT-TERM INTEREST GUARANTEES:** The DEFRA Blue Book noted at page 649 that *de minimis* guarantees in excess of the otherwise assumed floor rates may sometimes be disregarded. Generally, short-term guarantees (extending no more than one year) will be considered *de minimis* in the calculation of the guideline level premium but not in the calculation of the guideline single premium or the net single premium.

**SPECIFIED AMOUNT:** The death benefit for option 1 or traditional contracts, and the fixed risk amount in the case of option 2, which is the starting point in computing net premiums.

**STACKING RULES:** The ordering rules for determining whether a distribution is treated on an income out first (LIFO) or investment out first (FIFO) basis. See **FIFO taxation** and **LIFO taxation**.

**STANDARD NONFORFEITURE LAW FOR LIFE INSURANCE:** State nonforfeiture laws regulate the minimum cash surrender values that may be provided under a life insurance contract. Minimum cash value requirements are computed based on the expected future benefits under the contract assuming statutory maximum interest rates and mortality assumptions.

**SUBSTANDARD MORTALITY:** The interim rule of section 5011(c)(2) of TAMRA alludes to the need for reasonable mortality to take "into account any relevant characteristic of the insured of which the company is aware." Under the multiplicative method, the mortality assumption is set equal to the substandard rating applied to the reasonable mortality applicable to a standard contract. Under the additive approach, mortality for substandard contracts would take into account current substandard mortality charges that are increased over those which would be taken into account for a standard risk contract. A third approach, the current substandard method, allows the use of mortality charges that exceed reasonable mortality charges applicable to an otherwise similar standard risk contract, but only to the extent the insurance company actually expects to impose those higher charges.

**SURVIVORSHIP CONTRACT:** Unlike first-to-die contracts, which provide a death benefit on the first death, survivorship or last-to-die contracts provide a death benefit on the last death among the insureds. Survivorship contracts may be traditional, where the actuarial values are based on the three-status method and cash values are adjusted on the first death, or frasierised, where the actuarial values are based on the one-status method and cash values are not adjusted on the first death. See **Frasier method**.

**TAMRA:** Technical and Miscellaneous Revenue Act of 1988; cited as: Pub. L. No. 100-647. Section 7702A was enacted as part of TAMRA. In addition, TAMRA imposed restrictions on the mortality and expense charge assumptions used in setting the definitional limitations under section 7702.

**TAX PREFERENCE:** Provisions of the federal tax laws that allow a special exclusion, exemption or deduction from gross income or which provide a special credit, a preferential rate of tax or a deferral of tax liability.

**TAX REFORM ACT OF 1986:** Cited as Pub. L. No. 99-514. This act was notable in that one element of the Reagan Administration's proposal for a broader tax base was to tax the inside buildup of life insurance contracts. The 1986 act closed down many tax-favored investments and tax shelters, increasing the attractiveness of life insurance. Thus, in the 1986 act, life insurance benefited indirectly from changes affecting other financial instruments.

**TEFRA:** Tax Equity and Fiscal Responsibility Act of 1982; cited as: Pub. L. No. 97-248 (1982). Congress enacted section 101(f) as a part of TEFRA.

**TERM COVERAGE ON THE INSURED:** A rider to a permanent life insurance contract providing term life insurance coverage on the primary insured (in addition to the underlying contract's death benefit). Term coverage on the insured generally is treated as death benefit under both sections 7702 and 7702A if it is scheduled to continue to age 95.

**TERMINAL ILLNESS:** An individual is treated as a "terminally ill individual," within the meaning of section 101(g)(4)(A), if he or she has been certified by a physician, within the meaning of section 1861(r)(1) of the Social Security Act, as having an illness or physical condition which can reasonably be expected to result in death in 24 months or less after the date of the certification.

**TERMINATION DIVIDEND:** A dividend payable on the termination of a life insurance contract; reasonable termination dividends may be excluded from the contract's cash surrender value under section 7702. The legislative history for section 7702 observes that whether a termination dividend is reasonable in amount is to be determined with reference to the historical practice of the industry, giving as an example the New York insurance law's maximum of $35 per $1,000 of death benefit.

**TERMS OF THE CONTRACT:** Under both the cash value test of section 101(f) and the cash value accumulation test of section 7702, compliance must be guaranteed "by the terms of the contract." As a result, the CVAT is a prospective test that must be met at all times, as enforced by the terms of the contract. One should be able to read the contract at issue and know whether the requirement is satisfied (provided the contract is administered in accordance with its terms).

**TEST PLAN:** Conceptually, the actuarial limitations under sections 7702 and 7702A create a test or model plan that is used to determine the guideline premiums, net single premiums and 7-pay premiums. The test plan provides both premium and cash value limitations against which the actual plan is measured.

**TOLL CHARGE:** An informal term referring to the amount payable to the IRS under a closing agreement to remedy a failed life insurance contract or an inadvertent MEC or to obtain other relief.

**VARIABLE LIFE RULE:** For variable life plans, as defined under section 817, a special rule is provided in section 7702(f)(9). Under the rule, the determination of whether a variable life insurance contract falls within the requirements of section 7702(a) must be made whenever the death benefit changes but not less frequently than once during each 12-month period.

**WAIVER RULING:** The Congress, dating from the enactment of section 101(f)(3)(H), provided an extraordinary power to the IRS to waive noncompliance with the statute. A section 7702(f)(8) waiver of noncompliance may be granted by the National Office of the IRS where the admitted problem arises from reasonable error and where reasonable steps are being taken to correct it.

# APPENDIX A
## IRC SECTION 7702

## SECTION 7702. LIFE INSURANCE CONTRACT DEFINED

(a) General rule.—For purposes of this title, the term "life insurance contract" means any contract which is a life insurance contract under the applicable law, but only if such contract—

(1) meets the cash value accumulation test of subsection (b), or

(2)

(A) meets the guideline premium requirements of subsection (c), and

(B) falls within the cash value corridor of subsection (d).

(b) Cash value accumulation test for subsection (a)(1).—

(1) In general.—A contract meets the cash value accumulation test of this subsection if, by the terms of the contract, the cash surrender value of such contract may not at any time exceed the net single premium which would have to be paid at such time to fund future benefits under the contract.

(2) Rules for applying paragraph (1).—Determinations under paragraph (1) shall be made—

(A) on the basis of interest at the greater of an annual effective rate of 4 percent or the rate or rates guaranteed on issuance of the contract,

(B) on the basis of the rules of subparagraph (B)(i) (and, in the case of qualified additional benefits, subparagraph (B)(ii)) of subsection (c)(3), and

(C) by taking into account under subparagraphs (A) and (D) of subsection (e)(1) only current and future death benefits and qualified additional benefits.

(c) Guideline premium requirements.—For purposes of this section—

(1) In general.—A contract meets the guideline premium requirements of this subsection if the sum of the premiums paid under such contract does not at any time exceed the guideline premium limitation as of such time.

(2) Guideline premium limitation.—The term "guideline premium limitation" means, as of any date, the greater of—

(A) the guideline single premium, or

(B) the sum of the guideline level premiums to such date.

(3) Guideline single premium.—

(A) In general.—The term "guideline single premium'" means the premium at issue with respect to future benefits under the contract.

(B) Basis on which determination is made.—The determination under subparagraph (A) shall be based on—

(i) reasonable mortality charges which meet the requirements (if any) prescribed in regulations and which (except as provided in regulations) do not exceed the mortality charges specified in the prevailing commissioners' standard tables (as defined in section 807(d)(5)) as of the time the contract is issued,

(ii) any reasonable charges (other than mortality charges) which (on the basis of the company's experience, if any, with respect to similar contracts) are reasonably expected to be actually paid, and

(iii) interest at the greater of an annual effective rate of 6 percent or the rate or rates guaranteed on issuance of the contract.

(C) When determination made.—Except as provided in subsection (f)(7), the determination under subparagraph (A) shall be made as of the time the contract is issued.

(D) Special rules for subparagraph (B)(ii).—

(i) Charges not specified in the contract.—If any charge is not specified in the contract, the amount taken into account under subparagraph (B)(ii) for such charge shall be zero.

(ii) New companies, etc.—If any company does not have adequate experience for purposes of the determination under subparagraph (B)(ii), to the extent provided in regulations, such determination shall be made on the basis of the industry-wide experience.

(4) Guideline level premium.—The term "guideline level premium" means the level annual amount, payable over a period not ending before the insured attains age 95, computed on the same basis as the guideline single premium, except that paragraph (3)(B)(iii) shall be applied by substituting "4 percent" for "6 percent".

(d) Cash value corridor for purposes of subsection (a)(2)(B).—For purposes of this section—

(1) In general.—A contract falls within the cash value corridor of this subsection if the death benefit under the contract at any time is not less than the applicable percentage of the cash surrender value.

(2) Applicable percentage.—

| In the case of an insured with an attained age as of the beginning of the contract year of: | | The applicable percentage shall decrease by a ratable portion for each full year: | |
|---|---|---|---|
| More than: | But not more than: | From: | To: |
| 0 | 40 | 250 | 250 |
| 40 | 45 | 250 | 215 |
| 45 | 50 | 215 | 185 |
| 50 | 55 | 185 | 150 |
| 55 | 60 | 150 | 130 |
| 60 | 65 | 130 | 120 |
| 65 | 70 | 120 | 115 |
| 70 | 75 | 115 | 105 |
| 75 | 90 | 105 | 105 |
| 90 | 95 | 105 | 100 |

(e) Computational rules.—

(1) In general.—For purposes of this section (other than subsection (d)) -

(A) the death benefit (and any qualified additional benefit) shall be deemed not to increase,

(B) the maturity date, including the date on which any benefit described in subparagraph (C) is payable, shall be deemed to be no earlier than the day on which the insured attains age 95, and no later than the day on which the insured attains age 100,

(C) the death benefits shall be deemed to be provided until the maturity date determined by taking into account subparagraph (B), and

(D) the amount of any endowment benefit (or sum of endowment benefits, including any cash surrender value on the maturity date determined by taking into account subparagraph (B)) shall be deemed not to exceed the least amount payable as a death benefit at any time under the contract.

(2) LIMITED INCREASES IN DEATH BENEFIT PERMITTED.—Notwithstanding paragraph (1)(A) -

    (A) for purposes of computing the guideline level premium, an increase in the death benefit which is provided in the contract may be taken into account but only to the extent necessary to prevent a decrease in the excess of the death benefit over the cash surrender value of the contract,

    (B) for purposes of the cash value accumulation test, the increase described in subparagraph (A) may be taken into account if the contract will meet such test at all times assuming that the net level reserve (determined as if level annual premiums were paid for the contract over a period not ending before the insured attains age 95) is substituted for the net single premium, and

    (C) for purposes of the cash value accumulation test, the death benefit increases may be taken into account if the contract—

        (i) has an initial death benefit of $5,000 or less and a maximum death benefit of $25,000 or less,

        (ii) provides for a fixed predetermined annual increase not to exceed 10 percent of the initial death benefit or 8 percent of the death benefit at the end of the preceding year, and

        (iii) was purchased to cover payment of burial expenses, or in connection with prearranged funeral expenses.

For purposes of subparagraph (C), the initial death benefit of a contract shall be determined by treating all contracts issued to the same contract owner as 1 contract.

(f) OTHER DEFINITIONS AND SPECIAL RULES.—For purposes of this section -

(1) PREMIUMS PAID.—

    (A) IN GENERAL.—The term "premiums paid" means the premiums paid under the contract less amounts (other than amounts includible in gross income) to which section 72(e) applies and less any excess premiums with respect to which there is a distribution described in subparagraph (B) or (E) of paragraph (7) and any other amounts received with respect to the contract which are specified in regulations.

    (B) TREATMENT OF CERTAIN PREMIUMS RETURNED TO POLICYHOLDER.—If, in order to comply with the requirements of subsection (a)(2)(A), any portion of any premium paid during any contract year is returned by the insurance company (with interest) within 60 days after the end of a contract year, the amount so returned (excluding interest) shall be deemed to reduce the sum of the premiums paid under the contract during such year.

    (C) INTEREST RETURNED INCLUDIBLE IN GROSS INCOME.—Notwithstanding the provisions of section 72(e), the amount of any interest returned as provided in subparagraph (B) shall be includible in the gross income of the recipient.

(2) CASH VALUES.—

    (A) CASH SURRENDER VALUE.—The cash surrender value of any contract shall be its cash value determined without regard to any surrender charge, policy loan, or reasonable termination dividends.

    (B) NET SURRENDER VALUE.—The net surrender value of any contract shall be determined with regard to surrender charges but without regard to any policy loan.

(3) DEATH BENEFIT.—The term "death benefit" means the amount payable by reason of the death of the insured (determined without regard to any qualified additional benefits).

(4) FUTURE BENEFITS.—The term "future benefits" means death benefits and endowment benefits.

(5) QUALIFIED ADDITIONAL BENEFITS.—

(A) IN GENERAL.—The term "qualified additional benefits" means any -

   (i) guaranteed insurability,

   (ii) accidental death or disability benefit,

   (iii) family term coverage,

   (iv) disability waiver benefit, or

   (v) other benefit prescribed under regulations.

(B) TREATMENT OF QUALIFIED ADDITIONAL BENEFITS.—For purposes of this section, qualified additional benefits shall not be treated as future benefits under the contract, but the charges for such benefits shall be treated as future benefits.

(C) TREATMENT OF OTHER ADDITIONAL BENEFITS.—In the case of any additional benefit which is not a qualified additional benefit –

   (i) such benefit shall not be treated as a future benefit, and

   (ii) any charge for such benefit which is not prefunded shall not be treated as a premium.

(6) PREMIUM PAYMENTS NOT DISQUALIFYING CONTRACT.—The payment of a premium which would result in the sum of the premiums paid exceeding the guideline premium limitation shall be disregarded for purposes of subsection (a)(2) if the amount of such premium does not exceed the amount necessary to prevent the termination of the contract on or before the end of the contract year (but only if the contract will have no cash surrender value at the end of such extension period).

(7) ADJUSTMENTS.—

(A) IN GENERAL.—If there is a change in the benefits under (or in other terms of) the contract which was not reflected in any previous determination or adjustment made under this section, there shall be proper adjustments in future determinations made under this section.

(B) RULE FOR CERTAIN CHANGES DURING FIRST 15 YEARS.—If –

   (i) a change described in subparagraph (A) reduces benefits under the contract,

   (ii) the change occurs during the 15-year period beginning on the issue date of the contract, and

   (iii) a cash distribution is made to the policyholder as a result of such change, section 72 (other than subsection (e)(5) thereof) shall apply to such cash distribution to the extent it does not exceed the recapture ceiling determined under subparagraph (C) or (D) (whichever applies).

(C) RECAPTURE CEILING WHERE CHANGE OCCURS DURING FIRST 5 YEARS.—If the change referred to in subparagraph (B)(ii) occurs during the 5-year period beginning on the issue date of the contract, the recapture ceiling is -

   (i) in the case of a contract to which subsection (a)(1) applies, the excess of -

      (I) the cash surrender value of the contract, immediately before the reduction, over

      (II) the net single premium (determined under subsection (b)), immediately after the reduction, or

   (ii) in the case of a contract to which subsection (a)(2) applies, the greater of -

      (I) the excess of the aggregate premiums paid under the contract, immediately before the reduction, over the guideline premium limitation for the contract (determined under subsection (c)(2), taking into account the adjustment described in subparagraph (A)), or

(II) the excess of the cash surrender value of the contract, immediately before the reduction, over the cash value corridor of subsection (d) (determined immediately after the reduction).

(D) RECAPTURE CEILING WHERE CHANGE OCCURS AFTER 5TH YEAR AND BEFORE 16TH YEAR.—If the change referred to in subparagraph (B) occurs after the 5-year period referred to under subparagraph (C), the recapture ceiling is the excess of the cash surrender value of the contract, immediately before the reduction, over the cash value corridor of subsection (d) (determined immediately after the reduction and whether or not subsection (d) applies to the contract).

(E) TREATMENT OF CERTAIN DISTRIBUTIONS MADE IN ANTICIPATION OF BENEFIT REDUCTIONS.—Under regulations prescribed by the Secretary, subparagraph (B) shall apply also to any distribution made in anticipation of a reduction in benefits under the contract. For purposes of the preceding sentence, appropriate adjustments shall be made in the provisions of subparagraphs (C) and (D); and any distribution which reduces the cash surrender value of a contract and which is made within 2 years before a reduction in benefits under the contract shall be treated as made in anticipation of such reduction.

(8) CORRECTION OF ERRORS.—If the taxpayer establishes to the satisfaction of the Secretary that –

(A) the requirements described in subsection (a) for any contract year were not satisfied due to reasonable error, and

(B) reasonable steps are being taken to remedy the error,

the Secretary may waive the failure to satisfy such requirements.

(9) SPECIAL RULE FOR VARIABLE LIFE INSURANCE CONTRACTS.—In the case of any contract which is a variable contract (as defined in section 817), the determination of whether such contract meets the requirements of subsection (a) shall be made whenever the death benefits under such contract change but not less frequently than once during each 12-month period.

(g) TREATMENT OF CONTRACTS WHICH DO NOT MEET SUBSECTION (a) TEST.—

(1) INCOME INCLUSION.—

(A) IN GENERAL.—If at any time any contract which is a life insurance contract under the applicable law does not meet the definition of life insurance contract under subsection (a), the income on the contract for any taxable year of the policyholder shall be treated as ordinary income received or accrued by the policyholder during such year.

(B) INCOME ON THE CONTRACT.—For purposes of this paragraph, the term "income on the contract" means, with respect to any taxable year of the policyholder, the excess of -

(i) the sum of -

(I) the increase in the net surrender value of the contract during the taxable year, and

(II) the cost of life insurance protection provided under the contract during the taxable year, over

(ii) the premiums paid (as defined in subsection (f)(1)) under the contract during the taxable year.

(C) CONTRACTS WHICH CEASE TO MEET DEFINITION.—If, during any taxable year of the policyholder, a contract which is a life insurance contract under the applicable law ceases to meet the definition of life insurance contract under subsection (a), the income on the contract for all prior taxable years shall be treated as received or accrued during the taxable year in which such cessation occurs.

(D) Cost of life insurance protection.—For purposes of this paragraph, the cost of life insurance protection provided under the contract shall be the lesser of -

   (i) the cost of individual insurance on the life of the insured as determined on the basis of uniform premiums (computed on the basis of 5-year age brackets) prescribed by the Secretary by regulations, or

   (ii) the mortality charge (if any) stated in the contract.

(2) Treatment of amount paid on death of insured.—If any contract which is a life insurance contract under the applicable law does not meet the definition of life insurance contract under subsection (a), the excess of the amount paid by the reason of the death of the insured over the net surrender value of the contract shall be deemed to be paid under a life insurance contract for purposes of section 101 and subtitle B.

(3) Contract continues to be treated as insurance contract.—If any contract which is a life insurance contract under the applicable law does not meet the definition of life insurance contract under subsection (a), such contract shall, notwithstanding such failure, be treated as an insurance contract for purposes of this title.

(h) Endowment contracts receive same treatment.—

(1) In general.—References in subsections (a) and (g) to a life insurance contract shall be treated as including references to a contract which is an endowment contract under the applicable law.

(2) Definition of endowment contract.—For purposes of this title (other than paragraph (1)), the term "endowment contract" means a contract which is an endowment contract under the applicable law and which meets the requirements of subsection (a).

(i) Transitional rule for certain 20-pay contracts.—

(1) In general.—In the case of a qualified 20-pay contract, this section shall be applied by substituting "3 percent" for "4 percent" in subsection (b)(2).

(2) Qualified 20-pay contract.—For purposes of paragraph (1), the term "qualified 20-pay contract" means any contract which -

   (A) requires at least 20 nondecreasing annual premium payments, and

   (B) is issued pursuant to an existing plan of insurance.

(3) Existing plan of insurance.—For purposes of this subsection, the term "existing plan of insurance" means, with respect to any contract, any plan of insurance which was filed by the company issuing such contract in 1 or more States before September 28, 1983, and is on file in the appropriate State for such contract.

(j) Certain church self-funded death benefit plans treated as life insurance.—

(1) In general.—In determining whether any plan or arrangement described in paragraph (2) is a life insurance contract, the requirement of subsection (a) that the contract be a life insurance contract under applicable law shall not apply.

(2) Description.—For purposes of this subsection, a plan or arrangement is described in this paragraph if –

   (A) such plan or arrangement provides for the payment of benefits by reason of the death of the individuals covered under such plan or arrangement, and

   (B) such plan or arrangement is provided by a church for the benefit of its employees and their beneficiaries, directly or through an organization described in section 414(e)(3)(A) or an organization described in section 414(e)(3)(B)(ii).

(3) DEFINITIONS.—For purposes of this subsection –

(A) CHURCH.—The term "church" means a church or a convention or association of churches.

(B) EMPLOYEE.—The term "employee" includes an employee described in section 414(e)(3)(B).

(k) REGULATIONS.—The Secretary shall prescribe such regulations as may be necessary or appropriate to carry out the purposes of this section.

## SOURCE

(Added Pub. L. No. 98-369, div. A, title II, Sec. 221(a), July 18, 1984, 98 Stat. 767; amended Pub. L. No. 99-514, title XVIII, Sec. 1825(a)-(c), Oct. 22, 1986, 100 Stat. 2846-2848; Pub. L. No. 100-647, title V, Sec. 5011(a), (b), title VI, Sec. 6078(a), Nov. 10, 1988, 102 Stat. 3660, 3661, 3709.)

## AMENDMENTS

**1988** - Subsec. (c)(3)(B)(i), (ii). Pub. L. No. 100-647, Sec. 5011(a), added cls. (i) and (ii) and struck out former cls. (i) and (ii) which read as follows:

> (i) the mortality charges specified in the contract (or, if none is specified, the mortality charges used in determining the statutory reserves for such contract),
>
> (ii) any charges (not taken into account under clause (i)) specified in the contract (the amount of any charge not so specified shall be treated as zero), and.

Subsec. (c)(3)(D). Pub. L. No. 100-647, Sec. 5011(b), added subpar. (D).

Subsecs. (j), (k). Pub. L. No. 100-647, Sec. 6078(a), added subsec. (j) and redesignated former subsec. (j) as (k).

**1986** - Subsec. (b)(2)(C). Pub. L. No. 99-514, Sec. 1825(a)(2), substituted "subparagraphs (A) and (D)" for "subparagraphs (A) and (C)".

Subsec. (e)(1). Pub. L. No. 99-514, Sec. 1825(a)(3), inserted "(other than subsection (d))" after "section".

Subsec. (e)(1)(B). Pub. L. No. 99-514, Sec. 1825(a)(1)(A), substituted "shall be deemed to be no earlier than" for "shall be no earlier than".

Subsec. (e)(1)(C). Pub. L. No. 99-514, Sec. 1821(a)(1)(C), added subpar. (C). Former subpar. (C) redesignated (D).

Subsec. (e)(1)(D). Pub. L. No. 99-514, Sec. 1821(a)(1)(C), (D), redesignated subpar. (C) as (D) and substituted "the maturity date determined by taking into account subparagraph (B)" for "the maturity date described in subparagraph (B)".

Subsec. (e)(2)(C). Pub. L. No. 99-514, Sec. 1825(a)(4), added subpar. (C).

Subsec. (f)(1)(A). Pub. L. No. 99-514, Sec. 1825(b)(2), substituted "less any excess premiums with respect to which there is a distribution described in subparagraph (B) or (E) of paragraph (7) and any other amounts received" for "less any other amounts received".

Subsec. (f)(7). Pub. L. No. 99-514, Sec. 1825(b)(1), amended par. (7) generally. Prior to amendment, par. (7)(A), in general, read as follows: "In the event of a change in the future benefits or any qualified additional benefit (or in any other terms) under the contract which was not reflected in any previous determination made under this section, under regulations prescribed by the Secretary, there shall be proper adjustments in future determinations made under this section.", and par. (7)(B), certain changes treated as exchange, read as follows: "In the case of any change which reduces the future benefits under the contract, such change shall be treated as an exchange of the contract for another contract."

Subsec. (g)(1)(B)(ii). Pub. L. No. 99-514, Sec. 1825(c), amended cl. (ii) generally. Prior to amendment, cl. (ii) read as follows "the amount of premiums paid under the contract during the taxable year reduced by any policyholder dividends received during such taxable year."

**EFFECTIVE DATE OF 1988 AMENDMENT**

Section 5011(d) of Pub. L. No. 100-647 provided that: "The amendments made by this section (amending this section) shall apply to contracts entered into on or after October 21, 1988."

Section 6078(b) of Pub. L. No. 100-647 provided that: "The amendment made by subsection (a) (amending this section) shall take effect as if included in the amendment made by section 221(a) of the Tax Reform Act of 1984 (Pub. L. No. 98-369, which enacted this section)."

**EFFECTIVE DATE OF 1986 AMENDMENT**

Section 1825(a)(4) of Pub. L. No. 99-514, as amended by Pub. L. No. 100-647, title I, Sec. 1018(j), Nov. 10, 1988, 102 Stat. 3583, provided that the amendment made by that section is effective with respect to contracts entered into after Oct. 22, 1986.

Amendment by section 1825(a)(1)-(3), (b), (c) of Pub. L. No. 99-514 effective, except as otherwise provided, as if included in the provisions of the Tax Reform Act of 1984, Pub. L. 98-369, div. A, to which such amendment relates, see section 1881 of Pub. L. No. 99-514, set out as a note under section 48 of this title.

**EFFECTIVE DATE**

Section 221(d) of Pub. L. No. 98-369, as amended by Pub. L. No. 99-514,

Sec. 2, title XVIII, Sec. 1825(e), 1899A(69), Oct. 22, 1986, 100 Stat. 2095, 2848, 2962, provided that:

(1) IN GENERAL.—Except as otherwise provided in this subsection, the amendments made by this section (enacting this section and amending section 101 of this title and provisions set out as a note under section 101 of this title) shall apply to contracts issued after December 31, 1984, in taxable years ending after such date.

(2) SPECIAL RULE FOR CERTAIN CONTRACTS ISSUED AFTER JUNE 30 1984.—

(A) GENERAL RULE.—Except as otherwise provided in this paragraph, the amendments made by this section shall apply also to any contract issued after June 30, 1984, which provides an increasing death benefit and has premium funding more rapid than 10-year level premium payments.

(B) EXCEPTION FOR CERTAIN CONTRACTS.—Subparagraph (A) shall not apply to any contract if--

(i) such contract (whether or not a flexible premium contract) would meet the requirements of section 101(f) of the Internal Revenue Code of 1986 (formerly I.R.C. 1954),

(ii) such contract is not a flexible premium life insurance contract (within the meaning of section 101(f) of such Code) and would meet the requirements of section 7702 of such Code determined by—

(I) substituting '3 percent' for '4 percent' in section 7702(b)(2) of such Code, and

(II) treating subparagraph (B) of section 7702(e)(1) of such Code as if it read as follows: "the maturity date shall be the latest maturity date permitted under the contract, but not less than 20 years after the date of issue or (if earlier) age 95, or

(iii) under such contract -

(I) the premiums (including any policy fees) will be adjusted from time-to-time to reflect the level amount necessary (but not less than zero) at the time of such adjustment to provide a level death benefit assuming interest crediting and an annual effective interest rate of not less than 3 percent, or

(II) at the option of the insured, in lieu of an adjustment under subclause (I) there will be a comparable adjustment in the amount of the death benefit.

(C) CERTAIN CONTRACTS ISSUED BEFORE OCTOBER 1, 1984.—

(i) IN GENERAL.—Subparagraph (A) shall be applied by substituting 'September 30, 1984' for 'June 30, 1984' in the case of a contract -

(I) which would meet the requirements of section 7702 of such Code if '3 percent' were substituted for '4 percent' in section 7702(b)(2) of such Code, and the rate or rates guaranteed on issuance of the contract were determined without regard to any mortality charges and any initial excess interest guarantees, and

(II) the cash surrender value of which does not at any time exceed the net single premium which would have to be paid at such time to fund future benefits under the contract.

(ii) DEFINITIONS.—For purposes of clause (i)—

(I) IN GENERAL.—Except as provided in subclause (II), terms used in clause (i) shall have the same meanings as when used in section 7702 of such Code.

(II) NET SINGLE PREMIUM.—The term 'net single premium' shall be determined by substituting '3 percent' for '4 percent' in section 7702(b)(2) of such Code, by using the 1958 standard ordinary mortality and morbidity tables of the National Association of Insurance Commissioners, and by assuming a level death benefit.

(3) TRANSITIONAL RULE FOR CERTAIN EXISTING PLANS OF INSURANCE.—A plan of insurance on file in 1 or more States before September 28, 1983, shall be treated for purposes of section 7702(i)(3) of such Code as a plan of insurance on file in 1 or more States before September 28, 1983, without regard to whether such plan of insurance is modified after September 28, 1983, to permit the crediting of excess interest or similar amounts annually and not monthly under contracts issued pursuant to such plan of insurance.

(4) EXTENSION OF FLEXIBLE PREMIUM CONTRACT PROVISIONS.—The amendments made by subsection (b) (amending section 101 of this title and provisions set out as a note under section 101 of this title) shall take effect on January 1, 1984.

(5) SPECIAL RULE FOR MASTER CONTRACT.—For purposes of this subsection, in the case of a master contract, the date taken into account with respect to any insured shall be the first date on which such insured is covered under such contract."

## INTERIM RULES; REGULATIONS; STANDARDS BEFORE REGULATIONS TAKE EFFECT

Section 5011(c) of Pub. L. No. 100-647 provided that:

(1) REGULATIONS.—Not later than January 1, 1990, the Secretary of the Treasury (or his delegate) shall issue regulations under section 7702(c)(3)(B)(i) of the 1986 Code (as amended by subsection (a)).

(2) STANDARDS BEFORE REGULATIONS TAKE EFFECT.—In the case of any contract to which the amendments made by this section (amending this section) apply and which is issued before the effective date of the regulations required under paragraph (1), mortality charges which do not differ materially from the charges actually expected to be imposed by the company (taking into account any relevant characteristic of the insured of which the company is aware) shall be treated as meeting the requirements of clause (i) of section 7702(c)(3)(B) of the 1986 Code (as amended by subsection (a)).

**TREATMENT OF FLEXIBLE PREMIUM CONTRACTS ISSUED DURING 1984 WHICH MEET NEW REQUIREMENTS**

Section 221(b)(3) of Pub. L. No. 98-369, as added by Pub. L. No. 99-514, title XVIII, Sec. 1825(d), Oct. 22, 1986, 100 Stat. 2848, provided that: "Any flexible premium contract issued during 1984 which meets the requirements of section 7702 of the Internal Revenue Code of 1954 (now 1986) (as added by this section) shall be treated as meeting the requirements of section 101(f) of such Code."

# APPENDIX B
## IRC SECTION 7702A

## SECTION 7702A. MODIFIED ENDOWMENT CONTRACT DEFINED

(a) GENERAL RULE.—For purposes of section 72, the term "modified endowment contract" means any contract meeting the requirements of section 7702 -

  (1) which -

    (A) is entered into on or after June 21, 1988, and

    (B) fails to meet the 7-pay test of subsection (b), or

  (2) which is received in exchange for a contract described in paragraph (1) or this paragraph.

(b) 7-PAY TEST.—For purposes of subsection (a), a contract fails to meet the 7-pay test of this subsection if the accumulated amount paid under the contract at any time during the 1st 7 contract years exceeds the sum of the net level premiums which would have been paid on or before such time if the contract provided for paid-up future benefits after the payment of 7 level annual premiums.

(c) COMPUTATIONAL RULES.—

  (1) IN GENERAL.—Except as provided in this subsection, the determination under subsection (b) of the 7 level annual premiums shall be made -

    (A) as of the time the contract is issued, and

    (B) by applying the rules of section 7702(b)(2) and of section 7702(e) (other than paragraph (2)(C) thereof), except that the death benefit provided for the 1st contract year shall be deemed to be provided until the maturity date without regard to any scheduled reduction after the 1st 7 contract years.

  (2) REDUCTION IN BENEFITS DURING 1ST 7 YEARS.—

    (A) IN GENERAL.—If there is a reduction in benefits under the contract within the 1st 7 contract years, this section shall be applied as if the contract had originally been issued at the reduced benefit level.

    (B) REDUCTIONS ATTRIBUTABLE TO NONPAYMENT OF PREMIUMS.—Any reduction in benefits attributable to the nonpayment of premiums due under the contract shall not be taken into account under subparagraph (A) if the benefits are reinstated within 90 days after the reduction in such benefits.

  (3) TREATMENT OF MATERIAL CHANGES.—

    (A) IN GENERAL.—If there is a material change in the benefits under (or in other terms of) the contract which was not reflected in any previous determination under this section, for purposes of this section –

      (i) such contract shall be treated as a new contract entered into on the day on which such material change takes effect, and

      (ii) appropriate adjustments shall be made in determining whether such contract meets the 7-pay test of subsection (b) to take into account the cash surrender value under the contract.

    (B) TREATMENT OF CERTAIN BENEFIT INCREASES.—For purposes of subparagraph (A), the term "material change" includes any increase in the death benefit under the contract or any increase in, or addition of, a qualified additional benefit under the contract. Such term shall not include –

      (i) any increase which is attributable to the payment of premiums necessary to fund the lowest level of the death benefit and qualified additional benefits payable in the 1st 7 contract years (determined after taking into account death benefit increases described in subparagraph (A) or (B) of section 7702(e)(2)) or to crediting of interest or other earnings (including policyholder dividends) in respect of such premiums, and

(ii) to the extent provided in regulations, any cost-of-living increase based on an established broad-based index if such increase is funded ratably over the remaining period during which premiums are required to be paid under the contract.

(4) SPECIAL RULE FOR CONTRACTS WITH DEATH BENEFITS OF $10,000 OR LESS.—In the case of a contract –

(A) which provides an initial death benefit of $10,000 or less, and

(B) which requires at least 7 nondecreasing annual premium payments,

each of the 7 level annual premiums determined under subsection (b) (without regard to this paragraph) shall be increased by $75. For purposes of this paragraph, the contract involved and all contracts previously issued to the same policyholder by the same company shall be treated as one contract.

(5) REGULATORY AUTHORITY FOR CERTAIN COLLECTION EXPENSES.—The Secretary may by regulations prescribe rules for taking into account expenses solely attributable to the collection of premiums paid more frequently than annually.

(6) TREATMENT OF CERTAIN CONTRACTS WITH MORE THAN ONE INSURED.—If -

(A) a contract provides a death benefit which is payable only upon the death of 1 insured following (or occurring simultaneously with) the death of another insured, and

(B) there is a reduction in such death benefit below the lowest level of such death benefit provided under the contract during the 1st 7 contract years, this section shall be applied as if the contract had originally been issued at the reduced benefit level.

(d) DISTRIBUTIONS AFFECTED.—If a contract fails to meet the 7-pay test of subsection (b), such contract shall be treated as failing to meet such requirements only in the case of -

(1) distributions during the contract year in which the failure takes effect and during any subsequent contract year, and

(2) under regulations prescribed by the Secretary, distributions (not described in paragraph (1)) in anticipation of such failure.

For purposes of the preceding sentence, any distribution which is made within 2 years before the failure to meet the 7-pay test shall be treated as made in anticipation of such failure.

(e) DEFINITIONS.—For purposes of this section -

(1) AMOUNT PAID.—

(A) IN GENERAL.—The term "amount paid" means -

(i) the premiums paid under the contract, reduced by

(ii) amounts to which section 72(e) applies (determined without regard to paragraph (4)(A) thereof) but not including amounts includible in gross income.

(B) TREATMENT OF CERTAIN PREMIUMS RETURNED.—If, in order to comply with the requirements of subsection (b), any portion of any premium paid during any contract year is returned by the insurance company (with interest) within 60 days after the end of such contract year, the amount so returned (excluding interest) shall be deemed to reduce the sum of the premiums paid under the contract during such contract year.

# Life Insurance and Modified Endowments

(C) INTEREST RETURNED INCLUDIBLE IN GROSS INCOME.—Notwithstanding the provisions of section 72(e), the amount of any interest returned as provided in subparagraph (B) shall be includible in the gross income of the recipient.

(2) CONTRACT YEAR.—The term "contract year" means the 12-month period beginning with the 1st month for which the contract is in effect, and each 12-month period beginning with the corresponding month in subsequent calendar years.

(3) OTHER TERMS.—Except as otherwise provided in this section, terms used in this section shall have the same meaning as when used in section 7702.

## SOURCE

Added by Pub. L. No. 100-647, title V, Sec. 5012(c)(1), Nov. 10, 1988, 102 Stat. 3662; amended Pub. L. No. 101-239, title VII, Sec. 7647(a), 7815(a)(1), (4), Dec. 19, 1989, 103 Stat. 2382, 2414; Pub. L. No. 106-554, Sec. 1(a)(7), title III, Sec. 318(a)(1), (2), Dec. 21, 2000, 114 Stat. 2763, 2763A-645; Pub. L. No. 107-147, title IV, Sec. 416(f), Mar. 9, 2002, 116 Stat. 55.

## AMENDMENTS

**2002** -- Subsec. (c)(3)(A)(ii). Pub. L. No. 107-147, § 416(f), substituted "under the contract" for "under the old contract".

**2000** - Subsec. (a)(2). Pub. L. No. 106-554, Sec. 1(a)(7) (title III, Sec. 318(a)(1)), inserted "or this paragraph" before period at end.

Subsec. (c)(3)(A)(ii). Pub. L. No. 106-554, Sec. 1(a)(7) (title III, Sec. 318(a)(2)), substituted "under the old contract" for "under the contract".

**1989** - Subsec. (c)(3)(B). Pub. L. No. 101-239, Sec. 7815(a)(1), substituted "benefit increases" for "increases in future benefits" in heading and amended text generally. Prior to amendment, text read as follows:

"(B) For purposes of subparagraph (A), the term 'material change' includes any increase in future benefits under the contract. Such term shall not include –

(i) any increase which is attributable to the payment of premiums necessary to fund the lowest level of future benefits payable in the 1st 7 contract years (determined after taking into account death benefit increases described in subparagraph (A) or (B) of section 7702(e)(2)) or to crediting of interest or other earnings (including policyholder dividends) in respect of such premiums, and

(ii) to the extent provided in regulations, any cost-of-living increase based on an established broad-based index if such increase is funded ratably over the remaining life of the contract."

Subsec. (c)(4). Pub. L. No. 101-239, Sec. 7815(a)(4), substituted "of $10,000 or less" for "under $10,000" in heading and "the same policyholder" for "the same insurer" in concluding provisions.

Subsec. (c)(6). Pub. L. No. 101-239, Sec. 7647(a), added par. (6).

## EFFECTIVE DATE OF 2002 AMENDMENT

Pub.L. No. 107-147, Title IV, Sec. 416(f), Mar. 9, 2002, 116 Stat. 55, provided that: Pub.L. No. 106-554, Sec. 1(a)(7) [Title III, Sec. 318(a)(2),Dec. 2, 2000, 114 Stat. 2763, 2763A-645; amending subsec. (c)(3)(A)] is repealed, and clause (ii) of section 7702A(c)(3)(A) [subsec. (c)(3)(A) of this section] shall read and be applied as if the amendment made by such paragraph had not been enacted.

## EFFECTIVE DATE OF 2000 AMENDMENT

Pub. L. No. 106-554, Sec. 1(a)(7) (title III, Sec. 318(a)(3)), Dec. 21, 2000, 114 Stat. 2763, 2763A-645, provided that: "The amendments made by this subsection (amending this section) shall take effect as if included in the amendments made by section 5012 of the Technical and Miscellaneous Revenue Act of 1988 (Pub. L. No. 100-647)."

**EFFECTIVE DATE OF 1989 AMENDMENT**

Section 7647(b) of Pub. L. No. 101-239 provided that: "The amendment made by subsection (a) (amending this section) shall apply to contracts entered into on or after September 14, 1989." Amendment by section 7815(a)(1), (4) of Pub. L. No. 101-239 effective, except as otherwise provided, as if included in the provision of the Technical and Miscellaneous Revenue Act of 1988, Pub. L. No. 100-647, to which such amendment relates, see section 7817 of Pub. L. No. 101-239, set out as a note under section 1 of this title.

**EFFECTIVE DATE**

Section 5012(e) of Pub. L. No. 100-647, as amended by Pub. L. No. 101-239, title VII, Sec. 7815(a)(2), Dec. 19, 1989, 103 Stat. 2414, provided that:

(1) IN GENERAL.—Except as otherwise provided in this subsection, the amendments made by this section (enacting this section and amending sections 26 and 72 of this title) shall apply to contracts entered into on or after June 21, 1988.

(2) SPECIAL RULE WHERE DEATH BENEFIT INCREASES BY MORE THAN $150,000.—If the death benefit under the contract increases by more than $150,000 over the death benefit under the contract in effect on October 20, 1988, the rules of section 7702A(c)(3) of the 1986 Code (as added by this section) shall apply in determining whether such contract is issued on or after June 21, 1988. The preceding sentence shall not apply in the case of a contract which, as of June 21, 1988, required at least 7 level annual premium payments and under which the policyholder makes at least 7 level annual premium payments.

(3) CERTAIN OTHER MATERIAL CHANGES TAKEN INTO ACCOUNT.—A contract entered into before June 21, 1988, shall be treated as entered into after such date if –

(A) on or after June 21, 1988, the death benefit under the contract is increased (or a qualified additional benefit is increased or added) and before June 21, 1988, the owner of the contract did not have a unilateral right under the contract to obtain such increase or addition without providing additional evidence of insurability, or

(B) the contract is converted after June 20, 1988, from a term life insurance contract to a life insurance contract providing coverage other than term life insurance coverage without regard to any right of the owner of the contract to such conversion.

(4) CERTAIN EXCHANGES PERMITTED.—In the case of a modified endowment contract which –

(A) required at least 7 annual level premium payments,

(B) is entered into after June 20, 1988, and before the date of the enactment of this Act (Nov. 10, 1988), and

(C) is exchanged within 3 months after such date of enactment for a life insurance contract which meets the requirements of section 7702A(b), the contract which is received in exchange for such contract shall not be treated as a modified endowment contract if the taxpayer elects, notwithstanding section 1035 of the 1986 Code, to recognize gain on such exchange.

(5) SPECIAL RULE FOR ANNUITY CONTRACTS.—In the case of annuity contracts, the amendments made by subsection (d) (amending section 72 of this title) shall apply to contracts entered into after October 21, 1988.

# APPENDIX C
## IRC SECTION 7702B

## SECTION 7702B. TREATMENT OF QUALIFIED LONG-TERM CARE INSURANCE

(a) IN GENERAL.—For purposes of this title –

(1) a qualified long-term care insurance contract shall be treated as an accident and health insurance contract,

(2) amounts (other than policyholder dividends, as defined in section 808, or premium refunds) received under a qualified long-term care insurance contract shall be treated as amounts received for personal injuries and sickness and shall be treated as reimbursement for expenses actually incurred for medical care (as defined in section 213 (d)),

(3) any plan of an employer providing coverage under a qualified long-term care insurance contract shall be treated as an accident and health plan with respect to such coverage,

(4) except as provided in subsection (e)(3), amounts paid for a qualified long-term care insurance contract providing the benefits described in subsection (b)(2)(A) shall be treated as payments made for insurance for purposes of section 213 (d)(1)(D), and

(5) a qualified long-term care insurance contract shall be treated as a guaranteed renewable contract subject to the rules of section 816 (e).

(b) QUALIFIED LONG-TERM CARE INSURANCE CONTRACT.—For purposes of this title—

(1) IN GENERAL.—The term "qualified long-term care insurance contract" means any insurance contract if—

(A) the only insurance protection provided under such contract is coverage of qualified long-term care services,

(B) such contract does not pay or reimburse expenses incurred for services or items to the extent that such expenses are reimbursable under title XVIII of the Social Security Act or would be so reimbursable but for the application of a deductible or coinsurance amount,

(C) such contract is guaranteed renewable,

(D) such contract does not provide for a cash surrender value or other money that can be—

(i) paid, assigned, or pledged as collateral for a loan, or

(ii) borrowed, other than as provided in subparagraph (E) or paragraph (2)(C),

(E) all refunds of premiums, and all policyholder dividends or similar amounts, under such contract are to be applied as a reduction in future premiums or to increase future benefits, and

(F) such contract meets the requirements of subsection (g).

(2) SPECIAL RULES.—

(A) PER DIEM, ETC. PAYMENTS PERMITTED.—A contract shall not fail to be described in subparagraph (A) or (B) of paragraph (1) by reason of payments being made on a per diem or other periodic basis without regard to the expenses incurred during the period to which the payments relate.

(B) SPECIAL RULES RELATING TO MEDICARE.—

(i) Paragraph (1)(B) shall not apply to expenses which are reimbursable under title XVIII of the Social Security Act only as a secondary payor.

(ii) No provision of law shall be construed or applied so as to prohibit the offering of a qualified long-term care insurance contract on the basis that the contract coordinates its benefits with those provided under such title.

(C) REFUNDS OF PREMIUMS.—Paragraph (1)(E) shall not apply to any refund on the death of the insured, or on a complete surrender or cancellation of the contract, which cannot exceed the aggregate premiums paid under the contract. Any refund on a complete surrender or cancellation of the contract shall be includible in gross income to the extent that any deduction or exclusion was allowable with respect to the premiums.

(c) QUALIFIED LONG-TERM CARE SERVICES.—For purposes of this section—

(1) IN GENERAL.—The term "qualified long-term care services" means necessary diagnostic, preventive, therapeutic, curing, treating, mitigating, and rehabilitative services, and maintenance or personal care services, which –

(A) are required by a chronically ill individual, and

(B) are provided pursuant to a plan of care prescribed by a licensed health care practitioner.

(2) CHRONICALLY ILL INDIVIDUAL.—

(A) IN GENERAL.—The term "chronically ill individual" means any individual who has been certified by a licensed health care practitioner as—

(i) being unable to perform (without substantial assistance from another individual) at least 2 activities of daily living for a period of at least 90 days due to a loss of functional capacity,

(ii) having a level of disability similar (as determined under regulations prescribed by the Secretary in consultation with the Secretary of Health and Human Services) to the level of disability described in clause (i), or

(iii) requiring substantial supervision to protect such individual from threats to health and safety due to severe cognitive impairment.

Such term shall not include any individual otherwise meeting the requirements of the preceding sentence unless within the preceding 12-month period a licensed health care practitioner has certified that such individual meets such requirements.

(B) ACTIVITIES OF DAILY LIVING.—For purposes of subparagraph (A), each of the following is an activity of daily living:

(i) Eating.

(ii) Toileting.

(iii) Transferring.

(iv) Bathing.

(v) Dressing.

(vi) Continence.

A contract shall not be treated as a qualified long-term care insurance contract unless the determination of whether an individual is a chronically ill individual described in subparagraph (A)(i) takes into account at least 5 of such activities.

(3) MAINTENANCE OR PERSONAL CARE SERVICES.—The term "maintenance or personal care services" means any care the primary purpose of which is the provision of needed assistance with any of the disabilities as a result of which the individual is a chronically ill individual (including the protection from threats to health and safety due to severe cognitive impairment).

(4) LICENSED HEALTH CARE PRACTITIONER.—The term "licensed health care practitioner" means any physician (as defined in section 1861(r)(1) of the Social Security Act) and any registered professional

nurse, licensed social worker, or other individual who meets such requirements as may be prescribed by the Secretary.

(d) AGGREGATE PAYMENTS IN EXCESS OF LIMITS.—

(1) IN GENERAL.—If the aggregate of—

(A) the periodic payments received for any period under all qualified long-term care insurance contracts which are treated as made for qualified long-term care services for an insured, and

(B) the periodic payments received for such period which are treated under section 101 (g) as paid by reason of the death of such insured,

exceeds the per diem limitation for such period, such excess shall be includible in gross income without regard to section 72. A payment shall not be taken into account under subparagraph (B) if the insured is a terminally ill individual (as defined in section 101 (g)) at the time the payment is received.

(2) PER DIEM LIMITATION.—For purposes of paragraph (1), the per diem limitation for any period is an amount equal to the excess (if any) of—

(A) the greater of—

(i) the dollar amount in effect for such period under paragraph (4), or

(ii) the costs incurred for qualified long-term care services provided for the insured for such period, over

(B) the aggregate payments received as reimbursements (through insurance or otherwise) for qualified long-term care services provided for the insured during such period.

(3) AGGREGATION RULES.—For purposes of this subsection—

(A) all persons receiving periodic payments described in paragraph (1) with respect to the same insured shall be treated as 1 person, and

(B) the per diem limitation determined under paragraph (2) shall be allocated first to the insured and any remaining limitation shall be allocated among the other such persons in such manner as the Secretary shall prescribe.

(4) DOLLAR AMOUNT.—The dollar amount in effect under this subsection shall be $175 per day (or the equivalent amount in the case of payments on another periodic basis).

(5) INFLATION ADJUSTMENT.—In the case of a calendar year after 1997, the dollar amount contained in paragraph (4) shall be increased at the same time and in the same manner as amounts are increased pursuant to section 213 (d)(10).

(6) PERIODIC PAYMENTS.—For purposes of this subsection, the term "periodic payment" means any payment (whether on a periodic basis or otherwise) made without regard to the extent of the costs incurred by the payee for qualified long-term care services.

(e) TREATMENT OF COVERAGE PROVIDED AS PART OF A LIFE INSURANCE OR ANNUITY CONTRACT.—Except as otherwise provided in regulations prescribed by the Secretary, in the case of any long-term care insurance coverage (whether or not qualified) provided by a rider on or as part of a life insurance contract or an annuity contract—

(1) IN GENERAL.—This title shall apply as if the portion of the contract providing such coverage is a separate contract.

(2) DENIAL OF DEDUCTION UNDER SECTION 213.—No deduction shall be allowed under section 213 (a) for any payment made for coverage under a qualified long-term care insurance contract if such pay-

ment is made as a charge against the cash surrender value of a life insurance contract or the cash value of an annuity contract.

(3) PORTION DEFINED.—For purposes of this subsection, the term "portion" means only the terms and benefits under a life insurance contract or annuity contract that are in addition to the terms and benefits under the contract without regard to long-term care insurance coverage.

(4) ANNUITY CONTRACTS TO WHICH PARAGRAPH (1) DOES NOT APPLY.—For purposes of this subsection, none of the following shall be treated as an annuity contract:

(A) A trust described in section 401 (a) which is exempt from tax under section 501 (a).

(B) A contract—

(i) purchased by a trust described in subparagraph (A),

(ii) purchased as part of a plan described in section 403 (a),

(iii) described in section 403 (b),

(iv) provided for employees of a life insurance company under a plan described in section 818 (a)(3), or

(v) from an individual retirement account or an individual retirement annuity.

(C) A contract purchased by an employer for the benefit of the employee (or the employee's spouse).

Any dividend described in section 404 (k) which is received by a participant or beneficiary shall, for purposes of this paragraph, be treated as paid under a separate contract to which subparagraph (B)(i) applies.

(f) TREATMENT OF CERTAIN STATE-MAINTAINED PLANS.—

(1) IN GENERAL.—If—

(A) an individual receives coverage for qualified long-term care services under a State long-term care plan, and

(B) the terms of such plan would satisfy the requirements of subsection (b) were such plan an insurance contract,

such plan shall be treated as a qualified long-term care insurance contract for purposes of this title.

(2) STATE LONG-TERM CARE PLAN.—For purposes of paragraph (1), the term "State long-term care plan" means any plan—

(A) which is established and maintained by a State or an instrumentality of a State,

(B) which provides coverage only for qualified long-term care services, and

(C) under which such coverage is provided only to—

(i) employees and former employees of a State (or any political subdivision or instrumentality of a State),

(ii) the spouses of such employees, and

(iii) individuals bearing a relationship to such employees or spouses which is described in any of subparagraphs (A) through (G) of section 152 (d)(2).

(g) CONSUMER PROTECTION PROVISIONS.—

(1) IN GENERAL.—The requirements of this subsection are met with respect to any contract if the contract meets—

(A) the requirements of the model regulation and model Act described in paragraph (2),

(B) the disclosure requirement of paragraph (3), and

(C) the requirements relating to nonforfeitability under paragraph (4).

(2) REQUIREMENTS OF MODEL REGULATION AND ACT.—

(A) IN GENERAL.—The requirements of this paragraph are met with respect to any contract if such contract meets—

(i) MODEL REGULATION.—The following requirements of the model regulation:

(I) SECTION 7A (RELating to guaranteed renewal or noncancellability), and the requirements of section 6B of the model Act relating to such section 7A.

(II) Section 7B (relating to prohibitions on limitations and exclusions).

(III) Section 7C (relating to extension of benefits).

(IV) Section 7D (relating to continuation or conversion of coverage).

(V) Section 7E (relating to discontinuance and replacement of policies).

(VI) Section 8 (relating to unintentional lapse).

(VII) Section 9 (relating to disclosure), other than section 9F thereof.

(VIII) Section 10 (relating to prohibitions against post-claims underwriting).

(IX) Section 11 (relating to minimum standards).

(X) Section 12 (relating to requirement to offer inflation protection), except that any requirement for a signature on a rejection of inflation protection shall permit the signature to be on an application or on a separate form.

(XI) Section 23 (relating to prohibition against preexisting conditions and probationary periods in replacement policies or certificates).

(ii) MODEL ACT.—The following requirements of the model Act:

(I) Section 6C (relating to preexisting conditions).

(II) Section 6D (relating to prior hospitalization).

(B) DEFINITIONS.—For purposes of this paragraph—

(i) MODEL PROVISIONS.—The terms "model regulation" and "model Act" mean the long-term care insurance model regulation, and the long-term care insurance model Act, respectively, promulgated by the National Association of Insurance Commissioners (as adopted as of January 1993).

(ii) COORDINATION.—Any provision of the model regulation or model Act listed under clause (i) or (ii) of subparagraph (A) shall be treated as including any other provision of such regulation or Act necessary to implement the provision.

(iii) DETERMINATION.—For purposes of this section and section 4980C, the determination of whether any requirement of a model regulation or the model Act has been met shall be made by the Secretary.

(3) DISCLOSURE REQUIREMENT.—The requirement of this paragraph is met with respect to any contract if such contract meets the requirements of section 4980C(d).

(4) NONFORFEITURE REQUIREMENTS.—

(A) IN GENERAL.—The requirements of this paragraph are met with respect to any level premium contract, if the issuer of such contract offers to the policyholder, including any group policyholder, a nonforfeiture provision meeting the requirements of subparagraph (B).

(B) REQUIREMENTS OF PROVISION.—The nonforfeiture provision required under subparagraph (A) shall meet the following requirements:

(i) The nonforfeiture provision shall be appropriately captioned.

(ii) The nonforfeiture provision shall provide for a benefit available in the event of a default in the payment of any premiums and the amount of the benefit may be adjusted subsequent to being initially granted only as necessary to reflect changes in claims, persistency, and interest as reflected in changes in rates for premium paying contracts approved by the appropriate State regulatory agency for the same contract form.

(iii) The nonforfeiture provision shall provide at least one of the following:

(I) Reduced paid-up insurance.

(II) Extended term insurance.

(III) Shortened benefit period.

(IV) Other similar offerings approved by the appropriate State regulatory agency.

(5) CROSS REFERENCE.—For coordination of the requirements of this subsection with State requirements, see section 4980C(f).

## SOURCE

(Added and amended Pub. L. No. 104–191, title III, §§ 321(a), 325, Aug. 21, 1996, 110 Stat. 2054, 2063; Pub. L. No. 105–34, title XVI, § 1602(b), (e), Aug. 5, 1997, 111 Stat. 1094; Pub. L. No. 105–206, title VI, § 6023(28), July 22, 1998, 112 Stat. 826; Pub. L. No. 108–311, title II, § 207(25), Oct. 4, 2004, 118 Stat. 1178; Pub. L. No. 109–280, title VIII, § 844(c), (f), Aug. 17, 2006, 120 Stat. 1011, 1013.)

## INFLATION ADJUSTED ITEMS FOR CERTAIN YEARS

For inflation adjustment of certain items in this section, see Revenue Procedures listed in a table under section 1 of this title.

## REFERENCES IN TEXT

The Social Security Act, referred to in subsec. (b)(1)(B), (2)(B)(i), is act Aug. 14, 1935, ch. 531, 49 Stat. 620, as amended. Title XVIII of the Act is classified generally to subchapter XVIII (§ 1395 et seq.) of chapter 7 of Title 42, The Public Health and Welfare. Section 1861(r)(1) of the Act is classified to section 1395x (r)(1) of Title 42. For complete classification of this Act to the Code, see section 1305 of Title 42 and Tables.

## AMENDMENTS

2006—Subsec. (e). Pub. L. No. 109–280, § 844(c), amended subsec. (e) generally. Prior to amendment, subsec. (e) related to treatment of coverage provided as part of a life insurance contract.

Subsec. (e)(1). Pub. L. No. 109–280, § 844(f), substituted "title" for "section".

2004—Subsec. (f)(2)(C)(iii). Pub. L. No. 108–311 substituted "subparagraphs (A) through (G) of section 152 (d)(2)" for "paragraphs (1) through (8) of section 152 (a)".

1998—Subsec. (e)(2). Pub. L. No. 105-206 inserted "section" after "Application of" in heading.

1997—Subsec. (c)(2)(B). Pub. L. No. 105-34, § 1602(b), inserted "described in subparagraph (A)(i)" after "chronically ill individual" in concluding provisions.

Subsec. (g)(4)(B)(ii), (iii)(IV). Pub. L. No. 105-34, § 1602(e), substituted "appropriate State regulatory agency" for "Secretary".

1996—Subsec. (g). Pub. L. No. 104-191, § 325, added subsec. (g).

**Effective Date of 2006 Amendment**

Amendment by Pub. L. No. 109-280 applicable to contracts issued after Dec. 31, 1996, but only with respect to taxable years beginning after Dec. 31, 2009, except as otherwise provided, see section 844(g)(1) of Pub. L. No. 109-280, set out as a note under section 72 of this title.

Amendment by section 844(f) of Pub. L. No. 109-280 effective as if included in section 321(a) of Pub. L. No. 104-191, see section 844(g)(5) of Pub. L. No. 109-280, set out as a note under section 72 of this title.

**Effective Date of 2004 Amendment**

Amendment by Pub. L. No. 108-311 applicable to taxable years beginning after Dec. 31, 2004, see section 208 of Pub. L. No. 108-311, set out as a note under section 2 of this title.

**Effective Date of 1997 Amendment**

Amendment by Pub. L. No. 105-34 effective as if included in the provisions of the Health Insurance Portability and Accountability Act of 1996, Pub. L. No. 104-191, to which such amendment relates, see section 1602(i) of Pub. L. No. 105-34, set out as a note under section 26 of this title.

**Effective Date of 1996 Amendment**

Amendment by section 325 of Pub. L. No. 104-191 applicable to contracts issued after Dec. 31, 1996, with provisions of section 321(f) of Pub. L. No. 104-191, set out as an Effective Date note below, applicable to such contracts, see section 327 of Pub. L. No. 104-191, set out as an Effective Date note under section 4980C of this title.

**Effective Date**

Pub. L. No. 104-191, title III, § 321(f), Aug. 21, 1996, 110 Stat. 2059, provided that:

(1) GENERAL EFFECTIVE DATE.—

(A) IN GENERAL.—Except as provided in subparagraph (B), the amendments made by this section [enacting this section and amending sections 106, 125, 807, and 4980B of this title, section 1167 of Title 29, Labor, and section 300bb-8 of Title 42, The Public Health and Welfare] shall apply to contracts issued after December 31, 1996.

(B) RESERVE METHOD.—The amendment made by subsection (b) [amending section 807 of this title] shall apply to contracts issued after December 31, 1997.

(2) CONTINUATION OF EXISTING POLICIES.—In the case of any contract issued before January 1, 1997, which met the long-term care insurance requirements of the State in which the contract was issued at the time the contract was issued—

(A) such contract shall be treated for purposes of the Internal Revenue Code of 1986 as a qualified long-term care insurance contract (as defined in section 7702B(b) of such Code), and

(B) services provided under, or reimbursed by, such contract shall be treated for such purposes as qualified long-term care services (as defined in section 7702B(c) of such Code).

In the case of an individual who is covered on December 31, 1996, under a State long-term care plan (as defined in section 7702B(f)(2) of such Code), the terms of such plan on such date shall be treated for purposes of the preceding sentence as a contract issued on such date which met the long-term care insurance requirements of such State.

(3) EXCHANGES OF EXISTING POLICIES.—If, after the date of enactment of this Act [Aug. 21, 1996] and before January 1, 1998, a contract providing for long-term care insurance coverage is exchanged solely for a qualified long-term care insurance contract (as defined in section 7702B(b) of such Code), no gain or loss shall be recognized on the exchange. If, in addition to a qualified long-term care insurance contract, money or other property is received in the exchange, then any gain shall be recognized to the extent of the sum of the money and the fair market value of the other property received. For purposes of this paragraph, the cancellation of a contract providing for long-term care insurance coverage and reinvestment of the cancellation proceeds in a qualified long-term care insurance contract within 60 days thereafter shall be treated as an exchange.

(4) ISSUANCE OF CERTAIN RIDERS PERMITTED.—For purposes of applying sections 101(f), 7702, and 7702A of the Internal Revenue Code of 1986 to any contract—

(A) the issuance of a rider which is treated as a qualified long-term care insurance contract under section 7702B, and

(B) the addition of any provision required to conform any other long-term care rider to be so treated, shall not be treated as a modification or material change of such contract.

(5) APPLICATION OF PER DIEM LIMITATION TO EXISTING CONTRACTS.—The amount of per diem payments made under a contract issued on or before July 31, 1996, with respect to an insured which are excludable from gross income by reason of section 7702B of the Internal Revenue Code of 1986 (as added by this section) shall not be reduced under subsection (d)(2)(B) thereof by reason of reimbursements received under a contract issued on or before such date. The preceding sentence shall cease to apply as of the date (after July 31, 1996) such contract is exchanged or there is any contract modification which results in an increase in the amount of such per diem payments or the amount of such reimbursements."

## LONG-TERM CARE STUDY REQUEST

Pub. L. No. 104–191, title III, § 321(g), Aug. 21, 1996, 110 Stat. 2060, provided that: "The Chairman of the Committee on Ways and Means of the House of Representatives and the Chairman of the Committee on Finance of the Senate shall jointly request the National Association of Insurance Commissioners, in consultation with representatives of the insurance industry and consumer organizations, to formulate, develop, and conduct a study to determine the marketing and other effects of per diem limits on certain types of long-term care policies. If the National Association of Insurance Commissioners agrees to the study request, the National Association of Insurance Commissioners shall report the results of its study to such committees not later than 2 years after accepting the request."

# APPENDIX D
## IRC SECTION 101(f)

# Life Insurance and Modified Endowments

## SECTION 101(f). PROCEEDS OF FLEXIBLE PREMIUM CONTRACTS ISSUED BEFORE JANUARY 1, 1985 PAYABLE BY REASON OF DEATH

(1) IN GENERAL.—Any amount paid by reason of the death of the insured under a flexible premium life insurance contract issued before January 1, 1985 shall be excluded from gross income only if—

   (A) under such contract—

   (i) the sum of the premiums paid under such contract does not at any time exceed the guideline premium limitation as of such time, and

   (ii) any amount payable by reason of the death of the insured (determined without regard to any qualified additional benefit) is not at any time less than the applicable percentage of the cash value of such contract at such time, or

   (B) by the terms of such contract, the cash value of such contract may not at any time exceed the net single premium with respect to the amount payable by reason of the death of the insured (determined without regard to any qualified additional benefit) at such time.

(2) GUIDELINE PREMIUM LIMITATION.—For purposes of this subsection -

   (A) GUIDELINE PREMIUM LIMITATION.—The term "guideline premium limitation" means, as of any date, the greater of -

   (i) the guideline single premium, or

   (ii) the sum of the guideline level premiums to such date.

   (B) GUIDELINE SINGLE PREMIUM.—The term "guideline single premium" means the premium at issue with respect to future benefits under the contract (without regard to any qualified additional benefit), and with respect to any charges for qualified additional benefits, at the time of a determination under subparagraph (A) or (E) and which is based on -

   (i) the mortality and other charges guaranteed under the contract, and

   (ii) interest at the greater of an annual effective rate of 6 percent or the minimum rate or rates guaranteed upon issue of the contract.

   (C) GUIDELINE LEVEL PREMIUM.—The term "guideline level premium" means the level annual amount, payable over the longest period permitted under the contract (but ending not less than 20 years from date of issue or not later than age 95, if earlier), computed on the same basis as the guideline single premium, except that subparagraph (B)(ii) shall be applied by substituting "4 percent'" for "'6 percent".

   (D) COMPUTATIONAL RULES.—In computing the guideline single premium or guideline level premium under subparagraph (B) or (C) -

   (i) the excess of the amount payable by reason of the death of the insured (determined without regard to any qualified additional benefit) over the cash value of the contract shall be deemed to be not greater than such excess at the time the contract was issued,

   (ii) the maturity date shall be the latest maturity date permitted under the contract, but not less than 20 years after the date of issue or (if earlier) age 95, and

   (iii) the amount of any endowment benefit (or sum of endowment benefits) shall be deemed not to exceed the least amount payable by reason of the death of the insured (determined without regard to any qualified additional benefit) at any time under the contract.

   (E) ADJUSTMENTS.—The guideline single premium and guideline level premium shall be adjusted in the event of a change in the future benefits or any qualified additional benefit under the contract which was not reflected in any guideline single premiums or guideline level premium previously determined.

(3) OTHER DEFINITIONS AND SPECIAL RULES.—For purposes of this subsection –

(A) FLEXIBLE PREMIUM LIFE INSURANCE CONTRACT.—The terms "flexible premium life insurance contract" and "contract" mean a life insurance contract (including any qualified additional benefits) which provides for the payment of one or more premiums which are not fixed by the insurer as to both timing and amount. Such terms do not include that portion of any contract which is treated under State law as providing any annuity benefits other than as a settlement option.

(B) PREMIUMS PAID.—The term "premiums paid" means the premiums paid under the contract less any amounts (other than amounts includible in gross income) to which section 72(e) applies. If, in order to comply with the requirements of paragraph (1)(A), any portion of any premium paid during any contract year is returned by the insurance company (with interest) within 60 days after the end of a contract year –

(i) the amount so returned (excluding interest) shall be deemed to reduce the sum of the premiums paid under the contract during such year, and

(ii) notwithstanding the provisions of section 72(e), the amount of any interest so returned shall be includible in the gross income of the recipient.

(C) APPLICABLE PERCENTAGE.—The term "applicable percentage" means –

(i) 140 percent in the case of an insured with an attained age at the beginning of the contract year of 40 or less, and

(ii) In the case of an insured with an attained age of more than 40 as of the beginning of the contract year, 140 percent reduced (but not below 105 percent) by one percent for each year in excess of 40.

(D) CASH VALUE.—The cash value of any contract shall be determined without regard to any deduction for any surrender charge or policy loan.

(E) QUALIFIED ADDITIONAL BENEFITS.—The term "qualified additional benefits" means any –

(i) guaranteed insurability,

(ii) accidental death benefit,

(iii) family term coverage, or

(iv) waiver of premium.

(F) PREMIUM PAYMENTS NOT DISQUALIFYING CONTRACT.—The payment of a premium which would result in the sum of the premiums paid exceeding the guideline premium limitation shall be disregarded for purposes of paragraph (1)(A)(i) if the amount of such premium does not exceed the amount necessary to prevent the termination of the contract without cash value on or before the end of the contract year.

(G) NET SINGLE PREMIUM.—In computing the net single premium under paragraph (1)(B) –

(i) the mortality basis shall be that guaranteed under the contract (determined by reference to the most recent mortality table allowed under all State laws on the date of issuance),

(ii) interest shall be based on the greater of –

(I) an annual effective rate of 4 percent (3 percent for contracts issued before July 1, 1983), or

(II) the minimum rate or rates guaranteed upon issue of the contract, and

(III) the computational rules of paragraph (2)(D) shall apply, except that the maturity date referred to in clause (ii) thereof shall not be earlier than age 95.

(H) CORRECTION OF ERRORS.—If the taxpayer establishes to the satisfaction of the Secretary that –

(i) the requirements described in paragraph (1) for any contract year was not satisfied due to reasonable error, and

(ii) reasonable steps are being taken to remedy the error,

the Secretary may waive the failure to satisfy such requirements.

(I) REGULATIONS.—The Secretary shall prescribe such regulations as may be necessary or appropriate to carry out the purposes of this subsection.

## SOURCE

Added by Pub. L. No. 97-248, title II, § 266(a), Sept. 3, 1982, 96 Stat. 547.

## EFFECTIVE DATE OF 1982 AMENDMENTS

Section 266(c)(1) of Pub. L. No. 97-248, as amended by Pub. L. 98-369, Sec. 221(b)(1), July 18, 1984, 98 Stat. 772, provides that: "The amendments made by this section (amending this section) shall apply to contracts entered into before January 1, 1985."

## FLEXIBLE PREMIUM CONTRACTS ISSUED DURING 1984 WHICH MEET REQUIREMENTS OF SECTION 7702 TREATED AS MEETING THE REQUIREMENTS OF SECTION 101(F)

Flexible premium contracts issued during 1984 which meet requirements of section 7702 of this title treated as meeting requirements of subsec. (f) of this section, see section 221(b)(3) of Pub. L. No. 98-369, as added by Pub. L. No. 99-514, set out as a note under section 7702 of this title.

## SPECIAL RULES FOR CONTRACTS ENTERED INTO BEFORE JANUARY 1, 1983

Section 266(c)(2), (3) of Pub. L. No. 97-248, as amended by Pub. L. No. 97-448, title III, Sec. 306(a)(13), Jan. 12, 1983, 96 Stat. 2405; Pub. L. No. 99-514, Sec. 2, Oct. 22, 1986, 100 Stat. 2095, provided that:

(2) SPECIAL RULE FOR CONTRACTS ENTERED INTO BEFORE JANUARY 1, 1983.—Any contract entered into before January 1, 1983, which meets the requirements of section 101(f) of the Internal Revenue Code of 1986 (formerly I.R.C. 1954) on the date which is 1 year after the date of the enactment of this Act (Sept. 3, 1982) shall be treated as meeting the requirements of such section for any period before the date on which such contract meets such requirements. Any death benefits paid under a flexible premium life insurance contract (within the meaning of section 101(f)(3)(A) of such Code) before the date which is 1 year after such date of enactment (Sept. 3, 1982) shall be excluded from gross income.

(3) SPECIAL RULE FOR CERTAIN CONTRACTS.—Any contract entered into before January 1, 1983, shall be treated as meeting the requirements of subparagraph (A) of section 101(f)(1) of such Code if such contract would meet such requirements if section 101(f)(2)(C) of such Code were applied by substituting "3 percent" for "4 percent".

# APPENDIX E
## IRC SECTION 101(g)

**SECTION 101(g). TREATMENT OF CERTAIN ACCELERATED DEATH BENEFITS**

(1) IN GENERAL.—For purposes of this section, the following amounts shall be treated as an amount paid by reason of the death of an insured:

  (A) Any amount received under a life insurance contract on the life of an insured who is a terminally ill individual.

  (B) Any amount received under a life insurance contract on the life of an insured who is a chronically ill individual.

(2) TREATMENT OF VIATICAL SETTLEMENTS.—

  (A) IN GENERAL.—If any portion of the death benefit under a life insurance contract on the life of an insured described in paragraph (1) is sold or assigned to a viatical settlement provider, the amount paid for the sale or assignment of such portion shall be treated as an amount paid under the life insurance contract by reason of the death of such insured.

  (B) VIATICAL SETTLEMENT PROVIDER.—

   (i) IN GENERAL.—The term "viatical settlement provider" means any person regularly engaged in the trade or business of purchasing, or taking assignments of, life insurance contracts on the lives of insureds described in paragraph (1) if—

    (I) such person is licensed for such purposes (with respect to insureds described in the same subparagraph of paragraph (1) as the insured) in the State in which the insured resides, or

    (II) in the case of an insured who resides in a State not requiring the licensing of such persons for such purposes with respect to such insured, such person meets the requirements of clause (ii) or (iii), whichever applies to such insured.

   (ii) TERMINALLY ILL INSUREDS.—A person meets the requirements of this clause with respect to an insured who is a terminally ill individual if such person—

    (I) meets the requirements of sections 8 and 9 of the Viatical Settlements Model Act of the National Association of Insurance Commissioners, and

    (II) meets the requirements of the Model Regulations of the National Association of Insurance Commissioners (relating to standards for evaluation of reasonable payments) in determining amounts paid by such person in connection with such purchases or assignments.

   (iii) CHRONICALLY ILL INSUREDS.—A person meets the requirements of this clause with respect to an insured who is a chronically ill individual if such person—

    (I) meets requirements similar to the requirements referred to in clause (ii)(I), and

    (II) meets the standards (if any) of the National Association of Insurance Commissioners for evaluating the reasonableness of amounts paid by such person in connection with such purchases or assignments with respect to chronically ill individuals.

(3) SPECIAL RULES FOR CHRONICALLY ILL INSUREDS.—In the case of an insured who is a chronically ill individual—

  (A) IN GENERAL.—Paragraphs (1) and (2) shall not apply to any payment received for any period unless—

   (i) such payment is for costs incurred by the payee (not compensated for by insurance or otherwise) for qualified long-term care services provided for the insured for such period, and

(ii) the terms of the contract giving rise to such payment satisfy—

(I) the requirements of section 7702B (b)(1)(B), and

(II) the requirements (if any) applicable under subparagraph (B).

For purposes of the preceding sentence, the rule of section 7702B (b)(2)(B) shall apply.

(B) OTHER REQUIREMENTS.—The requirements applicable under this subparagraph are—

(i) those requirements of section 7702B (g) and section 4980C which the Secretary specifies as applying to such a purchase, assignment, or other arrangement,

(ii) standards adopted by the National Association of Insurance Commissioners which specifically apply to chronically ill individuals (and, if such standards are adopted, the analogous requirements specified under clause (i) shall cease to apply), and

(iii) standards adopted by the State in which the policyholder resides (and if such standards are adopted, the analogous requirements specified under clause (i) and (subject to section 4980C (f)) standards under clause (ii), shall cease to apply).

(C) PER DIEM PAYMENTS.—A payment shall not fail to be described in subparagraph (A) by reason of being made on a per diem or other periodic basis without regard to the expenses incurred during the period to which the payment relates.

(D) LIMITATION ON EXCLUSION FOR PERIODIC PAYMENTS.—For limitation on amount of periodic payments which are treated as described in paragraph (1), see section 7702B (d).

(4) DEFINITIONS.—For purposes of this subsection—

(A) TERMINALLY ILL INDIVIDUAL.—The term "terminally ill individual" means an individual who has been certified by a physician as having an illness or physical condition which can reasonably be expected to result in death in 24 months or less after the date of the certification.

(B) CHRONICALLY ILL INDIVIDUAL.—The term "chronically ill individual" has the meaning given such term by section 7702B (c)(2); except that such term shall not include a terminally ill individual.

(C) QUALIFIED LONG-TERM CARE SERVICES.—The term "qualified long-term care services" has the meaning given such term by section 7702B (c).

(D) PHYSICIAN.—The term "physician" has the meaning given to such term by section 1861(r)(1) of the Social Security Act (42 U.S.C. 1395x (r)(1)).

(5) EXCEPTION FOR BUSINESS-RELATED POLICIES.—This subsection shall not apply in the case of any amount paid to any taxpayer other than the insured if such taxpayer has an insurable interest with respect to the life of the insured by reason of the insured being a director, officer, or employee of the taxpayer or by reason of the insured being financially interested in any trade or business carried on by the taxpayer.

## SOURCE

Added by Pub. L. No. 104–191, title III, § 331(a), Aug. 21, 1996, 110 Stat. 2067.

## EFFECTIVE DATE

Pub. L. No. 104–191, title III, § 331(b), Aug. 21, 1996, 110 Stat. 2069, provided that: "The amendments made by [§ 331(a)] shall apply to amounts received after December 31, 1996."

# APPENDIX F
## IRC SECTION 4980C

## SECTION 4980C. REQUIREMENTS FOR ISSUERS OF QUALIFIED LONG-TERM CARE INSURANCE CONTRACTS

(a) GENERAL RULE.—There is hereby imposed on any person failing to meet the requirements of subsection (c) or (d) a tax in the amount determined under subsection (b).

(b) AMOUNT.—

(1) IN GENERAL.—The amount of the tax imposed by subsection (a) shall be $100 per insured for each day any requirement of subsection (c) or (d) is not met with respect to each qualified long-term care insurance contract.

(2) WAIVER.—In the case of a failure which is due to reasonable cause and not to willful neglect, the Secretary may waive part or all of the tax imposed by subsection (a) to the extent that payment of the tax would be excessive relative to the failure involved.

(c) RESPONSIBILITIES.—The requirements of this subsection are as follows:

(1) REQUIREMENTS OF MODEL PROVISIONS.—

(A) MODEL REGULATION.—The following requirements of the model regulation must be met:

(i) Section 13 (relating to application forms and replacement coverage).

(ii) Section 14 (relating to reporting requirements), except that the issuer shall also report at least annually the number of claims denied during the reporting period for each class of business (expressed as a percentage of claims denied), other than claims denied for failure to meet the waiting period or because of any applicable preexisting condition.

(iii) Section 20 (relating to filing requirements for marketing).

(iv) Section 21 (relating to standards for marketing), including inaccurate completion of medical histories, other than sections 21C(1) and 21C(6) thereof, except that—

(I) in addition to such requirements, no person shall, in selling or offering to sell a qualified long-term care insurance contract, misrepresent a material fact; and

(II) no such requirements shall include a requirement to inquire or identify whether a prospective applicant or enrollee for long-term care insurance has accident and sickness insurance.

(v) Section 22 (relating to appropriateness of recommended purchase).

(vi) Section 24 (relating to standard format outline of coverage).

(vii) Section 25 (relating to requirement to deliver shopper's guide).

(B) MODEL ACT.—The following requirements of the model Act must be met:

(i) Section 6F (relating to right to return), except that such section shall also apply to denials of applications and any refund shall be made within 30 days of the return or denial.

(ii) Section 6G (relating to outline of coverage).

(iii) Section 6H (relating to requirements for certificates under group plans).

(iv) Section 6I (relating to policy summary).

(v) Section 6J (relating to monthly reports on accelerated death benefits).

(vi) Section 7 (relating to incontestability period).

(C) DEFINITIONS.—For purposes of this paragraph, the terms "model regulation" and "model Act" have the meanings given such terms by section 7702B (g)(2)(B).

(2) DELIVERY OF POLICY.—If an application for a qualified long-term care insurance contract (or for a certificate under such a contract for a group) is approved, the issuer shall deliver to the applicant (or policyholder or certificateholder) the contract (or certificate) of insurance not later than 30 days after the date of the approval.

(3) INFORMATION ON DENIALS OF CLAIMS.—If a claim under a qualified long-term care insurance contract is denied, the issuer shall, within 60 days of the date of a written request by the policyholder or certificateholder (or representative)—

(A) provide a written explanation of the reasons for the denial, and

(B) make available all information directly relating to such denial.

(d) DISCLOSURE.—The requirements of this subsection are met if the issuer of a long-term care insurance policy discloses in such policy and in the outline of coverage required under subsection (c)(1)(B)(ii) that the policy is intended to be a qualified long-term care insurance contract under section 7702B (b).

(e) QUALIFIED LONG-TERM CARE INSURANCE CONTRACT DEFINED.—For purposes of this section, the term "qualified long-term care insurance contract" has the meaning given such term by section 7702B.

(f) COORDINATION WITH STATE REQUIREMENTS.—If a State imposes any requirement which is more stringent than the analogous requirement imposed by this section or section 7702B (g), the requirement imposed by this section or section 7702B (g) shall be treated as met if the more stringent State requirement is met.

## SOURCE

Added by Pub. L. No. 104–191, title III, § 326(a), Aug. 21, 1996, 110 Stat. 2065.

## EFFECTIVE DATE

Pub. L. No. 104–191, title III, § 327, Aug. 21, 1996, 110 Stat. 2066, provided that:

"(a) IN GENERAL.—The provisions of, and amendments made by, this part [part II (§§ 325–327) of subtitle C of title III of Pub. L. No. 104–191, enacting this section and amending section 7702B of this title] shall apply to contracts issued after December 31, 1996. The provisions of section 321(f) [set out as an Effective Date note under section 7702B of this title] (relating to transition rule) shall apply to such contracts.

"(b) ISSUERS.—The amendments made by section 326 [enacting this section] shall apply to actions taken after December 31, 1996."

# APPENDIX G
## DEFRA BLUE BOOK:

## GENERAL EXPLANATION OF THE REVENUE PROVISIONS OF THE DEFICIT REDUCTION ACT OF 1984

[JOINT COMMITTEE PRINT]

# GENERAL EXPLANATION OF THE REVENUE PROVISIONS OF THE DEFICIT REDUCTION ACT OF 1984

(H.R. 4170, 98TH CONGRESS; PUBLIC LAW 98-369)

PREPARED BY THE STAFF

OF THE

## JOINT COMMITTEE ON TAXATION

DECEMBER 31, 1984

U.S. GOVERNMENT PRINTING OFFICE
WASHINGTON : 1985

40-926 O

JCS-41-84

For sale by the Superintendent of Documents, U.S. Government Printing Office
Washington, D.C. 20402

645

## 3. Taxation of Life Insurance Products

### a. Definition of a life insurance contract (sec. 221 of the Act and new sec. 7702 of the Code) [49]

*Prior Law*

Generally, there was no statutory definition of life insurance under prior law. A life insurance contract was defined generally in section 1035 (relating to tax-free exchanges) as a contract with a life insurance company which depended in part on the life expectancy of the insured and which was not ordinarily payable in full during the life of the insured.

Under prior and present law, income earned on the cash surrender value of a contract is not taxed currently to the policyholder, but it is taxed upon termination of the contract prior to death to the extent that the cash surrender value exceeds the policyholder's investment in the contract, i.e., the sum of all premiums paid on the contract. Gross income does not include amounts received by a beneficiary under a life insurance contract, if the amounts are paid because of the death of the insured.

In TEFRA, Congress enacted temporary guidelines for determining whether flexible premium life insurance contracts (e.g., universal life or adjustable life) qualified as life insurance contracts for purposes of the exclusion of death benefits from income. Violation of the guidelines at any time during the contract caused the contract to be treated as providing a combination of term life insurance and an annuity or a deposit fund (depending on the terms of the contract). In the event of the death of the insured, only the term life insurance component is excluded from gross income.

*1982 and 1983 temporary guidelines*

Under the temporary guidelines which apply to contracts issued in 1982 and 1983, death proceeds from flexible premium life insurance contracts are treated as life insurance if either of two tests are met.

*Alternative 1*

Under the first of the two alternative tests, a contract qualifies if:

(a) The sum of the premiums paid for the benefits at any time does not exceed the net single premium (based on interest rates at 6 percent) or the sum of the net level premiums (based on interest rates at 4 percent), assuming the policy matures no earlier than in 20 years or at age 95, (if earlier); and

(b) the death benefit is at least 140 percent of cash value at age 40, phasing down one percentage point each year to 105 percent.

---

[49] For legislative background of the provision, see: H.R. 4170, committee amendment approved by the House Committee on Ways and Means on March 1, 1984, sec. 221; H. Rep. No. 98-432, Pt. 2 (March 5, 1984), pp. 1442-1450; "Deficit Reduction Act of 1984," as approved by the Senate Committee on Finance on March 21, 1984, sec. 221; S. Prt. 98-169, Vol. I (April 2, 1984), pp. 571-580; and H. Rep. No. 98-861 (June 23, 1984), pp. 1074-1076 (Conference Report).

### Alternative 2

Under the second of the two alternative tests, a contract qualifies if the cash surrender value does not exceed the net single premium (based on interest rates at 4 percent and the most recent mortality table) for the amount payable at death, assuming the policy matures no earlier than age 95.

### Explanation of Provision

The Act adopts a definition of a life insurance contract for purposes of the Internal Revenue Code. This provision extends to all life insurance contracts rules that are similar to those contained in the temporary provisions of TEFRA. Because there was a general concern with the proliferation of investment-oriented life insurance products, the definition was narrowed in some respects.

### Definition of life insurance

A life insurance contract is defined as any contract, which is a life insurance contract under the applicable State or foreign law, but only if the contract meets either of two alternatives: (1) a cash value accumulation test, or (2) a test consisting of a guideline premium requirement and a cash value corridor requirement. Whichever test is chosen, that test must be met for the entire life of the contract in order for the contract to be treated as life insurance for tax purposes. The choice of test will be evident on issuance of the contract. Because the cash value accumulation test must be met at all times *by the terms of the contract*, failure of a contract meeting this requirement will mean that the contract must meet, at all times, the guideline premium/cash value corridor test.[50] Rather than being a requirement on the terms of the contract, the latter test (guideline premium/cash value corridor test) is one that is applied in practice and calls for specific corrective actions if a contract fails to meet it at any time. Although the guideline premium/cash value corridor test does not have to be met by the terms of the contract, the test limitations could be built into a contract to make compliance therewith automatic and to avoid inadvertent violation of those test limitations.

The term "life insurance contract" does not include that portion of any contract that is treated under State law as providing any annuity benefits other than as a settlement option. Thus, although a life insurance contract may provide by rider for annuity benefits, the annuity portion of the contract is not part of the life insurance contract for tax purposes and such annuity benefits may not be reflected in computing the guideline premiums. Thus, an insurance arrangement written as a combination of term life insurance with an annuity contract, or with a premium deposit fund, is not a life insurance contract for purposes of the alternative tests because all of the elements of the contract are not treated under State law as

---

[50] A change from the guideline premium test to the cash value accumulation test may occur, however, in those limited circumstances under which a contract need not continue to meet the guideline premium test because by the election of a nonforfeiture option, which was guaranteed on issuance of the contract, the contract meets the cash value accumulation test by the terms of the contract. However, any reinstatement of the original terms of such a contract would also reinstate the application of the original guideline premium test to the contract.

providing a single integrated death benefit. As a result, only the term portion of any such contract can meet the tests and be treated as life insurance proceeds upon the insured's death. However, any life insurance contract that is treated under State law as a single, integrated life insurance contract and that satisfies these tests will be treated for Federal tax purposes as a single contract of life insurance and not as a contract that provides separate life insurance and annuity benefits. For example, for purposes of this definition, a whole life insurance contract that provides for the purchase of paid-up or deferred additions is treated as a single life insurance contract.

In the case of variable life insurance contracts (as defined in sec. 817), the determination of whether the contract meets the cash value accumulation test, or meets the guideline premium requirements and falls within the cash value corridor, must be made whenever the amount of the death benefits under the contract change, but not less frequently than once during each 12-month period. Further, if a contract is checked to see if it satisfies the requirements once a year, the determination must be made at the same time each year.

*Cash value accumulation test*

The first alternative test under which a contract may qualify as a life insurance contract is the cash value accumulation test. This test is intended to allow traditional whole life policies, with cash values that accumulate based on reasonable interest rates, to continue to qualify as life insurance contracts. Certain contracts that have been traditionally sold by life insurance companies, such as endowment contracts, will not continue to be classified as life insurance contracts because of their innate investment orientation.

Under this test, the cash surrender value of the contract, by the terms of the contract, may not at any time exceed the net single premium which would have to be paid at such time in order to fund the future benefits under the contract assuming the contract matures no earlier than age 95 for the insured. Thus, this test allows a recomputation of the limitation (the net single premium) at any point in time during the contract period based on the current and future benefits guaranteed under the contract at that time. The term future benefits under the Act means death benefits and endowment benefits. The death benefit is the amount that is payable in the event of the death of the insured, without regard to any qualified additional benefits.

Cash surrender value is defined in the Act as the cash value of any contract (i.e., any amount to which the policyholder is entitled upon surrender and, generally, against which the policyholder can borrow) determined without regard to any surrender charge, policy loan, or a reasonable termination dividend. For these purposes, termination dividends are considered reasonable based on what has been the historical practice of the industry in paying such dividends. Historically, termination dividends have been modest in amount. For example, the Congress understood that New York State prescribes a maximum termination dividend of $35 per $1,000 of face amount of the policy. Just as termination dividends are not reflected in the cash surrender value, any policyholder dividends

648

left on deposit with the company to accumulate interest is not part of the cash surrender value of a contract; interest income on such dividend accumulations is currently taxable to the policyholder because the amounts are not held pursuant to an insurance or annuity contract. Likewise, amounts that are returned to a policyholder of a credit life insurance policy because the policy has been terminated upon full payment of the debt are not considered part of any cash surrender value because, generally, such amount is not subject to borrowing under the policy.

Whether a contract meets this test of a life insurance contract will be determined on the basis of the terms of the contract. In making the determination that a life insurance contract meets the cash value accumulation test, the net single premium for any time is computed using a rate of interest that is the greater of an annual effective rate of 4 percent or the rate or rates guaranteed on the issuance of the contract. To be consistent with the definitional test reference to the cash surrender value, the "rate or rates guaranteed on the issuance of the contract" means the interest rate or rates reflected in the contract's nonforfeiture values (i.e., the cash surrender value), assuming the use of the method in the Standard Nonforfeiture Law.[51] With respect to variable contracts that do not have a guaranteed rate, the 4-percent rate applies. The mortality charges taken into account in computing the net single premium are those specified in the contract or, if none are specified in the contract, the mortality charges used in determining the statutory reserves for the contract.[52]

The statutory reference to the rate or rates of interest guaranteed on the issuance of the contract serves the same role as the "minimum rate or rates" referred to in the TEFRA provision of section 101(f). Thus, although the company may guarantee a higher interest rate from time to time, either by contractual declaration or by operation of a formula or index, generally, the rate guaranteed on the issuance of the contract refers to the floor rate, that is, the rate below which the interest credited to the cash surrender value of the contract cannot fall. The statutory reference to "rate or rates" recognizes that a contract may guarantee different floor rates for different periods of the contract, although each is guaranteed upon issuance and remains fixed for the applicable period for the life of the contract. Likewise, the reference to multiple rates indicates that the comparison of the statutorily prescribed rate (e.g. 4 percent or 6 percent) to the rate or rates guaranteed, and the selection of the higher one, must be done for each period for which an interest rate is guaranteed in the cash surrender value. Specifically, it should be noted that when the initial interest rate guaranteed to be credited to the contract is in excess of the generally applicable floor rate assumed in the contract, the higher initial interest rate is the rate guaranteed on the issuance of the contract with

---

[51] Discussions herein relating to the determination of the "rate or rates guaranteed on issuance of the contract" and mortality and other charges are generally applicable for purposes of computing definitional test limitations under both the cash value accumulation test and the guideline premium/cash value corridor test.

[52] The term "mortality charges" refers to the amounts charged for the pure insurance risk, even though they may be labeled differently in the contract (e.g. cost of insurance, monthly deduction, mortality deduction, etc.).

649

respect to the initial period of that guarantee. *De minimis* guarantees (i.e., guarantees of short durations) in excess of the otherwise assumed floor rates may be ignored in certain situations; generally short-term guarantees (extending no more than one year) will be *de minimis* in the calculation of the guideline level premium, but will not be considered *de minimis* in the calculation of the guideline single premium or the net single premium.

The rate or rates guaranteed on issuance of the contact may be explicitly stated in the contract or may be implicitly stated by a guarantee of particular cash surrender values. Since the rate or rates guaranteed are those reflected in the nonforfeiture/cash surrender values (assuming the use of the Standard Nonforfeiture Method), a company will not be considered to guarantee a lower interest rate by failing to state a mortality charge. In such a case the mortality charges used for statutory reserves will be assumed, and the interest rate or rates implicit in the guaranteed cash surrender values (assuming such charges) will be the rate or rates guaranteed on issuance of the contract. Also, if the contract's nonforfeiture values for any duration are determined by a formula that uses the highest value produced by alternative combinations of guaranteed interest rate or rates and specified mortality (and other) charges, the combination of such factors used, on a guaranteed basis, in the highest cash surrender value for such duration should be used for such duration in determining either the net single premium or the guideline premium limitation.[53]

Finally, the amount of any qualified additional benefits will not be taken into account in determining the net single premium. However, the charge stated in the contract for the qualified additional benefit will be treated as a future benefit, thereby increasing the cash value limitation by the discounted value of that charge. For life insurance contracts, qualified additional benefits are guaranteed insurability, accidental death or disability, family term coverage, disability waiver, and any other benefits prescribed under regulations. In the case of any other additional benefit which is not a qualified additional benefit and which is not prefunded, neither the benefit nor the charge for such benefit will be taken into account. For example, if a contract provides for business term insurance as an additional benefit, neither the term insurance nor the charge for the insurance will be considered a future benefit.

*Guideline premium and cash value corridor test requirements*

The second alternative test under which a contract may qualify as a life insurance contract has two requirements; the guideline premium limitation and the cash value corridor. The guideline premium portion of the test distinguishes between contracts under which the policyholder makes traditional levels of investment

---

[53] For example, under a so-called fixed premium universal life contract, if the cash surrender value on a guaranteed basis (ignoring nonguaranteed factors such as excess interest) is not determined by the guaranteed interest rate and the specified mortality and expense charges used to determine the policy value for some duration, but is instead determined by a secondary guarantee using the guaranteed interest rate and specified mortality and expense charges associated with an alternate State law minimum nonforfeiture value for such duration, the guaranteed interest rate and the mortality and expense charges for the secondary guarantee are to be used with respect to such duration in determining either the net single premium or the guideline premium limitation.

through premiums and those which involve greater investments by the policyholder. The cash value corridor disqualifies contracts which allow excessive amounts of cash value to build up (i.e., premiums, plus income on which tax has been deferred) relative to the life insurance risk. In combination, these requirements are intended to limit the definition of life insurance to contracts which require only relatively modest investment and permit relatively modest investment returns.

The specifics of these requirements are described below.

*Guideline premium limitation.*—A life insurance contract meets the guideline premium limitation if the sum of the premiums paid under the contract does not at any time exceed the greater of the guideline single premium or the sum of the guideline level premiums to such date. The guideline single premium for any contract is the premium at issue required to fund future benefits under the contract. The computation of the guideline single premium must take into account (1) the mortality charges specified in the contract, or used in determining the statutory reserves for the contract if none is specified in the contract, (2) any other charges specified in the contract (either for expenses or for supplemental benefits), and (3) interest at the greater of a 6-percent annual effective rate or the rate or rates guaranteed on the issuance of the contract. The guideline level premium is the level annual amount, payable over a period that does not end before the insured attains age 95, which is necessary to fund future benefits under the contract.[54] The computation is made on the same basis as that for the guideline single premium, except that the statutory interest rate is 4 percent instead of 6 percent. See also the discussion under the cash value accumulation test relating to "rate or rates guaranteed on issuance of the contract" and guaranteed mortality and other charges for use in computing the definitional test limitations.

A premium payment that causes the sum of the premiums paid to exceed the guideline premium limitation will not result in the contract failing the test if the premium payment is necessary to prevent termination of the contract on or before the end of the contract year, but only if the contract would terminate without cash value but for such payment. Also, premium amounts returned to a policyholder, with interest, within 60 days after the end of a contract year in order to comply with the guideline premium requirement are treated as a reduction of the premiums paid during the year. The interest paid on such return premiums is includible in gross income.

*Cash value corridor.*—A life insurance contract falls within the cash value corridor if the death benefit under the contract at any time is equal to at least the applicable percentage of the cash surrender value. Applicable percentages are set forth in a statutory table. Under the table, an insured person, who is 55 years of age at the beginning of a contract year and has a life insurance contract

---

[54] To the extent the guideline level premium includes a charge for an additional benefit that is scheduled to cease at a certain age (i.e., there are discrete payment periods for separate policy benefits), the charges for such benefit should be reflected in a level manner over the period such charges are being incurred. This prevents post-funding of the qualified additional benefit.

with $10,000 in cash surrender value, must have a death benefit at that time of at least $15,000 (150 percent of $10,000).

As the table shows, the applicable percentage to determine the minimum death benefit starts at 250 percent of the cash surrender value for an insured person up to 40 years of age, and the percentage decreases to 100 percent when the insured person reaches age 95. Starting at age 40, there are 9 age brackets with 5-year intervals (except for one 15-year interval) to which a specific applicable percentage range has been assigned. The applicable percentage will decrease by the same amount for each year in that age bracket. For example, for the 55 to 60 age bracket, the applicable percentage falls from 150 to 130 percent, or 4 percentage points for each annual increase in age. At 57, the applicable percentage will be 142.

The statutory table of applicable percentages follows:

| In the case of an insured with an attained age as of the beginning of the contract year of: | | The applicable percentages shall decrease by a ratable portion for each full year: | |
|---|---|---|---|
| More than: | But not more than: | From: | To: |
| 0 | 40 | 250 | 250 |
| 40 | 45 | 250 | 215 |
| 45 | 50 | 215 | 185 |
| 50 | 55 | 185 | 150 |
| 55 | 60 | 150 | 130 |
| 60 | 65 | 130 | 120 |
| 65 | 70 | 120 | 115 |
| 70 | 75 | 115 | 105 |
| 75 | 90 | 105 | 105 |
| 90 | 95 | 105 | 100 |

For purposes of applying the cash value corridor and the guideline premium limitation (as well as the computational rules described below), the attained age of the insured means the insured's age determined by reference to contract anniversaries (rather than the individual's actual birthdays), so long as the age assumed under the contract is within 12 months of the actual age.

## Computational rules

The Act provides three general rules or assumptions to be applied in computing the limitations set forth in the definitional tests. These rules restrict the actual provisions and benefits that can be offered in a life insurance contract only to the extent that they restrict the allowable cash surrender value (under the cash value accumulation test) or the allowable funding pattern (under the guideline premium limitation). By prescribing computation assumptions for purposes of the definitional limitations, Congress limited the investment orientation of contracts while avoiding the regulation of the actual terms of insurance contracts.

652

First, in computing the net single premium under the cash value accumulation test or the guideline premium limitation under any contract, the death benefit is deemed not to increase at any time during the life of the contract (qualified additional benefits are treated in the same way). Thus, a contract cannot assume a death benefit that decreases in earlier years and increases in later years in order to avoid the guideline premium limitation.

Second, irrespective of the maturity date actually set forth in the contract, the maturity date (including the date on which any endowment benefit is payable) is deemed to be no earlier than the day on which the insured attains age 95 and no later than the day on which the insured attains age 100. Thus, the deemed maturity date generally is the termination date set forth in the contract or the end of the mortality table. In applying this rule to contracts that are scheduled to automatically mature or terminate prior to age 95, the benefits should also be deemed to continue to age 95 for purposes of computing both the net single premium and the guideline premium limitations. This rule will generally prevent contracts endowing at face value before age 95 from qualifying as life insurance. However, it will allow an endowment benefit at ages before 95 for amounts less than face value. Similarly, a contract written with a termination date before age 95 (e.g. term life insurance to age 65), which otherwise satisfies the requirements of section 7702, will qualify as a life insurance contract for tax purposes. Also, an actual contract maturity date later than age 100 (e.g., in the case of contract issued on a mortality basis that employs an age setback for females insureds) will qualify with application of this computational rule.

Third, the amount of any endowment benefit, or the sum of any endowment benefits, is deemed not to exceed the least amount payable as a death benefit at any time under the contract. For these purposes, the term endowment benefits includes the cash surrender value at the maturity date.

Notwithstanding the first computational rule, an increase in the death benefit that is provided in the contract, and which is limited to the amount necessary to prevent a decrease in the excess of the death benefit over the cash surrender value, may be taken into account for purposes of meeting the two definitional tests provided under the Act. Specifically, for a contract qualifying under the guideline premium requirement, this type of increasing death benefit can be taken into account in computing the guideline level premium. Thus, in such a case, the premium limitation is the greater of the guideline single premium computed by assuming a nonincreasing death benefit or the sum of the guideline level premiums computed by assuming an increasing death benefit. In the case of a contract qualifying under the cash accumulation test, the above described increasing death benefit can be taken into account if the cash surrender value of the contract cannot exceed at any time the net level reserve. For this purpose, the net level reserve will be determined as though level annual premiums will be paid for the contract until the insured attains age 95, and the net level reserve is substituted for the net single premium limitation in the cash value accumulation test. These modifications to the computational rules allow the sale of contracts in which the death benefit is defined as the cash surrender value plus a fixed amount of pure life insurance protection.

The special computational rule for certain contracts with increasing death benefits allows flexible premium contracts using the guideline premium/cash value corridor test to have a higher internal rate of investment return than otherwise would be allowed under the general computational rules. Although the special computational rule expands the investment orientation allowed for flexible premium contracts, it does not provide a comparable expansion for contracts using the cash value accumulation test over that which is already allowed under the general computational rules.[55]

Finally, it was understood that in computing actual cash surrender values that rounding differences or other computational variations could produce minor variations in results. For example, it has been standard practice for most companies to round all cash values up to the next whole dollar per thousand of face amounts. This simplifies displays and assures compliance with minimum nonforfeiture standards under State law. Thus, it is expected that, in addition to the application of the above described computational rules, reasonable approximations (e.g., $1.00 per $1,000 of face amount) in the calculation of the net single premium or the guideline premiums will be permitted.

*Adjustments*

The Act provides that proper adjustments be made for any change in the future benefits or any qualified additional benefit (or in any other terms) under the contract, which was not reflected in any previous determination made under the definitional section. Changes in the future benefits or terms of a contract can occur at the behest of the company or the policyholder, or by the passage of time. However, proper adjustments may be different for a particular change, depending on which alternative test is being used or on whether the changes result in an increase or decrease of future benefits. In the event of an increase in current or future benefits, the limitations under the cash value accumulation test must be computed treating the date of change, in effect, as a new date of issue for determining whether the changed contract continues to qualify as life insurance under the definition prescribed in the Act. Thus, if a future benefit is increased because of a scheduled change in death benefit or because of the purchase of a paid-up addition (or its equivalent), the change will require an adjustment and new computation of the net single premium definitional limitation. Under the guideline premium limitation, an adjustment is required under similar circumstances, but the date of change for increased benefits should be treated as a new date only with respect to the

---

[55] The discrepancy between the tax treatment of flexible premium contracts and that of the more traditional life insurance products (which is embodied in the differences between the cash value corridor and cash value accumulation test) reflect the general concern over the investment orientation of certain life insurance products and recognition of the fact that for an investment-oriented purchase of traditional life insurance products, the after-tax rate of return can be boosted through the use of the policy loan provisions. Whereas, flexible premium contracts might have slightly more generous limitations under the new definitional provisions, it is generally understood that the owner of such a contract is not able to leverage his investment in the contract, and boost the after-tax rate of return, through the use of policyholder loans.

changed portion of the contract. Likewise, no adjustment shall be made if the change occurs automatically, for example, a change due to the growth of the cash surrender value (whether by the crediting of excess interest or the payment of guideline premiums) or changes initiated by the company. If the contract fails to meet the recomputed limitations, a distribution of cash to the policyholder may be required. Under the Act, the Secretary of the Treasury has authority to prescribe regulations governing how such adjustments and computations should be made. Such regulations may revise, prospectively, some of the adjustment rules described above in order to give full effect to the intent of the definitional limitations.

Further, for purposes of the adjustment rules, any change in the terms of a contract that reduces the future benefits under the contract will be treated as an exchange of contracts (under sec. 1035). Thus, any distribution required under the adjustment rules will be treated as taxable to the policyholder under the generally applicable rules of section 1031. This provision was intended to apply specifically to situations in which a policyholder changes from a future benefits pattern taken into account under the computational provision for policies with limited increases in death benefits to a future benefit of a level amount (even if at the time of change the amount of death benefit is not reduced). If the adjustment provision results in a distribution to the policyholder in order to meet the adjusted guidelines, the distribution will be taxable to the policyholder as ordinary income to the extent there is income in the contract. The provision that certain changes in future benefits be treated as exchanges was not intended to alter the application of the transition rules for life insurance contracts (explained below); Thus, section 7702 will not become applicable to a contract that was issued before January 1, 1985, because a reduction of the contracts future benefits resulted in the application of this adjustment provision. Likewise, this adjustment provision was not intended to repeal indirectly the application of section 72(e) to life insurance contracts.

### *Endowment contracts treated as life insurance contracts*

Endowment contracts which meet the requirements of the definition of a life insurance contract will receive the same treatment as a life insurance contract.

### *Contracts not meeting the life insurance definition*

If a life insurance contract does not meet either of the alternative tests under the definition of a life insurance contract, the income on the contract for any taxable year of the policyholder will be treated as ordinary income received or accrued by the policyholder during that year.[56] For this purpose, the income on the contract is the amount by which the sum of the increase in the net surrender value of the contract during the taxable year and the

---

[56] Under a special rule for correction of errors (new sec. 7702(f)(8)), if it is established to the satisfaction of the Secretary that the requirements of the definitional tests were not met due to reasonable error and reasonable steps are being taken to remedy the error, the Secretary may waive the failure to satisfy the requirements.

cost of life insurance protection provided during the taxable year under the contract exceed the amount of premiums paid less any policyholder dividends paid under the contract during the taxable year. The term premiums paid means the amounts paid as premiums under a contract less amounts to which the rules for allocation between income and investment under annuity and other contracts in section 72(e) apply. Because the income on the contract is treated as received by the policyholder, the income would be a distribution subject to the recordkeeping, reporting, and withholding rules under present and prior law relating to commercial annuities (including life insurance). It is hoped this will provide the policyholder with adequate notice that disqualification has occurred, thus giving some protection against underpayment of estimated taxes.

The income on the contract for all prior taxable years is treated as received or accrued during the taxable year in which a life insurance contract ceases to meet the definition of a life insurance contract. The cost of life insurance protection provided under any contract is the lesser of the cost of individual insurance on the life of the insured as determined on the basis of uniform premiums, computed using 5-year age brackets, as prescribed by the Secretary by regulations, or the mortality charge stated in the contract.

The excess of the amount of death benefit paid over the net surrender value of the contract will be treated as paid under a life insurance contract for purposes of the exclusion from income with respect to the beneficiary.

If a life insurance contract fails to meet the tests in the definition, it will nonetheless be treated as an insurance contract for tax purposes. This insures that the premiums and income credited to failing policies will continue to be taken into account by the insurance company in computing its taxable income. In addition, it insures that a company that issues failing policies continue to qualify as an insurance company.

### Effective Date

#### General effective date

Generally, the new definition of life insurance applies to contracts issued after December 31, 1984. See, however, the discussion below regarding certain increasing death benefit contracts issued after June 30, 1984. Also, the TEFRA provisions for flexible premium contracts (that is, sec. 101(f)) were extended through 1984. For purposes of applying the effective date provisions (new sec. 7702(i) of the Code and secs. 221(b)(c) and (d) of the Act) the issue date of a contract is generally the date on the policy assigned by the insurance company, which is on or after the date the application was signed.[57] With respect to group or master contracts, the date taken into account for any insured is the first date on which the insured is covered under the contract and not the date of the master contract. Thus, except in the case of certain increasing death benefit policies, the law in effect prior to the 1984 Act will apply to any

---

[57] The use of the date on the policy would not be considered the date of issue if the period between the date of application and the date on which the policy is actually placed in force is substantially longer than under the company's usual business practice.

contract issued during 1984. Also, any product that meets the definitional requirements of new section 7702 will be treated as life insurance if the contract is issued during 1984.

Contracts issued in exchange for existing contracts after December 31, 1984, are to be considered new contracts issued after that date. The exercise of an option or right granted under the contract as originally issued does not result in an exchange and thus does not constitute the issuance of a new contract for purposes of new section 7702 and any applicable transition rules if the option guaranteed terms that might not otherwise have been available when the option is exercised. Similarly, a substitution of insured (for example, in a key man insurance policy) pursuant to a binding obligation will not be considered to create a new contract subject to the terms of section 7702; this treatment would not extend to an individual who becomes a new insured under a group master contract after the effective date of section 7702. In addition, a change in an existing contract will not be considered to result in an exchange, if the terms of the resulting contract (that is, the amount or pattern of death benefit, the premium pattern, the rate or rates guaranteed on issuance of the contract, or mortality and expense charges) are the same as the terms of the contract prior to the change. Thus, a change in minor administrative provisions or a loan rate generally will not be considered to result in an exchange. See also the discussion below on contracts issued pursuant to existing plans of insurance.

*Certain increasing death benefit policies issued after June 30, 1984.*—The new definitional provisions for life insurance apply to any contract issued after June 30, 1984, if the contract has an increasing death benefit and premium funding more rapid than 10-year level premium payments, unless the contract meets one of three transition rules. An otherwise level death benefit policy is not subject to this earlier effective date merely because the death benefit may increase with the crediting of excess interest or paid-up additions. The premium funding in this instance refers generally to the premium payment pattern and requires that the pattern not allow an annual premium payment by the policyholder in the first 10 years of the policy in excess of the level amount for a 10-pay premium pattern for the increasing death benefit, based on mortality and expense charges and interest rate(s) guaranteed on issuance of the contract.

Increasing death benefit contracts with premium funding more rapid than 10-year level premium payments are not subject to the new definitional provision unless issued after December 31, 1984, if: (1) the contract (whether or not a flexible premium contract) meets the requirements of the temporary provisions for flexible premium contracts (sec. 101(f) enacted in TEFRA); (2) the contract (that is not a flexible premium contract as defined in sec. 101(f)) meets the requirements set forth in the new section 7702 by substituting 3 percent for 4 percent as the minimum interest rate to be used in the cash value accumulation test and the maturity date is deemed to be the latest permitted under the contract (but not less than 20 years after the date of issue or, if earlier, age 95); or (3) the contract meets certain definitional requirements as an irreplaceable life insurance contract.[58]

*Certain contracts issued before October 1, 1984.*—There is an additional transition rule for certain increasing death benefit policies, which makes the new definitional provisions of new section 7702 applicable only for a contract issued after September 30, 1984, if the contract would meet the new definition by substituting "3 percent" for "4 percent" as the minimum interest rate in the cash value accumulation test (assuming that the rate or rates guaranteed on issuance of the contract can be determined without regard to any mortality charges, and without regard to any initial interest rate guaranteed in excess of the stated minimum rate),[59] and if (with the same "3 percent" for "4 percent" substitution) the cash surrender value of the contract does not at any time exceed the net single premium which would have to be paid at such time to fund future benefits at the then current level of benefits.

*Contracts issued pursuant to existing plans of insurance.*—Under a transition rule, certain qualified contracts under existing plans of insurance qualify as life insurance contracts under the cash value accumulation test, discussed above, if the contracts would meet the test using 3-percent, instead of 4-percent, as the statutorily prescribed minimum interest rate. A "qualified contract" will mean any contract that requires at least 20 nondecreasing annual premium payments and is issued pursuant to an existing plan of insurance. An existing plan of insurance is any plan of insurance or policy blank that has been filed by the issuing company in one or more States before September 28, 1983.

It is intended that the 20-pay requirement will not be violated by a plan of insurance that provides for the purchase of insurance by means of paid-up additions, if the additional amounts are modest and reasonable compared with the basic benefit under the contract. Similarly it was not intended that administrative changes made as part of the ongoing maintenance of the plan of insurance should result in forfeiture of the special transition rule for existing plans of insurance if the changes do not significantly affect the fundamental terms and economics of contracts sold under such plan. For example, a company may clarify the wording of its contracts, slightly modify its loan rate provisions, conform its contracts to state readability standards, or modify the plan of insurance in order to accommodate other state requirements of an administrative nature. Generally, such modifications will not result in forfeiture of an existing plan of insurance because they do not affect the fundamental terms and economics of the insurance plan described by the amount or pattern of death benefit available, the premium paying patterns available, the rate or rates guaranteed on issuance of the contract, or the mortality and expenses charges to be used.

---

[58] That is, under such contract, (i) the premiums (including any policy fees) will be adjusted from time to time to reflect the level amount necessary (but not less than zero) at the time of such adjustment to provide a level death benefit assuming interest crediting and an annual effective interest rate of not less than 3 percent, or (ii) at the option of the insured, in lieu of an adjustment under clause (i), there will be a comparable adjustment in the amount of the death benefit.

[59] This latter point is not presently specified in the statute, but was intended . Also, the special transition rule erroneously refers to a "clause (i)" of subparagraph (A) that does not exist.

658

There is a further transitional rule for the application of the definition of an existing plan of insurance. That is, a plan of insurance on file in one or more States before September 28, 1983, will continue to be treated as such even though the plan of insurance is modified after September 28, 1983, to permit the crediting of excess interest or similar amounts annually and not monthly. Because of this specific statutory exception, such a change will not result in a forfeiture of the grandfather for an otherwise qualified contract even though it alters the fundamental economics of the plan of insurance.

### b. Treatment of certain annuity contracts (sec. 222 of the Act and sec. 72 of the Code) [60]

*Prior Law*

Cash withdrawals prior to the annuity starting date were includible in gross income to the extent that the cash value of the contract (determined immediately before the amount was received and without regard to any surrender charge) exceeds the investment in the contract. A penalty tax of 5 percent was imposed on the amount of any such distribution that is includible in income, to the extent that the amount is allocable to an investment made within 10 years of the distribution. The penalty was not imposed if the distribution is made after the contractholder attains age 59½, when the contractholder becomes disabled, upon the death of the contractholder or as a payment under an annuity for life or at least 5 years. No income was recognized to the recipient of an annuity on the death of the contractholder. However, since the recipient had the same investment in the contract as the deceased contractholder, the recipient was subject to income tax on the income accumulated in the contract prior to death when it was distributed from the contract.

*Explanation of Provision*

*Penalty on premature distributions*

The Act generally retains the prior-law provisions for annuity contracts. However, the 5-percent penalty on premature distributions applies to any amount distributed to the taxpayer, without regard to whether the distribution is allocable to an investment made within 10 years, unless the taxpayer owner has attained age 59½.[61] This is consistent with a general objective of the Act to encourage the use of annuities as retirement savings as opposed to short-term savings.

---

[60] For legislative background of the provision, see: H.R. 4170, committee amendment approved by the House Committee on Ways and Means on March 1, 1984, sec. 222; H. Rep. No. 98-432, Pt. 2 (March 5, 1984), pp. 1450-1451; "Deficit Reduction Act of 1984," as approved by the Senate Committee on Finance on March 21, 1984, sec. 222; S. Prt. 98-169, Vol. I (April 2, 1984), pp. 580-581; and H. Rep. No. 98-861 (June 23, 1984), pp. 1076-1078 (Conference Report).

[61] The Act adopts a technical correction to the TEFRA annuity provisions which allows any investment in a multiple premium annuity contract (issued prior to the effective date of the new penalty provisions) to be treated as having been made on January 1 of the year of investment. This technical correction was intended to simplify the accounting requirements of the 10-year-aging rule in TEFRA for the penalty on early distributions from annuity contracts.

# APPENDIX H
## TAMRA HOUSE REPORT:

**MISCELLANEOUS REVENUE ACT OF 1988—REPORT OF THE COMMITTEE ON WAYS AND MEANS**

| 100TH CONGRESS 2d Session | HOUSE OF REPRESENTATIVES | REPORT 100-795 |

# MISCELLANEOUS REVENUE ACT OF 1988

## REPORT

OF THE

## COMMITTEE ON WAYS AND MEANS HOUSE OF REPRESENTATIVES

[Including cost estimate of the Congressional Budget Office]

JULY 26, 1988.—Committed to the Committee of the Whole House on the State of the Union and ordered to be printed

U.S. GOVERNMENT PRINTING OFFICE
WASHINGTON : 1988

87-311

The fact that the Treasury Secretary is required to prescribe regulations under this provision is not to be construed as indicating that related parties, pass-through entities, intermediaries, options, and other similar arrangements may be used under present law to avoid the application of the long-term contract rules.

### *Effective Date*

The provision generally is effective for contracts entered into on or after June 21, 1988. The provision, however, does not apply to any contract entered into pursuant to a written bid or proposal that was submitted by a taxpayer to the other party to the contract before June 21, 1988, if the bid or proposal could not have been revoked or altered by the taxpayer at any time during the period beginning on June 21, 1988, and ending on the date that the contract was entered into.

### 3. Treatment of modified endowment contracts (secs. 313 and 348 of the bill and secs. 72 and 7702A of the Code)

### *Present Law*

#### *In general*

Under present law, the undistributed investment income ("inside buildup") earned on premiums credited under a contract that satisfies a statutory definition of life insurance is not subject to current taxation to the owner of the contract. In addition, death benefits paid under a contract that satisfies the statutory definition are excluded from the gross income of the recipient, so that neither the owner of the contract nor the beneficiary of the contract is ever taxed on the inside buildup.

Amounts received under a life insurance contract prior to the death of the insured generally are not includible in gross income to the extent that the amounts received are less than the taxpayer's investment in the contract. Amounts borrowed under a life insurance contract generally are not treated as received under the contract and, consequently, are not includible in gross income.

#### *Definition of life insurance*

##### *In general*

The favorable income tax treatment accorded to life insurance is only available for contracts that satisfy a statutory definition of life insurance. Under this definition a life insurance contract is any contract that is a life insurance contract under the applicable State or foreign law, but only if the contract satisfies either of two alternative tests: (1) a cash value accumulation test, or (2) a test consisting of a guideline premium requirement and a cash value corridor requirement.

A contract satisfies the cash value accumulation test if the cash surrender value of the contract may not at any time exceed the net single premium that would have to be paid at such time to fund future benefits under the contract. A contract satisfies the guideline premium/cash value corridor test if the premiums paid under the contract do not exceed certain guideline levels, and the death benefit under the contract is not less than a varying statutory percentage of the cash surrender value of the contract.

If a contract does not satisfy the statutory definition of life insurance, the sum of (1) the increase in the net surrender value of the contract during the year and (2) the cost of insurance coverage provided under the contract during the year, over the premiums paid during the year (less any nontaxable distributions) is treated as ordinary income received or accrued by the owner of the contract during the year. In addition, only the excess of the amount of the death benefit paid over the net surrender value of the contract is treated as paid under a life insurance contract for purposes of the gross income exclusion that applies to the recipient of the death benefit.

*Cash value accumulation test*

Under the cash value accumulation test, the cash surrender value of the contract, by the terms of the contract, may not at any time exceed the net single premium that would have to be paid at such time in order to fund the future benefits under the contract assuming the contract matures no earlier than the day on which the insured attains age 95. The net single premium under this test is recomputed at any point in time during the contract period used on the current and future benefits guaranteed under the contract at that time. The term future benefits means death benefits and endowment benefits.[160]

Cash surrender value is defined as the cash value of the contract (i.e., any amount to which the owner of the contract is entitled upon surrender and, generally, against which the owner of the contract can borrow) determined without regard to any surrender charge, policy loan, or reasonable termination dividend.

The determination of whether contract satisfies the cash value accumulation test is made on the basis of the terms of the contract. In making this determination, the net single premium as of any date is computed using a rate of interest that equals the greater of an annual effective rate of 4 percent or the rate or rates guaranteed on the issuance of the contract. The mortality charges taken into account in computing the net single premium are those specified in the contract, or, if none are specified in the contract, the mortality charges used in determining the statutory reserves for the contract. Expense charges are not taken into account in determining the net single premium for a contract.

*Guideline premium and cash value corridor test*

The second alternative test under which a contract may qualify as a life insurance contract has two requirements: the guideline premium limitation and the cash value corridor.

A life insurance contract satisfies the guideline premium limitation if the sum of the premiums paid under the contract does not at any time exceed the greater of the guideline single premium or

---

[160] The amount of any qualified additional benefit is not taken into account in determining the net single premium. The charge stated in the contract for the qualified additional benefit, however, is treated as a future benefit, thereby increasing the cash value limitation by the discounted value of that charge. Qualified additional benefits include guaranteed insurability, accidental death or disability, family term coverage, disability waiver, and any other benefits prescribed under Treasury regulations.

the sum of the guideline level premiums as of such time. The guideline single premium for any contract is the premium at issue required to fund future benefits under the contract. The computation of the guideline single premium takes into account (1) the mortality charges specified in the contract, or, if none are specified, the mortality charges used in determining the statutory reserves for the contract, (2) any other charges specified in the contract (either for expenses or for qualified additional benefits), and (3) interest at the greater of a 6-percent annual effective rate or the rate or rates guaranteed on the issuance of the contract.

The guideline level premium is the level annual amount, payable over a period that does not end before the insured attains age 95, which is necessary to fund future benefits under the contract. The computation is made on the same basis as that for the guideline single premium, except that the statutory interest rate is 4 percent instead of 6 percent.

A premium payment that causes the sum of the premiums paid to exceed the guideline premium limitation will not result in the contract failing the test if the premium payment is necessary to prevent termination of the contract on or before the end of the contract year, but only if the contract would terminate without cash value but for such payment. Also, premiums returned to a policyholder with interest within 60 days after the end of a contract year in order to comply with the guideline premium requirement are treated as a reduction of the premiums paid during the year. The interest paid on such return premiums is includible in gross income.

A life insurance contract satisfies the cash value corridor if the death benefit under the contract at any time is equal to or greater than the applicable percentage of the cash surrender value. As the table below illustrates, the applicable percentage starts at 250 percent of the cash surrender value for an insured person up to 40 years of age and decreases to 100 percent for an insured person that is age 95. Beginning at age 40, there are 9 age brackets with 5-year intervals (except for one 15-year interval) to which a specific applicable percentage range has been assigned.

### Cash Value Corridor

| In the case of an insured with an attained age as of the beginning of the contract year of— | | The applicable percentage shall decrease by a ratable portion for each full year— | |
|---|---|---|---|
| More than: | But not more than: | From: | To: |
| 0 | 40 | 250 | 250 |
| 40 | 45 | 250 | 215 |
| 45 | 50 | 215 | 185 |
| 50 | 55 | 185 | 150 |
| 55 | 60 | 150 | 130 |
| 60 | 65 | 130 | 120 |
| 65 | 70 | 120 | 115 |

474

## Cash Value Corridor—Continued

| In the case of an insured with an attained age as of the beginning of the contract year of— | | The applicable percentage shall decrease by a ratable portion for each full year— | |
|---|---|---|---|
| More than: | But not more than: | From: | To: |
| 70 | 75 | 115 | 105 |
| 75 | 90 | 105 | 105 |
| 90 | 95 | 105 | 100 |

*Computational rules*

Present law provides four general rules or assumptions that are applied in computing the net single premium, guideline single premium, and guideline level premium. First, the death benefit and any qualified additional benefits generally are deemed not to increase during the life of the contract. Second, irrespective of the maturity date actually set forth in the contract, the maturity date (including the date on which any endowment benefit is payable) is deemed to be no earlier than the day on which the insured attains age 95 and no later than the day on which the insured attains age 100. Third, the death benefits are deemed to be provided until the maturity date described in the second computational rule. Fourth, the amount of any endowment benefit, or the sum of any endowment benefits, is deemed not to exceed the least amount payable as a death benefit at any time under the contract.

*Adjustments*

Under present law, if there is a change in the future benefits or other terms of a contract that was not reflected in any previous determination or adjustment made under the definitional rules, proper adjustments must be made in future determinations under the definition. If the change reduces future benefits under the contract, the adjustments may include a required cash distribution in an amount that is necessary to enable the contract to meet the applicable definitional test. A portion of the cash distributed to a policyholder as a result of a reduction in future benefits is treated as being paid first out of income in the contract, rather than as a return of the policyholder's investment in the contract, if the reduction in future benefits occurs during the 15-year period following the issue date of the contract.

*Contracts not meeting the life insurance definition*

If a contract does not satisfy the definition of life insurance, the income on the contract for any taxable year of the policyholder is treated as ordinary income received or accrued by the policyholder during that year. In addition, the income on the contract for all prior taxable years is treated as received or accrued during the taxable year in which the contract ceases to meet the definition.

For this purpose, the income on a contract is the amount by which (1) the sum of the increase in the net surrender value of the contract during the year and the cost of life insurance protection provided under the contract during the year exceeds (2) the amount of premiums paid during the year less any amounts distributed under the contract during the year that are not includible in income. The cost of life insurance protection provided under any contract is the lesser of the cost of individual insurance on the life of the insured as determined on the basis of uniform premiums computed using 5-year age brackets, or the mortality charge stated in the contract.

Finally, if a contract does not satisfy the definition of life insurance, only the excess of the amount of the death benefit paid over the net surrender value of the contract is treated as paid under a life insurance contract for purposes of the gross income exclusion that applies to the recipient of the death benefit.

*Treatment of amounts received under life insurance contracts*

Amounts received under a life insurance contract prior to the death of the insured are subject to income inclusion rules that depend on the nature of the payment received. In the case of amounts received as an annuity under a life insurance contract, a portion of each payment is excludable from gross income as a return of the taxpayer's investment in the contract and the remainder is subject to tax as ordinary income. The amount that is excludable from gross income is determined on the basis of an exclusion ratio, the numerator of which is the taxpayer's investment in the contract as of the annuity starting date and the denominator of which is the expected return under the contract.

Amounts received under a life insurance contract that are not received as an annuity, such as dividends, cash withdrawals, and amounts received upon a partial or total surrender of the contract, are subject to different income inclusion rules. Under these rules, amounts received that do not exceed the taxpayer's investment in the contract are excludable from gross income. Amounts received in excess of the taxpayer's investment in the contract are includible in the gross income of the recipient as ordinary income.[161] For purposes of these rules, a taxpayer's investment in a contract as of any date equals (1) the aggregate amount of premiums or other consideration paid for the contract as of such date, minus (2) the aggregate amount received under the contract before such date that was excludable from gross income.

The receipt of a loan under a life insurance contract or the assignment or pledging of any portion of a life insurance contract is not treated as an amount received under the contract for purposes of the income inclusion rules. In addition, any amount in the nature of a dividend or similar distribution under a life insurance contract that is retained by the insurer as a premium or other con-

---

[161] As indicated above, a portion of any amount received under a life insurance contract as a result of a reduction in future benefits under the contract is treated as being paid first out of income in the contract, rather than as a return of the taxpayer's investment in the contract, if the reduction in future benefits occurs during the 15-year period following the issue date of the contract.

sideration paid for, the contract is not includible in the gross income of the owner of the contract.

*Treatment of amounts received under annuity contracts*

Amounts received as an annuity under an annuity contract are treated in the same manner as amounts received as an annuity under a life insurance contract. Thus, a portion of each payment is excludable from gross income as a return of the taxpayer's investment in the contract and the remainder is subject to tax as ordinary income.

Amounts received under an annuity contract that are not received as an annuity, such as dividends, cash withdrawals and amounts received upon a partial surrender of the contract, are subject to income inclusion rules that differ from the rules applicable to similar amounts received under life insurance contracts. First, amounts received prior to the annuity starting date are includible in gross income to the extent that the cash surrender value of the annuity contract (determined immediately before the amount is received and without regard to any surrender charge) exceeds the taxpayer's investment in the contract. To the extent that amounts received are greater than the excess of the cash surrender value over the taxpayer's investment in the contract, the excess amounts are treated as a return of capital to the taxpayer and reduce the taxpayer's investment in the contract.[162]

Second, the receipt of any amount (directly or indirectly) as a loan under an annuity contract or the assignment or pledge of any portion of the value of an annuity contract is treated as an amount received under the contract for purposes of the income inclusion rules.

Finally, an additional 10-percent income tax is imposed on the portion of any amount received under an annuity contract that is includible in gross income. This additional income tax does not apply to any amount that is (1) paid on or after the date that the taxpayer attains age 59½; (2) paid on or after the death of the owner of the contract; (3) attributable to the taxpayer becoming disabled; or (4) one of a series of substantially equal periodic payments (not less frequently that annually) made for the life (or life expectancy) of the taxpayer or the joint lives (or joint life expectancies) of the taxpayer and the taxpayer's beneficiary.

### Reasons for Change

In recent years, single premium life insurance and other forms of life insurance have been widely marketed as tax-sheltered investment vehicles. The owner of a life insurance contract is able to defer tax on the investment earnings that are credited under the contract and may never pay tax on such earnings if the contract is held until death. In addition, the owner of a life insurance contract is able to withdraw or borrow the investment earnings without incurring a Federal income tax liability.

---

[162] Amounts received under a life insurance or annuity contract that are not received as an annuity and that are received after the annuity starting date are includible in gross income without regard to the taxpayer's investment in the contract

The attractiveness of single premium life insurance as an investment vehicle is illustrated by the sales growth of such contracts. Preliminary data indicates that the volume of single premium life insurance sold has increased by more than 800 percent since 1984, while the volume of all other whole life insurance sold since 1984 has increased by only 22 percent.

The committee believes that the favorable income tax treatment accorded life insurance is inappropriate for contracts purchased for investment purposes and that in order to discourage the purchase of life insurance as tax-sheltered investment vehicles, the favorable income tax treatment of pre-death distributions under certain life insurance contracts, which are recharacterized as modified endowment contracts under the bill, should be modified. In addition, the committee believes that the tax treatment of life insurance and annuity contracts should be studied by the Treasury Department and the General Accounting Office to determine whether further legislative change in the treatment of such contracts is warranted.

### *Explanation of Provision*

#### *Treatment of modified endowment contracts*

##### In general

The bill alters the Federal income tax treatment of loans and other amounts received under a class of life insurance contracts that are statutorily defined as "modified endowment contracts." Under the bill, amounts received under modified endowment contracts are treated first as income and then as recovered basis. In addition, loans under modified endowment contracts and loans secured by modified endowment contracts are treated as amounts received under the contract for purposes of the income inclusion rules. Finally, an additional 10-percent income tax is imposed on certain amounts received under modified endowment contracts to the extent that the amounts received are includible in gross income.

##### *Reversal of basis ordering rule*

Amounts received under a modified endowment contract that are not received as an annuity, such as dividends, cash withdrawals, and amounts received upon a partial surrender of the contract, are includible in gross income to the extent that the cash surrender value of the modified endowment contract (determined immediately before the amount is received and without regard to any surrender charge) exceeds the taxpayer's investment in the contract. To the extent that amounts received are greater than the excess of the cash surrender value over the taxpayer's investment in the contract, the amounts are treated as a return of capital to the taxpayer and reduce the taxpayer's investment in the contract.[163]

In determining whether an amount is received under a modified endowment contract, the present-law rules applicable to annuity contracts apply. Thus, for example, any amount received that is in

---

[163] Amounts received under a modified endowment contract that are not received as an annuity and that are received after the annuity starting date are includible in gross income without regard to the taxpayer's investment in the contract.

the nature of a dividend or similar distribution is includible in gross income to the extent that the cash surrender value exceeds the taxpayer's investment in the contract. As under present law, any amount in the nature of a dividend or similar distribution that is retained by the insurer as a premium or other consideration paid for the contract is not includible in the gross income of the owner of the contract. Because such amounts are excludable from gross income, these retained policyholder dividends do not increase the taxpayer's investment in the contract.

### Treatment of loans under modified endowment contracts

The receipt of any amount (directly or indirectly) as a loan under a modified endowment contract or the assignment or pledge of any portion of the value of a modified endowment contract is treated as an amount received under the contract for purposes of the income inclusion rules. Thus, for example, the amount of any loan that is received under a modified endowment contract is includible in gross income to the extent that the cash surrender value of the contract exceeds the taxpayer's investment in the contract.

The assignment or pledge of any portion of a modified endowment contract is not treated as an amount received under a modified endowment contract if the contract (1) has an initial death benefit of $5,000 or less and a maximum death benefit of $25,000 or less, (2) provides for a fixed predetermined annual increase in the death benefit not to exceed 10 percent of the initial death benefit or 8 percent of the death benefit at the end of the preceding year, and (3) was purchased to cover payment of burial expenses or in connection with prearranged funeral expenses, but only if the assignment or pledge is solely to cover the current or future payment of burial expenses or prearranged funeral expenses.[164]

### Additional tax on certain pre-death distributions

The portion of any amount received under a modified endowment contract that is includible in gross income is subject to an additional 10-percent income tax. This additional tax does not apply to any amount that is (1) received on or after the date that the taxpayer attains age 59½; (2) attributable to the taxpayer becoming disabled; or (3) one of a series of substantially equal periodic payments (not less frequently than annually) made for the life (or life expectancy) of the taxpayer or the joint lives (or joint life expectancies) of the taxpayer and the taxpayer's beneficiary.

## Definition of modified endowment contract

### In general

A modified endowment contract is defined as any contract that satisfies the present-law definition of a life insurance contract but fails to satisfy a 7-pay test. In addition, a modified endowment contract includes any life insurance contract that is received in exchange for a modified endowment contract.

---

[164] For purposes of this rule, the initial death benefit is determined by treating all life insurance and modified endowment contracts that cover the payment of burial expenses or prearranged funeral expenses and that are issued to the same contract owner as a single contract

### Description of 7-pay test

A contract fails to satisfy the 7-pay test if the cumulative amount paid under the contract at any time during the first 7 contract years exceeds the sum of the net level premiums that would have been paid on or before such time had the contract provided for paid-up future benefits after the payment of 7 level annual premiums.

Thus, in order for a contract to satisfy the 7-pay test, the contract must provide greater insurance protection per premium dollar during the first 7 years of the contract than is required under the present-law definition of life insurance. Or, stated differently, the amount of the death benefit for the first 7 years of the contract must be greater than the death benefit that is required under present law for the same premium dollar. By requiring increased insurance protection during the first 7 years of the contract, the committee believes that the purchase of life insurance as an investment vehicle will be reduced.

The net level premiums under the 7-pay test ("7-pay premiums") are computed by applying the computational rules used in determining the net single premium under the cash value accumulation test, except that the death benefit that is provided under the contract for the first contract year is deemed to be provided until the deemed maturity date of the contract. Thus, the 7-pay premiums are computed using a rate of interest that equals the greater of an annual effective rate of 4 percent or the rate or rates guaranteed on the issuance of the contract. The mortality charges taken into account in computing the 7-pay premiums must be reasonable as determined under Treasury regulations and, except as provided in Treasury regulations, cannot exceed the mortality charges taken into account in determining the Federal income tax reserve for the contract.[165] Finally, expense charges are not taken into account in determining the 7-pay premiums.

The 7-pay premiums for any contract are determined at the time that the contract is issued. If there is a scheduled or unscheduled reduction in the death benefit under a contract during the first 7 contract years, however, the 7-pay premiums are redetermined as if the contract had originally been issued at the reduced death benefit level and the new limitation is applied to the cumulative amount paid under the contract for each of the first 7 contract years.[166] If, under this recomputation of the 7-pay premiums, a contract fails to satisfy the 7-pay test for any prior contract year, the contract is considered a modified endowment contract for (1) distributions that occur during the contract year that the death benefit reduction takes effect and all subsequent contract years, and (2) distributions that are made in anticipation of such death benefit reduction as determined under Treasury regulations.[167]

---

[165] For a more detailed discussion of the mortality charges that are taken into account for purposes of the definition of a life insurance contract, see the discussion in III G 4., below.

[166] This rule applies to any reduction in death benefits occurring during the first 7 contract years whether or not the reduction is considered an exchange of the original contract for a new contract.

[167] For this purpose, any distribution that reduces the cash surrender value of a contract and that is made within 2 years before a reduction in death benefits under the contract is treated as made in anticipation of such reduction.

For purposes of the 7-pay test, the term "amounts paid" means the premiums paid under the contract reduced by amounts received under the contract that are not received as an annuity to the extent that such amounts are not includible in gross income and are not attributable to a reduction in the originally scheduled death benefits. If, in order to comply with the 7-pay test, the amount of any premium payment is returned by the insurance company with interest within 60 days after the end of a contract year, the amount of the premium returned reduces the amount paid under the contract for such contract year. The interest that is required to be paid with the returned premium is includible in the gross income of the recipient.

Under the bill, the term "contract year" means the 12-month period beginning with the first month that the contract is in effect and each 12-month period beginning with the corresponding month in subsequent calendar years. Other terms used in defining a modified endowment contract have the same meaning as used in defining a life insurance contract.

*Material changes*

If there is a material change in the benefits or other terms of the contract at any time that a life insurance contract is outstanding that was not reflected in any previous determination under the 7-pay test, the contract is considered a new contract that is subject to the 7-pay test as of the date that the material change takes effect. In applying the 7-pay test to a contract that is materially changed, appropriate adjustments as described below are to be made in the application of the 7-pay test to take into account the greater of (1) the premiums previously paid under such contract or (2) the cash surrender value of such contract.

For purposes of this rule, a material change does not include a reduction in the death benefit under the contract during the first 7 contract years.[168] A material change does include the exchange of a life insurance contract for another life insurance contract (other than an exchange of a contract for another contract with a reduced death benefit if the exchange occurs during the first 7 contract years of the original contract) and the conversion of a term life insurance contract into a whole life insurance contract (whether or not the conversion is considered an exchange of contracts). In addition, an increase in the future benefits provided under a life insurance contract constitutes a material change unless the increase is required to satisfy the cash value accumulation test or the guideline premium/cash corridor test and the increase is attributable to (1) the payment of premiums necessary to fund the lowest death benefit payable in the first 7 contract years,[169] or (2) the crediting of interest or other earnings with respect to such premiums.

The payment of any premium is not necessary to fund the lowest death benefit payable during the first 7 contract years to the extent that the amount of the premium exceeds the excess, if any,

---

[168] If there is a reduction in the death benefit during the first 7 contract years, the rules provided above in the description of the 7-pay test apply.
[169] In the case of a contract that was materially changed as of a prior date, the death benefit taken into account is the lowest death benefit payable during the most recent 7 contract-year period that the 7-pay test applied.

of (1) the single premium for the contract immediately before the premium payment, over (2) the deemed cash surrender value of the contract immediately before the premium payment.

For this purpose, the single premium for a contract is determined by applying the computational rules under the cash value accumulation test or the guideline premium requirement, whichever is applicable, except that the lowest death benefit that is provided during the first 7 contract years is deemed to be provided until the deemed maturity date of the contract. Thus, for example, in the case of a contract that satisfies the cash value accumulation test, the single premium is computed using a rate of interest that equals the greater of 4 percent or the rate or rates guaranteed on the issuance of the contract, and expense charges are not taken into account.

The deemed cash surrender value of any contract equals the cash surrender value (determined without regard to any surrender charge or policy loan) that would result if the premiums paid under the contract [170] had be credited with interest at the policy rate and had been reduced by the applicable mortality and expense charges. For this purpose, in the case of a contract that satisfies the cash value accumulation test, the policy rate equals the greater of 4 percent or the rate or rates guaranteed on the issuance of the contract. In the case of a policy that satisfies the guideline premium requirement, the policy rate equals the greater of 6 percent or the rate or rates guaranteed on the issuance of the contract. The applicable mortality and expense charges for any contract are those charges that were taken into account for prior periods under the cash value accumulation test or the guideline premium requirement, whichever is applicable.

If a life insurance contract is materially changed, in applying the 7-pay test to any new premiums paid under the contract, the 7-pay premium for each of the first 7 contract years is to be reduced by the product of (1) the greater of the premiums previously paid under the contract or the cash surrender value of the contract as of the date that the material change takes effect, and (2) a fraction, the numerator of which equals the 7-pay premium for the future benefits under the contract and the denominator of which equals the net single premium for such benefits computed using the same assumptions used in determining the 7-pay premium.

This rule can be illustrated by the following example. Assume that a contract with a death benefit of $30,000, a cash surrender value of $10,000, and total premiums paid of $9,000 is materially changed by increasing the death benefit to $100,000. In addition, assume that after the material change, the 7-pay premium for such contract equals $4,774 and the net single premium equals $29,502. Under the adjustment rule, the cash surrender value of $10,000 is first multiplied by a fraction the numerator of which is the $4,774 7-pay premium and the denominator of which is the $29,502 net single premium. The result of this calculation, $1,618 is then sub-

---

[170] For this purpose, premiums paid under a contract include all premiums other than premiums that are returned within 60 days after the end of a taxable year in order to satisfy the guideline premium requirement or the 7-pay test.

tracted from $4,774 to yield a 7-pay premium of $3,156 that is applied for purposes of the 7-pay test.[171]

### Study of life insurance and annuity contracts

The bill requires the Secretary of the Treasury and the Comptroller General of the United States to each conduct a study of (1) the effectiveness of the revised tax treatment of life insurance and annuity contracts in preventing the sale of life insurance primarily for investment purposes, and (2) the policy justification for, and the practical implications of, the present-law treatment of earnings on the cash surrender value of life insurance and annuity contracts in light of the reforms made by the Tax Reform Act of 1986. The results of each study, as well as any recommendations that are considered advisable, are required to be submitted to the House Ways and Means Committee and the Senate Finance Committee not later than March 1, 1989.

### Effective Date

The provision applies to contracts that are entered into or that are materially changed on or after June 21, 1988. For purposes of this effective date, a contract is considered entered into no earlier than the date that (1) the contract is endorsed by both the owner of the contract and the insurance company; or (2) an application is executed by both the applicant and the insurance company and a premium payment is made by the applicant to the insurance company. The backdating of an application or an insurance contract shall be disregarded for purposes of this effective date.

In determining whether a contract has been materially changed, the rules described above are to apply, except that in determining whether an increase in future benefits constitutes a material change, the death benefit payable under the contract as of June 20, 1988, is to be taken into account rather than the lowest death benefit payable during the first 7 contract years. If a contract entered into before June 21, 1988, is materially changed, the 7-pay test is to be applied to the contract with the adjustments described above.

### 4. Corporate estimated tax payments (sec. 314 of the bill and sec. 6655 of the Code)

#### Present Law

Under present law, corporations are required to make estimated tax payments four times a year (sec. 6655). For small corporations, each installment is required to be based on an amount equal to the lesser of (1) 90 percent of the tax shown on the return or (2) 100 percent of the tax shown on the preceding year's return. For large corporations, each installment is required to be based on an amount equal to 90 percent of the tax shown on the return (except that the first payment may be based on 100 percent of the tax shown on the preceding year's return). For both large and small corporations, the amount of any payment is not required to exceed

---

[171] This example is based on a male who is 43 years old on the date of the material change. The assumed mortality charges equal 80 percent of the 1980 Commissioners' Standard Ordinary Mortality Table.

545

## 4. Limitation on unreasonable mortality and expense charges for definition of life insurance (sec. 346 of the bill and sec. 7702 of the Code)

### *Present Law*

Under present law, the undistributed investment income ("inside buildup") earned on premiums credited under a life insurance contract generally is not subject to current taxation to the owner of the contract. In addition, death benefits paid under a life insurance contract are excluded from the gross income of the recipient.

The favorable tax treatment accorded to life insurance is available only for contracts that satisfy a statutory definition of life insurance. Under this statutory definition, a contract must satisfy either a cash value accumulation test or a test consisting of a guideline premium requirement and a cash value corridor requirement. In determining whether a contract satisfies the cash value accumulation test or the guideline premium requirement, the mortality charges taken into account are the charges specified in the contract, or, if none are specified in the contract, the mortality charges used in determining the statutory reserve for the contract. In determining whether a contract satisfies the guideline premium requirement, the expense charges taken into account are the charges specified in the contract.

### *Reasons for Change*

Concerns have been raised that some insurance companies are taking aggressive positions with respect to mortality and expense charges. Specifically, companies may be overstating mortality and expense charges and then rebating them to policyholders, or not charging the stated amounts. By overstating mortality and expense charges, insurance companies can increase the investment orientation of life insurance products, contrary to the intent of Congress when the definition of life insurance was enacted. The committee believes that it is appropriate to clarify that such practices with respect to mortality and expense charges are not reasonable.

### *Explanation of Provision*

For all life insurance contracts, the mortality charges taken into account for purposes of the definition of life insurance are required to be reasonable as determined under Treasury regulations and, except as provided in Treasury regulations, may not exceed the mortality charges required to be used in determining the Federal income tax reserve for the contract. The expense charges taken into account for purposes of the guideline premium requirement are required to be reasonable based on the experience of the company and other insurance companies with respect to similar life insurance contracts.

### *Effective Date*

The provision generally is effective for all life insurance contracts issued on or after July 13, 1988, and for all life insurance contracts that are materially changed on or after July 13, 1988. A material change for this purpose has the same meaning as a material change under the provisions relating to modified endowment contracts (see III.B.3, above).

### 5. Valuation of group-term life insurance (sec. 347 of the bill and sec. 79 of the Code)

*Present Law*

Under present law, the cost of employer-provided group-term life insurance generally is included in an employee's income to the extent that such cost exceeds the cost of $50,000 of group-term life insurance. In addition, the cost of employer-provided group-term life insurance generally is includible in the income of highly compensated employees to the extent that such insurance is provided on a basis that discriminates in favor of such employees.

In general, the cost of employer-provided group-term life insurance is determined under a table prescribed by the Secretary, which is set forth below. Section 79(c) provides that the cost with respect to any employee older than 63 is to be determined as if such employee were 63. (Because of the 5-year age brackets established by the Secretary, individuals over age 64 are the ones actually receiving special treatment under the table.)

*Cost per $1,000 of protection for 1-month period*

5-year age bracket:
| | |
|---|---|
| Under 30 | $0.08 |
| 30 to 34 | .09 |
| 35 to 39 | .11 |
| 40 to 44 | .17 |
| 45 to 49 | .29 |
| 50 to 54 | .48 |
| 55 to 59 | .75 |
| 60 to 64 | 1.17 |

In the case of discriminatory group-term life insurance, the amount includible in a highly compensated employee's income is the greater of the table cost or the actual cost of the employer-provided group-term life insurance.

Group-term life insurance provided by an employer to certain former employees is subject to special treatment pursuant to a grandfather rule included in the Deficit Reduction Act of 1984. Pursuant to this grandfather rule, the cost of employer-provided group-term life insurance generally is not includible in income without regard to whether it exceeds the cost of $50,000 of insurance or is discriminatory. The former employees entitled to such treatment are (1) any individual who attained age 55 on or before January 1, 1984, and was employed by the employer (or a predecessor employer) at any time during 1983; and (2) any individual who retired on or before January 1, 1984, and who was, when he or she retired, covered by the plan (or a predecessor plan). This grandfather rule is limited to group-term life insurance plans of the employer (or a successor employer) that were in existence on January 1, 1984, or are comparable successor plans to such plans. In addition, the grandfather rule does not apply to a discriminatory plan with respect to an individual retiring after December 31, 1986.

# APPENDIX I
## TAMRA CONFERENCE REPORT:

## TECHNICAL AND MISCELLANEOUS REVENUE ACT OF 1988—CONFERENCE REPORT

| 100TH CONGRESS 2d Session | HOUSE OF REPRESENTATIVES | REPORT 100-1104 |

# TECHNICAL AND MISCELLANEOUS REVENUE ACT OF 1988

## CONFERENCE REPORT

TO ACCOMPANY

## H.R. 4333

**Volume II of 2 Volumes**

OCTOBER 21, 1988.—Ordered to be printed

U.S. GOVERNMENT PRINTING OFFICE
WASHINGTON : 1988

89-860

For sale by the Superintendent of Documents, U.S. Government Printing Office
Washington, DC 20402

would be due if the total payments for the year up to the required payment equal 90 percent of the tax which would be due if the income already received during the current year were placed on an annual basis. Any reduction in a payment resulting from using this annualization rule must be made up in the subsequent payment if the corporation does not use the annualization rule for that subsequent payment. However, if the subsequent payment makes up at least 90 percent of the earlier shortfall, no penalty is imposed.

### House Bill

A corporation that uses the annualization method for a prior payment is required to make up the entire shortfall (rather than 90 percent of the shortfall) in the subsequent payment in order to avoid an estimated tax penalty. The provision is effective for estimated tax payments required to be made after December 31, 1988.

### Senate Amendment

The Senate amendment is the same as the House bill, effective for estimated tax payments required to be made after September 30, 1988.

### Conference Agreement

The conference agreement follows the House bill.

### B. Life Insurance Provisions

### 1. Treatment of single premium and other investment-oriented life insurance contracts

### Present Law

Under present law, the undistributed investment income ("inside buildup") earned on premiums credited under a contract that satisfies a statutory definition of life insurance is not subject to current taxation to the owner of the contract. In addition, death benefits paid under a contract that satisfies the statutory definition are excluded from the gross income of the recipient, so that neither the owner of the contract nor the beneficiary of the contract is ever taxed on the inside buildup if the insured dies before the contract is surrendered.

Amounts received under a life insurance contract prior to the death of the insured generally are not includible in gross income to the extent that the amount received does not exceed the taxpayer's investment in the contract. Amounts borrowed under a life insurance contract generally are not treated as received and, consequently, are not includible in gross income.

### House Bill

*Treatment of modified endowment contracts*

*Distribution rules*

In order to discourage the purchase of life insurance as a tax-sheltered investment vehicle, the House bill alters the Federal income tax treatment of loans and other amounts received under a class of life insurance contracts that are statutorily defined as "modified endowment contracts." Under the House bill, amounts received under modified endowment contracts are treated first as income and then as recovered basis. In addition, loans under modified endowment contracts and loans secured by modified endowment contracts are treated as amounts received under the contract. Finally, an additional 10-percent income tax is imposed on certain amounts received under modified endowment contracts to the extent that the amounts received are includible in gross income.

Under the House bill, the assignment or pledge of any portion of a modified endowment contract is not treated as an amount received under the contract if the assignment or pledge is solely to cover the payment of burial expenses or prearranged funeral expenses and the contract satisfies special rules relating to the definition of life insurance (sec. 7702(e)(2)(C)).

In determining whether amounts payable or borrowed under a modified endowment contract are received under the contract, the House bill adopts the present-law rules applicable to annuity contracts. Under these rules, any amount in the nature of a dividend or similar distribution that is retained by the insurer as a premium or other consideration paid for the contract is not includible in the gross income of the owner of the contract. Because such amounts are excludable from gross income, these retained policyholder dividends do not increase the taxpayer's investment in the contract.

*Definition of modified endowment contract*

A modified endowment contract is defined as any contract that satisfies the present-law definition of a life insurance contract but fails to satisfy a 7-pay test. In addition, a modified endowment contract includes any life insurance contract that is received in exchange for a modified endowment contract.

A contract fails to satisfy the 7-pay test if the cumulative amount paid under the contract at any time during the first 7 contract years exceeds the sum of the net level premiums that would have been paid on or before such time had the contract provided for paid-up future benefits after the payment of 7 level annual premiums.

The net level premiums under the 7-pay test ("7-pay premiums") are computed by applying the computational rules used in determining the net single premium under the cash value accumulation test, except that the death benefit that is provided under the contract for the first contract year is deemed to be provided until the deemed maturity date of the contract. Under the House bill, the mortality charges taken into account in computing the 7-pay premiums must be reasonable as determined under Treasury regulations and, except as provided in Treasury regulations, cannot exceed the mortality charges taken into account in determining the Federal income tax reserve for the contract. Expense charges are not taken into account in determining the 7-pay premiums.

For purposes of the 7-pay test, the term "amount paid" means the premiums paid under the contract reduced by amounts received under the contract that are not received as an annuity to the extent that such amounts are not includible in gross income and are not attributable to a reduction in the originally scheduled death benefit.

*Material change rules*

If there is a material change in the benefits or other terms of a contract that was not reflected in any previous determination under the 7-pay test, the contract is considered a new contract that is subject to the 7-pay test as of the date that the material change takes effect and adjustments are made in the application of the 7-pay test to take into account the greater of the cash surrender value of the contract or the premiums paid under the contract.

For purposes of this rule, a material change includes the exchange of a life insurance contract for another life insurance contract and the conversion of a term life insurance contract into a whole life insurance contract. In addition, an increase in the future benefits provided under a life insurance contract constitutes a material change unless the increase is required to satisfy the statutory definition of life insurance and the increase is attributable to (1) the payment of premiums necessary to fund the lowest death benefit payable in the first 7 contract years, or (2) the crediting of interest or other earnings with respect to such premiums.

The payment of any premium is not necessary to fund the lowest death benefit payable during the first 7 contract years to the extent that the amount of the premium exceeds the excess, if any, of (1) the single premium for the contract immediately before the premium payment, over (2) the deemed cash surrender value of the contract immediately before the premium payment.

For this purpose, the single premium for a contract is determined by applying the computational rules under the cash value accumulation test or the guideline premium requirement, whichever is applicable, except that the lowest death benefit that is provided during the first 7 contract years is deemed to be provided until the deemed maturity date of the contract.

The deemed cash surrender value of any contract equals the cash surrender value (determined without regard to any surrender charge or policy loan) that would result if the premiums paid under the contract had been credited with interest at the policy rate and had been reduced by the applicable mortality and expense charges. For this purpose, in the case of a contract that satisfies the cash value accumulation test, the policy rate equals the greater of 4 percent or the rate or rates guaranteed on the issuance of the contract. In the case of a contract that satisfies the guideline premium requirement, the policy rate equals the greater of 6 percent or the rate or rates guaranteed on the issuance of the contract. The applicable mortality and expense charges for any contract are those charges that were taken into account for prior periods under the cash value accumulation test or the guideline premium requirement, whichever is applicable.

If a life insurance contract is materially changed, in applying the 7-pay test to any new premiums paid under the contract, the 7-pay premium for each of the first 7 contract years is to be reduced by the product of (1) the greater of the premiums previously paid under the contract or the cash surrender value of the contract as of the date that the material change takes effect, and (2) a fraction, the numerator of which equals the 7-pay premium for the future benefits under the contract and the denominator of which equals the net single premium for such benefits computed using the same assumptions used in determining the 7-pay premium.

*Studies of life insurance and annuity contracts*

The House bill requires the Secretary of the Treasury and the Comptroller General of the United States to each conduct a separate study of (1) the effectiveness of the revised tax treatment of life insurance in preventing the sale of life insurance primarily for investment purposes, and (2) the policy justification for, and the practical implications of, the present-law treatment of earnings on the cash surrender value of life insurance and annuity contracts in light of the reforms made by the Tax Reform Act of 1986. The results of each study, as well as any recommendations that are considered advisable, are required to be submitted to the House Ways and Means Committee and the Senate Finance Committee not later than March 1, 1989.

*Effective date*

The provision of the House bill relating to modified endowment contracts applies to contracts that are entered into or that are materially changed on or after June 21, 1988. In determining whether a contract has been materially changed, the rules described above are to apply, except that in determining whether an increase in future benefits constitutes a material change, the death benefit payable under the contract as of June 20, 1988, is to be taken into account rather than the lowest death benefit payable during the first 7 contract years. If a contract entered into before June 21, 1988, is materially changed, the 7-pay test is to be applied to the contract with the adjustments described above.

### Senate Amendment

The Senate amendment is the same as the House bill with the following clarifications and modifications.

*Treatment of modified endowment contracts*

   *Distribution rules*

The Senate amendment is the same as the House bill with respect to the treatment of assignments solely to pay burial or prearranged funeral expenses, except that the Senate amendment applies to all life insurance contracts, rather than only those contracts satisfying the special definition of life insurance for burial contracts, and the Senate amendment clarifies that the treatment of assignments to cover the payment of burial or prearranged funeral expenses applies only if the policyholder does not receive cash directly or indirectly in connection with the assignment.

The Senate amendment also provides that any amount payable or borrowed under a modified endowment contract is not included in gross income to the extent that the amount is retained by the insurance company as a premium or other consideration paid for the contract or as interest or principal paid on a loan under the contract. Because amounts retained by the insurer are not included in the gross income of the taxpayer, the taxpayer's investment in the contract is not increased by the amount retained.

Under the Senate amendment, the cash surrender value of a modified endowment contract is reduced by the amount of any loan that is treated as received under the contract under the revised income inclusion rules. In addition, the investment in the contract and the cash surrender value of the contract are each increased by the amount of payments on a loan to the extent attributable to loans treated as received under the contract under the revised income inclusion rules.

The Senate amendment extends the provision of the House bill relating to the treatment of distributions from a contract that is a modified endowment contract on account of a reduction in death benefits to all modified endowment contracts without regard to the reason that the contract fails to satisfy the 7-pay test. Thus, under the Senate amendment, a contract is considered a modified endowment contract for (1) distributions that occur during the contract year that the contract fails (whether due to a death benefit reduction or otherwise) to satisfy the 7-pay test and all subsequent contract years, and (2) distributions that are made in anticipation of the contract failing to satisfy the 7-pay test as determined by the Treasury Department.

*Definition of modified endowment contract*

Under the Senate amendment, the mortality charges taken into account in computing the 7-pay premiums equal the mortality charges specified in the prevailing commissioners' standard table (as defined in sec. 807(d)(5)) at the time that the contract is issued or materially changed (currently 1980 CSO) except to the extent provided otherwise by the Treasury Department (e.g., with respect to substandard risks).

In the case of a contract that provides an initial death benefit of $10,000 or less and that requires at least 20 nondecreasing annual premium payments, the Senate amendment provides that the amount of the 7-pay premium for each year is increased by an expense charge of $75. All contracts issued by the same insurance company to the same policyholder are treated as a single contract for purposes of applying this rule.

Under the Senate amendment, riders to contracts are considered part of the base insurance contract for purposes of the 7-pay test. In addition, the complete surrender of a life insurance contract during the first 7 years of the contract does not in itself cause the contract to be treated as a modified endowment contract.

The Senate amendment provides that the lapse of a contract resulting in paid-up insurance in a reduced amount due to the nonpayment of premiums is not considered in applying the 7-pay test if the contract is reinstated to the original face amount within 180 days after the lapse. Finally, under the Senate amendment, the amount paid under a contract is reduced by nontaxable distributions to which section 72(e) applies whether or not attributable to a reduction in the originally scheduled death benefit.

101

*Material change rules*

The Senate amendment deletes the rule in the House bill that a death benefit increase must be required in order to satisfy the statutory definition of life insurance. Thus, under the Senate amendment, an increase in the future benefits provided under a life insurance contract constitutes a material change unless the increase is attributable to (1) the payment of premiums necessary to fund the lowest death benefit payable in the first 7 contract years or (2) the crediting of interest or other earnings with respect to such premiums.

Under the Senate amendment, the definition of necessary premium for guideline premium contracts is modified to allow aggregate premium payments equal to the greater of (1) the guideline single premium or (2) the sum of the guideline level premiums to date (without regard to the deemed cash value). In determining the necessary premiums under a contract, an increase in the death benefit provided in the contract may be taken into account to the extent necessary to prevent a decrease in the excess of the death benefit over the cash surrender value of the contract.

The Senate amendment provides that a decrease in future benefits under a contract is not considered a material change. In addition, policyholder dividends are considered other earnings that may increase the death benefit without triggering a material change.

Under the Senate amendment, the Treasury Department is granted authority to provide circumstances under which a de minimis death benefit increase is not a material change (e.g., a death benefit increase that is attributable to a reasonable cost of living adjustment determined under an established index specified in the contract).

In the case of a contract that is materially changed, the new 7-pay premium is adjusted to take into account only the cash surrender value of the contract as of the date of the material change. Thus, under the Senate amendment, in applying the 7-pay test to any new premiums paid under a contract that has been materially changed, the 7-pay premium for each of the first 7 contract years after the change is to be reduced by the product of (1) the cash surrender value of the contract as of the date that the material change takes effect, and (2) a fraction the numerator of which equals the 7-pay premium for the future benefits under the contract, and the denominator of which equals the net single premium for such benefits computed using the same assumptions used in determining the 7-pay premium.

*Studies of life insurance and annuity contracts*

The Senate amendment does not follow the House bill provision requiring studies on the taxation of life insurance and annuity contracts.

*Effective date*

The provision of the Senate amendment relating to modified endowment contracts applies to contracts entered into on or after June 21, 1988. A contract is considered entered into on or after June 21, 1988, if (1) on or after June 21, 1988, the death benefit under the contract is increased or a qualified additional benefit is increased or added to the contract and, prior to June 21, 1988, the owner of the contract did not have a unilateral right under the contract to obtain such increase or addition without providing additional evidence of insurability, or (2) the contract is converted from a term life insurance contract into a life insurance contract providing coverage other than term insurance coverage after June 20, 1988, without regard to any right of the owner under the contract to obtain such conversion.

In addition, a modified endowment contract that is entered into on or after June 21, 1988, and before the date of enactment and that is exchanged within 3 months after the date of enactment for a life insurance contract that satisfies the 7-pay test is not considered a modified endowment contract if gain (if any) is recognized on the exchange.

### Conference Agreement

The conference agreement follows that Senate amendment with the following modifications and clarifications.

#### Treatment of modified endowment contracts

##### Distribution rules

The conference agreement provides that the assignment or pledge of any portion of a modified endowment contract is not treated as an amount received under the contract if the assignment or pledge is solely to cover the payment of burial expenses or prearranged funeral expenses and the maximum amount of the death benefit provided under the contract does not exceed $25,000.

In determining whether amounts payable or borrowed under a modified endowment contract are received under the contract, only an amount in the nature of a dividend or similar distribution that is retained by the insurer as a premium or other consideration paid for the contract is not includible in the gross income of the owner of the contract. Thus, for example, any amount borrowed under a modified endowment that is retained by the insurer as a premium under the contract is considered an amount received under the contract. In addition, any dividend under a modified endowment contract that is retained by the insurer as principal or interest on a loan under the contract is considered an amount received under the contract. On the other hand, any dividend under a modified endowment contract that is retained by the insurer to purchase an additional amount of paid-up insurance or a qualified additional benefit is not considered an amount received under the contract.

The conference agreement also provides rules with respect to the determination of a taxpayer's investment in the contract in the case of any loan that is treated as received under a modified endowment contract or an annuity contract. Under these rules, the investment in the contract is increased by the amount of any loan that is treated as received under the contract to the extent that the loan is includible in the gross income of the taxpayer. In addition, unlike the present-law rule for other amounts received that are excludable from gross income, the amount of any loan that is treated as received under the contract but is excludable from gross income does not affect the calculation of the taxpayer's investment in the contract. Under the conference agreement, the cash surrender value of a contract is determined without regard to the amount of any loan and the repayment of a loan (as well as any interest under the loan) does not affect a taxpayer's investment in the contract whether or not the loan was treated as received under the contract.

In order to stop the marketing of serial contracts that are designed to avoid the rules applicable to modified endowment contracts, the conference agreement provides that all modified endowment contracts issued by the same insurer (or affiliates) to the same policyholder during any 12-month period are to be aggregated for purposes of determining the amount of any distribution that is includible in gross income. In addition, all annuity contracts issued by the same insurer (or affiliates) to the same policyholder during any 12-month period are to be aggregated for purposes of determining the amount of any distribution that is includible in gross income. Finally, the Treasury Department is provided regulatory authority to prevent the avoidance of the rules contained in section 72(e) through the serial purchase of contracts or otherwise.

*Definition of modified endowment contract*

Under the conference agreement, the mortality charges taken into account in computing the 7-pay premiums are the same as those taken into account for purposes of the definition of a life insurance contract (as modified by this conference agreement). Thus, the mortality charges are to be reasonable as determined under Treasury regulations and, except as provided in Treasury regulations, cannot exceed the mortality charges specified in the prevailing commissioners' standard table (as defined in sec. 807(d)(5)) at the time that the contract is issued or materially changed (currently 1980 CSO).[1]

The conference agreement also modifies the provision in the Senate amendment relating to the $75 expense charge for small contracts. Under the conference agreement, in the case of a life insurance contract that provides an initial death benefit of $10,000 or less and requires at least 7 annual level premium payments (rather than 20 nondecreasing annual premium payments as provided in the Senate amendment), the amount of the 7-pay premium for each year is increased by an expense charge of $75. For purposes of determining whether a contract provides an initial death benefit of $10,000 or less, any life insurance contract previously issued by the same insurer (or affiliates) to the same policyholder is to be treated as part of such contract, except that any contract that under the effective date provisions is not treated as entered into on or after June 21, 1988, is not to be taken into account.

The conference agreement also authorizes the Treasury Department to prescribe rules for taking into account expenses solely attributable to the collection of premiums paid more frequently than annually. For example, it may be appropriate to take into account the increased expenses that are often charged under smaller con-

---

[1] For a more detailed discussion of the mortality charges that are taken into account for this purpose, see the discussion in IV. B. 2., below.

tracts (e.g., those with a death benefit of $25,000 or less) and that are attributable to the required payment of premiums more frequently than annually.

Under the conference agreement, a reduction in benefits associated with the lapse of a contract due to the nonpayment of premiums is not considered in applying the 7-pay test if the benefits are reinstated within 90 days after the lapse (rather than 180 days after the lapse as provided in the Senate amendment).

The conference agreement provides that for purposes of the 7-pay test, the term "amount paid" means the premiums paid under the contract reduced by amounts received under the contract that are not received as an annuity to the extent that such amounts are not includible in gross income. The receipt of any amount as a loan or the repayment of a loan (as well as any interest under the loan) is not to be taken into account in determining the amount paid under a contract.

### Material change rules

Under the conference agreement, a material change includes any increase in the future benefits provided under a life insurance contract with two exceptions. First, a material change does not include an increase in the future benefits provided under a contract if the increase is attributable to (1) the payment of premiums necessary to fund the lowest death benefit payable in the first 7 contract years (except that certain limited death benefit increases described in sec. 7702(e)(2)(A) and (B) may be taken into account), or (2) the crediting of interest or other earnings (including policyholder dividends) with respect to such premiums.

Second, to the extent provided in Treasury regulations, a material change does not include a death benefit increase attributable to a cost-of-living adjustment that is based on an established broad-based index (such as the Consumer Price Index) specified in the contract if (1) the period over which the cost-of-living increase is determined does not exceed the remaining period over which premiums will be paid under the contract and (2) any additional premiums required to fund the increased death benefit are paid ratably over the remaining life of the contract.

In determining whether the payment of any premium is necessary to fund the lowest death benefit payable in the first 7 contract years (taking into account the limited death benefit increases described in section 7702(e)(2(A) and (B)), the conference agreement provides one standard for contracts that satisfy the cash value accumulation test and a second standard for contracts that satisfy the guideline premium requirement. In the case of a contract that satisfies the cash value accumulation test, a premium is necessary to fund the lowest death benefit payable during the first 7 contract years to the extent that the net amount of the premium (i.e., the amount of the premium reduced by any expense charge) does not exceed the excess, if any, of (1) the attained age net single premium for the contract immediately before the premium payment,[2] over

---

[2] The attained age net single premium for a contract is to be determined by applying the computational rules under the cash value accumulation test and by assuming that the lowest death

Continued

(2) the deemed cash surrender value of the contract immediately before the premium payment.[3]

In the case of a contract that satisfies the guideline premium requirement, a premium is necessary to fund the lowest death benefit payable during the first 7 contract years to the extent that the premium paid does not exceed the excess, if any, of (1) the greater of the guideline single premium or the sum of the guideline level premiums to date,[4] over (2) the sum of the premiums previously paid under the contract.

In the case of a contract that is materially changed due to an increase in future benefits that is attributable to a premium that is not necessary to fund the lowest death benefit payable in the first 7 contract years, the amount of the premium that is not necessary to fund such death benefit is to be subject to the 7-pay test without regard to the timing of the premium payment. In applying the 7-pay test to any premiums paid under a contract that has been materially changed, the 7-pay premium for each of the first 7 contract years after the change is to be reduced by the product of (1) the cash surrender value of the contract as of the date that the material change takes effect (determined without regard to any increase in the cash surrender value that is attributable to the amount of the premium payment that is not necessary), and (2) a fraction the numerator of which equals the 7-pay premium for the future benefits under the contract, and the denominator of which equals the net single premium for such benefits computed using the same assumptions used in determining the 7-pay premium.

*Studies of life insurance and annuity contracts*

The conference agreement follows the House bill in requiring studies on the taxation of life insurance and annuity contracts. The results of the studies are required to be submitted to the House Ways and Means Committee and the Senate Finance Committee not later than June 1, 1989.

*Effective date*

The provision of the conference agreement relating to modified endowment contracts applies to contracts entered into on or after June 21, 1988. In determining whether a contract is entered into on or after June 21, 1988, for purposes of this effective date, if the death benefit payable under the contract as of October 20, 1988, increases by more than $150,000, the material change rules generally applicable under the conference agreement are to apply. In determining whether an increase in future benefits constitutes a materi-

---

benefit that is provided during the first 7 contract years is provided until the deemed maturity date of the contract, except that the limited death benefit increases described in section 7702(e)(2)(B) may be taken into account.

[3] In the case of a life insurance contract with a deemed cash surrender value in excess of the actual cash surrender value (determined without regard to any surrender charge or policy loan), the actual cash surrender value is to be substituted for the deemed cash surrender value in determining whether a premium is necessary to fund the lowest death benefit payable during the first 7 contract years.

[4] The guideline single premium and the guideline level premiums for a contract are to be determined by applying the computational rules applicable to guideline premium contracts and by assuming that the lowest death benefit that is provided during the first 7 contract years is provided until the deemed maturity date of the contract, except that the limited death benefit increases described in section 7702(e)(2)(A) may be taken into account.

al change, however, the death benefit payable under the contract as of June 20, 1988, is to be taken into account rather than the lowest death benefit payable during the first 7 contract years.

A contract is not to be considered entered into on or after June 21, 1988, under the effective date provision that applies the material change rules to a contract with a death benefit increase of more than $150,000, if as of June 21, 1988, the terms of the contract required at least 7 annual level premium payments and the policyholder continues to make the level annual premium payments in accordance with the terms of the contract as of June 21, 1988. Consequently, an ordinary whole life insurance contract that is entered into before June 21, 1988, will not be subject to the modified endowment contract provisions of the conference agreement.

In addition, under the conference agreement, a contract is considered entered into on or after June 21, 1988, for purposes of this effective date if (1) on or after June 21, 1988, the death benefit under the contract is increased or a qualified additional benefit is increased or added to the contract and, prior to June 21, 1988, the owner of the contract did not have a unilateral right under the contract to obtain such increase or addition without providing additional evidence of insurability, or (2) the contract is converted after June 20, 1988, from a term life insurance contract into a life insurance contract providing coverage other than term insurance coverage, without regard to any right of the owner under the contract to obtain such conversion.

If a contract entered into before June 21, 1988, is considered entered into on or after such date under these rules, the 7-pay test is to be applied to the contract by taking into account the cash surrender value of the contract under the material change rules of the conference agreement.

The conference agreement also provides that in the case of a modified endowment contract that (1) required at least 7 annual level premium payments on the date that the contract was entered into, (2) is entered into on or after June 21, 1988, and before the date of enactment, and (3) is exchanged within 3 months after the date of enactment for a life insurance contract that satisfies the 7-pay test, the contract that is received in exchange for the modified endowment contract is not to be considered a modified endowment contract if the taxpayer elects to recognize the gain (if any) that is realized on the exchange.

Finally, the conference agreement provides that the provision relating to the determination of a taxpayer's investment in the contract in the case of a loan under an annuity contract and the antiabuse provision applicable to the serial purchase of annuity contracts are to apply to annuity contracts entered into after October 21, 1988. No inference is intended by this provision concerning the treatment of annuity contracts under present law.

## 2. Limitation on unreasonable mortality and expense charges for purposes of the definition of life insurance

### *Present Law*

For purposes of the statutory definition of a life insurance contract, the mortality charges taken into account are the charges

107

specified in the contract, or, if none are specified in the contract, the mortality charges used in determining the statutory reserve for the contract. For purposes of one of the alternative provisions of the statutory definition of life insurance (the guideline premium requirement), the expense charges taken into account are the expense charges specified in the contract.

### *House Bill*

For all life insurance contracts, the mortality charges taken into account for purposes of the definition of life insurance are required to be reasonable as determined under Treasury regulations and, except as provided in Treasury regulations, may not exceed the mortality charges required to be used in determining the Federal income tax reserve for the contract. The expense charges taken into account for purposes of the guideline premium requirement must be specified in the contract and must be reasonable charges which, on the basis of the company's experience, are reasonably expected to be actually paid. If a company does not have adequate experience for purposes of determining whether expense charges are reasonably expected to be made, the determination is to be made on the basis of the experience of other insurance companies with respect to similar life insurance contracts.

The provision applies to contracts entered into or materially changed on or after July 13, 1988.

### *Senate Amendment*

The Senate amendment does not contain a provision relating to the mortality and expense charges that are taken into account for purposes of the definition of life insurance. The Senate amendment provides that, in determining whether a contract that satisfies the statutory definition of life insurance is a modified endowment contract, the mortality charges taken into account are the mortality charges specified in the prevailing commissioners' standard tables (as determined pursuant to sec. 807(d)(5)) at the time the contract is issued or materially changed (currently 1980 CSO), except to the extent provided otherwise by the Treasury Department (e.g., with respect to substandard risks).

The provision applies to contracts entered into on or after June 21, 1988 (i.e., the effective date of the Senate amendment with respect to the treatment of modified endowment contracts). A contract is considered entered into on or after June 21, 1988, if (1) on or after that date, the death benefit is increased or qualified additional benefits are increased or added and, prior to that date, the owner of the contract did not have a unilateral right under the contract to obtain the increase or addition without providing evidence of insurability; or (2) the contract is converted from term insurance coverage to other than term insurance coverage after June 20, 1988, without regard to any right of the owner under the contract to obtain such conversion.

108

*Conference Agreement*

The conference agreement follows the House bill, with modifications.

For all life insurance contracts, the mortality charges taken into account for purposes of the definition of life insurance are required to be reasonable as determined under Treasury regulations and, except as provided in Treasury regulations, may not exceed the mortality charges specified in the prevailing commissioners' standard tables (within the meaning of section 807(d)(5)) as of the time the contract is issued. The Treasury Department is directed to issue regulations by January 1, 1990, setting forth standards for determining the reasonableness of mortality charges, including standards with respect to substandard risks. Standards set forth in such regulations that limit mortality charges to amounts less than those specified in the prevailing commissioners' standard tables are to be prospective in application. Pending the issuance of such regulations, mortality charges are to be considered reasonable if such charges do not differ materially from the charges actually expected to be imposed by the company, taking into account any relevant characteristics of the insured of which the company is aware.

For example, in determining whether it is appropriate to take into account mortality charges for any particular insured person as a substandard risk, a company should take into account relevant facts and circumstances such as the insured person's medical history and current medical condition. Other relevant factors include the applicability, if any, of State or local law prohibiting or limiting the company's inquiry into some or all aspects of the insured person's medical history or condition, increasing the potential unknown insurance risk with respect to insured persons in the jurisdiction.

The expense charges taken into account for purposes of the guideline premium requirement of the definition of life insurance are to be reasonable and are to be charges which, on the basis of the company's experience, if any, with respect to similar contracts, are reasonably expected to be actually paid. If any company does not have adequate experience to determine whether expense charges are reasonably expected to be paid, then to the extent provided in regulations, the determination is to be made on the basis of industry-wide experience. The conferees do not intend by this rule, however, that a company will be required to make an independent determination with respect to industry-wide experience. Rather, the conferees expect that regulations will provide guidance on what constitutes reasonable expense charges for similar contracts.

No inference is intended by this provision that present law does not require mortality and expense charges specified in a life insurance contract to be reasonable.

The provision is effective with respect to contracts entered into on or after October 21, 1988.

# APPENDIX J

## 1989 OBRA HOUSE REPORT:

### OMNIBUS BUDGET RECONCILIATION ACT OF 1989—REPORT OF THE COMMITTEE ON THE BUDGET

| 101st Congress  1st Session | HOUSE OF REPRESENTATIVES | Report 101-247 |

# OMNIBUS BUDGET RECONCILIATION ACT OF 1989

## REPORT

OF THE

## COMMITTEE ON THE BUDGET HOUSE OF REPRESENTATIVES

TO ACCOMPANY

## H.R. 3299

A BILL TO PROVIDE FOR RECONCILIATION PURSUANT TO SECTION 5 OF THE CONCURRENT RESOLUTION ON THE BUDGET FOR THE FISCAL YEAR 1990

together with

SUPPLEMENTAL AND ADDITIONAL VIEWS

SEPTEMBER 20, 1989.—Committed to the Committee of the Whole House on the State of the Union and ordered to be printed

U.S. GOVERNMENT PRINTING OFFICE
WASHINGTON : 1989

21-826

For sale by the Superintendent of Documents, U.S. Government Printing Office
Washington, DC 20402

### c. Valuation date for transfer for which gift tax return not required (sec. 11811(i)(4) of the bill, sec. 1014 of the 1988 Act, and sec. 2642(b) of the Code)

*Present Law*

If an allocation of GST exemption is made on a timely filed gift tax return required under the Federal gift tax, the value of property for generation-skipping transfer tax purposes is the same as its value for gift tax purposes, and the allocation is effective on and after the date of transfer. No gift tax return is required to be filed for gift tax purposes for a transfer of less than $10,000.

*Explanation of Provision*

The requirement that GST exemption be allocated on a gift tax return required for gift tax purposes is eliminated. The gift tax return must nonetheless be "timely." Thus, under the bill, if an allocation for a transfer of less than $10,000 is made on a gift tax return that would be timely filed were a return required, the value of property for generation-skipping transfer tax purposes is the same as its value for gift tax purposes and the allocation is effective on and after the date of transfer.

### 7. Estimated taxes of trusts and estates (sec. 11811(i)(5),(6) of the bill, sec. 1014 of the 1988 Act, and sec. 6654(l) of the Code)

*Present Law*

Trusts and estates generally are required to pay estimated taxes in the same manner as individuals. Estates, however, do not pay estimated taxes for taxable years ending within two years of the decedent's death. Likewise, a grantor trust that receives the residue of the probate estate under the grantor's will is exempted from payment of estimated taxes with respect to such taxable years. No exemption is available if the decedent lacks a will.

*Explanation of Provision*

If there is no will, a grantor trust that is primarily responsible for paying taxes, debts and expenses of administration is not required to pay estimated taxes for taxable years ending within two years of the decedent's death. For purposes of this rule, there is no will if the will is invalid under local law.

### 8. Insurance provisions

#### a. Treatment of modified endowment contracts (sec. 11815 of the bill, sec. 5012 of the 1988 Act, and secs. 72 and 7702A of the Code)

*Present Law*

Under present law, amounts received under modified endowment contracts are treated first as income and then as recovered basis. In addition, loans under modified endowment contracts and loans secured by modified endowment contracts are treated as amounts received under the contract. Finally, an additional 10-percent income tax is imposed on certain amounts received under modified endowment contracts to the extent that the amounts received are includible in gross income.

A modified endowment contract is defined as any contract that satisfies the definition of a life insurance contract but fails to satisfy a 7-pay test. A contract fails to satisfy the 7-pay test if the cumulative amount paid under the contract at any time during the first 7 contract years exceeds the sum of the net level premiums that would have been paid on or before such time had the contract provided for paid-up benefits after the payment of 7 level annual premiums.

## Explanation of Provision

### Distribution rules

In determining whether certain amounts received under a modified endowment contract are includible in gross income, all modified endowment contracts issued by the same insurer to the same policyholder during any 12-month period are aggregated. A similar aggregation rule applies to certain amounts received under annuity contracts. The bill provides that contracts under qualified pension plans are not subject to the aggregation rules which generally apply to modified endowment contracts and annuity contracts.

### Material change rules

If there is a material change in the benefits or other terms of a contract that was not reflected in any previous determination under the 7-pay test, the contract is considered a new contract that is subject to the 7-pay test as of the date that the material change takes effect and adjustments are made in the application of the 7-pay test to take into account the cash surrender value of the contract as of the date of the material change.

The bill clarifies that an increase in the charge for a qualified additional benefit is not a material change in the benefits under a contract, and, consequently, the 7-pay test is not to be reapplied at such time. An addition of, or an increase in, a qualified additional benefit, however, is a material change in the benefits under the contract and requires a reapplication of the 7-pay test.

A material change also does not include an increase in the death benefit provided under a contract if the increase is attributable to (1) the payment of premiums necessary to fund the lowest death benefit payable in the first 7 contract years (and certain prescribed death benefit increases), or (2) the crediting of interest or other earnings (including policyholder dividends) with respect to such premiums. For this purpose, a death benefit increase may be considered as attributable to the payment of premiums necessary to fund the lowest death benefit payable in the first 7 contract years or the crediting of interest or other earnings with respect to such premiums if each premium paid prior to the death benefit increase is necessary to fund the lowest death benefit payable in the first 7 contract years. Any death benefit increase that is not considered a material change under the preceding sentence, however, is to be considered a material change as of the date that a premium is paid that is not necessary to fund the lowest death benefit payable in the first 7 contract years.

The bill also clarifies that, to the extent provided in regulations, a material change does not include a death benefit increase attributable to a cost-of-living adjustment that is based on an established broad-based index specified in the contract if the increase is funded ratably over the remaining period during which premiums are required to be paid under the contract (rather than over the remaining life of the contract).

Finally, it is intended that a contract which is materially changed is not to be considered a modified endowment contract if the calculation of the 7-pay premium after the material change results in a negative amount provided that no additional premiums are paid during the first 7 years after the material change.

*Effective date*

The modified endowment contract provisions generally apply to contracts entered into on or after June 21, 1988. In determining whether a contract is entered into on or after June 21, 1988, for purposes of this effective date, if the death benefit under a contract increases by more than $150,000 over the death benefit under the contract as of October 20, 1988, the material change rules apply as of the date that the death benefit exceeds the threshold. In determining whether the death benefit increase constitutes a material change, the death benefit payable under the contract as of October 20, 1988, increased by $150,000 is to be taken into account rather than the lowest death benefit payable during the first 7 contract years.

A contract is not to be considered entered into on or after June 21, 1988, under this $150,000 increase provision, if, as of June 21, 1988, the terms of the contract required at least 7 level annual premium payments and under which the policyholder makes at least 7 level annual premium payments.

Finally, the 7-pay premium for an insurance contract that is entered into before June 21, 1988, and that is exchanged on or after such date for another contract or that is otherwise treated under the effective date provisions as entered into on or after such date is to be reduced by the cash surrender value of the contract in the same manner as a contract that is materially changed.

### b. Treatment of certain workers' compensation funds (sec. 11816 of the bill and sec. 6076 of the 1988 Act)

*Present Law*

Under the Technical and Miscellaneous Revenue Act of 1988, a qualified group self-insurers' fund is not to be assessed a deficiency (and, if assessed, the collection of the deficiency is not to occur) for taxable years beginning before January 1, 1987, to the extent that the deficiency is attributable to the timing of the deduction for policyholder dividends. For taxable years beginning on or after January 1, 1987, a fund's deduction for policyholder dividends is allowed no earlier than the date that the State regulatory authority determines the amount of the policyholder dividend that may be paid by the fund.

# APPENDIX K
## 1986 TECHNICAL CORRECTIONS BLUE BOOK:

## EXPLANATION OF TECHNICAL CORRECTIONS TO THE TAX REFORM ACT OF 1984 AND OTHER RECENT TAX LEGISLATION

[JOINT COMMITTEE PRINT]

# EXPLANATION OF TECHNICAL CORRECTIONS TO THE TAX REFORM ACT OF 1984 AND OTHER RECENT TAX LEGISLATION

## (TITLE XVIII OF H.R. 3838, 99TH CONGRESS; PUBLIC LAW 99-514)

Prepared by the Staff

of the

## JOINT COMMITTEE ON TAXATION

MAY 13, 1987

U.S. GOVERNMENT PRINTING OFFICE
WASHINGTON : 1987

72-502

JCS-11-87

For sale by the Superintendent of Documents, U.S. Government Printing Office
Washington, DC 20402

tion of this rule, a company must have been using the net level reserve method to compute at least 99 percent of its statutory reserves for directly written noncancellable accident and health insurance contracts as of December 31, 1982, and for the 1982 calendar year must have received more than half its premium income from directly written noncancellable accident and health insurance.

After December 31, 1983, the company will be treated as using the prescribed reserve method for a taxable year if through such taxable year, the company has continuously used the net level method for computing at least 99 percent of its tax and statutory reserves on its directly written noncancellable accident and health contracts. This requires a complete and continuous use of the net level method for tax and statutory purposes for all but one percent of directly written noncancellable accident and health contracts; for contracts for which the company does not use the net level method, the company should use the method used for statutory purposes, for purposes of computing tax reserves.

### 23. Underpayments of estimated tax (sec. 1824 of the Act and sec. 218 of the 1984 Act)

*Prior Law*

Under prior law, no addition to tax was made under the provision relating to failure by a corporation to pay estimated tax with respect to any underpayment of an installment required to be paid before July 18, 1984, to the extent that such underpayment was created or increased by any provision of the insurance tax subtitle and such underpayment is paid in full on or before the last date prescribed for payment of the first installment of estimated tax required to be paid after July 18, 1984.

*Explanation of Provision*

The Act repeals section 218 of the 1984 Act in favor of the application of the broader general relief granted by the Act under which no addition to tax shall be made for underpayments of estimated tax by corporations for any period before March 16, 1985 (by individuals, for any period before April 16, 1985), to the extent that such underpayment was created or increased by a provision of the 1984 Act.

### 24. Definition of life insurance contract; computational rules (sec. 1825(a) of the Act and sec. 7702(e)(1) of the Code)

*Prior Law*

Under prior and present law, a life insurance contract is defined as any contract, which is a life insurance contract under the applicable State or foreign law, but only if the contract meets either (1) a cash value accumulation test, or (2) a test consisting of a guideline premium limitation requirement and a cash value corridor requirement. Under both tests, prior and present law prescribe minimum interest assumptions and mortality assumptions that must be taken into account in computing the limitations.

Under the cash value accumulation test, the cash surrender value of the contract, by the terms of the contract, may not at any time exceed the net single premium which would have to be paid at such time in order to fund the future benefits under the contract assuming the contract matures no earlier than age 95 for the insured.

Under the guideline premium limitation/cash value corridor test, a contract continues to be treated as life insurance so long as it does not violate its guideline premium limitation or the cash value corridor. A life insurance contract meets the guideline premium limitation if the sum of the premiums paid under the contract does not at any time exceed the greater of the guideline single premium or the sum of the guideline level premiums to such date.

In addition, prior and present law provide three general rules or assumptions to be applied in computing the limitations set forth in the definitional tests. These computational rules restrict the actual provisions and benefits that can be offered in a life insurance contract only to the extent that they restrict the allowable cash surrender value (under the cash value accumulation tests) or the allowable funding pattern (under the guideline premium limitation). First, in computing the net single premium (under the cash value accumulation test) or the guideline premium limitation for any contract, the death benefit generally is deemed not to increase at any time during the life of the contract (qualified additional benefits are treated the same way). It is unclear under prior law whether this computational rule applies for purposes of determining the satisfaction of the cash value corridor test.

Second, the maturity date, including the date on which any endowment benefit is payable, shall be no earlier than the day on which the insured attains age 95, and no later than the day on which the insured attains age 100. Third, the amount of any endowment benefit (or sum of endowment benefits, including any cash surrender value on the maturity date described in the second computational rule) shall be deemed not to exceed the least amount payable as a death benefit at any time under the contract.

Under prior law, the term "premiums paid" meant the premiums paid under the contract minus amounts to which section 72(e) applies (other than amounts includible in income) and any other amounts specified in regulations.

### *Explanation of Provision*

The Act clarifies the second computational rule by specifically stating that the maturity date shall be deemed to be no earlier than age 95 and no later than age 100.

The Act also adds an additional computational rule which provides that for purposes of applying the second computational rule and for purposes of determining the cash surrender value on the maturity date under the third computational rule, the death benefits shall be deemed to be provided until the maturity date described in the second computational rule. This rule combined with the second computational rule will generally prevent contracts endowing at face value before age 95 from qualifying as life insurance. However, it will allow an endowment benefit at ages before 95 for amounts less than face value.

Finally, the Act amends the computational rules to clarify that these rules do not apply for purposes of determining qualification under the cash value corridor test.

### 25. Treatment of policies to cover prearranged funeral expenses (sec. 1825(a)(4) of the Act and sec. 7702(e)(2) of the Code)

*Prior Law*

A life insurance contract generally is defined as a contract which meets either (1) a cash value accumulation test, or (2) a test consisting of a guideline premium requirement and a cash value corridor requirement. Future increases in death benefits may cause a contract not to qualify under these tests.

*Explanation of Provision*

The Act amends the definition of a life insurance contract to provide that future increases in death benefits may be taken into account in determining whether the definition of a life insurance contract is satisfied with respect to certain policies to cover payment of burial expenses or in connection with prearranged funeral expenses. Such contracts can qualify as a life insurance contract provided that (1) the initial death benefit under the contract is $5,000 or less (treating all contracts issued to the same contract owner as one contract), (2) the contract provides for fixed annual increases in the death benefit not exceeding 10 percent of the initial death benefit or 8 percent of the death benefit at the end of the preceding year, and (3) the death benefit under the contract (treating all contracts issued to the same owner as one contract) does not exceed $25,000.

*Effective Date*

The provision is effective on the date of enactment of the 1986 Act (October 22, 1986).[4]

### 26. Reduction in future benefits (sec. 1825(b) of the Act and sec. 7702(f)(7) of the Code)

*Present Law*

Under prior and present law, proper adjustments must be made for any change in the future benefits or any qualified additional benefit (or any other terms) under a life insurance contract, which was not reflected in any previous determination made under the definitional section. Changes in the future benefits or terms of the contract can occur by an action of the company or the policyholder or by the passage of time. However, proper adjustments may be made for a particular change, depending on which alternative test is being used or whether the changes result in an increase or decrease of future benefits.

---

[4] A technical correction may be needed so the statute reflects this intent.

In the event of an increase in current or future benefits, the limitations under the cash value accumulation test must be computed by treating the date of change, in effect, as a new date of issue for determining whether the changed contract continues to qualify as life insurance under the prescribed definition. Thus, if a future benefit is increased because of a scheduled change in death benefit or because of the purchase of a paid-up addition (or its equivalent) the change will require an adjustment in the new computation of the net single premium definitional limitation. Under the guideline premium limitation, an adjustment is required under similar circumstances, but the date of change for increased benefits should be treated as a new date of issue only with respect to the changed portion of the contract. Likewise, no adjustment shall be made if the change occurs automatically, for example, a change due to the growth of the cash surrender value (whether by the crediting of excess interest or the payment of guideline premiums) or changes initiated by the company. If the contract fails to meet the limitations after proper adjustments have been made, a distribution of cash to the policyholder may be required in order to maintain qualification of the contract as life insurance.

Under prior law, the Secretary of the Treasury had the authority to prescribe regulations governing how such adjustments in computations of the definitional limitations were to be made. Such regulations could revise, prospectively, some of the adjustment rules described above in order to give full effect to the intent of the definitional limitations.

Further, under prior and present law, for the purpose of the adjustment rules, any change in the terms of a contract that reduces the future benefits under the contract will be treated as an exchange of contracts (under sec. 1035). Thus, any distribution required under the adjustment rules will be treated as taxable to the policyholder under the generally applicable rules of section 1035. This provision was intended to apply specifically to situations in which a policyholder changes from a future benefits pattern taken into account under the computational provision for policies with limited increases in death benefits to a future benefit of a level amount (even if at the time of change the amount of death benefit is not reduced). If the adjustment provision results in a distribution to a policyholder in order to meet the adjusted guidelines, the distribution will be taxable to the policyholder as ordinary income to the extent there is income in the contract.

The provision that certain changes in future benefits be treated as exchanges was not intended to alter the application of the transition rules for life insurance contracts and only applies with respect to such changes in contracts issued after December 31, 1984. Likewise, this adjustment provision was not intended to repeal indirectly the application of section 72(e) to life insurance contracts.

*Explanation of Provision*

*In general.*—The Act modifies the provision of prior law that governs how adjustments of future benefits will be treated under section 7702. The Act retains the requirement that, in determining whether the contract continues to qualify as life insurance, proper adjustments be made when future benefits are changed. However, the express delegation of authority to the Secretary of the Treasury to issue regulations governing adjustments has been deleted. In its place, the Act contains specific rules governing the extent to which a reduction in future benefits will cause income to be recognized to the policyholder.

Specifically, the Act provides that if there is a change in the benefits under (or in other terms of) the contract which was not reflected in any previous determination or adjustment made under the definitional section, there shall be proper adjustments in future determinations made under the definitional section. If the change reduces benefits under the contract, the adjustments may include a required distribution in an amount determined under the adjustment regulations for purposes of enabling the contract to meet the applicable definitional test. A portion of the distribution required by application of the definitional tests will be taxed as ordinary income to the extent there is income in the contract.

In stating the "income characterization" portion of the adjustment provision, the Act refers directly to the provisions governing the taxation of distributions from annuity and life insurance contracts, pointing out that the provision which allows withdrawals from life insurance contracts to be treated as withdrawal of investment first does not apply under certain circumstances.

Under the Act, a portion of the cash distributed to a policyholder as a result of a change in future benefits will be treated as being paid first out of income in the contract, rather than as a return of the policyholder's investment in the contract, only if the reduction in future benefits occurs during the 15-year period following the issue date of the contract.

Congress intended that, if a contract originally issued before December 31, 1984, is changed after that date in such a manner or extent that it is treated as newly issued after December 31, 1984, then the 15-year period is to commence on the date (after December 31, 1984) on which the contract is considered as newly issued. If the 15-year period were considered to commence when the contract was originally issued, then contracts issued before 1985 could become vehicles for circumvention of the distribution rules described below, regardless of how substantially such contracts were changed after 1984.

*Changes during first 5 years.*—For the first 5 years following the issuance of the contract, the amount that will be treated as having been paid first out of income in the contract will be equal to the amount of the required distribution under subparagraph (A) of section 7702(f)(7). This amount will depend on whether the contract meets the cash value accumulation test or the guideline premium/cash value corridor test of section 7702(a). In the case of a contract to which the cash value accumulation test applies, the excess of the cash surrender value of the contract over the net single premium determined immediately after the reduction shall be required to be distributed to the policyholder. In the case of a contract to which the guideline premium/cash value corridor test applies, the amount of the required distribution is equal to the greater of (1) the excess of the aggregate premiums paid under the contract over the redetermined guideline premium limitation, or (2) the excess of the cash surrender value of the policy immediately before the reduction over the redetermined cash value corridor. The guideline premium limitation shall be redetermined by using an "attained-age-decrement" method.

Under this method, when benefits under the contract are reduced, the guideline level and single premium limitations are each adjusted and redetermined by subtracting from the original guideline premium limitation a "negative guideline premium limitation" which is determined as of the date of the reduction in benefits and at the attained age of the insured on such date. The negative guideline premium limitation is the guideline premium limitation for an insurance contract that, when combined with the original insurance contract after the reduction in benefits, produces an insurance contract with the same benefit as the original contract before such reduction.

To the extent that the redetermined guideline premium limitation requires a distribution from the contract, the amount of the distribution will also be an adjustment to premiums paid under the contract (within the meaning of sec. 7702(f)(1)(A), to be specified in regulations). It is understood that any adjustments to premiums paid as part of the definitional determinations will be independent of, and may differ in amount from, the determination of investment in the contract for purposes of computing the amount of income in the contract (under sec. 72).

*Changes during years 6 to 15.*—For cash distributions occurring between the end of the fifth year and the end of the fifteenth year from the issuance date of the policy, a single rule applies for all contracts. Under this rule, the maximum amount that will be treated as paid first out of income in the contract will equal the amount by which the cash surrender value of the contract (determined immediately before the reduction in benefits) exceeds the maximum cash surrender value that would not violate the cash value corridor (determined immediately after the reduction in benefits).

*Distribution in anticipation of a reduction.*—The Act also provides that certain distributions of cash made in anticipation of a reduction in benefits under the contract shall be treated as a cash distribution made to the policyholder as a result of such change in order to give full effect to the provision. Any distribution made up to two years before a reduction in benefits occurs will be treated as having been made in anticipation of such a reduction. The Secretary of the Treasury is authorized to issue regulations specifying other instances when a distribution is in anticipation of a reduction of future benefits. In addition, the regulations may specify the extent to which the rules governing the calculation of the maximum amount that will be treated as paid first out of income in the contract will be adjusted to take account of the prior distributions made in anticipation of reduction of benefits.

*Definition of premiums paid.*—The Act modifies the definition of the term "premiums paid." Under the Act, premiums paid are computed in the same manner as under prior law, except that the premiums actually paid under the contract will be further reduced by amounts treated as paid first out of income in the contract under the revised adjustment rule. This reduction in premiums paid is limited to the amounts that are included in gross income of the policyholder solely by reason of the fact that a reduction in benefits has been made.

### 27. Treatment of contracts that do not qualify as life insurance contracts (sec. 1825(c) of the Act and sec. 7702(g) of the Code)

*Prior Law*

If a life insurance contract does not meet either of the alternative tests under the definition of a life insurance contract, the income on the contract for the taxable year of the policyholder will be treated as ordinary income received or accrued by the policyholder during that year. For this purpose, the income on the contract is the amount by which the sum of the increase in the net surrender value of the contract during the taxable year and the cost of insurance protection provided during the taxable year exceed the amount of premiums paid less any policyholder dividends paid under the contract during the taxable year. The term premiums paid means the amount paid as premiums under a contract less amounts to which the rules for allocation between income and investment under annuity and other contracts in section 72(e) apply.

*Explanation of Provision*

Under the Act, income in the contract is computed without reduction by the amount of policyholder dividends paid under the contract during the taxable year. This change was necessary to avoid overstating the income in the contract, which otherwise would occur due to the fact that policyholder dividends are treated as a nontaxable return of basis under section 72(e) and reduce premiums paid directly. If these dividends were also added to the amount of income on the contract, income would be overstated because policyholder dividends would reduce premiums paid twice.

### 28. Treatment of flexible premium contracts issued during 1984 which meet new requirements (sec. 1825(d) of the Act and sec. 221(d)(1) of the 1984 Act)

*Present Law*

Under the 1984 Act, the new definition of life insurance generally applies to contracts issued after December 31, 1984, except in the case of certain increasing death benefit contracts issued after June 30, 1984. Also, the TEFRA provisions for flexible premium contracts (that is, prior-law sec. 101(f) applicable during 1982 and 1983) were extended through 1984.

*Explanation of Provision*

The Act clarifies the transition rules for the definition of life insurance so that any contract issued during 1984 which meets the definitional requirements of section 7702 will be treated as meeting the requirements of prior-law section 101(f), which was extended through 1984.

### 29. Treatment of certain contracts issued before October 1, 1984 (sec. 1825(e) of the Act and sec. 221(d)(2)(C) of the 1984 Act)

*Prior Law*

Under the 1984 Act, a transition rule was provided for certain increasing death benefit policies. This rule made the new definitional provisions of section 7702 applicable only for a contract issued after September 30, 1984, if (1) the contract would meet the new definition by substituting 3 percent for 4 percent as the minimum interest rate in the cash value accumulation test (assuming that the rate or rates guaranteed on issuance of a contract can be determined without regard to any mortality charges), and (2) if the cash surrender value of the contract did not at any time exceed the net single premium which would have to be paid at such time to fund future benefits at the then current level of benefits (with the same 3 percent for 4 percent substitution).

*Explanation of Provision*

The Act clarifies the transition rule so that, in applying the cash value accumulation test by substituting 3 percent for 4 percent as the minimum interest rate, the taxpayer should not only assume that the rate or rates guaranteed on issuance of the contract can be determined without regard to any mortality charges, but should also assume that the rate or rates should be determined without regard to any initial interest rate guaranteed in excess of the stated minimum rate.

### 30. Amendments related to annuity contracts (sec. 1826 of the Act and sec. 72(q) and (s) of the Code)

*Prior Law*

Under prior and present law, cash withdrawals from an annuity contract prior to the annuity starting date are includible in gross income to the extent that the cash value of a contract (determined immediately before the amount was received and without regard to any surrender charge) exceeds the investment in the contract. An additional income tax of 5 percent was imposed, under prior law, on the amount of any such distribution that was includible in income, to the extent that the amount was allocable to an investment made on or after August 14, 1982. This tax was not imposed if the distribution was made after the contractholder attained age 59½, after the contractholder became disabled, upon the death of the contractholder, or as payment under an annuity for life or for at least 5 years.

An annuity contract must provide specific rules for distribution in the event of the contractholder's (owner's) death in order to be treated as an annuity contract for income tax purposes under prior and present law. These after-death distribution rules generally conform to those rules applicable to qualified pension plans and IRAs. To be treated as an annuity contract, the contract must provide that, if the contractholder dies on or after the annuity starting date and before the entire interest in the contract has been distributed, the remaining portion of such interest will be distributed at

# APPENDIX L

## TEFRA BLUE BOOK:

## GENERAL EXPLANATION OF THE REVENUE PROVISIONS OF THE TAX EQUITY AND FISCAL RESPONSIBILITY ACT OF 1982

[JOINT COMMITTEE PRINT]

# GENERAL EXPLANATION

## OF THE

# REVENUE PROVISIONS OF THE TAX EQUITY AND FISCAL RESPONSIBILITY ACT OF 1982

(H.R. 4961, 97TH CONGRESS; PUBLIC LAW 97-248)

PREPARED BY THE STAFF OF THE

## JOINT COMMITTEE ON TAXATION

DECEMBER 31, 1982

U.S. GOVERNMENT PRINTING OFFICE
WASHINGTON : 1983

11-324 O  JCS-38-82

For sale by the Superintendent of Documents, U.S. Government Printing Office
Washington, D.C. 20402

### 8. Flexible premium life insurance contracts (sec. 266 of the Act and sec. 101 of the Code) *

*Prior law*

Gross income does not include amounts received (whether in a single sum or otherwise) under a life insurance contract, if the amounts are paid by reason of the death of the insured (sec. 101(a)).

In addition, prior to the death of the insured, amounts credited to the cash value of a life insurance contract are taxed only when withdrawn and to the extent the withdrawals exceed the aggregate premiums paid by the policyholder for the contract (sec. 72(e)).

In recent years, life insurance companies have marketed flexible premium life insurance contracts (referred to as "universal life" or "adjustable life"). These contracts are similar in some respects to traditional whole life policies, but typically permit the policyholder to change the amount and timing of the premiums and the size of the death benefit automatically as the policyholder's needs change. These contracts may permit the policyholder to invest a substantial cash fund without a related increase in the amount of pure insurance protection offered by the contracts.

In a letter ruling (January 23, 1981), the Internal Revenue Service concluded that the entire amount paid upon the death of the insured under a universal life insurance contract is excluded from gross income as proceeds of a life insurance contract under section 101(a), even though the death benefit may reflect a large cash fund and a relatively small amount of pure insurance protection. If the contract is treated as a life insurance contract, the interest on the cash fund is not subject to tax, unless the contract is surrendered prior to the death of the insured. Subsequent to the letter ruling, the Service announced that it was reconsidering its position on such life insurance contracts. Thus, it was unclear whether such contracts will be treated as life insurance contracts for tax purposes.

*Reasons for Change*

Congress believed that flexible premium life insurance contracts should have the same tax treatment as traditional level-premium whole life insurance contracts if they are substantially comparable to traditional contracts. However, Congress was concerned by the fact that some flexible premium contracts can be overly investment oriented by allowing large cash value build-ups without requiring a continued reasonable amount of pure insurance protection. In the

---

*For legislative background of the provision, see: H.R. 4961, as reported by the Senate Finance Committee, sec. 268; S. Rep. No. 97-494, Vol. 1 (July 12, 1982), pp. 352-354; and H. Rep. No. 97-760 (August 17, 1982), pp. 647-649 (Joint Explanatory Statement of the Committee of Conference).

case of such contracts, the traditional use of life insurance as financial protection against early death could be overshadowed by the use of the contract as a vehicle for tax-favored investment.

Because the uncertain tax treatment of flexible premium life insurance contracts has caused significant confusion among consumers and life insurance companies, Congress believed that it should resolve the tax treatment of these contracts, at least temporarily, by legislation.

*Explanation of Provisions*

The Act provides mandatory guidelines that flexible premium life insurance contracts must meet in order to be treated as life insurance for tax purposes. If these guidelines are violated at any time over the duration of the contract, the contract will not be treated as providing only life insurance for tax purposes. Rather, the contract may be treated as providing a combination of term life insurance with an annuity or a deposit fund (depending upon the terms of the policy).

A flexible premium life insurance contract is a life insurance contract which provides for the payment of one or more premiums that are not fixed by the company as to both timing and amount. Thus, under such a contract, the insurance company may fix the timing of the premium payments but not the amount, the amount of the premiums but not the timing, or neither the timing nor the amount of the premiums. For example, an indeterminate premium policy would not come within the definition of a flexible premium life insurance contract because, typically, the insurance company fixes the timing of the premium payments upon issuance of the contract and the insurance company, not the policyholder, fixes (and periodically adjusts) the amount of each future premium payment. The policyholder must pay the amount that the company prescribes, neither more nor less, and must pay it at the time prescribed in order to prevent the contract from being in default. The term "flexible premium life insurance contract" also includes contracts that provide for certain qualified additional benefits, specifically, family term life insurance (e.g., for the insured, a spouse or a child), an accidental death benefit, a waiver of premium benefit, and a guaranteed insurability benefit. The terms used in listing the four specific qualified additional benefits are generally descriptive. Thus, the "waiver of premium" benefit is intended to include, also, a waiver of the cost of insurance charge benefit. However, the inclusion of an additional benefit that does not come within these generally descriptive terms can disqualify the contract for purposes of the new guidelines. For example, if a benefit rider providing term life insurance for a nonfamily member is added to the contract, such contract does not qualify as a flexible permium life insurance contract under these provisions.

The statute states that the term "flexible premium life insurance contracts" does not include that portion of any contract that is treated under State law as providing any annuity benefits other than as a settlement option. Thus, although a flexible premium life insurance contract may provide by rider for annuity benefits, the annuity portion of the contract is not part of the flexible premium contract for tax purposes and such annuity benefits may not be reflected in computing the guideline premiums. Likewise, an insurance arrangement *written* as a combination of term life insurance with an annuity contract, or with a premium deposit fund, is not a flexible premium life insurance contract for purposes of the guidelines because all the elements of the contract provisions and contract values are not subject to the provisions of State law regulating life insurance. However, any flexible premium contract that is treated under State law as a single integrated life insurance contract and that satisfies these guidelines will be treated for Federal tax purposes as a single contract of life insurance and not as a contract that provides separable life insurance and annuity benefits.

Finally, the guidelines contain alternative tests which a contract may meet in order for the death proceeds therefrom to be treated as life insurance for tax purposes.

*Alternative 1—guideline premium with limited cash value*

The first test provides that two requirements be met at all times: (1) the sum of the premiums paid under the contract at any time cannot exceed a specifically computed guideline premium limitation; and (2) the amounts payable on the death of the insured cannot be less than a certain multiple of the contract's cash value as of the date of death. For purposes of applying the first requirement, the sum of the premiums paid includes premiums for any additional qualified benefits as well as the primary death benefit. However, the amount of premiums paid should be reduced by any amounts received by the policyholder and not includible in income under section 72(e).

A premium payment that causes the sum of the premiums paid to exceed the guideline premium limitation will not result in the contract failing the guidelines if the premium payment is necessary to prevent termination of the contract on or before the end of the contract year. Also, if it is established to the satisfaction of the Secretary that the first requirement was not met due to reasonable error and reasonable steps are being taken to remedy the error, the Secretary may waive the first requirement. If a premium that causes the first test to be violated is returned (together with interest allocable thereto) within 60 days after the end of any policy year, the first test will be deemed to have been satisfied at all times during the contract year preceding the return of the premium. The interest returned with such a premium is includible in the policyholder's income currently notwithstanding the general rules of section 72(e).

The premium limitation in the first test is intended to prevent investment motivated contributions of large cash amounts to the contract. The guideline premium limitation means, on any date, the greater of: (1) the single premium at issue necessary to fund the future benefits provided under the contract, based on mortality and other charges fixed in the contract (including expense charges) and based on interest at the greater of 6 percent or the minimum rate or rates guaranteed in the contract; or (2) the sum of the level annual amounts payable over the longest period permitted under the contract (but not less than 20 years from date of issue or not later than age 95, if earlier), computed on the same basis as the single premium except that the interest rate used cannot be less than 4 percent. For purposes of computing the guideline premium, charges for qualified additional benefits are appropriately discounted and taken into account as part of the guideline premium.

In calculating the guideline premiums, on a single premium basis and in certain other situations, the inclusion of a qualified additional benefit can have an impact on the value of the future benefits relating to the basic life coverage of the contract. For example, under a universal life policy with a death benefit equal to a specified amount (as opposed to a benefit equal to a level risk amount plus the cash value at death), the addition of a single premium for a qualified additional benefit will tend to increase the policy's cash value and thereby to reduce the "net amount at risk" with respect to the basic life coverage under the policy. In computing the guideline premiums, it would be appropriate to reflect this interaction in the computation.

Likewise, the inclusion of a qualified additional benefit can also impact on the computation of the guideline level premium. If a qualified additional benefit is scheduled to cease at a certain age, the charges for such qualified additional benefit should be reflected in a level manner in the guideline level premium only over the period such charges are being incurred, despite the fact that the longest premium payment period under the policy, in general, extends beyond that period. This interpretation recognizes that separate policy benefits can have discrete payment periods. Likewise, it prevents the anomalous result of requiring some degree of postfunding of charges for certain qualified additional benefits should the longest (though inapplicable) premium payment period be used. Hence, if premiums are payable to age 95, and a qualified additional benefit ceases at age 65, the guideline level premium up to age 65 will be higher (reflecting the charges for the qualified additional benefit) than it will be over the period from age 65 to age 95.

In defining the guideline single premium the statute refers (1) to the mortality and other charges guaranteed under the contract and (2) to interest at the minimum rate or rates guaranteed upon issue of the contract. In order to give meaning to these phrases as definitional limitations on the contract obligations of the issuing insurance company, the term "the mortality and other charges" means the maximum charges guaranteed at issue for the life of the contract, and the term "minimum rate or rates" means the floor rate or rates of interest guaranteed at issue of the contract. Thus, although the company may guarantee a higher interest rate from time to time, either by contractual declaration or by operation of a formula or index, the minimum rate still should be taken to be the floor rate, that is, the rate below which the interest credited to the contract cannot fall. The statutory reference to minimum rate or rates recognizes that a contract may guarantee different floor rates for different periods of the contract, although each is guaranteed at issue and remains fixed for the applicable period for the life of the contract. However, it should be noted that when the initial interest rate guaranteed to be credited to the contract is in excess of the generally applicable floor rate assumed in the contract, the higher initial interest rate is the minimum or floor rate with respect to the initial period of that guarantee. This is because that rate is guaranteed at issue and, for the initial guarantee period, the interest rate cannot fall below that guaranteed rate. Similarly, although the contract may have generally applicable assumptions for mortality and other charges, any deviations in these charges that are guaranteed at issue, though even for a short time, would be the maximum charges with respect to the initial guarantee period. Aside from taking into account initial guarantees that are different from the generally applicable charges and interest rates assumed in the contract, the Act does not require that any "excess interest" (interest credited at a rate in excess of any rate or rates guaranteed in the contract at the time of issue), or any reduction in the mortality charge below the maximum chargeable, be taken into account in the computation of the guideline premiums.

The Act also contains three computational rules for the guideline premiums, which are designed to limit the range of future benefits that may be assumed in computing such premiums. First, the net amount at risk assumed to exist at any time in the future of the contract cannot exceed the comparable amount existing when the contract is issued. Absent such a rule, the guideline premiums could be artificially raised by assuming increased future death benefits even though there is no intention to keep the contract in force until those benefits are actually effective. For purposes of this rule, the net amount at risk upon issue would be the face amount of the policy when it is issued, reduced by the cash value resulting from the initial premium. This would be true whether the death proceeds of the contract are defined as a level face amount or as a level specified amount plus the policy's cash value at death. Also, the cash value of the contract (one of the factors that determines the net amount at risk) is the cash value accumulated by using the same assumptions concerning interest rates, mortality charges, and other charges used to compute the guideline premiums. Second, the maturity date of the contract is the latest date permitted under the contract, which cannot be less than 20 years after the contract is issued or age 95, if earlier. Third, the amount of any endowment benefit (*i.e.*, the benefit payable if the insured survives to the contract's maturity date) cannot exceed the smallest death benefit (determined without regard to any qualified additional benefits) at any time under the contract. This rule is designed to require that guideline premiums be computed on a basis consistent with premium computations for a traditional endowment policy, where the endowment benefit generally equals the death benefit. Under this rule, if the death proceeds of a policy equal a level specified amount plus the policy's cash value at death the endowment benefit will reflect the cash value produced by the initial premium payment because under such a policy, presumably, the death benefit upon issue will be the lowest death benefit payable over the life of the policy.

At the start of the contract the guideline premiums are based on the future benefits specified in the contract as of such date. If future contract benefits are changed at a subsequent date, the guideline premiums must be adjusted (upward or downward) to reflect the change. Such adjustments should not be made for increases in the death benefit that reflect excess interest that has been credited. A colloquy between Senator Dole and Senator Bentsen (128 Cong. Rec. S10943, August 19, 1982) explained that the guideline premiums are to be adjusted only in two circumstances. First, they are to be adjusted if the amount or pattern of a policy's benefits (including qualified additional benefits) is changed by the policy owner. For this purpose, if a qualified additional benefit ceases for any reason, including the death of an individual (such as the insured's spouse) insured thereunder, this is considered a change in benefits requiring an adjustment of the guideline premiums. Second, the guideline premiums are to be adjusted upon the occurrence of a change in benefits previously scheduled under the contract that could not earlier be taken into account in the calculation of the guideline premiums because of the "computational" rules set forth in section 101(f)(2)(D). The colloquy further noted that these adjustments are to be computed in the same manner as the initial guideline premiums, but based on the change in the amount or pattern of the benefits and the insured's attained age at the time of the change. The computational rules apply to the change in amount at the time of change independently of their application at issue or for a previous change. The colloquy recognized, however, that the Treasury may determine in regulations that some other method of computing adjustments is to be used instead. This adjustment rule is consistent with the statutory language of the premium test that the sum of the premiums paid at any time not exceed the guideline limitation at such time.

The second requirement provides a restriction on the death benefit in order to ensure that flexible premium contracts offer at least a minimum amount of pure insurance protection at all times. For purposes of meeting the second requirement, the death benefit under a flexible premium contract must be 140 percent of the cash value if the insured has an attained age of 40 or less at the beginning of the contract year; thereafter, the percentage is reduced by one percent for each year until the insured has an attained age of 76. In this context "attained age" can appropriately be read as meaning the insured's age determined by reference to contract anniversaries rather than the individual's actual birthdays. So long as the age assumed by the contract is within 12 months of the insured's actual age, then it is reasonable to use that age as the "attained age". The sliding scale for the death benefit ensures that the policy provide a minimum amount of pure insurance protection at all times.

*Example for computing the guideline premium limitation*

*Option 1 death benefit.*—Assume that a flexible premium life insurance contract is issued on the life of a male, age 35, for a death benefit defined as a "specified amount" equal to $100,000 (or, if greater, the contract's cash value at the time of the insured's death multiplied by the applicable percentage as set forth in section 101(f)(1)(A)(ii) and (3)(C)). The contract's guaranteed rate of interest at issue is 10 percent in the first contract year and 4 percent thereafter; the contract matures when the insured reaches age 95. The contract's guaranteed charges for mortality are based on the 1958 CSO Mortality Table, age last birthday, curtate functions, except that the rates in the first contract year are based on 75 percent of 1958 CSO mortality; for expenses, the charges are 10 percent of gross premiums plus $3.00 per $1,000 of specified amount at issue (or $3.00 per $1,000 of increase in the specified amount at the time of increase). These charges and credits are processed on an annual basis.

The guideline premium limitation means, as of any date, the greater of the guideline single premium, or the sum of the guideline level premiums to such date. The statute provides that the guideline single premium is the premium at issue necessary to fund future benefits under the contract, based on the mortality and other charges (including expense charges) guaranteed under the contract and based on interest at the greater of 6 percent or the minimum rate or rates guaranteed upon issue of the contract. Therefore, under the facts of the example, the guideline single premium is equal to the net single premium for a life insurance contract with an endowment at age 95, plus the expense charges specified under the contract. The net single premium is computed on the basis of assumed rates of interest of 10 percent for the first policy year and 6 percent thereafter and on the basis of a mortality charge of 75 percent of the 1958 CSO mortality for the first policy year and the 1958 CSO mortality thereafter. The statute provides that the guideline level premium is the level annual amount that is payable over the longest period permitted under the contract (ending not less than 20 years from the date of issue or not later than age 95, if earlier), computed on the same basis as the guideline single premium, except the interest rate must be the greater of 4 percent or the minimum rate or rates guaranteed in the contract. Thus, under the facts of the example, the guideline level premium is equal to the guideline single premium divided by the annuity value of the contract, where the annuity value is computed on the same basis as the guideline single premium except that the assumed rate of interest for the second policy year and later is 4 percent.

Based on the facts of the example, the guideline premiums and the guideline premium limitation are:

| Contract duration | Guideline single premium | Sum of guideline level premiums | Guideline premium limitation |
|---|---|---|---|
| At issue | $17,219 | $1,590 | $17,219 |
| Year 10 | 17,219 | 15,900 | 17,219 |
| Year 20 | 17,219 | 31,800 | 31,800 |
| Year 30 | 17,219 | 47,700 | 47,700 |

Assume that ten years later the specified amount is increased to $125,000 (the insured is age 45). The contract's guaranteed rate of interest in the first contract year after the increase is 8 percent, and in that year the mortality rates are guaranteed to be 75 percent of the 1958 CSO mortality. The statute provides that the guideline single premium and the guideline level premium must be adjusted if there is a change in future benefits under the contract that was not reflected in the guideline premiums previously determined. Any adjustment is computed in the same manner as the initial guideline premium computations, but taking into account any changes. Thus, under the facts of the example, the guideline single premium of $17,219 is adjusted by $6,774, to become $23,993. Also, the guideline level premium of $1,590 is adjusted by $631, to become $2,221. The guideline premiums and the guideline premium limitation then will be:

| Contract duration | Guideline single premium | Sum of guideline level premiums | Guideline premium limitation |
|---|---|---|---|
| Year 10 (before increase) | $17,219 | $15,900 | $17,219 |
| Year 11 | 23,993 | 18,121 | 23,993 |
| Year 20 | 23,993 | 38,110 | 38,110 |
| Year 30 | 23,993 | 60,320 | 60,320 |

*Option 2 death benefit.*—Also, many flexible premium life insurance contracts provide for a death benefit that is defined as the contract's cash value at death plus a level "specified amount" (though never less than the cash value multiplied by the applicable percentage under section 101(f)(1)(A)(ii) and (3)(C)). Assume that all other facts remain as stated under option 1, except that an option 2 death benefit is chosen. Assume that the specified amount is $100,000 and that a premium of $20,000 is paid at issue. After the payment of the $20,000 premium, the cash value of the contract is $17,524 (which is the premium paid less the expenses charges and the mortality charge for the first policy year). The statute provides that any endowment benefit assumed in computing the guideline premiums cannot exceed the least death benefit payable at any time under the contract. As the cash value will generally increase over the life of the contract, the initial death benefit is the least death benefit in this example. Thus, the endowment assumed in computing the guideline premiums cannot exceed $117,524 (the specified amount plus the initial cash value).[12] Assuming an endowment benefit of $117,524 at age 95, under option 2, the guideline single premium is equal to that endowment benefit discounted at interest and mortality to the date at issue, plus the expense charges specified.[13] It should be noted that the computation for option 2 assumes a pattern of benefits in which the death benefit always consists of the specified amount ($100,000) plus the cash value. The guideline level premium is computed, as under option 1,

---

[12] Based on the facts assumed, for an option 2 death benefit with a specified amount of $100,000, the maximum guideline single premium that may be computed is $40,713, assuming the payment of such amount as the premium at issue. If the maximum guideline single premium were paid initially, the maximum endowment benefit that can be assumed is equal to $136,166.

[13] The assumed interest rates, mortality charges and other charges are the same used under option 1.

374

by dividing the guideline single premium by the annuity value. Thus, upon issue of the contract with the option 2 death benefit, the guideline premiums and the guideline premium limitation are:

| Contract duration | Guideline single premium | Sum of guideline level premiums | Guideline premium limitation |
|---|---|---|---|
| At issue................ | $40,108 | $3,934 | $40,108 |
| Year 10................. | 40,108 | 39,340 | 40;108 |
| Year 20................. | 40,108 | 78,680 | 78,680 |
| Year 30................. | 40,108 | 118,020 | 118,020 |

When the specified amount in the option 2 case is later increased to $125,000 (again, when the insured is age 45), and an additional premium of $10,000 is paid at such time, the guideline single premium is adjusted by $17,210, and the guideline level premium is adjusted by $1,510. The new figures are:

| Contract duration | Guideline single premium | Sum of guideline level premiums | Guideline premium limitation [14] |
|---|---|---|---|
| Year 10 (before increase).................. | $40,108 | $39,340 | $40,108 |
| Year 11................. | 57,318 | 44,784 | 57,318 |
| Year 20................. | 57,318 | 93,780 | 93,780 |
| Year 30................. | 57,318 | 148,220 | 148,220 |

[14] The endowment benefit, after the adjustment, is assumed to equal $151,352. The maximum guideline single premium adjustment that may be computed is $17,616, based upon the payment of such amount as a premium at the time of adjustment (and assuming an endowment benefit of $176,849).

*Alternative 2–cash value computation*

The second test is a specific cash value test patterned after a traditional whole life policy. That is, death proceeds paid from a flexible premium life insurance contract will be excluded from the beneficiary's gross income if, by the terms of the contract, the cash value may not exceed at any time the net single premium for the amount payable by reason of the death of the insured (without regard to any qualified additional benefit) at such time. Thus, the net single premium must be adjusted (upward or downward) to reflect increases or decreases in the death benefit provided under the policy. This is required by the language of the cash value test itself, even though the statute does not specifically call for the adjustment as it does with the first alternative test. For these purposes, the net single premium must be computed by using the mortality basis guaranteed under the contract but determined by reference to the most recent mortality table allowed under all State laws on the date of issue; an interest factor that is the greater of 4 percent (3 percent for contracts issued before July 1, 1983) or the rate guaranteed in the contract; and the computational rules for the guideline premium, except that the maturity date of the contract cannot be earlier than age 95. The phrase "the most recent mortality table allowed under all State laws" should be read literally and refers to that mortality table, appropriate to the particular insurance plan, that has been adopted and is permitted to be used by companies in all fifty States. The requirement of referring to the most recent mortality table is intended to prevent a company from using a guaranteed mortality basis which, on the date of issuance, is outdated and is replaceable by a more modern basis. Thus, the statute requires that the most recent mortality table be used as a measuring rod, that is, that the net single premium computed on the guaranteed mortality basis cannot exceed that which would result if it were computed on the basis of the most recent mortality table. For example, in addition to the most recent mortality table adopted and permitted to be used in all fifty states, a company may use a more recent table adopted and permitted in the State in which a contract is issued, or any other table that results in a smaller net single premium.

### *Effective Dates*

In general, the provisions regarding flexible premium life insurance contracts apply to all such contracts issued before January 1, 1984.

The Act provides two special transition rules for contracts issued before January 1, 1983. First, any such contract that is in compliance with the new provisions on the date one year after the date of enactment of the Act will be treated as meeting all the requirements of the provisions retroactively. For purposes of bringing a contract into compliance with the new provisions, it will be sufficient for the guideline premium limitation to be computed on the assumption that the benefits at the time of the computation have been in effect since the time of issue. Such an assumption avoids the necessity of reconstructing guideline premiums and adjustments for past benefit changes under a policy for which historical data may be limited and implements the spirit of the grandfather provisions applicable to existing contracts. Likewise, in bringing a contract into compliance, if on the date of computation of the guideline premium limitation the sum of the premiums paid exceeds such limitation, amounts removed from the policy and returned to the policyholder need not include interest paid on such amounts. Although the new guideline provisions require that interest be paid on premiums returned to a policyholder in order to maintain compliance with the guidelines, such provisions are inapplicable until an existing contract is brought into compliance with the guidelines. Second, any such contract shall be treated as meeting the first alternative test if it would meet the requirements of the provision by using 3 percent instead of 4 percent for computing the guideline level premium. Finally, the Act provides a grandfa-

376

ther provision for any death benefits paid within the first year of enactment under a flexible premium contract issued before January 1, 1983; such benefits are excluded from gross income whether or not the contract is in compliance with the guidelines.

# APPENDIX M
## 104<sup>TH</sup> CONGRESS BLUE BOOK:

## GENERAL EXPLANATION OF TAX LEGISLATION ENACTED IN THE 104<sup>TH</sup> CONGRESS

[JOINT COMMITTEE PRINT]

# GENERAL EXPLANATION OF TAX LEGISLATION ENACTED IN THE 104TH CONGRESS

Prepared by the Staff

of the

## JOINT COMMITTEE ON TAXATION

December 18, 1996

U.S. GOVERNMENT PRINTING OFFICE
WASHINGTON : 1996

36-319

JCS-12-96

cludability of payments under arrangements having the effect of accident or health insurance under prior law.

### Revenue Effect

The provision is estimated to reduce Federal fiscal year budget receipts by $64 million in 1997, $238 million in 1998, $340 million in 1999, $377 million in 2000, $410 million in 2001, $445 million in 2002, $537 million in 2003, $824 million in 2004, $1,290 million in 2005, and $1,827 million in 2006.

## C. Treatment of Long-Term Care Insurance and Services (secs. 321-327 of HIPA and secs. 106, 125, 213, 4980B, 4980C, 6050Q, and 7702B of the Code)

### Present and Prior Law

#### In general

Prior law generally did not provide explicit rules relating to the tax treatment of long-term care insurance contracts or long-term care services. Thus, the treatment of long-term care contracts and services was unclear. Prior and present law do provide rules relating to medical expenses and accident or health insurance.

#### Itemized deduction for medical expenses

In determining taxable income for Federal income tax purposes, a taxpayer is allowed an itemized deduction for unreimbursed expenses that are paid by the taxpayer during the taxable year for medical care of the taxpayer, the taxpayer's spouse, or a dependent of the taxpayer, to the extent that such expenses exceed 7.5 percent of the adjusted gross income of the taxpayer for such year (sec. 213). For this purpose, expenses paid for medical care generally are defined as amounts paid: (1) for the diagnosis, cure, mitigation, treatment, or prevention of disease (including prescription medicines or drugs and insulin), or for the purpose of affecting any structure or function of the body (other than cosmetic surgery not related to disease, deformity, or accident); (2) for transportation primarily for, and essential to, medical care referred to in (1); or (3) for insurance (including Part B Medicare premiums) covering medical care referred to in (1) and (2).

#### Exclusion for amounts received under accident or health insurance

Amounts received by a taxpayer under accident or health insurance for personal injuries or sickness generally are excluded from gross income to the extent that the amounts received are not attributable to medical expenses that were allowed as a deduction for a prior taxable year (sec. 104).

#### Treatment of accident or health plans maintained by employers

Contributions of an employer to an accident or health plan that provides compensation (through insurance or otherwise) to an employee for personal injuries or sickness of the employee, the employee's spouse, or a dependent of the employee, are excluded from the gross income of the employee (sec. 106). In addition, amounts received by an employee under such a plan generally are excluded from gross income to the extent that the amounts received are paid, directly or indirectly, to reimburse the employee for expenses for the medical care of the employee, the employee's spouse, or a dependent of the employee (sec. 105). For this purpose, expenses incurred for medical care are defined in the same manner as under the rules regarding the deduction for medical expenses.

A cafeteria plan is an employer-sponsored arrangement under which employees can elect among cash and certain employer-provided qualified benefits. No amount is included in the gross income of a participant in a cafeteria plan merely because the participant has the opportunity to make such an election (sec. 125). Employer-provided accident or health coverage is one of the benefits that may be offered under a cafeteria plan.

A flexible spending arrangement (FSA) is an arrangement under which an employee is reimbursed for medical expenses or other nontaxable employer-provided benefits, such as dependent care, and under which the maximum amount of reimbursement that is reasonably available to a participant for a period of coverage is not substantially in excess of the total premium (including both employee-paid and employer-paid portions of the premium) for such participant's coverage. Under proposed Treasury regulations, a maximum amount of reimbursement is not substantially in excess of the total premium if such maximum amount is less than 500 percent of the premium. An FSA may be part of a cafeteria plan or provided by an employer outside a cafeteria plan. FSAs are commonly used to reimburse employees for medical expenses not covered by insurance. If certain requirements are satisfied,[234] amounts reimbursed for nontaxable benefits from an FSA are excludable from income.

### *Health care continuation rules*

The health care continuation rules require that an employer must provide qualified beneficiaries the opportunity to continue to participate for a specified period in the employer's health plan after the occurrence of certain events (such as termination of employment) that would have terminated such participation (sec. 4980B). Individuals electing continuation coverage can be required to pay for such coverage.

### *Reasons for Change*

The long-term care rules of HIPA provide an incentive for individuals to take financial responsibility for their long-term care needs. HIPA therefore generally provides favorable tax treatment with respect to long-term care insurance contracts and services meeting HIPA's requirements.

---

[234] These requirements include a requirement that a health FSA can only provide reimbursement for medical expenses (as defined in sec. 213) and cannot provide reimbursement for premium payments for other health coverage and that the maximum amount of reimbursement under a health FSA must be available at all times during the period of coverage.

337

## Explanation of Provision

### Tax treatment and definition of long-term care insurance contracts and qualified long-term care services

#### Exclusion of long-term care proceeds

A long-term care insurance contract generally is treated as an accident and health insurance contract. Amounts (other than policyholder dividends or premium refunds) received under a long-term care insurance contract generally are excludable as amounts received for personal injuries and sickness, subject to a cap of $175 per day, or $63,875 annually, as indexed, on per diem contracts only. The dollar cap is indexed by the medical care cost component of the consumer price index.

#### Employer-provided long-term care coverage

A plan of an employer providing coverage under a long-term care insurance contract generally is treated as an accident and health plan. Employer-provided coverage under a long-term care insurance contract is not, however, excludable by an employee if provided through a cafeteria plan; similarly, expenses for long-term care services cannot be reimbursed under an FSA.[235] Thus, employer contributions (other than through a cafeteria plan) for long-term care insurance for the employee, his or her spouse, and his or her dependents (as defined for tax purposes) are excludable from income and wages for employment tax purposes. Employer contributions for long-term care insurance are deductible by the employer. Amounts received from long-term care insurance purchased by the employer are excludable from income in accordance with the rules relating to excludability of proceeds of accident or health insurance (and subject to the cap on per diem contracts).

#### Definition of long-term care insurance contract

A long-term care insurance contract is defined as any insurance contract that provides only coverage of qualified long-term care services and that meets other requirements. The other requirements are that (1) the contract is guaranteed renewable, (2) the contract does not provide for a cash surrender value or other money that can be paid, assigned, pledged or borrowed, (3) refunds (other than refunds on the death of the insured or complete surrender or cancellation of the contract) and dividends under the contract may be used only to reduce future premiums or increase future benefits, and (4) the contract generally does not pay or reimburse expenses reimbursable under Medicare (except where Medicare is a secondary payor, or the contract makes per diem or other periodic payments without regard to expenses).

A contract does not fail to be treated as a long-term care insurance contract solely because it provides for payments on a per diem or other periodic basis without regard to expenses incurred during the period.

---

[235] HIPA does not otherwise modify the requirements relating to FSAs. An FSA is defined as a benefit program providing employees with coverage under which specified incurred expenses may be reimbursed (subject to maximums and other reasonable conditions), and the maximum amount of reimbursement that is reasonably available to a participant is less than 500 percent of the value of the coverage.

### State-maintained plans

Under HIPA, an arrangement is treated as a qualified long-term care insurance contract if an individual receives coverage for qualified long-term care services under a State long-term care plan, and the terms of the arrangement would satisfy the requirements for a long-term care insurance contract under the provision, were the arrangement an insurance contract. For this purpose, a State long-term care plan is any plan established and maintained by a State (or instrumentality of such State) under which only employees (and former employees, including retirees) of a State or of a political subdivision or instrumentality of the State, and their relatives, and their spouses and spouses' relatives, may receive coverage only for qualified long-term care services. "Relative" is defined as under section 152(a)(1)-(8). No inference was intended with respect to the tax consequences of such arrangements under prior law.

### Medicare duplication rules

HIPA provides that no provision of law shall be construed or applied so as to prohibit the offering of a long-term care insurance contract on the basis that the contract coordinates its benefits with those provided under Medicare. Thus, long-term care insurance contracts are not subject to the rules requiring duplication of Medicare benefits.

### Definition of qualified long-term care services

Qualified long-term care services means necessary diagnostic, preventive, therapeutic, curing, treating, mitigating and rehabilitative services, and maintenance or personal care services that are required by a chronically ill individual and that are provided pursuant to a plan of care prescribed by a licensed health care practitioner. Maintenance and personal care services may include meal preparation, household cleaning, and other similar services which the chronically ill individual is unable to perform. It is anticipated that the scope of maintenance and personal care services will be defined in Treasury regulations.

A chronically ill individual is one who has been certified within the previous 12 months by a licensed health care practitioner as (1) being unable to perform (without substantial assistance) at least 2 activities of daily living for at least 90 days [236] due to a loss of functional capacity, (2) having a similar level of disability as determined under regulations prescribed by the Secretary of the Treasury in consultation with the Secretary of Health and Human Services, or (3) requiring substantial supervision to protect such individual from threats to health and safety due to severe cognitive impairment. Activities of daily living are eating, toileting, transferring, bathing, dressing and continence.[237]

---

[236] The 90-day period is not a waiting period. Thus, for example, an individual can be certified as chronically ill if the licensed health care practitioner certifies that the individual will be unable to perform at least 2 activities of daily living for at least 90 days. The certification of an insured as a chronically ill individual may occur at any time, and is intended to take into account the sum of continuous prior days when the insured was chronically ill and future days when the insured is expected to remain chronically ill.

[237] HIPA provides that, for purposes of determining whether an individual is chronically ill, the number of activities of daily living that are taken into account under the contract may not be less than five. For example, a contract could require that an individual be unable to perform

It was intended that an individual who is physically able but has a cognitive impairment such as Alzheimer's disease or another form of irreversible loss of mental capacity be treated similarly to an individual who is unable to perform (without substantial assistance) at least 2 activities of daily living. Because of the concern that eligibility for the medical expense deduction not be diagnosis-driven, the provision requires the cognitive impairment to be severe. It was intended that severe cognitive impairment mean a deterioration or loss in intellectual capacity that is measured by clinical evidence and standardized tests which reliably measure impairment in: (1) short- or long-term memory; (2) orientation to people, places or time; and (3) deductive or abstract reasoning. In addition, it was intended that such deterioration or loss place the individual in jeopardy of harming self or others and therefore require substantial supervision by another individual.

A licensed health care practitioner is a physician (as defined in sec. 1861(r)(1) of the Social Security Act) and any registered professional nurse, licensed social worker, or other individual who meets such requirements as may be prescribed by the Secretary of the Treasury. A licensed social worker includes any social worker who has been issued a license, certificate, or similar authorization to act as a social worker by a State or a body authorized by a State to issue such authorizations.

*Expenses for long-term care services treated as medical expenses*

Unreimbursed expenses for qualified long-term care services provided to the taxpayer or the taxpayer's spouse or dependent are treated as medical expenses for purposes of the itemized deduction for medical expenses (subject to the present-law floor of 7.5 percent of adjusted gross income). For this purpose, amounts received under a qualified long-term care insurance contract (regardless of whether the contract reimburses expenses or pays benefits on a per diem or other periodic basis) are treated as reimbursement for expenses actually incurred for medical care.

For purposes of the deduction for medical expenses, qualified long-term care services do not include services provided to an individual by a relative or spouse (directly, or through a partnership, corporation, or other entity), unless the relative is a licensed professional with respect to such services, or by a related corporation (within the meaning of Code section 267(b) or 707(b)).[238]

---

(without substantial assistance) two out of any five of the activities listed in HIPA. By contrast, a contract does not meet this requirement if it required that an individual be unable to perform two out of any four of the activities listed in HIPA. This requirement does not apply to the determination of whether an individual is a chronically ill individual either (1) by virtue of severe cognitive impairment, or (2) if the insured satisfies a standard (if any) that is not based upon activities of daily living, as determined under regulations prescribed by the Secretary of the Treasury in consultation with the Secretary of Health and Human Services.

[238] The rule limiting such services provided by a relative or a related corporation does not apply for purposes of the exclusion for amounts received under a long-term care insurance contract, whether the contract is employer-provided or purchased by an individual. The limitation is unnecessary in such cases because it is anticipated that the insurer will monitor reimbursements to limit opportunities for fraud in connection with the performance of services by the taxpayer's relative or a related corporation.

340

*Long-term care insurance premiums treated as medical expenses*

Long-term care insurance premiums that do not exceed specified dollar limits are treated as medical expenses for purposes of the itemized deduction for medical expenses.[239] The limits are as follows:

| In the case of an individual with an attained age before the close of the taxable year of: | The limitation on premiums paid for such taxable years is: |
|---|---|
| Not more than 40 | $200 |
| More than 40 but not more than 50 | 375 |
| More than 50 but not more than 60 | 750 |
| More than 60 but not more than 70 | 2,000 |
| More than 70 | 2,500 |

For taxable years beginning after 1997, these dollar limits are indexed for increases in the medical care component of the consumer price index. The Secretary of the Treasury, in consultation with the Secretary of Health and Human Services, is directed to develop a more appropriate index to be applied in lieu of the foregoing. Such an alternative might appropriately be based on increases in skilled nursing facility and home health care costs. It is intended that the Treasury Secretary annually publish the indexed amount of the limits as early in the year as they can be calculated.

*Deduction for long-term care insurance of self-employed individuals*

The present-law 30 percent deduction for health insurance expenses of self-employed individuals is phased up to 80 percent under HIPA. Because HIPA treats payments of eligible long-term care insurance premiums in the same manner as medical insurance premiums, the self-employed health insurance deduction applies to eligible long-term care insurance premiums under HIPA.

The deduction for health insurance expenses of a self-employed individual is not available for a month for which the individual is eligible to participate in any subsidized health plan maintained by any employer of the individual or the individual's spouse. The fact that an individual is eligible for employer-subsidized health insurance is not intended to affect the ability of such an individual to deduct long-term care insurance premiums, so long as the individual is not eligible for employer-subsidized long-term care insurance.[240]

*Long-term care riders on life insurance contracts*

In the case of long-term care insurance coverage provided by a rider on or as part of a life insurance contract, the requirements applicable to long-term care insurance contracts apply as if the por-

---

[239] Similarly, within certain limits, in the case of a rider to a life insurance contract, charges against the life insurance contract's cash surrender value that are includible in income are treated as medical expenses (provided the rider constitutes a long-term care insurance contract).

[240] A technical correction may be necessary so that the statute reflects this intent.

tion of the contract providing such coverage were a separate contract. The term "portion" means only the terms and benefits that are in addition to the terms and benefits under the life insurance contract without regard to long-term care coverage. As a result, if the applicable requirements are met by the long-term care portion of the contract, amounts received under the contract as provided by the rider are treated in the same manner as long-term care insurance benefits, whether or not the payment of such amounts causes a reduction in the contract's death benefit or cash surrender value. The guideline premium limitation applicable under section 7702(c)(2) is increased by the sum of charges (but not premium payments) against the life insurance contract's cash surrender value, the imposition of which reduces premiums paid for the contract (within the meaning of sec. 7702(f)(1)). In addition, it is anticipated that Treasury regulations will provide for appropriate reduction in premiums paid (within the meaning of sec. 7702(f)(1)) to reflect the payment of benefits under the rider that reduce the cash surrender value of the life insurance contract. A similar rule should apply in the case of a contract governed by section 101(f) and in the case of the payments under a rider that are excludable under section 101(g) of the Code (as added by HIPA).

*Health care continuation rules*

The health care continuation rules do not apply to coverage under a long-term care insurance contract. The health care continuation rules do not apply to coverage under a plan, substantially all of the coverage under which is for qualified long-term care services.

### Inclusion of excess long-term care benefits

HIPA provides for the following calculation of the dollar cap applicable to aggregate payments under per diem type long-term care insurance contracts and amounts received with respect to a chronically ill individual pursuant to a life insurance contract.[241] The amount of the dollar cap with respect to any one chronically ill individual (who is not terminally ill) is $175 per day ($63,875 annually, as indexed), reduced by the amount of reimbursements and payments received by anyone for the cost of qualified long-term care services for the chronically ill individual. If more than one payee receives payments with respect to any one chronically ill individual, then everyone receiving periodic payments with respect to the same insured is treated as one person for purposes of the dollar cap. The amount of the dollar cap is utilized first by the chronically ill person, and any remaining amount is allocated in accordance with Treasury regulations. If payments under such contracts exceed the dollar cap, then the excess is excludable only to the extent of actual costs (in excess of the dollar cap) incurred for long-term care services. Amounts in excess of the dollar cap, with respect to which no actual costs were incurred for long-term care services, are fully includable in income without regard to rules relating to return of basis under Code section 72.

---

[241] See item D, below, relating to "Treatment of Accelerated Death Benefits Under Life Insurance Contracts."

A grandfather rule is provided under HIPA in the case of a per diem type contract issued to a policyholder on or before July 31, 1996. Under the grandfather rule, the amount of the dollar cap with respect to such a per diem contract is calculated without any reduction for reimbursements for qualified long-term care services under any other contract issued with respect to the same insured on or before July 31, 1996. The other provisions of the dollar cap are not affected by the grandfather rule. The grandfather rule ceases to apply as of the time that any of the contracts issued on or before July 31, 1996, with respect to the insured are exchanged, or benefits are increased.

Congress wished to clarify that, although the legislation imposes a daily (or equivalent) dollar cap on the amount of excludable benefits under certain types of long-term care insurance in certain circumstances, this limitation is not intended to suggest a preference or otherwise convey or facilitate a competitive advantage to one type of long-term care insurance compared to another type of long-term care insurance.

The Chairmen of the House Committee on Ways and Means and the Senate Finance Committee are directed jointly to request that the NAIC, in consultation with representatives of the insurance industry and consumer organizations, develop and conduct a study to determine the marketing and other effects, if any, of the dollar limit on excludable long-term care benefits under certain types of long-term care insurance contracts under the bill. Such Chairmen are to request that the NAIC, if it agrees to such request, shall submit the results of its study to the such Committees by no later than two years after agreeing to the request.

The $175 per day limit is indexed for inflation after 1997 for increases in the medical care component of the consumer price index. The Treasury Secretary, in consultation with the Secretary of Health and Human Services, is directed to develop a more appropriate index, to be applied in lieu of the foregoing. Such an alternative might appropriately be based on increases in skilled nursing facility and home health care costs. It is intended that the Treasury Secretary annually publish the indexed amount of the limit as early in the year as it can be calculated.

A payor of long-term care benefits (defined for this purpose to include any amount paid under a product advertised, marketed or offered as long-term care insurance) is required to report to the IRS the aggregate amount of such benefits paid to any individual during any calendar year, and the name, address and taxpayer identification number of such individual. In addition, a payor is required to report the name, address, and taxpayer identification number of the chronically ill individual on account of whose condition such amounts are paid, and whether the contract under which the amount is paid is a per diem-type contract. A copy of the report must be provided to the payee by January 31 following the year of payment, showing the name of the payor and the aggregate amount of benefits paid to the individual during the calendar year. Failure to file the report or provide the copy to the payee is subject to the generally applicable penalties for failure to file similar information reports.

343

*Life insurance company reserves*

In determining reserves for insurance company tax purposes, HIPA provides that the Federal income tax reserve method applicable for a long-term care insurance contract issued after December 31, 1996, is the method prescribed by the NAIC (or, if no reserve method has been so prescribed, a method consistent with the tax reserve method for life insurance, annuity or noncancellable accident and health insurance contracts, whichever is most appropriate). The method currently prescribed by the NAIC for long-term care insurance contracts is the one-year full preliminary term method. As under prior and present law, however, in no event may the tax reserve for a contract as of any time exceed the amount which would be taken into account with respect to the contract as of such time in determining statutory reserves.

*Consumer protection provisions*

Under HIPA, long-term care insurance contracts, and issuers of contracts, are required to satisfy certain provisions of the long-term care insurance model Act and model regulations promulgated by theNAIC (as adopted as of January 1993).

The contract requirements relate to disclosure, nonforfeitability, guaranteed renewal or noncancellability, prohibitions on limitations and exclusions, extension of benefits, continuation or conversion of coverage, discontinuance and replacement of policies, unintentional lapse, post-claims underwriting, minimum standards, inflation protection, preexisting conditions, and prior hospitalization. HIPA also provides disclosure and nonforfeiture requirements. The nonforfeiture provision gives consumers the option of selecting reduced paid-up insurance, extended term insurance, or a shortened benefit period in the event a policyholder who elects a nonforfeiture provision is unable to continue to pay premiums.[242] The requirement that insurers offer policyholders a nonforfeiture benefit does not preclude the imposition of a reasonable delay period. The consumer protection provisions that apply with respect to the terms of the contract apply only for purposes of determining whether a contract is a qualified long-term care insurance contract (within the meaning of HIPA).

The requirements for issuers of long-term care insurance contracts relate to application forms, reporting requirements, marketing, appropriateness of purchase, format, delivering a shopper's guide, right to return, outline of coverage, group plans, policy summary, monthly reports on accelerated death benefits, and incontestability period. A tax is imposed equal to $100 per insured per day for failure to satisfy these requirements. The consumer protection requirements for issuers of contracts apply with respect to contracts that are qualified long-term care insurance contracts (within the meaning of HIPA).

---

[242] The nonforfeiture provision shall provide for a benefit available in the event of a default in the payment of any premiums and the amount of the benefit may be adjusted subsequent to being initially granted only as necessary to reflect changes in claims, persistency, and interest as reflected in changes in rates for premium paying policies approved by the appropriate State regulatory authority for the same contract form. A technical correction may be necessary so that the statute reflects this intent.

HIPA provides that, for purposes of both the requirements as to contract terms and the requirements relating to issuers of contracts, the determination of whether any requirement of a model regulation or model Act has been met is made by the Secretary of the Treasury. It was not intended that the Secretary create a Federal standard, but rather, look to applicable or appropriate State standards or to those provided specifically in the model regulation or model Act.

HIPA provides that an otherwise qualified long-term care insurance contract will not fail to be a qualified long-term care insurance contract, and will not be treated as failing to meet the analogous requirement under HIPA, solely because it satisfies a consumer protection standard imposed under applicable State law that is more stringent than the analogous standard provided in HIPA. HIPA does not preclude States from enacting more stringent consumer protection provisions than the analogous standards under HIPA.

### *Effective Date*

The provisions defining long-term care insurance contracts and qualified long-term care services apply to contracts issued after December 31, 1996. Any contract issued before January 1, 1997, that met the long-term care insurance requirements of the State in which the contract was sitused at the time it was issued is treated as a qualified long-term care insurance contract, and services provided under or reimbursed by the contract are treated as qualified long-term care services. Solely for purposes of this grandfather rule, and not for other purposes, it is intended that in the case of a group contract that was issued before January 1, 1997, the contract will not cease to be treated as issued before January 1, 1997, solely by reason of the addition after December 31, 1996, of individuals to the coverage (as of December 31, 1996) under the contract. It is intended that a contract be treated as meeting the long-term care insurance requirements of the State, if it meets the insurance requirements of the State with respect to insurance contracts covering types of long-term care services (such as only nursing home care, or only home health care), even though such State requirements are separate from long-term care insurance requirements, or prohibit the contract from being labeled a long-term care contract. Similarly, a State waiver of a long-term care insurance requirement (such as the loss ratio requirement) in the case of a long-term care rider or provision under a life insurance contract is not intended to cause the contract to be treated as not meeting the long-term care insurance requirements of the State.

A contract providing for long-term care insurance may be exchanged for a long-term care insurance contract (or the former canceled and the proceeds reinvested in the latter within 60 days) tax free between the date of enactment and January 1, 1998. Taxable gain would be recognized to the extent money or other property is received in the exchange.

The issuance or conformance of a rider to a life insurance contract providing long-term care insurance coverage is not treated as a modification or a material change for purposes of applying sections 101(f), 7702 and 7702A of the Code.

The provisions relating to treatment of eligible long-term care premiums and long-term care services as a medical expense generally are effective for taxable years beginning after December 31, 1996.

The provisions relating to the maximum exclusion for certain long-term care benefits and reporting are effective for taxable years beginning after December 31, 1996. Thus, the initial year in which reports will be filed with the IRS and copies provided to the payee will be 1998, with respect to long-term care benefits paid in 1997.

The provision relating to life insurance company reserves is effective for contracts issued after December 31, 1997.

### Revenue Effect

The provisions are estimated to reduce Federal fiscal year budget receipts by $108 million in 1997, $667 million in 1998, $645 million in 1999, $663 million in 2000, $743 million in 2001, $827 million in 2002, $905 million in 2003, $1,009 million in 2004, $1,103 million in 2005, and $1,205 million in 2006.

## D. Treatment of Accelerated Death Benefits Under Life Insurance Contracts (secs. 331-332 of HIPA and secs. 101(g), 818(g), 6050Q, and 7702B of the Code)

### Present and Prior Law

#### Treatment of amounts received under a life insurance contract

If a contract meets the definition of a life insurance contract, gross income does not include insurance proceeds that are paid pursuant to the contract by reason of the death of the insured (sec. 101(a)). In addition, the undistributed investment income ("inside buildup") earned on premiums credited under the contract is not subject to current taxation to the owner of the contract. The exclusion under section 101 applies regardless of whether the death benefits are paid as a lump sum or otherwise.

Under prior law, amounts received under a life insurance contract (other than a modified endowment contract) prior to the death of the insured were includible in the gross income of the recipient to the extent that the amount received constitutes cash value in excess of the taxpayer's investment in the contract. Generally, the investment in the contract is the aggregate amount of premiums paid less amounts previously received that were excluded from gross income.

If a contract fails to be treated as a life insurance contract under section 7702(a), inside buildup on the contract is generally subject to tax (sec. 7702(g)).

#### Requirements for a life insurance contract

To qualify as a life insurance contract for Federal income tax purposes, a contract must be a life insurance contract under the applicable State or foreign law and must satisfy either of two alternative tests: (1) a cash value accumulation test or (2) a test consisting of a guideline premium requirement and a cash value corridor requirement (sec. 7702(a)). A contract satisfies the cash value accumulation test if the cash surrender value of the contract may not at any time exceed the net single premium that would have to be paid at such time to fund future benefits under the contract. A contract satisfies the guideline premium and cash value corridor tests if the premiums paid under the contract do not at any time exceed the greater of the guideline single premium or the sum of the guideline level premiums, and if the death benefit under the contract is not less than a varying statutory percentage of the cash surrender value of the contract.

### Proposed regulations on accelerated death benefits

The Treasury Department issued proposed regulations [243] under which certain "qualified accelerated death benefits" paid by reason of the terminal illness of an insured would have been treated as paid by reason of the death of the insured and therefore qualify for exclusion under section 101. In addition, the proposed regulations would have permitted an insurance contract that includes a qualified accelerated death benefit rider to qualify as a life insurance contract under section 7702. Thus, the proposed regulations would have provided that including this benefit would not cause an insurance contract to fail to meet the definition of a life insurance contract.

Under the proposed regulations, a benefit would have qualified as a qualified accelerated death benefit only if it met three requirements. First, the accelerated death benefit could be payable only if the insured becomes terminally ill. Second, the amount of the benefit had to equal or exceed the present value of the reduction in the death benefit otherwise payable.[244] Third, the cash surrender value and the death benefit payable under the policy had to be reduced proportionately as a result of the accelerated death benefit.

For purposes of the proposed regulations, an insured would have been treated as terminally ill if he or she had an illness that, despite appropriate medical care, the insurer reasonably expected to result in death within twelve months from the payment of the accelerated death benefit. The proposed regulations would not have applied to viatical settlements.

### Reasons for Change

Congress wished to extend the present-law rule permitting an exclusion from income for amounts paid under a life insurance contract by reason of the death of the insured to accelerated death benefits paid with respect to certain terminally ill and chronically ill insured individuals. In addition, Congress believed that this exclusion from income should be extended to certain sales or assignments of all or a portion of a life insurance contract to a viatical settlement provider. Congress believed that a single set of rules should apply to benefits received with respect to a chronically ill individual to the extent possible. To provide parity in treatment,

---

[243] Prop. Treas. Reg. Secs. 1.101-8, 1.7702-0, 1.7702-2, and 1.7702A-1 (December 15, 1992).
[244] For purposes of determining the present value under the proposed regulations, the maximum permissible discount rate would be the greater of (1) the applicable Federal rate that applies under the discounting rules for property and casualty insurance loss reserves, and (2) the interest rate applicable to policy loans under the contract. Also, the present value would be determined assuming that the death benefit would have been paid twelve months after payment of the accelerated death benefit.

the same definition of a chronically ill individual applies for purposes of the rules under this provision and the rules governing long-term care insurance contracts. Further, the $175 per day ($63,875 annual) limit on excludability of benefits under per diem type long-term care insurance contracts applies for chronically ill individuals.

## *Explanation of Provision*

HIPA provides an exclusion from gross income as an amount paid by reason of the death of an insured for (1) amounts received under a life insurance contract and (2) amounts received for the sale or assignment of any portion of the death benefit under a life insurance contract to a qualified viatical settlement provider, provided that the insured under the life insurance contract is either terminally ill or chronically ill.[245] For example, the sale or assignment to a viatical settlement provider of a life insurance contract that has a long-term care insurance rider (payments under which are funded by and reduce the death benefit) is considered the sale or assignment of the death benefit. Sale or assignment of a stand-alone rider providing for long-term care insurance (where payments under the rider are not funded by reductions in the death benefit), however, is not considered the sale or assignment of the death benefit.

The provision does not apply in the case of an amount paid to any taxpayer other than the insured, if such taxpayer has an insurable interest by reason of the insured being a director, officer or employee of the taxpayer, or by reason of the insured being financially interested in any trade or business carried on by the taxpayer.

A terminally ill individual is defined as one who has been certified by a physician as having an illness or physical condition that reasonably can be expected to result in death within 24 months of the date of certification. A physician is defined for this purpose in the same manner as under the long-term care insurance rules of HIPA.[246] An individual who meets the definition of a terminally ill individual is not treated as chronically ill, for purposes of this provision.

A chronically ill individual is defined under the long-term care provisions of HIPA.[247] HIPA clarifies the rules for chronically ill insureds so that the tax treatment of payments with respect to

---

[245] If the amount is received under a rider or other provision of the contract that is treated as a long-term care insurance contract under section 7702B (as added by HIPA), the rules of section 7702B apply.

[246] A physician is defined for these purposes as in section 1861(r)(1) of the Social Security Act, which provides that a physician means a doctor of medicine or osteopathy legally authorized to practice medicine and surgery by the State in which he performs such function or action (including a physician within the meaning of section 1101(a)(7) of that Act). Section 1101(a)(7) of that Act provides that the term physician includes osteopathic practitioners within the scope of their practice as defined by State law.

[247] Thus, a chronically ill individual is one who has been certified within the previous 12 months by a licensed health care practitioner as (1) being unable to perform (without substantial assistance) at least 2 activities of daily living for at least 90 days due to a loss of functional capacity, (2) having a similar level of disability as determined under regulations prescribed by the Secretary of the Treasury in consultation with the Secretary of Health and Human Services, or (3) requiring substantial supervision to protect such individual from threats to health and safety due to severe cognitive impairment. Activities of daily living are eating, toileting, transferring, bathing, dressing and continence. The number of activities of daily living that are taken into account for this purpose may not be less than five.

chronically ill individuals is reasonably similar under the long-term care rules of HIPA and under this provision. In the case of a chronically ill individual, the exclusion under this provision with respect to amounts paid under a life insurance contract and amounts paid in a sale or assignment to a viatical settlement provider applies if the payment received is for costs incurred by the payee (not compensated by insurance or otherwise) for qualified long-term care services (as defined under the long-term care rules) for the insured person for the period, and two other requirements (similar to requirements applicable to long-term care insurance contracts) are met. The first requirement is that under the terms of the contract giving rise to the payment, the payment is not a payment or reimbursement of expenses reimbursable under Medicare (except where Medicare is a secondary payor under the arrangement, or the arrangement provides for per diem or other periodic payments without regard to expenses for qualified long-term care services). HIPA provides that no provision of law shall be construed or applied so as to prohibit the offering of such a contract giving rise to such a payment on the basis that the contract coordinates its payments with those provided under Medicare. The second requirement is that the arrangement complies with those consumer protection provisions applicable to long-term care insurance contracts and issuers that are specified in Treasury regulations. It was intended that such guidance incorporate rules similar to those of section 6F (relating to right to return, permitting the payee 30 days to rescind the arrangement) of the NAIC Long-Term Care Insurance Model Act, and section 13 (relating to requirements for application, requiring that the payee be asked if he or she already has long-term care insurance, Medicaid, or similar coverage) of the NAIC Long-Term Care Insurance Model Regulations. If the NAIC or the State in which the policyholder resides issues standards relating to chronically ill individuals, then the analogous requirements under Treasury regulations cease to apply.

Payments made on a per diem or other periodic basis, without regard to expenses incurred for qualified long-term care services, are nevertheless excludable under this provision, subject to the $175 per day ($63,875 annually, as indexed) dollar cap on excludable benefits that applies for amounts that are excludable under per diem type long-term care insurance contracts. HIPA provides as follows with respect to the calculation of the dollar cap applicable to aggregate payments under per diem type long-term care insurance contracts and amounts received with respect to a chronically ill individual pursuant to a life insurance contract. The amount of the dollar cap with respect to the aggregate amount received under per diem type long-term care insurance contracts and this provision with respect to any one chronically ill individual (who is not terminally ill) is $175 per day ($63,875 annually), as indexed, reduced by the amount of reimbursements and payments received by anyone for the cost of qualified long-term care services for the chronically ill individual. If more than one payee receives payments with respect to any one chronically ill individual, the amount of the dollar cap is utilized first by the chronically ill person, and any remaining amount is allocated in accordance with Treasury regulations. If payments under such contracts exceed the dollar cap, then the excess is excludable only to the extent of actual costs incurred for long-term care services. Amounts in excess of the dollar cap, with respect to which no actual costs (in excess of the dollar cap) were incurred for long-term care services, are fully includable in income without regard to rules relating to return of basis under Code section 72.

The payor of a payment with respect to an individual who is chronically ill is required to report to the IRS the aggregate amount of such benefits paid to any individual during any calendar year, and the name, address and taxpayer identification number of such individual. In addition, the payor is required to report the name, address, and taxpayer identification number of the chronically ill individual on account of whose condition such amounts are paid, and whether the contract under which the amount is paid is a per diem-type contract. A copy of the report must be provided to the payee by January 31 following the year of payment, showing the name of the payer and the aggregate amount of such benefits paid to the individual during the calendar year. Failure to file the report or provide the copy to the payee is subject to the generally applicable penalties for failure to file similar information reports.

HIPA provides that a viatical settlement provider is any person regularly engaged in the trade or business of purchasing or taking assignments of life insurance contracts on the lives of insured individuals who are terminally ill or chronically ill, so long as the viatical settlement provider meets certain requirements. The viatical settlement provider must either (1) be licensed, in the State where the insured resides, to engage in such transactions with terminally ill individuals (if the insured is terminally ill) or with chronically ill individuals (if the insured is chronically ill), or (2) if such licensing with respect to the insured individual is not required in the State, meet other requirements depending on whether the insured is terminally or chronically ill. If the insured is terminally ill, the viatical settlement provider must meet the requirements of sections 8 and 9 of the Viatical Settlements Model Act, relating to disclosure and general rules (issued by the NAIC, and also meet the section of the NAIC Viatical Settlements Model Regulation relating to standards for evaluation of reasonable payments, including discount rates, in determining amounts paid by the viatical settlement provider. If the insured is chronically ill, the viatical settlement provider must meet requirements similar to those of sections 8 and 9 of the NAIC Viatical Settlements Model Act, and also must meet the standards, if any, promulgated by the NAIC for evaluating the reasonableness of amounts paid in viatical settlement transactions with chronically ill individuals.

For life insurance company tax purposes, HIPA provides that a life insurance contract is treated as including a reference to a qualified accelerated death benefit rider to a life insurance contract (except in the case of any rider that is treated as a long-term care insurance contract under section 7702B, as added by HIPA). A qualified accelerated death benefit rider is any rider on a life insurance contract that provides only for payments of a type that are excludable under this provision.

### Effective Date

The provision applies to amounts received after December 31, 1996. The provision treating a qualified accelerated death benefit rider as life insurance for life insurance company tax purposes takes effect on January 1, 1997. The issuance of a qualified accelerated death benefit rider to a life insurance contract, or the addition of any provision required to conform an accelerated death benefit rider to these provisions, is not treated as a modification or material change of the contract (and is not intended to affect the issue date of any contract under section 101(f)).

### Revenue Effect

The provision is estimated to reduce Federal fiscal year budget receipts by $10 million in 1997, $107 million in 1998, $166 million in 1999, $214 million in 2000, $265 million in 2001, $316 million in 2002, $376 million in 2003, $446 million in 2004, $527 million in 2005, and $599 million in 2006.

## E. Exemption From Income Tax for State-Sponsored Organizations Providing Health Coverage for High-Risk Individuals; Exemption from Income Tax for State-Sponsored Workers' Compensation Reinsurance Organizations (secs. 341-342 of HIPA and secs. 501(c)(26) and (27) of the Code)

### Present and Prior Law

In general, the Internal Revenue Service ("IRS") takes the position that organizations that provide insurance for their members or other individuals are not considered to be engaged in a tax-exempt activity. The IRS maintains that such insurance activity is either (1) a regular business of a kind ordinarily carried on for profit, or (2) an economy or convenience in the conduct of members' businesses because it relieves the members from obtaining insurance on an individual basis.

Certain insurance risk pools have qualified for tax exemption under Code section 501(c)(6). In general, these organizations (1) assign any insurance policies and administrative functions to their member organizations (although they may reimburse their members for amounts paid and expenses); (2) serve an important common business interest of their members; and (3) must be membership organizations financed, at least in part, by membership dues.

State insurance risk pools may also qualify for tax exempt status under section 501(c)(4) as a social welfare organizations or under section 115 as serving an essential governmental function of a State. In seeking qualification under section 501(c)(4), insurance organizations generally are constrained by the restrictions on the provision of "commercial-type insurance" contained in section 501(m). Section 115 generally provides that gross income does not include income derived from the exercise of any essential governmental function and accruing to a State or any political subdivision thereof. However, the IRS may be reluctant to rule that particular State risk-pooling entities satisfy the section 501(c)(4) or 115 requirements for tax-exempt status.

# INDEX

## A

Accelerated death benefits (ADBs), 2, 338. *See also* Death benefits
    consequences of, under sections 7702, 7702A, and 72, 247-251
    critical illness and, 212-213
    federal tax rules for, 207-213
    life insurance tax rules and, 11
    origin and characteristics of, 205-207
    terminal illness and, 211-212

Accelerated death benefit (ADB) riders
    accounting for, 247-251
    grandfather considerations for, 251
    section 1035 exchanges involving, 251-252

Activities of daily living (ADLs), 207, 226, 338

Actuarial assumptions, 21, 338

Additive method in substandard mortality, 98

Adjustable whole life, 309, 313

Adjustment event, 338

Adjustments, 53-56
    cash value accumulation test (CVAT), 54, 104-105
    guideline premium test, 54-55, 105-122
    rules for, 54, 338
    role of, 162
    under section 7702, 103-104
    7-pay test, 55-56

Age
    adjustments for substandard mortality, 99
    attained, 25, 339
    defining, 72-76
    mortality rates beyond 100, 92-96

Age 121 terminal values, 92-93

Aggregation rule, 14-15, 338

Alternate death benefit rules, 52, 338

Alternative forms of life insurance, 8

Amount paid, 34, 35, 338

Amounts retained rule, 14, 338

Anderson, James C. H., 310

Annual approach to adjusting guideline premiums, 116

Applicable law, 6, 338
    requirement of section 7702, 6-9

Assumption eras, 168-169

At-issue calculations, 57-59

At-issue compliance, 167

Attained age, 25, 339

Attained-age increment and decrement method, 55, 107, 99-112, 339

Attained-age net single premium, applying computational rules for cash value accumulation test and, 134

Attained-age regulations, 73, 339

Automatic waivers, 267, 283

## B

Bank-owned life insurance (BOLI), 340

Basic actuarial principles, 59, 339

Blue Book, 19, 339

Bond fund total return, 289

Burial contracts, 195-197, 339

## C

Calculation methods, 59-63
    basic actuarial principles, 59-60
    commutation functions, 60-61
    equivalence of, 62-63
    processing frequency, 62
    projection-based, 61
    rounding of values, 63

Canadian Income Tax Regulations, 10

Case law, 20

Cash surrender value (CSV), 21, 25, 69, 339
    cash value accumulation test and, 25
    deemed, 129-130, 134, 341
    deferral of tax on increments, 323
    defining, 69-72
    development of, 297-298
    early cases, 302
    legislative history relating to, 72
    1992 proposed regulation defining, 70-71
    private letter rulings defining, 71-72
    product-specific issues and, 186-192

Cash value, 22, 339
    defining, 69-72

Cash value accumulation test (CVAT), 6, 23-25, 339-340
    adjustments, 54, 104-105
    cash surrender value, 25
    necessary premiums under, 133-137
    net single premium, 24-25
    under section 7702, 32-34
    terms of contract, 25

Cash value bonuses, 198-199

Cash value corridor, 6, 26, 340

*Century Wood Preserving Co.* v. *Commissioner,* 302

Chronic illness, 225, 228-232, 340

Chronic illness riders, 207, 240-247
    qualified long-term care insurance riders, 223-240
    reporting requirements for, 246-247
    requirements for, under section 101(g), 241-244
    separate contract rule for long-term care riders, 235-236
    tax treatment of, from section 101(g) riders, 241

Church-related death benefit plans, 198, 340

Closing agreements, 34, 262, 264, 340

Colloquies, 19, 340

Combination plans, 185

*Commissioner* v. *Keller's Estate,* 303-305

Commutation functions, 59, 60, 340

Computational rules, 22, 51, 340
    restrictions on future benefits and, 24-25

for 7-pay premium, 82-83
Constructive Receipt Doctrine, 325, 340
Consumer protection qualification rules, 252-260
   extension of benefits, 254
   group policy requirements, 254
   guaranteed renewability, 253
   home and community care coverage, 256
   inflation protection, 256-257
   permitted limitations and exclusions, 254
   pre-existing condition limitations, 252-253
   prior hospitalization and institutionalization requirements, 253
   prohibition against pre-existing conditions and probationary periods in replacement policies, 257
   prohibition on post-claims underwriting, 255-256
   protection against unintentional lapse, 255
   renewability and certain disclosures, 255
   renewal, waiting periods and coverage of less than skilled care, 252
Contract adjustments, material changes and effective date rules, 103, 122, 169-174
Contract changes, loss of grandfathers and new-issuance treatment, 151-152
Contract exchanges, 2, 152-154
   life insurance income tax treatment, 16-17
Contract period method, long-term care period, 219
Contracts
   burial, 195-197
   failed, 6, 261, 341
   first-to-die, 180-181
   foreign-issued life insurance, 9-10
   grandfathered, 157-158
   intentionally failed, 200
   joint life insurance, 74, 180-181, 344
   last-to-die, 181
   material changes in, 151

   new issue treatment of, 159-162
   preneed, 195-197
   review of, 293
   survivorship, 184, 351-352
   variable, 3, 17-18, 289
Contract sales
   gifts, 2
   life insurance tax rules, 17
Contract year, 29, 340
Corporate-owned life insurance (COLI), 340
   best practices rules, 12
   policies, 7-8
Cost of insurance (COI), 41, 340-341
*Cottage Savings Association* v. *Commissioner,* 156-157
Critical illness, other accelerated death benefits, 212-213
Crossover duration, 187
Curtate, 63, 341

# D

Death benefit exclusion, 2, 322-323
   life insurance tax rules, 11
Death benefits. *See also* Accelerated death benefits (ADBS)
   accelerated, 2, 12
   alternative rules, 79-82
   church-related plans, 198, 340
   discount rate, 41, 341
   least endowment rule, 81
   net level reserve test, 80-81, 345
   payout, over time, 2, 11
   under section 7702A, 83
   target, 185
Deduction of loss on surrender or sale, life insurance tax rules, 17
Deemed cash surrender value, 134, 341
   necessary premiums, 129-130
Deemed exchange, 155, 341
Deemed maturity date, 52, 341
Deficit Reduction Act of 1984 (DEFRA), enactment of section 7702, 341
   applicable law requirement, 6-7
   Blue Book footnote 49, 186
   cash surrender value, 69-70

   cash value accumulation test (CVAT), adjustments, 104
   introduction of section 7702, 19
   life insurance contracts, 4
   variable life insurance, 175
*De minimis* overage earnings rule, 288
Diversification rules, 176, 341
   for variable contract separate account, 18
Dividends, 1, 341
Dole-Bentsen colloquy, 109, 110, 341
   *Congressional Record* inclusion of, 106-107
   repeating elements of, 54
*Dow Chemical Co.* v. *United States,* 8
Dual cash surrender values, 186-192

# E

Economically equivalent to policyholder dividends, 39
Economic income, associated with inside buildup, 323-324
Effective date rules
   administering, 167-174
   material changes, contract adjustments, 169-174
Employer-owned life insurance
   death benefit exclusion, 2
   life insurance tax rules, 12-13
Equal payment rate method, long-term care period, 219
Equity fund total return, 289
Equity-indexed universal life insurance (EIUL) contract, 179-180
*Evans* v. *Commissioner,* 306
Exact approach to adjusting guideline premium, 113-114, 116-117
Excess earnings approach, 281
Excess interest, 39, 341
Expense charges, 27, 49-50, 341
   in calculating guideline premiums, 50
   defining reasonable, 49-50
Extension rider, 239
Extraordinary life, 309

## F

Face amount plans, decreasing, 199
Failed contracts, 6, 261, 341
Failed contracts and inadvertent modified endowment contracts, 261-294
    remediation processes, 265-266
    remediation revolution, 274-294
    section 101(f) and 7702 failures, 262-265
    "self-help" corrections, 261-262
    waivable errors and causes of noncompliance, 269-274
    waiver and closing agreement processes, 266-269
Fail-safe provision, 33, 341-342
Federal tax rules for accelerated death benefits, 207-215
FIFO taxation, 18n, 342
Financed life insurance, limitations on, 306-309
First-to-die contracts, 180-181
Fixed premium universal life (FPUL), 186-192, 342
Floor interest rate, 37, 342
Footnote 49, 342
Force-out approach, accounting for ADBs, 31, 248-249
Foreign Account Tax Compliance Act (2010) (FATCA), 10
Foreign-issued life insurance contracts, 9-10
Frasier method, 181-182, 342
Future benefits, 21, 50-53, 342
    computational rules, 51-53
    limiting, 76-79
    qualified additional benefits, charges for, 53
    under section 7702A, 83
Future limitations, 334-335

## G

General account total return rate, 289
General Counsel Memorandum (GCM) 38934, 312
General Counsel Memorandum (GCM) 39022, 313-314
Gifts, contract sales and, 2
Grandfather considerations for accelerated death benefits (ADB) riders, 251
Grandfathered contracts, changes made to, 157-158
Grandfathering, 109, 151, 167
Gross-up rule, 41, 193-195, 342
Group universal life (GUL), 192-193
GSP to 7-pay ratio, 36
Guaranteed minimum withdrawal benefits, 178-179
Guaranteed mortality, 41-42, 342
Guideline level premium (GLP), 342
    qualified additional benefits in, 87-89
Guideline premium/cash value corridor test, 26-32
Guideline premium limitation (GPL), 6, 26, 342
Guideline premium test (GPT), 26, 342-343
    applying, 31-32
    necessary premiums under, 131-133
    treatment of premiums returned to policyholders to comply with, 30-31
Guideline premium test adjustments, 54-55, 105-122
    decrease in death benefit example, 117-119
    increase in death benefit example, 115
    off-anniversary changes, 115-117
    problems in applying, 119-120
    reinstatements, 120-122
    section 101(f) adjustment events and methods, 105-107
    section 7702 adjustment events, 107-109
    section 7702 adjustment method, attained-age increment and decrement rule, 109-112
    timing of adjustments to, 112-114
Guideline single premium (GSP), 26, 343
    treatment of, under option 2 plans, 138-139

## H

Haig-Simons income, 343
Hands-on assistance, 229
Health Insurance Portability and Accountability Act of 1996 (HIPAA), 12, 343
    federal tax rules, 207
    grandfather considerations for accelerated death benefits (ADBs), 251
    tax treatment for refund of premium, 222
*Helvering* v. *Le Gierse,* 3-4, 343
    developments after, 305-306
    economic definition of life insurance, 295-296
    estate tax exemption and, 303
    federal common law definition of insurance, 303-305
    life insurance and annuity combinations, 200
    standard of, 8, 9
Henningsen, Victor E., 306
High early cash value policies, 308-309
Hutton Life rulings, 311-312

## I

Illustration-based projection, 48, 49, 343
Immediate payment of claims (IPC), 63, 343
Implied guarantees, 41, 343
Inadvertent MEC, 261, 343
Income
    on the contract, 262, 343
    Haig-Simons, 343
Income tax, tax policy and ideal of comprehensive, 321-323
Income tax treatment of life insurance contracts, 1-3
    contract sales and gifts, 2
    death benefits, 2
    deduction of loss on surrender or sale, 3
    exchanges, 2
    inside buildup, 2
    lifetime distributions, 2

premium and interest deduction limits, 2
variable, and investor control, 3
In-force management, 167
Initial guarantees, 38, 343
Inside buildup, 1, 262, 343
　economic income associated with, 323-324
　life insurance tax rules, 13
　lifetime distributions and, 2
　limitations on, 326-335
　of permanent life insurance contracts, 323-326
　reasons for tax deferral on, 324-326
Insurable interest, 3, 7-8, 343-344
Insurance company rehabilitations, 167
Insurance risk, associated with accelerated death benefits, 206
Insurance value concept, 296-297
Intentionally failed contracts, 200
Interest, 37-41
　implied guarantees, 41
　initial guarantee of, 38
　monthly assumption and death benefit discount rate, 40-41
　policyholder dividends and guarantees, 39-40
　relationship of statutory rates to contractual guarantees, 40
　short-term guarantees of, 38-39
Interest-sensitive whole life, 186-192
Inter-governmental agreements (IGAs), 10
Interim mortality rules, 42, 344
Investment in the contract, effect of charges for
　qualified long-term care insurance, 214
Investment orientation, 327, 344
　efforts to limit, on life insurance contracts, 4
Investor control, variable contracts and, 3
Investor control doctrine, 17-18
Irreplaceable Life, 310

## J

Joint industry proposal, 317-318
Joint life insurance contracts, 74, 180-181, 344

## L

Last-to-die contracts, 181
Layered approach to adjusting guideline premium, 107, 113, 116
Least endowment rule, 344
　for death benefits, 81
Legislative history, 6, 344
Licensed health care practitioner (LHCP), 344
　chronically ill individuals and, 208, 226-227
Life insurance, 3, 344
　alternative forms of, 8-9
　common law rules, 3-4
　Deficit Reduction Act of 1984, 4
　development of economic definition of, 302-306
　rise of statutory definition of, 309-312
　Tax Equity and Fiscal Responsibility Act of 1982, 4
　Tax Reform Act of 1986, 4-5
　tax treatment of, 322-323
　Technical and Miscellaneous Revenue Act of 1988, 5
Life insurance contracts
　Canadian restrictions on, 10
　foreign-issued, 9-10
　gift of, 17
　income tax treatment of, 1-3
　　contract sales and gifts, 2
　　death benefits, 2
　　deduction of loss on surrender or sale, 3
　　exchanges, 2
　　inside buildup, 2
　　lifetime distributions, 2
　　premium and interest deduction limits, 2
　　variable, and investor control, 3
　inside buildup of permanent, 323-326
　issue date of, 154-155
　tax policy and taxation of, 321-335

Life insurance taxation, role of sections 7702 and 7702A in, 5-6
Life insurance tax rules, 10
　accelerated death benefits, 12
　contract exchanges, 16-17
　contract sales, 17
　death benefit exclusion, 11
　deduction of loss on surrender or sale, 17
　employer-owned, 12-13
　inside buildup, 13
　lifetime distributions, 13-14
　payout of death benefit over time, 11
　policy loans applied to pay premiums, 16
　premium and interest deduction limits, 15
　transfer for value rule, 11
　variable contracts, 17-18
Lifetime distributions
　inside buildup and, 2
　life insurance tax rules and, 13-14
LIFO taxation, 18n, 344
*London Shoe Co.* v. *Commissioner*, 302
Look-back rules, 123, 344
Loss, deduction of, on surrender or sale, 3

## M

Material changes, 129, 152, 345
　of benefits, 124-127
　in contracts, 151
　double meaning of, 124
　effective date rules, contract adjustments, 169-174
　examples of, 128-129
　rules on, 56
　　administering, 167-174
　section 7702 effective date rule, 155-159
　seven contract years following under section 7702A, 34
M&E and asset-based expenses, 177-178
Minimum deposit, 345
Minimum deposit life insurance plans, 308-309
Minimum interest rate, 345

under cash value accumulation test (CVAT), 29

Minimum premium, 200

Model or test plan concept, 21-23

Model-plan values, 22

Modified endowment contract (MEC), 1, 345
- effective date rule, 152
- under section 7702A, 34-36

Monthly mortality rates, 47-48, 345

Mortality, 41-49
- cost of insurance rates, 48-49
- interim rule, 43
- monthly assumption, 47-48, 345
- Notice 2006-95, 44-47
- permanent rule, 42-43
- proposed regulation on reasonable, 66-67
- rates beyond age 100, 92-96
- reasonable, prevailing commissioners' standard tables and Notice 88-128, 43-44
- reasonable standard, 42
- substandard, 97-100

Multiple-life plans, 180-184

Multiplicative method (or ratio method), in substandard mortality, 98

# N

NALU-AALU proposal, 316

Necessary premiums, 129-137, 345
- under cash value accumulation test (CVAT), 133-137
- under guideline premium test (GPT), 131-133

Necessary premium test (NPT), 345

Negative income, 264

Net amount of risk (NAR), 6, 345

Net level reserve test
- for death benefits, 80-81, 345

Net premium, 21, 345

Net rate products, 41, 345

Net single premiums (NSPs), 21-22, 345
- cash value accumulation test (CVAT), 24-25

Net surrender value (NSV), 25, 345-346

New-issuance treatment, contract changes and, 151-152

No-lapse guarantees, 200-203

Nonforfeiture Law for Life Insurance, 333-334

Nonguaranteed element, 346

Nonqualified additional benefit (Non-QAB), 53, 346

Nonqualified long-term care insurance, 346
- federal income tax treatment of, 208

Notice 88-128, 43-44, 65-66, 346

Notice 99-48, 346

Notice 2006-95, 44-47, 346

Notice 2011-68, 346

# O

Off-anniversary, 346

Offshore contract, 176-177, 346

100 percent of error approach, 281

Option 1, 346

Option 2, 346
- death benefit option changes and, 138-139
- treatment of guideline single premium under plans, 138-139

Overage earnings, 269, 287

# P

Packwood-Baucus colloquy, 51, 346-347

Paid-up additions riders, 184-185

Partial exchange concept, applying, to life insurance contract, 17

Partial extinguishment approach, accounting for ADBs, 249

Partial withdrawals, 2, 347

Payment of death claims assumptions, 63-65

Payout of death benefit over time, life insurance tax rules, 11

Pay premiums, policy loans applied to, 16

Penalty tax, 2, 347

*Penn Mutual Life Insurance Co.* v. *Lederer,* 302

Per diem benefits, 217, 347

Per diem limitation, 207

Permanent mortality rule, 42-43, 347

Pike, Andrew, 23

Plan of care, 347

Policy loans, 2, 347
- life insurance tax rules and, 16

Policy value, 48, 347

Postfunding, 87
- of QABs, 347

Pre-DEFRA contracts, 168

Premium and interest deduction limits, life insurance tax rules, 2, 15

Premium deposit funds, 201

Premiums paid, 23, 29-30, 347-348
- treatment of, returned to policyholder to comply with guidelines premium test (GPT), 30-31

Preneed contracts, 195-197

Preneed model, 196

Prevailing tables, 43, 348

Private letter ruling (PLR), 19, 348
- death benefits, 9
- defining cash surrender value, 71-72

Private placement, 348

Private placement variable life, sale of, 177

Processing frequency, 348

Product review, 292

Product-specific issues, 175-203
- burial or preneed contracts, 195-197
- cash value bonuses, 198-199
- church-related death benefits plans, 198, 340
- combination plans, 185
- decreasing face amount plans, 199
- determining insureds "age," 182-184
- dual cash surrender values, 186-192
- equity-indexed universal life insurance (EIUL) contract, 179-180

fixed-premium universal life, 186-192
group universal life, 192-193
intentionally failed contracts, 200
interest-sensitive whole life (ISWL), 186-192
joint-life, or first-to-die, contracts, 180-181
multiple-life plans, 180-184
no-lapse guarantees, 200-203
paid-up additions riders, 184-185
premium deposit funds, 201
reduction in benefits under survivorship contracts, 184
return of premium plans, 201-203
reversionary annuity plans, 198
single premium net rate products, 193-195
survivorship, 181-182
variable life insurance, 175-179
Projection-based approach, 59, 348
Proposed mortality regulations, 43, 348
Proposed regulation defining cash value, 70, 348
Pro rata approach to adjusting guideline premium, 113, 116
Prospective calculation, 348

## Q

Qualified additional benefits (QABs), 24-25, 348
application of reasonable expense charge limitations to, 100-101
in guideline level premium (GLP), 87-89
postfunding of, 347
Qualified long-term care insurance (QLTCI) contracts, 223-240, 348
considerations relating to definition of chronically ill individual, 228-232
plan of care, 228
scope of QLTC services, 227
section 7702B(b)(1), insurance contract requirement, 224-225
section 7702B(b)(1)(A), coverage of only QLTC services, 225
section 7702B(b)(1)(B), coordination with Medicare, 232

section 7702B(b)(1)(C), guaranteed renewability, 232
section 7702B(b)(1)(D), (E), and (2)(C), limitations on cash and loan values and allowance of return of premium benefits, 233-234
section 7702B(b)(2)(A), special rule for per diem benefits, 234-235
section 7702B(e), special rule for long-term care riders, 235-236
section 7702B(g) and 4980C, consumer protection rules for, 236-240
tax treatment of benefits, 215-223
tax treatment of premiums and charges and, 213-215
Qualified long-term care insurance (QLTCI) riders, refunds from, 222-223
Qualified medical expenses, 214

## R

Rate or rates guaranteed on issuance, 37
Reasonable charge effective date rule, 152
Reasonable error, 261, 348-349
Reasonable expense charges, 349
application of limitations, to qualified additional benefits (QABs), 100-101
Reasonable expense rule, 264
Reasonable mortality charges, 27, 44-47, 264, 349
reapplication of rule, 164-166
Recapture rules, 349
under section 7702(f)(7)(B)-(E), 145-150
Reclocking, 294, 349
Reduction-in-benefits rule, 55-56, 349
Reinstatements, 84
qualified additional benefits (QABs), 84-90
Return attachment, 283
Return of premium plans, 201-203
Rev. Proc. 99-27, 275, 284, 349
Rev. Proc. 2001-42, 275, 285, 349
Rev. Proc. 2008-38, 275-278, 349

Rev. Proc. 2008-39, 275, 285-292, 349-350
Rev. Proc. 2008-40, 275, 278-283, 350
Rev. Proc. 2008-41, 275, 350
Rev. Proc. 2008-42, 275, 283-284, 350
Rev. Proc. 2010-28, 93-95, 350
observations on, 95-96
Rev. Proc. 92-57, 167, 349
Rev. Rul. 91-17, 262, 267, 274-275, 350
Rev. Rul. 2003-95, 147-150, 350
Rev. Rul. 2005-6, 100, 276-278, 350
Revenue Act (1913), 298-302, 323
tax treatment of inside buildup and, 325
Reversionary annuity plans, 184
Risk distribution, case law on, 20
Risk shifting, 3
case law on, 20
Rollover rule, 56, 127-128, 350
Rounding rule, 25n
Rule eras, 168-169

## S

Safety net, Nonforfeiture Law for Life Insurance as, 333-334
Sale, deduction of loss on, 3
Section 72(e), 350
Section 101(a), 350
Section 101(f), 350
Section 101(g), 350
Section 1035, 350-351
Section 1035 exchanges, involving accelerated death benefits riders, 251-252
Section 7702, 351
adjustments under, 103-104
applicable law requirement of, 6-9
choice of tests under, 32-34
material changes and effective date rule, 155-159
reapplication of reasonable mortality rule, 164-166
reapplying, 159-162
relationship between State Nonforfeiture Law for Life Insurance and, 331-332

role of, in life insurance taxation, 5-6
Section 7702(f)(7)(B)-(E), recapture ceiling rules under, 145-150
Section 7702A, 315-319, 351
    death benefits under, 83
    future benefits under, 83
    modified endowment contracts (MECs) under, 34
    role of, in life insurance taxation, 5-6
Section 7702A adjustments, 122-129
    material changes, 124-127, 128-129
    reduction in benefits, 122-124
    rollover rule, 127-128
Section 7702B, 351
Segregated asset account, 18
"Self-help" corrections, 261-262, 351
Separate account total return, 289
Separate contract rule, 215-217, 235-236
7-pay premiums, 21
    computational rules for, 82-83
    defined, 351
7-pay test, 5, 34-36, 351
    applying, 36
    applying to contract on future benefits, 124
7-pay test adjustments, 55-56
Severe cognitive impairment, 225n, 229
Shadow account, 200
Short-term interest guarantees, 38, 105, 351
Simons, Henry, 324
Simplified underwriting, substandard mortality and, 100
Single life, 73
Single premium net rate products, 193-195
16th Amendment, 323
Specified amount, 351
Split Life, 310
Stacking rules, 14n, 351
*Standard Brewing Company, Appeal of*, 302

Standard Nonforfeiture Law for Life Insurance (SNFL), 329, 351
Standby assistance, 229
Stark-Gradison bill, 315-316
Stark-Moore proposal, 314-315
State Nonforfeiture Law for Life Insurance
    relationship between section 7702 and, 331-332
Substandard mortality, 22, 97-100, 351
    additive method in, 98
    age adjustments in, 99
    multiplicative method (or ratio method) in, 98
    simplified underwriting and, 100
Substantial assistance, 225n
Substantial supervision, 225n
Supplee-Biddle Hardware, 301-302
Surrender, deduction of loss on, 3
Survivorship, 181-182
Survivorship contracts, 351-352
    reduction in benefits under, 184

## T

Target death benefits, 185
Tax authorities, 19-20
Tax deferral, reasons for, on insider buildup, 324-326
Tax Equity and Fiscal Responsibility Act of 1982 (TEFRA), 352
    life insurance contracts in, 4
    section 101(f), 312-314
Tax policy, ideal of comprehensive income tax and, 321-323
Tax preference, 352
Tax Reform Act of 1986 (TRA), 352
    enactment of, 315
    life insurance contracts in, 4-5
    technical corrections to DEFRA, 195
Tax treatment of life insurance, 322-323
Technical advice memoranda (TAMs), 19
Technical and Miscellaneous Revenue Act of 1988 (TAMRA), 352
    effective date rules, 162-164

    life insurance contracts in, 5
    reasonable expense charge limitation in, 100-101
    reasonable mortality and expense charge rules in, 98
    revision of life insurance product tax rules in, 315
    section 7702A, 318-319
    substandard mortality under, 97
Term coverage on the insured, 352
Terminal illness accelerated death benefits, 211-212
Terminally ill individual, 211, 352
Termination dividend, 352
Term insurance, 310
    application of test plan to, 59
    riders on insured, 91-92
Terms of the contract, 352
Test plan, 21, 352
Test plan values, 22
Toll charge, 352
Transfer for value rule, 2
    life insurance tax rules and, 11
Trust-owned life insurance (TOLI), 340

## U

Universal life, 310-311

## V

Variable contracts
    earnings rate on, 289
    investor control and, 3
    life insurance tax rules and, 17-18
Variable life, 175-179, 310
Variable life rule, 352

## W

Waiver rulings, 34, 352
Waiver statement, 283
Whole life
    adjustable, 309
    interest-sensitive, 186-192
Wright, Elizur, 296-297